(Continued on back endsheets)

Canadian Writers
Before 1890

Dictionary of Literary Biography • Volume Ninety-nine

Canadian Writers
Before 1890

8407

Edited by
W. H. New
University of British Columbia

A Bruccoli Clark Layman Book
Gale Research Inc.
Detroit, New York, London

Matthew J. Bruccoli and Richard Layman, *Editorial Directors*
C. E. Frazer Clark, Jr., *Managing Editor*

Printed in the United States of America

Published simultaneously in the United Kingdom
by Gale Research International Limited
(An affiliated company of Gale Research Inc.)

The paper used in this publication meets the minimum requirements
of American National Standard for Information Sciences—Permanence
Paper for Printed Library Materials, ANSI Z39.48-1984.   ∞™

ISBN 0-8103-4579-X
90-43445 CIP

Contents

Plan of the Series

. . . Almost the most prodigious asset of a country, and perhaps its most precious possession, is its native literary product—when that product is fine and noble and enduring.

Mark Twain*

The advisory board, the editors, and the publisher of the *Dictionary of Literary Biography* are joined in endorsing Mark Twain's declaration. The literature of a nation provides an inexhaustible resource of permanent worth. We intend to make literature and its creators better understood and more accessible to students and the reading public, while satisfying the standards of teachers and scholars.

To meet these requirements, *literary biography* has been construed in terms of the author's achievement. The most important thing about a writer is his writing. Accordingly, the entries in *DLB* are career biographies, tracing the development of the author's canon and the evolution of his reputation.

The purpose of *DLB* is not only to provide reliable information in a convenient format but also to place the figures in the larger perspective of literary history and to offer appraisals of their accomplishments by qualified scholars.

The publication plan for *DLB* resulted from two years of preparation. The project was proposed to Bruccoli Clark by Frederick G. Ruffner, president of the Gale Research Company, in November 1975. After specimen entries were prepared and typeset, an advisory board was formed to refine the entry format and develop the series rationale. In meetings held during 1976, the publisher, series editors, and advisory board approved the scheme for a comprehensive biographical dictionary of persons who contributed to North American literature. Editorial work on the first volume began in January 1977, and it was published in 1978. In order to make *DLB* more than a reference tool and to compile volumes that individually have claim to status as literary history, it was decided to organize volumes by topic, period, or genre. Each of these freestanding volumes provides a biographical-bibliographical guide and overview for a particular area of literature. We are convinced that this organization—as opposed to a single alphabet method—constitutes a valuable innovation in the presentation of reference material. The volume plan necessarily requires many decisions for the placement and treatment of authors who might properly be included in two or three volumes. In some instances a major figure will be included in separate volumes, but with different entries emphasizing the aspect of his career appropriate to each volume. Ernest Hemingway, for example, is represented in *American Writers in Paris, 1920-1939* by an entry focusing on his expatriate apprenticeship; he is also in *American Novelists, 1910-1945* with an entry surveying his entire career. Each volume includes a cumulative index of subject authors and articles. Comprehensive indexes to the entire series are planned.

With volume ten in 1982 it was decided to enlarge the scope of *DLB*. By the end of 1986 twenty-one volumes treating British literature had been published, and volumes for Commonwealth and Modern European literature were in progress. The series has been further augmented by the *DLB Yearbooks* (since 1981) which update published entries and add new entries to keep the *DLB* current with contemporary activity. There have also been *DLB Documentary Series* volumes which provide biographical and critical source materials for figures whose work is judged to have particular interest for students. One of these companion volumes is entirely devoted to Tennessee Williams.

We define literature as the *intellectual commerce of a nation:* not merely as belles lettres but as that ample and complex process by which ideas are generated, shaped, and transmitted. *DLB* entries are not limited to "creative writers" but extend to other figures who in their time and in their way influenced the mind of a people. Thus the series encompasses historians, journalists, publishers, and screenwriters. By this means readers of *DLB* may be aided to perceive litera-

*From an unpublished section of Mark Twain's autobiography, copyright © by the Mark Twain Company.

ture not as cult scripture in the keeping of intellectual high priests but firmly positioned at the center of a nation's life.

DLB includes the major writers appropriate to each volume and those standing in the ranks immediately behind them. Scholarly and critical counsel has been sought in deciding which minor figures to include and how full their entries should be. Wherever possible, useful references are made to figures who do not warrant separate entries.

Each *DLB* volume has a volume editor responsible for planning the volume, selecting the figures for inclusion, and assigning the entries. Volume editors are also responsible for preparing, where appropriate, appendices surveying the major periodicals and literary and intellectual movements for their volumes, as well as lists of further readings. Work on the series as a whole is coordinated at the Bruccoli Clark Layman editorial center in Columbia, South Carolina, where the editorial staff is responsible for accuracy of the published volumes.

One feature that distinguishes *DLB* is the illustration policy–its concern with the iconography of literature. Just as an author is influenced by his surroundings, so is the reader's understanding of the author enhanced by a knowledge of his environment. Therefore *DLB* volumes include not only drawings, paintings, and photographs of authors, often depicting them at various stages in their careers, but also illustrations of their families and places where they lived. Title pages are regularly reproduced in facsimile along with dust jackets for modern authors. The dust jackets are a special feature of *DLB* because they often document better than anything else the way in which an author's work was perceived in its own time. Specimens of the writers' manuscripts are included when feasible.

Samuel Johnson rightly decreed that "The chief glory of every people arises from its authors." The purpose of the *Dictionary of Literary Biography* is to compile literary history in the surest way available to us–by accurate and comprehensive treatment of the lives and work of those who contributed to it.

The *DLB* Advisory Board

Foreword

This is the sixth volume in a series devoted to Canadian writers whose main language of composition is English or French. (The others are volumes 53, 60, 68, 88, and 92.) This volume covers the long period of Canadian literary history that stretches from the seventeenth century to 1890. It stops just as Canadians were beginning to think of themselves as a coherent national community. Hence in effect it not only surveys a group of literary figures but also examines the several intellectual movements and economic and political aspirations that turned a collection of trading territories, Indian lands, and European colonies into a modern nation-state.

The biocritical essays assembled here concern those writers who had established their literary reputations by 1890. Several lived well past this date–the poet Charles Mair and the social reformer Emily Murphy, for example. But the focus of this book remains on the literary paradigms of colony and early nationhood.

In this volume are to be found accounts of explorers, travelers, teachers, missionaries, settlers, newspaper journalists, lawyers, politicians, civil servants, and assorted literary poseurs. The range is wide. Writers came from many walks of life. Their voices also range widely–stylistically as well as spiritually; it is important to recognize from the outset the degree to which religion underpinned the culture of these years. From the (variously liberal or ultramontane) Catholicism of such Quebec writers as Louis-Antoine Dessaulles and Arthur Buies, the conventional Church of England practices of Frances Brooke, and the millenarianism of Louis Riel, to the Methodist enthusiasm of Susanna Moodie and the Presbyterian didacticism of Thomas McCulloch, religious experience directed and preoccupied writers for more than three centuries. It took multiple forms not only in theological matters but also in patterns of literary expression, ultimately affecting how writers imagined God, how they perceived the land and conceived of society, and how they saw their role as writers. From the beginning (indeterminate as this date must be), European connections with Canada linked place and language with

power, both spiritual and civil. The shaping of Canada is in great part, therefore, a record of a series of efforts to extend an existing authority into new territory. Because religion and law are neither recognized nor received in uniform fashion, however, a parallel record involves a series of unanticipated transformations of authority that stemmed from uncontrolled and unexpected quarters.

Early Canadian writing in European languages primarily takes documentary form. The explorers who predate Canadian literature but who nonetheless had an impact upon it (and an impact upon many of the place-names on contemporary Canadian maps)–Samuel de Champlain, Jacques Cartier, Gabriel Sagard, William Baffin, Henry Hudson, John Davis, George Vancouver, Luke Foxe, and James Cook–left diaries and logbooks and other records that chart the measurable, observable world. So do the early mission records, especially those of the *Jesuit Relations*: reports home to authorities in France, measuring both the annual progress in cultivation and salvation and the annual losses in disappointments and lives. Yet these records were all couched in conventional literary forms, recurrently turning mapmaking into invention, experience into strange adventure, event into moral fable. History was being fabricated even while it was being lived. Hence the literary bequest to subsequent generations involves the shapes of romance as well as the illusion of documentary authenticity. The character of the blend between these two literary features matters acutely. For the one impulse–to declare the realities of place and experience–repeatedly hid beneath the other one, meaning that "reality" was recurrently taking on the masks of familiar European tropes. One result was that Canada came to seem to the foreign reader to be merely an extension of the already familiar; another was that Canada came to seem unfamiliar to those Canadian writers for whom the local language of expression was a foreign medium. It was a predicament out of which twentieth-century Canadian writing would later grow.

To read many early Canadian works is to see something of this predicament in embryo, depending often on a writer's chosen market, on literary intention, and on birthplace and education. (The immigrant writer, the settler, and the traveler, all frequently found the new world inhospitable and uncivilized, while at the same time–recurrently–"sublime"; but native-born writers not uncommonly cast Canada in a "wilderness mold," too, not because the land was exotic to them but because it had to conform to an overseas market's conventional expectations.) Hence in all genres language was a measure of both experience and preconception–a way, like the maps that figure so prominently in early European definitions of Canada, of dressing the fanciful in credibility and shaping reality to serve the figures of romance.

In the journals of Samuel Hearne, for example, the contrary iconography of the sublime and the picturesque served not only to portray differences in landscape (the wilderness barrens, the controllable garden) but also to distinguish racially between savage and civilized behavior. For modern readers, Hearne has become something of an icon himself, a historical figure epitomizing the ambivalent relation between person and place, the defensive posture so often adopted against physical and psychological reality. (Other historical figures–Fr. Jean de Brébeuf, Susanna Moodie, and Louis Riel–carry a similar symbolic resonance for many subsequent readers and writers.) Hearne's journal of his trip to the mouth of the Coppermine River, moreover, is now read more for its psychological revelations, its tacit defensiveness, than for its "accuracy." "Accuracy" is in constant dispute. The captivity journals of John Gyles and John Jewitt also carry about them an aura of invention. But there were other works–notably the exploration journals of Alexander Mackenzie and David Thompson–that rooted themselves more openly in detailed empirical annotations and frank opinion. While European readers responded conventionally to these works, too, identifying them on publication as uplifting adventures in exotic territory, more recent estimations have stressed the way in which, say, Thompson's travels (and his record of them) altered not only the reality that was perceived to exist in the distances of Canada but also the manner of perceiving. When the narratives of settlement subsequently appeared in the 1850s and after–those of Moodie and her sister Catharine Parr Traill are particularly noteworthy–the shift

from romantic to reportorial conventions (using distant landscape as a backdrop to moral education, using experience as a model for practical advice) had become approved in practice as well as attitude.

Such a change in literary method can be traced through other genres as well, apparent in diction, structural pattern, handling of idiom, and moral design. In poetry and drama, for example, Marc Lescarbot's early seventeenth-century masque celebrates the French political hierarchy in formal rhymed verse; formal rhyme also characterizes Robert Hayman's poetic tribute to the orderly virtues of English Newfoundland. Literary order continued to serve political ends. In the eighteenth century, Loyalist poets such as Jonathan Odell, who had moved north after the American Declaration of Independence, formally and satirically attacked the political presumptions of the new United States. In the early nineteenth century, Oliver Goldsmith in "The Rising Village" was even imitating the formal order of his (namesake) great-uncle's work; but by then other poets were redefining order in progressive terms. (In the inimitable work of James McIntyre a formal idiom soon became unintentionally parodic.) By the end of the nineteenth century, the anglophone "Confederation Poets" were seeking to balance an ideal of Classical verities with a vision of Romantic change. (Local history, local speech, detailed local observation: all developed into lyrics of social orderliness and controlled sensation.) At the same time, francophone poets were variously adapting to Canada both the landscape aesthetics and the symbolist practice of French poets from Alfred de Musset and Alphonse de Lamartine to Paul Verlaine and Stéphane Mallarmé. By the 1890s the land had shifted from being a setting for imaginative adventure to being an empirical phenomenon and an implicitly political symbol. The nineteenth-century dramas of Sarah Anne Curzon, Charles Heavysege, and Louis Fréchette further demonstrate how a formal mode gradually gives way to a vernacular one, and how the pressures of experience (of women, of minorities) find one form of political and literary expression through the analogues of history.

In prose, the multiple tensions between trope and trauma reveal a society in the throes of political and social change, and also one in which the writers were severally struggling to free themselves from the limits of convention. The nineteenth-century religious writers–John Carroll among them–were trying in the face of Social Darwinism to locate the divine in a version of nature and (largely male) human experience. The travel writers (many of them female, such as Anna Jameson and Anne Langton) were frequently rebelling—to a degree—against the status quo, seeking to reconcile received order with their personal resistance to intellectual conventionality. The letter writers—Elisabeth Bégon, Frances Brooke (especially in her 1769 epistolary novel *The History of Emily Montague*)—adapted a further mode of discourse to their own purposes, revealing the social strictures women faced and their political perspicacity.

Satire was yet another broadly political literary technique. While the most influential political satirists—Thomas McCulloch and Thomas Chandler Haliburton—espoused conservative social values, they too sought change. McCulloch perhaps sought change most by resisting it: that is, by seeking a return to past values, as in his didactic moral narratives of a character named Mephibosheth Stepsure. Haliburton, however, resistant to the political liberalism of his publisher Joseph Howe and of the society around them, nonetheless encouraged active economic development. Through his dialogues of "Sam Slick" (an itinerant Yankee clock peddler, whom some have claimed as the original of the figure of "Uncle Sam"), Haliburton used vernacular speech as an agent to espouse progress of particular kinds (a railroad, economic self-reliance) and to encourage social reform.

By 1867, the year of Confederation, when Canada gained its independence from Britain, this desire for and resistance to social change were expressing themselves differently in English and French. Much hinges on particular features of social history. For example, the political regime when Canada was a French colony had prevented any newspapers from being locally published, the governors thinking thereby to suppress dissent. But after the British acquired Quebec in 1759, journals became commonplace, and the newspaper served as a major outlet for political comment, much of it critical of the governing powers: W. L. Mackenzie's *Colonial Advocate*, for example, or Howe's *Novascotian*, or George Brown's *Globe*. While nineteenth-century literary journals—those of the Moodies and George Stewart, or John Lovell's *Literary Garland*—tended to house conventional lyrics, romantic tales, and sentimental moral lessons, the newspapers focused more sharply on opinion and empirical data. And as the newspapers increased their readership, the literary journals tended to fade. Moreover—although by the 1890s the situation had changed—the newspaper long remained the focusing agent for English-Canadian political dissent. (Indeed, many anglophone writers of the later nineteenth century, from Edward Thomson to Sara Duncan, were practicing newspaper journalists). In French Canada dissent had necessarily learned to take another form. Under the old regime in Quebec, experience had made oral rather than written forms the main agency of political comment. Hence there (and, later, in the West, too), the forms of folk song, folktale, and theatrical performance all rapidly became political in function. These were forms taken up by Aubert de Gaspé *père*, J. C. Taché, Louis Fréchette, Honoré Beaugrand, and others, all concerned to make the popular idiom a medium of resistance to external political design.

By 1890 several moments in history had come to be collectively identified as critical markers of social development. The years 1759, 1812, 1837, 1867 and 1885 all changed the way Canadians thought about themselves: 1759 marked the formal end of the ancien régime and the arrival of the British in Quebec; 1812 marked Canada's collective resistance to political absorption by the United States, an act which indirectly gave social precedence to the Loyalist culture of Ontario; 1837, the year of the W. L. Mackenzie and Louis Papineau "Rebellions," was marked by the selective resistance in Canada to political orthodoxy, leading subsequently toward independence and to a particular form of monarchical democracy; 1867 was the year of formal independence; 1885 was the year of the completion of the Canadian Pacific Railroad between Montreal and the West Coast, solidifying the transcontinental character of the new nation, and also the year of the hanging of Louis Riel, which turned a millenarian Métis rebel into a francophone cultural martyr. Riel's death, that is, hinted at a continuing resistance to the then-dominant version of nationalism, and of changes still to come; the events of 1837 also resulted in the forms of exile that followed the rebellions (an exile made especially eloquent in Antoine Gérin-Lajoie's folk-melody "Un canadien errant," which voiced the loss of any Quebeckers forcibly denied their land and culture). The shared dates, in other words, also constitute moments of internal cultural divisiveness, moments of misapprehensions about how the dates and the experiences they represent have come to be reconstructed in Canadian social mythologies. In English Canada they represented a collective independence based on a British model; in French Canada they represented a more locally defined collective independence that would be shaped apart from an English connection. Such separate presumptions fed at once the anglophone beliefs of the Canada First Movement (involving Charles Mair, George Monro Grant, and others) and the ultramontane Catholic nationalism of Jules-Paul Tardivel and Henri Bourassa. During World War I these two positions flared in opposition, and Canada emerged from that conflict substantially changed.

These positions also affected the determinations of history and fiction. Following the historical writing of François-Xavier Garneau, many nineteenth-century Quebec novelists devised historical fictions about conquest and martyrdom, shaping narrative as a device of cultural resistance. Among these writers were Aubert de Gaspé *fils*, Pierre Chauveau, Napoléon Bourassa, Georges Boucher de Boucherville, and Pamphile Lemay. Among anglophone historical novelists, however–John Richardson, William Kirby, or, later, Gilbert Parker (whose source was more likely to be the American historian Francis Parkman than it would be Garneau)–history was reconstructed as a psychological conflict between (francophone, Gothic) decadence and (anglophone, civil) order, not, notably, between good and evil. Virtue was allowed to equate with Protestant civility, but whenever goodness was assigned to a francophone environment, it was equated with pastoral sentimentalism. Theirs was a version of history that romanticized nature, distorted the dynamics of political change, and especially left women and cities out of account. But as with fictions of martyrdom in Quebec, it was pervasive.

For many modern critics, the fascination of the early writers lies less in the literary quality they were once presumed to possess than in the palpable bias that shaped the literary conventions they employed. Among the most persistently compelling writers to contemporary eyes, moreover, are the women: Frances Brooke and Laure Conan, Catharine Traill and Rosanna Leprohon, Susanna Moodie and Anna Leonowens. The men on the whole contented themselves with redefining the borders of systems of closure; the women devised ways to deal with the pressures of experience and the inadequacies of speech. Wilderness may have lain around them all, and an inherited language constrained them. But in the women's works are the real signs of indirection and reconstruction, of dissatisfaction with the empires of the mind in which as citizens and writers they were being asked to live. In their life stories one finds recurrent records of large families, infant mortality, penury, duty, patriotism, faith, and a determined resistance to parental control. In their works (though not in their works alone), the old maps of the European explorers were being redrawn and a local history was coming to life.

–W. H. New

Acknowledgments

This book was produced by Bruccoli Clark Layman, Inc. Karen L. Rood is senior editor for the *Dictionary of Literary Biography* series. Jack Turner was the in-house editor.

Production coordinator is James W. Hipp. Systems manager is Charles D. Brower. Photography editor is Susan Brennen Todd. Permissions editor is Jean W. Ross. Layout and graphics supervisor is Penney L. Haughton. Copyediting supervisor is Bill Adams. Typesetting supervisor is Kathleen M. Flanagan. Information systems analyst is George F. Dodge. Charles Lee Egleston is editorial associate. The production staff includes Rowena Betts, Anne L. M. Bowman, Polly Brown, Teresa Chaney, Patricia Coate, Marie Creed, Allison Deal, Holly L. Deal, Sarah A. Estes, Mary L. Goodwin, Cynthia Hallman, Susan C. Heath, David Marshall James, Kathy Lawler Merlette, Laura Garren Moore, John Myrick, Gina D. Peterman, Cathy J. Reese, Edward Scott, Laurrè Sinckler, Maxine K. Smalls, John C. Stone III, and Betsy L. Weinberg.

Walter W. Ross and Parris Boyd did the library research with the assistance of the following librarians at the Thomas Cooper Library of the University of South Carolina: Gwen Baxter, Daniel Boice, Faye Chadwell, Cathy Eckman, Gary Geer, Cathie Gottlieb, David L. Haggard, Jens Holley, Jackie Kinder, Thomas Marcil, Marcia Martin, Laurie Preston, Jean Rhyne, Carol Tobin, and Virginia Weathers.

The editor expresses special thanks to Joe Jones and the staff of the University of British Columbia Library Humanities Division, and to Robin Van Heck, Carole Gerson, and Beverly Westbrook. Kenneth Landry of the *Dictionnaire des œuvres littéraires du Québec* has provided valuable assistance in securing illustrative materials.

Dictionary of Literary Biography • Volume Ninety-nine

Canadian Writers
Before 1890

Dictionary of Literary Biography

Graeme Mercer Adam

(25 May 1839 - 30 October 1912)

Carole Gerson
Simon Fraser University

BOOKS: *History of Toronto and County of York, Ontario; Containing an Outline of the History of the Dominion of Canada; A History of the City of Toronto and the County of York, with the Townships, Towns, Villages, Churches, Schools; General and Local Statistics, Etc., Etc. . . .* (Toronto: Robinson, 1885);

The Canadian North-west: Its History and Its Troubles, From the Early Days of the Fur-trade to the Era of the Railway and the Settler, with Incidents of Travel in the Region, and the Narrative of Three Insurrections (Toronto: Rose / Whitby, Ont.: Robertson, 1885);

Public School History of England and Canada (Toronto: Copp, Clark, 1886);

An Algonquin Maiden: A Romance of the Early Days of Upper Canada, by Adam and Agnes Ethelwyn Wetherald (New York: Lovell, 1886; Montreal: Lovell / Toronto: Williamson, 1887; London: Low, Marston, Searle & Rivington, 1887);

Illustrated Quebec (Montreal: McConniff, 1891);

Illustrated Toronto (Montreal: McConniff, 1891);

Toronto, Old and New: A Memorial Volume, Historical, Descriptive and Pictorial, Designed to Mark the Hundredth Anniversary of the Passing of the Constitutional Act of 1791, Which Set Apart the Province of Upper Canada and Gave Birth to York (Now Toronto) . . . (Toronto: Mail Printing Company, 1891);

Makers of American History: The Lewis & Clark Exploring Expedition, 1804-'06, published with *John Charles Fremont* by Charles Wentworth Upham (New York: University Society, 1904);

The Life of General Robert E. Lee: The Life-Career and Military Achievements of the Great Southern General (New York: Burt, 1905).

OTHER: *Prominent Men of Canada,* edited by Adam (Toronto: Canadian Biographical, 1892).

An enterprising Scotsman who, according to Henry Morgan, "may almost be said to have been cradled among books," Graeme Mercer Adam already possessed considerable experience in the book trade when he came to Canada in 1858 at the age of nineteen. From then until he went to New York in 1892, his activities as bookseller and importer, publisher, editor, and author, as well as his association with the *Canadian Monthly* and the *Week,* influenced and encouraged the growth of Canadian letters. Adam "had much to do with almost all the literary undertakings which originated in Toronto between the years 1872 and 1892," says Morgan, and wrote, edited, or contributed to many books, including school texts, fiction, history, and travel narratives.

Upon his arrival in Canada Adam became manager of Cunningham Geikie, a book and stationery business in Toronto, and within two years he established, with a partner, the publishing firm of Rollo and Adam. One of their major productions was the *British American Magazine* (May 1863-April 1864), for which Adam wrote book reviews. Upon the dissolution of this partnership in

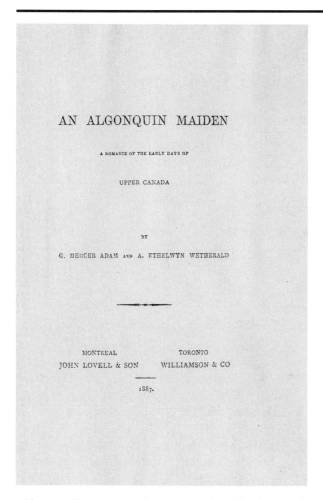

AN ALGONQUIN MAIDEN

A ROMANCE OF THE EARLY DAYS OF

UPPER CANADA

BY

G. MERCER ADAM AND A. ETHELWYN WETHERALD

MONTREAL   TORONTO
JOHN LOVELL & SON   WILLIAMSON & CO

1887.

Title page for the first Canadian edition of Adam's only novel, a collaboration with the poet Agnes Ethelwyn Wetherald

1866 Adam formed a new firm, Adam, Stevenson and Company, which lasted for ten years. In 1863 Adam further cemented his ties with the Canadian publishing community when he married Jane Beazley, a daughter of John Gibson, the man who had edited the *Literary Garland* (1838-1851), English Canada's most enduring pre-Confederation literary periodical. From 1876 to 1878, in alliance with John Lovell, Adam operated a publishing business at Rouse's Point in New York State. The shock of his first wife's death in 1884 and his subsequent courtship and remarriage in 1891 (to Frances Isabel Brown) inspired Adam to write five unremarkable poems, which appeared in the *Week* from 1884 to 1888. During this period he ventured also into fiction,

co-authoring with the poet Agnes Ethelwyn Wetherald *An Algonquin Maiden: A Romance of the Early Days of Upper Canada* (1886).

However, it was not as a writer but as an editor and publisher that Adam left his deepest mark on Canadian culture. The firm of Adam, Stevenson, and Company encouraged Canadian authors, and, in 1872, with the cooperation of the prominent educator, historian, and journalist Goldwin Smith, it launched the *Canadian Monthly and National Review* (1872-1878), Canada's most important periodical of the time, which published work on literary, political, and religious matters by leading Canadian writers and intellectuals, as well as fiction, poetry, and reviews. In 1878, to resolve financial difficulties, the *Canadian Monthly and National Review* merged with *Belford's Monthly Magazine* to form *Rose-Belford's Canadian Monthly and National Review*, which Adam edited from 1879 until its demise in 1882. In addition, he edited and wrote nearly all the material for the trade journal the *Canada Bookseller* (1865?-1872); founded and edited the *Canadian Educational Monthly* (1879-1885?); aided Goldwin Smith with the *Bystander* (which appeared irregularly from 1880 to 1890); and contributed to the *Week* and the Toronto newspapers the *Nation*, the *Globe*, and the *Mail*. Many of his pieces advocated greater support for Canadian writers and attacked the existing international copyright laws, which favored British and American publishers to the detriment of Canadians.

In 1892 Adam left Canada permanently, spending four years in New York, six in Chicago, then returning to New York, where he died in 1912. During these years he transferred his literary energy to the United States, contributing to reference books and periodicals, editing the Chicago-based journal *Self-Help*, and writing biographies, such as his *Life of General Robert E. Lee* (1905).

References:

Marilyn Flitton, *An Index to the Canadian Monthly and National Review and Rose-Belford's Canadian Monthly* (Toronto: Bibliographical Society of Canada, 1976);

Henry James Morgan, ed., *The Canadian Men and Women of the Time: A Handbook of Canadian Biography* (Toronto: Briggs, 1898), pp. 5-7.

Levi Adams
(17 March 1802? - 21 June 1832)

Mary Lu MacDonald

BOOK: *Jean Baptiste: A Poetic Olio. In II Cantos* (Montreal: Printed for the author, 1825; modern edition, Ottawa: Golden Dog, 1978).

SELECTED PERIODICAL PUBLICATIONS–
UNCOLLECTED: "The Young Lieutenant. A Tale," *Canadian Magazine and Literary Repository*, 4 (June 1825): 495-500;
"The Wedding," *Canadian Magazine and Literary Repository*, 4 (June 1825): 523-524.

As the earliest volume of Upper or Lower Canadian writing to which the author signed his name, Levi Adams's *Jean Baptiste* (1825) has received some critical attention. The work, which was printed for the author and then reprinted in *Canadian Review and Literary and Historical Journal* in 1826, was part of a minor writing and publishing boom in Montreal in the mid 1820s. A well-known 1960 article by Carl F. Klinck brought Adams's name to the attention of many students, but unfortunately connected it with an extensive body of anonymous works subsequently proved to have been written by another Canadian, George Longmore. Adams's own work appears to consist only of *Jean Baptiste*, two short stories that appeared in the *Canadian Magazine* (June 1825), and a few poems published in the *Montreal Herald* in 1825 and 1826, all signed simply "L. A."

Very little is known of Adams's life. The documents attached to his 1827 petition for license as an advocate and his newspaper obituary (*Montreal Gazette*, 21 June 1832) produce the only surviving factual evidence. His brother Austin signed Adams's original articles of indenture on 23 October 1822 as his guardian, and on 17 March 1823 Adams, "being of age," signed a further document consenting to the articles. It is for this reason that 17 March 1802 is given as the probable date of his birth. If Adams and his master, François Pierre Bruneau, were not precise to the day about such legal details, then the correct date lies somewhere in the preceding five

months. A further document in the petition states that "at the time of his birth there was no regular record of Baptisms kept in the Parish."

Unfortunately, the name of the parish is not mentioned. His place of residence at the time of becoming an articled clerk is given as the Seigneury of Noyan in Quebec. Since some of his works are signed "L. A., Henryville," and since the village of Henryville is situated in that seigneury, it seems likely that he lived there before moving to Montreal, but there is no firm indication that he was born there, or even that he was born in Canada.

Adams articled in the office of Bruneau. All the documents relating to his clerkship are in French, so it would appear that French was the language in which he worked and studied. His petition for admission to the bar was granted on 2 November 1827.

On 10 July 1830 Adams married Elizabeth Wright of Northampton, Massachusetts. He died of cholera in Montreal on 21 June 1832, and his wife died the following day, leaving a three-week-old son.

All the works that appear to have been written by Levi Adams were published in the years 1825 and 1826 when he was still a law student. In that respect he is typical of his time and place. Many early Canadian writers in both languages were students in the professions who ceased to publish as soon as they had finished their training. Adams was atypical in that he signed his name or his initials, while others remained anonymous.

The story of *Jean Baptiste,* told in verse, is simple. An old bachelor, rejected by his true love, Lorrain, settles, after much poetic despair, for the willing Rosalie. In the short story "The Young Lieutenant," Launcelot sees action with the militia in the War of 1812. He is captured at Plattsburgh and does not return home until the end of hostilities. His true love, Isabelle, thinking him dead, has pined away. Launcelot, seeking to forget the past, takes ship for the West Indies, where he dies. "The Wedding" describes a happy occasion, followed in two months by the bride's funeral.

The two stories, told in the third-person omniscient, are melancholic after the fashion of young men of that period. Although Canada is specifically named as the locale, almost any other place names could be substituted without any change in detail. *Jean Baptiste,* on the other hand, is comic, bathetic, and full of small details about Montreal life and politics, as well as the conventional stanzas of philosophizing about life, love, and human nature. The author's legal training is frequently apparent. Adams had read George Gordon, Lord Byron's *Beppo* (1818) and *Don Juan* (1819-1824) closely and follows Byron's verse form carefully, often at the expense of logical speech patterns.

All Adams's works are those of a young man for whom writing was a hobby rather than a vocation. Much of his writing has the unevenness of something dashed off in a moment of inspiration. Of the 160 mock-heroic stanzas of *Jean Baptiste,* some come off perfectly, while others seem to be the work of an enthusiastic but untalented schoolboy. Whether he would have returned to literary endeavors as a mature adult, we will never know, but he did at least leave works that give us a good indication of the *mentalité* of a young Canadian of his day.

References:

Carl F. Klinck, "The Charivari and Levi Adams," *Dalhousie Review,* 40 (Spring 1960): 34-42;

Klinck, Introduction to *Jean Baptiste* (Ottawa: Golden Dog, 1978), pp. 1-9;

M. L. MacDonald, "George Longmore: A New Literary Ancestor," *Dalhousie Review,* 59 (Summer 1979): 265-285.

Henry Alline

(14 January 1748 - 28 January 1784)

Thomas B. Vincent
Royal Military College of Canada

BOOKS: *Two Mites* (Halifax: A. Henry, 1781);
Hymns and Spiritual Songs (Halifax: A. Henry, 1782);
A Sermon Preached to a Religious Society of Young Men (Halifax: A. Henry, 1782);
A Sermon on a Day of Thanksgiving (Halifax: A. Henry, 1782);
The Anti-Traditionalist (Halifax: A. Henry, 1783);
A Sermon Preached at Fort Medway (Halifax: A. Henry, 1783);
Hymns and Spiritual Songs (Boston: Edes, 1786);
The Life and Journal of the Rev. Mr. Henry Alline (Boston: Gilbert & Dean, 1806).

Henry Alline is best known to historians as a dynamic evangelical preacher who precipitated a major religious revival of great social and political significance in late-eighteenth-century Nova Scotia. But during his brief preaching career, he also produced numerous "hymns and spiritual songs" (as he called them), together with a sizable body of theological prose works. While his theology has not withstood the test of time, his poetry has come to represent one of the few significant canons of verse from this period of Canadian literature. Although originally intended as an adjunct to his religious mission, his poetry is most meaningful today as a sensitive expression of the range and nature of his religious experience.

Alline was born in Newport, Rhode Island, on 14 January 1748 into an old New England family whose roots lay in Massachusetts; his parents were William and Rebecca Clark Alline. He received some formal schooling in Newport, but when he was eleven, his family moved to Nova Scotia to settle at Falmouth at the head of the Annapolis Valley. The lands they occupied had recently been made vacant by the expulsion of the French Acadians. But even though these farms had been previously cultivated, life was very difficult for the new settlers and entirely lacked the kinds of social and cultural institutions, such as schools and churches, that were an integral part of the communal life of New England. It is amazing that such thin religious and cultural soil was able to nurture the poetic talent and theological vision of Henry Alline.

Alline's life on his father's farm and with his friends in Falmouth was quite ordinary until Sunday, 26 March 1775. It was on that day that he experienced his personal conversion to Jesus Christ, as he reports in his *Life and Journal* (1806), "that instant in time when I gave up all to him, to do with me, as he pleased, and was willing that God should reign in me and rule over me at his pleasure." Alline's conversion brought with it not only an intense personal commitment to Christ but also a desire to serve Christ as a preacher. Although initially concerned that he had no formal theological training, he overcame his hesitation and in April 1776 began a career as an itinerant preacher in Nova Scotia (which then included New Brunswick). Until his death in 1784, he traveled through most of the Maritimes, raising the religious consciousness of all who listened to him preach. In that brief time, he helped establish several independent churches, which subsequently formed the basis of the Baptist movement in the Maritime Provinces.

While best remembered as a charismatic preacher, Alline sought to broaden his theological influence through the written word. In the four years between 1780 and his death, he produced two substantial theological works, three sermons, and two volumes of religious verse, as well as keeping a detailed journal of his travels. Most of his publications were printed at the press of Anthony Henry in Halifax, except for the second book of verse and his journal, which were published in Boston. In the late 1790s most of his works were reprinted for use among the Free-Will Baptists of New England.

Alline's theological views, articulated in *Two Mites* (1781) and *The Anti-Traditionalist* (1783), are not particularly original, nor are they coherently and systematically presented in these books. He was apparently heavily influenced by the works of the English theologian William Law. He found the pietistical nature of Law's theology as well as its mystical and ascetic elements very attractive. Yet Alline's theology also asserts the need for enthusiastic evangelism, requiring a conscious commitment to the proclamation of the gospel to others. The spirit of his evangelism is essentially non-Calvinist, but Universalist and Arminian in nature. The grace of God was free to all men, a truth proclaimed by Christ and made manifest in his Crucifixion; only Christians who had truly received the gift of grace knew this truth and were bound to proclaim it to all mankind.

The tug in Alline's theology toward asceticism on the one hand and evangelism on the other resulted in a logical inconsistency and emotional tension that he never really resolved. His passion for the experience of inner spiritual reality and his commitment to spreading his vision of spiritual truth seem strangely incompatible, creating a figure who always seems to be struggling to articulate truths that lie beyond words. In his own day he was attacked for his rather blurred theological views. The strongest of his detractors was Jonathan Scott, a Calvinistic Congregationalist minister at Yarmouth, Nova Scotia. Scott published a religious tract (*A Brief View of . . . Mr. Henry Alline,* 1784) in which he minutely dissected Alline's theology.

But the dichotomy that apparently undermines Alline's theology enhances the effect of his religious poetry and hymns. His verse is characterized by a sense of struggle in human religious experience. Thus the irreconcilable emotional tension between his inclination to experience his inner self and the need to preach religious truths reflects the dichotomous nature of religious experience as Alline understood it. In Alline's view, the Christian was caught in a world that had the potential for both good and evil, a potential the Christian himself embodied in his own being, because, like his world, he was divinely created yet fallen. Man's religious awareness, then, stretches across a broad spectrum from the agony of damnation and sinfulness to the ecstasy of salvation through grace. While Alline's verse usually presents one of these extremes at a time, the other is never far off. This coexistence of agony and ecstasy is perhaps best exemplified in Alline's vision of Christ and the Crucifixion: as Savior, Christ is the supreme manifestation of God's grace, but his role as Savior was necessitated by man's sin. Christ is symbolically and historically an expression of the agony and ecstasy of man's lot.

If there is a resolution of this religious struggle in Alline's verse, it lies in another element of his Christology. As the manifestation of God's grace in the act of accepting the burden of man's sin, Christ is the source of peace through faith. Ultimately, the Christian's struggle is resolved through simple faith in Christ, open to all men who are prepared to resign themselves totally to the will of God. This vision of peace-in-Christ has a special, mysterious evocativeness all its own in Alline's verse and is all the more surprising when it emerges out of tension and struggle.

These themes of struggle and peace in Alline's poetry are perhaps most clearly displayed in *Hymns and Spiritual Songs* (1786), which was probably written during his last illness in the spring and summer of 1783. In some ways, this collection of over 480 hymns amounts to a spiritual autobiography, although repetition of themes and subjects tends to blur that perception. Alline viewed the work as an adjunct to his preaching, and was traveling to Boston to have it published when his health finally gave out. He died far from friends and family at North-Hampton, New Hampshire, on 28 January 1784.

Today, Alline tends to be seen as another singular figure in early Canadian verse whose influence petered out somewhere among the minor hymnists of the nineteenth century. In fact, when placed beside the other Canadian poets of his time, his work emerges as a significant part of the broad spectrum of poetic perspectives and styles that formed the foundation of poetic development in Canada.

References:

Maurice W. Armstrong, *The Great Awakening in Nova Scotia* (Hartford: American Society of Church History, 1948);

J. M. Bumsted, *Henry Alline* (Toronto: University of Toronto Press, 1971);

Thomas B. Vincent, "Alline and Bailey," *Canadian Literature,* 68-69 (1976): 124-133;

Vincent, "Henry Alline: Problems of Approach and Reading the Hymns as Poetry," in *They Planted Well: New England Planters in Maritime Canada,* edited by M. Conrad (Fredericton: Acadiensis, 1988), pp. 201-210.

Philippe-Ignace-François Aubert de Gaspé

(8 April 1814 - 7 March 1841)

Mary Lu MacDonald

BOOK: *L'Influence d'un livre* (Quebec: Cowan, 1837); revised by H.-R. Casgrain as *Le Chercheur de trésors* (Quebec: Desbarats, 1864; modern edition, Montreal: Réédition Québec, 1968).

Philippe-Ignace-François Aubert de Gaspé, the author of the first Canadian novel written in French, was the eldest son of Philippe-Joseph Aubert de Gaspé, whose own novel, *Les Anciens Canadiens* (1863), was published more than twenty-five years later. To distinguish him from his more famous father he is usually referred to as Aubert de Gaspé *fils*. His father's family were hereditary seigneurs of Saint-Jean-Port-Joli, Quebec. His mother, Suzanne Allison Aubert de Gaspé, was the daughter of a British officer and one of the well-to-do Baby family, so on both sides of his family the young Aubert de Gaspé was connected to prominent families of what was then Lower Canada. What should have been a privileged childhood in his native Quebec City was interrupted in 1822 by his father's disgrace and removal from office for defaulting on his accounts as sheriff of the city. The family then moved to Saint-Jean-Port-Joli. Except for two years, 1827 to 1829, when he was noted as a brilliant student at the Collège de Nicolet, the young man was educated at home by his father.

There is evidence in a petition he presented to the Legislative Assembly of Lower Canada that he worked as a parliamentary reporter from about 1832. In 1835 he was definitely employed in that capacity by two Quebec City papers of opposing political views, *Le Canadien* and the *Mercury*. When the *Vindicator*, a radical Montreal newspaper owned by a member of the Assembly, E. B. O'Callaghan, criticized the honesty of parliamentary reports in the two papers, Aubert de Gaspé confronted him in the Assembly building. Accounts of the confrontation vary, but the legislator triumphed over the reporter, having him confined to jail for a month. The matter became a momentary cause célèbre, with all newspapers and political factions taking sides. Because he acted

against the radical O'Callaghan, it is generally assumed today that his political views were as conservative as those of his father. There is no evidence to prove the matter one way or another, but his closest friends were certainly all well-known reformers. Several months after his release Aubert de Gaspé revenged himself by pouring a bottle of asafetida over the heating stove of the Assembly, forcing its members to flee the awful smell. He was seen in the act and convicted a second time of breach of privilege, but this time he fled to Saint-Jean-Port-Joli and was not jailed. The newspapers again had a field day with the events—witty puns and clever verse abounded.

Keeping a low profile in the country over the winter, he passed the time by writing the novel that was to become French Canada's first (*L'Influence d'un livre*, 1837). Back in Quebec City, between March and June 1837 he edited, with Napoléon Aubin, a bilingual newspaper, *Le Télégraph-The Telegraph*. The paper did not last long, but he seems to have remained in the city until at least 1839. The next record of his whereabouts places him in Halifax in late 1840. An old school friend of his father found him a teaching job, which he kept for three months before accepting a job as parliamentary reporter for the *Halifax Morning Post*. He died after an illness of only a few days and was buried, it appears, in an unmarked grave in the poorhouse cemetery. Many years later Abbé H.-R. Casgrain wrote that he died of drink, but there is no evidence to support either this assertion or other negative comments Casgrain made about the character of Aubert de Gaspé *fils*. There is also no justification for Casgrain's extensive revision of the text, published with a new title, *Le Chercheur de trésors*, in 1864. It is from Casgrain as well that we have the information that chapter five was written by Aubert de Gaspé *père*. Much critical ink has been spilt subsequently in building cases for other parts of the novel as the work of the father. Little has been written about the work itself.

The original novel contains three intertwined plots: Charles Amand's attempts to make

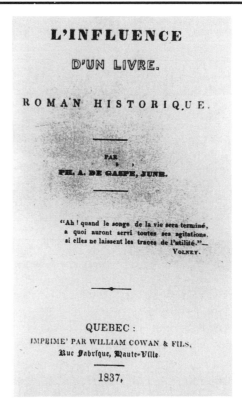

Title page and preface for Aubert de Gaspé's novel, the first written and published in French Canada

PREFACE.

CEUX qui liront cet ouvrage, le cours de Littérature de Laharpe d'une main, et qui y chercheront toutes les règles d'unités requises par la critique du dix-huitième Siècle, seront bien trompés. Le Siècle des unités est passé ; la France a proclamé Shakspeare le premier tragique de l'univers et commence à voir qu'il est ridicule de faire parler un valet dans le même style qu'un Prince. Les Romanciers du dix-neuvième Siècle ne font plus consister le mérite d'un Roman en belles phrases fleuries ou en incidents multipliés ; c'est la nature humaine qu'il faut exploiter pour ce Siècle positif, qui ne veut plus se contenter de Bucoliques, de tête-à-têtes sous l'ormeau, ou de promenades Solitaires dans les bosquets. Ces galanteries pouvaient amuser les cours oisives de Louis XIV et de Louis XV ; maintenant c'est le cœur humain qu'il faut développer à notre âge industriel. La pensée ! voilà son livre——Il y a quelques années, j'avais jeté sur le papier le plan d'un ouvrage, où, après avoir fait passer mon héros par toutes les tribulations d'un amour contrarié, je terminais en le rendant heureux durant le reste de ses jours. Je croyais bien faire ; mais je me suis aperçu que je ne faisais que reproduire de vieilles idées, et des sensations qui nous sont toutes connues. J'ai détruit mon manuscrit et j'ai cru voir un champ plus utile s'ouvrir devant moi. J'offre à mon pays le premier Roman de Mœurs canadien, et en le présentant à mes compatriotes je réclame leur indulgence à ce titre. Les mœurs pures de nos campagnes sont une vaste mine à exploiter; peut-être serais-je assez heureux pour faire naître, à quelques uns de mes concitoyens, plus habiles que moi, le désir d'en enrichir ce pays. L'INFLUENCE

D'UN LIVRE est historique comme son titre l'annonce. J'ai décrit les évènemens tels qu'ils sont arrivés, m'en tenant presque toujours à la réalité, persuadé qu'elle doit toujours remporter l'avantage sur la fiction la mieux ourdie. Le Canada, pays vierge, encore dans son enfance, n'offre aucun de ces grands caractères marqués, qui ont fourni un champ si vaste au génie des Romanciers de la vieille Europe. Il a donc fallu me contenter de peindre des hommes tels qu'ils se rencontrent dans la vie usuelle. Le Page et Amand font seuls des exceptions : le premier, par sa soif du sang humain ; le second, par sa folie innocente. L'opinion publique décidera si je dois m'en tenir à ce premier essai. En attendant, j'espère qu'en terminant cet ouvrage mon lecteur aura une pensée plus consolante, pour l'auteur, que celle de Voltaire :

Tout ce fatras fut du chanvre en son tems.

The Aubert de Gaspé manor house at Saint-Jean-Port-Joli, Quebec

gold by using formulas found in a book of alchemy, the *Petit Albert*; the murder of the pedlar Guillemette by Joseph Mareuil; and young Saint-Ceźran's winning of his beloved Amélie, Amand's daughter. Two legends, that of "Rose la Tulipe" and "L'homme du Labrador," are also brought into the text as stories told by elderly men to a group of young listeners. Although Aubert de Gaspé claimed in his preface to be writing a realistic novel, and although it has been established that an individual like Amand did live in the seigneury, and that a pedlar named Gilmet was murdered there by a man named Marois in 1829, the novel still seems more fantastic than realistic, at least in part because coincidence plays such a major role in events. Scenic description is rare, and female characters exist only offstage. Nonetheless, however unrealistic the events, dialogue is written in the ordinary language of the people.

The novel was not particularly well received, a fact possibly related to Aubert de Gaspé's problems of the previous year. "Pierre André" (André-Romuald Cherrier) claimed in the pages of *Le Populaire* that alchemy and ava-

rice were not *canadien* traits, that the novelist had not preserved the traditional unities, and that popular legends and quotations in English had no part in a proper French novel. The author replied that he knew both alchemists and misers, that the story was true, that legends were part of the culture of his corner of the country, and that all literature was universal, regardless of language. Like most early Canadian literature, *L'Influence d'un livre* is the single work of a very young man. His stylistic models were the popular contemporary novels of England and France, but the actual story is uniquely *canadien*.

References:

David M. Hayne, "La Première edition de notre premier roman," *Bulletin des Recherches Historiques*, 59 (1953): 49-50;

Luc Lacourcière, "Aubert de Gaspé fils (1814-1841)," *Les cahiers des dix*, 40 (1975): 275-302;

Léopold Leblanc, Preface to *Le Chercheur de trésors* (Montreal: Réédition Québec, 1968), pp. i-vii.

Philippe-Joseph Aubert de Gaspé

(30 October 1786 - 29 January 1871)

Barbara Godard
York University

BOOKS: *Les Anciens Canadiens* (Quebec: Desbarats & Derbishire, 1863; revised edition, Quebec: Desbarats, 1864); translated by Georgiana M. Pennée as *The Canadians of Old* (Quebec: Desbarats, 1864); translated by Charles G. D. Roberts, also as *The Canadians of Old* (New York: Appleton, 1890; Toronto: Hart, 1891); Roberts's translation republished as *Cameron of Lochiel* (Boston: Page, 1905);

Mémoires (Ottawa: Desbarats, 1866); translated by Jane Brierley as *A Man of Sentiment: The Memoirs of Philippe-Joseph Aubert de Gaspé 1786-1871* (Montreal: Véhicule, 1988);

Divers (Montreal: Beauchemin, 1893).

Inverting the usual pattern of things, Philippe-Ignace-François Aubert de Gaspé *fils* was instrumental in starting his father's literary career, with their collaboration on *L'Influence d'un livre* (1837), the first novel written in French Canada. With its embedded narratives from the oral tradition and its historical aim, this novel also inaugurated the dominant mode of nineteenth-century Quebec fiction. These strains reached a high degree of finish and attained great popular success in one of the best-loved Quebec classics, *Les Anciens Canadiens* (1863), the work of Philippe-Joseph Aubert de Gaspé *père*.

Through both his parents–Pierre-Ignace-François and Catherine Tarien de Lanaudière Aubert de Gaspé–Philippe-Joseph belonged to the most illustrious aristocratic families in Canada. Conscious of this tradition, he became one of its most authoritative recorders in his historical fiction and memoirs. Born at the family manor of Saint-Jean-Port-Joli, he was sent to Quebec City at the age of seven for his education, boarding first with the Misses Cholet before commencing his classical studies at the seminary of Quebec in a class composed of such future notables as Louis-Joseph Papineau, leader of the 1837 revolt. In his final years he lived in a boarding school kept by an Anglican minister, where he per-

Philippe-Joseph Aubert de Gaspé (Archives Nationales du Québec)

fected his English. Afterward he studied law under the future chief justice Jonathan Sewell and Jean-Baptiste-Olivier Perreault, being called to the bar in 1811. In the same year he married Suzanne Allison, with whom he had thirteen children.

Aubert de Gaspé had every advantage at the beginning of his career–high birth, excellent education, advantageous connections, and financial sufficiency. He was active in all aspects of Quebec society: the Jockey Club, the Quebec Bank, the Quebec and District Militia, and the executive of the Literary Society. In 1812 he was ap-

Suzanne Allison, whom Aubert de Gaspé married in 1811
(Archives Nationales du Québec)

pointed deputy judge advocate of Lower Canada, becoming sheriff of the district of Quebec in 1816. This brilliant career plummeted in 1822, when, heavily in debt to the Crown, he was removed from office and forced into retirement at the family manor. Ultimately he was imprisoned for this debt from 1838 to 1841, the intervening years having been spent in anxiety and legal proceedings. Society's loss was literature's gain, for he spent his days reading and teaching his large family, as well as finding pleasure in the society of the habitants, lending an ear to their legends, tales, and songs, which were to pour forth from the storehouse of his prodigious memory in the books he wrote in the final years of his life. They were also evident in the section "Rose la Tulipe" that he wrote for inclusion in his son's novel.

(Philippe-Ignace-François was the second of Aubert de Gaspé's children.)

Aubert de Gaspé *père* was able to participate fully in the nationalist literary flowering of the "Ecole de 1860" and may indeed have been instrumental in resurrecting interest in his son's book with the subsequent appearance of his best-selling novel. In 1842 the deaths of his mother and aunt made Aubert de Gaspé *père* at last heir to the fortunes of two seigneuries, Port Joli and La Pocatière, effacing his financial disgrace and allowing him to return to the social life in Quebec, where he frequented the Club des Anciens, swapping yarns with such figures as the historian François-Xavier Garneau, whose work inspired this generation of writers. Here, too, he met old literary friends such as Octave Crémazie, who was to write a poem to be included in *Les Anciens Canadiens,* and J. C. Taché, who published its first chapter in *Les Soirées Canadiennes* (1862).

When Aubert de Gaspé took up his pen after many long years, he returned to the convoluted manner of his section of *L'Influence d'un livre,* this time mindful of the critics. He wrote a preface showing his own awareness of the unconventionalities of his narrative: "call it a novel, memoirs, a chronicle, a mish-mash, a hotch-potch; I care little!" His disclaimer to the contrary, *Les Anciens Canadiens* has more coherency than the earlier novel, its enveloping narrative being a historical episode drawn from his family's past. Set in Quebec and the manor of Haberville at the time of the conquest, the novel dramatizes the conflict between French and English and explores the social consequences of the French defeat. Aubert de Gaspé had read widely in the works of Sir Walter Scott, whom he quotes in this book, and although *Les Anciens Canadiens* is not up to the best of Scott in its manner, its maintaining of pace, and its illuminating of character, it certainly rivals Scott in the nature of its matter—the lore and legend of preconquest Quebec. As his mentor had done for the conquered Scots, Aubert de Gaspé was to do for the defeated *Canadiens,* to elevate and ennoble the common, eccentric people and events of his country's past. Moreover, his plotting, like Scott's, while centering on a crucial moment in the history of the nation—the conquest, in this case—outlines its evolution, based ultimately on compromise and sealed in that metaphor of marriage beloved to both Scott and Canadian politicians. (The joining of Quebec and English Canada is popularly referred to as a shotgun marriage.)

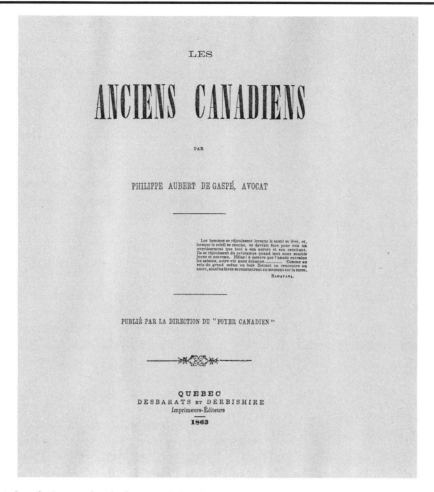

Title page for Aubert de Gaspé's first book, a novel that dramatizes the forced unification of Quebec and English Canada

The action is simple, involving the relationship of two college friends, one *Canadien*, the other Scots, as it is affected by the war. Jules d'Haberville in the spring of 1757 invites his friend Archibald Cameron of Lochiel (son of a Jacobite) to visit his father's manor at the conclusion of their studies with the Jesuits. In the company of an old servant, José Dubé, modeled on one of Aubert de Gaspé's own servants, the two cross to the south shore of the St. Lawrence during the spring ice breakup. The journey serves as a frame for a series of picaresque episodes, not least of which is Archie's rescue of a man stranded on an ice floe. The first part introduces several folktales and descriptions of folk customs associated with manor life. Part two, set during the war of 1759, depicts the climaxes of individual and collective dramas, when Jules and Archie find themselves enemies, forced to choose between the cries of their hearts and their military honor. Archie both destroys the Haberville

manor and saves his friend's life on the battlefield. The last part relates the difficulties of reconciliation and the trials of choosing a country. Aubert de Gaspé's conclusion outlines the broad sweep of the future, the merging of English and French within the country, when Jules marries an English girl (as Aubert de Gaspé's father had), while the spiritual independence of the generation of 1837 is suggested in the refusal of Blanche to accept Archie's hand in marriage.

Much of the delight for the reader lies in the verve with which Aubert de Gaspé relates the seigneurial customs. His familiarity with the habitants has made his record of their lives valuable for historians. Moreover, he has absorbed their narrative tradition. Like José he is a skilled raconteur, providing fresh embellishments of classic legends. Indeed, he is virtually unrivaled as a storyteller in this mode, which he introduced into Quebec literature, by far the most popular form in the nineteenth century. And the discontinuous narrative he inherited from the oral tradition expands infinitely to allow tale to follow tale with great ingenuity.

His skill is demonstrated in the many editions of this novel, which was an immediate success and has been almost continuously in print in French and in English translations—each modifying the emphases of the original—since it was published. In 1865 it was adapted for the stage. A generation of historical novelists adopted the period of the conquest and the Corneillian conflict between love and duty made popular by *Les Anciens Canadiens*. When historical fiction lost its vogue, Camille Roy gave the novel new life by placing it in the tradition of rural idylls, reading it as a eulogy to the simple but picturesque manners of country life. Luc Lacourcière values it for the personal recollections of the author, overflowing into footnotes in an essentially confessional novel. It seems permanently enthroned as a classic of Quebec literature.

In his next book, *Mémoires* (1866), Aubert de Gaspé abandoned fictional form and allowed his memory (which he judged outstanding) to range freely. In a steady stream of anecdotes he introduces more than one thousand people he has known or heard of, bathing them in his humor and charity, qualities making this book a fount of insight into human nature as well as an irreplaceable historical document. Mostly the author himself stands revealed—his unquenchable curiosity, his wit—in sum a brilliant if rambling conversationalist. Concentrating on the period of his youth before 1822, he introduces ancestors and the figures of Quebec society he knew. Of his wife and children we learn little. Only when speaking of the habitants does he move forward in time to the present. Here, too, he is describing a dying way of life. One of the best portraits of Canadian society, urban and rural, aristocratic and popular, this book is of perennial value and is also an exemplary Romantic autobiography.

Aubert de Gaspé's active old age came to an end in Quebec City in 1871, but his popularity lasted. A posthumous book, *Divers* (1893), includes four legends. More amply developed in their detail than such tales within the novels, they reveal the author's skill in the genre and his predilection for the story, the foundation of his longer works. "Femme de la tribu des Renards," "Le loup-jaune," and "La jeune Lorette," moreover, reveal his knowledge of Indian legends and customs. Like his other tales, these are unrivaled descriptions of popular traditions.

As a pioneer in a literary tradition and as a social historian, Aubert de Gaspé enjoys a secure position in Quebec literary history. But the enchantment of his storytelling has made him beloved as well.

References:

Henri-Raymond Casgrain, *De Gaspé et Garneau* (Montreal: Beauchemin, 1912);

Jacques Castonguay, *La Seigneurie de Philippe Aubert de Gaspé* (Montreal: Fides, 1977);

James Reaney, "Tales of the Great River: Aubert de Gaspé and John Richardson," *Proceedings and Transactions of the Royal Society of Canada*, fourth series, 17 (1979);

Pierre-Georges Roy, *A travers les* Mémoires *de Philippe Aubert de Gaspé* (Montreal: Ducharme, 1943);

Roy, *La Famille Aubert de Gaspé* (Levis, Que.: Mercier, 1907).

Napoléon Aubin
(9 November 1812 - 12 June 1890)

Mary Lu MacDonald

BOOKS: *Le Fantasque,* 8 volumes (Quebec, August 1837-May 1845, June 1848-February 1849);

La Chimie agricole mise à la portée de tout le monde (Quebec: Fréchette, 1847);

Cours de Chimie (Quebec, 1850).

SELECTED PERIODICAL PUBLICATIONS—
UNCOLLECTED: "La lucarne d'un vieux garçon," *La Minerve,* 11 June 1835, p. 1;

"Une Entrée dans le monde," *La Minerve,* 22 June 1835, pp. 1-2;

"Une Chanson—un songe—un baiser," *La Minerve,* 13 July 1835, pp. 1-2;

"Histoire qui n'a pas de nom ou plutôt mélanges," *La Minerve,* 6 August 1835, p. 1.

Influential though he was in the history of French-Canadian literature, Napoléon Aubin produced no literary books. His two books are chemistry texts related to his parallel career as an inventor and scientist. His literary bibliography consists of a few poems and short stories, most of the content of the satirical review *Le Fantasque,* and various articles published in the newspapers he edited. Although he never ran for public office his journalistic career made him influential in politics.

Although he married a French-Canadian Roman Catholic (Marie-Luce-Emilie Sauvageau) and raised his children in that faith, Aubin himself was a Swiss Protestant. Son of Pierre-Louis-Charles and Elizabeth Escuyer Aubin, he was born Aimé-Nicolas Aubin at Chêne-Bougeries in the suburbs of Geneva, and was baptized a Calvinist. The fact of his Swiss birth and upbringing was generally known, but his Protestantism was not common knowledge in Quebec. His Protestant funeral and burial came as a surprise to most of the community.

When Aubin was only sixteen he left Switzerland for the United States. A little over five years later he moved to Montreal and then to Quebec City. Four of the eight short stories as well as

Lithograph by Napoléon Aubin, based on a portrait by T. Hamel (C 92694, National Archives of Canada). The portrait was identified by the Archives Nationales du Québec as being a likeness of Aubin.

most of the poetry for which he is known appeared in the Montreal newspaper *La Minerve* between June and August of 1835. Three of the stories were later collected in volume 1 of *Le Répertoire national* in 1848.

In Quebec City he edited various short-lived newspapers and periodicals, all devoted to a liberal, democratic point of view, but he is best known as the editor, publisher, as well as writer of most of the content of *Le Fantasque,* which he published, with five breaks of several months each, from August 1837 to May 1845, and again from June 1848 to February 1849. The remainder of his known poems and stories appeared in this periodical. The principal objective of *Le Fantasque*, however, was not literature but political satire. There was a great deal of scope for a satirist in the Lower Canada of 1837-1848, and Aubin had the talent necessary to make full use of the opportunities offered by the twists and turns of both politics and individual behavior.

Aubin appears to have been a liberal reformer but not a revolutionary. He supported the *patriote* party, but did not support the armed rebellions of 1837 and 1838. Initially he welcomed John George Lambton, Lord Durham, the new governor-general, as a fellow liberal, but Durham did not measure up to Aubin's expectations and soon became the object of the editor's ridicule. Durham's successor, Charles Poulett Thomson, Lord Sydenham, found no favor with Aubin. Thomson's middle name being close to the French *poulet* (chicken) gave Aubin the opportunity to write some very witty lines at his expense. Charles Bagot and his ministry gained Aubin's approval, but Charles Metcalfe, his successor, was again the target of disapproving jibes. In each of these instances Aubin's stance was in accord with that of liberal French Canadians.

Aubin had never had much good to say about Louis-Joseph Papineau, perceiving him as a man who had led his supporters into dangerous folly and then saved his own skin. However, when *Le Fantasque* was revived for about nine months beginning in 1848, it was to support Papineau and his *rouge* colleagues who remained outside the reform mainstream that had come to power. Aubin continued to edit newspapers devoted to the *rouge* cause for several years.

As a printer and publisher Aubin was involved in two cases of official censorship in the postrebellion period. He and J.-G. Barthe were jailed for six weeks in 1839 for a poem of Barthe's, published by Aubin, "Aux exilés politiques canadiens." Questions of freedom of the press aside, the poem was intended, and perceived, as an incitement to further rebellion. In 1842 Aubin published Regis de Trobriand's novel *Le Rebelle*, a work in which all characters are portrayed as black or white, depending on whether they opposed or supported the *patriotes*. A Montreal bookseller was charged and briefly jailed

for uttering a seditious libel in selling the book. Aubin rejoiced publicly that the affair had served only to increase sales.

Although Aubin's personal involvement in politics was limited to lending the support of his pen to individuals and groups of whom he approved, he was nonetheless recognized as a potent force in the political life of the colony. Similarly, he encouraged the young literary gentlemen of Quebec City. Many biographies and autobiographies from this period mention Aubin as the center of a literary circle in that community. He found time before 1850 to teach chemistry in the Quebec School of Medicine and to write and publish his two chemistry textbooks. As the inventor of a machine for pressing bricks, he was a partner in a brick factory located on the Isle d'Orléans.

Between 1853 and 1863 Aubin lived in the United States, but he returned to Quebec City briefly, finally settling in Montreal in 1866. While in the States he patented a gaslighting process that was widely used. For most of the decade after his return to Canada he was associated as editor and journalist with several newspapers. In 1875 he was appointed gas inspector for the city of Montreal.

Aubin is remembered today more for his scientific and journalistic contributions to Quebec society than for his actual literary production. Philosophically he remained a Swiss democrat throughout his life. His veneration for Napoléon Bonaparte is evidenced by the name he chose for himself, by some of his poetry, and by his involvement in La Société des Français en Canada, which held its annual dinner on the feast of Saint-Napoléon. Although his imaginative prose does not have a specific Quebec setting and his poetry deals with those aspects of human life that transcend national borders, his literary works are nevertheless of very high quality. His often brilliant political satire, specifically rooted in Quebec society, unfortunately requires a specialist's knowledge of early-nineteenth-century Quebec history in order to be fully appreciated.

Reference:

Jean-Paul Tremblay, *A la recherche de Napoléon Aubin* (Quebec: Presses de l'Université Laval, 1969).

Jacob Bailey

(16 April 1731 - 25 July 1808)

Thomas B. Vincent
Royal Military College of Canada

BOOK: *The Frontier Missionary,* edited by W. S. Bartlett (Boston: Ide & Dutton, 1853).

SELECTED PERIODICAL PUBLICATIONS–
UNCOLLECTED: "Observations and Conjectures on the Antiquities of America," *Massachusetts Historical Society: Collections,* first series 4 (1795): 100-105;
"Letter from Rev. Jacob Bailey in 1775, Describing the Destruction of Falmouth, Me.," *Collections of the Maine Historical Society,* first series 5 (1857): 437-450.

Jacob Bailey was one of the most prolific writers in late-eighteenth-century North America and perhaps the finest practitioner of Hudibrastic verse satire after Samuel Butler himself. However, he published few of his works (a collection was published posthumously). He was content to circulate them in manuscript form among close friends. Today his papers represent perhaps the largest and most significant collection of eighteenth-century Canadian literary writings.

Bailey, the son of David and Mary Hodgkins Bailey, was born in Rowley, Massachusetts, to a poor family but received a good education, which prepared him to enter university; he received an A.B. from Harvard in 1755 and an M.A. there in 1758. After graduating he taught school for a while and served briefly as a congregationalist minister. However, he soon converted to the Church of England and in 1760 was ordained a priest in London, England. He was appointed by the Society for the Propagation of the Gospel to its mission parish at Pawnalborough (now West Dresden), Maine. In August 1761 Bailey married Sally Weeks, and he worked hard to build up his parish, but it was a predominantly congregationalist community that resented the presence of the tax-supported Church of England. As the country moved toward civil war after 1774, much of the resentment of the community was focused on Bailey, who openly supported the Crown. After considerable persecu-

Engraving of Jacob Bailey's silhouette used as the frontispiece for The Frontier Missionary, *edited by W. S. Bartlett, in 1853 (C 16337, National Archives of Canada)*

tion he and his family were permitted to flee to Nova Scotia in 1779.

Bailey dabbled in poetry during his college years and while working as a young teacher. His early verse was mostly of a lyrical nature, often pastoral in its imagery, reflecting a refined literary taste. But as he became involved in building his parish, Bailey turned more to prose. He composed many sermons, but his two most ambitious projects were a prose description of Maine and a novel. In his description, he developed as compre-

18

hensive a picture as possible of the geography, ecology, society, and history of the area, under what amounts to subject headings. He wrote as an essayist, a knowledgeable generalist presenting a composite view of his subject. His unpublished novel "The Flower of the Wilderness" is a mixture of narrative, letter, and dialogue, centered on the journeys of the protagonist Thomas Watkins in New England and the romantic concerns of Miss Ann Rosedale, with frequent digressions into moral and philosophical subjects. It was left incomplete and is something of a shambles; nevertheless, it is of some interest as an early effort in the history of the American novel.

In the late 1770s Bailey's antirebel views were reflected in some rather sentimental verse deploring the injustices and atrocities of civil war, the best known of which was his valedictory "Farewell to Kennebec" (written in 1779). His forte, however, lay in verse satire, a form he turned to with a vengeance upon arriving in Nova Scotia. Between 1779 and 1784 he vigorously and savagely attacked the American rebels and their aims in such satires as "The Character of a Trimmer" and "America." In these poems and in shorter pieces he used Hudibrastic verse satire as a trenchant and incisive instrument for clarifying and articulating the fears, frustrations, and moral indignation aroused in him by the American rebellion. In addition he worked on an epistolary novel entitled "Serena," which dealt with the kidnapping of a Loyalist girl from Nova Scotia by rebel privateers. The novel remains incomplete, as does the satire "America" (over forty-one hundred lines long); in the wake of the Peace of 1784, such subjects were no longer relevant politically or artistically.

After the rebellion Bailey (like other Loyalists) turned his attention to local concerns, particularly those dealing with the building of a stable and prosperous society. In his "Description of various journeys through Nova Scotia," he surveys the geography, economy, and people of Nova Scotia. But his most ambitious work (over ninety-two hundred lines) is his satiric poem "The Adventures of Jack Ramble, the Methodist Preacher." In it, he attacked itinerant preachers whose evangelical religious beliefs and activities (he believed) promoted irrationality and immorality among the common people and inculcated a disrespect for order, all of which led inevitably to social and political upheaval. The intensity of his attack reflects a deeply felt commitment to the creation of a stable and orderly society in Nova Scotia.

It is difficult to estimate Bailey's importance and influence in his own day because little is known about the extent of his readership. There is no doubt, however, that his views reflected those of a significant element of the population and that his papers now represent one of the most important collections of late-eighteenth-century literary activity in Canada. He is a central figure in the earliest period of our literature.

References:

Ray Palmer Baker, "The Poetry of Jacob Bailey, Loyalist," *New England Quarterly,* 2 (1929): 58-92;

Thomas B. Vincent, "Alline and Bailey," *Canadian Literature,* 68-69 (1976): 124-133;

Vincent, "Keeping the Faith: The Poetic Development of Jacob Bailey," *Early American Literature,* 14 (1979): 3-14.

Papers:

The Jacob Bailey Papers, Public Archives of Nova Scotia, include major poems, such as "Farewell to Kennebec," "Character of a Trimmer," "America," and "The Adventures of Jack Ramble, the Methodist Preacher"; works of fiction, including "The Flower of the Wilderness, or the History of Miss Ann Rosedale" and "Serena"; and prose pieces such as "A Description and Natural History of the new entered Province between New Hampshire and Nova Scotia" and "Descriptions of various journeys through Nova Scotia."

Honoré Beaugrand

(24 March 1848 - 7 October 1906)

John Stockdale
Laval University

BOOKS: *Jeanne la fileuse: Episode de l'emigration Franco-Canadienne aux Etats Unis* (Fall River, Mass.: 1878; Montreal: La Patrie, 1888);
De Montréal à Victoria par le transcontinental Canadien (Montreal, 1887);
Mélanges (Montreal: La Patrie, 1888);
Lettres de voyage: France–Italie–Sicilie–Malte–Tunisie–Algérie–Espagne (Montreal: La Patrie, 1889);
Six mois dans les Montagnes Rocheuses: Colorado–Utah–Nouveau-Mexique (Montreal: Granger, 1890);
La Chasse-Galerie: Légendes Canadiennes, published with *La Chasse-Galerie, and Other Canadian Stories* (Montreal: Pelletier, 1900);
New Studies of Canadian Folklore (Montreal: Renouf, 1904).

OTHER: *Le Vieux Montreal,* edited by Beaugrand (Montreal, 1884).

Honoré Beaugrand (PA 29018, National Archives of Canada)

Honoré Beaugrand was a genuine man of letters, and his volcanic energy, practical skills as a journalist, cosmopolitan views, and talents as a writer in French and in English brought him recognition and made him a figure to emulate in the great bilingual experiment that was early Canada. He was also a successful municipal politician.

Born in Lanoraie, Quebec, on 24 March 1848, Honoré Beaugrand was educated at the Seminaire de Joliette, run by the Clercs de Saint-Viateur. At fifteen he began his religious training, but left without taking his first vows to become a sailor on the St. Lawrence River. He next completed a brief officers' training course in Montreal and, upon graduation in August 1865, enlisted in the French army and went to Mexico as part of Napoleon III's expeditionary force in aid of Emperor Maximilian. At eighteen Beaugrand had been wounded, captured, promoted, and decorated, and had learned to smoke, drink, curse, and chase girls like many of the other soldiers.

He accompanied his regiment back to France, and from 1867 to 1869 he seems to have wandered through Europe supporting himself as a typesetter, a photographer, and perhaps a journalist. Beaugrand absorbed the main currents of thought in France during that period and became a liberal, anticleric freethinker.

He surfaced in New Orleans in 1869, first as a laborer and then as an employee of the French-language newspaper *L'Abeille,* where he was valued for his facility in French, English, and Spanish. After a short time he returned to Mex-

Henri Julien's illustration of a magic flying canoe from the 1900 edition of Beaugrand's La Chasse-Galerie:
Légendes Canadiennes

ico as an accountant and translator for a railway company. From there he found his way to Fall River, Massachusetts, where many French Canadians worked in the textile mills. He was first a housepainter and a fiddler and then a sign painter. Beaugrand married a Protestant girl, Eliza Walker, on 5 October 1873 and then became a member of the Masonic Lodge and alienated himself from the Roman Catholic community.

In 1873 he and Dr. Alfred Mingnault founded the first French-language newspaper in Fall River, a weekly called *L'Echo du Canada,* dedicated to the protection of their compatriots, and for a time Beaugrand kept his true sentiments in check. In 1874, at a celebration of the Feast of St. John the Baptist in Montreal, he publicly suggested that Ottawa and Quebec set up a fund for the repatriation of French Canadians working in the United States. In Fall River, the same year, he was appointed justice of the peace for Bristol County and began to support the idea of an independent Quebec for the preservation of the French language and race. In the following three

years he moved to St. Louis, to Boston, back to Fall River, back to St. Louis, and again to Fall River, always working in the newspaper trade. In 1879 he ended his self-imposed exile by returning to Montreal to found and edit *La Patrie,* a liberal-reformist publication.

In addition to his duties as an editor and a journalist, Beaugrand began to publish books and to take part in municipal politics. He was elected mayor of Montreal in 1885 and again in 1886, and although the conservative Catholic element opposed him, he energetically attacked problems of public hygiene, fire protection, water purification, public parks, sidewalks, and lighting, and organized the first great Montreal Carnival. He also organized the successful containment of a flood and led a campaign for compulsory vaccination against smallpox during a severe epidemic that killed some three thousand in the city. During the epidemic his office was stoned by an angry mob shouting "No compulsory vaccination!," but he continued his campaign. He was such a successful mayor that when the modern city of Montreal was building its subway, it remembered him by naming one of its subway stations "Honoré Beaugrand."

Beaugrand remained editor of *La Patrie* until 1897 and also founded the *Daily News,* though he edited it only briefly. Besides a flood of journalism, Beaugrand produced several stories and poems in English and published in the *Canadian Magazine of Politics, Science, Art and Literature* (Toronto), the *Forum* (New York), and the *Century Illustrated Magazine* (New York). He also edited an archeological work, *Le Vieux Montréal* (1884), and gave many public speeches. He traveled in Europe and in 1892 visited Japan and China. He was also active in several literary and scientific organizations. Beaugrand retired in 1897 at the age of forty-nine because of ill health and died in 1906. A rebellious anticleric to the last, he ordered in his will that his remains be cremated, and when his Protestant wife tried to have them buried in a Catholic cemetery, she was turned away and was forced to bury them in the Mount Royal Protestant Cemetery.

Jeanne la fileuse (1878) is the only one of Beaugrand's published books that could be called a novel, and even the author himself said it was less a novel than it was a pamphlet, which attempts to explain the economic forces that drove so many French Canadians across the border into the United States to seek employment. At another point in the book he wonders why more of his compatriots had not followed, even though the exodus significantly depopulated Quebec. The plot suffers from the intrusion of so much commentary, but the book was widely read. His last book, *New Studies of Canadian Folklore* (1904), with a foreword by W. D. Lighthall, contains two legends, "Macloun" and "A Legend of the North Pacific," plus two scholarly articles, "The Goblin Lore of French Canada" and "Indian Picture and Symbol Writing." In his collecting and rewriting of French-Canadian legends, Beaugrand was part of a move to preserve the art of the rural storytellers before urban sophistication destroyed its last remnants.

Biographies:

Lucie Lafrance, *Bio-bibliographie de M. Honoré Beaugrand, 1849-1906* (Montreal: Ecole de Bibliothécaires, 1948);

Pierre Bance, "Beaugrand et son temps," Ph.D. dissertation, University of Ottawa, 1964.

Elisabeth Bégon
(27 July 1696 - 1 November 1755)

Eva-Marie Kröller
University of British Columbia

BOOK: *Lettres au cher fils: Correspondance d'Elisabeth Bégon avec son gendre (1748-1753)*, edited by Nicole Deschamps (Montreal: HMH, 1972).

OTHER: "La Correspondance de Madame Bégon 1748-1753," edited, with a translation into modern French, by Claude de Bonnault, *Rapport de l'Archiviste de la Province de Quebec* (1934-1935): 1-277.

A lively and perceptive letter writer, Elisabeth Bégon, as a member of the Montreal elite under the French regime, furnishes the contemporary reader with an eyewitness account of the mundane problems of eighteenth-century colonial life. As her correspondence–addressed to her son-in-law, Honoré-Michel de Villebois de la Rouvilliére–moreover reveals a private passion barely masked as maternal affection, she is also a psychologically intriguing figure appealing to the modern interest in journals and autobiographies, and a prefiguration of the *mater dolorosa* dominating the fictions of Gabrielle Roy, Marie-Claire Blais, and other writers from Quebec.

Born in Montreal in 1696, Marie-Elisabeth Rocbert de la Morandière married in 1718 the sub-lieutenant Claude-Michel Bégon–a man whose various adventures at sea had left him with one eye gone and his fingers mutilated–against the wishes of his brother, Quebec's intendant Michel Bégon, who considered their liaison socially unacceptable. After thirty years of marriage, during which the Bégons, installed in several high-ranking posts, became famous for their lavish hospitality, Madame Bégon was widowed in 1748, moving into her family home on Rue Saint-Paul in Montreal. Here she devoted herself to the education of her granddaughter, Marie-Cathérine de Villebois, whose mother had died young, and wrote daily reports of progress to the girl's father, then stationed as financial commissary in Louisiana. Besides chronicling details of her granddaughter's acquisition of the social graces

deemed necessary in her class, Bégon–exceptionally well informed because of her intimate acquaintance with such officials as Roland-Michel-Barrin de La Galissonière, acting governor-general of the colony (whom she plied with "vin de la Champagne")–also passed on news and gossip about New France's leading families. She paid equal attention to La Galissonière's glamorous sleigh-ride parties, balls, and dinners (the extravagance of which was later said to have contributed to the downfall of the colony) and to the often merciless realities of life in a harsh climate: even for the affluent, firewood was prohibitively expensive, food supplies limited, and illnesses such as pneumonia often deadly. Occasionally, questions of limited resources, the difficulty of survival, and etiquette have a pathetic encounter in her descriptions, as when she depicts a little girl's funeral as having been enacted with unduly limited pomp.

Although many individuals sought to benefit from her connections and influence, Bégon generally refrained from political commentary apart from brief references to exchanges of prisoners among the English, French, and various Indian tribes. A devout Roman Catholic who attended Mass even on the coldest of winter days, she still felt that the church's interference with citizens' lives was sometimes unduly repressive, criticizing for instance the clergy's decision to withhold absolution from party-goers. Her independence of mind had earlier been signaled when, lacking the intendant's approval, she had married her husband *à la gaumine*, a pseudo-marriage later regularized, and when she participated in a charivari, a practice the church condemned.

Although born a Canadian, Bégon longed to "return" to her mother country, France, a dream she fulfilled in 1749, when, having sold her house to the intendant François Bigot, she moved to Rochefort, where, much to her disappointment, she found herself ridiculed by her husband's family as "une Iroquoise," a disillusioning

Elisabeth Bégon (painting by Henri Beau; C 10599, National Archives of Canada)

experience prefiguring that of many later French-Canadian visitors to France. Her life, active despite her widowhood in Montreal, became very quiet and withdrawn in France, and she soon began to draw comparisons between her former and present existence to the disadvantage of the latter. Her letters, brief and sketchy while written in Canada, now became long and discursive, expressive of the isolation she must have felt.

Bégon's only true solace after her husband's death appears to have been her love for her son-in-law (an obese, unattractive man almost her own age), whom she advised equally anxiously on his health and his career. From the first editor of her papers, Claude de Bonnault, onward, all historians dealing with the Bégon papers have agreed that Bégon's concern was that of an amorous woman rather than of a mother-in-law; variously addressing him as "cher fils," "mon ange bouffi," and "mon gros cochon," she assured de Villebois of her undying love, longed for the days when only a wall separated them, and eagerly antici-

pated their reunion. The poignancy of her passion derives from its hopelessness: de Villebois failed to join her in France as she had planned. Their relationship became strained when, embroiled in career difficulties, he responded with bad-tempered, almost paranoid letters to the epistles Bégon assiduously sent with almost every vessel leaving France for the colonies. De Villebois died in New Orleans in 1752, and Bégon died three years later. They had never seen each other again.

In keeping with a general effort in recent Québecois literature to revitalize older documents, contemporary critics of Bégon's letters have perceived her as a French-Canadian Iocasta, a mythological character who, although limited in her self-expression by the exigencies of her historical existence, combines important elements of Québecois womanhood.

References:

Marie-Aimeé Cliche, "Correspondence de Madame Bégon, 1748-1753," in *Dictionnaire des* oeuvres littéraires du Québec, volume 1, edited by Maurice Lemire (Montreal: Fides, 1978), pp. 156-158;

Nicole Deschamps, Preface to Lettres au cher fils (Montreal: HMH, 1972), pp. 13-27;

Isabel Landels, "La Correspondance de Madame Bégon," Ph.D. dissertation, Laval University, 1947.

Michel Bibaud
(19 January 1782 - 3 August 1857)

Mary Lu MacDonald

BOOKS: *L'Arithmétique en quatre parties* (Montreal: Printed for the author by N. Mower, 1816);

Epîtres, satires, chansons, épigrammes, et autres pièces de vers (Montreal: L. Duvernay, 1830);

L'Arithmétique a l'usage des écoles élémentaires (Montreal: Workman & Bowman, 1832);

Histoire du Canada, sous la domination française (Montreal: J. Jones, 1837);

Histoire du Canada, et des Canadiens, sous la domination anglaise (Montreal: Lovell & Gibson, 1844).

OTHER: Gabriel Franchère, *Relation d'un voyage à la côte du nord-ouest de l'Amérique septentrionale*, edited by Bibaud (Montreal: C. B. Pasteur, 1820);

La Bibliothèque Canadienne, 9 volumes, edited by Bibaud (Montreal: J. Lane, 1825-1830);

L'Observateur, edited by Bibaud (Montreal: L. Duvernay, 1831-1832);

Le Magasin du Bas-Canada, edited by Bibaud (Montreal: L. Duvernay, 1832);

L'Encyclopédie Canadienne, edited by Bibaud (Montreal: J. Lovell, 1842-1843).

Michel Bibaud (C 81497, National Archives of Canada)

As historian, journalist, poet, and editor, Michel Bibaud was almost a one-man literary scene in Montreal between 1815 and 1844. He was the son of a farmer, Michel-Ange Bibaud and his wife, Cécile-Clémence Fresne Bibaud. He did not enter classical college until he was almost nineteen–the age at which most of his fellow students were graduating. After college he immedi- ately started to earn his living as a teacher, unlike the sons of more prosperous families who continued their studies in one of the liberal professions. In 1813, still working as a tutor, as well as a free-lance translator, he added journalism to his list of activities. Three years later he published an arithmetic textbook, and the following year started *L'Aurore*, his own newspaper. *L'Aurore* lasted from 1817 to 1819 when it was finally sold to Charles-Bernard Pasteur, the proprietor of *Le Spectateur Canadien*. Part of the agreement was that Bibaud, although he was free to work for others, would not start any other publication of his own before 1825. He served as editor of *Le Spectateur Canadien* from September 1819 to July 1827.

June 1825 saw the first number of the first of Bibaud's literary and scientific periodicals, *La Bibliothèque Canadienne* (1825-1830), in many ways the most successful of them all. It was followed by *L'Observateur* (1831-1832), *Le Magasin du Bas-Canada* (1832), and *L'Encyclopédie Canadienne* (1842-1843). All of the periodicals were dedicated to the scientific and cultural advancement of his fellow citizens. Each prospectus in turn spoke of the need for education in science, arts, and letters, and of the lack of French-Canadian periodicals to publish what local works had been produced. As editor Bibaud pushed and prodded his people toward greater intellectual endeavors, at the same time publishing many locally written contributions—most notably, in *La Bibliothèque Canadienne*, installments of Jacques Viger's "Ma Saberdache." Although Bibaud declared himself anxious to please as well as instruct his readers, all the periodicals are strongly oriented toward the transmission of serious, educational information.

In 1830 *Epîtres, satires, chansons, épigrammes, et autres pièces de vers*, a collection of Bibaud's poems printed in newspapers and periodicals in the previous fifteen years, became the first collection of poetry by a French Canadian to be published in Canada. Despite this distinction, it received little attention at the time. A year later a disparaging review by Isidore Lebrun, a French critic, sparked a controversy in the pages of *La Minerve*, with Bibaud defending himself vigorously against several opponents. Until late in 1830 Bibaud had been on good terms with Ludger Duvernay and the reformers of *La Minerve*. A quarrel with Duvernay and the bad reviews of the book took place at the same time. The long poems in the collection are in the style of Nicolas Boileau-Despréaux and Horace. The four satires condemn French-Canadian society

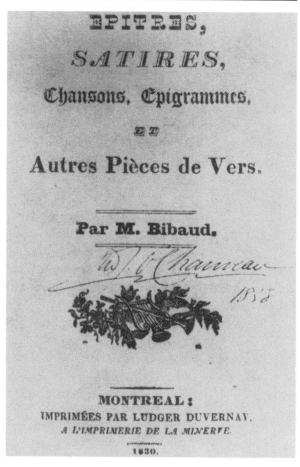

Title page for Bibaud's 1830 collection, the first anthology of poetry by a French Canadian to be published in Canada

for its avarice, envy, laziness, and hostility to education. Most of the shorter poems also deal with aspects of French-Canadian life. The outdated form and pedantic content of most of the poems ensured that they would not be enthusiastically received in their own day or in the years to follow.

Bibaud also wrote two volumes of history—*Histoire du Canada, sous la domination française* (1837) and *Histoire du Canada, et des Canadiens, sous la domination anglaise* (1844). These represent the first attempts by a French Canadian to put together a history of his people. The titles are revealing. At the center is Canada; the two controlling powers are external. Both of Bibaud's volumes concentrate on political history, generally recounted through the activities of individuals. The first volume is critical of French policy and French governors. The second is much less critical of English policy and English governors, but very critical of the *patriotes*. Such an attitude was not a popular one then or now, so Bibaud's second volume, and by reflection the first as well, has been severely criticized from its first date of publication. The conservative *Les Mélanges Religieux*, owned by Roman Catholic clergy, also found it anticlerical. The charge was withdrawn when Bibaud threatened action for libel. Critics in reform newspapers accused him of a lack of both patriotism and impartiality.

In 1837 Bibaud was appointed a justice of the peace, and in 1838 he became clerk of the Hay Market and inspector of weights and measures. In 1843 the city of Montreal took over administration of the market and reduced his salary by two-thirds. Bibaud resigned. His application for a pension, on the grounds that he had been deprived of a job granted to him by royal commission, was denied by the city councillors because he had resigned of his own accord. The councillors who supported him were solidly French; the majority that denied his application was entirely English. In 1844 he became translator for the Geological Survey of Canada, a post he held until suffering a stroke in 1856.

Although his nationalism did not take the same political form as that of the *patriotes* and their followers, Bibaud had as proud a sense of national identity as any man of his day. His political position, however, affected his literary reputation both in his own day and in our own. He was certainly not a great writer, but he was considerably better than his present reputation would indicate.

No better poet or historian had emerged in French Canada before his works were published. His history was soon eclipsed by François-Xavier Garneau's work and by the works of those who wrote to prove that Garneau was wrong about many things. It would be many years before another poet published a volume of his own poetry in Quebec. It is probably with *La Bibliothèque Canadienne* that Bibaud made his greatest contribution to French-Canadian culture. Periodical editors were very important in the development of early Canadian literature–providing a medium for publication and circulation of their compatriots' work. *La Bibliothèque Canadienne* was the first French-Canadian periodical to be mostly written in Canada, and it played a role in encouraging the development of French-Canadian literature.

References:

Bernardine Bujila, "Michel Bibaud's Encyclopédie Canadienne," *Culture*, 21, no. 2 (1960): 117-132;

Jeanne d'Arc Lortie, "Les Origines de la poésie au Canada français," in *Archives des lettres canadiennes*, volume 4 (Montreal: Fides, 1969), pp. 11-49;

Vincent Schonberger, "Le Journalisme littéraire de Michel Bibaud," *Revue de l'Université d'Ottawa*, 47, no. 4 (1977): 488-505;

Claude Tousignant, "Michel Bibaud: sa vie, son oeuvre et son combat politique," *Recherches Sociographiques*, 15 (1974): 21-30.

Margaret Agnew Blennerhassett

(1773? - 20 June 1842)

Mary Lu MacDonald

BOOK: *The Widow of the Rock, and Other Poems* (Montreal: E. V. Sparhawk, 1824).

Most of the details of Margaret Agnew Blennerhassett's life remain obscure. What is known of her is derived from information about the males in her life: that she was a "daughter of the Lieutenant Governor of the Isles of Man, and grand-daughter of General Agnew, killed in the battle of Germantown, a young lady of high family connexion, great beauty and accomplishments" (*Montreal Gazette*, 28 January 1841). She married Harman Blennerhassett sometime between 1796 and 1800 and either went with him to the United States or joined him there (accounts vary). Much has been written about her husband and his seemingly naive involvement in the "Aaron Burr affair" in 1806, as a result of which he lost his home and possessions, his estate on an island in the Ohio River, and a large portion of his considerable fortune. After living for some years on a plantation he then purchased in Mississippi, the Blennerhassetts, apparently almost bankrupt, moved to Montreal. Harman Blennerhassett was admitted to the Lower Canada bar in 1819. In 1822 he left Montreal for London expecting to be appointed a judge in Lower Canada, but his sponsor, Charles Lennox, Duke of Richmond and governor-general of Canada had died in 1819, so Blennerhassett was unsuccessful. However, a spinster sister settled her share of the family fortune on him, so he remained in England and sent for his family.

Margaret Blennerhassett's book was published in Montreal in the spring of 1824, so she was most likely still living in the city then. It seems that she may have been one of the genteel early female writers whose books were published as a means of alleviating their economic distress. Although the book was published anonymously, according to the practice of the time, it was generally referred to in the Montreal press as "Mrs. Blennerhassett's poems," and the author was treated with considerable personal and literary respect.

Margaret Blennerhassett (by permission of the Missouri Historical Society)

The date she left Montreal has not been recorded. Her husband died on the island of Guernsey in 1831, and she was reported as living there in 1837. In 1842 she went to the United States to seek compensation from Congress for the family's earlier losses in that country. After she died in New York in June, she was reported (in the *Toronto Examiner*, 6 July 1842) as having been "in the 70th year of her age," which would make the Library of Congress catalogue entry of 1777 for her birth date incorrect.

Blennerhassett's one book of poetry falls into three parts. The last three poems are "by an

Engraving of the Blennerhassett Mansion on Backus's Island in the Ohio River, near Parkersburg. The family lived there from 1800 to 1806; it was destroyed by fire in 1811.

American gentleman," and of little interest. The initial section uses a variety of verse forms to express fairly standard sentiments. The lines are all end-stopped, and the basic thought is frequently obscured by the necessity of producing rhyme. There are occasional flashes of wit, as in the mock-heroic poem "To a Beloved Object" (her stove), and a certain asperity when dealing with the subject of human love. Toward the end of her section of the book two poems, "The Desert Isle" and "The Jackal President"–the latter with a lengthy prose introduction–are completely different from the preceding ones. In these she gives free rein to her anger at the events and people responsible for her destitution almost twenty years earlier. In "The Desert Isle" her feeling for the beauty of the island comes through as strongly as does her shock at finding a "plunder-greedy," "infuriate populace" in control of her home. She sees the ideals of Washingtonian democracy set aside by anarchy and violence and in the final couplet asks "spare me from that phantom of *equality,* That *equals* men in knavery and brutality!"

"How the Song Was Made," a prose dialogue between Sambo and Jonathan, mockingly imitating a black drawl in the first case and a northern twang in the second, leads into the song "The Jackal President to the tune of 'Possum up dee Gum-tree,' " which satirizes President James Madison. The satire is directed at Jonathan and Sambo– both North and South–as well as at the president. The language is vicious and the indignation evident, but most of the references are obscure today.

Because of its early date and the author's romantic history, Margaret Blennerhassett's one book has perhaps received more notice than it should in the history of Canadian literature. She lived only briefly in Canada, and the subjects that brought forth the greatest evidence of her talent as a poet were ones concerning the United States. She remains in the public eye for reasons that are essentially nonliterary. Although *The Widow of the Rock* is briefly mentioned as a "first" in many surveys of Canadian literary history, there have been no critical studies devoted to this book.

Georges Boucher de Boucherville

(21 October 1814 - 6 September 1894)

Mary Lu MacDonald

BOOK: *Une de perdue, deux de trouvées*, 2 volumes
(Montreal: E. Senécal, 1874; modern edition, Montreal: HMH, 1973).

SELECTED PERIODICAL PUBLICATIONS–
UNCOLLECTED: "La Tour de Trafalgar," *L'Ami
du Peuple*, 3 (2 May 1835): 1;
"Louise Chawinikisique," *L'Ami du Peuple*, 4 (23
and 26 September 1835);
Une de perdue, deux de trouvées [early, incomplete
version], anonymous, *L'Album Littéraire et
Musical de la Minerve* (January 1849-June
1851);
*Nicolas Perrot ou les Coureurs de bois sous la domina-
tion française*, anonymous, *Revue de Québec*,
10 October 1889.

Remembered today as the author of one of
the earliest French-Canadian novels, Georges Boucher de Boucherville (whose full first name was
Pierre-Georges-Prévost) was the son of Pierre-
Amable Boucher de Boucherville, Seigneur of
Boucherville and member of the Executive Council of Lower Canada, and his wife, née Marguerite-
Emilie Sabrevois de Bleury. Thus, on both sides
of his family, the writer was related to two of the
most prominent and powerful families in Quebec. Georges was educated at the Montreal Seminary and admitted to the bar in January 1837.

In 1835, while still a law student, he published two short stories, "La Tour de Trafalgar"
and "Louise Chawinikisique," in *L'Ami du Peuple*.
The latter work was accorded first prize in a competition for Canadian writers sponsored by that
newspaper. The stories differ markedly from
each other. "La Tour de Trafalgar" is a tale of
ghosts, murder, and vengeance, all taking place
in a specific setting on the slopes of Mount Royal
in Montreal. "Louise Chawinikisique," in which
all but one of the protagonists are Indians, was intended as a story of love and piety triumphant.
In its resolution the heroine, a Christian convert,
and the warrior she loves are finally united in religion, marriage, and death–in that order. *L'Ami*

*Georges Boucher de Boucherville (pencil-and-charcoal draw-
ing by Jean-Joseph Girouard; C 18461, National Archives
of Canada)*

du Peuple was owned by the Sulpician order. The
subject was sure to please the contest judges.

Boucherville was involved, as were so many
other writers of his generation, in the rebellion
of 1837. As secretary of Les Fils de la Liberté, a
paramilitary organization supporting the *patriote*
cause, he was arrested in mid November 1837
and was thus in jail when the insurrection actually took place, so he was able to be associated
with the rebellion without actually having fought
in it. Released in July 1838 through the intervention of his father, he was sent off in November

to visit a distant relative in New Orleans. There he remained until it was safe for him to return to Canada in 1841. In 1847 he married Louise Gregory, daughter of a Poughkeepsie, New York, doctor. After the fashion of the time where mixed-religion marriages were concerned, the couple was married by both Protestant and Roman Catholic rites. In *La Minerve* in the same year, using the pseudonym José, he published a series of articles on economics entitled "Les sophismes de M. Bastiat."

In addition to saving him from the difficulties that participation in the 1838 rebellion would have caused, Boucherville's stay in New Orleans provided him with the raw material for his novel *Une de perdue, deux de trouvées* (One Lost, Two Found, 1874), the first thirty-three chapters of which were published in installments between January 1849 and June 1851 in *L'Album Littéraire*. The plot, much too complex for any brief summary, concerns the supposedly orphaned Pierre de St-Luc's discovery of the identity of his parents and sisters, his acquisition of the fortune left by his father, and his courtship and marriage. In the tradition of the serial publishing genre, the novel is punctuated by abductions and rescues, mistaken identities, and evil men thwarted in their villainy by the hero and his friends at the last possible moment.

The novel is clearly divided into two parts. In the first the action takes place principally in the area around New Orleans. In the second the action takes place in Quebec at the time of the 1837 rebellion. The latter part, which did not appear in *L'Album Littéraire*, was not published until 1864 (in *La Revue Canadienne*). It is generally considered to have been written later than the first. This section is better known for its account of the rebellion and its causes, and for Boucherville's own apologia, than it is for its literary qualities. In it the Quebecois are portrayed as peacefully seeking the redress of just grievances and taking up arms only to defend themselves from attack. The author's alter ego, the hero, is portrayed as a neutral outsider on good terms with both sides in the conflict.

Despite stereotyped characterization, *Une de perdue* is an interesting novel: there is so much action taking place that it is impossible for the reader not to be carried along. Some critics have referred to it as the first French-Canadian *roman policier*, but, although many of the literary devices are similar, it is hardly that. As with the novels Charles Dickens published in installments, the plot is constructed so as to keep the reader's interest at a high enough pitch to ensure the purchase of a magazine each month.

After his return to Canada in 1841 Boucherville had practiced law. In 1867 he entered public service, first as secretary to the lieutenant-governor of Quebec, and subsequently as clerk of the Legislative Council, a post he held until his retirement in 1890. The critic Maurice Lemire has written that in 1889 a second novel by Boucherville, *Nicolas Perrot ou les Coureurs de bois sous la domination française* was published anonymously in installments in *La Revue de Québec*. It appears that only one installment has survived.

Boucherville's personal and literary career is typical of many others of the time. Writers were amateurs who did not make their living by the pen. In French Canada they were generally well-educated males, who did their writing when they were young before settling into careers in one of the professions. Many of them, like Boucherville, showed promise of a talent that remained undeveloped. The principal reason for reading their works today is for the insight they give us into the *mentalité* of nineteenth-century Canada. Georges de Boucherville's two stories and his novel are fine examples of the literary manners of his day.

Reference:

Réginald Hamel, ed., Introduction to *Une de perdue, deux de trouvées* (Montreal: HMH, 1973), pp. 9-33.

Napoléon Bourassa

(21 October 1827 - 27 August 1916)

Mary Lu MacDonald

BOOKS: *Jacques et Marie. Souvenirs d'un peuple dispersé* (Montreal: Senécal, 1866);

Nos Grand'mères (Montreal: Cadieux & Dionne, 1887);

Mélanges littéraires. Causeries et discours (Montreal: Beauchemin, 1887);

Mélanges littéraires. Souvenirs de voyage (Montreal: Beauchemin, 1889);

Lettres d'un artiste canadien: N. Bourassa, edited by Adine Bourassa (Bruges & Paris: Brouwer, 1929).

SELECTED PERIODICAL PUBLICATIONS–
UNCOLLECTED: "Discours d'introduction au cours de dessin pratique de M. Bourassa à l'école normale Jacques-Cartier," *Journal de l'instruction publique,* December 1861, February 1862;

"Du développement du goût dans les arts en Canada," *Revue Canadienne,* 5, nos. 1 and 3 (January and March 1868): 67-80, 207-215.

As painter, architect, writer, editor, and teacher, Napoléon Bourassa was an important figure in French-Canadian society in the second half of the nineteenth century. Today his many accomplishments are often forgotten by those who see him only as a link between his father-in-law, the political leader Louis-Joseph Papineau, and youngest son, the editor and political leader Henri Bourassa.

Napoléon Bourassa was the fifth child of a prosperous farmer, François Bourassa, and his wife, Geneviève Patenaude Bourassa. Born in the village of L'Acadie, Lower Canada (Quebec), he was educated at the Collège de Montréal. In the course of his studies he became interested in art and literature. However, to please his parents, on graduation he began law studies. After several years he abandoned law in favor of art, which he studied under Théophile Hamel. From 1852 to 1855 he continued his art education in Paris, Florence, and Rome.

In the decade following his return to Canada, Bourassa painted portraits, gave public lec-

Napoléon Bourassa (photograph by H. Dagenais; PA 74155, National Archives of Canada)

tures, and taught art. His sketch for a large historical painting, "L'Apothéose de Christophe Colomb," was displayed at the Paris Exhibition of 1863. His early interest in literature had continued, and in 1864 he was elected president of the editorial board of *La Revue Canadienne,* a post he held until 1870. Lacking a suitable novel for serial publication, Bourassa himself sat down to write one. *Jacques et Marie* (1866) was the result.

This tale of true love triumphing over many trials, set against the Acadian deportation and the final battle for New France, has remained in print through the years more because of its thematic content than its literary qualities, although the writing is competent and the plot well constructed. Two youthful lovers in Grand Pré swear to marry. The family of Jacques Hébert is about to move to Chignecto, where they will be farther from British jurisdiction. Marie Landry and her family will remain. An English lieutenant, George Gordon, is attracted to Marie, whose mother encourages his attentions to her daughter. Jacques believes Marie to have been unfaithful and rejects her. Marie refuses to save her family by marrying the lieutenant, and they are all deported. After her mother's death, Marie, in company with Jacques' father, walks from Boston to Canada, where, in the village of L'Acadie, she is united with Jacques, who has in the meantime been fighting the English. On the Plains of Abraham he has accepted the conversion to Catholicism of the dying George Gordon. Refusing to leave Canada with his regiment, Jacques chooses to remain in the New World. He and Marie marry and live happily ever after.

Given their symbolic nature, the characters are reasonably well drawn. Marie's mother is a foolish woman, not the perfect Acadian matron Bourassa might have portrayed. George Gordon is pleasant and likable until the moment when Marie rejects him, when he is transformed into a villain. Even he is redeemed by Jacques' forgiveness and his Catholic death. Jacques develops from an impulsive, hotheaded youth to a mature man during his years spent fighting in the forest. The Indian allies of the French are not gentle children of nature, but savage fighting men. Although Marie's character is revealed by authorial comment rather than by action, she, too, is more than a cardboard heroine.

Jacques et Marie is the first instance in Canadian literature of the linking of Acadian and Quebec historical mythmaking. The survivors of the two French-speaking colonies, rejecting the Old World, unite to form their own country in the New. Two defeats are turned into a positive myth of identity and survival. The linkage has perhaps been more satisfying to the Québecois than to the Acadians. *Jacques et Marie* was a great success in its own day, but some modern Acadian critics have suggested that in absorbing Acadian history into Quebec history, the Québecois have deprived Acadians of an important element in the development of a distinct culture. Bourassa, raised in a Quebec village inhabited by many descendants of Acadians, would not have understood their point.

Illustration showing the forced evacuation of the Acadians by British forces, from an 1886 edition of Jacques et Marie *(engraving by L. Mouchot)*

Bourassa was a devout ultramontane Catholic. Catholicism is triumphant both in his writing and in his art. The buildings he designed were churches, his major works of art were ecclesiastical, and the English characters of his novel were bad more because of their Protestant impiety than because of their mother country or mother tongue. In one of his lectures on art he deprecated Dutch genre painting because the artists lost inspiration and idealism when the country ceased to be Catholic and thus lost the ability to elevate the mind and spirit. In his long lecture *Nos Grand'mères*, published in book form in 1887, Bourassa illustrated with historical examples his conception of the ideal woman as a pious mother devoted to the Christian education of her children. The book is dedicated to his own mother. His wife, Azélie Papineau, died in 1869 after almost twelve years of marriage. She had been ill for increasingly long periods after the birth of each of their five children and never recovered from the birth of Henri, the youngest.

In the thirty years after he gave up his formal connection with *La Revue Canadienne*, Bourassa painted, taught, traveled, and designed buildings. His travel writings and some of his lectures were published in book form (*Mélanges littéraires*, 1887, 1889). He was also active in the management of the Papineau estate after his father-in-law's death in 1871. In public life he served on the executive committee of many worthy cultural causes and was highly respected by the conservative elements in French-Canadian society.

Today, as with so many other nineteenth-century figures, his painting, writing, and social attitudes are out of fashion. The themes of *Jacques et Marie*–the triumph over English oppression and the deep roots of a distinctive French culture in North America–have ensured that his one work of fiction has continued to have a place in Quebec literary history.

References:

Roger LeMoine, *Napoléon Bourassa* (Montreal: Fides, 1972);

LeMoine, *Napoléon Bourassa, artiste et écrivain* (Ottawa: Presses de la Université d'Ottawa, 1973);

Gérard Morisset, "Napoléon Bourassa et son école," in his *La Peinture Traditionnelle au Canada français* (Montreal: Cercle du Livre de France, 1960), pp. 157-162.

John George Bourinot

(24 October 1837 - 13 October 1902)

Michèle Lacombe
Trent University

BOOKS: *The Intellectual Development of the Canadian People* (Toronto: Hunter, Rose, 1881);

Parliamentary Procedure and Practice in Canada (Montreal: Dawson, 1884; revised and enlarged, 1892); revised by Thomas Bernard Flint (Toronto: Canada Law Book, 1916);

Local Government in Canada (Montreal: Dawson, 1886; Baltimore: Johns Hopkins University Press, 1887);

A Manual of the Constitutional History of Canada (Montreal: Dawson, 1888; revised and enlarged edition, Toronto: Copp, Clark, 1901);

Federal Government in Canada (Baltimore: Johns Hopkins Press, 1889);

Canadian Studies in Comparative Politics (Montreal: Dawson, 1890);

Historical and Descriptive Account of the Island of Cape Breton (Montreal: Brown, 1892);

Our Intellectual Strength and Weakness; a Short Historical and Critical Review of Literature, Art and Education in Canada (Montreal: Brown, 1893; modern edition, Toronto: University of Toronto Press, 1973);

Bibliography of the Members of the Royal Society of Canada (Ottawa: Royal Society of Canada, 1894);

A Canadian Manual on the Procedure at Meetings of Municipal Councils, Shareholders and Directors of Companies, Synods, Conventions, Societies and Public Bodies Generally (Toronto: Carswell, 1894); republished as *Rules of Order* (Toronto: McClelland, Goodchild & Stewart, 1918); revised by J. Gordon Dubroy and republished as *Bourinot's Rules of Order* (Toronto: McClelland & Stewart, 1963);

How Canada Is Governed (Toronto: Copp, Clark, 1895; Boston: Ginn, 1895); revised by Arnold W. Duclos (Toronto: Copp, Clark, 1909); revised by Francis H. Gisborne (Toronto: Copp, Clark, 1918); revised by Arthur S. Bourinot (Toronto: Copp, Clark, 1928);

John George Bourinot, Chief Clerk of the House of Commons, June 1888 (PA 25659, National Archives of Canada)

The Story of Canada (New York: Putnam's, 1896); published in England as *Canada* (London: Unwin, 1896); revised as *Canada*, with an additional chapter by Edward Porritt (London: Unwin / New York: Putnam's, 1898 [i.e., 1897]); revised again (as *Canada*), with an additional chapter by W. H. Ingram (London: Unwin, 1922);

Builders of Nova Scotia (Toronto: Copp, Clark, 1900);

Canada under British Rule 1760-1900 (Cambridge: Cambridge University Press, 1900; Toronto: Copp, Clark, 1901); revised edition, with an additional section by G. M. Wrong (Cambridge: Cambridge University Press, 1909);

Lord Elgin (Toronto: Morang, 1903; London: Jack, 1903).

SELECTED PERIODICAL PUBLICATIONS—
UNCOLLECTED: "Gentlemen Adventurers of

Acadia," *New Dominion Monthly* (March-June 1869);

Marguerite; A Tale of Forest Life in the New Dominion [novel], *New Dominion Monthly* (January-June 1870);

"Canadian Materials for History, Poetry and Romance," *New Dominion Monthly* (April 1871): 193-204;

"Canada's Relations with the United States and her Influence in Imperial Councils," *Forum*, 25 (May 1898): 329-340.

Although he earned his reputation in the 1880s as an expert on British and especially on Canadian parliamentary procedure, John George Bourinot is remembered today as one of nineteenth-century Canada's most prominent and incisive cultural critics. As a man of letters, he promoted Canadian interests by writing historical fiction and essays, by helping to establish and administer the Royal Society of Canada, and by involving himself in the popular cause then known as imperial federation. Yet his major publications, still consulted by statesmen and students of constitutional law, do not reflect the breadth of his interests or the scope of his reputation. Many of his purely literary contributions, for example, remain buried in the unindexed pages of Canadian monthly magazines and weekly belles-lettres reviews, such as *Stewart's*, the *New Dominion*, the *Canadian Monthly*, and the *Week*. In his day, however, even his legal and political commentaries were read by the educated middle classes who subscribed to *Blackwood's* and the other great quarterlies based in London and Edinburgh.

Bourinot was born on 24 October 1837 in Sydney, on Nova Scotia's Cape Breton Island. His father, a prominent citizen of French Huguenot descent, was a member of the provincial legislature, while his mother, whose ancestry boasted a Loyalist Ulster army captain, was the granddaughter of an English jurist known for his temperance beliefs and pamphlets on social and religious issues. Shortly after graduating from Toronto's Trinity College with a Bachelor of Arts degree in 1857, Bourinot asserted his literary and intellectual interests by working as a parliamentary reporter. In 1860 he founded and began editing the *Halifax Reporter*, serving as chief correspondent for the Nova Scotia legislative assembly until 1867. Confederation and his father's appointment to the Dominion senate inspired his move to Ottawa as a member of the *Hansard* staff in 1868. His first civil-service duties date from this period, and in 1880 he was finally promoted from assistant to chief clerk of the House of Commons, a position he retained until his death in 1902. Bourinot's involvement with the Royal Society of Canada, the Royal Colonial Institute of London, and the Imperial Federation League also dates to the 1880s. He was appointed the first secretary of the Royal Society of Canada upon its formation in 1882, promoted to president in 1892, and remained honorary secretary for life; largely responsible for collating its *Proceedings*, he contributed regularly to its equally prestigious *Transactions*. Bourinot received an honorary LL.D. from Queen's University in 1887 and from Trinity in 1889, an honorary D.C.L. from the University of New Brunswick in 1890 and from Bishop's in 1895, and an honorary D. ès L. from Laval University in 1893. He was married three times: to Delia Hawke in 1858, to Emily Pillsbury Alden (daughter of the American

consul in Halifax) in 1865, and to Isabelle Cameron in 1889. He was survived by one daughter and four sons, one of whom (Arthur S. Bourinot) is known as a poet and critic.

Bourinot's political ideas were mostly consistent with those of his fellow intellectuals and accurately reflect the spirit of the age: his importance lies not in originality of thought so much as in the ability to define and evaluate contemporary intellectual currents with clarity and grace. In one area, that of French-English relations, he was more progressive than his age, although today he might be considered benignly paternalistic. Bourinot's Protestant French origins and deep respect for the Catholic culture of Quebec combined to convince him that the British parliamentary system was the only one that could ensure the rights and promote the interests of French Canadians or for that matter of any ethnic or religious group. While he was perhaps too eager to prescribe the direction of growth francophone culture should take, his recognition of the need for equality and cooperation anticipates the findings of the Massey Commission in 1951. Bourinot's imperialist affiliations, countering the annexationist views of Goldwin Smith, are more representative of English-Canadian currents of thought. As one of the group of intellectuals led by Col. George Denison, George Parkin, and George Grant, Bourinot believed that his country's interests were best served by strong economic and cultural links with the British Empire. He foresaw an age in which Canada would not only compete on an equal footing with the mother country, but even rejuvenate the dying empire. Bourinot joined his contemporaries in a rather paradoxical brand of nationalism devoted to the imperial cause, examined by Carl Berger in *A Sense of Power* (1970).

Bourinot's fascination with the French regime as a glamorous era in Canada's past provides one link between his political and literary credos. His aesthetic beliefs, like his politics, largely reflected those of his contemporaries, but were also shaped by personal preferences and a sense of tradition derived from his Maritime roots. Bourinot believed that great historical movements, events, and personalities constituted a rich tradition and potential literary heritage best expressed in epic rather than lyrical verse and, to a lesser extent, in romantic fiction that would both amuse and instruct. For him, Henry Wadsworth Longfellow's *Evangeline* (1847) was living proof that Canada possessed the stuff of romance, and that it was her history rather than her geography that inspired human drama, what today's critics would term narrative appeal. Bourinot by no means denied the importance of a sense of place, but he preferred the essay to landscape poetry and always stressed the link between significant past events and their specific locales in his own descriptive sketches of Nova Scotia, placing the emphasis on events. In his opinion historical fiction was of some value as long as it did not sacrifice authenticity, based on rigorous research, to mere sensationalism; such historical novels at their best combined true romance with a vision of Canada's people, their spirit, and their future greatness.

Bourinot's political ideas are expressed throughout his numerous books and pamphlets about the government of Canada. *Our Intellectual Strength and Weakness* (1893), by far his most important publication to students of Canadian culture, revisits some of these themes but concentrates on Bourinot's literary ambitions for his country. As Clara Thomas notes in her critical introduction to the 1973 edition, Bourinot was not the first nor the last to uphold literature as the embodiment of a nation's spirit. She identifies the main parts of his argument, necessarily shaped by the fact that it originated as his 1892 presidential address to the Royal Society: it incorporates a general cultural survey, comparing Canada's literary history to that of the United States; an analysis of contemporary Canadian writing in French and English; a history of the Royal Society; and finally an evaluation of Canada's educational and cultural resources and facilities. The first two sections amplify the ideas expressed as early as 1871 in "Canadian Materials for History, Poetry and Romance" (*New Dominion Monthly*) and outlined above. The fourth section tempers his more positive observations with an honest statement of his fear that commercial success might substitute for true culture and education in a country that was only beginning to emerge from its colonial status. It is characteristic of Bourinot that he tempers praise with criticism and advice in a style noted for its clarity and elegance.

Bourinot's most valuable contribution to Canadian fiction is the novel *Marguerite; A Tale of Forest Life in the New Dominion*, serialized in the *New Dominion Monthly* from January to June 1870, which has yet to be reprinted. Set in Halifax and adjacent forts in the period between 1757 and the cessation of the Seven Years' War, a period during which the French and the English were still struggling for sole dominion of the Maritime colonies, it dramatizes Bourinot's beliefs about the happy in-

termarriage of racial characteristics. The novel also constitutes the author's riposte to John Richardson's *Wacousta* (1832), a novel he considered too sensational and derivative of James Fenimore Cooper's romances. Unlike Wacousta, Bourinot's hero/villain Black Cloud derives his identity from Acadian history rather than the novels of Sir Walter Scott, thus representing a more "Canadian" viewpoint. Bourinot skillfully avoids taking sides in the political struggles of the day, instead choosing to romanticize all aspects of colonial life, depicting soldiers, savages, and frontiersmen equally as colorful rogue-heroes within a conventional romance plot of mistaken identity and thwarted love. The plot's denouement, unlike the descriptive interludes, articulates Bourinot's somewhat naive political optimism concerning race relations: the heroine Marguerite, as an English child abducted by Indians, rescued and adopted by French Acadians, and wooed and wedded by the colonial officer Col. Evelyn in London, "belongs" in all three settings but casts her future fortunes with the English, as do her adoptive French parents, who survive military defeat without loss of humor, manners, or status. While the novel suffers from hasty writing, melodramatic excesses, and a rather pat ending, it is worth rereading for its local color and dramatization of the author's literary credo, embodying Canadian materials for romance.

Undoubtedly the nineteenth-century reader of *Marguerite* did not share the modern reader's desire for greater credibility of plot and character within the romance genre; our criticisms of Bourinot's limited talents as a novelist should perhaps be tempered by a reminder of the breadth of his vision and the scope of his scholarship in several diverse areas. Ranging from the technicalities of constitutional law, to the tenets of Arnoldian criticism in the wilderness, to the complexities of Canadian literature in both official languages, his commentaries transcend the simple patriotism of his audience and the rather singleminded imperial rhetoric adopted by so many of his intellectual contemporaries. *Our Intellectual Strength and Weakness* alone would stand as a testimony to his intelligence, knowledge, and wit, generously placed in the service of his country and its future as a considerable cultural force.

References:

Carl C. Berger, "Race and Liberty: The Historical Ideas of Sir John George Bourinot," *Cana-*

dian Historical Association Annual Report (1965): 87-104;

C. B. Koester, Introduction to Bourinot's *Parliamentary Procedure and Practice in the Dominion of Canada* (Shannon, Ireland: Irish University Press, 1971), pp. 5-12;

The Library of the Late Sir John Bourinot (New York: Anderson Auction Company, 1906);

Madge Macbeth, "A Great Canadian: Sir John Bourinot," *Dalhousie Review*, 34 (Summer 1954): 173-180;

Clara Thomas, Introduction to *Our Intellectual Strength and Weakness* (Toronto: University of Toronto Press, 1973), pp. vii-xvii.

Papers:

The J. G. Bourinot Collection is in the Public Archives of Nova Scotia.

Frances Brooke

(January 1724 - 23 January 1789)

Lorraine McMullen
University of Ottawa

See also the Frances Brooke entry in *DLB 39: British Novelists, 1660-1800.*

BOOKS: *The Old Maid*, as Mary Singleton, 37 issues (London, 15 November 1755 - 24 July 1756; collected edition, London: Printed for A. Millar, 1764);

Virginia, a Tragedy, with Odes, Pastorals, and Translations (London: Printed for the author & sold by A. Millar, 1756);

The History of Lady Julia Mandeville, anonymous, 2 volumes (London: Printed for R. & J. Dodsley, 1763; modern edition, London: Scholartis, 1930);

The History of Emily Montague, anonymous, 4 volumes (London: Printed for J. Dodsley, 1769; modern edition, Toronto: McClelland & Stewart, 1961; another modern edition, edited by Mary Jane Edwards, Ottawa: Carleton University Press, 1985);

All's Right at Last; or, The History of Miss West, anonymous, attributed to Brooke, 2 volumes (London: F. & J. Noble, 1774);

The Excursion, 2 volumes (London: Printed for T. Cadell, 1777);

The Siege of Sinope. A Tragedy (London: T. Cadell, 1781);

Rosina: A Comic Opera, in Two Acts, anonymous (London: T. Cadell, 1783; Boston: William P. Blake, 1795);

The History of Charles Mandeville, 2 volumes (London: Printed for W. Lane, 1790);

Marian: A Comic Opera, in Two Acts (London: Printed by A. Strahan for T. N. Longman & O. Rees, 1800).

PLAY PRODUCTIONS: *The Siege of Sinope*, London, Theatre Royal in Covent Garden, 31 January 1781;

Rosina, London, Theatre Royal in Covent Garden, 3 December 1782;

Marian, London, Theatre Royal in Covent Garden, May 1788.

OTHER: *Gustabus Vasa*, in *The British Drama*, 3 volumes (London & Edinburgh: Printed for W. Miller by J. Ballantine, 1804).

TRANSLATIONS: Marie Jeanne Riccoboni, *Letters from Juliet, Lady Catesby, to Her Friend, Lady Henrietta Campley* (London: Printed for R. & J. Dodsley, 1760);

Nicolas Etienne Framéry, *Memoirs of the Marquis de St. Forlaix*, 4 volumes (London: Printed for J. Dodsley, 1770);

Claude François Xavier Milot, *Elements of the History of England, from the Invasion of the Romans to the Reign of George the Second* (London: Printed for J. Dodsley & T. Cadell, 1771).

Frances Brooke in the early 1770s (portrait by Catherine Read; National Archives of Canada)

SELECTED PERIODICAL PUBLICATION–
UNCOLLECTED: "Authentic Memoirs of Mrs. Yates," *Gentleman's Magazine*, 58 (July 1787).

Frances Brooke, novelist, dramatist, essayist, translator, and poet, is best remembered today for her fiction, especially for the first Canadian novel, *The History of Emily Montague* (1769), written during her years in Quebec when her husband was military chaplain to the British garrison there. Her highly successful comic opera, *Rosina* (1783), first produced at London's Covent Garden on 3 December 1782, appears often in anthologies of eighteenth-century drama.

She was baptized Frances Moore on 24 January 1724 at Claypole, England, where her father, Rev. Thomas Moore, was curate. On his death in 1727 Frances moved with her mother and two

younger sisters to the home of Mrs. Moore's mother. Ten years later, after their mother's death, the daughters went to live with their mother's sister, Sarah, and her husband, Rev. Roger Steevens, at the rectory of Tydd St. Mary. By the 1750s Frances was writing poetry and plays in London, and by the summer of 1756 she was married to Rev. John Brooke, D.D., rector of Colney, Norfolk.

Despite her early and continuing interest in drama, Mrs. Brooke was most successful with her novels. Her skillful handling of the epistolary mode, and the wit and liveliness of her style brought immediate success. While her plots revolve around the usual theme of courtship and its complications, her real concern is often the role of women in society, a concern developed usually through contrasting women characters, one lively and independent minded, the other a traditional eighteenth-century woman of decorum and sensibility. Within the tradition of the novel of sensibility Brooke moves toward a more realistic attitude and style and to an integration of setting into theme and plot, and, perhaps because of her own background, consistently asserts the value of rural life over that in the city.

During her early years in London, Brooke became acquainted with many theatrical figures, including dramatist Arthur Murphy; Tate Wilkinson, actor and later actor-manager at York; actors James Quin, Henry Woodward, and Peg Woffington; and Peg's sister Mary (Polly), who married the Honourable Robert Cholmondeley, second son of Hugh, Lord Cholmondeley and nephew of Horace Walpole. Polly Cholmondeley, who remained a close friend of Brooke, was a member of Samuel Johnson's circle and, through her sister Peg, close to David Garrick, actor-manager of Drury Lane Theatre. By 1756 Brooke was also a friend of Johnson. There are no clear links between novelist Samuel Richardson and Brooke at this time, although she was in later years a friend of John Duncombe, author of *The Feminead* (1754), and his wife Susanna Highmore, both of whom had been among the young admirers of Richardson who gathered in the novelist's North End garden to hear him read from the manuscript of *Sir Charles Grandison* (1753-1754) in the early 1750s.

Brooke first attracted public attention with a weekly periodical, the *Old Maid*, which she wrote under the pseudonym of Mary Singleton from 15 November 1755 to 24 July 1756, for a total of thirty-seven issues. In the vein of Joseph Addison and Richard Steele's *Spectator*, the *Old Maid* included essays and letters commenting on theater, politics, religion, and society. In this venture she had the assistance of several friends, including John Boyle, Earl of Cork and Orrery, earlier a friend of Jonathan Swift, later of Richardson and Johnson. The variety of writing styles in the letters of fictional characters to the editor and the reported conversations of a fictitious group of friends provided an apprenticeship for Brooke's dramas and epistolary novels. Her observations on theater mark her as an astute drama critic. Her observations on society reveal her feminist outlook. Singleton's fictitious niece, Julia, is a forerunner of Julia Mandeville, the youthful heroine of marked sensibility of Brooke's first novel (1763), while Singleton herself has the shrewd, ironic voice belonging to Anne Wilmot in the same novel and continued with Arabella Fermor

Reverend John Brooke, the author's husband, whom she married in the 1750s (anonymous portrait; National Archives of Canada)

in *The History of Emily Montague* and with the narrator of *The Excursion* (1777). The tension between acceptance of eighteenth-century social mores and questioning of these mores, notably those pertaining to women, continued throughout Brooke's career. The undertaking of a venture such as the *Old Maid* was itself unusual for a woman.

In 1756 Brooke gave up attempts to have her tragedy *Virginia*, written some years earlier, produced by either of the two London theaters licensed to produce plays, Covent Garden and Drury Lane. Both theaters had produced plays on the same theme, neither particularly successful, within the past few years. Brooke published some poems and translations along with the tragedy. *Virginia* is based on an incident in Livy's *Early History of Rome*, Virginia choosing to die at her father's hand rather than surrender herself to the lustful tyrant Appius. The play ends on a note of victory, as it becomes apparent that Virginia's death will lead to the overthrow of the tyrant. Classical in form, the tragedy adheres to the unities of time, place, and action. Brooke's dramatic skill, developed later in her novels, is evident in the skillful interweaving of several themes within a single incident and her alternating of the emotional rhythms of the play.

In 1757 Brooke's husband, John, left for America as a military chaplain. She remained in London, continuing to write for the theater, and hoping to have her work accepted by one of the actor-managers. Her only son, John Moore Brooke, was born that year.

Three years later, turning to fiction, Brooke translated Marie Jeanne Riccoboni's *Lettres de milady Juliette Catesby à milady Henriette Campley, son amie,* a novel of sensibility published in France only the previous year (1759). Riccoboni and her novel were already popular, and the translation proved equally successful; by 1780 six editions had been published. It is evident upon reading this novel that Riccoboni and the French novel of sensibility, of which she was at this time a leading exponent, were, along with Richardson, influences on Brooke's first novel.

The sensibility and didacticism of *Letters from Juliet, Lady Catesby*—Brooke's translation—are evident in her *History of Lady Julia Mandeville,* a very successful first novel. Written in the epistolary mode, *Julia Mandeville* revolves around the ill-fated romance of Harry Mandeville and his cousin Julia. The climax occurs when Harry is mortally wounded in a duel and Julia dies of a broken heart. The two main correspondents, Harry and Julia's lively friend, Lady Anne Wilmot, present the central situation from different viewpoints. Harry's excessive sensibility is balanced by Anne's wit. At the same time, Anne's lively, coquettish manner contrasts with Julia's delicacy and sensibility. Through the witty and independent Anne, Brooke adds a humor and liveliness not markedly evident in Richardson or Riccoboni.

Julia Mandeville was highly praised on publication. The *Monthly Review* (August 1763), while regretting, as did general readers as well as critics, the unhappy ending, praised the style and the sentiments expressed: "This performance is distinguished from the common production of the novel tribe, by ease and elegance of style, variety and truth of character, delicacy and purity of sentiment. The plan is simple and natural, the incidents are interesting and important, the catastrophe highly affecting and exemplary." The *Critical Review* (July 1763) called the author "as sentimental as Rousseau, and as interesting as Richardson, without the caprice of one, or the tediousness of the other," but adding, "We cannot recommend the catastrophe." The novel was soon translated into French and highly praised in French jour-

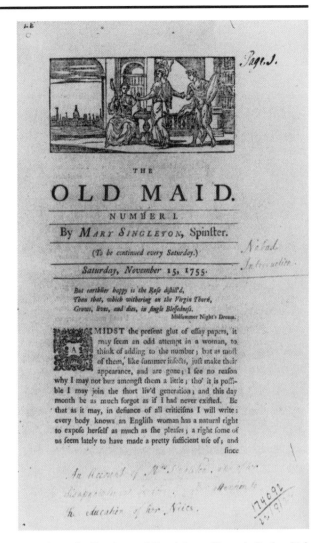

Page from the first issue of Brooke's weekly periodical, which ran from 15 November 1755 to 24 July 1756 (Thomas Fisher Library, Toronto)

nals. So popular was it in England that three editions appeared the first year, a fourth in 1765, and later editions in 1769, 1773, 1775, and 1782. Later references to Brooke usually began by identifying her as the author of *Julia Mandeville.*

For six years, from 1757 to 1763, Brooke had continued her literary activities in London while her husband was absent and acting as army chaplain. In 1760 Gen. James Murray, military governor of Quebec, had appointed John Brooke chaplain to the British garrison there and minister to the town. In October 1761 his appointment as garrison chaplain became official. When in 1763 France formally ceded Canada to Britain by the Treaty of Paris, Brooke sailed to Quebec to join her husband. Her son, John, and her sister Sarah accompanied her.

Brooke's experiences in Canada provided the material for her next novel, *The History of Emily Montague*. This novel, too, revolves around courtship and its complications. Three sets of lovers are involved, the first two pairs in Canada: Emily, a woman of sensibility and decorum, and Ed Rivers, a young retired colonel planning to settle in Canada; Arabella (Bell) Fermor, the witty and perceptive friend of Emily, and Captain Fitzgerald; and Ed's sister Lucy and his friend John Temple, both in England. By the end of the novel the three couples are happily married and settled in England.

Most of the 228 letters that make up the novel are written from Canada to England, providing opportunities to describe the scenery, customs, and inhabitants of the new colony to the reader in England. Brooke manipulates the epistolary method to provide variety. The letters are of different lengths; none are long, chapterlike letters as in Richardson and, later, Fanny Burney's *Evelina* (1778). Rarely is dialogue included; instead, some letters are so brief as to appear to be parts of conversational exchanges. In using multiple points of view, the author exploits opportunities for dramatic irony. The mood and tempo of the novel vary with the letter writers. The two central viewpoints are those of Arabella and the sentimental Ed Rivers. Arabella's father, Sir William Fermor, reports in formal, essaylike letters to England on the political, religious, and social situations in Canada. The novel was more interesting to the eighteenth-century reader for its observations of Canada than for its conventional plot.

Climate is, of course, of great interest. The author describes the alarm with which her protagonists view the coming of winter: "I have been seeing the last ship go out of port, Lucy," writes Arabella to her friends in England; "you have no notion what a melancholy sight it is; we are now left to ourselves, and shut up from all the world for the winter; somehow we seem so forsaken, so cut off from the rest of human kind, I cannot bear the idea." On 1 January she writes, "I no longer wonder the elegant arts are unknown here; the rigour of the climate suspends the very powers of the understanding: what then must become of those of the imagination?" Soon, however, Arabella and her friends begin to enjoy winter. She writes, "I begin not to disrelish the winter here; now I am used to the cold, I don't feel it so much: as there is no business done here in the winter, 'tis the season of general dissipation; amusement is the study of every body, and

the pains people take to please themselves contribute to the general pleasure: upon the whole, I am not sure it is not a pleasanter winter than that of England."

Brooke's feminism is more evident in this novel than in *Julia Mandeville* and is voiced by Ed Rivers and Arabella Fermor. Ed is attracted to women of intelligence and personality. "I persist in my opinion, that women are most charming when they join the attraction of the mind to those of the person," he writes. He speaks of women as "the sex we have so unjustly excluded from power in Europe," and writes of marriage: "Equality is the soul of friendship; marriage, to give delight, must join two minds, not devote a slave to the will of an imperious lord; whatever conveys the idea of subjection necessarily destroys that of love, of which I am so convinced, that I have always wished the word OBEY expunged from the marriage ceremony." Both Ed and Arabella speak of the importance of choice in marriage. Arabella says, "Parents should chuse our company, but never even pretend to direct our choice. . . ." Equally interesting is the view of sensibility expressed by Arabella in this age of sensibility. Arabella warns Emily, "Take care, my dear Emily, you do not fall into the common error of sensible and delicate minds, that of refining away your happiness." Dividing women into two classes, "the tender and the lively," Arabella writes, "The former, at the head of which I place Emily, are infinitely more capable of happiness; but, to counterbalance this advantage, they are capable of misery in the same degree. We of the other class, who feel less keenly, are perhaps upon the whole as happy, at least I would fain think so."

Although early sales of *Emily Montague* seem to have been disappointing, reviews were generally favorable, and in France the novel was received enthusiastically: two French translations appeared in 1770. British travelers to Canada noted their familiarity with it. Baroness Friedricka von Massow Riedesel, wife of the commander of Brunswick troops fighting with Britain during the American revolution, wrote on her arrival at Quebec on 11 June 1777: "Quebec presents a fine view from the water, and as I gazed upon it I thought of Emily Montague's letters, in which she gives a lovely description of it with which I fully agree."

In Quebec the Brookes were acquainted with Governor James Murray and members of his government, such as Adam Mabane, Hector

Theophilus Cramahé, and Henry Caldwell, and members of the merchant class, such as James Taylor Bondfield and George Allsopp, as well as officers of the British regiment. By the time of his wife's arrival at Quebec, John Brooke had acquired a reputation for interfering in affairs not his concern. Toward the end of 1764, Murray wrote of Brooke and his wife, "he cannot govern his tongue, and will perpetually interfere with things that do not concern him; I was in hopes the Ladys would have wrought a change, but on the Contrary they meddle more than he does" (Murray Papers, volume 2, National Archives of Canada). Brooke aligned himself with the British merchants at Quebec in opposition to Murray's policy of conciliation of the French Canadians and in support of a policy of linguistic and religious assimilation. When Murray was recalled in 1766 to give an account of his administration, Guy Carleton, who replaced him, was at first sympathetic to the merchants, but soon, like Murray, saw the value of a more conciliatory approach to the Canadians. The Brookes got along better with Carleton and left on good terms with him. Carleton's attorney general wrote of the Brookes, "The doctor is a very sensible agreeable companion, and Mrs. Brooke is a very sensible agreeable woman, of a very improved understanding and without any pedantry or affectation (*The Maseres Letters*, edited by W. Stewart Wallace, 1919). She dedicated *Emily Montague* to Carleton.

In the fall of 1768 the Brookes returned to England. They settled in London, where Frances renewed her acquaintance with Johnson and other members of the literary world. Music historian Charles Burney was an acquaintance at this time, and his young daughter Fanny recounted in her diary her impression of Mrs. Brooke on first meeting her at the studio of the celebrated portrait painter Catherine Read: "Mrs. Brooke is very short and fat, and squints; but has the art of showing agreeable ugliness. She is very well bred, and expresses herself with much modesty upon all subjects; which in an *authoress*, a woman of *known* understanding, is extremely pleasing."

Soon after her return Brooke published two translations. The first was a translation of Nicolas Framéry's melodramatic and sentimental novel *Histoire de M. le Marquis de S. Forlaix* (1770), the second of Abbé Claude François Xavier Milot's *Histoire de l'Angleterre* in 1771.

In 1773 Brooke and her close friend the great tragic actress Mary Ann Yates took on the management of an opera house, the King's The-

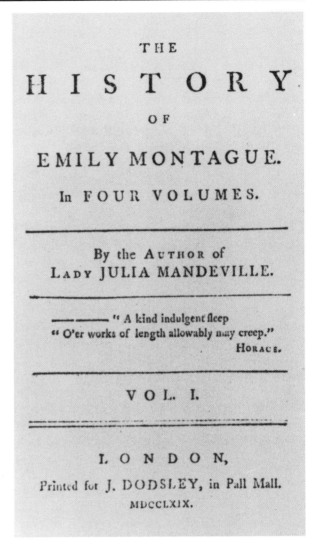

Title page for the first Canadian novel

atre in the Haymarket. The King's Theatre had been bought by Mary Ann's husband, actor Richard Yates, and Frances's brother-in-law, James Brooke. The two women remained comanagers of the opera house until it was sold in 1778 to Richard Brinsley Sheridan and Thomas Harris.

A second novel of Canada, *All's Right at Last; or, The History of Miss West*, published anonymously in 1774, may have been written by Brooke. Although it contains several factual errors, the novel has themes, attitudes, and elements of style that suggest her as author. The French translation ascribes authorship of the original to her. Set first in London, then moving to Trois-Rivières, Quebec, and Montreal, the novel focuses upon the trials of young Frances West, an innocent young country girl, as she moves from London to Canada and back to England, to marriage at last to the man she loves, but only after he and she have married other partners, who conveniently die, freeing their spouses to achieve happiness together. Like *Emily Montague*, *All's Right at Last* describes the life of the upper class in Canada. The heroine is a conventional eighteenth-century young woman. Characters include a handsome British colonel reminiscent of Ed Rivers, and two lively French-Canadian women.

With her next novel, *The Excursion* (1777), Brooke alters her narrative technique, using an omniscient narrator to recount events. Like the heroine of Fanny Burney's *Evelina*, Maria Villiers is a naive young gentlewoman brought up in the country who finds her way into London society. Maria's adventures as she learns the ways of the world make of this novel a bildungsroman. The narrator takes on the persona of a witty, ironic, and worldly wise woman. Maria's naivete is set in opposition to this narrator's worldly wisdom. While she lacks the sophistication of Anne Wilmot and the wit and perception of Arabella Fermor, Maria, unlike the conventional heroine of the time, is self-confident, intelligent, and ambitious. Assisted by her friends, the young protagonist extricates herself from various difficulties, and the novel ends with a romantic wedding back in the countryside. The intrusive narrator and mildly picaresque adventures of Maria suggest that Brooke is moving out of Richardson's sphere of influence toward that of Henry Fielding.

For years Brooke had been disappointed at having her plays rejected by David Garrick, and the most celebrated incident in *The Excursion* involves a lampoon of Garrick. Young Maria, a would-be dramatist, submits her tragedy to him through an intermediary acquaintance. In conversation with Maria's advocate, Garrick reveals, after some evasion, that he has not in fact read the play, although he purports to judge and reject it. In letters to friends at the time of the publication of *The Excursion* Garrick revealed his angry reaction to this incident in the novel. A scathing review of the novel, strongly supporting Garrick, was published in the *Monthly Review* and, as it turns out, was written by Garrick himself.

The Excursion is Brooke's shortest novel. It is made up of chapters ranging in length from a few lines to several pages. The scene shifts frequently; for example, moving from Maria to her erstwhile London friends gossiping about her, to her would-be seducer plotting against her, to her guardian uncle in his country garden thinking about her. Brooke's theatrical proclivities are evi-

dent in such rapid scene shifting and in her use of dialogue to act out some scenes. Despite Maria's mishaps and the didactic nature of the novel, the tone remains light. Unlike Burney's *Evelina*, *The Excursion* does not demonstrate the rewards for adhering to the eighteenth-century standards of decorum and propriety for women, but criticizes the corrupt London world of bon ton and of the Chesterfieldian young man; comments on the dangers lying in wait for young women who seek to bring their intelligence, warmth, and wit to such a society; and looks at the unfortunate theatrical situation in which playwrights must depend on the good will of the only two theater managers in London. This novel did not have the contemporary popularity of the earlier *Julia Mandeville* and *Emily Montague*, although reviews other than that in the *Monthly Review* and one in *Town and Country* (which felt its "Tête-à-Tête" gossip column attacked) were favorable. It was 1785 before a second edition appeared.

In the meantime Brooke was at last successful in her attempts to have a theatrical work produced. On 31 January 1781 Thomas Harris produced *The Siege of Sinope* at Covent Garden, with Mrs. Mary Ann Yates in the title role of Thamyris. Like *Virginia*, *The Siege of Sinope* is based on a historical event in the classical world. Brooke's immediate source is Giuseppi Sarti's opera *Mitridate a Sinope*, first produced at Florence in 1779. Brooke's play is a pseudoclassic tragedy written in blank verse and adhering to the classical unities. Thamyris, queen of Sinope, displays strength and courage as she faces a conflict between her loyalties to her husband, ruler of Sinope, and her father, who is besieging the city. The play was reasonably successful, with a run of ten nights.

A much greater success was Brooke's comic opera *Rosina*. It, too, was produced by Harris, opening to great applause on 3 December 1782. *Rosina* is charming entertainment, and William Shield's music contributed to its popularity. Set in a village in the north of England, the play involves Rosina, the local squire who falls in love with her, and the squire's dissolute brother, who tries to seduce her and, failing that, to kidnap her. Two rustics, William and Phoebe, act as foils for the lovers and provide comic relief. When Rosina, brought up among the peasants, is discovered to be the daughter of a gentleman, she is a suitable bride for the squire.

Scenes are brief, action lively. The idyllic setting, attractive music, quick humor, and brisk plot combine to produce highly successful entertainment, Brooke's most successful theatrical production, and the period's most popular comic opera. While the author mentions in her preface that sources of her plot include the book of Ruth, the episode of Palaemon and Lavinia in James Thomson's *Seasons* (1730), and C. S. Favart's opera *Les Moissonneurs* (1768), it is Favart's opera which is the direct source.

During these years Brooke was living in London, but she made frequent visits to Lincolnshire, most often visiting her sister Sarah, now wife of Rev. Joseph Digby, rector of Tinwell. John Brooke seems to have divided his time between London and his livings in Norfolk. In the meantime, their only son, John Moore Brooke, was educated at Cambridge and, like his forefathers, entered the ministry. He took up livings at Helpringham and Folkingham in Lincolnshire. Before the production of her second comic opera, *Marian*, in May 1788 at Covent Garden, Mrs. Brooke, who had been in failing health for some time, moved to Sleaford, Lincolnshire, to live with her son, returning to London from time to time as necessary.

Marian is similar to *Rosina* in its pastoral setting and its happy resolution of the complications of courtship. A young country girl, Marian is engaged to be married to a penniless young man. Upon her inheritance of a small sum of money, her father wants her to forego her lover for someone more equal in fortune. Happily Marian's fiancé learns that he has inherited an estate so that his planned marriage to Marian once more meets with her father's approval. Shield's music once more enhances Brooke's opera, which met with an excellent reception. It did not, however, meet with the long-lasting popularity of the earlier *Rosina*. The pastoral settings of both operas suggest, as do Brooke's novels, that true happiness is to be found in the simple virtues and pleasures of rural life.

Brooke died at Sleaford on 23 January 1789. She is buried in the chancel of St. Denys's church, Sleaford, and her son, who died in 1798, is buried beside her. Her husband, who died at Colney, Norfolk, just two days before her, is buried in Colney Cathedral.

Brooke's last novel, *The History of Charles Mandeville*, was published the year following her death. With this novel she returns to the epistolary mode but, unlike her earlier method, writes the novel almost entirely from one point of view, with two important exceptions: almost half the novel is made up of two long accounts of past events–Charles's own account of the fantastic land where he spent his youth, and his late wife's account of his exploits in that land. Extensive reporting of conversations places the style closer to Fanny Burney's than that of Brooke's earlier works.

The novel, a utopian one, is in one sense a completion of the much earlier *Julia Mandeville*. Harry Mandeville's brother, Charles, believed lost at sea as a child of eleven, was sole survivor of a shipwreck and now returns to England a wealthy young man. At the conclusion of the novel he marries Emily Howard, Julia's best friend, who had become a surrogate daughter to Julia's bereaved parents. By providing Charles to replace the dead Harry and Emily to replace Julia, Brooke gives her readers the happy ending she refused them with the earlier novel.

Of most interest to the reader is the account by Charles and his late wife, Agnes, of the fantastic land where Charles was shipwrecked. It is a utopian land with a communal society, an advanced system of justice, and an antimaterialistic outlook. The reward for service to the state is honor; gold, jewels, and other forms of wealth are meaningless. With this novel Brooke transfers her Eden from pastoral England and primitive Canada to a fantastic, futuristic world.

Frances Brooke's most enduring work is her novels, while her plays, except for *Rosina*, are long forgotten. Nevertheless, her theatrical interests contributed to the development of her novelistic technique. Her way of using the epistolary mode and her exploitation of opportunities for dramatic irony owe much to her theatrical bent. With her skillful interweaving of a complex of voices in *Emily Montague* and her manipulation of setting to echo the actions and emotions of her protagonists, she took the novel in new directions. Her use of an ironic and intrusive narrator in *The Excursion* reveals yet another facet of her talent. At a time when most novelists were excessively sentimental, Brooke combined wit and sensibility, moving toward realism in plot, dialogue, and characterization. An astute and witty observer, in balancing sensibility with sense she moved in the direction of Jane Austen.

References:

Marvin L. Brown, ed., *Baroness von Riedesel and the American Revolution: Journal and Correspon-*

dence of a Tour of Duty 1776-1783 (Chapel Hill: University of North Carolina Press, 1965);

Frances (Fanny) Burney, *The Early Diary of Fanny Burney*, edited by A. R. Ellis, 2 volumes (London: Bell, 1889);

Carl F. Klinck, Introduction to *The History of Emily Montague* (Toronto: McClelland & Stewart, 1961);

Lorraine McMullen, "*All's Right at Last*: An Eighteenth-Century Canadian Novel," *Journal of Canadian Fiction*, 21 (1977-1978): 95-104;

McMullen, *An Odd Attempt in a Woman: The Literary Life of Frances Brooke* (Vancouver: University of British Columbia Press, 1983);

Gwendolyn B. Needham, "Mrs. Frances Brooke: Dramatic Critic," *Theatre Notebook*, 15 (Winter 1960-1961): 47-52;

W. H. New, "Frances Brooke's Chequered Garden," *Canadian Literature*, 52 (Spring 1972): 24-38;

New, "The Old Maid: Frances Brooke's Apprentice Feminism," *Journal of Canadian Fiction*, 2 (Summer 1973): 9-12;

John Nichols, *Literary Anecdotes of the Eighteenth Century*, volume 2 (London: Nichols, Son & Bentley, 1812-1815);

E. Phillips Poole, Introduction to *Lady Julia Mandeville* (London: Eric Partridge / Scholaris Press, 1930);

Katherine M. Rogers, "Sensibility and Feminism: the Novels of Frances Brooke," *Genre*, 11 (Summer 1978): 159-171;

Edmund Royds, "Stubton Strong-Room-Stray Notes (2nd Series) Moore and Knowles Families–Two Sisters," *Reports and Papers of the Architectural Societies of the County of Lincoln, County of York* (Lincoln, England, 1926-1927), pp. 97-99, 213-312;

W. Stewart Wallace, ed., *The Maseres Letters 1766-1768* (Toronto: University of Toronto Press, 1919).

Papers:

The Houghton Library, Harvard University, holds an extensive collection of Brooke's letters and manuscripts, most notably her correspondence with Richard Gifford. Other letters and family papers are deposited in the Lincolnshire Archives, Lincoln. Other miscellaneous letters and papers are in the manuscript collections of the British Library, the Bodleian Library, Oxford, and the Northamptonshire Record Office in Northampton.

Richard Maurice Bucke

(18 March 1837 - 19 February 1902)

James Doyle
Wilfrid Laurier University

BOOKS: *Man's Moral Nature: An Essay* (New York: Putnam's / Toronto: Willing & Williamson, 1879; London: Trübner, 1879);

Walt Whitman (Philadelphia: McKay, 1883; London: Trübner, 1883); enlarged edition, edited by Edward Dowden (London: Gardner, 1883);

Cosmic Consciousness: A Study in the Evolution of the Human Mind (Philadelphia: Innes, 1901).

OTHER: *In Re Walt Whitman,* edited by Bucke, Horace L. Traubel, and Thomas B. Harned (Philadelphia: McKay, 1893);

Walt Whitman, *Calamus: A Series of Letters Written during the Years 1868-1880, by Walt Whitman to a Young Friend (Peter Doyle),* edited, with an introduction, by Bucke (Boston: Maynard, 1897);

Whitman, *The Wound Dresser; Letters Written to His Mother from the Hospitals in Washington During the Civil War,* edited by Bucke (Boston: Small, Maynard, 1898);

Whitman, *Notes and Fragments,* edited by Bucke (London, Ont.: Printed for the editor, 1899);

Whitman, *The Complete Writings of Walt Whitman,* edited by Bucke, Traubel, and Harned, 10 volumes (New York & London: Putnam's, 1902);

Whitman, *Leaves of Grass,* edited by Bucke, Traubel, and Harned (New York: Putnam's, 1902).

Richard Maurice Bucke, physician, hospital administrator, adventurer, scholar, mystic, editor, and author, is mainly remembered in literary history as the friend, first biographer, and literary executor of the American poet Walt Whitman. Besides editing or coediting several volumes of Whitman's writings, Bucke was the author of three books and dozens of articles reflecting a wide variety of interests. His best-known book, *Cosmic Consciousness,* has been continuously in print since its first publication in 1901, and his life and writings have been the subjects of articles, theses, and books by literary scholars, philosophers, and historians. The list of international authors who have expressed admiration for Bucke's work includes William James, P. D. Ouspensky, Edward Carpenter, Algernon Blackwood, Aldous Huxley, and Henry Miller. In spite of this extensive recognition, however, he remains largely neglected by English-Canadian literary history. This neglect can be related to the diversity of his writings, which elude categorization, to the derivative and eccentric qualities of much of his work, and to his detachment from dominant Victorian-Canadian literary trends.

Bucke was born in Methwold, Norfolk, England on 18 March 1837, one of seven children of Rev. Horatio Walpole Bucke and his wife, Clarissa Andrews Bucke. The family immigrated to Canada the following year and settled on a farm near London, Upper Canada (Ontario). "Maurice" was educated at home by his father, who introduced him to a wide range of philosophy, religion, and literature. At the age of seventeen he left home to join the California gold rush, during which he experienced a series of adventures, including an arduous trek over the Sierra Nevadas in mid winter, resulting in frostbite and permanent disfigurement of both feet. Returning to Canada, Bucke enrolled in the medical faculty of McGill University, from which he graduated in 1862 with an M.D. After two years in Europe studying psychiatry, he set up a general practice in Sarnia, Ontario, and in 1865 he married Jesse Maria Gurd. In 1876 he was appointed superintendent of the Asylum for the Insane in Hamilton, Ontario, but only a few months later he became superintendent of the new asylum in London, Ontario, a position he held for the rest of his life.

During the years of medical school and early practice, Bucke found time to pursue his literary and philosophical interests, learning German in order to read Johann Wolfgang von Goethe, keeping up with contemporary British

Richard Maurice Bucke, circa 1901

poets–such as Alfred, Lord Tennyson, Robert and Elizabeth Barrett Browning, and Algernon Charles Swinburne–and reading such thinkers as Joseph Renan, Voltaire, Charles Darwin, and Auguste Comte. These readings contributed to his formulation of the intellectual problem that had obsessed him since his student days, the relationship between the material and spiritual aspects of human experience. His interest in this subject was stimulated when he discovered the poetry of Walt Whitman and had his first experience of what he was to call "cosmic consciousness." In 1868 he read with great enthusiasm Whitman's *Leaves of Grass* (1855). On a visit to London, England, in 1872 he experienced an "intellec-

tual illumination," as he explained in *Cosmic Consciousness* in words echoing section 5 of Whitman's "Song of Myself": "I saw and knew that the Cosmos is not dead matter but a living Presence, that the soul of man is immortal, that the universe is so built and ordered that without any peradventure all things work together for the good of each and all, that the foundation principle of the world is what we call love and that the happiness of every one is in the long run absolutely certain."

In 1877 Bucke traveled to Camden, New Jersey, to visit Whitman. Two years later Bucke published his first book, *Man's Moral Nature,* a rather turgid attempt to relate human emotional and

Walt Whitman, Bucke's friend for whom Bucke was literary executor (from Richard Maurice Bucke, Medical Mystic, *edited by Artem Lozynsky, 1977)*

moral experience to the principles of physiology. Around the same time, he began researching and writing a much more important literary venture, an authorized biography of Whitman. Although this biography, published in 1883, was reputedly revised or even partly written by Whitman himself, it is still valuable as a representation of Whitman's life and work by a contemporary who knew him. Most of the facts remain undisputed, and its exposition of the mystical qualities of Whitman's imagination has influenced subsequent evaluations of the poet.

Bucke's most ambitious literary effort was *Cosmic Consciousness,* consisting of a series of chap-

ters on various notable persons from philosophy, literature, and religion, with excerpts from their works and with a long general introduction. According to Bucke various people in past ages and modern times have experienced a mystical state that releases their individual genius and reveals the potential of the human race to move toward increasingly higher intellectual and spiritual levels. The supreme example of "cosmic consciousness" is Whitman, who is the subject of the longest chapter.

Cosmic Consciousness is, on the whole, an earnest but naive work. Its concept of moral and spiritual evolution and its "great men" theory of history are staples of nineteenth-century thought. Its analyses of literature and philosophy are often clumsy in their determination to wrest from the works of various authors hidden clues to their experience of cosmic consciousness. As far as literary history is concerned, Bucke's most important achievement besides his biography of Whitman consists of the various volumes of the poet's letters, miscellaneous papers, and poetry that he edited or coedited after Whitman's death. As an editor Bucke was careful and unobtrusive, never allowing his own philosophical and artistic notions to interfere with the words and ideas of Whitman.

In addition to these writing and editing tasks, Bucke wrote many articles on a variety of literary and scientific topics, all the while pursuing a distinguished career as psychiatrist and hospital administrator. His life came to an abrupt and tragic end on 19 February 1902, when he slipped on a patch of ice on the front porch of his home, struck his head, and died instantly. Well known internationally by the end of the nineteenth century for his innovative work with the insane, and subsequently acknowledged by American literary history as one of the more important members of the Whitman circle, Bucke also deserves a place in Canadian literature, for the intrinsic interest of his life and career and for his conscientious, if limited, efforts to contribute to nineteenth-century philosophical and literary issues.

Letters:

A Series of Letters which Passed Between Dr. Richard Maurice Bucke and William Douglas O'Connor 1880-1888 (Toronto, 1912?);
Richard Maurice Bucke, Medical Mystic: Letters of Dr. Bucke to Walt Whitman and His Friends, ed-ited by Artem Lozynsky (Detroit: Wayne State University Press, 1977).

References:
E. G. Berry, "Whitman's Canadian Friend," *Dalhousie Review,* 24 (April 1944): 77-82;
John Robert Colombo, "A Doctor of Mysticism: Richard Maurice Bucke," *Canadian Theosophist,* 41 (January 1961): 133-139;
James H. Coyne, "Richard Maurice Bucke: A Sketch," *Transactions of the Royal Society of Canada,* second series 12 (1906): 159-196;
James Doyle, "R. M. Bucke," *Canadian Literature,* 83 (Winter 1979): 201-206;
Cyril Greenland, "Richard Maurice Bucke, M.D., a Pioneer of Scientific Psychiatry," *Canadian Medical Association Journal,* 91 (22 August 1964): 385-391;
Mary Ann Jameson, ed., *Richard Maurice Bucke: A Catalogue Based upon the Collection of the University of Western Ontario Libraries* (London, Ont.: UWO Libraries, 1978);
Brian Lauder, "Two Radicals: Richard Maurice Bucke and Lawren Harris," *Dalhousie Review,* 56 (Summer 1976): 307-318;
W. Mitchinson, "R. M. Bucke: A Victorian Asylum Superintendent," *Ontario History,* 73 (December 1981): 239-254;
Samuel E. Shortt, *Victorian Lunacy: Richard M. Bucke and the Practice of Late Nineteenth-Century Psychiatry* (Cambridge: Cambridge University Press, 1986).

Papers:
A collection of Bucke's literary, philosophical, scientific, and administrative papers is in the library of the University of Western Ontario, London, Ontario.

Arthur Buies
(24 January 1840 - 26 January 1901)

Paul Matthew St. Pierre
Simon Fraser University

BOOKS: *Lettres sur le Canada*, 3 volumes (Montreal: Printed for the author, 1864-1867);

Chroniques: Humeurs et caprices (Quebec: Darveau, 1873);

Chroniques: Voyages etc., etc. (Quebec: Darveau, 1875);

Petites Chroniques pour 1877 (Quebec: Darveau, 1878);

Le Saguenay et la vallée du Lac St. Jean (Quebec: Coté, 1880); enlarged as *Le Saguenay et le bassin du Lac Saint-Jean* (Quebec: Brousseau, 1896);

Chroniques canadiennes: Humeurs et Caprices (Montreal: Sénecal, 1884);

La Lanterne (Montreal, 1884);

Anglicismes et canadienismes (Quebec: Darveau, 1888);

L'Outaouais supérieur (Quebec: Darveau, 1889);

Les Comtés de Rimouski de Matane et de Témiscouata (Quebec: Belleau, 1890); translated by Buies, H. A. Turgeon, and C. E. Damours as *Reports on the Counties of Rimouski, Matane and Temiscouata* (Quebec: Langlois, 1890);

Récits de voyages (Quebec: Darveau, 1890);

La Région de Lac Saint-Jean, grénier de la province de Québec: Guide des colons (Quebec: Chemin de Fer de Quebec, 1890); translated as *The Lake St. John Region, the Granary of the Province of Quebec: A Guide for Settlers* (Quebec: Morning Chronicle, 1891);

Au Portiques des Laurentides. Une Paroisse moderne. Le Curé Labelle (Quebec: Darveau, 1891);

Réminiscences. Les Jeunes Barbares (Quebec: Electeur, 1892);

Québec en 1900. Conférence donnée à l'Académie de Musique de Québec, lundi, le 29 mai 1893 (Quebec: Brousseau, 1893);

Le Chemin de fer du Lac Saint-Jean (Quebec: Brousseau, 1895);

La Vallée de la Matapédia (Quebec: Brousseau, 1895);

Les Poissons et les animaux à fourrures au Canada (Ottawa: Ministère de l'Agriculture, 1900); translated as *Animals of Canada: Fishes, Birds*

Arthur Buies (photograph by Jules-Ernest Livernois; Collection Léopold-Lamontagne, Centre de Recherche en Civilisation Canadienne-Française, Université d'Ottawa)

and Furred Animals (Ottawa: Ministry of Agriculture, 1900);

La Province de Québec (Quebec: Départment de l'Agriculture, 1900).

Editions and Collections: *Arthur Buies, 1840-1961,* edited by Léopold Lamontagne (Montreal & Paris: Fides, 1959);

La Lanterne d'Arthur Buies: Propos révolutionnaires et chroniques scandaleuses, confessions publiques, edited by Marcel A. Gagnon (Montreal: Editions de l'Homme, 1964);

Anthologie d'Arthur Buies, edited by Laurent Mailhot (Montreal: HMH, 1978).

Like many nineteeth-century Quebec writers, Arthur Buies is memorable less for the
brillance of his career and for the clarity of his
ideas than for the light he shed on the Quebecois
struggle to earn a living from writing, even at the
expense of sacrificing permanent artistic worth.
His evidently selfless and unspectacular professional life has indirectly freed contemporary
francophone writers not just to develop exclusively artistic careers but to realize that there is
an artistic dignity in writing to support oneself,
which is to be distinguished from the indignity of
hackwork. Buies ushered in the modern age for
Quebec writers, surveying through a variety of
journalistic forms the physical and cultural geogra-
phies of his province in the context of Confederation, as writers today use the journalistic forms of
literary and critical articles to analyze the sociolo-
gies of a province testing the waters of distinct society status and sovereignty association.

Born on 24 January 1840 in Montreal to William Buies, a Scotsman who had immigrated to
Canada fifteen years earlier, and Marie Antoinette Leocadie d'Estmauville Buies, Arthur truly
entered into his vicissitudinary life when in 1841
his parents went to live in British Guiana, placing
him in the care of his Quebec aunts. He began
his education at the seminaries of Nicolet and
Ste. Anne de la Pocatière, but after a visit to British Guiana in 1856, continued it abroad: at Trinity College, Dublin (1856), and at the Lycée
Impérial Saint Louis in Paris (1857-1859, and sporadically until 1862). In 1860 he served briefly
with Giuseppe Garibaldi's army in Turin, Italy,
an experience that deeply influenced his professional and journalistic careers when, upon returning to Montreal in 1862 and entering the Institut
Canadien, he published an article praising Garibaldi, whose push against the Papal States was
very unpopular in Canada. He made his anticlerical stance and his position on secularizing education clear in letters published in *Lettres sur le Canada* (1864-1867) and, after he was called to the
bar in 1866, in the journal *Le Pays.* After an unsuccessful sojourn in Paris in 1867, Buies made his religious and political views concrete and public in
three journals that he founded: *La Lanterne*
(1868-1869, collected in 1884), *L'Indépendant*
(1870), and *Le Réveil* (1876). His success in writing newspaper articles on the Quebec region led
him to collect them in a sequence of books of cul-

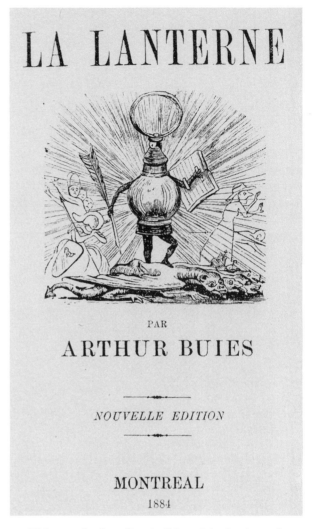

*Title page for the collected edition of the first journal
Buies founded*

tural geography: *Chroniques: Humeurs et caprices*
(1873); *Chroniques: Voyages etc., etc.* (1875); *Petites
Chroniques pour 1877* (1878); and *Chroniques
canadiennes: Humeurs et Caprices* (1884).

Realizing that his journalistic future lay not
in denigrating the clergy but in promoting French-
Canadian culture, Buies went on to write a series
of books on the Saguenay and Outaouais rivers:
Le Saguenay et la vallée du Lac St. Jean (1880); and
L'Outaouais supérieur (1889); on the Great Lakes:
Récits de voyages (1890); and on the Laurentian
mountains: *Au Portiques des Laurentides* (1891). *Au
Portique* is in part a tribute to the curé Antoine
Labelle, who helped redirect Buies's journalism
away from accusation and toward provocation,
away from the descriptive and toward the interpre-
tive.

In the midst of his prosperity, in 1887, Buies married. He took as his wife Marie-Mila Catellier, the daughter of Canada's under secretary of state. They were to have five children.

Just as his preoccupation with great waterways anticipated the fascination that such serious modern writers as Hugh MacLennan and Roderick Haig-Brown would have, so his concerns about linguistic and stylistic standards among French-Canadian journalists–in *Anglicismes et canadienismes* (1888)–foreshadowed the fears that francophones throughout Canada and particularly in Quebec would have regarding the protection and extension of their language rights.

Arthur Buies expressed his cultural views most articulately, emphatically, and memorably in *Réminiscences. Les Jeunes Barbares* (1892). He died on 26 January 1901 shortly after the birth of the new century.

Bibliography:

Rachel Tessier, *Bio-Bibliographie d'Arthur Buies* (Montreal: Ecole des Bibliothécaires de l'Université de Montréal, 1943).

Biographies:

Raymond Donville, *La Vie adventureuse d'Arthur Buies* (Montreal: Lévesque, 1933);

Léopold Lamontagne, *Arthur Buies: Homme de lettres* (Quebec: Presses Universitaires Laval, 1957).

References:

René Dionne, "Buies chez lui hier aujourd'hui ou le Québec chez Buies," *Relations,* 38 (December 1978): 344-346;

Marcel A. Gagnon, "Arthur Buies: L'Enfant terrible," *Maclean,* 5 (November 1965): 30, 32-34, 36, 38;

Gagnon, *Le Ciel et l'enfer d'Arthur Buies* (Quebec: Presses de l'Université Laval, 1965);

John Hare, "Arthur Buies, essayiste: Une Introduction à la lecture de son oeuvre," in *L'Essai et la prose d'idées au Québec,* edited by Paul Wyczynski, François Gallays, and Sylvain Simard (Montreal: Fides, 1985), pp. 295-310;

Laurent Mailhot, "Aux frontières (à l'horizon) de l'essai québécois," *Nouvelle Barre du Jour,* 63 (February 1978): 69-86;

Francis Parmentier, "Arthur Buies et la littérature nationale," *Revue d'Histoire Littéraire du Québec et du Canada Français,* 7 (Winter-Spring 1984): 57-59;

Parmentier, "Réception de *La Lanterne* par la presse canadienne-française," *Revue d'Histoire de l'Amerique-Francaise,* 34 (September 1980): 269-274;

Pierre-Georges Roy, "Les Ouvrages d'Arthur Buies," *Bulletin des Recherches Historiques,* 7, no. 5 (1901): 150-153;

Sylvain Simard, "L'Essai québécois aux XIXe siècle," *Voix et Images,* 6 (Winter 1981): 264-265;

Jean-Pierre Tousseau, "La Fin 'édifiante' d'Arthur Buies," *Etudes Françaises,* 9 (February 1973): 45-54;

Tousseau, "Quelques Aspects idéologiques de l'oeuvre d'Arthur Buies," *Stratégies,* 9 (Summer 1975): 73-80;

G.-André Vachon. "Arthur Buies, écrivain," *Etudes Françaises,* 6 (August 1970): 283-295.

Papers:

Buies's papers are in the Archives Nationale du Québec and in the Bibliothèque de Collège de Lèvis.

Adam Hood Burwell

(4 June 1790 - 2 November 1849)

George L. Parker
Royal Military College of Canada

BOOKS: *Doctrine of the Holy Spirit* (Toronto: W. J. Coates, 1835);

A Voice of Warning and Instruction Concerning the Signs of the Times.... (Kingston, Ont.: Upper Canada Herald, 1835);

On the Philosophy of Human Perfection and Happiness (Montreal: Lovell & Gibson, 1849);

Summer Evening Contemplations (Montreal: Lovell & Gibson, 1849);

The Poems of Adam Hood Burwell, Pioneer Poet of Upper Canada, edited by Carl F. Klinck (London, Ont.: Lawson Memorial Library, University of Western Ontario, 1963).

SELECTED PERIODICAL PUBLICATIONS–
UNCOLLECTED: "Ultimate Destination of the Earth; or, What Was It Made for?," *Literary Garland*, new series 7 (May 1849): 215-221;

"On the Doctrine of Social Unity," *Literary Garland*, new series 7 (September and October 1849): 403-409, 448-457.

The first native-born poet in Western Ontario, Adam Hood Burwell was the earliest writer to mythologize the pioneer Loyalist past and the War of 1812. He was born near Fort Erie, Upper Canada (Ontario), to Loyalist parents–Adam and Sarah Veal Burwell–who had emigrated from New Jersey in the 1780s. Soon after the War of 1812 Burwell joined Col. Thomas Talbot's settlement on the north shore of Lake Erie, but farming did not appeal to him, and in 1818 (according to an August 1831 letter he wrote to John Macaulay) he had a vision that he was to be "a poet who should be a great man." He published poems under his pseudonym Erieus in local newspapers, and from 1821 to 1825 *Scribbler* (Montreal), Canada's first literary weekly, and the *Canadian Review* (Montreal) published a total of twenty-one of his poems.

The poems catch fire when he describes first-hand the Talbot settlement or Niagara Falls and its environs. The long poem "Talbot Road" (1820; collected in *The Poems*, 1963) celebrates

Talbot's transformation of the wilderness into a bountiful society firmly based on those British principles that had been successfully tested by the American invasions of 1812-1814. In "A Summer's Evening" (1821) and "Journal of A Day's Journey in Upper Canada, in October, 1816" (1822; both collected in *The Poems*), Burwell records the sights and sounds of his beloved countryside, which stirred his creative imagination, enlarged his heart, and strengthened his faith, for he saw in the natural world the signs of eternity and man's reconciliation with God. Burwell's is a poetry not of loss and pain but of affirmation.

After theological training in England, he returned to Canada and was ordained in the Church of England in 1828; he explains in "Farewell to the Shores of Lake Erie" (1827; collected in *The Poems*) how his poetic muse has led him to God and away from Upper Canada. At Trois-Rivières, Lower Canada (Quebec), he combined preaching with the editorship of the the short-lived *Christian Sentinel* (1830-1831), to the detriment of his nerves and frail health. Despite his bishop's objections, he wanted the *Sentinel* to be an organ for the British Constitutionalist party in the growing provincial conflicts over the political shape of Canada, and he contributed several anti-republican letters (signed "One of the People") to the *Kingston Chronicle* in 1831 and a series of letters on church-and-state relations in 1834. During his Ottawa-Hull curacy (1832-1836), he gravitated toward Rev. Edward Irving's apocalyptic sect, which he defended in two monographs in 1835 (*Doctrine of the Holy Spirit* and *A Voice of Warning*). Burwell then left the church to serve as minister of the Irvingite Catholic Apostolic Church at Kingston, Canada West (Ontario), until his death. He apparently published little poetry after 1830–although more may come to light in contemporary newspapers–until in 1849 he produced three religious essays (including *On the Philosophy of Human Perfection and Happiness*, separately published later that year) and three poems for the *Lit-*

erary Garland (the poems being collected in the 1963 anthology); in these works his visionary and mystical side has become long-winded.

For a century after his death, Burwell was all but forgotten until Lawrence Lande's 1957 appreciation and Carl Klinck's 1963 edition of his poems restored him to a modest but distinctive place in colonial Canadian poetry. Burwell always used the poetic diction, iambic couplets, and blank verse that are characteristic of late-eighteenth-century verse. Thus he typifies a dichotomy in colonial poets, whose techniques were borrowed from English poets like Thomas Gray and Thomas Campbell but whose perceptions and subjects were shaped by their North American experiences and cultural life. Despite the clash between form and content in his poetry, his own particular sensibility, which fuses his faith and his response to nature, often emerges with charm and vitality.

References:

Mary Jane Edwards, ed., *The Evolution of Canadian Literature in English: Beginnings to 1867* (Toronto: Holt, Rinehart & Winston, 1973), pp. 59-69;

Carl F. Klinck, ed., *Literary History of Canada*, second edition, revised (Toronto: University of Toronto Press, 1976), p.139;

Klinck and R. E. Watters, eds., *Canadian Anthology*, third edition, revised (Toronto: Gage, 1974), pp.15-17;

Lawrence M. Lande, *Old Lamps Aglow. An Appreciation of Early Canadian Poetry* (Montreal: The author, 1957), pp. 243-253;

Mary Lu MacDonald, " 'New' Poems of Adam Hood Burwell," *Canadian Poetry*, 18 (Spring/Summer 1986): 99-117;

Thomas Millman, *The Life of the Right Reverend, the Honourable Charles James Stewart* (London, Ont.: Huron College, 1953), pp. 69, 194.

Papers:
Burwell's correspondence is in the Macaulay Papers, MS 78, housed at the Archives of Ontario, Toronto.

George Frederick Cameron

(24 September 1854 - 17 September 1885)

John Parr

BOOKS: *Lyrics on Freedom, Love and Death,* edited by Charles J. Cameron (Kingston, Ont.: Shannon, 1887; Boston: Moore, 1887);

Leo, the Royal Cadet. An Entirely New and Original Military Opera in Four Acts, libretto by Cameron, music by Oscar Telgmann, edited by C. J. Cameron (Kingston, Ont.: Henderson, 1889).

Definitely a subject for further study is the poet George Frederick Cameron, much of whose work not only is unpublished at present but never was in print even during his lifetime. In fact the only volume of Cameron's poetry ever to appear, *Lyrics on Freedom, Love and Death* (1887), was published two years after his death. Chronologically, Cameron belongs to the Confederation generation of poets, along with Charles G. D. Roberts, Archibald Lampman, and Bliss Carman; but the nature of his work is different from theirs. Furthermore, opinion is still divided as to exactly what he accomplished in his departure from the mainstream of Canadian poetry.

George Frederick Cameron, the son of James Grant Cameron, a carpenter, and his wife, Jessie Sutherland Cameron, was born in New Glasgow, Nova Scotia, on 24 September 1854. His maternal grandfather had been New Glasgow's first shipbuilder. Before age fourteen Cameron had read most of Virgil and Cicero in Latin and was spending most of his spare time creating his own poetry. In 1869 the family moved to Boston, where, three years later, Cameron entered the Boston University of Law. After graduating he joined a local law firm but continued with his writing, contributing to various Boston periodicals, such as the *Courier* and the *Transcript*. In 1882, now in his late twenties, Cameron evidently decided to make a fresh start by returning to Canada and enrolling in Queen's University, Kingston, to study for the ministry. Unfortunately, Cameron did not do well academically, although he did gain some distinction with his poetry, pub-

lishing in the *Queen's College Journal* and winning third prize in the university poem competition.

In March 1883 Cameron left Queen's to become editor of the *Kingston News.* Then in August he married Ella Amey of Millhaven, Ontario, with whom he had a daughter, Jessie. During 1884 and 1885 Cameron, afflicted with insomnia, slept only two or three hours a night; finally, on 17 September 1885, one week short of his thirty-first birthday, he died of heart disease.

The few contemporary glimpses of Cameron that are available suggest an individual very much in keeping with the customary image of the nineteenth-century romantic poet. The author's brother, Charles J. Cameron, who edited *Lyrics on Freedom, Love and Death,* says in the preface: "Young, as the world counts time, at thirty years of age he had run the whole *gamut* of its pleasures and its pains. There was to him a terrible sameness to it all." And then he adds cryptically: "It was impossible, being what he was, that his poetry should be free from occasional pessimism. This was the natural product of the circumstances of his life. It was necessary from the character of the age in which he wrote: it was inevitable from the quality of his own mind." Exactly what these circumstances were that caused "occasional pessimism" has never been revealed. A university classmate of Cameron's, S. W. Dyde, also hinted of a darkness in Cameron's personality: "Few, possibly none, of us realized what music there was behind those quiet eyes, and too, what sadness."

Other personal recollections are found in a letter to critic Arthur S. Bourinot from the poet's daughter, Mrs. Jessie Cameron Alison:

> He was very fond of the study of Astronomy–my Mother said a group used to often spend hours lying upon a rooftop studying the stars. (I think he must have put this study to good advantage in courtship days, for in one of his love letters–into which, as a child, I surreptitiously peeped!)–there was some reference to a 'first kiss,' stolen while pointing out certain planets,

(probably Venus!) . . . (To my shame and chagrin, those letters all disappeared . . . what good reading they would have made!). . . .

He wrote many love songs–addressed to many names. When I asked my mother about this, she said that he had said, "One must explain not only one's own feelings–but those of others."

It is not stated what the response was to this justification of the variety of addressees in the love poems (Adelle, Miss Iasigi, the "Beacon Hill Coquette," Isabel, and Lurline), although possibly Mrs. Cameron's reaction had something to do with her husband's "occasional pessimism."

Charles J. Cameron says in the preface to *Lyrics on Freedom, Love and Death*, "This volume represents about one fourth of his life work. If it is well received, the rest will follow in due course." Evidently the reception was not satisfactory, for the only remaining work ever to be published was the opera *Leo, the Royal Cadet* (1889), an uncharacteristically light-hearted creation that played successfully in Kingston, Ottawa, Guelph, Toronto, and Woodstock and Utica, New York.

In regard to the degree of achievement in Cameron's sole book of poetry, a considerable variety of judgments have been issued. E. K. Brown dismisses Cameron's 296 pages of lyrics as irrelevant for their time and place. Cameron was not concerned with Canadian nationalism (his poems about freedom deal with the identity struggles of foreign lands), and he did not depict nature in the precise fashion of his esteemed contemporary Archibald Lampman. For instance, Cameron's description of a bird as a "silver-throated singer" represents to Brown "a rhetorician's nature." Curiously, though, Brown's favorite writer, Lampman, holds Cameron's literary attributes in high regard. In "Two Canadian Poets: A Lecture, 1891" Lampman states: "There is a strong Byronic quality in Cameron's genius, and his utterance has the Byronic nerve and imperious directness. . . . Cameron's gift was a purely lyric one. He was a poet of life, and his work rings with the truth of experience. . . . He has left us in his own degree the same sort of gift that Heine left to the world, the picture of a brilliant, passionate, imperfect human soul, and the record of its eager contact with the world."

Despite all that enthusiasm from the generally well-respected Lampman, the usual present-day approach is to go along with the strictures of Brown, as can be seen in the curt assessment of Desmond Pacey: "George Frederick Cameron

[was] a rather too shrill disciple of the Swinburne of *Songs Before Sunrise* and the Tennyson of 'Maud'. . . . " Nevertheless, Cameron has had one modern champion, A. J. M. Smith, who included Cameron in his anthology *The Book of Canadian Poetry* (1957) with the accompanying endorsement: "His command of metrics is admirable. . . . There are literary echoes here and there–of Poe in the earlier poems and sometimes of Swinburne, and the influence of *Maud* can be felt in the background of the remarkable lyrical monodrama 'Ysolte.' Yet this is of little importance, for the literary influences are generally well assimilated. . . . There is nothing . . . of the conscious effort to be 'Canadian'. . . . There is, instead, an awareness of classical culture. . . . "

So the case of George Frederick Cameron is still up in the air, with no ultimate decision having been made thus far about whether he was a peripheral and derivative writer or a major creative force in late-nineteenth-century Canadian poetry. Luckily the evidence is available for a definitive assessment. *Lyrics on Freedom, Love and Death* has been reprinted recently in McClelland & Stewart's New Canadian Library Series (1973), and Cameron's remaining unpublished work is now housed in the library of the University of British Columbia. Everything is all set for some discerning scholar thoroughly to assess the worth of such lines as:

Ah, me! the mighty love that I have borne
   To thee, sweet Song! A perilous gift was it
My mother gave me that September morn
   When sorrow, song, and life were at one altar lit.

A careful, competent evaluation of the art of this mysterious, melancholy Canadian is long overdue.

References:
Arthur S. Bourinot, "George Frederick Cameron (Some notes on his opera and his life)," *Canadian Author and Bookman*, 29 (Winter 1954): 3-5; republished in his *Five Canadian Poets* (Montreal: Quality Press, 1956), pp. 22-26;

E. K. Brown, *On Canadian Poetry* (Toronto: Ryerson, 1943), pp. 37-41;

S. W. Dyde, "The Two Camerons," *Queen's Review*, 3 (August 1929): 196-198;

Hazel Ferguson, "Let Not This Poet Fade into Oblivion," *Atlantic Advocate*, 65 (August 1975): 51-52;

Archibald Lampman, "Two Canadian Poets: A Lecture, 1891" *University of Toronto Quarterly,* 13 (July 1944): 406-423; republished in *Masks of Poetry,* edited by A. J. M. Smith (Toronto: McClelland & Stewart, 1962), pp. 26-44;

Desmond Pacey, *Creative Writing in Canada,* second edition, revised (Toronto: Ryerson, 1961), p. 68;

A. J. M. Smith, ed., *The Book of Canadian Poetry,* third edition, revised and enlarged (Toronto: W. J. Gage, 1957), pp. 15-16, 144-157.

Papers:
Unpublished poetry by Cameron is in the University of British Columbia Library, Vancouver.

William Bleasdell Cameron
(26 July 1862 - 4 March 1951)

Harry Prest
Camrose Lutheran University College

BOOKS: *The War Trail of Big Bear, Being the Story of the Connection of Big Bear and Other Cree Indian Chiefs and their Followers with the Canadian North-West Rebellion of 1885, the Frog Lake Massacre and Events Leading up to and Following it, and of Two Month's Imprisonment in the Camp of the Hostiles* (London: Duckworth / Toronto: Ryerson, 1926; revised edition, London: Duckworth, 1927; Boston: Small, Maynard, 1927); revised as *Blood Red the Sun* (Calgary: Kenway, 1950);

When Fur Was King, by Cameron and Henry John Moberly (London & Toronto: Dent, 1929; New York: Dutton, 1929);

The Yarn of the Howling Gale, anonymous (Athabasca, Alta.: Cameron Shipyards, 1938);

Eyewitness to History: William Bleasdell Cameron, Frontier Journalist, edited by R. H. Macdonald (Saskatoon: Western Producer, 1985).

OTHER: Cecil E. Denny, *The Law Marches West,* edited by Cameron (Toronto: Dent, 1939; London: Dent, 1939).

That William Bleasdell Cameron should be included in a collection such as this is largely the result of a strange trick of fate, a classic instance of someone being in the wrong place at the right time. Had he not been serving as a clerk at a Hudson's Bay Company store in a small settlement near Fort Pitt on 2 April 1885, he would not have been witness to one of the bloodiest incidents of the North-West Insurrection, the Frog Lake Massacre. Up to that moment Cameron had shown not the least inclination toward a literary career; indeed, it would be another six years before he actually turned his hand to writing. But on that day he narrowly escaped death at the hands of the wild young men of Big Bear's band of Plains Cree, led by their fierce war chief, Wandering Spirit. For the next two months Cameron, along with a few other survivors, remained the closely guarded prisoners of the band, often under threat of violent death. During his captivity he witnessed the sacking of Fort Pitt and the inconclusive Battle of Frenchman's Butte. He was present at some of the band's war councils, including those called to decide his own fate, and heard Big Bear speak eloquently on behalf of the prisoners. On 1 June 1885 Cameron escaped and joined Gen. Thomas Strange's Alberta Field Force, volunteering as a guide and scout in the pursuit of his former captors. After the insurrection Cameron testified at the trials of those accused of responsibility for the massacre and spoke on behalf of Big Bear. Thirteen years later he produced a manuscript describing all those events and his own part in them. Twenty-seven years after that it finally appeared in print under the striking but misleading title *The War Trail of Big Bear* (1926), a nonfiction narrative of such compelling power that it assured its author a

William Bleasdell Cameron, circa 1925 (Chambury's Studio, Saskatoon; NA-1193-1, Glenbow Archives, Calgary, Alberta)

place in the history of Canadian letters.

William Bleasdell Cameron was born in Trenton, Ontario, on 26 July 1862, the son of John C. and Agnes Emma Cameron. He was named for his maternal grandfather, Canon William Bleasdell, who served as rector of St. George's Anglican Church in Trenton for forty years. His father, who worked in the lumber trade, died while Cameron was still a child. Cameron was an early and avid reader, a pursuit encouraged by his grandfather, who lent him many books from his own extensive library. He attended public and high school in Trenton, graduating in 1879. A two-year apprenticeship in a local drugstore owned by a member of the Bleasdell family followed. In 1881, however, he grew tired of the pharmacy business and headed west to Winnipeg, perhaps inspired by the tales of his cousin Joe Woods, a veteran of the North-West Mounted Police who had encountered Sitting Bull's band of Sioux when they crossed the Canadian border after their defeat of Gen. George

Armstrong Custer at Little Big Horn. Cameron then traveled by Red River cart brigade to Battleford, Northwest Territories, where he went to work for a local merchant. After learning the rudiments of trade with the native population and acquiring considerable proficiency in the Cree language, Cameron drifted south, then west, and finally back north again, picking up odd jobs along the way. The restlessness and rootlessness that were to dominate his life were already much in evidence.

In 1884 Cameron was at Frog Lake trading with the Woodland and Plains Cree in partnership with another Ontarian, George Dill. Cameron dissolved their partnership in the spring of 1885 and joined the Hudson's Bay Company, an act that probably saved his life, for Dill was slain in the ensuing massacre while the Hudson's Bay Company employees were spared. During his year-long stay at Frog Lake, Cameron came to know all the major players in the drama that was soon to unfold before his eyes. In particular he grew to be on friendly terms with Big Bear, the last great Plains Cree chief to sign a treaty with the Canadian government and the only one still refusing to settle on a reservation. Cameron, whom the Cree called *N'Chawamis*, or "My Little Brother," later proved to be both a keen observer and a sensitive, if not totally objective, interpreter of Cree life.

Cameron finally took up writing in the early 1890s while working for the Hudson's Bay Company at Fort Alexander. He sold articles based on his own frontier experiences to several leading journals, including *Waverly Magazine, Harper's Weekly*, and *Toronto Saturday Night*. At this time he also began a lifelong correspondence with Owen Wister, an American writer whose collection of cowboy stories, *The Virginian* (1902), subsequently made him famous. When Cameron's first book was published thirty years later, Wister wrote the foreword to the American edition. By 1896 Cameron had become a full-time journalist. In the fall of that year he joined the staff of a fledgling periodical, *Western Field and Stream*, and within a short time became its editor. There he discovered an obscure cowboy artist from Montana and signed him to a contract to provide the magazine with cover illustrations on Western themes. This arrangement provided the artist, C. M. "Charley" Russell, with some much-needed exposure. When in 1898, at Cameron's promptings, the magazine assumed a more national profile, dropping "Western" from its name and moving from St. Paul to New York, Cameron moved with it but soon had a dispute with his publisher and resigned. After a brief stay in Toronto, Cameron again headed west where he remained for the rest of his life. Thus ended the first phase of Cameron's literary career, in which he had produced numerous articles for leading periodicals, edited a sports and outdoor magazine that was rapidly acquiring a national reputation, and completed a manuscript version of his memoirs of the Frog Lake Massacre, the latter finished sometime in 1898.

The next twenty-seven years were very different. Though he married Mary Maud Atkins, a woman thirteen years his junior, in 1902, he did not settle down. He continued his nomadic life, and the marriage, while it produced two sons, yielded little else in the way of stability: Cameron for the most part traveled alone. He still did freelance writing when he could, but increasingly he became preoccupied with a succession of none-too-successful business ventures. All this changed be-

cause of a chance meeting in 1925 at the unveiling of a cairn marking the site of the Frog Lake Massacre. Cameron showed the manuscript of his memoirs to Howard A. Kennedy, an influential author and member of the Canadian Authors' Association. As reported by R. H. MacDonald, Kennedy was impressed; he told an association meeting in Winnipeg soon after: "I did not know of any book published in or on Canada in the last twenty years that so thrilled me." The manuscript was sent to Ryerson Press, which arranged for its publication as *The War Trail of Big Bear* by Duckworth's in London, reserving a portion of the original run for sale in Canada. This initial run quickly sold out as did a second printing. Duckworth's also printed an American edition with Wister's foreword but misfortune dogged that venture. The American publisher (Small, Maynard of Boston) went bankrupt while the pages were in transit, and on their arrival they were sold to a New York jobber to pay the customs duties. Though the book enjoyed brisk sales in New York, neither Cameron nor his publisher reaped any financial benefit.

The War Trail of Big Bear was well received. F. W. Howay, writing in the *Canadian Historical Review*, lauded its "simple but arresting style." He also praised Cameron's scrupulous honesty: "Everywhere he is fair to the Indians: apportioning the responsibility and placing the blame upon the proper persons, Wandering Spirit and Imasees." The *Times* of London also commended Cameron for having "preserved a most interesting record of the mode of life of his captors." For the most part such praise was deserved. Cameron's style is one of the book's chief strengths. Generally lucid and straightforward, it is yet capable of rising to moments of high drama when the occasion demands—the massacre itself or the trial of Big Bear, for example. Fortunately Cameron usually resisted the tendency to overwrite or melodramatize and instead allowed even the most terrifying, horrific, or pathetic events to speak for themselves. To say it is merely the style of a capable journalist would not do Cameron justice. He knew well how to set a scene, build suspense, and capture a mood or character. His action scenes are tense and exciting, his moments of pathos moving and not merely sentimental. In the hands of a less talented writer much of the power of the story itself—and it is undoubtedly one of the great stories of the Canadian West—would have been squandered.

Cameron (right) with his friend Harry Adams, circa 1945 (photograph by Everett Baker; NA-119-2, Glenbow Archives, Calgary, Alberta)

Cameron's depiction of the Cree is certainly another great strength. He was a perceptive observer who knew the language well. He lived and traded among them for a sufficient time to acquire some notion of their customs, rituals, and individual personalities. In the crucible of a two-month captivity, never far from death, he learned much more since his life depended on it. His sense of his captors as individuals is notable. As Macdonald has observed, Cameron does not think in stereotypes: "there is none of the white superiority over the 'child-like' native." Particularly memorable are his portraits of the main instigators of the uprising: the implacable old war chief, Wandering Spirit, and Big Bear's crafty and unscrupulous son, Imasees. They come wonderfully to life in Cameron's hands—as mysterious, treacherous, and always dangerous. But the work's undisputed masterpiece is clearly the portrait of Big Bear himself, a figure both heroic and pathetic, a tragic victim of his young warriors' rashness, who tries to stop the massacre and pleads eloquently for its survivors, yet finds himself charged with felony-treason—a charge he cannot understand—and sentenced to three years' imprisonment. His eloquent plea for mercy not for himself but for his people at the conclusion of his trial, after his sentencing, is the true climax of the book; it is one of the most moving speeches ever recorded.

It is little wonder then that Cameron, when he came to revise and reissue his book in the last years of his life, chose to rename the work *Blood Red the Sun*, attempting, albeit too late, to undo the impression his original title may have given that somehow the "war trail" was Big Bear's.

Doubt has more recently been raised about Cameron's objectivity. Canadian novelist Rudy Wiebe, for instance, who freely acknowledges the profound debt his own superb fictionalized version of the events (in *The Temptations of Big Bear*, 1973) owes Cameron's book, has noted the work's "personal biases." There is, of course, no denying Cameron's ethnocentricity; while he carefully assigns blame among the natives and Métis (Wandering Spirit, Imasees, and Louis Riel clearly being in his mind the chief culprits), he never seriously considers the part played by the Indian Affairs Department and, behind it, the John A. Macdonald government, in provoking the uprising. In this regard Wiebe's novel is a valuable counter voice, though it, too, is not without its own biases (but then again, as Wiebe shrewdly puts it, even supposedly objective scholars are "biased by their seemingly unbiased scholarliness"). Suffice it to say Cameron's account is sympathetic if not wholly free from bias.

Cameron's writing career did not end with *The War Trail of Big Bear*. In 1929 he collaborated with Henry John Moberly, a retired Hudson's Bay Company factor, in editing and expanding a version of the latter's well-kept diary of his experiences as a fur trader in the West long before white settlement. The resulting work, entitled *When Fur Was King*, was published by J. M. Dent. A few years later Cameron edited the journals of the late Cecil Denny, a former member of the original North-West Mounted Police, which were published as *The Law Marches West* in 1939. While both these works contain fascinating details of frontier life and numerous exciting incidents, neither has the powerful drama nor the compelling portraits of his first book. Thereafter Cameron continued his nomadic existence and, despite failing health, continued his free-lance writing al-

most to the time of his death, which occurred in Meadow Lake, Saskatchewan, on 4 March 1951.

Biographies:

Hugh A. Dempsey, "Foreword to Fifth Edition," in *Blood Red the Sun* (Edmonton: Hurtig, 1977), pp. ix-xvii;

R. H. Macdonald, Introduction to *Eyewitness to History: William Bleasdell Cameron, Frontier Journalist*, edited by Macdonald (Saskatoon: Western Producer, 1985), pp. xii-xxvi.

Reference:

W. J. Keith, ed., *A Voice in the Land: Essays by and about Rudy Wiebe* (Edmonton: NeWest, 1981), pp. 132-141, 163-169.

John Carroll

(8 August 1809 - 13 December 1884)

Paul Matthew St. Pierre
Simon Fraser University

BOOKS: *The Stripling Preacher; or, A Sketch of the Life and Character, with the Theological Remains of the Rev. Alexander S. Byrne* (Toronto: Green, 1852);

Past and Present; or, A Description of Persons and Events Connected with Canadian Methodism for the Last Forty Years (Toronto: Dredge, 1860);

Reasons for Wesleyan Belief and Practise Relative to Water Baptism (Peterborough, Ont.: White, 1862); revised as *Reasons for Methodist Belief and Practise Relative to Water Baptism* (Toronto: Wesleyan Conference Office, 1870);

Case and His Cotemporaries; or, The Canadian Itinerants' Memorial: Constituting a Bibliographical History of Methodism in Canada, 5 volumes (Toronto: Rose, 1867-1877);

The School of the Prophets; or, Father McRorey's Class and 'Squire Firstman's Kitchen Fire: A Fiction Founded on Facts, first series (Toronto: Burrage & Magurn, 1876); second series (Toronto: Magurn, 1876);

A Needed Exposition; or, The Claims and Allegations of the Canada Episcopals Calmly Considered by One of the Alleged "Seceders" (Toronto: Rose, 1877);

"Father Corson"; or, The Old Style Canadian Itinerant: Embracing the Life and Gospel Labours of the Rev. Robert Corson (Toronto: Rose, 1879);

Thoughts and Convictions of a Man of Years (Toronto: Briggs, 1879);

The "Exposition" Expounded, Defended, and Supplemented (Toronto: Methodist Book & Publishing House, 1881);

My Boy Life, Presented in a Succession of True Stories (Toronto: Briggs, 1882).

Collection: *Salvation! O the Joyful Sound: The Selected Writings of John Carroll*, edited by John Webster Grant (Toronto: Oxford University Press, 1967).

SELECTED PERIODICAL PUBLICATION– UNCOLLECTED: "James Evans, the Planter of Methodist Missions in Rupert's Land," *Canadian Methodist Magazine*, 16, no. 4 (1882): 329-340.

History has proven John Carroll to have been a kind of Parson Adams of the real, an itinerant minister who actually did manage to publish his sermons to universal acclaim. His exchange with history was so thorough, in fact, that his various writings have assumed a profound historical significance that in no way detracts from their theological astuteness. Whether he wrote Methodist biography, history, or apologetics, Carroll invariably documented the evangelization of Canadian society and bore witness to the process of Canadian Confederation, but, even more important, he held up a flawless homiletic glass to himself, revealing as much about his own character as an overactive missionary as about the character of a land founded through missionary hyperactivity. His biographical portraits of Alexander Byrne, William Case, Robert Corson, a host of supporting Methodists, and even the fanciful Father Mc-Rorey and Squire Firstman are also an inadvertent self-portrait, just as his autobiography, *My Boy Life* (1882), gives an inclusive impression of his whole life by offering a subjective account of a mere part of it. In these respects, Carroll's unique contribution to Canadian letters lies in the area of vicarious biography and subjective history. But his more traditionally ministerial literary offerings to Canadian ecclesiastical history are nevertheless startlingly singular, distinguishing Carroll–in the select company of perhaps only one other preacher-writer, William Withrow (1839-1908)–as a prophetic archivist of Methodism in nineteenth-century Canada.

The transitory circumstances of his birth and early life–"Father's changeableness led to a great many wearisome moves," he writes in *My Boy Life*–anticipate the peripatetic nature of his clerical and authorial maturity. Born on 8 August 1809 on Saltkill Island, Passamaquoddy Bay, New Brunswick, to Joseph and Molly Rideout Carroll in the middle of his parents' journey from Fredericton to their thousand-acre grant in Upper Canada (Ontario), John Saltkill Carroll and his twin brother, Isaac (the last of twelve children), found themselves on the road only three weeks into their lives and for a further three weeks before finally reaching their destination. Realizing later that the grant of land was no longer available to his family was John Carroll's early introduction to moving on as an answer to disappointment. Later, ministerial itinerancy would be his unceasing response not to his own misfortunes but to those of his dispersed congregations.

The most influential incidents of Carroll's boyhood were his first encounters with native people, his exposure to the Battle of Fort Niagara (1813), the deaths of his eldest brother and of his twin brother, and his mother's conversion from a Quaker background to the aggressive foreground of Methodism. At the time of the Carrolls' arrival in York (Toronto), at the cessation of the War of 1812, only the Church of England was in operation, but the foundation of a Methodist meeting-house there in 1818 marked both the "spiritual birth-place" of Mrs. Carroll and her son's own passage "from death unto life" (*My Boy Life*), an innocently arduous passage that concluded in 1824, when John Carroll took up his mother's lead and officially converted to the Methodism with which previously he had only flirted. Despite having only the rudiments of a formal education, he seriously considered pursuing careers as a lawyer and as a physician before choosing the Christian ministry and then becoming a Methodist preacher in 1829. It was precisely as a circuit preacher crisscrossing hundreds of miles of newly settled territory north of Toronto that Carroll fulfilled his ministerial commitment, not only by meeting the spiritual needs of isolated Canadians but also by making the personal contacts and the personal observations that were to be the subject-matter of his theological and creative writing, of what has come to be acknowledged as his authorial ministry.

In his first book, *The Stripling Preacher* (1852), Carroll addressed himself to both biography and eulogy, the study focusing on the precocious life and the premature death of Rev. Byrne, the romantically charismatic Irish convert whom Carroll (while stationed at London, one of his many pastoral appointments in Ontario) had met in the winter of 1848-1849, and who had died in 1851 as a result of a chill caught during his Canadian preaching tour. Carroll's fascination with Byrne was due partly to his premature death (at the mere age of majority), but mainly to what Carroll recognized as their shared precocity: Byrne's adolescent conversion and ministry seemed at once to recall and to anticipate Carroll's own conversion at the age of fifteen and his own ministry begun at the age of twenty-one.

This early identification with the subject of his writing set an important precedent for his subsequent books on Methodist preachers in Canada and the United States. In *Past and Present* (1860), for example, Carroll offers quasi-impressionistic descriptions of his encounters with the proponents of Methodism, rather than pretending to offer historically objective descriptions. His approach to the common ground of theology, biography, and history is, in a telling word, unorthodox, the focus of his impressions and encounters repeatedly shifting back to himself. "I well remember my first sight of [Rev. William Gill]. It was at a camp-meeting, the presiding officer at which asked Gill to preach," he writes, concluding: "Ever after he was a favourite preacher with me" (*Salvation!*, 1967). Carroll's portraits are detailed and precise, imaginable and memorable, powerfully suggesting the corporate ministry in which he himself had an equal share. As the perceived and the perceiver coexist in the single act of perception, so the congregation and the preacher share in the oneness of spiritual reality: this is a basic truth Carroll expresses throughout his writing, both thematically and technically.

Perhaps the greatest of his works in this respect is his concurrent memoir of Methodists and history of Methodism, *Case and His Cotemporaries* (1867-1877). Carroll's striking use of the word "cotemporaries" (a seventeenth-century variant of "contemporaries" that went out of fashion early in the eighteenth century, and that was only barely current in Carroll's own day) suggests his characteristic view of his fellow itinerants as temporary coworkers coexisting in the history of salvation. His introductory description of this ambitious five-volume study as "a biographical history" has the permanence of Methodism to back it up, a permanence to which Carroll contributed immeasurably through multiple processes of documentation. His observations of Rev. Case and his confreres on the road to Confederation are invaluable and irreplaceable, profound declarations of Canadian religious history. The study's greatest distinguishing features are its meticulous organization, from table of contents through to index, and its engaging biographical rhythm of conversion-to-superannuation, counterpointing the traditional birth-to-death biographical cycle.

During the 1870s and until his death, Carroll's publications alternated between precisely this kind of "biographical history" and a more theologically orthodox kind of evangelical apologetics, although his publications in the latter style—*Reasons for Wesleyan Belief and Practise Relative to Water Baptism* (1862), *A Needed Exposition* (1877), and *The "Exposition" Expounded* (1881)—do not figure directly in his reputation as an author. In *The School of the Prophets* (1876), Carroll extended his biographical-historical approach into a more subjective and idiosyncratic fictional-factual

compact, facetiously casting himself as William Warble, and casting Beulah Adams, daughter of War of 1812 veteran Capt. Joshua Adams, as Miss Hephzibah Firstman. Based on his ministerial tenure at Perth, Ontario, from 1830 to 1832, the work is a gentle roman à clef, its characters modeled on easily identifiable historical personages, but exaggerated to the prickly point of the comically ridiculous. Carroll's self-caricature as an unassuming new minister and an ingenuous young lover is especially appealing and revealing. In Warble one sees a Methodist minister as representative as Carroll's peculiar vision can make him, and thus readers come to see Carroll himself in the role of a representative Methodist minister. History has come to see him in a similar way, as a man in his own mold.

Although the point of view of his other major "biographical history" of the 1870s, *"Father Corson"; or, The Old Style Canadian Itinerant* (1879), is characteristically his own, his focus is unusually precise and other-centered, Carroll representing the great itinerant minister Corson (whose long career had ended with his death the year before the book's publication) less as a mere clergyman among clergy than as an individual man and a model minister.

That John Carroll never made as direct a likeness of himself as he made of every one of his biographical-historical subjects is the greatest indication of his own other-centeredness and of his otherworldly kind of exile in language and time. The sketchy details of his adult life—which his single volume of straightforward autobiography, *My Boy Life*, and his cameo roles in his other writings do little to clarify—contrast with the subjective precision of his authorial expression. His disappearance into the ranks of Methodist ministers, the byways of itinerancy, the labyrinth of history, and the plethora of words simply makes his largely documentary and testimonial existence all the more authentic and memorable. John Carroll was indisputably one of the greatest religious observers of nineteenth-century Canada, his books occupying a place in Methodist history analogous to that of *The Jesuit Relations* (1632-1672) in Catholic history. He saw and visualized in prose what very few thought to record.

References:

John Webster Grant, Introduction to *Salvation! O the Joyful Sound: The Selected Writings of John Carroll*, edited by Grant (Toronto: Oxford

University Press, 1967), pp. 9-31;

William Pirritte, *A Vindication of the Methodist Episcopal Church in Canada* (Hamilton, Ont.: Methodist Episcopal Book Room, 1879).

Papers:

Several of Carroll's letters are located at the United Church of Canada Central Archives in Toronto.

William Chapman

(13 September 1850 - 23 February 1917)

Jack Warwick
York University

BOOKS: *Les Québecquoises* (Quebec: Darveau, 1876);

Mines d'or de la Beauce (Levis, Que.: Mercier, 1881); translated as *Gold Mines of Beauce* (Levis, Que.: Mercier, 1881);

Guide et souvenir de la St-Jean-Baptiste (Montreal: Post, 1884);

Les Feuilles d'érable. Poésies canadiennes (Montreal: Gebhardt-Berthiaume, 1890);

Le Lauréat; Critique des oeuvres de M. Louis Fréchette (Quebec: Brousseau, 1894);

Deux Copains; Réplique à Mm. Fréchette et Sauvalle (Quebec: Brousseau, 1894);

A propos de la guerre hispano-américaine (Quebec: Brousseau, 1898);

Les Aspirations (Paris: Motteroz, Martinet, 1904);

Les Rayons du nord (Paris: Revue des Poètes, 1909);

Les Fleurs de givre (Paris: Revue des Poètes, 1912).

William Chapman is best known as a nationalistic French-Canadian poet of the late nineteenth and early twentieth centuries. His worst poetry, often ridiculed for its bombast and technical clumsiness, makes him an easy scapegoat for a literary fashion that has long since declined. Nevertheless, no anthology of French-Canadian poetry is complete without some of Chapman's best poems, which were greatly admired in his day and still stand as robust expressions of national sentiment.

George William Alfred Chapman was born in Saint-François de Beauce (Quebec), a prosperous rural region. His father, George William Alfred Chapman, was a businessman from England who had settled in what was then Lower Canada; his mother, Caroline Angers Chapman, was the daughter of a French-Canadian military and legal family. Chapman studied in Levis and Quebec City, without distinction, but well enough to gain a place at Laval University, where he entered his poem "L'Algonquine" in a competition in 1873. Chapman was awarded a "mention honorable"; it is thought that he might well have won the prize had his poem not offended religious susceptibilities by portraying a priest in physical combat with an Indian woman.

Chapman immersed himself in the French-Canadian literature of the day. Later he was to remark that he had read nothing else, but the influence of major French Romantics is also recognizable in his work. He abandoned law studies to take up writing, including journalism, and in 1876 he published a volume of collected verse, *Les Québecquoises*. This was the second such volume in Canada (the first being Louis Fréchette's *Mes Loisirs,* 1863) and earned the congratulations of François Coppée, at that time possibly the most popular of the Romantic poets in France.

The prominent themes in this first collection are national history, Canadian scenery, and nature in general. There is also much comment on world events–showing Chapman's ultramontane Catholicism and arch-conservatism–as well as a few conventional love poems. Occasional verse in the tradition of Octave Crémazie plays a large part. The quality of the versification and

William Chapman (C 9747, National Archives of Canada)

style is uneven, and the poet himself later dismissed much of the collection as youthful errors.

During the next ten years, Chapman turned his hand to various types of writing. He translated poems by Henry Wadsworth Longfellow, he worked for newspapers, and he published two volumes in prose. *Mines d'or de la Beauce* (*Gold Mines of Beauce,* 1881) is a well-documented report on local gold mining. *Guide et souvenir de la St-Jean-Baptiste* (1884) gives an account of the Montreal feast of Saint John the Baptist (Canada's patron saint).

Les Feuilles d'érable (The Maple Leaves, 1890) is Chapman's second poetry collection; despite characteristic weaknesses, it is considerably better than the first. The best verse, in the manner of Coppée, contains moving evocations of the life of simple people. The celebration of nature gives the New World a place in the aesthetic consciousness. "L'Aurore boréale" (first version), a word painting of the northern lights, is a reveling in spectacular beauty. A feature imitated in Cana-

dian tourist illustrations ever since is the placing of a moose in the foreground of the symphony of light and color. In other poems, the search for effect is all too visible. Religion, patriotism, and folk tales are the basis of other poems, which thus continue Chapman's tradition, including his didacticism.

The year 1894 seems to have included considerable bitterness for Chapman. He had given up regular journalism, and his hopes of success as a writer were seriously threatened by criticism; his subscription campaign to publish another volume was disappointing; and he was short of money. Meanwhile, Fréchette had been honored by the Académie Française in 1880 with the title of "laureate" and was lionized in Montreal. Chapman had been one of his devoted admirers and imitators. Jealousy was exacerbated by ideological differences, and Chapman attacked Fréchette's support for secular education in Quebec. (Opposition to secular schools was a powerful rallying cry until 1966.) In the ensuing quarrel Chapman attacked Fréchette's verse, using (with some justification) the very complaints that had been levelled against his own poetry: plagiarism and clumsiness. Fréchette riposted and Chapman then published his own collected articles in a volume entitled *Le Lauréat* (1894). These complicated maneuvers constituted a major literary event, doing little for the reputation of Chapman.

Continuing to write on controversial topics, he produced *A propos de la guerre hispano-américaine* (1898), a condemnation in verse of the American invasion of Cuba. Chapman upholds the bond of the Latin peoples, their sense of chivalry, and a Romantic notion of the hispanic character, contrasted with the materialism and bellicosity of Americans. A milder version was published in his next collection, *Les Aspirations* (1904).

After working as a civil servant and as an insurance salesman in the Eastern Townships, Chapman returned to Ottawa as a translator. He at last traveled overseas and saw France in 1903. Renewed contact with the soil and with France inspired the poetry he was now composing for his next three volumes, generally considered his best.

Les Aspirations was published in Paris. While it seems obvious that Chapman was seeking recognition in France such as his rival Fréchette had enjoyed, there can be no doubt of the strong feeling for the land of his cultural ancestry. "Notre langue," first published in *Le Monde Illustré* in 1890, gives vigorous and varied expression to the French Canadians' attachment to their mother tongue. "A la Bretagne" is a movingly explicit revelation of nostalgia for the country of origin, whose landscapes, legends, and ancient traditions are cherished, while evocations of sea and ships link the two countries. The collection also contains a high proportion of rural Quebec scenes, including "Le Laboureur," probably Chapman's most anthologized poem; in a colorful Parnassian description, the ploughman is first identified with his land, and then his productive activity is sanctified by association with God. Again Chapman produced an image that was to be. much repeated, degenerating into a literary and political

cliché. This volume's best poems earned it a good reception and it was honored by the Académie Française.

Two more of Chapman's collections were to be honored by the Académie. *Les Rayons du nord* (The Northern Lights, 1909) and *Les Fleurs de givre* (Frost Flowers, 1912) continue Chapman's well-established themes, stressing the Canadian landscape and further developing scenes with Amerindians, lumbermen, trappers, and hunters, as well as relating folktales. Word pictures of wildlife express the poet's yearning for the noble, the pure, and the grandiose. They probably also reveal the yearnings of his generation for escape and greater personal freedom, but such intimations must have been mainly unconscious; Chapman remained a conservative and conforming Roman Catholic. One finds no reference to his late and somewhat unhappy marriage to Emma Gingras (1909).

With his strengths and his weaknesses, William Chapman is characteristic of French-Canadian poetry at the turn of the century. From a modern critical distance, the stylistic difference between him and Fréchette seems unimportant. Chapman may well have been more clumsy more often, but they speak the same grandiloquence. Meanwhile, the *symboliste* movement was at its height in France, and in Canada, Emile Nelligan's work was highly appreciated by the Montreal avant-garde. Yet Chapman's nationalistic vision of the Canadian land with its muscular inhabitants and symbolic fauna is a lasting contribution, anticipating by ten years the *terroir* (Quebec rural) school of writing. His unequivocal support for a supranational French-language community remains an important part of Quebec's identity in a more complex cultural and political scene.

Biography:
Jean Ménard, *William Chapman* (Montreal: Fides, 1968).

Reference:
Jane Turnbull, *Essential Traits of French-Canadian Poetry* (Chicago, 1935).

Pierre-Joseph-Olivier Chauveau

(30 May 1820 - 4 April 1890)

Mary Lu MacDonald

BOOKS: *Charles Guérin* (Montreal: Cherrier, Lovell, 1852);

L'Instruction publique au Canada (Québec: Côté, 1876);

Souvenirs et Légendes (Québec: Côté, 1877);

François-Xavier Garneau. Sa Vie et ses oeuvres (Montreal: Beauchemin & Valois, 1883);

Bertrand de la Tour, suivi de Les Plaines d'Abraham (Levis, Que.: Roy, 1898).

Pierre-Joseph-Olivier Chauveau was one of nineteenth-century Quebec's greatest men of letters as well as one of its best-known public figures. Born in Charlesbourg, on the outskirts of Quebec City, he was the son of Pierre-Charles and Marie-Louise Roy Chauveau. His father died when he was four, and the young Chauveau was raised in the home of his maternal grandfather, Joseph Roy, a prosperous and well-connected Quebec merchant. As a student at the Quebec Seminary, Chauveau was evidently brilliant, so that great achievements were expected of him from an early age. He had just begun his legal studies in 1837 when the first Lower Canada Rebellion broke out. His first published work, the poem "L'Insurrection" (*Le Canadien*, 6 April 1838), praising the rebel *patriotes*, appeared the next spring. "L'Insurrection" and the few additional poems on the same theme that followed it indicate that the teenaged Chauveau was already an accomplished poet as well as a political partisan. In 1841 he was admitted to the bar and immediately became a partner in the firm of his uncle Louis-David Roy.

The remainder of his life falls readily into three distinct periods. In the first of these he busied himself with matters both literary and political. In the early 1840s he was one of the founders of the Société Saint Jean-Baptiste de Québec and of the Société Canadienne d'Etudes Littéraires et Scientifiques. He also was president of the prestigious and largely anglophone Quebec Literary and Historical Society in 1843. Although he was never a prolific poet, his poems continued to appear from time to time in newspapers

Pierre-Joseph-Olivier Chauveau (C 4267, National Archives of Canada)

and periodicals. The first installment of his novel *Charles Guérin* appeared in *L'Album Littéraire* in February 1846. Despite his personal literary production in the 1840s he was best known in intellectual circles for his lectures on French literature and history, given before various literary and patriotic societies. These were always extensively reported and were praised by all except his political enemies.

Although there were loose "reform" and "Tory" groupings, no firm party system existed in the Canadas at this time. Coalitions that had developed in relation to one issue often collapsed when confronting another. Chauveau was a philosophical liberal. As a nationalist he had supported the *patriotes* and opposed the union of Upper and Lower Canada. However, he entered the Legislative Assembly in 1844 as a supporter of Louis-Hippolyte Lafontaine, a reformer who had chosen to work within the system. Chauveau maintained his political independence, particularly in advancing the interests of Quebec City against those of Montreal. Consequently, although the reformers came to power in 1848, it was not until 1851 that Chauveau was admitted to the cabinet. There he remained until dropped by a new ministry in 1855. He campaigned vigorously for a government appointment and was rewarded a few months later with the post of superintendent of the Board of Education.

While he sat in the Legislative Assembly *Charles Guérin* had been published, initially in installments and subsequently in book form (1852). This work is considered by many today to be the finest nineteenth-century Quebec novel. Certainly it is the best of those written in the pre-1860 period. Influenced by Honoré de Balzac, it attempts to present in the form of fiction a realistic account of Quebec life in the early 1830s. The principal protagonists are young French-speaking males, thwarted in their attempts to establish themselves in the world by an English-speaking ruling class that controls political, commercial, and administrative advancement. The overcrowded legal, medical, and clerical professions are their only options if they remain in Quebec. Exile is the only other possibility. Ultimately they establish a new French-speaking colony in Eastern Quebec, where everyone lives happily ever after.

In addition to the larger themes of Quebec society, *Charles Guérin* depicts small details of life in both town and country. There are mid-Lent and May Day festivals, auctions, student social events, and scenes with servants who speak lower-class dialects. The cholera epidemic of 1832 is one of the central episodes of the plot. As is generally the case with nineteenth-century novels, none of the characters is particularly lifelike, although some of them are fairly complex. The various elements of the plot are generally well controlled, although coincidence is allowed to play a much greater role than is acceptable today. As an example of historical mythmaking the novel is unusual in that it deals with the recent, rather than distant, past.

Title page for Chauveau's first book, now considered one of the best novels published in nineteenth-century Quebec

In the next period of his life, the twelve years Chauveau spent as superintendent of the Department of Public Instruction for Canada East (Quebec), he published little other than articles on education topics in the *Journal de l'Instruction Publique*. He continued to be known for his public addresses on national and literary themes, and he entered into correspondence with many of the leading intellectual figures in France, thus bringing Canadian cultural progress to the attention of Europeans.

An impasse in the selection of the first premier of Quebec at the time of Confederation in 1867 resulted in the appointment of Chauveau to the post, as a moderate figure acceptable to all the contending interests. Shifts in political alliances within the Canadas meant that he was now officially a Conservative. The job was probably an impossible one, but Chauveau managed to win the first election with a large majority, and a second one in 1871 with a reduced majority. Unable to control his divided party, he resigned in

1873 and was appointed speaker of the Senate, a post he had to leave the following year when the Conservatives were defeated. Unsuccessful in his attempt to win a seat in the federal parliament, in debt, and suffering from the deaths between 1870 and 1875 of his wife–Marie-Louise-Flore, née Massé, whom he had married in 1840–and three of his eight daughters, he tried to reenter provincial politics. Again he was rebuffed. Eventually, in 1877, he was given the post of sheriff of Montreal–a lucrative and powerful position. He also began to teach in the law faculty of what became the University of Montreal. He was dean of the faculty from 1884 to 1890, during which time he was frequently attacked by ultramontane social forces for his liberal views.

In this last period of his life he was able to devote more time to his role as a man of letters. In the three years (1874-1877) when he had no regular income, he produced two books, *L'Instruction publique au Canada* (1876) and *Souvenirs et Légendes* (1877), and wrote the manuscript of another, *Bertrand de la Tour*, published in 1898 after his death. He also gave more public addresses. His work on François-Xavier Garneau was included in the fourth edition of the *Histoire du Canada* in 1883 and was published separately later that year. He was president of the Royal Society of Canada in 1883 and 1884. The Chauveau Medal, established in 1951, is now awarded biennially by the Royal Society to honor a distinguished contribution to the humanities.

In his own day Chauveau's literary works were generally well received. When they were not, it is important to investigate the political and social motivation of the critic. The Quebec literary world of his day was a small one in which Montreal-Quebec City rivalries played an important part. Within each city there were competing literary groups, each of which usually had access to the pages of a newspaper or periodical. Since all writers were amateurs who made their living in some other activity, there were often professional rivalries, as well as literary and personal ones. Some of this ad hominem criticism persists today in the critical writing of those who feel that Chauveau's later political career demonstrates a reprehensible abandonment of his youthful principles.

Nonetheless, his poetry, his public addresses, his nonfiction works, and his one novel were all of unusually high quality for their time. As a man of culture and intelligence he left a considerable legacy to future generations.

References:

Jean-Charles Falardeau, "Le Désir du départ dans quelques anciens romans canadiens," *Recherches Sociographiques* (May-August 1963): 219-223;

T.-L. Hébert, *Bio-bibliographie de Pierre-Joseph-Olivier Chauveau*, Thèse de bibliothéconomie, Université de Montréal, 1944;

Maurice Lebel, "P.-J.-O. Chauveau, humaniste de dix-neuvième siècle," *Mémoires de la Société Royale du Canada*, third series 56 (1962): 1-10.

Papers:

The Archives Nationales de Québec in Quebec City hold Chauveau's personal papers in file no. AP-G-41. Correspondence may also be found in other papers both there and at the National Archives of Canada, Ottawa.

Harriet Vaughan Cheney

(9 September 1796 - 14 May 1889)

Mary Lu MacDonald

BOOKS: *A Peep at the Pilgrims in sixteen hundred thirty-six. A Tale of Olden Times*, 2 volumes (Boston: Wells & Lilly, 1824; London: G. B. Whittaker, 1825);

The Rivals of Acadia, an Old Story of the New World (Boston: Wells & Lilly, 1827);

Sketches from the Life of Christ (Boston: Crosby, 1844);

Confessions of an Early Martyr (Boston: Benjamin H. Greene, 1846).

Harriet Vaughan Cheney is an interesting anomaly in Canadian literary history. Although she wrote four books, none of them are considered "Canadian Literature," because they were published in the United States, despite the fact that the Canadian canon incorporates many works published in other countries by residents of what is now Canada. Cheney is known only as a periodical writer and editor whose importance stems from her association with the *Literary Garland* and the *Snow Drop*. Even in this context, her name but not her writing is what is familiar to scholars.

Cheney was the daughter of the distinguished American Unitarian theologian John Foster and his wife, Hannah Webster Foster, one of the first American novelists. She was born in Brighton, Massachusetts, but her permanent residence for most of her life was in Montreal, where she was married to Edward Cheney in 1830, bore at least four children, and died in 1889. Her family's Boston-Montreal axis and the literary and theological interests she absorbed from her parents are the dominant features of her life and writing.

Mrs. Cheney's first two books were published before her marriage and probably before her move to Montreal, although exactly when she settled there is not known. Members of the Foster family went back and forth between Montreal and Boston with regularity, as did her dry-goods merchant husband, who also came from a Boston family. She may have met Cheney in Boston, or in Montreal at the home of her older sister, who

had married a Montreal hardware dealer. Edward Cheney died in Boston in 1845, so Mrs. Cheney may have been residing there when her last book was published, but she was back in Montreal by at least 1847 and seems to have resided there for the last forty-two years of her life.

Harriet Cheney, her sister Elizabeth Lanesford Cushing, and their cousin Elizabeth Hedge are credited in Montreal Unitarian history with keeping the fledgling congregation together during the difficult period of the rebellions of 1837 and 1838, when some of their fellow members' *patriote* sympathies had forced them to flee. A third Foster sister married Rev. Henry Giles, one of the ministers who served the Montreal church during this time.

Although she published four books in the United States, in Canada Cheney is best known for her contributions to the *Literary Garland* and for her editorship, with Cushing, of the first Canadian children's periodical, the *Snow Drop*. The two sisters also edited the *Garland* for the last year of its publication, and the demise of that periodical may have been linked to a dispute with the distributor over the ownership of the *Snow Drop* mailing list. In both publications Cheney's interest in fiction based on North American history, first evident in her books, can also be found. Although nothing in the *Snow Drop* was signed, the two long series, "Conversations on History" and "Stories from the History of Canada" that appeared there are almost certainly her work. Most of the sixteen stories by "H.V.C." in the *Garland* are set in the past, particularly in the period of New France.

Cheney was a sound, if unexciting writer, more concerned in prose with describing events than with creating atmosphere or character. Her poetry is typical of the time, metrically and morally correct but not exceptional in any way. Moral precepts were important to her. She also valued progress and believed in human perfectability. When writing about Canadian history she was sympathetic to native peoples, taking the view, enlightened for her time, that when they had absorbed the ways of Western European civilization they would take their place as equals in Canadian society. Equally enlightened for 1850 was her view that children were inherently good and needed only encouragement and education to help them follow the correct moral path.

Many passing references have been made in literary histories to the *Snow Drop* as the first publication of its kind, but there have been no extended studies of the periodical. It merits detailed attention as evidence of the ideas liberal women considered important in the education of their children in mid-nineteenth-century Canada.

Similarly, as one of Canada's earliest writers of historical fiction, whose works were produced in a period when many of her contemporaries did not even think of Canada as having a history, Cheney's work in that genre merits scholarly study.

Reference:
Carol Gerson, "*The Snow Drop* and *The Maple Leaf*: Canada's First Periodicals for Children," *Canadian Children's Literature*, 18/19 (1980).

Laure Conan
(Félicité Angers)
(9 January 1845 - 6 June 1924)

Dawn Thompson
University of British Columbia

and

Lorraine Weir
University of British Columbia

BOOKS: *Un amour vrai* (Montreal: Leprohon & Leprohon, 1879); republished as *Larmes d'amour* (Montreal: Leprohon & Leprohon, 1897);

Angéline de Montbrun (Quebec: Brousseau, 1884); translated by Yves Brunelle (Toronto & Buffalo: University of Toronto Press, 1974);

Si les canadiennes le voulaient! Aux canadiennes-françaises (à l'occasion de la nouvelle année) (Quebec: Darveau, 1886); republished as *Si les canadiennes le voulaient! suivi par Aux jours de Maisonneuve* [theatrical adaptation of *L'Oublié*] (Montreal: Leméac, 1974);

A l'oeuvre et à l'épreuve (Quebec: Darveau, 1891); translated by Edward J. Devine, under the pseudonym of Theresa A. Gethin, as *The Master Motive: A Tale of the Days of Champlain* (St. Louis: Herder, 1909);

L'Oublié (Montreal: Revue Canadienne, 1900);

Elisabeth Seton (Montreal: Revue Canadienne, 1903);

Physionomies de Saints (Montreal: Beauchemin, 1913);

Silhouettes canadiennes (Quebec: Action Sociale, 1917);

L'Obscure Souffrance (Quebec: Action Sociale, 1919);

La Vaine Foi (Montreal: Maisonneuve, 1921);

La Sève immortelle (Montreal: Bibliothèque de l'Action Française, 1925);

Oeuvres romanesques, 3 volumes, edited by Roger Le Moine (Montreal: Fides, 1974-1975).

Quebec's first woman novelist and author of the first psychological novel in Canadian literature, Félicité Angers, who published all her works

Laure Conan

under the pseudonym Laure Conan, is a transitional figure in the history of Quebec literature. In her novel *Angéline de Montbrun* (1884) she moves beyond the patriotic themes typical of much nineteenth-century fiction in Quebec and takes as her center of interest—as André Brochu has shown in a 1963 article—the interior climate of her characters. Whereas writers of the *terroir* school later concerned themselves with the idea of the land itself, Conan attempts to explore symbolic wounds, the movements of love and loss, and the compensatory life of religious devotion in a conservative Catholic society.

Conan, the daughter of Elie and Marie Perron Angers, was born at La Malbaie, Quebec, on 9 January 1845 and studied for five years at the Ursuline convent in Quebec City. Shortly after she left the convent, she fell in love with Pierre-Alexis Tremblay, a surveyor and member of Parliament, but for reasons which remain obscure, she never married him. The rest of her life she devoted to writing: to journalism as well as to works of fiction and drama. It is generally believed that her first experience of love and loss provided her with the central theme for her fiction. With the exception of a five-year stay (1893-1898) at the convent of the Soeurs de Precieux-Sang at Maska, Conan remained at the family home at La Malbaie. In October 1923 she moved to a home

for the aged attached to a convent in Sillery. On 6 June 1924 she died at the Hôtel-Dieu in Montreal, of pulmonary congestion following surgery.

Angéline de Montbrun is considered by most critics to be the finest of Conan's novels. It consists of a threefold narrative structure: an initial epistolary section, followed by a brief third person narrative, then extracts from Angéline's journal. The exchange of letters (in which Angéline figures only briefly) introduces Maurice Darville, a young man who is in the process of courting Angéline; his sister Mina, confidante of both Maurice and Angéline; and Charles de Montbrun, Angéline's father, who finally gives his consent to the engagement. The young couple's relationship and the first section of the novel are interrupted by Charles's violent death.

This event produces severe consequences. Mina, who has been portrayed as a slightly headstrong young socialite attracted to the much older Charles, enters a convent. Angéline's health declines rapidly. In the first (serially published) version of the novel, a facial tumor develops, and the operation to remove it leaves her disfigured. In the second version (the 1884 book) a more obviously symbolic fall necessitates an operation with the same results. Believing that Maurice's ardor has cooled, Angéline releases him from his commitment to marry her. Alone at the Montbrun home, she enters a protracted period of mourning, characterized in her journal by confusion between grief for her father and for the lost love of Maurice. A product of the Jansenist society of nineteenth-century Quebec, Angéline eventually achieves a preference for the abiding presence of her dead father over the transitory love of a mortal man. Once again rejecting Maurice at the end of the novel, Angéline chooses to live (and write) her life on her own terms; however, the difficulty of her decision and the ambiguity with which it is expressed reveal those terms to be the conditions of her own psychosocial imprisonment within a patriarchal culture.

While Conan's contemporaries were most impressed with the spirit of Christian renunciation they perceived in *Angéline de Montbrun*, more recent critics have been concerned with the motifs of symbolic disfigurement and self-sacrifice, by what some have seen as Angéline's Electra complex, and by Conan's depiction of the dichotomy of flesh and spirit, an opposition regarded as one of the great neuroses of premodern Quebec. Attention has also been given to the structure of this novel, with at least one commentator arguing

Illustration by Marc Antigna for a 1904 edition of Conan's L'Oublié, *a patriotic love story*

that the tension between the initial epistolary mode and the fragmented form of Angéline's journal extracts constitutes the true interest of the novel.

More recently, the publication of Conan's *Oeuvres romanesques* (1974-1975), beginning on the fiftieth anniversary of her death, has encouraged readings of her work. Critics such as René Dionne, E. D. Blodgett, and Patricia Smart have attempted to separate author from character, a juxtaposition that, as Gabrielle Poulin showed in a 1983 article, was already evident at the time of Louis Fréchette's 1906 commentary on the novel. In addition, the feminist analyses by Blodgett and Smart have pointed toward the novel's potential for resistance to the patriarchal system in which it works. However, the systematic reassessment not only of *Angéline de Montbrun* but also of Conan's oeuvre within the sociopolitical and literary contexts of nineteenth-century Quebec literature is still in its early stages. It is a much-needed labor, as is indicated by the views of Gérard Tougas expressed in his *Histoire de la littérature canadienne-française* (1960). Conan, Tougas remarks, "concevait le roman comme un genre d'apostolat [et] ne pouvait écrire que des catéchèses" ("thought of the novel as a kind of apostolate [and] was able to write only catechisms" [1966 translation]). Although thirty years

old, this view remains in place, categorizing Conan as a religious apologist and rendering the considerable body of her nationalistic and religious journalism, much of it an attempt to inspire the women of Quebec to action, virtually incomprehensible. It also relegates to the shadows some of her other novels, such as *A l'oeuvre et à l'épreuve* (1891; translated as *The Master Motive: A Tale of the Days of Champlain*, 1909), the story of Charles Garnier, one of the Jesuit martyrs of Canada. Conan's patriotic works also include her historical novel *L'Oublié* (The Forgotten One, 1900), which received a prize from the French Academy and was later adapted into a play under the title *Aux jours de Maisonneuve* (In the Days of Maisonneuve). Telling the story of the love of Lambert Closse and Elizabeth Moyen, *L'Oublié* is set against a backdrop of Iroquois violence and the early days of the settlement of Ville-Marie, which later became Montreal. *La Sève immortelle* (The Immortal Sap, 1925), written by Conan on her deathbed and published posthumously, is another historical fiction. Set in 1760, it turns upon the conflict of Jean de Tilly, a hero in the Battle of Sainte-Foy, who must decide whether to marry Thérèse d'Antrée and go to France or remain true to the cause of patriotism and stay in Canada.

Those whose concerns are primarily evaluative and biographical have persisted in seeing these novels primarily as expressions of Conan's lifelong fascination with the sorrows of love, even in light of the activist, individualist stance of some of her more argumentative writing. As recent revisionist critiques begin to challenge views such as those expressed in Tougas's history, further reassessment of Conan's work is likely to provide a new understanding of her contribution to Quebec literature as well as to the development of the novel and of feminist polemic in Canada.

References:

Alexandre Amprimoz, "Signification de la multiplicité formelle de *Angéline de Montbrun* de Laure Conan," *Studies in Canadian Literature*, 9, no. 2 (1984): 144-147;

Francine Belle-Isle, "La Voix-séduction–A propos de Laure Conan," *Etudes littéraires*, 11, no. 3 (1978): 459-472;

E. D. Blodgett, "The Father's Seduction: The Example of Laure Conan's *Angéline de Montbrun*," in *A Mazing Space: Writing Canadian Women Writing*, edited by Shirley Neuman and Smaro Kamboureli (Edmonton: Longspoon/NeWest, 1986), pp. 17-30;

André Brochu, "Le Cercle et l'évasion verticale dans *Angéline de Montbrun*," *Etudes Françaises*, 1 (February 1965): 90-100; reprinted in his *L'Instance critique, 1961-1973*, pp. 121-132;

Brochu, "La Technique romanesque dans *Angéline de Montbrun*," *Le Quartier Latin*, 155, no. 37 (19 February 1963): 7; and no. 41 (5 March 1963): 11; reprinted in his *L'Instance critique, 1961-1973* (Montreal: Leméac, 1974), pp. 112-120;

Jacques Cotnam, "*Angéline de Montbrun*: Un Cas patent de masochisme moral," *Journal of Canadian Fiction*, 2 (Summer 1973): 152-160;

René Dionne, "Entre terre et ciel. Pour une lecture littéraire de l'oeuvre de Laure Conan," *Lettres Québécoises*, 1 (March 1976): 19-21;

Louis Fréchette, "*Angéline de Montbrun* par Laure Conan," *Le Journal de Française*, 7 April 1906, p. 4;

Madeleine Gagnon-Mahony, "*Angéline de Montbrun*: Le Mensonge historique et la subversion de la métaphore blanche," *Voix et Images du Pays*, 5 (1972): 57-68;

François Gallays, "*Angéline de Montbrun*: Reflets et rédoublements–L'infra-textuel," *Incidences*, 4 (January-April 1980): 51-66; translated as "Reflections in the Pool: The Subtext of Laure Conan's *Angéline de Montbrun*," in *Traditionalism, Nationalism, & Feminism–Women Writers of Québec*, edited by Paula Gilbert Lewis (Westport, Conn.: Greenwood, 1985), pp. 11-26;

Rosmarin Heidenreich, "Narrative Strategies in Laure Conan's *Angéline de Montbrun*," *Canadian Literature*, 81 (Summer 1979): 37-46;

Pierre H. Lemieux, "Le Plan du roman *Angéline de Montbrun*," *Revue de l'Université d'Ottawa/University of Ottawa Quarterly*, 54 (January-March 1984): 55-64;

Suzanne Paradis, *Femme Fictive, Femme réelle* (Ottawa: Garneau, 1966);

Gabrielle Poulin, "*Angéline de Montbrun* ou les abîmes de la critique," *Revue d'Histoire Littéraire du Québec et du Canada Français*, 5 (1983): 125-132;

Patricia Smart, "*Angéline de Montbrun* ou la chute dans l'écriture," in her *Ecrire dans la maison du pére: l'émergence du féminin dans la tradition littéraire du Québec* (Montreal: Editions Québec/Amérique, 1988): 41-86;

Gérard Tougas, *Histoire de la littérature canadienne-française* (Paris: Presses Universitaires de France, 1960); translated by Alta Lind Cook as *History of French-Canadian Literature* (Toronto: Ryerson, 1966).

Papers:

Félicité Angers's correspondence with Abbé H.-R. Casgrain is in the Fonds Casgrain at the Archives du Séminaire de Québec.

Octave Crémazie
(16 April 1827 - 16 January 1879)

Kathy Mezei
Simon Fraser University

BOOKS: *Oeuvres complètes* (Montreal: Beauchemin & Valois, 1882);
Lettres et fragments de lettres (Montreal: Beauchemin & Valois, 1886);
Poésies (Montreal: Beauchemin & Valois, 1886);
Oeuvres, 2 volumes, edited by Odette Condemine (Ottawa: Editions de l'Université d'Ottawa, 1972, 1976).

OTHER: *La Littérature canadienne de 1850 à 1860*, volume 2, includes 25 poems by Crémazie (Quebec: Desbarats, 1864).

With the appearance of his celebrated poem "Le Drapeau de Carillon" (The Flag of Carillon) in *Le Journal de Quebec* in 1858, Octave Crémazie was hailed as the national poet of Quebec. The first important poet to emerge in that province, he also became the major representative of French-Canadian romanticism. Attracted both by his poetry and his lively presence, a literary circle—the earliest in Quebec—formed around him. For these reasons Crémazie inspired continued admiration during his lifetime, rising, after his death, to the height of a legendary figure.

Born on 16 April 1827 in Quebec City, he was baptized Claude-Joseph-Olivier Crémazie. In admiration for the bishop of Quebec, Joseph-Octave Plessis, his mother added the name Octave. He was the eleventh of twelve children born to Jacques and Marie-Anne Miville Crémazie. Appropriately for a poet obsessed by ancestors and a heroic past, his grandfather had arrived in Quebec in 1759 on a ship in a flotilla sailing to the assistance of Marquis de Montcalm in his doomed battle with the English. Crémazie's family was in trade, and when the poet abruptly ended his studies at the Pétit Séminaire de Québec at the age of sixteen, he also entered the world of commerce. In 1844, with his brother Joseph, he opened the famous bookstore Librairie Ecclésiastique de J. & O. Crémazie. Within ten years the bookstore had developed into a successful commercial establishment, importing not only

Octave Crémazie (photograph by Albert Ferland; C 6717, National Archives of Canada)

religious texts, artifacts, wine, and cheese from France, but also a wide and formerly unavailable range of books. Crémazie dipped enthusiastically into the many books that stocked his shop, and became renowned for his erudition, prodigious memory, and subtle wit. In keeping with his interest in cultural affairs, he helped found L'Institut Canadien de Québec in 1847.

Crémazie acquired his reputation of national poet of Quebec because he explored subjects close to French-Canadian hearts: the hero-

The building on Rue la Fabrique in Quebec City that housed the Crémazies' bookstore, a popular meeting place for young writers in the 1850s

ism of their ancestors, the soldiers, explorers, missionaries, and settlers of New France; and fidelity to the French-Canadian soil, traditions, language, and Catholic religion. In at least two succeeding generations of poets, the patriotic mode that he perfected dominated the content of their verse. Many of his poems were occasional poems, commemorating some event of note, often a military battle, for he reveled in dreams of military glory. Other poems extolled his love for France, the estranged motherland and beloved repository of French culture, traditions, and Catholicism. In these poems he attempted to attain an epic quality, but they more often rang the tones of an impassioned and nostalgic patriotism. He also turned his hand to the lyric, and here the tone darkened as he dwelled, in macabre and morbid fashion, on death. Writing in the tradition of Alphonse de Lamartine, Alfred de Musset, Lord

Byron, and Victor Hugo, Crémazie firmly aligned himself with Romanticism. Stylistically he was conventional, resorting frequently to the classical alexandrine within quatrains or sestets. In politics he was a conservative and an imperialist, believing strongly in the entrenched powers of monarchical governments and abhorring the upheavals of 1848 revolutionary Europe, although he approved of the emergence of responsible government in Canada. A devout Catholic, he sided with the ultramontanes and ardently supported the Pope and his mission.

From 1849–when his first poem, "Premier jour de l'an, 1849" (New Year's Day, 1849), appeared in the broadsheet *L'Ami de la Réligion et de la Patrie*–until 1855, Crémazie was testing the wings of creativity and published seven poems in local papers (later collected in *Oeuvres complètes*, 1882). In "Colonisation" (1853) the patriotic theme is trumpeted as the poet encourages colonists settling new lands in Quebec (in response to the colonization movement begun in 1848), while extolling the past glories of Quebec and France, and reminds them of the sanctity and messianic significance of their task. Already the mournful complaint of the exile, a recurring motif in his work, is sounded in his address to a French-Canadian who must leave "la patrie" for Californian goldfields.

Attracted by the splendor of military combat and the vision of France as savior of the oppressed, Crémazie shifted his desire for epic material to the Crimean War in three poems–"Guerre" (War, 1854), "La Guerre d'Orient" (The War in the Orient, 1855), and "Sur les ruines de Sébastopol" (On the Ruins of Sebastopol, 1856). However, when in 1855 *La Capricieuse*, the first French ship to arrive since 1759, sailed down the St. Lawrence, and its captain began to negotiate direct commercial ties between France and Canada, Crémazie captured the exuberance of the French-Canadians in his topical "Le Vieux Soldat canadien" (The Old Canadian Soldier). In the first part of the poem, composed of sestets in an alexandrine meter, the old soldier longs for the days of the French regime, dreams of the glories of France and Napoleon's victories, trembles under the yoke of a foreign race (the English), and leaning fraility on his son, waits upon the ramparts of Quebec City for the French flag to appear victoriously on the horizon. The second part is a song, "Chant du vieux Soldat canadien," later set to music by the organist Antonin Dessane. As the speaker describes the

77

arrival of *La Capricieuse,* the trembling ghost of the soldier appears. And finally in the "Envoi" to the sailors of *La Capricieuse* the "barde inconnu" (unknown poet) rejoices in the reestablishment of ties with France. This poem, which aroused immediate and enthusiastic response from the critics and the public, was published in *Le Journal de Québec* on 21 August 1855, the day before the ship's departure.

The patriotism, the attachment to France, the tragedy of the conquest, and the cult of French military glory, all compactly symbolized by a flag, were also the dominant themes of "Le Drapeau de Carillon," written to celebrate the victory in July 1758 by Montcalm at Fort Carillon. On his deathbed a Récollet brother apparently revealed that he had saved one of the flags of Fort Carillon from fire in 1796; this ragged cloth then held the place of honor in the Saint-Jean-Baptiste Day parades. In Crémazie's poem the flag symbolizes a glorious and noble past and fidelity to Catholicism and the French language. Once again an old soldier sadly describes his heroic adventures in Quebec, later cruelly neglected by the decadent Louis XV. Four verses of this poem, too, were set to music–by Charles Sabatier as "O Carillon!"–and received praise from poets and critics. According to Abbé H.-R. Casgrain, "Le Drapeau de Carillon" was behind the origin of the literary movement of 1860. However, English-Canadian military personnel were annoyed by this flagrant attack on the English presence in Quebec, an almost treasonous attachment to France, and consequently did not allow the flag of Carillon in the Saint-Jean-Baptiste Day parade, all of which only increased the fame of Crémazie's song.

Other later poems also celebrated heroic figures or events from Quebec's past: "Aux Canadiens français" (1859), "La Fiancée du marin" (1859), "Les Mille-Iles" (1860), and "Le Potowatomis" (1860). "Le Chant des voyageurs" (1862) was set to music by Dessane.

In 1856 Crémazie departed on the last of three business trips to France; however, his demeanor and experience differed on this voyage. Introduced by Madame de Grandfort, a Parisian lady of letters who had been on a lecture tour in Quebec in 1854, to the elegant literary and artistic salons of the Second Empire, Crémazie passed himself off as a millionaire bookseller. His misogyny was often remarked upon, though, and there is no evidence that he showed any other attachment–romantic or intellectual–to women. During this visit a Paris-printed edition of "Le Vieux Soldat canadien" was available in French bookstores, and his poem "Sur les ruines de Sébastopol" appeared in a French journal.

Just after his return from Paris he published "Les Morts" (The Dead, *Le Journal de Québec,* 31 October 1856), in which he turned to a different theme–that of death and graves–which had begun to preoccupy him in earlier poems: in "Le Vieux Soldat canadien," he had presented a haunting picture of the soldier as a ghost. Addressed to the dead, this elegy, in twenty-six sestets, evokes the peace and calm of the grave in contrast to the selfish and lustful pursuits of the living (perhaps an expression of his disgust at the loose morals and debauchery of French salon life). The poet imagines the dead leaving their graves to wander among the ungrateful and forgetful living. He requests that the reader give "Une fleur à la tombe" (a flower to the grave) and pray for friends and relatives and for the exile far from his homeland so that when the dead reach heaven their names will already be familiar. This poem, with its echoes from Dante and the Psalms, although praised for its Catholic orthodoxy, was received less warmly than his patriotic poems.

During this time, a group of intellectuals began gathering in the back room of Crémazie's bookstore to engage in informal literary discussions. Among them were prominent politicians, lawyers, doctors, civil servants, and writers, including the historians François-Xavier Garneau and Abbé Jean-Baptiste-Antoine Ferland; the poets Pamphile Le May, Louis Fréchette, and Alfred Garneau; the novelist Antoine Gérin-Lajoie; the writer of legends and tales Joseph-Charles Taché; and the indomitable man of letters Abbé Casgrain. This group, later called the literary movement of 1860, or inflated to the Patriotic School of Quebec, founded two literary journals, *Les Soirées Canadiennes* (1861) and *Le Foyer Canadien* (1863). Like Crémazie they were interested in discovering and promoting the noble heritage and traditions of Quebec through their writings.

In 1862 *Les Soirées Canadiennes* published the first of the promised three parts of Crémazie's "Promenade de trois morts" (Parade of Three Corpses). The theme of death is morbidly presented in this "Fantaisie" commemorating, as did "Les Morts," All-Saints' Day. A boy, a young man, and an elderly man emerge from their graves to wander amid the shadows of

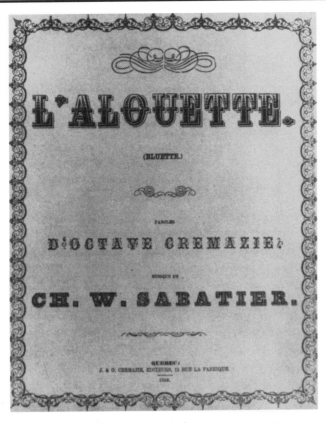

Title page for one of Crémazie's poems as set to music by Charles W. Sabatier in 1858

"l'éternelle nuit" (the eternal night), seeking prayers from the living. The rest of the poem of 638 lines consists of a disturbing, indeed, gruesome, dialogue between a worm, King of the Dead, and a dead man, fresh in his grave, whose flesh is being painfully gnawed by the worm. Crémazie suggests that the torments of the flesh continue even after death to add to the torments suffered by the spirit, creating a horrifying picture of purgatory. He was criticized for abandoning his patriotic poems and turning to realism and romanticism; the reading public seemed confused by the poem's bleak realism. Although he had planned out the rest of the poem and claimed to hold 2000 lines in his head (Crémazie's method of composition was to commit the poem to memory and then write the entire poem at once), he never completed it.

On 11 November 1862 Crémazie's life changed dramatically. The gloom of "Promenade des trois morts" seemed fulfilled when suddenly he was cast into the role of the exile, "loin de sa patrie," so often pitied in his verse. Over the years he had accumulated debts in his bookstore that he could not honor and for which he had friends sign promissory notes. It is possible that he may have forged some notes and signatures in order to extend his credit. When inquiries were initiated, a group of his friends met on 10 November to discuss the situation and decided that it was sufficiently grave for Crémazie to depart the next day. Under the pseudonym Jules Fontaine, Crémazie fled via New York to Paris, where he lived in exile for sixteen years, subsisting on loans from his family and, later, on jobs in Bordeaux and Le Havre in an export agency run by a family called Bossange, who showed him kindness and hospitality. It was a pathetic and friendless existence, and he often complained of ill health. Although he took some courses at the Sorbonne and Collège de France, Crémazie did not participate in French literary life. In Quebec efforts were made to assist Crémazie, including an appeal with 73 signatures for a royal pardon, but none came to fruition. During his exile he wrote only three poems, which are of little interest, and he spoke of his literary career as finished. In a 29 January letter to Casgrain he wrote: "Les poèmes les plus beaux sont ceux que l'on rêve mais que l'on n'écrit pas" (The most beautiful poems are the ones that one dreams but that one never writes).

The first verse of Crémazie's "Le Drapeau de Carillon," as set to music by Sabatier (from John Hare, Anthologie de la poèsie québécoise du XIXᵉ siècle, *1979)*

However, he maintained a voluminous correspondence with his family and an exchange of letters with Abbé Casgrain in which he made astute literary and social comments. There are only twelve letters (held at the Séminaire de Québec), and although they do not constitute a comprehensive literary theory, they nevertheless intimate the beginnings of a French-Canadian literary criticism, which he himself pointed out Quebec desperately needed. In one letter describing Quebec as a society of grocers in pursuit of material gain with no sensitivity to literature, he wonders how "the grocers" could appreciate or encourage the budding literature of Quebec; in another he asserts that Canada lacks its own language, which hinders its literary development.

During the Franco-Prussian war (1870-1871), the siege of Paris, and the Commune, Crémazie kept an extensive, detailed daily account of events in his "Journal du siège de Paris" (in *Oeuvres complètes*), which is of historical as well as literary interest. At the age of 52 he died at Le Havre of a respiratory ailment.

Although Crémazie's poetry was popular both in his lifetime and for several generations following because of its incantatory and patriotic vein and fluid verse, his style reveals severe limitations. Often resorting to classical and artificial clichés rather than to vivid metaphor, and to vague epithets, abstract or general images, and exclamatory phrases, it lacks moving description, personal lyricism, or emotion, despite its fervent patriotism and concrete images from nature or life in Quebec. Moreover, his rhymes were often heavy and unoriginal. The prose of his letters and journal, however, was laced with irony, wit, and intricate and engaging descriptions of people and events; his letters, in particular to his family, were wrought with heartrending emotions and touching expressions of self-pity and despair.

Crémazie remained for many years an inspirational figure in the world of Quebec letters. Poems were dedicated to him by other well-known Quebec poets; monuments were erected in his honor; his poems and songs were taught to schoolchildren; and his poems and letters were collected and published posthumously. Since he so adeptly captured that tone of alienation and melancholy that pervades much of Quebec poetry, he initiated what the critic Gilles Marcotte has called the poetry of exile in Quebec literature. Although only three or four of his poems have stood the test of time and continue to be read and studied, the tragic and exiled Crémazie is undoubtedly one of the fathers of French-Canadian literature.

References:

Gérard Bessette, *Les Images en poésie canadienne-française* (Montreal: Beauchemin, 1960);

Lise Brunet, *Octave Crémazie, Bio-bibliographie* (Montreal: Ecole de Bibliothécaires, Université de Montréal, 1945);

H.-R. Casgrain, "Le mouvement littérature en Canada," in Crémazie's *Oeuvres complètes*, volume 2 (Montreal: Beauchemin & Valois, 1884), pp. 352-375;

Thomas Chapais, "Octave Crémazie," in his *Nouvelles Soirées canadiennes* (Quebec: Demers, 1883);

Odette Condemine, "Octave Crémazie," in *La Poésie canadienne-française, Archives des Lettres canadiennes*, volume 4 (Montreal: Fides, 1969);

Condemine, *Octave Crémazie* (Montreal: Fides, 1980);

Michel Dassonville, "Crémazie, le romantisme et nous," *Revue de l'Université de Laval*, 9 (November 1954): 210-221;

Jean Ethier-Blais, *Signets II* (Montreal: Cercle du Livre de France, 1967);

Soeur Jeanne-Leber, "L'amitié de Crémazie et Casgrain," in *Archives des lettres canadiennes*, volume 1 (Ottawa: Editions de l'Université d'Ottawa, 1961);

Maurice Lebel, *D'Octave Crémazie à Alain Grandbois* (Quebec: Editions de L'Action, 1963);

Gilles Marcotte, *Une littérature qui se fait* (Montreal: HMH, 1962);

Seraphin Marion, *Octave Crémazie, Précurseur du romantisme canadien-français, Les Lettres canadiennes d'autrefois*, volume 5 (Ottawa: Editions de l'Université, 1946);

Bernard Muddiman, "Octave Crémazie," *Queen's Quarterly*, 27 (January-February-March 1920): 240-251;

Fernand Rinfret, "Octave Crémazie," *Etudes sur la littérature canadienne-française*, volume 1 (St-Jerome, Que.: Prévost, 1906);

Réjean Robidoux and Paul Wyczynski, eds., *Crémazie et Nelligan* (Montreal: Fides, 1981);

Pierre-Georges Roy, *A propos de Crémazie* (Quebec: Garneau, 1945);

M. Torres, "Octave Crémazie and His Return to Mother Death," *Canadian Literature* (Summer 1985): 69-97.

Papers:

The Archives du Séminaire de Québec, Quebec City, in the Fonds Casgrain holds letters from Crémazie to Casgrain and drafts of Casgrain's letters to Crémazie.

Sarah Anne Curzon

(1833 - 6 November 1898)

Anton Wagner
York University

BOOK: *Laura Secord, the Heroine of 1812: A Drama, and Other Poems* (Toronto: Robinson, 1887)–includes *The Sweet Girl Graduate*.

SELECTED PERIODICAL PUBLICATIONS– UNCOLLECTED: "Historical Societies," *Wentworth Historical Society: Journal and Transactions*, 1 (1892);
"Mrs. Curzon's Address," *Pioneer and Historical Association of the Province of Ontario, Canada: Proceedings* (1894-1895);
"The Battle of Queenston Heights, October 13th, 1812," *Women's Canadian Historical Society of Toronto: Transactions*, 2 (1899).

Sarah Anne Curzon was one of the first English-Canadian playwrights to dramatize Canadian historical subject matter and public social issues of the day. Her drama *Laura Secord, the Heroine of 1812* (1887) and the comedy *The Sweet Girl Graduate* (originally published in *Grip-Sack* in 1882) stand in marked contrast to the prevalent poetic dramas with non-Canadian settings, melodramas, parodies, burlesques, comic operettas, and political satires of other nineteenth-century English-Canadian writers.

Curzon was born near Birmingham, England, in 1833. Her parents, Mary Jackson Vincent and George Phillips Vincent, a well-educated glass manufacturer, took a strong interest in the upbringing of their children. Curzon was educated in ladies' schools in Birmingham and studied music and languages with private tutors. Her lifelong preoccupation with literature, history, and politics was undoubtedly stimulated by her early family environment. In her youth she submitted poetry and stories to popular family periodicals. In 1858 Sarah Anne married Robert Curzon of Norfolk and immigrated with him to Toronto in 1862. She contributed verse, essays, and fiction to Goldwin Smith's *Canadian Monthly*, to the *Dominion Illustrated*, *Grip*, the *Week*, *Evangelical Churchman*, and *Canadian Magazine* and also wrote in support of women's suffrage in Canadian, English, and American newspapers.

Curzon was a leading member of the Toronto Women's Literary Club, Canada's first ongoing women's rights group, founded in November of 1876 by Dr. Emily Howard Stowe. It agitated for better sanitary conditions in stores and factories, organized the first deputation to lobby the provincial government for women's suffrage in 1881, and lobbied for the admission of women to University College. Curzon edited a women's page and worked for two years as an associate editor of the *Canada Citizen*, the prohibitionist weekly that placed a column at the disposal of the club in 1881. The club became the Toronto Women's Suffrage Association on 9 March 1883 and functioned nationally as the Canadian Women's Suffrage Association until February 1889, when it was reorganized as the Women's Enfranchisement Association of Canada. Stowe again served as president and Curzon as recording secretary. In 1895 Curzon and Mary Agnes Fitzgibbon founded the Women's Canadian Historical Society of Toronto, with Curzon serving as president until 1897.

Laura Secord, the Heroine of 1812 is Curzon's major literary achievement. Written in 1876, the drama was not published until eleven years later, as the author notes in the play's preface, because of the "inertness of Canadian interest in Canadian literature at that date." The work thus predates the writing of Charles Mair's more widely known poetic drama *Tecumseh*, published in 1886, by nearly a decade. In her preface Curzon also states that "during the first few years of her residence in Canada the author was often astonished to hear it remarked, no less among educated than uneducated Canadians, that 'Canada has no history'; and yet on every hand stories were current of the achievements of the pioneers, and the hardships endured and overcome by the United Empire Loyalists." Her aim in writing *Laura Secord* was "to rescue from oblivion the name of a brave woman, and set it in its proper place

Sarah Anne Curzon (C 25817, National Archives of Canada)

among the heroes of Canadian history" and to "inspire other hearts with loyal bravery such as hers." The difficulty Curzon faced in her dramatization was that the historical facts of her story, though full of pathos, were "barren of great incidents." Nevertheless, Curzon was largely successful in transforming the historical Laura Secord into a traditional heroic literary character. She accomplished this transformation by enlarging the concept of heroism–"to save from the sword is surely as great a deed as to save with the sword"– and through the first extensive use of gender-role reversal in English-Canadian drama.

Because James Secord in the play has already been seriously wounded fighting the invading Americans at the Battle of Queenston Heights, Laura convinces her husband that she herself must go to warn Lieutenant Fitzgibbon of the impending attack on Beaver Dam, "a task at which a man might shrink." Secord's heroism is emphasized through accounts of her rescuing her wounded husband from the battlefield, outwitting the American sentries, and enduring the hazards of the unchartered forest with its wild animals and Indians on her nine-mile-long journey. Yet the play also presents an idyllic rhapsody of the woods and country being fought for, implicitly making the land a character in the action. The invading Americans are compared to Satan in the form of a snake seeking to defile this Eden. Secord is depicted as St. George, who will crush the serpent approaching to destroy the Canadians. "Ah, little recks he that a woman holds / The power to draw his fangs!" Warned by Secord, Fitzgibbon succeeds in forcing the surrender of the much larger American detachment, "thanks to a brave woman's glorious deed."

Through its celebration of Canadian heroism during the War of 1812, *Laura Secord* succeeds in instilling national patriotism and pride in the accomplishments of Canada's early pioneers. Intended for reading rather than stage production, the play's characterization, rapid exposition, and development of action and plot is nevertheless theatrically effective.

Based on the public controversy surrounding the admission of women to University College in Toronto, Curzon's comedy *The Sweet Girl Graduate* was first published in John Wilson Bengough's satirical *Grip-Sack* in 1882. As in *Laura Secord*, in which the heroine exchanges traditional male-female roles with her husband, Kate Bloggs tells her father "I'll make you proud of me as if I were a son" and literally assumes male attire to obtain her Master of Arts degree and top honors in traditionally male subjects such as mathematics, natural science, and the classics. Having proved "that Canadian girls are equal in mental power with Canadian boys," Kate is able to drop her disguise as Tom Christopher and wins the support of her fellow students and teachers to petition the provincial government for women's rights. Compared to the frequently heavy rhetorical language and seriousness of *Laura Secord*, the dialogue, tone, and characterization of *The Sweet Girl Graduate* is charmingly lighthearted and graceful. The play humorously satirizes the stereotyped roles of both sexes and effectively punctures the arguments then being made to deny women admission to university studies.

In addition to her two plays, Curzon's *Laura Secord, the Heroine of 1812: A Drama, and Other Poems* also contains her "Memoir of Mrs. Secord," "A Ballad of 1812," twenty-two poems, two fables, and fourteen translations of fables and poetry by Pamphile Lemay, Claris de Florian, Jean Rameau, François René de Chateaubriand, Victor Hugo, and Phillipe Desportes. Her poetry, undistinguished in form and imagery, conveys standard moral messages appealing to the concerns of her Victorian reading public. Her subject matter ranges from patriotic verse extolling the grandeur of the British Empire and the celebration of heroic historical figures to the quiet heroism of common soldiers, immigrants, and family loved ones, as well as encompassing nature, death, and religious faith. One of her best poems is "On Queenston Heights," written in 1881, an effective poetic evocation of the feelings aroused in the author by the locale and recollection of events during the War of 1812. Curzon's translations are actually better than her own poetry. Her inclusion of Lemay's French-Canadian patriotic poems "A Memory of the Heroes of 1760" and "The Song of the Canadian Voltigeurs" exemplifies Curzon's attempt to reconcile the many diverse elements of Canadian society and to create a strong, genuine sense of nationhood.

Sarah Anne Curzon is a figure of historical importance for her cultural and political nationalism, her activism on behalf of women's rights, and for demonstrating that women could also successfully enter the largely male-dominated field of poetic and dramatic writing. Before her death in Toronto on 6 November 1898, Thomas O'Hagan declared Curzon, together with Agnes Maule Machar, "two of the strongest women writers in Ontario" and asserted that *Laura Secord* had "a masculinity and energy found in the work of no other Canadian woman."

References:

Lady Edgar, "Sketch of Mrs. Curzon's Life and Work," *Women's Canadian Historical Society of Toronto: Transactions*, 2 (1899);

Thomas O'Hagan, "Canadian Women Writers," in *Canada. An Encyclopaedia of the Country*, volume 5, edited by J. Castelle Hopkins (Toronto: Linscott, 1899);

O'Hagan, "Some Canadian Women Writers," *Catholic World*, 63 (September 1896);

Anton Wagner, ed., *Women Pioneers. Canada's Lost Plays*, volume 2 (Toronto: Canadian Theatre Review Publications, 1979), pp. 8-10, 93-94, 141-142.

Eliza Lanesford Cushing
(19 October 1794 - 4 May 1886)

Anton Wagner
York University

BOOKS: *The Sunday School or Village Sketches*, by Cushing and Harriet Vaughn Foster [Cheney] (Andover, Mass.: Flagg & Gould, 1820);

Saratoga: A Tale of the Revolution, 2 volumes (Boston: Cummings, Hillard, 1824);

Yorktown: An Historical Romance, 2 volumes (Boston: Wells & Lilly, 1826);

Esther, a Sacred Drama; with Judith, a Poem (Boston: Dowe, 1840);

Saratoga: A Story of 1787 (New York: Fetridge / Boston: Williams, 1856).

OTHER: *The Fatal Ring*, in *Women Pioneers. Canada's Lost Plays*, volume 2, edited by Anton Wagner (Toronto: Canadian Theatre Review, 1979), pp. 22-91.

SELECTED PERIODICAL PUBLICATIONS– UNCOLLECTED: "Deaf Molly," *Lady's Book,* 18 (March 1839): 104-107;

"A Tale of the Richelieu," *Lady's Book,* 19 (July-August 1839): 13-19, 73-80;

"The Fairies' Fountain," *Lady's Book,* 19 (November-December 1839): 210-216, 245-251;

"The Neglected Wife," *Literary Garland,* new series 1 (April-July 1843): 159-168, 213-224, 249-261, 289-300;

"Dramatic Sketch from Scripture History," *Literary Garland,* new series 2 (April 1844): 177-188.

Eliza Lanesford Cushing's dramatic sketches and full-length plays, originally published in *Lady's Book* and the *Literary Garland* between 1839 and 1845, mark the beginning of playwriting as a literary art form in English Canada. Born on 19 October 1794 in Brighton, Massachussetts, Cushing was already an established writer before moving to Montreal with her husband, Dr. Frederick Cushing, in 1833. Her mother, Hannah Webster Foster, was the author of one of the earliest American novels, *The Coquette; or, The History of Eliza*

Wharton (1797). Her father, John Foster, the popular pastor of the Congregationalist Unitarian Church in Brighton, published seventeen sermons from 1799 to 1821.

The Foster daughters, Eliza, Harriet, and T. D. Foster, who became the wife of the lecturer and essayist Rev. Henry Giles of Boston, were greatly influenced by the literary and religious work of their parents. Eliza and Harriet collaborated on *The Sunday School or Village Sketches*, written for "the Sabbath readings of children," published in 1820. Cushing's historical novels, *Saratoga: A Tale of the Revolution* and *Yorktown: An Historical Romance*, were published in Boston in 1824 and 1826.

Cushing's most important literary works are the biblical play *Esther* (1840) and the romantic drama *The Fatal Ring* (*Literary Garland*, 1840; collected in 1979). *Esther*, a five-act religious drama, was first published in Sarah J. Hale's *Lady's Book* from June to December 1838. It vividly depicts how the humble Jewish maiden becomes queen of Persia as God's instrument for saving His people from destruction. The same theme is treated in Cushing's "Judith," appearing in the November 1839 issue of the *Literary Garland* and republished in *Esther, a Sacred Drama; with Judith, a Poem*. Reviewing *Esther* in the August 1840 *Literary Garland*, John Gibson, its editor, noted the "ease and elegance which characterise the writings of the gifted authoress of this beautiful drama," praised the "delicate riches of its poetic thought," and concluded that its "language is eloquent and beautiful–deeply imbued with the spirit of poesy." Next to Susanna Moodie, Cushing was the most frequent contributor to the *Garland* with seventy publications of verse, prose, and dramatic works from 1838 to 1850. Her sisters also frequently wrote for the publication, the most important Canadian cultural periodical of the period.

Cushing's most significant dramatic works in the *Literary Garland* are her one-act "Dramatic Sketch from Scripture History" (April 1844) and the three-act *Fatal Ring* (July-September 1840). Like Esther's foil Vashti, once queen of Persia, who is banished from the throne and her husband's bed after defying the king, Athaliah in the "Dramatic Sketch from Scripture History" is the incarnation of woman morally and physically destroyed by lust for power. She is the first English-Canadian dramatic antihero, a pagan "she-wolf " who has deceived and murdered her husband and his heirs to seize the throne of Judah.

Set in early-sixteenth-century France, *The Fatal Ring* is Cushing's best dramatic work in terms of the richness of its language, characterization, and action. The play's characters are more "modern" in that their motivations and moral character are more complex than the stark moral juxtapositions of Cushing's shorter historical and biblical dramatic sketches. The innocent young Estelle, falsely lured to her destruction at the French court, is Cushing's only tragic heroine and the first tragic heroine in English-Canadian drama. *The Fatal Ring*'s theme of woman destroyed by contact with a corrupt society is echoed in many of Cushing's prose and dramatic works. Nowhere else is this process of victimization more convincingly portrayed, however. Surprisingly, King Francis, Estelle's seducer, emerges as a colorful and even sympathetic figure, who arouses sympathy because he openly admits his weakness for female beauty. At the close of act 2, Estelle is at the height of her temporal power, the mistress of the king, who has become "love's slave." The fact that she was largely powerless to resist his amorous advances, her self-awareness of her moral guilt, and her decision to renounce the king and his court to seek penance in a convent contribute to Estelle's tragic stature. Her fall from pastoral innocence and subsequent violent death at the hands of her maddened husband are vivid demonstrations of the moral of *The Fatal Ring*: "They who prize / A heart of purity, a home of peace, / Should crave not worldly honours, / Shun the court, its dangers and its strifes."

Cushing's numerous tales, whether in a distant historical or more contemporary setting, almost invariably feature a romantic plot and contrasting characterization sharply depicting the conflict between virtue and sensual passion, love and duty, vice and religious faith, morality and jealousy, and violence and greed. Stylistically her stories range from the exotic, Arabian "The Fairies' Fountain" (*Lady's Book*, November-December

1839; *Literary Garland,* July 1844) to the more realistically drawn character study "Deaf Molly" (*Lady's Book*, March 1839; *Literary Garland*, April 1848) and her melodramatic study of marital breakdown, infidelity, and death "The Neglected Wife" (*Literary Garland,* April-July 1843.) Few of Cushing's stories have a distinctly Canadian setting. The most interesting of these is "A Tale of the Richelieu" (*Lady's Book*, July-August 1839), in which the daughter of a French-Canadian seigneur loses her father, lover, and her own life in the 1837 rebellion.

In 1846 Dr. Frederick Cushing, then a physician at the Montreal Emigrant Hospital, died from ship fever while treating immigrants, forcing his wife to support herself through literary work. With her sister Harriet she founded and coedited the monthly *Snow Drop* (1847-1853), the first children's literary magazine with Canadian and U.S. distribution. In 1850 she also became editor of the *Literary Garland*, until its demise in December of 1851 due to excessive competition from cheaper American monthlies.

The persistent moral and religious focus in Cushing's work is partly the result of the influence of her parents and partly a reflection of the great evangelical revival sweeping the United States in the 1830s and the subsequent influence of Victorian cultural values in the United States and Canada. Cushing's literary universe is essentially a religious and moral one in which the temptations of worldly existence are but a trial to be endured until the attainment of the greater reality of the next world. Besides her rich, poetic language and imagery, it is this genuine religious conviction that distinguishes her literary work from the often merely fashionable sentiment in the work of other Victorian writers.

References:

Carol Gerson, "*The Snow Drop* and *The Maple Leaf*: Canada's First Periodicals for Children," *Canadian Children's Literature*, 18/19 (1980): 10-23;

Vernon R. Lindquist, "The Soil and the Seed. The Birth of the Canadian Short Story In English: Haliburton, Moodie, and Others 1830-1867," Ph.D. dissertation, University of New Brunswick, 1979 pp. 208-292;

Robert Law McDougall, "A Study of Canadian Periodical Literature of the Nineteenth Century," Ph.D. dissertation, University of Toronto, 1950.

Nicholas Flood Davin

(13 January 1840? - 18 October 1901)

Neil K. Besner
University of Winnipeg

SELECTED BOOKS: *British versus American Civilization: A Lecture* (Toronto: Adam, Stevenson, 1873);

The Earl of Beaconsfield, with Disraeli Anecdotes Never Before Published (Toronto: Belford, 1876);

The Fair Grit; or The Advantages of Coalition; a Farce (Toronto: Belford, 1876);

The Irishman in Canada (London: Low, Marston / Toronto: Maclear, 1877; facsimile, Shannon, Ireland: Irish University Press, 1969);

Great Speeches (Toronto: Hunter, Rose, 1881);

Album Verses and Other Poems (Ottawa: MacLean, Roger, 1882);

Eos: A Prairie Dream and Other Poems (Ottawa: Citizen, 1884);

Eos: An Epic of the Dawn, and Other Poems (Regina: Leader, 1889).

OTHER: *Homes for Millions. The Great Canadian North-West*, edited by Davin (Ottawa: Chamberlain, 1891).

SELECTED PERIODICAL PUBLICATIONS—
UNCOLLECTED: "The London and Canadian Press," *Canadian Monthly and National Review*, 5 (February 1874);

"The Bennett Murder Case," *Rose-Belford's Canadian Monthly and National Review*, 5 (July-December 1880);

"The North-West Farmer," *Week*, 6 (7 December 1888 and 4 January 1889).

Although Nicholas Flood Davin was a prolific writer whose works include poems, speeches, journalistic writings, and numerous literary, legal, historical, political, and socioeconomic studies, he is now more widely known as one of the most prominent figures in the early political and cultural life of the Northwest Territories. Davin's professional activities and accomplishments, all pursued with characteristic energy and flair, ranged widely: he was a noted lawyer; an able and adventurous reporter and columnist; an edi-

tor and founder in 1883 of one of the Territories' first newspapers, the *Regina Leader*; in 1887, the first Member of Parliament to represent Assiniboia West, and thereafter, an impassioned advocate of regional interests in Ottawa. Davin was an acclaimed speaker and debater, whose quick wit and articulateness in the House of Commons and on the podium were celebrated across Canada; a man committed to education, the arts, and the fostering of a literary culture; and above all, a mercurial personality who alternately charmed and outraged his friends and enemies in public and private life. In 1939 Roy St. George Stubbs, in his *Lawyers and Laymen of Western Canada*, described Davin's career with a typical reservation: "Canada is under obligation to Ireland, that land where genius is indigenous to the soil, for Nicholas Flood Davin, a man who had every talent save that of making the best use of his talents: and who, as lawyer, legislator, orator and man of letters, just missed achieving the heights which only genius can climb."

Davin was born in the Irish village of Kilfinane, County Limerick, to Nicholas Flood and Eliza Lane Davin. In his 1980 biography, *Mr. Davin, M.P.*, C. B. Koester sees it as a mark of his ambition and insecurity that Davin, christened Nicholas Francis, seems to have adopted the middle name Flood not to affirm his father's name, but his Protestant upbringing with the family of his uncle James Flood Davin. Koester also suspects that Davin's real birth year was 1840 but that Davin claimed to have been born in 1843 to disguise "the supposed disadvantages of a late start." After a six-year stint as an ironmonger's apprentice, Davin attended Queen's College, Cork, in 1864 and 1865 before leaving Ireland for London, seeking to better his lot. In 1865 he began his training as a lawyer when he was admitted to the Honourable Society of the Middle Temple in London, where he also began editing and writing for a periodical, the *Monthly Journal*. About 1867 Davin became a member of the press gallery of the House of Commons, working for the London

Nicholas Flood Davin (R-A 6665, Saskatchewan Archives Board)

Star and writing columns and letters for several other papers. Later in his life, Davin would frequently allude to his time in the press gallery in London as a major formative influence; Koester notes that Charles Dickens, William Hazlitt, and Samuel Coleridge worked in the gallery early in their careers, and that Davin was probably acquainted with Benjamin Disraeli and John Stuart Mill, among others, during his time there.

Although he was called to the bar in 1868, Davin became a war correspondent for the *Irish Times* and the London *Star* in 1870, reporting on the Franco-Prussian War. Toward the end of 1871 Davin returned to Ireland to edit a new paper, the *Belfast Times*, but the position proved disastrous, with Davin, unhappy with the owners' policies and already under pressure because of his drinking problem, finally dismissed in May of 1872 for running a piece he had already written for another paper in 1871. In July of 1872, Davin came to Canada to report on Canadian af-

fairs for the *Pall Mall Gazette*.

Davin worked in Toronto for George Brown on the *Globe*, but left in 1875 and worked for another Toronto newspaper, the *Mail*. His first several years in Canada were busy ones; he quickly established a reputation as a gifted speaker, became involved in political life, and published several books. *British versus American Civilization* (1873), a spirited reply to an unabashedly pro-American speech of Rev. O. H. Tiffany in Toronto, launched Davin's career in Canada. Davin's book on Disraeli, *The Earl of Beaconsfield*, appeared in 1876, as did *The Fair Grit*, a political satire. But the most significant of Davin's early works is *The Irishman in Canada* (1877), a history in which Davin shows the major contributions of the Irish, and through which Davin began to articulate what was to become his own lifelong commitment to Canada. Davin's accomplished prose style, his driving ambition, and his perspective on the opportunities late-nineteenth-century Canada

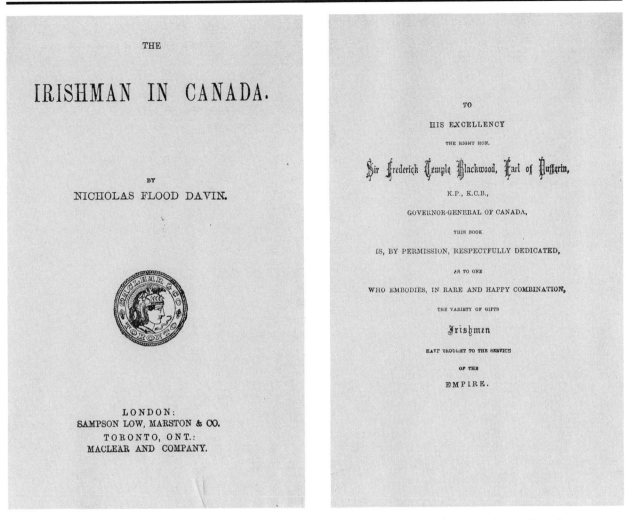

THE

IRISHMAN IN CANADA.

BY

NICHOLAS FLOOD DAVIN.

LONDON:
SAMPSON LOW, MARSTON & CO.
TORONTO, ONT.:
MACLEAR AND COMPANY.

TO

HIS EXCELLENCY

THE RIGHT HON.

Sir Frederick Temple Blackwood, Earl of Dufferin,

K.P., K.C.B.,

GOVERNOR-GENERAL OF CANADA,

THIS BOOK

IS, BY PERMISSION, RESPECTFULLY DEDICATED,

AS TO ONE

WHO EMBODIES, IN RARE AND HAPPY COMBINATION,

THE VARIETY OF GIFTS

Irishmen

HAVE BROUGHT TO THE SERVICE

OF THE

EMPIRE.

Title page and dedication for Davin's 1877 history of Irish immigrants and their contributions to Canada

offered to a man like himself can be measured in a passage from this book: "In such a country . . . it would be an extraordinary thing if the Irishman did not rise to a high level. Here, all that his fathers ever struggled for he has. He is a controlling part of the present; he is one of the architects of the future, and he has nothing to do with the disasters of the past, only so far as they teach him lessons for the present. Nothing to do with the glories of the past, save to catch their inspiration."

Davin's stay in Toronto culminated with two milestones: his celebrated, although inevitably unsuccessful, defense of George Bennett, the disgruntled ex-employee of the *Globe* who shot George Brown (Brown died of complications from the wound six weeks later); and his first election bid, an unsuccessful one as the Conservative candidate for Haldimand in the 1878 election. Koester sees this fight as a "triumphant defeat"

for Davin; he was not expected to win, but the Conservatives quickly recognized his potential.

In pursuit of opportunity and nurturing his political ambitions, Davin made his decisive move in Canada in the fall of 1882, when he came West to Regina, established as Pile of Bones and renamed that year in honor of the Queen. Supported by Prime Minister John A. Macdonald's Conservatives, Davin founded the *Regina Leader*, which would be a staunch Conservative paper under his editorship, printing the first issue on 1 March 1883. Regina and the *Leader* were the bases for Davin's political, editorial, and literary activities; and he quickly became a well-known figure in the Territories, celebrated for his style, urbanity, and wit as much as for his enterprise. In 1886 in Regina Davin met Mrs. Kate Simpson-Hayes, who was separated from her husband; Davin was strongly attracted to her and encouraged her in her early career as a writer, but they never married, because Kate never attained a divorce from her husband. Davin and Kate had two children, a son born in 1889 and a daughter two years later. His son later joined the Canadian army and was killed in action during World War I; through a series of misadventures, his daughter, whom Davin and Simpson-Hayes had left at an orphanage, was baptized under another name and never knew her father. On 25 July 1895, Davin married Eliza Jane Reid of Ottawa, who moved with him to Regina.

The most significant of Davin's many publications in Regina was his book *Eos: An Epic of the Dawn, and Other Poems* (1889), sometimes cited as the first literary work published in the Canadian Northwest. Although the poetry is sometimes stilted and overly ornate, there are passages, particularly in the title poem, which clearly show Davin's descriptive gifts as the poet gazes down on the prairie, borne aloft by Eos:

A sunny sky of blue arching
A plain in verdure drowned, and floating thick
Upon the emerald sea sweet wild flowers gay:
Their stately queen the light-pink prairie rose.
The whirr of insects loud on every side,
And loud and clear the prairie lark, deep hid
In those vast fragrant meadows, sang; the creek
Sent thousand-voiced upon the sultry air
The bull-frog's weary canticle.

Davin wrote this volume of poetry, he explained in the preface, because he believed "the cultivation of taste and imagination as important as the raising of grain" and hoped that the book would be "a step towards the creation of a Canadian literature," "a small beginning of great things." "Before a great poet can arise," he wrote, "there must be a large number of writers to prepare, not merely the mind of the nation for him, but to accumulate material on which his more plastic hand shall work." Koester justly remarks that although "Eos" is "not great poetry," it is "unique . . . because it sets forth very competently, in a carefully integrated poetical illusion, the terms of reference of the life of its author, who would admit to no anomaly in being a poet in politics." In 1906 Archibald MacMurchy, in his *Handbook of Canadian Literature*, assessed Davin's verse with a typical reference to Davin's wide range of activity: "These poems reveal the man, scholarly, witty, with fine touches, yet, at times, sacrificing nature, or true art, to the requirements of classical rules. Mr. Davin was too successful in other fields of literary effort to be wholly successful as

Elizabeth Reid Davin, who married Davin in July 1895

a poet. The Muse of poetry bestows her rare honors only upon the ardent and life-long devotee."

The most celebrated episode in Davin's career as a journalist, and an exemplary indication of his panache and ingenuity, came in 1885 when Louis Riel was tried for treason in Regina and condemned to hang. Davin, who covered the trial for the *Leader*, was at once firm in his conviction that Riel must hang for treason, but, characteristically, also sympathetic to the man himself, whom he saw as flawed, failed but possessed of nobility and great potential—perhaps in some measure a dim and premonitory reflection of his own character and achievements. Davin was determined to interview Riel in his cell, but Riel was under close guard and no one was allowed access to him; disguising himself as a French priest and posing as Riel's confessor, Davin was allowed in to speak with him and published his famous interview with Riel in the *Leader*.

Davin was elected to parliament three times—in 1887 and 1901 as part of the Conservative government, and in 1896, when he won by a single vote, in opposition against Wilfrid Laurier's Liberals. The turbulence in the progress and decline of his political career was symptomatic of Davin's many contradictions: although he was a staunch supporter of the Northwest Territories, he was also deeply committed to Federal policy and to the Conservative party, and he was often pulled between the demands of the region and the national party, particularly in the bitter and drawn-out battle over the Manitoba separate-school issue (1890-1896), which raised the question of whether there should be a return to a dual system of education—Protestant and Catholic—a system that had been abolished in 1892. The debate pitted Ottawa against Manitoba, Protestant against Catholic, and forced Davin to take positions that were bound to be controversial, if not misinterpreted by some in his constituency. Davin's stand on this issue, combined with the lingering distrust that some of his supporters felt for him and the rise of the Liberals in Ottawa and the regions, led to his fall in the election of 1900, when he was defeated by Walter Scott, whom Davin had originally employed at the *Leader*. The defeat, although predictable, was a bitter disappointment to Davin, one that he might have seen as the last in a series of failures: he was never appointed to cabinet, although frequently mentioned as an able candidate; he could never marry Kate Simpson-Hayes; and although

he was brilliant in several fields and celebrated for some of his accomplishments, his career had been spotted with bitter rivalries and petty feuds. On 8 October 1901, Davin traveled to Winnipeg, hoping to find work with the Manitoba government of Rodmond Roblin; on Friday, 18 October 1901, Davin shot himself in his room at the Clarendon Hotel in Winnipeg. Koester suggests that the real tragedy of Davin's career was that there were "so few like him"; certainly very few contemporaries of Davin's were so passionately involved and so closely identified with their times.

Biography:

C. B. Koester, *Mr. Davin, M.P.: A Biography of Nicholas Flood Davin* (Saskatoon: Western Producer, 1980).

Reference:

Ken Mitchell, *Davin: The Politician* [play], introduction by C. B. Koester (Edmonton: NeWest, 1979).

Papers:

The major collection of material by and about Davin is at the Archives of Saskatchewan, Regina. It includes unpublished Davin manuscripts, clippings, letters, and other miscellaneous items.

James De Mille

(23 August 1833 - 28 January 1880)

Patricia Monk
Dalhousie University

BOOKS: *Andy O'Hara*, anonymous (New York: Carlton & Porter, 1861);

The Martyr of the Catacombs, anonymous (New York: Carlton & Porter, 1865);

Helena's Household; A Tale of Rome in the First Century, anonymous (New York: Carter, 1867);

The "B. O. W. C." A Book for Boys (Boston: Lee & Shepard, 1869);

Cord and Creese (New York: Harper, 1869);

The Dodge Club; or, Italy in 1859 (New York: Harper, 1869);

The Cryptogram (New York: Harper, 1870);

The Lady of the Ice (New York: Appleton, 1870);

Lost in the Fog (Boston: Lee & Shepard, 1870);

The Boys of Grand Pré School (Boston: Lee & Shepard, 1871);

Fire in the Woods (Boston: Lee & Shepard, 1871);

The American Baron (New York: Harper, 1872);

Among the Brigands (Boston: Lee, 1872);

A Comedy of Terrors (Boston: Osgood, 1872);

Picked Up Adrift (Boston: Lee & Shepard, 1872);

An Open Question (New York: Appleton, 1873);

The Seven Hills (Boston: Lee & Shepard, 1873);

The Treasure of the Seas (Boston: Lee & Shepard, 1873);

The Lily and the Cross. A Tale of Acadia (Boston: Lee & Shepard, 1874);

The Living Link (New York: Harper, 1874);

The Babes in the Wood: A Tragic Comedy. A Story of the Italian Revolution of 1848 (Boston: Gill, 1875);

The Winged Lion; or, Stories of Venice (Boston: Lee & Shepard / New York: Dillingham, 1877);

A Castle in Spain (New York: Harper, 1878);

The Elements of Rhetoric (New York: Harper, 1878);

A Strange Manuscript Found in a Copper Cylinder, anonymous (New York: Harper, 1888; London: Chatto & Windus, 1888).

Working at night and very fast, James De Mille wrote over twenty popular novels–"potboilers"–between 1861 and 1877. By day, he was the respected and respectable professor of rhetoric and history at Dalhousie University, Halifax, who taught his classes competently, and was working on a textbook of rhetoric for use in universities. The dichotomy is somewhat disturbing–as disturbing now, in fact, as it was to his colleagues, who barely knew what to make of him, although his students all remembered him with affection. De Mille does not reveal himself easily to the enquiring reader.

According to the best authority available, his tombstone, he was born on 23 August 1833, the third child of the ten born to Elizabeth and Nathan Smith De Mill (the original spelling of the name, which James changed sometime before 1865). His father had helped to found Horton Academy, a Baptist school that prepared boys to go on to university, and it was to Horton that James, in due course, was sent. From Horton, De Mille followed his elder brother, Elisha, to Acadia College (now Acadia University). On leaving Acadia in 1850, he was given, at his father's expense, a trip to Europe with Elisha, which Elisha's journal rather primly records. In 1852, on their return, De Mille entered Brown University, from which he graduated in 1854 with an M.A. After several unsettled years, during which he made a business trip to Cincinnati for his father, opened a bookstore (which failed, although the fault was not entirely De Mille's), and married (in 1859) Elizabeth Anne Pryor, he finally found a position that suited him, when he was appointed professor of classics at Acadia.

In 1865 he resigned from Acadia to take up the chair of history and rhetoric at Dalhousie University. He had already started writing his popular fiction, and although some of the novels are still only tentatively dated, it is known that at least one (*Andy O'Hara*) had appeared in 1861. But it was not until the year of his appointment to Dalhousie that his second book appeared: *The Martyr of the Catacombs*, a pious tale of the early Christian church. Two years later, a similar novel, *Helena's Household*, was published in New York. From 1869 to 1875 he published at least

James De Mille (Nova Scotia Archives)

one popular novel each year, and sometimes as many as three. His last published fiction during his lifetime was *A Castle in Spain* (1878).

In 1878 he also published *The Elements of Rhetoric*, which he had worked on—for eight years, according to his wife—during his daytime avatar as professor of rhetoric. This book was clearly designed for use in his rhetoric class at Dalhousie. By modern criteria it would be classified as a handbook rather than a textbook, since it contains no exercises. In this aspect it agrees with the recollection of De Mille's pupils, who recalled that the class was given a great deal of theory, but not very many exercises. The range of material on which De Mille draws (not only poetry and fiction but also, for example, history, philosophy, political theory, and oratory) demonstrates in him a wide-ranging and enquiring mind, as well as a lively and intelligent one. The full implications of De Mille's theory of rhetoric, as contrasted with the older texts on rhetoric that *The Elements of Rhetoric* was designed to supplant, have not yet been fully investigated, but will almost certainly repay investigation.

His most famous novel, *A Strange Manuscript Found in a Copper Cylinder*, was ironically itself found in manuscript among his papers after his death and was published anonymously, after some delay, by Harper of New York in 1888. A lively and satirical tale of a marooned sailor in a South Pole utopia, it is sometimes regarded as an early piece of science fiction, in the same light as the early works of H. G. Wells and Jules Verne. Whatever its source, and however it be classified, it makes good reading today, for it is fast-moving, free of pomposity, and full of sharp humor and vitality. The satire of Adam More's sojourn among the Kosekin people is, however, less simple than apparent at first glance. It is true, certainly, that the way of the Kosekin directly reverses the customs of Europe and North America with which De Mille, his narrator, and his readers were all familiar. The Kosekin seek poverty instead of wealth, misery instead of happiness, darkness instead of light, and death instead of life. But they are curiously like westerners in other ways, as Adam finds out when he tries to solve the problem of an offer of marriage from one woman when he has already agreed to marry another. His solution is to suggest that he marry both of them, but bigamy, he discovers, is as immoral among the Kosekin as it is in the western society from which he has come. The land of the Kosekin is not, strictly speaking, a utopia; within their own moral code, they also backslide and have doubts about their values. The net effect of this is to throw into doubt not just western codes of values but the concept of codes of value as such. This is a remarkably subtle notion from a writer who contemptuously dismissed his own fiction as "pot-boilers"–a judgment his contemporaries and critics seem for the most part to have agreed with. In *A Strange Manuscript*, however, De Mille's social perceptions, imagination, humor, and craftsmanship blend to produce a remarkably engaging tale.

His popular fiction was not a secret among his circle in Halifax, but when he died there in January 1880, at the early age of forty-six, it was as the respected professor of Dalhousie University that he was mourned, not only by his wife and family of three sons and a daughter, but also by his colleagues, students, and many Dalhousie graduates. His importance as a writer rests at the moment on *A Strange Manuscript*, which is one of the best and most entertaining pieces of social criticism by a Canadian writer of his period.

Reference:

Kenneth J. Hughes, "*A Strange Manuscript*: Source, Satire, a Positive Utopia," in *The Canadian Novel*, volume 2, edited by John Moss, revised edition (Toronto: NC Press, 1984), pp. 111-125;

Janice Kulyk Keefer, *Under Eastern Eyes* (Toronto & Buffalo: University of Toronto Press, 1987), pp. 129-137;

Patricia Monk, *The Gilded Beaver: An Introduction to the Life and Work of James De Mille* (Toronto: ECW, 1990);

George Woodcock, "De Mille and the Utopian Vision," in *The Canadian Novel*, volume 2, revised edition, pp. 99-110.

Papers:

The De Mille Papers are housed at the Dalhousie University Library Archives.

Louis-Antoine Dessaulles

(31 January 1819 - 5 August 1895)

Julie LeBlanc
Carleton University

BOOKS: *Papineau et Nelson. Blanc et noir . . . et la lumière fut* (Montreal: Avenir, 1848);
Six Lectures sur l'annexion du Canada aux Etats-Unis (Montreal: Gendron, 1851; modern edition, New York: Johnson, 1968);
Galilée, ses travaux scientifiques et sa condamnation (Montreal: Avenir, 1856);
Discours sur l'Institut canadien prononcé par L'Hon. L.-A. Dessaulles (Montreal: Le Pays, 1863);
La Guerre américaine, son origine et ses vraies causes (Montreal: Le Pays, 1865);
La Grande Guerre ecclésiastique. La Comédie infernale et les noces d'or. La Suprématie Ecclésiastique sur l'ordre temporel (Montreal: Doutre, 1873);
Réponse honnête à une circulaire assez peu chrétienne (Montreal: Doutre, 1873);
Les Erreurs de l'église en droit naturel et canonique sur le mariage et le divorce (Paris: Pedone, 1894).

Described by some as the most dangerous enemy of religion in Canada and by others as a great philosopher, an eminent sociologist, a universal scholar, and the victim of the Canadian clergy, Louis-Antoine Dessaulles is best remembered as a journalist and a political figure, as a prominent leader of the Institut Canadien, and as a fierce opponent of the clergy. Since Dessaulles's literary career arose from his religious and philosophical convictions, it is only by taking into account the social and political context of his writings that one can succeed in understanding the contribution of this controversial figure to the revolutionary spirit of nineteenth-century French-Canadian literature.

Dessaulles was born in Saint-Hyacinthe, Quebec, on 31 January 1819. His mother, Marie-Rosalie née Papineau–sister of the prominent patriot leader Louis-Joseph Papineau–and his father, Jean Dessaulles–a militia officer, seigneur, and politician–had been married on 9 May 1816. They had five children, three of whom survived them: Louis-Antoine, Rosalie, and Georges-Casimir. In February 1850 Louis-Antoine Dessaulles

Louis-Antoine Dessaulles (C 7550, National Archives of Canada)

married Zéphirine Thomson and on 13 October 1852 Caroline, their only child, was born.

Politics dominated Dessaulles's entire life: his father sat on the legislative council, a position Louis-Antoine would later occupy; his brother Georges-Casimir was mayor of Saint-Hyacinthe and a senator; and his uncle, Louis-Joseph Papineau, was a controversial politician who greatly influenced Dessaulles's political and religious convictions. Papineau was not only leader of the Patriotes but also a prominent member of the Institut Canadien and a strong opponent of the clergy, so strong an opponent that the clergy sent him into exile in France from 1839 to 1845. Many historians regard Dessaulles's visits to Paris with Papineau as crucial events that greatly contributed to strengthening his liberal and anticlerical convictions.

Papineau's influence on his nephew can best be seen in Dessaulles's support of his uncle's annexation proposal. In a series of conferences entitled *Six Lectures sur l'annexion du Canada aux Etats-Unis* (1851), delivered to the members of the Institut Canadien from 1850 to 1851, Dessaulles presented the economic and political advantages of Canada's annexation with the United States: it would have offered Canadians a way to access American capital resources and given them the opportunity to participate in the policy of the central government. Dessaulles's pro-annexation position was also published in one of Montreal's major French newspapers, *L'Avenir,* and in *Le Pays,* a newspaper Dessaulles helped found in 1852 and ran as editor-in-chief from 1861 to 1863. One of the harshest critics of the annexationist movement and one of Dessaulles's long-standing opponents was Monseigneur Bourget, the man who would later inspire Dessaulles to write several anticlerical works: *Galilée, ses travaux scientifiques et sa condamnation* (1856), *La Grande Guerre ecclésiastique. La Comédie infernale et les noces d'or. La Suprématie Ecclésiastique sur l'ordre temporel* (1873), and *Réponse honnête à une circulaire assez peu chrétienne* (1873).

As an elected member of the legislative council for Rougemont from 1856 to 1863 and as a prominent member and president of the Institut Canadien in 1862, Dessaulles was always regarded as a controversial figure, greatly criticized by the French clergy and the conservatives for his anticlerical views and his radical liberal ideologies. Described in a parliamentary decree as a literary and artistic association whose main objective was to provide an open education through courses and public lectures, the Institut Canadien became the scene of extensive struggles between the liberals and the clergy. The institute's publications were not only indexed by the church but Bourget declared that all members of the Institut Canadien and anyone involved in publishing, distributing, or reading their publications would be refused the last sacrament.

One of Dessaulles's best-known publications, *Discours sur l'Institut canadien* (1863), written for the eighteenth anniversary of the institute, is a refutation of the French clergy's practice of censorship, which Dessaulles perceived as another example of the Church's autocratic and oppressive disposition toward nonconformists. In addition to the publication of *Discours,* Dessaulles's anticlerical stand on the well-known "Affaire Guibord" (concerning a member of the Institut Canadien to whom the church had refused a proper Catholic burial because of his political affiliations) intensified his fiery relationship with Bourget.

La Grande Guerre ecclésiastique, Dessaulles's most anticlerical and controversial essay and perhaps the work that is most extensively referred to by historians, was described by Philippe Sylvain as Dessaulles's "last intellectual testament." Written as a reaction to the "Affaire Guibord" and to a clerical publication, *La Comédie infernale ou Conjuration libérale,* Dessaulles's *La Grande Guerre* is made up of two letters addressed to Bourget, the first dated 31 July 1872 and the second dated 14 December 1872. It is in this document that Dessaulles emphatically criticizes every aspect of clerical life, the clergy's doctrines, "supremacist" and "ultramontane" attitudes toward their parishioners, and their ongoing practice of censorship: "the objective of the clergy is to impose the idea of their ultimate superiority . . . it is against this audacious project of clerical domination that I must protest." For no known official reasons, three years after the publication of *La Grande Guerre,* Dessaulles went into exile in France, where he remained until his death in Paris on 5 August 1895.

References:

F. L. (Dessaulles) Béique, *Quatre-vingts ans de souvenirs* (Montreal: Valiquette, (1939);

Pierre Berthiaume, "Les Rouges au XIXe siècle: lecture des pamphlets de Louis-Antoine Dessaulles," *Etudes Littéraires,* 2 (August 1978): 333-380;

Jean-Paul Bernard, *Les Rouges: libéralisme, nationalisme et anticléricalisme au XIXe siècle* (Montreal: Presses de l'Université du Québec, 1971);

Joseph Costisella, *L'Esprit révolutionnaire dans la littérature canadienne-française de 1837 à la fin du XIXe siècle* (Montreal:Beauchemin, 1968);

Théophile Hudon, *L'Institut Canadien de Montréal et l'Affaire Guibord* (Montreal: Fides, 1976);

Yvon Lamonde, *Inventaire chronologique et analytique d'une correspondance de Louis-Antoine Dessaulles (1817-1895)* (Quebec: Ministère des Affaires Culturelles, Archives Nationales, 1978);

Gérard Parizeau, *Les Dessaulles. Seigneurs de Saint-Hyacinthe* (Montreal: Fides, 1976);

Phillipe Sylvain, "Un Disciple canadien de Lamenais: Louis-Antoine Dessaulles," *Les Cahiers des dix*, 34 (1969): 61-83;

Sylvain, "Libéralisme et ultramontisme au Canada français: affrontement idéologique et doctrinal (1840-1865)," in his *The Shield of Achilles/Le Bouclier d'Achille* (Toronto & Montreal: McClelland & Stewart, 1968), pp. 11-138;

Marcel Trudel, "Les Chefs de l'Institut Canadien," in his *L'Influence de Voltaire au Canada,* volume 2 (Montreal: Fides, 1945), pp. 45-54.

Papers:

Dessaulles's papers are in the Thomas Fisher Rare Book Library and the St. Michael's University Rare Book Collection, both at the University of Toronto; in the Bibliothèque du Séminaire de Sherbrooke; and in the Institut Canadien de Microreproduction Historique at the University of Ottawa.

Edward Hartley Dewart

(30 March 1828 - 17 June 1903)

Mary Lu MacDonald

BOOKS: *Songs of Life: A Collection of Poems* (Toronto: Dudley & Burns, 1869);

Living Epistles; or, Christ's Witnesses in the World (Toronto: Christian Guardian, 1878);

Jesus the Messiah in Prophecy and Fulfillment (Toronto: Briggs, 1890; Cincinnati: Cranston & Stowe/New York: Hunt & Eaton, 1891);

Brief Outlines of Christian Doctrine (Toronto: Briggs/Montreal: Coates/Halifax: Huestis, 1898);

Essays for the Times; Studies of Eminent Men and Important Living Questions (Toronto: Briggs, 1898);

The Bible Under Higher Criticism (Toronto: Briggs, 1900).

OTHER: *Selections from Canadian Poets; with Occasional Critical and Biographical Notes, and an Introductory Essay on Canadian Poetry,* edited by Dewart (Montreal: Lovell, 1864; modern edition, Toronto: University of Toronto Press, 1973);

The Canadian Speaker and Elocutionary Reader . . . with Introductory Remarks on the Principles of Elocution, edited by Dewart (Toronto: Miller, 1868).

Edward Hartley Dewart was born on 30 March 1828 in Stradone, County Cavan, Ireland, the son of James and Margaret Hartley Dewart. When he was four his father immigrated to Canada, sending for his wife and children two years later. Edward was educated in the local Ontario schools of Dummer Township and at the provincial Normal School, then taught briefly before entering a career in the church. He was ordained into the Wesleyan Methodist ministry in 1855 after a four-year probation. The following year he married Matilda Hunt, and they apparently had three sons. For twenty-five years, from 1869 to 1894, he edited the *Christian Guardian*, the Methodists' weekly newspaper in Toronto. He received an honorary Doctor of Divinity degree from the Methodist-sponsored Victoria University in 1879. He was still writing columns for the *Christian Guardian* up until his fatal heart attack.

Although a fine writer himself, always interested in literature and acquainted with many of the Canadian writers of his day, he nonetheless saw his literary pursuits as an extension of his theological endeavors. The first two poems in his *Songs of Life* (1869), "Prologue" and "The Poet's Mission," make his position clear: "A nobler task be mine. To wake within / The dreaming soul a higher view / Of life's mysterious worth" rather than "To silver over selfishness and wrong, /

Title page and preface for Dewart's best-known work, still used as a textbook in some Canadian schools

SELECTIONS

FROM

CANADIAN POETS;

WITH OCCASIONAL

CRITICAL AND BIOGRAPHICAL NOTES,

AND AN

Introductory Essay on Canadian Poetry.

BY

EDWARD HARTLEY DEWART.

Montreal:
PRINTED BY JOHN LOVELL, ST. NICHOLAS STREET.
1864.

PREFACE.

MY object in compiling this volume has been to rescue from oblivion some of the floating pieces of Canadian authorship worthy of preservation in a more permanent form; and to direct the attention of my fellow-countrymen to the claims of Canadian poetry. The fact that I entered on an untrodden path, without any way-marks to guide me, necessarily caused me a vast amount of labor, and an extensive correspondence; as, in many instances, both poets and poetry had to be discovered by special research. This will, I hope, be duly considered by readers in judging of the work, should it be found less perfect than they had anticipated.

As I do not wish to be judged by a wrong standard, I must remind my readers that this is not "a work on the Poets and Poetry of Canada." Such a work may be highly desirable and necessary; and there is valuable material, in the poetic effusions of the past fifty years, with which to enrich such a work. But this collection makes no pretension to such a character: it is simply " SELECTIONS FROM CANADIAN POETS." With the hope of enhancing the interest and usefulness of the work, I have subjoined occasional brief notes; but the plan and scope of the work precluded any lengthy biographical sketches. It is easy for persons who

viii   PREFACE.

have neither literary nor financial responsibility, to suggest changes in the plan of such a work. But the same persons might, in a different position, fail to act on their own suggestions. To those who may feel disappointed, because selections are not made from their poetry, I have no apology to offer. An immense quantity of verse, much of it of high merit, has passed under my notice. Financial reasons compelled me to limit the size of the volume. I could not put in everything that I approved of. I have made a selection, according to the best of my judgment, without partiality, or sectional feeling of any kind. If any are dissatisfied with me, I am sorry; but, conscious of the integrity of my motives, I have nothing to regret. Nearly all the pieces in this volume are published by special permission of the authors; and many of them have never been published before.

My warmest thanks are due to the authors for the courtesy and liberality with which, without exception, they placed their poems at my disposal; and to editors of newspapers throughout the country for their friendly notice of my project. They are also due to the subscribers—many of whom I recognize as personal friends—for their confidence and patronage, by which I have been encouraged to place the work before the public. Should it secure their approbation, and be instrumental in awakening a more extensive interest in the Poets and Poetry of our beloved country, my humble labors will be amply rewarded.

ST. JOHNS, CANADA EAST, Jan., 1864.

With the soft grace and witchery of song. . . . "

Almost every Canadian student has read some part of Dewart's introductory essay to *Selections from Canadian Poets* (1864), but very few have read *Songs of Life,* which is one of the neglected masterpieces of early Canadian writing. Given the poetic conventions of his day and his deep religious convictions, the poems nonetheless compel a reader's attention. The forms are varied, he eschews the then-popular singsong rhyme schemes, and he handles iambic pentameter with great assurance. His subject matter is also varied. The book is divided into an initial general section, followed by "Songs of the World Without," "Songs of the World Within," "Songs of Home and Heart," "National and Patriotic Pieces," and finally "Miscellaneous Pieces." The "World Without" includes poems addressed to Niagara Falls and to the Atlantic cable, to various natural phenomena, and "Ocean Musings" on the occasion of his first adult sea voyage. The poems of the "World Within" are largely devotional, and those of "Home and Heart" are works of sentiment. The patriotic poems indicate a deep love of Canada as well as token nostalgia for the Ireland of his birth. At least one of the miscellaneous poems, "Deacon Grimes," depicting a man of moral and doctrinal rigidity, shows Dewart to have been, in the context of his time, broad and charitable in his definition of Christianity.

The long-term scholarly value of *Selections from Canadian Poets* lies in its overview of Canadian poetry as seen from the vantage point of 1864. Although a few of the works included come from the 1820s and 1830s, most are by writers known to Dewart, who published their work after he reached adulthood. His occasional biographical and publishing notes are also helpful to modern scholars. The introductory essay defends poetry at some length and speaks of the need for a national literature, but it is the section in which he condemns the perceived "colonial mentality" of the Canadian reader that has touched a responsive chord in late-twentieth-century critics, keeping his name before the public in modern times.

In his preface to *Essays for the Times* (1898) Dewart returns at the end of his life to themes that first occupied his attention thirty years earlier. He thinks a national literature is important as a record of a country's thought, and he wants to make sure that some of that record includes "the thoughts of the thoughtful on subjects of living interest. . . . " The essays, with the exception of one on Charles Sangster, all have theological subjects. The Sangster essay is an "appreciation" of the poet's work rather than a critique.

Almost all of what has been written about Edward Hartley Dewart focuses on him as the compiler of *Selections from Canadian Poets.* More attention should be paid to him as a writer. His papers, which are in the National Archives, contain some autobiographical fragments that merit publication.

Reference:
Douglas Lochhead, Introduction to Dewart's *Selections from Canadian Poets* (Toronto: University of Toronto Press, 1973), pp. vii-xvii.

Papers:
Dewart's papers are in the National Archives of Canada, Ottawa, in file MG29 D107.

William "Tiger" Dunlop

(19 November 1792 - 28 June 1848)

Elizabeth Waterston
University of Guelph

BOOKS: *Statistical Sketches of Upper Canada, for the Use of Emigrants: By a Backwoodsman* (London: Murray, 1832);
Recollections of the American War, 1812-14 (Toronto: Historical Publishing, 1905);
Tiger Dunlop's Upper Canada (Toronto: McClelland & Stewart, 1967).

OTHER: T. R. Beck, *Elements of Medical Jurisprudence*, includes notes and appendix by Dunlop (Edinburgh: Blackwood, 1825).

SELECTED PERIODICAL PUBLICATIONS–UNCOLLECTED "Writers and Writerism," *Blackwood's*, 11 (April 1822): 432-437;
"The Indian Press," *Blackwood's*, 12 (August 1822): 133-139;
"A Paper on Peat Mosses," *Canadian Literary Magazine*, 1 (May 1833): 98-100;
"Letter from Dr. Dunlop," *The Canadian, British American, and West Indian Magazine*, 1 (December 1839): 458-460.

"Tiger" Dunlop's *Statistical Sketches* (1832) will not provide statistics on the Canadian settlements in the years before the 1837 rebellion. Nor will his *Recollections* (1905) give insight into the causes and implications of the 1812 War between the British Canadas and the United States. They *will* give a sense of the huge, energetic, eccentric author, glorying in his own oddities as well as in the raw, envigorating life of the frontier. They give also the pleasure of seeing the writer wrestle his experiences in battle and in the backwoods into vivid, sophisticated style.

William Dunlop was born in Greenock, Scotland, and received a medical education at the University of Glasgow in a time when Scotland was bursting with creativity and achievement in science, political thought, architecture, and engineering, as well as literature. Self-confidence and self-discipline were in the air. They impelled young Dunlop first into a career in the army as surgeon. At the end of the Napoleonic Wars he was

slated for Spain but sent instead to the Canadian frontier in 1813.

At Ganonoque, Fort Erie, and Niagara, he saw action; in 1815 he volunteered to lead a party from Lake Simcoe to Penetanguishene, cutting a military road from December to March to the potential northern shipbuilding center. Then he was shipped back to England with the dim prospect of half pay at the age of twenty-four.

Shipped next, through family business interests, as a civilian to India, Dunlop tried journalism in Calcutta (taking an important stand against censorship). Next he undertook to prepare Saugog Island, near Calcutta, for settlement by clearing it of tigers. He conquered innumerable tigers by throwing snuff in their faces and then shooting them point-blank–or so his tale ran. The tale earned him the sobriquet "Tiger." The exploits also earned him "jungle fever"; he was invalided home in 1819 via South Africa. After his convalescence, from 1820 to 1824 he sent articles to *Blackwood's* and was welcomed by the magazine's brilliant circle including John Galt.

Dunlop moved to London, carrying his Edinburgh reputation for wit and energy. He edited the *British Press* and *Telescope*, (magazines focusing on affairs in India), helped edit a medical textbook, and dabbled, like Galt, in business management.

Galt, excited about the settlement of Canada, talked Dunlop into going to the New World in 1826. As "Warden of Woods and Forests," Dunlop had the job of inspecting Canada Company lands. Diving into the woods west of Toronto, he was in at the founding of Guelph, and was himself the founder of Goderich. "Founding" involved chopping a hundred-mile road from Guelph to the beautiful harbor on Lake Huron, building a rough receiving house, pacing out a wheel of roads for an elegant townsite, and claiming and clearing a fine holding across the river. Here he would build "Gairbraid," the fabulous

AUTHOR OF "SKETCHES OF UPPER CANADA".

Portrait from the Fraser's Magazine *"Gallery of Illustrious Literary Characters" (1830-1838)*

bachelors' hall visited by many travelers in the next twenty years.

When Galt fell out with the Canada Company and was recalled in 1829, Dunlop stayed on, eventually becoming general superintendent of the Huron Tract. Meantime, roaring through the bush, hunting, drinking, and fraternizing, he collected materials for *Statistical Sketches*. Journals in England—especially *Blackwood's* and *Fraser's* (which had featured his portrait and feats in 1830 and 1833)—hailed *Statistical Sketches* as the best of its multitudinous kind. Dunlop wrote on the climate, the cookery, the canals, the soil, the sects, and the sports, always with gusto, frankly re-

porting drawbacks, but openly calling working-class immigrants to come to Huron. Far from the folk art of a raw frontier, Dunlop's book controls his own turbulence with style and self-conscious structure.

Dunlop settled into local and provincial politics in the later 1830s as the colony moved toward splitting among the Family Compact, William Lyon Mackenzie's radicals, the colonial governors, and the Canada Company. In spite of lack of support from compact, company, and government, Dunlop raised a militia, "The Huron Invincibles," to patrol western frontiers against American attacks fomented by Mackenzie's rebels. Wearied by his subsequent effort to get pay for his militia, Dunlop resigned from the company, and stood for Parliament, for the seat first held by his now-deceased brother Robert. He won a bitter contest. In Parliament at Kingston and later Montreal, he paced, roared, and pounced, delighting the gallery, wearying opponents, and sometimes flabbergasting his party.

Though returned in a series of elections, he was gradually weakened in constitution by the pace of his travels, his drinking bouts, and his political rages. In 1846 he resigned his seat, accepting a well-paid sinecure as "Superintendent of the Lachine Canal." He then worked on a memoir of his earliest, most energetic foray through Canadian life. In *Recollections of the American War* he recalls landing in Quebec, the eager dash upriver, the "brigandish" exploits, and the dreadful scenes of horror and sorrow as he mopped up after battle. The aging writer rekindled a great narrative force as he moved from the natural drive of travel account through the anecdotal richness of pungent war scenes to the culminating energy of the Penetanguishene road building. Dunlop died at Lachine, Quebec, and his body was brought back by Louisa McColl Dunlop, his devoted, ferocious sister-in-law, to Goderich.

Dunlop had contributed literary distinction as well as legendary leadership to early Canada. Consciously a "backwoodsman," he was also a "*Blackwood's* man." John Wilson, *Blackwood's* editor, described him thus: "Gruff but gracious, he was at once one of the most forbidding, and one of the most winning of men." Carl F. Klinck and W. H. Graham refueled interest in this remarkable man in the late 1950s and early 1960s.

References:

W. H. Graham, *The Tiger of Canada West* (Toronto: Clarke, Irwin, 1962);

Carl F. Klinck, *William "Tiger" Dunlop* (Toronto: Ryerson, 1958);

Roberta and K. M. Lizars, *Humours of '37* (Toronto: Briggs, 1897);

Lizarses, *In the Days of the Canada Company* (Toronto: Briggs, 1896);

William Maginn "Canada—by Tiger—Galt—Picken," *Fraser's*, 5 (July 1832): 635-642;

Maginn, "Gallery of Literary Characters . . . The Tiger," *Fraser's*, 7 (April 1833): 436;

John Wilson, "Upper Canada. By a Backwoodsman," *Blackwood's*, 32 (July 1832): 238-262.

Papers:

Dunlop's papers are in the National Library of Scotland; the Galt Papers, Public Archives of Canada; the Crown Land Papers, Provincial Archives of Ontario; and the Lizars Papers, University of Western Ontario.

May Agnes Fleming

(14 November 1840 - 24 March 1880)

Lorraine McMullen
University of Ottawa

BOOKS: *Silver Star; or, the Mystery of Fontelle Hall*, as Cousin May Carleton (New York: Brady, 1861); republished as *The Dark Secret; or, The Mystery of Fontelle Hall* (New York: Beadle & Adams, 1875);

Sybil Campbell; or, The Queen of the Isle, as Carleton (New York: Brady, 1861); republished as *An Awful Mystery* (New York: Beadle & Adams, 1875); republished as *The Queen of the Isle* (New York: Dillingham, 1886);

Erminie; or, The Gipsy's Vow, as Carleton (New York: Brady, 1862);

La Masque; or, The Midnight Queen (New York: Brady, 1863); republished as *The Midnight Queen* (New York: Dillingham, 1888);

The Twin Sisters; or, the Wronged Wife's Hate (New York: Beadle & Adams, 1864); republished as *The Rival Brothers; or, The Wronged Wife's Hate* (New York: Beadle & Adams, 1875);

Victoria; or, The Heiress of Castle Cliffe (New York: Brady, 1864); republished as *Unmasked; or, The Heiress of Castle Cliffe* (New York: Beadle, 1870);

Eulalie; or, A Wife's Tragedy, as M. A. Earlie (New York: Brady, 1866);

The Baronet's Bride; or, A Woman's Vengeance, edited by W. J. Benners, Jr. (New York: Munro, 1868);

The Heiress of Glen Gower; or, The Hidden Crime, edited by Benners (New York: Munro, 1868);

Estella's Husband; or, Thrice Lost, Thrice Won (New York: Munro, 1869); republished as *Thrice Lost, Thrice Won* (New York: Street & Smith, 1900);

The Unseen Bridegroom; or, Wedded for a Week, edited by Benners (New York: Munro, 1869);

Lady Evelyn; or, The Lord of Royal Rest (New York: Street & Smith, 1870);

Who Wins?; or, The Secret of Monkswood Waste (New York: Donohue, 1870);

Magdalen's Vow, edited by Benners (New York: Munro, 1871);

Guy Earlscourt's Wife (New York: Carleton / London: Low, 1873);

A Wonderful Woman (New York: Carleton, 1873);

A Terrible Secret (New York: Carleton / London: Low, 1874);

A Mad Marriage (New York: Carleton / London: Low, 1875);

Norine's Revenge, [and] *Sir Noel's Heir* (New York: Carleton, 1875);

Kate Danton; or, Captain Danton's Daughters (New York: Carleton, 1876; Toronto: Rose-Belford, 1878);

One Night's Mystery (New York: Carleton / London: Low, 1876);

The Ghost of Riverdale Hall (New York: Lupton, 1877);

Silent and True; or, A Little Queen (New York: Carleton, 1877);

Carried by Storm (New York: Street & Smith, 1878);

The Heir of Charlton (New York: Carleton, 1878);

Lost for a Woman (New York: Carleton / London: Low, 1880);

A Changed Heart (New York: Carleton / London: Low, 1881);

Fated to Marry; A Night of Terror; Kathleen (New York: Ogilvie, 1881);

The Three Cousins, [and] *One Summer Month* (New York: Ogilvie, 1881);

The Secret Sorrow (New York: Ogilvie, 1883); republished as *A Fateful Abduction; or, The Secret Sorrow* (New York: Dillingham, 1907);

Sharing Her Crime (New York: Carleton / London: Low, 1883);

Maud Percy's Secret (New York: Carleton, 1884);

The Actress' Daughter (New York: Carleton, 1886);

The Virginia Heiress (New York: Street & Smith, 1888);

Married for Money, and Other Stories (New York: Ogilvie, 1891);

A Pretty Governess, and Other Stories (New York: Ogilvie, 1891);

Edith Percival (New York: Dillingham, 1893);

The Sisters of Torwood (New York: Dillingham, 1898).

May Agnes Fleming

May Agnes Early (later Fleming) was born in the Portland area of Saint John, New Brunswick, on 14 November 1840, to Bernard and Mary Doherty Early, Irish immigrants. While still a schoolgirl, at the Convent of the Sacred Heart, she began to publish in the weekly story papers. Using the pseudonym Cousin May Carleton, she was soon contributing regularly to three or four papers. She quickly progressed from short stories to longer stories, becoming proficient in developing complex plots and in combining romantic and sentimental elements with such gothic elements as mystery, disguise, startling events, and murder so that the weekly episodes of her stories left her readers in suspense. By the time she was twenty her novels were being serialized in the story papers, then published in cheap paperbacks. By the time of her marriage, on 24 August 1865, to John William Fleming, she was established as a popular writer of serialized novels.

Fleming's success coincided with the rapid expansion of the weekly story papers and the con-comitant demand for writers. As a writer of gothic and sentimental serials she became Canada's first best-selling novelist. At the peak of her career she published in the most widely read of the story papers in England and the United States and in hardcover in London and New York. Royalties and serial rights brought her an income of over fifteen thousand dollars a year. After her death, the demands of her readers led to frequent reprints of her books, including lesser-known short stories and serials published early in her career before she became so popular.

The very successful *Sybil Campbell; or, The Queen of the Isle* (1861) exemplifies Fleming's early style. It is an intricately plotted story of a young brother and sister who return to their ancestral home, a small island off the coast of North America. The novel concludes happily for the protagonists, who find true love, but only after a series of startling and harrowing events. The complicated, fast-moving plot leaves no room for character development, nor is there any sense of a specific time or place. Like many of Fleming's novels this one, frequently republished, also appeared under different titles, among them *An Awful Mystery* (1875) and *The Queen of the Isle* (1886). This cavalier treatment of titles, combined with the ephemeral nature of some of the papers in which she published, makes the compiling of an accurate bibliography of Fleming's writings a difficult task.

In 1868 Fleming's success led to an exclusive contract with the Philadelphia weekly *Saturday Night* (circulation one hundred thousand), writing three stories a year for two thousand dollars. Her first novel for that paper, *The Baronet's Bride; or, a Woman's Vengeance* (published serially in 1868 and in book form later that year), has all the gothic elements her most eager readers could desire: hidden identities, attempted murder, family secrets, and mysterious meetings. The plot hinges on the search for vengeance of a Spanish gypsy woman, seduced and abandoned by an English baronet. Unknown to the baronet, the liaison resulted in a daughter. The daughter and later the granddaughter continue the vendetta, designed to bring disgrace and death to the baronet's only son. The villainous woman—dark, passionate, and exotically foreign—had made her first appearance in *Eulalie; or, A Wife's Tragedy* (1864; published as a book in 1866) and was to continue as one of Fleming's stock characters.

After five years with *Saturday Night* Fleming moved to the New York *Weekly*, which claimed its circulation of three hundred thousand to be the largest of any of the American story papers. Here she was paid six thousand dollars for two stories a year. She soon arranged for simultaneous publication in the London *Journal*, which had earlier pirated one of her stories from *Saturday Night*, and for hardcover publication by George W. Carleton immediately after serialization. She was now making well over fifteen thousand dollars a year. The Flemings moved with their two children to New York to be near her publishers and bought a house in Brooklyn.

Fleming's novels, after this move to the *Weekly*, became to a degree more realistic, less gothic and melodramatic. Most are set in New York and New England, areas familiar to her, rather than, as in much of her earlier work, in an England she never knew. At times she included episodes set in Canada, usually Quebec.

While retaining mystery and romance she moved to a less involved plot, allowing for more character development. By 1877 ill health forced her to reduce her output to one novel a year.

Fleming's last novel published in her lifetime, *Lost for a Woman* (1880), is possibly her best. It follows the protagonist from her childhood to an unhappy marriage from which she runs away, an ensuing period of independence, and then her marriage to the childhood friend she loves. The young woman displays courage, liveliness, and initiative—qualities generally seen in Fleming's earlier novels only in the villainous woman. Most interesting today is the episode in which the heroine leads the life of a career woman, sharing an apartment in New York with her former maid, now her companion and equal, and making a living as tutor to the children of socialites. Although many of the conventions of the sentimental novel are retained, the attractive protagonist is more fully developed. She finds happiness not in wealth and title, which she has rejected, but in the simple life. Her own initiative rather than a handsome hero rescues her from her difficulties. The novel is interesting for the episodes Fleming chose to develop: the heroine gives insight into the mind of a woman trapped in an unhappy marriage; her servant portrays life on a lower scale than usually enters into the sentimental novel, which is characteristically set in upper-class society; and the period of independence indicates the possibility of a satisfying life for a single woman.

Fleming has been likened to E.D.E.N. Southworth, the immensely popular American novelist of the time, and Mary Elizabeth Braddon, the well-known British novelist. Fleming knew her readers and gave them the kind of novel they demanded—complex and ingenious plots with gothic and melodramatic elements that lent themselves admirably to serialization. Along with ingenious plots, her skillful dialogue and underlying humor help to explain her popularity. Fleming was a talented woman who chose her area and developed her craft early in life. In what she set out to do she was eminently successful.

Reference:

Henry J. Morgan, ed., *Types of Canadian Women* (Toronto: Briggs, 1903).

John Franklin

(16 April 1786 - 11 June 1847)

I. S. MacLaren
University of Alberta

BOOKS: *Narrative of a Journey to the Shores of the Polar Sea, in the Years 1819, 20, 21, and 22* (London: John Murray, 1823; Philadelphia: Carey & Lea, 1824; facsimile, New York: Greenwood, 1969; another facsimile, Edmonton: Hurtig, 1969);

Narrative of a Second Expedition to the Shores of the Polar Sea, in the Years 1825, 1826, and 1827 . . . Including an Account of the Progress of a Detachment to the Eastward, by John Richardson, M.D., Surgeon and Naturalist to the Expedition (London: John Murray, 1828; Philadelphia: Carey & Lea, 1828; facsimile, New York: Greenwood, 1969; another facsimile, Edmonton: Hurtig, 1971).

John Franklin will always be better known, deservedly, for the events of his life than for his narratives of them; yet his two books of early-nineteenth-century arctic travels present some of the best examples in the literature of Canadian exploration of the duty-bound officer's highly disciplined, factual, and unadorned style, as called for in the genre by the Royal Society's Thomas Sprat in 1664. Literary flourish, even metaphor, was nearly a stranger to Franklin's reportorial pen; still, the events at least of the first arctic expedition rendered his first narrative one of the most captivating ever written about early Canada.

John Franklin was born on 16 April 1786 at Spilsby, Lincolnshire, England, the twelfth child of Willingham Franklin, a banker (his mother's name is unknown). By the age of thirteen he was at sea aboard a ship of Britain's prodigious merchant fleet. He joined the navy a year later and saw action with Adm. Horatio Nelson's fleet at Copenhagen (1801) and Trafalgar (1804). In between these two famous naval battles, Franklin sailed with Matthew Flinders to chart the coast of Australia. His first arctic service came in 1818, an indifferent voyage amid the ice-choked waters off Spitsbergen, Norway. However, it made way for his first major arctic expedition–a search for a

Sir John Franklin (portrait by Stephen Pearce, circa 1837, based on the portrait attributed to J. M. Negelen; by permission of the Scott Polar Research Institute, Cambridge)

northwest passage–which started a year later from York Factory in Hudson Bay.

Lasting through the summer of 1822, this expedition had only a slight naval dimension: Franklin was charged with directing a twenty-man party to the Arctic Ocean at the mouth of the Coppermine River (seen by Samuel Hearne in July 1771) by following, not oceans in ships, but inland fur-trade routes in boats and canoes. Once at the ocean, which he reached in July 1821, he was to follow the continent's northern coast eastward until arriving, it was hoped, back in Hudson Bay. In 1825 his second expedition continued the coastal charting begun by the first, starting from the delta of the Mackenzie River (reached by Alexander Mackenzie in 1789) and, by splitting into two detachments, going both westward, nearly to a planned rendezvous with a navy ship that had sailed around South America and up through Bering Strait, and eastward, to the mouth of the Coppermine. Nearly two full decades passed after this successful expedition–seven years of which Franklin spent as governor of Britain's penal colony Van Diemen's Land (Tasmania)–before he sailed into the Canadian Arctic again, in 1845. This last expedition, an utter catastrophe, claimed the lives of Franklin and every one of his 139 men; although he died, it appears, from natural causes, his crew's deaths remain an actively researched question today. But because no narratives survived this tragic voyage, it offers the student of exploration literature nothing directly. Several literary works have, however, been created from the events of the tragedy: for example, Sten Nadolny's 1983 novel *Die Entdeckung der Langsamkeit* (translated in 1987 as *The Discovery of Slowness*) and Gerald St. Maur's poem "John Franklin, His Enterprise" (in his *Odyssey Northwest*, 1983).

Franklin's first expedition passed winters on the Saskatchewan River, at Cumberland House (Saskatchewan), and on Winter River, at Fort Enterprise (Northwest Territories), before descending the Coppermine River by birchbark canoes during the late spring and early summer of 1821. Then the four officers (the others were Dr. John Richardson and Midshipmen Robert Hood and George Back), one British seaman, two Indian interpreters, two Inuit guides, and eleven fur-trade voyageurs set out on the waters and ice floes of Coronation Gulf. Although all survived the perilous summer's charting of the continental coastline, Franklin had waited too long before admitting to himself that his hopes of reaching Hudson Bay were wildly impracticable: during the feverish return trip overland to Fort Enterprise, eleven of the twenty men died, some from starvation, others, it is believed, by murder at the hands of a starvation-crazed voyageur, Michel Teroahauté. One of the officers, Hood, perished at his hands. Those who reached the fort crawled to it. They survived to tell their tale only because the Copper Indians of the district nursed them back from the edge of death.

That tale is for the most part impersonally rendered in *Narrative of a Journey to the Shores of*

Jane Griffin, who became Franklin's second wife in 1828 (from the drawing by Miss Romilly, 1816); his first wife, Eleanor Porden Franklin, had died in 1825.

the *Polar Sea* (1823). Occasionally Franklin betrays his anxiety over the tragedy playing itself out before him, but such utterances are conventional even at that: "our infinite disappointment and grief"; "the most melancholy communications from our companions"; and so on. Typically his narrative presents not a fascinating, profound literary character, but an officer impassively recording the events of his duty. Writing for the Admiralty necessarily precluded the expression of ultimate hopes and fears or the pronouncements of recrimination and remorse at failures. Franklin was seeking security in his professional career at a time–during the peace that ensued at the defeat of Napoleon–when few men found security in active military or naval service. While in the employ of the Admiralty, therefore, he adopted a tight-lipped demeanor. Even so, it is excessively tight and colorless, or so it appears when his narrative is compared to those of his fellow officers, Richardson and Hood, whose trainings had been similar, but who did not share Franklin's ultimate responsibility for the expedition's success or its failure.

The contents of Franklin's first book are, apart from the drama brought to the tale by starvation, paralleled by those of his second (published in 1828). Typical for his age's literature of travel and exploration, it includes logistical, cartographical, geographical, and ethnographical information but almost no personal contemplation, speculation, or literary flourish. Attitudes are mainly directed by Christian and British imperial senses of spiritual, racial, and economic superiority over other peoples. (Franklin thereby produces unintentional irony when he openly thanks the Copper Indians and their chief, Akaitcho, for rescuing him and eight of his men but attributes their finding him and his fellows to the providence of God.) Like the first narrative, as well, the second is not entirely by Franklin: because the second expedition divided at the Mackenzie River Delta, the report of the eastward detachment, which charted as much coastline as Franklin's westward party, is the work of Richardson, whose additional interests in geology, biology, and botany afforded him greater interest in the tundra and greater opportunity to see it as more than a sterile waste (because treeless).

Franklin's westward detachment failed to rendezvous with the HMS *Blossom*, though he would later learn the two parties came within 160 miles of each other on the ice-packed coast of modern Alaska before Franklin turned back to the Mackenzie Delta–he had no intention of staying out on the ocean for too long on a second expedition. But if he thought himself a failure, Great Britain did not, bestowing a knighthood on him. He and Richardson also received honorary degrees from Oxford. His third voyage being the consummate tragedy, Franklin never realized a successful expedition in the Arctic, but like Robert Falcon Scott in the Antarctic sixty years later, his failure seemed to guarantee his lasting fame: the story of the Northwest Passage is linked more often with Franklin's name than with that of any other explorer.

Letters:

Some Private Correspondence of Sir John and Lady Jane Franklin, 2 volumes, edited by George Mackaness (Sydney, Australia: Ford, 1947).

References:

Richard C. Davis, "Vision and Revision: John Franklin's Arctic Landscapes," *Australian-Canadian Studies*, 6, no. 2 (1989): 23-33;

Robert Hood, *To the Arctic by Canoe 1819-1821: The Journal and Paintings of Robert Hood Midshipman with Franklin*, edited by C. Stuart Houston (Montreal & London: McGill-Queen's University Press, 1974);

I. S. MacLaren, "The Aesthetic Mapping of Nature in the Second Franklin Expedition," *Journal of Canadian Studies*, 20 (Spring 1985): 39-59;

MacLaren, "Retaining Captaincy of the Soul: Response to Nature in the First Franklin Expedition," *Essays on Canadian Writing*, 28 (Spring 1984): 57-92;

Roderic Owen, *The Fate of Franklin* (London: Hutchinson, 1978);

John Richardson, *Arctic Ordeal: The Journal of John Richardson, Surgeon-Naturalist with Franklin 1820-1822* (Kingston, Ont. & Montreal: McGill-Queen's University Press, 1984).

Louis-Honoré Fréchette
(16 November 1839 - 31 May 1908)

John E. Hare
University of Ottawa

BOOKS: *Mes Loisirs* (Quebec: Brousseau, 1863); republished in the modern edition of *La Voix d'un exilé* (Montreal: Leméac / Paris: Aujourd'hui, 1979);

La Voix d'un exilé (Chicago: Privately printed, 1866; Montreal: Privately printed, 1868); enlarged as *La Voix d'un exilé: Poésies canadiennes* (Chicago: Imprimeries de l'Amérique, 1869; modern edition, Montreal: Leméac/ Paris: Aujourd'hui, 1979);

Félix Poutré (Montreal: Privately printed, 1871; modern edition, Montreal: Leméac, 1974);

Lettres à Basile à propos des Causeries du dimanche de A.-B. Routhier (Quebec: L'Evénement, 1872);

Pêle-Mêle (Montreal: Lovell, 1877);

Les Fleurs Boréales (Quebec: Darveau, 1879; Paris: Rouveyre, 1881);

Les Oiseaux de neige (Quebec: Darveau, 1879);

Poésies choisies (Quebec: Darveau, 1879);

Papineau, Drame historique canadien (Montreal: Chapleau & Lavigne, 1880; modern edition, Montreal: Leméac, 1974); translated by Eugene Benson and Renate Benson as *Papineau: A Canadian Historical Drama, Canadian Drama*, 7 (Spring 1981): 51-110;

Le Retour de l'exilé (Montreal: Chapleau & Lavigne, 1880; modern edition, Montreal: Leméac, 1974);

Petite Histoire des rois de France, as Cyprien (Montreal: La Patrie, 1881);

La Légende d'un peuple (Paris: Librairie Illustrée, 1887; revised edition, Quebec: Darveau, 1890);

Feuilles volantes (Quebec: Darveau, 1890);

Originaux et Détraqués: Douze types québécois (Montreal: Patenaude, 1892; modern edition, Montreal: Editions du Jour, 1972);

A propos d'éducation (Montreal: Desaulniers, 1893);

Christmas in French Canada (Toronto: Morang, 1899; London: Murry, 1899; New York: Scribners, 1899); translated into French as *La Noël au Canada (contes et récits)* (Toronto: Morang, 1900); modern edition published as *La Noël au Canada français* (Montreal: Stanké, 1986);

Poésies choisies, 3 volumes (Montreal: Beauchemin, 1908);

Histoire de chantiers (Montreal:Beauchemin: 1919);

Cent morceaux choisis, selected by Pauline Fréchette (Montreal: Privately printed, 1924);

L'Abonneux, as Cyprien (Trois Rivières, Que.: Privately printed, 1935);

Voix de Noël (San Francisco: Grabhorn, 1936);

Contes d'autrefois (Montreal: Beauchemin, 1946);

Fréchette, selected by Michel Dassonville (Montreal & Paris: Fides, 1959);

Mémoires intimes, edited by George A. Klinck (Montreal: Fides, 1961);

Contes de Jos Violon (Montreal: L'Aurore, 1974);

Véronica (Montreal: Leméac, 1974);

Contes, 2 volumes (Montreal: Fides, 1974, 1976);

Masques et Fantômes (Montreal: Fides, 1976);

Noël d'autrefois, by Fréchette and Robertine Barry (Montreal: Communications Match, 1982);

Margot (Trois Rivières, Que.: L'Association Catholique des Voyageurs de Commerce, n.d.).

PLAY PRODUCTIONS: *Félix Poutré*, Quebec, La Salle de Musique, 22 November 1862;

La Confédération, Montreal, College Bourget de Rigaud, 3 January 1878;

Le Retour de l'exilé, Montreal, Académie de Musique, 1 June 1880;

Papineau, Montreal, Académie de Musique, 7 June 1880;

Un dimanche matin à l'hôtel du Canada, Quebec, Académie de Musique, 26 December 1881;

Change pour change, Nicolet, Quebec, Séminaire de Nicolet, 1886;

Veronica, Montreal, Théâtre des Nouveautés, 2 February 1903.

OTHER: Honoré Beaugrand, *Six mois dans les Montagnes-rocheuses*, preface by Fréchette (Montreal: Granger, 1890);

The Louis Fréchette postage stamp

William Henry Drummond, *The Habitant and Other French-Canadian Poems*, introduction by Fréchette (Toronto: Musson, 1897);

Albert Ferland, *Femmes rêvées*, preface by Fréchette (Montreal: Ferland, 1899).

Louis-Honoré Fréchette (who occasionally used the pseudonym Cyprien) is remembered today for his short stories and recollections of the picturesque characters he met during his youth. During the last quarter of the nineteenth century, however, he was considered the most important poet that French Canada had produced, and a considerable essayist and playwright. A friend and patron of the literary and cultural movements of the period, he represented to his generation–despite the literary quarrels in which he became embroiled–the ideal man of letters.

Born in Lévis, Quebec, across the Saint Lawrence River from Quebec City, Fréchette was the son of Louis-Marthe and Marguerite Martineau Fréchette. In his memoirs he recalls these years as a time of joyous adventure, but from his earliest years, he was also drawn to the United States.

At the age of fifteen he ran away from home to spend several weeks there and was later to return there to work. (His younger brother Achille, who later married Annie Howells, the sister of the American writer William Dean Howells, was also to be strongly influenced by America in his own literary career.) Louis Fréchette returned to Quebec after this first fling abroad, however, to complete his formal schooling. He was educated first by the Christian Brothers, then (from 1854 to 1857) at the Séminaire de Québec, finishing his secondary training–after having been expelled from two other schools–at the Collège de Sainte-Anne-de-la-Pocatière (1857-1859). It was during this period that he came under the spell of Lamartine and other French Romantic poets, and his first published poem, "A une jeune fille" (To a Young Lady) appeared in *L'Abeille* in April 1859. After a second trip to the United States, later that year, he again returned to Quebec, to study law at Laval University from 1860 to 1861, after which he became a clerk in the law offices of Lemieux and Rémillard. He was called to the bar in 1864, opened an unsuccessful office in Lévis,

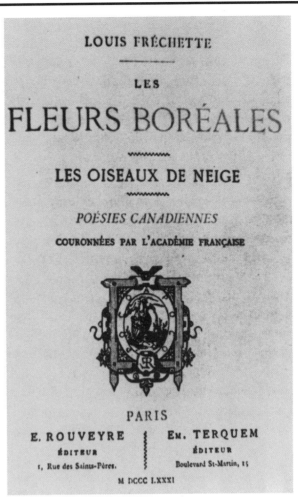

Frontispiece and title page for the Paris edition of Fréchette's 1879 collection, which won the Montyon Prize from the French Academy

and that year and the next founded two newspapers, neither of which lasted more than a few months.

During his student years Fréchette lived in a garret, a "mansarde de palais," with other aspiring lawyers and doctors, one of whom was Pamphile Lemay. They spent many evenings discussing literature, dreaming of future success, and beginning to write. Fréchette and Lemay were both to publish in *Les Soirées Canadiennes* from 1861 onward, and Fréchette, who would compose more than four hundred poems by the time of his death almost fifty years later–and publish nine books of poetry as well as dozens of chapbooks–was already writing the poems for his first collection, *Mes Loisirs* (In My Spare Time, 1863). The forty-five poems of this volume are romantic songs about the exploits of Canadian heroes and lyrical celebrations of the young women of the author's dreams: Flora, Louise, Juliette,

and Corinne. When it appeared in print, the book proved to be a challenge to readers. In a short preface, in the form of a dialogue, Fréchette attempted to subvert those who felt that poetry should have utilitarian value. But the experimental nature of this work and its personal lyricism evoked few echoes in the Quebec of the 1860s. Some of the poet's friends were sympathetic, but the general public seemed indifferent. The book was too modern for its time, and two years later Fréchette had still not sold enough copies even to pay for its printing. In the early 1870s the remaining copies were destroyed in a fire. By that time, however, he had again left Canada.

During the early 1860s Fréchette was also turning his hand to drama. The memoirs of Félix Poutré, who claimed to have been one of the leaders of the 1837-1838 Rebellion in Lower Canada, created quite a stir when they were published in 1862. Within a few months, Fréchette had taken the disjointed text of the memoirs and turned it into a successful play entitled *Félix Poutré*, which was first performed in Quebec City on 22 November 1862. A popular historical drama, it variously inspired patriotic fervor and appealed to the contemporary taste for melodrama and vaudeville. In spite of the many characters–over thirty–and the six scene changes, it was performed hundreds of times during the nineteenth century. Surprisingly, however, Fréchette himself took little interest in the text, perhaps suspecting that Poutré was not the hero he claimed to be. Today it is known that in fact Poutré was a paid informer working for the military police against the Patriotes. When the play was published in 1871, Poutré himself claimed all royalties.

As some of the scenes in this play indicate, Fréchette was discovering a talent for comedy as well as for romantic lyricism, and he would return to the comic mode in the later short stories for which he is now best known. But he was also becoming skilled as a political journalist. An active political campaigner during the early 1860s, he was an ardent defender of liberalism, and his radical opinions were expressed openly in the columns of his two short-lived newspapers: *Le Drapeau de Lévis* (1864) and *Le Journal de Lévis* (1865). Yet by 1866 he had become discouraged both with literature and with politics. There seemed little future for an aspiring writer in Quebec, and the approaching Canadian Confederation signaled for him the end of the French-Canadian nationality. Once again he turned south, leaving in July 1866 for Chicago, where his brother Achille had a law practice. Louis Fréchette worked there for the Illinois Central Railway and took part in the cultural life of the French community in the city, in part by participating in the publication of French-language newspapers, of which few traces remain. From the moment of his arrival in Chicago he felt invigorated by the energy and idealism of America. He wrote the libretto for an opera, *Les Fiancés de l'Outaouais* (The Betrothed of the Ottawa), and a play called *Tête à l'envers* (Confused), which was apparently performed in Chicago; unfortunately neither of these texts has survived.

Fréchette also found, however, that he could not easily turn his back on his countrymen, and in the fall of 1866 he wrote and published a twenty-five-verse poem called *La Voix d'un exilé* (An Exile's Voice), which was addressed to the Liberals of Canada, inciting them to struggle for the glorious day of liberty to come. *Le Pays*, a Liberal

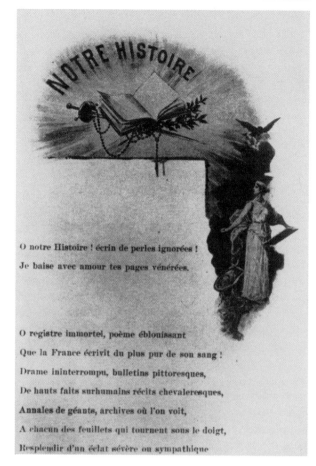

First page of Fréchette's "Notre Histoire," illustrated by Henri Julien, in the 1908 edition of La Légende d'un peuple

newspaper resolutely opposed to the proposed Confederation of 1867, published *La Voix d'un exilé* as part of its propaganda war against the Conservatives. The verses were then reproduced in many other publications and circulated by the Liberal Party, making Fréchette suddenly very well known in his home country. In 1868 he added a second part to the poem, the following year added a third, and he then published the definitive edition (1869). But then his life took another turn. In 1871, because of his pro-French stand during the Franco-Prussian War, he was obliged to leave the United States. He returned for a short visit to Quebec, and when, while he was there, the Chicago fire destroyed all his manuscripts, he decided to remain.

In 1870 Adolphe-Basile Routhier, who had studied with Fréchette, published the first of his *Causeries du dimanche*, which came out as a book the following year. Routhier attacked the liberal ideas that were dear to Fréchette and took his former friend to task for his beliefs. Fréchette could not accept these criticisms; so he wrote a series of letters exposing the weaknesses in Routhier's arguments and defending his own work. This polemic, which lasted from November 1871 to February 1872, had a positive effect on the careers of both men. Fréchette, through his *Lettres à Basile* (Letters to Basile, 1872), became known as an arch liberal and radical, whereas Routhier became one of the society's leading conservatives. Fréchette defended, for example, the right of an individual to differ with members of the clergy, a theme he would return to in his 1893 letters on education. At the same time, he was trying after his return to Canada to erase the memory–or at least soften the effect–of the strong political stance he had taken in *La Voix d'un exilé*. In 1877 he prepared a revised edition, which he had printed in a small private publication. Later he felt it more prudent simply to ignore the work, and consequently this poem, one of the most important of the period, was not reprinted until 1979.

In 1874 Fréchette had been elected to the Parliament of Canada, and in 1876 he married Emma Baudry, the daughter of a rich Montreal merchant. His future seemed assured. He was even considered as a future leader of the Liberal Party, and his 1877 book of verse, *Pêle-Mêle* (Miscellany), was designed as his farewell to poetry. His defeat in the 1878 election forced a return to a literary career, however, and from that time on Fréchette settled with his family in Montreal and wrote for the newspapers of that city.

Of the forty-eight poems in *Pêle-Mêle*, ten had already appeared in *Mes Loisirs*; another dozen had been written during his exile in Chicago. The perspective of the book is that of a man in his thirties, one who is aware that his youth is over and the young women he had loved gone forever, but who has learned that these are replaced by a wonderment at the restorative powers of nature and the joys of friendship and family life. The cult of great men, popular in his era, becomes more marked in this volume, as in poems addressed to Henry Wadsworth Longfellow and Louis-Joseph Papineau. The epic vein that he had exploited in *La Voix d'un exilé* is accentuated, and his long poem "Jolliet"–about Louis Jolliet, the explorer of the Mississippi Basin–expresses his faith in the role of man in the conquest of nature. His description of the immensity of the Mississippi remains among the best verse written in the nineteenth century.

The success of this volume, which was well received in France, paved the way for the triumphs of 1880, clearly the high point of his writing career. In June his two plays *Le Retour de l'exilé* (Exile's Return) and *Papineau* were performed before enthusiastic audiences, and on 5 August he received the Montyon Prize from the French Academy, at a ceremony in Paris, for his new book of poetry, *Les Fleurs Boréales* (Northern Flowers, 1879). This first French recognition of a work by a Quebec writer created a strong current of publicity in France, where Fréchette was lionized, and the event captured the imagination of French Canada. On his return home Fréchette was received as a hero and invited to a series of banquets held in major cities and towns throughout the province. While his popularity would be short-lived in France, he remained the best-known writer in his native Quebec for many years.

Specially prepared for the Montyon Prize competition, *Les Fleurs Boréales* was made up of poems from *Pêle-Mêle* together with fifty-two sonnets under the general title "Les Oiseaux de neige" (Snow Birds, published separately in 1879). The most interesting are the twelve poems of "L'Année canadienne," detailing the passing of the year, and those under the heading "Paysage" (Countryside). Several of these word paintings are among the best of his work, including those describing "Le Cap Tourment" and "Le Niagara."

Other works followed. He wrote a one-act comedy called "Une Journée à l'Hôtel du Canada" (One Day in the Hotel Canada) in 1881 (performed as *Un dimanche matin à l'hôtel du Canada* later that year), and in 1882 he began work on "The Last Creole," a play to be set in Louisiana. Although he never finished this latter work, he did continue with drama, and *Change pour change*, another vaudeville, was performed by the students of Séminaire de Nicolet in 1886.

Rapidly acquiring social stature, Fréchette became one of the founding members of the Royal Society of Canada in 1882, and increasingly he immersed himself in studying his country's past. Already he had celebrated Jolliet in verse; and his 1880 play, *Papineau*, which glorified the Patriote resistance leader of the 1837 Rebellion and his efforts to gain political control, had been performed to rave reviews in Montreal. The play carries several political implications. The third act presents the armed confrontation at St. Denis and the defeat of the Patriotes, followed by their escape to the United States. But to this narrative

Illustrations by Frederick Simpson Coburn for Fréchette's Christmas in French Canada *(1899; translated as* La Noël au Canada, *1900)*

Fréchette adds a romantic interest, in the person of Rose Laurier, who loves a young English lord, and in the end, Papineau gives his benediction to this union between the two races.

At this point in his career Fréchette decided to tell the history of his people in a long epic poem or series of poems. It might have been the fourth edition of François-Xavier Garneau's *Histoire du Canada* that inspired this desire; Fréchette contributed a meditative poem called "Notre Histoire" (Our History) to this volume when it appeared in 1882, and he wrote approximately twenty more poems concerning French-Canadian history over the next few years. These poems took book form in 1887: Fréchette spent the summer of 1887 in France, at the Nantes villa of Madame Eugène Riom, a patron of the arts, preparing *La Légende d'un peuple* (The Legend of a People); the book was published in Paris at the end of the year.

Victor Hugo's 1862 *La Légende des siècles* (The Story of the Centuries) was undoubtedly the book that focused Fréchette's attention on the way epic poetry could forcefully present the panorama of history. *La Légende d'un peuple* alludes to this sweep of time through the structure and sequence it adopts. The dedication–"A la France"–proclaims the poet's love for the mother country of his ancestors. The prologue then goes on to hail the New World. Emerging from the mists of time, "L'Amérique" subsequently serves as the call of God to the people of Europe. Fréchette sees North America as a force of liberty for all humanity. The history of Canada, Fréchette's native land, is then seen in three successive and interlocking periods or waves. The first involves the discoverers and pioneers; it is a record of primeval forests, the heroism of Adam Dollard des Ormeaux (the soldier who vainly helped to defend the fort at the Battle of the Long Sault, a battle that nineteenth-century writers depicted as a religious cause), and the solitary struggle of Pierre Cadieux (the eighteenth-century voyageur, whom ballads describe as having been aided by the Virgin Mary). The second period of Fréchette's poetic history centers on the struggle against the English for control of the continent, from before the 1759 Battle of the Plains of Abraham to the resistance during the American Revolution. Finally, in the third period, Fréchette praises the heroic struggles against British oppressors after the Conquest: from the Rebellion of 1837-1838 and the repression that followed, to the fanaticism of the Orangists and the hanging of Louis Riel in 1885. *La Légende d'un peuple* ends with an epilogue entitled "France," which corresponds in theme and structure to the prologue. Fréchette here sees France as the light and conscience of the civilized world.

This vast fresco was saluted by Premier Honoré Mercier of Quebec as the incarnation of the spirit of Quebec. In 1889 Mercier named Fréchette clerk of the legislative council, a largely honorary post. Other readers considered the book the most important work of French-Canadian literature yet to appear; the three editions published during Fréchette's lifetime assured its wide diffusion. In the twentieth century, because epic poetry has lost its critical appeal, *La Légende d'un peuple* is rarely read, but Fréchette's vision of history nonetheless played an important role in the development of the Quebec nationalist movement.

Some years earlier, Henri-Raymond Casgrain had encouraged Quebec writers to use legends and popular traditions as the basis for their works, and Fréchette, who had collaborated with Casgrain in the publication of *Les Soirées Canadiennes* between 1861 and 1865, had written a few short stories in the popular vein as early as 1861. But it was only in 1888 that he seems to have discovered his talent in this genre. That year he became a founding member of the Montreal chapter of the American Folklore Society and published seven stories based on popular themes.

In 1890 he gathered together the approximately thirty poems he had written after *Pêle-Mêle* and published them under the title of *Feuilles volantes* (Flying Leaves), but these added little to his poetic reputation. Although a few poems stand out–"La Louisiana," "Le Rêve de la vie" (The Dream of Life), and "La Manoir de Montebello" (The Manor House at Montebello [Papineau's estate])–critics tend to regard this collection as his weakest. Until his last years, it was also his final extended attempt to write poetry. Increasingly he was turning to fiction. In 1892 he published more than twenty stories, and in that same year his book *Originaux et Détraqués* (The Eccentric and the Unbalanced) appeared. Here Fréchette draws twelve portraits of some of the strange characters who inhabited Quebec and Lévis during his youth. He tells of the cruel ways in which bands of young people treated eccentric old men. Yet each old person in his own way had a delicious store of anecdotes to tell.

Fréchette's increasing success, however, created problems for him. Some people began to attack him, and his tendency to respond vehemently to any attack led to a series of tiresome polemical articles. These seldom resolved the disputes in question; unfortunately they did begin to raise questions in the public mind about the integrity of his authorship. It is true that Fréchette sometimes followed the models of others, as in his 1880 play *Le Retour de l'exilé*, which was based on Elie Berthet's novel *La Bastide Rouge*, but Fréchette's enemies used the similarity of plots to charge him with flagrant plagiarism, and the play, though successfully performed and published, had to be withdrawn. His antimonarchical pamphlet, *Petite Histoire des rois de France* (A Short History of the Kings of France, 1881) also embroiled him in controversy, as did his articles in *La Patrie* (Montreal). In his later years he also conceived the verse drama *Véronica* (1903; published in 1974), which he wrote for Sarah Bernhardt, but again he came to grief over the use of another man's work. Much of the background for this Italian melodrama had been prepared by a French writer named Maurice de Pradel. The play was not performed until a year after the French author's death, but in spite of a lavish production by the Théâtre de Nouveautés, it was not a success.

However, it was Fréchette's 1893 series of letters on the problems of education in the province of Quebec that led to his greatest difficulties with opponents. These thirteen letters, published under the title *A propos d'éducation* (About Education), present a penetrating analysis of the weaknesses of the *collège classique* system as it was then being directed by the Catholic clergy. In these writings Fréchette upholds the rights of parents to examine the curriculum and to question the competence of the teachers–he is particularly virulent when discussing the quality of the French spoken and written by school graduates–and he thereby challenges the prevailing authoritarianism of the system.

This polemic on education became the pretext for the most destructive attack against him. In June 1893 William Chapman, his onetime admirer, published the first of a long series of articles that attempted to demonstrate that Fréchette was nothing more than a plagiarist. Although the motivation for this attack was professional jealousy, Fréchette could not but be somewhat tarnished by the two volumes that Chapman subsequently published: *Le Lauréat. Critique des oeuvres de M. Louis Fréchette* (The Winner: A Critique of the Works of Fréchette, 1894) and *Deux Copains. Réplique à MM Fréchette et Sauvalle* (Two Chums: A Retort to Messrs. Fréchette and Sauvalle, 1894). Chapman examines each of Fréchette's works and purports to find parallels in the works of other French and Quebec writers; the "parallels," however, are often absurd, sometimes amounting to similarities between no more than a word or two in a verse. Fréchette wrote only one letter in response to this attack, allowing his friends to answer for him. Henri Roullaud and Paul-Marc Sauvalle, in defending him, used Chapman's methods to show that (on these grounds) Chapman himself could be accused of plagiarism. Unfortunately for Fréchette, Chapman's accusations continue to be given currency and used to denigrate his literary work.

Fréchette did not, however, withdraw from the public eye. He was awarded four honorary doctorates and made a Chevalier of the Légion d'Honneur and a Companion of the Order of St. Michael. President of the Royal Society in 1900 and 1901, Fréchette was also honorary president of L'Ecole Littéraire de Montréal. Each year he also published three or four more stories and anecdotes, some of which he grouped in an English-language volume called *Christmas in French Canada* (1899), which he also rendered in a French version, *La Noël au Canada*, the following year. He planned for another volume, to be called *Masques et Fantômes* (Masks and Phantoms), but this was not published till 1976. In 1900 he wrote serially for *Le Monde Illustrée* some autobiographical sketches, under the title *Mémoires intimes*, which tell of his youth and happiness in Lévis. Published as a volume in 1961, these provide a sympathetic account of life as it was lived in the 1840s. The long section devoted to Papineau reiterates the importance of this great hero for Fréchette as a young French Canadian. During his last year Fréchette also prepared the definitive, three-volume edition of his poetry, which was published in 1908, a few months before his death in May of that year. The volume was called *Poésies choisies* (Selected Poems).

Several selections from his work appeared following his death, and in recent years his more than seventy short stories have been carefully re-edited. While some critics judge his use of popular dialect severely, others praise it as a mark of his authenticity. The two volumes of *Contes* appeared in 1974 and 1976. In 1974 his eight stories attributed to the legendary storyteller Jos

Violon were published in a separate volume. All of these stories take their inspiration from the legends told during Fréchette's youth.

Over the course of time, Louis-Honoré Fréchette's place in the theater history of French Canada has not proved to be a solid one; and while his poetic use of patriotic themes in the epic style of Hugo was in tune with nineteenth-century tastes, it seems out of place today. Even by the end of his life, his Romanticism was deemed archaic. But his personal anecdotes, his reminiscences, and his short stories are still being read and studied. All his literary efforts must nevertheless be recognized as important contributions to the development of a literary tradition in Quebec. His immense output and his participation in the cultural and political life of Quebec made him a well-known and influential figure. Indeed, he marked the coming of age of French-Canadian letters in the last decades of the nineteenth century.

Biographies:

L.-O. David, *Souvenirs et Biographies* (Montreal: Beauchemin, 1911), pp. 153-178;

Henri d'Arles, *Louis Fréchette* (Toronto: Ryerson, 1923);

Lucien Serre, *Louis Fréchette* (Montreal: Fréres des Ecoles Chrétiennes, 1928);

Marcel Dugas, *Un Romantique Canadien: Louis Fréchette* (Paris: Revue Mondiale, 1934; Montreal: Beauchemin, 1946);

François Ricard, "Notre contemporain Louis Fréchette," *Liberté*, 16 (July-August 1974): 125-137;

James Doyle, *Annie Howells and Achille Fréchette* (Toronto: University of Toronto Press, 1979).

References:

Charles ab der Halden, "Louis-Honoré Fré-chette," in his *Etudes de littérature cana-dienne-française* (Paris: Rudeval, 1904), pp. 227-256;

Pierre Berthiaume, "Les Mémoires intimes de Louis Fréchette ou Actualisation du passé," *Lecture Québec*, 9 (February 1978): 42-44;

Jean-Ethier Blais, "Louis Fréchette," *Cahiers de l'Académie Canadienne-Française*, 7 (1963): 73-85;

Aurélien Boivin, "Louis Fréchette," in his *Le Conte littérature québécois au XIXe siècle* (Montreal: Fides, 1975), pp. 162-194;

Lise Gauvin, "Fréchette: des quiproquos dramatiques à l'ironie de conteur," *Livres et Auteurs Québécois* (1974): 338-348;

Pierre Gobin, "Le Papineau de Fréchette: absence de chef, absence de pays," *Canadian Drama*, 7 (Spring 1981): 12-18;

George A. Klinck, *Louis Fréchette, prosateur* (Lévis, Que.: Quotidien, 1955);

Séraphin Marion, "Louis Fréchette et le Canada français d'autrefois," *Cahiers des Dix*, no. 37 (1972): 123-157;

Guy Monette, "La Polémique autour de La Voix d'un exilé ou Le Chant du cygne de l'immanentisme au Québec," *Voix et images du pays*, 2 (April 1974): 334-357;

Camille Roy, "Louis Fréchette," in his *Nouveaux Essais de littérature canadienne* (Quebec: Action Sociale, 1914), pp. 135-215;

Paul Wyczynski, "Dans les coulisses du théâtre de Fréchette," in *Le Mouvement littéraire de Québec, 1860*, Archives des Lettres, volume 1 (Ottawa: University of Ottawa Press, 1961), pp. 100-128;

Wyczynski, "Louis Fréchette et le théâtre," in *Le Théâtre canadien-français*, Archives des Lettres, volume 5 (Montreal: Fides, 1976), pp. 137-166.

John Galt

(2 May 1779 - 11 April 1839)

Elizabeth Waterston
University of Guelph

BOOKS: *Voyages and Travels in the Years 1809, 1810, and 1811* (London: Cadell & Davies, 1812);

The Life and Administration of Cardinal Wolsey (London: Cadell & Davies, 1812); enlarged as *Life of Cardinal Wolsey* (London: Bogue, 1846);

The Tragedies of Maddalen, Agamemnon, Lady Macbeth, Antonia and Clytemnestra (London: Cadell & Davies, 1812);

Letters from the Levant (London: Cadell & Davies, 1813);

The Majolo: A Tale (London: Colburn, 1815);

The Life and Studies of Benjamin West (London: Cadell & Davies, 1816; Philadelphia: Thomas, Maxwell, 1816); enlarged as *The Life, Studies, and Works of Benjamin West* (London: Cadell & Davies, 1820);

All the Voyages Around the World, as Capt. Samuel Prior (London: Lewis, Phillips, 1820; enlarged edition, 1827; New York: Colyer, 1840);

George the Third, His Court, and Family, 2 volumes (London: Colburn, 1820);

The Earthquake, a Tale, 3 volumes (Edinburgh: Blackwood, 1820; 2 volumes, New York: Van Winkle, 1821);

Glenfell; or, MacDonalds and Campbells (London: Phillips, Sams, 1820);

The Wandering Jew, as Rev. T. Clark (London: Souter, 1820);

The Ayrshire Legatees (Edinburgh: Blackwood, 1821; New York: Gilley, Bliss & White, 1823); republished with *The Gathering of the West* (Edinburgh: Blackwood, 1823);

Annals of the Parish, as Rev. Micah Balwhidder (Edinburgh: Blackwood, 1821; Philadelphia: Carey, 1821);

Pictures, Historical and Biographical (London: Lewis, 1821);

The Provost (Edinburgh: Blackwood, 1822; New York: Duyckinck, Harper, 1822);

The Steam-boat (Edinburgh: Blackwood, 1822; New York: Campbell, 1823);

John Galt (portrait by Charles Grey; by permission of the Trustees of the National Museums of Scotland)

Sir Andrew Wylie, of that Ilk, 3 volumes (Edinburgh: Blackwood, 1822; 2 volumes, New York: Gratton, 1822);

The Entail; or, The Lairds of Grippy, 3 volumes (Edinburgh: Blackwood, 1823; 2 volumes, New York: Harper, 1823);

Ringan Gilhaizie; or, The Covenanters, 3 volumes (Edinburgh: Oliver & Boyd, 1823; 2 volumes, New York: Duyckinck, 1823);

The Spaewife, 3 volumes (Edinburgh: Oliver & Boyd, 1823; 2 volumes, Philadelphia: Carey & Lea, 1824);

118

The Bachelor's Wife; A Selection of Curious and Interesting Extracts (Edinburgh: Oliver & Boyd, 1824);

Rothelan, 3 volumes (Edinburgh: Oliver & Boyd / London: Whittaker, 1824; 1 volume, New York: Collins, 1825);

The Universal Traveller, as Prior (London: Whittaker, 1824);

The Omen (Edinburgh: Blackwood / London: Cadell, 1825);

The Last of the Lairds (Edinburgh: Blackwood / London: Cadell, 1826; New York: Harper, 1827);

Lawrie Todd; or, The Settlers in the Woods, 3 volumes (London: Colburn & Bentley, 1830; 2 volumes, New York: Harper, 1830; revised edition, London: Bentley, 1832; New York: Farmer & Daggers, 1845);

The Life of Lord Byron (London: Colburn & Bentley, 1830; New York: Harper, 1830);

Southennan, 3 volumes (London: Colburn & Bentley, 1830; 2 volumes, New York: Harper, 1830);

Bogle Corbet; or, The Emigrants, 3 volumes (London: Colburn & Bentley, 1831; volume 3 published in a modern edition, Toronto: McClelland & Stewart, 1977);

The English Mother's Catechism for Her Children, as Rev. T. Clark (London: J. Souter, 1831);

The Lives of the Players, 2 volumes (London: Colburn & Bentley, 1831; Boston: Hill, 1831);

The Member: An Autobiography (London: Fraser, 1832);

Stanley Buxton; or, The Schoolfellows, 3 volumes (London: Colburn & Bentley, 1832; 2 volumes, Philadelphia & Baltimore: Carey & Hart, 1833);

The Canadas, by Galt and Andrew Pickens (London: Wilson, 1832);

The Radical: An Autobiography (London: Fraser, 1832);

Stories of the Study, 3 volumes (London: Cochrane & M'Crone, 1833);

The Stolen Child (London: Smith, Elder, 1833; Philadelphia: Carey, Lea & Blanchard, 1833);

Eben Erskine; or, The Traveller, 3 volumes (London: Bentley, 1833; 2 volumes, Philadelphia: Carey, Lea & Blanchard, 1833);

The Ouranoulogos; or, The Celestial Volume (Edinburgh: Blackwood, 1833);

Poems (London: Cochrane & M'Crone, 1833);

The Autobiography of John Galt, 2 volumes (London: Cochrane & M'Crone, 1833; Philadelphia: Key & Biddle, 1833);

The Literary Life and Miscellanies, 3 volumes (Edinburgh: Blackwood / London: Cadell, 1834);

The Gambler's Dream, 3 volumes (London: Bull, 1837);

The Demon of Destiny; and Other Poems (Greenock, Scotland: Johnston, 1839);

The Howdie and Other Tales, edited by William Roughead (Edinburgh & London: Foulis, 1923);

A Rich Man and Other Stories, edited by Roughead (London & Edinburgh: Foulis, 1925).

Editions and Collections: *Works of John Galt*, 8 volumes, edited by D. Storrar Meldrum (Boston: Roberts, 1895-1896); enlarged as *The Works of John Galt*, 10 volumes, edited by Meldrum and William Roughead (Edinburgh: Grant, 1936);

The Gathering of the West, edited by Bradford Allen Booth (Baltimore: John Hopkins Press, 1939);

Poems of John Galt: A Selection, edited by G. H. Needler (Toronto: Burns & MacEachern, 1954);

Collected Poems, edited by H. B. Timothy (Toronto: University of Toronto Press, 1969.

OTHER: *The New British Theatre: A Selection of Original Dramas*, 4 volumes, edited by and including plays by Galt, (London: Colburn, 1814-1815);

Diary Illustrative of the Times of George the Fourth, Interspersed with Original Letters from the Late Queen Caroline, edited by Galt (London: Colburn, 1838-1839).

SELECTED PERIODICAL PUBLICATIONS–
UNCOLLECTED: "A Bandana on Emigration," *Blackwood's*, 24 (April 1826): 470-478;

"Colonial Discontent in Upper Canada," *Blackwood's*, 26 (August 1829): 332-337;

"The Hurons, a Canadian Tale," *Fraser's*, 1 (February 1830): 90-93;

"American Traditions," *Fraser's*, 2 (October 1830): 321-323;

"Guelph in Upper Canada," *Fraser's*, 2 (November 1830): 456-457;

"Canadian Affairs," *Fraser's*, 1 (June 1832): 389-398;

"Pere LaClaire," *Fraser's*, 7 (January 1835): 409-415;

"Sketches of Savage Life," *Fraser's*, 8 (March 1835): 160-166;

"Shaa-naan-Lillit, the Last of the Boeothics," *Fraser's*, 8 (May 1835): 316-323;

"Tecumseh, Chief of the Shawnees," *Fraser's*, 8 (June 1835): 499-511.

Annals of the Parish (1821) was the Scottish novel that established John Galt as a major proponent of regional realism; along with books such as Mary Russell Mitford's *Our Village* (1824), *Annals* offered a model for early Canadian sketch writers such as Susanna Moodie. John Galt contributed more directly to early Canadian literature with *Bogle Corbet* (1831); the third volume of this novel, set in southwestern Ontario, combines the ironic perspective of the *Annals* with details drawn from Galt's experience as colonizer in the 1820s. Galt's *Autobiography* (1833) is another essential source for students of politics, landscape, and the daily management of life in the Canadas.

John Galt was born on 2 May 1779 at Irvine, in west-coast Scotland, the son of John and Jean Thomson Galt. His father was a sea captain, and young John was early apprenticed to business in Greenock, in spite of a childhood flair for writing blank-verse tragedies. He left for London at the age of twenty-five. Among his first publications was "Statistical Account of Upper Canada" in the *Philosophical Magazine* (October 1807), owned by Dr. Alexander Tilloch, whose daughter Elizabeth he married on 20 April 1813. Galt's early experiences included business bankruptcy, legal studies, travels in Europe during the Napoleonic embargo–he became involved with George Gordon, Lord Byron in some smuggling enterprises–and prodigious writing of travel books, plays, biographies, and poems. In 1818 he returned to Glasgow to work as political lobbyist for the Glasgow-Edinburgh canal; this led in 1820 to another lobbying assignment, as agent for United Empire Loyalists hoping for government reimbursement for losses sustained during the War of 1812.

Galt's era of fame as a novelist also began in 1820. Ten novels about West Scotland life poured out in the next five years. Meantime, however, Galt continued his business life, pressing the claims of the Loyalists. His brief for them incorporated the suggestion that funds could be found by selling Canadian crown and church lands, a position offensive to Canadian clerics such as John Strachan. The Canadian Company was nevertheless formed, with Galt as one of its

The building in Irvine, Scotland, where Galt spent his early childhood, living with his parents in the upper flat. The building has since been demolished.

commissioners, and he made his first transatlantic visit in 1825 to arrange the takeover of vast tracts of land, to be sold by the company to immigrants. After visits to New York State to study methods of land settlement and town planning he returned to London in June 1825.

Galt came to Canada again in 1826 as superintendent of the Canada Company. Descriptions of his travels with William "Tiger" Dunlop from Quebec to York, Guelph, Penetanguishene, and Goderich make Galt's *Autobiography* an excellent source of information on roads, shipping, social life, and climate. Reports of his tussles with Lieutenant-Governor Peregrine Maitland and secretary Wilmot Horton (distorted by a misconception of Galt's connections with William Lyon Mackenzie) add a rich sense of politics in the mid 1820s. His production of novels momentarily ceased, although *The Last of the Lairds* (1826), arguably his best work, was published in London during his absence overseas.

Galt brought his wife and three sons to Canada in 1828 with the intention of permanent establishment there, but his dealings with the Canada Company became strained, and he was recalled April 1829, accused of mismanagement. Debts for his sons' schooling had piled up, and he was incarcerated in London debtors' prison from July to November, 1829. Here he wrote the following to clear his debts: *Lawrie Todd* (1830), a novel about settlement life in the United States; a biography of Byron (1830); *Southennan* (1830), a romance set in the time of Mary Queen of Scots; and articles for *Fraser's Magazine* including "The Hurons, a Canadian Tale," "Canadian Sketches," "American Traditions," and "Guelph in Upper Canada."

The popularity of *Lawrie Todd* brought financial relief, and the rise in value of Canada Company stock restored faith in Galt's management abilities. In 1831 he became secretary for the British-American Land Company. Settling his family in cheap lodgings in London, he continued to produce work on his Canadian experiences: *Bogle Corbet* and further articles on Canada published in *Fraser's*, *Tait's*, and *Blackwood's*.

His always precarious health deteriorated. A first stroke in 1832 was followed by another in 1834 and a third in 1836. Galt, now settled in Scotland, his debts paid off by Herculean efforts to publish, lived until 11 April 1839, writing and dictating until his last hours. Canada was still among his topics in late poetry and prose; important ethnographic articles in *Fraser's* included "Shaa-naan-Lillet, Last of the Boeothics," and "Tecumseh, Chief of the Shawnees" (both 1835).

The Autobiography and *The Literary Life and Miscellanies* (1834), partly dictated to his son when Galt was incapacitated, are sometimes rambling and inconsistent, but they are rewarding resources for students interested in early life in the Canadas or in the artistic strategies devised by a perceptive observer straining for ways to reveal and assess that life. *Lawrie Todd* and especially *Bogle Corbet*, however, constitute Galt's main claim for Canadian attention. The New World section of *Lawrie Todd* is set in upstate New York, but contains many details of settlement life drawn directly from Galt's Canadian experiences. Lively in tone and incisive in characterization, *Lawrie Todd* deserved its contemporary popularity; it also deserves a modern reprinting. The third volume of *Bogle Corbet* has been reissued in a New Canadian Library Edition. This part of the pseudoautobiography of a generally unsuccessful entrepreneur is set in a new Upper-Canadian community, sixty miles from York. Details of the founding and organization of this village replicate facts about Guelph, Ontario. In middle age, Bogle brings his unwilling wife, Urseline, and his family into the bush in order to set out a town de-

Capt. John Galt, shipmaster, the author's father (from Jennie W. Aberdein, John Galt, *1936)*

signed to satisfy modern economic and aesthetic principles. Like a bundle of sticks, the settlers will be tied by common ownership and cooperative work on roads, mills, and public buildings. Like the "New Town" in Edinburgh, the village will be laid out with vistas and green spaces, attention being paid to the picturesque aspects of cityscape as well as to practical needs for public gathering places, markets, schools, churches, and business facilities.

One recurring theme is the difference between life in such a planned colony and life in the United States, where the will-o'-the-wisp of freedom attracts radical members of the pioneer group away from the settlement of "Nox." Other points about life in a new country are slyly made by the portraiture of religious charlatans, such as Mr. Faggotter, the Methodist preacher who pursues the less respectable wives in the town, and the feckless farmer who stands helplessly by in

THE AUTHOR OF A "LIFE OF BYRON."

Portrait by Daniel Maclise in the Fraser's Magazine *"Gallery of Illustrious Literary Characters" (1830-1838)*

the face of disaster. As for Bogle himself, like the narrators of Galt's Scottish novels, he is untrustworthy, a persona whose oddities beckon the reader into rectifying his unbalanced account. In *Bogle Corbet* Galt inaugurates a new genre, a narrative form of loosely linked sequential sketches pointing the way not only to Susanna Moodie, but also to later writers such as Duncan Campbell Scott, Stephen Leacock, and Alice Munro.

Bibliographies:

Harry Lumsden, "The Bibliography of John Galt," *Records of the Glasgow Bibliographical Society*, 9 (1931): 1-41;

B. A. Booth, "A Bibliography of John Galt," *Bulletin of Bibliography*, 16 (1936).

Biographies:

D. M. Moir, *Biographical Memoir of John Galt*

(Edinburgh: Ballantyne, 1841);

R. K. Gordon, *John Galt* (Toronto: University of Toronto Press, 1920);

Jenny Aberdein, *John Galt* (London: Oxford University Press, 1936);

Ian A. Gordon, *John Galt, the Life of a Writer* (Edinburgh: Oliver & Boyd, 1972).

References:

Erik Frykman, *John Galt's Scottish Stories* (Upsalla: University of Upsalla Press, 1959);

Henri Gibault, *John Galt romancier ecossais* (Grenoble: Publications de l'Université des Langues et Lettres de Grenoble, 1979);

C. F. Klinck, "John Galt's Canadian Novels," *Ontario History*, 49 (Autumn 1957): 187-194;

F. H. Lyell, *A Study of the Novels of John Galt* (Princeton: Princeton University Press, 1942);

P. H. Scott, *John Galt* (Edinburgh: Scottish Academic Press, 1985);

Scottish Literary Journal, Galt issue (May 1981);

H. B. Timothy, *The Galts, A Canadian Odyssey*, 2 volumes (Toronto: McClelland & Stewart, 1977, 1984);

Elizabeth Waterston, Introduction to *Bogle Corbet* (Toronto: McClelland & Stewart, 1977);

Waterston, ed., *John Galt: Reappraisals* (Guelph: University of Guelph, 1985);

Christopher Whatley, ed., *John Galt, 1779-1979* (Edinburgh: Ramsay Head, 1979).

Papers:
The Public Archives of Canada hold the Galt Family Papers (MG 24, 1, 4), which include drafts and working copies of poems, narratives, plays, fiction, articles, and essays. The National Library of Scotland has manuscripts of *Ringan Gilhaizie* (1823), *The Last of the Lairds* (1826), and *The Howdie* (1923); and letters in the Blackwood Papers (4005-4044), Cadell and Davis Papers (9818), Moir Papers (6522), Oliver and Boyd Papers, and Walter Scott papers. Other papers are in the Bodleian Library, Oxford (Ms. Pigott, d.6); the Public Record Office, State Papers for Upper Canada; the Scottish Record Office (GD/45/226); the Baldwin Room, Toronto Metropolitan Library; the Greenock Public Library; the Irvine Public Library; and the Edinburgh University Library.

François-Xavier Garneau
(15 June 1809 - 2 February 1866)

David R. Mawer
Saint Paul University

BOOKS: *Histoire du Canada depuis sa découverte jusqu'à nos jours*, 3 volumes (Quebec: Aubin, 1845-1848; enlarged, 4 volumes, 1852; revised and abridged edition, 1 volume, Quebec: Coté, 1856); translated by Andrew Bell as *History of Canada, from the Time of Its Discovery till the Union Year*, 3 volumes (Montreal: Lovell, 1860);

Voyage en Angleterre et en France, dans les années 1831, 1832 et 1833 (Quebec: Coté, 1855; abridged edition, Quebec: Brousseau, 1878); modern edition, edited by Paul Wyczynski (Ottawa: Editions de l'Université d'Ottawa, 1968).

OTHER: James Huston, ed., *Le Répertoire national*, 4 volumes, includes poems by Garneau in volumes 1-3 (Montreal: Lovell & Gibson, 1848).

François-Xavier Garneau of Quebec City was the first major Canadian historian to write in either English or French. In his one great work, a liberal-nationalist history of Canada (4 volumes,

1845-1852), he took the story of French Canada only as his central theme, beginning with the earliest explorers and ending with the legislative union of Upper and Lower Canada in 1840. This latter event was regarded by Garneau as an affront to French-Canadian national hopes. His interpretation of it determined the thrust of his entire work, which was intended to provide French Canadians with a written history of which they could be proud. This view of history influenced subsequent historical writing in French Canada for more than a century. The best-known modern historian writing in the Garneau tradition was Lionel Groulx, and he, too, has had influential successors.

Garneau, the son François-Xavier and Gertrude Amiot-Villeneuve Garneau, received little formal education after the age of fourteen, but like many other distinguished Victorians, he was fortunate in the interest certain able individuals took in him during his formative years, J.-F. Perrault and Archibald Campbell among them. He was also introduced into the circle of French-Canadian politicians and public figures who were

François-Xavier Garneau

to be active in the politics of the "Patriote" era. They included such men as Etienne Parent, Denis-Benjamin Viger, and also Louis-Joseph Papineau, who took part in the rebellion of 1837. As a young adult Garneau was well informed and possessed considerable independence of mind.

For men of the professional class jobs were few. Garneau became a notary. His precarious means of livelihood was eventually put on a sounder footing when he became an official translator to the Quebec legislature in 1842. Garneau traveled little, his major traveling being to London and Paris as Viger's secretary from 1831 to 1833. The effect of these visits can be seen not merely in his grasp of English politics but also in the fear of violent revolution that always marked him; according to his *Voyage en Angleterre et en France* (1855), the London mob at the time of the 1832 Reform Bill debates made a profound impression upon him. Throughout these formative years Garneau continued to read widely in both classical and contemporary literature and history. He read the most recent French historians, Augustin Thierry being the most influential on Garneau's thinking. Thierry's theme of unending struggle between conqueror and conquered, both occupying the same territory, seemed to Garneau to have clear Canadian parallels, especially after 1840.

With his comparatively limited experience behind him and restricted also in access to the materials needed for his projected *Histoire*, his achievement was the more remarkable. In the "Discours préliminaire" prefixed to his first volume, he displays his grasp of the liberal historian's task, and throughout his work he marshals the evidence in effective support of his major thesis. Simply stated, French-Canadian history has been about struggle and conflict against overwhelming odds, against the intractable forces of nature confronting settlers in North America, against Indians, against indifference from metro-

The house on Rue Saint-Flavien, Quebec City, where Garneau lived during the last four years of his life

Garneau's work a messianic note, and Catholic readers soon abstracted theological themes of their own. There emerged in popular understanding the notion that Garneau had told the story of a "Catholic people," struggling, suffering, and at last rising to bear enduring witness to the eternal higher verities, little valued by the more numerous, prosperous, and commercially successful Anglo-Saxon Protestant Canadians. His tale of harsh struggle against vast odds was thus vindicated.

Garneau's work was in itself a solid achievement worthy to have survived on its own merits, but the appeal of the Catholic-nationalist view of him cannot be disassociated from his long-continuing popularity. Certainly in the countless histories, novels, and poems his work inspired, the Catholic element is more in evidence than in Garneau himself. He was, nonetheless, in his own right French Canada's most influential writer for a full century after his death.

Garneau's minor works deserve some notice. His poems are regarded today as among the best French-Canadian poetry of the time. He followed some outmoded and some contemporary French models, and in many of his poems the heroic picture of French Canada's past that was to appear in the *Histoire* is already present. They belong mainly to the 1830s. The *Voyage* has little in it that is authentically personal. It is of great interest for Garneau's views on politics in France and England in the 1830s, but it is overcrowded by quotations from his reading. It is a disappointing little work.

Garneau's writing as a whole has little stylistic verve. His most deliberately provocative judgments do not alter the tone of his writing, but he deals well with social and economic matters and is a good narrator. He engaged in much editing of his text in response to hostile Catholic critics, but only a certain laconic humor may be gathered from such passages, changed as they are in form but never in substance. In a historian he seems to have valued "gravity" above all.

In 1835 Garneau married Marie-Esther Bilodeau. His son Alfred and his grandson Hector Garneau both produced major editions of his *Histoire*. Writers descended from Garneau include Saint-Denys Garneau, Simone Routier, Anne Hébert, and Sylvain Garneau.

politan France, against clerical domination of colonial life, and, finally, against the English, a conflict that came to its tragic climax in 1760. The second half of Garneau's *Histoire* turns attention to that same conflict now diverted into political rather than military channels. From his work emerged the individual themes that were to be pursued by French-Canadian writers for decades: heroism, survival, endurance, struggle, and French and Catholic civilization. There was in

References:
Serge Gagnon, *Le Québec et ses historiens de 1840 à*

1920 (Quebec: Presses de l'Université Laval, 1978);

Paul Wyczynski, ed., *François-Xavier Garneau, Aspects littéraires de son oeuvre* (Ottawa: Editions de l'Université d'Ottawa, 1966).

Antoine Gérin-Lajoie

(4 August 1824 - 7 August 1882)

Barbara Godard
York University

BOOKS: *Le Jeune Latour. Tragédie en trois actes* (Montreal: Cinq-Mars, 1844; modern edition, Montreal: Réedition-Québec, 1969);

Catéchisme politique; ou Eléments du droit public et constitutionnel du Canada, mis à la portée du peuple (Montreal: Perrault, 1851; modern edition, New York: Johnson, 1967);

Jean Rivard, le défricheur. Recit de la vie réelle (Montreal: Rolland, 1874);

Jean Rivard, l'économiste, pour faire suite à Jean Rivard, le défricheur (Montreal: Rolland, 1876); translated by Vida Bruce as *Jean Rivard* (Toronto: McClelland & Stewart, 1977);

A. Gérin-Lajoie d'après ses mémoires, edited by Abbé Casgrain (Montreal: Beauchemin & Valois, 1886);

Dix Ans au Canada, de 1840 à 1850. Histoire de l'établissement du gouvernement responsable (Quebec: Demers, 1888).

OTHER: "Le Proscrit" ["Un Canadien errant"], in *Les Chansons populaires du Canada*, edited by Ernest Gagnon (Quebec: Morgan, 1865).

C 1475, National Archives of Canada

A member of the first generation of Quebec romantics imbued with the fervor of political revolution and historical nationalism, Antoine Gérin-Lajoie is remembered for his plaintive lament "Un Canadian errant" (1865) and his classic of nineteenth-century Quebec fiction, *Jean Rivard* (1874, 1876; originally published serially in 1862 and 1864), a "roman du terroir," preaching the nationalist myth of agriculturalism.

Gérin-Lajoie was born at Sainte-Anne-de-Yamachiche into the habitant family of Antoine and Marie Gélinas Gérin-Lajoie, whose house is today a museum, a monument to their traditional rural life that was to inspire *Jean Rivard*, a book full of nostalgic memories. Early in his career at the local school, Gérin-Lajoie won prizes and, with the priest's encouragement, was sent to the classical college at Nicolet for what his son, Léon Gérin, has described as a "brilliant career," his mark on college life made through his literary efforts. Always an avid reader of French classics, by fifteen he had made "attempts at rhyme," which were discouraged by his teachers. Nonetheless, he contributed occasional verse on college events, thus becoming laureate de facto.

The crowning creation of his college career, *Le Jeune Latour* (1844), a verse drama in the French classical mode, is based on an episode in Michel Bibaud's *L'Histoire du Canada, sous la domination française* (1843), depicting the conflict between a son and father on opposing sides in the battle for Acadia. The father, in exchange for a young English bride, has promised the English that he will hand over to them the last fort in Acadia under French control, a fort under the charge of his son, Roger Latour. The young man remains faithful to the French, despite his father's entreaties. The latter is rejected by his men. Although the appearance of the play earned the author twenty-five dollars from the governor-general, its fortunes declined after publication. Baudoin Berger, in the preface to a reedition (1969), reveals the historical interest of the play for, despite Gérin-Lajoie's inability to delve into the psychology of his characters and produce dramatic tension, he locates in the Corneillian conflict between familial love and patriotic duty a subject that has been of continuing interest to Quebec novelists and cineasts.

Ill-prepared to earn his living, Gérin-Lajoie's life declined upon leaving college. Plans to learn English in New York before further studies in Paris collapsed when he failed to find work immediately. He then took up legal studies in Montreal and entered on a period of his life recorded in letters of his character Gustave Charmenil (in *Jean Rivard*), a legal student, sometime teacher, translator, and hack writer, whose excessive timidity and scruples, lack of connections, and poverty are those of his creator. A journalist at *La Minerve*, Gérin-Lajoie was very active in the intellectual life of Montreal as founder, president, and active speaker of the Institut Canadien. Called to the bar in 1848, he made several abortive attempts to set up practice, followed by several tries at journalism and different administrative posts, finally entering the public service in 1852 as a translator. In 1860 he became parliamentary librarian, a post he held until his death.

During this period of occupational uncertainty, Gérin-Lajoie wrote *Catéchisme politique* (1851), the first guide to the parliamentary institutions of the Canadian union in a question-and-answer form. The young poet in Gérin-Lajoie was dead: his literary productions became increasingly didactic and practical. A move from Toronto to Quebec in 1860 with his new wife, Josephine née Parent, whom he had married in 1858, ushered in a period of intense literary activity with Gérin-Lajoie becoming coeditor of two significant literary periodicals, *Les Soirées Canadiennes* (1861), and *Le Foyer Canadien* (1863). Demonstrating his belief in the need for practical rather than imaginative literature, Gérin-Lajoie published serially in these journals his *Jean Rivard, le défricheur* (in *Les Soirées Canadiennes*) and *Jean Rivard, l'économiste* (in *Le Foyer Canadien*). The realism of the novel manifests itself in its autobiographical component and its balance sheets—statements of prices paid, agricultural earning, and statistics from economic publications—designed to prove farming an attractive financial proposition. Fortunately for the reader the author does not always follow his precepts, and this didacticism is merged in an epic that has proven enduring, and often repeated in Quebec literature, the story of the conquest of "virgin soil." Living out Gérin-Lajoie's dream, in contrast to Gustave, who shares the author's life style, Jean Rivard, an enterprising but poor college graduate, procures land in the eastern townships and, felling trees to grow wheat, orchards, and flowers, makes himself a "paradis terrestre." The first part follows his success on the land up to his marriage with a sensible farm girl, the narrative punctuated with the classic rituals of such rural idylls—husking bees, barn raising, and sugaring off. Characterization is flat and wooden, events serving as demonstrations of the heroism of Jean, who overcomes every difficulty.

Part 2 depicts the social action of this hero, who founds the village of Louiseville, setting up a model community, giving priority to producers (inspired by the theories of Frédéric Le Play), and instituting public education. For his work Jean is elected to Parliament, where he helps to shape the nation's destiny. Gérin-Lajoie, too, made an impact on his people: his novel was reprinted continuously for distribution to students and became, in Camille Roy's words, "une sorte d'évangile rustique de la race" (a sort of rustic Bible for our people). Today it is of most interest to historians, since, as Maurice Lemire says, it is

JEAN RIVARD

LE DÉFRICHEUR

———

Les pensées d'un homme fort et laborieux produisent toujours l'abondance ; mais tout paresseux est pauvre.

SALOMON.

La hardiesse et le travail surmontent les plus grands obstacles.

FÉNÉLON.

———

AVANT-PROPOS.

Jeunes et belles citadines qui ne rêvez que modes, bals et conquêtes amoureuses ; jeunes élégants qui parcourez, joyeux et sans soucis, le cercle des plaisirs mondains, il va sans dire que cette histoire n'est pas pour vous.

Le titre même, j'en suis sûr, vous fera bâiller d'ennui.

En effet, « Jean Rivard »....... quel nom commun ! que pouvait-on imaginer de plus vulgaire ? Passe encore pour Rivard, si au lieu de Jean c'était Arthur, ou Alfred, ou Oscar, ou quelque petit nom tiré de la mythologie ou d'une langue étrangère.

Puis un défricheur...... est-ce bien chez lui qu'on trouvera le type de la grâce et de la galanterie ?

Mais, que voulez-vous ? Ce n'est pas un roman que j'écris, et si quelqu'un est à la recherche d'aventures

First page of Gérin-Lajoie's preface to the 1874 edition of his best-known novel, originally published serially in 1862 in Les Soirées Canadiennes

"one of the most complete expressions of an ideology that for a long time supported the ideal of 'survivance.' "

Invalided by a stroke in 1880, Gérin-Lajoie succumbed to another one in 1882. Two posthumous works appeared: *Dix Ans au Canada* (1888), a lucid, impartial history of the period of struggle for responsible government that established his reputation in academic circles. Abbé Casgrain selected episodes from the journals Gérin-Lajoie had kept since 1849, including observations on his writing, and published them as *A. Gérin-Lajoie d'après ses mémoires* (1886). Whether it was the poor economic conditions for writers in Quebec or the conflicts of his personality that led to a suspicion of his own imagination, the promise of the enthusiastic student was never realized in his mature works. His claim to historical interest lies in his pioneering ability to detect significant plot outlines for Quebec literature and to understand the social and intellectual movements of his own time.

Biographies:

Louvigny de Montigny, *Antoine Gérin-Lajoie* (Toronto: Ryerson, 1925);

René Dionne, *Antoine Gérin-Lajoie* (Sherbrooke, Que.: Naaman, 1978).

References:

Beaudoin Berger, Introduction to *Le Jeune Latour* (Montreal: Réedition-Québec, 1969);

Léon Gérin, *Antoine Gérin-Lajoie: La Résurrection d'un patriote canadien* (Montreal: Devoir, 1925);

Edmond Lareau, *Histoire de la littéraire canadienne* (Montreal: Lovell, 1874), pp. 72-75, 303-306, 333-335;

Camille Roy, *Pour conserver notre héritage français* (Montreal: Beauchemin, 1937), pp. 174-185.

Oliver Goldsmith
(6 July 1794 - 1861)

Robert Gibbs
University of New Brunswick

BOOKS: *The Rising Village* (London: Printed for John Sharpe, 1825; modern edition, Montreal: Delta, 1968);

The Rising Village, with Other Poems (Saint John, N.B.: M'Millan, 1834);

The Autobiography of Oliver Goldsmith, edited by Wilfrid E. Myatt (Toronto: Ryerson, 1943);

The Manuscript Book, edited by E. Cockburn Kyte (Toronto: Bibliographical Society of Canada, 1950).

Oliver Goldsmith has a historical place in Canadian letters as the first published native-born poet. His poem *The Rising Village* (1825) is the first extended treatment in verse of the difficulties encountered by settlers in what are now the Maritime Provinces and of the development of colonial village life. As a response and a sequel to his namesake and great-uncle's *The Deserted Village* (1770), it presents contrasts with the decaying life of the Old World but in doing so offers ironies, not all of them conscious, and complexities of its own. Recent critical studies have shown it to be a far more interesting poem than literary history had previously acknowledged.

Third son and ninth child of Henry Goldsmith, an Irish-born Loyalist officer, Oliver was born in St. Andrew's, New Brunswick. Following a fire that destroyed their property near that town, Henry moved with his family in 1896 first to Annapolis Royal and then to Halifax, where he had secured a post as assistant commissary. (The commissariat was a civilian department of the British Army charged with providing regiments with food, fuel, forage, and quarters.) Educated at home, Oliver by 1808 had been placed by his father in five successive occupations with a view to launching him on a suitable career. These included jobs at the Naval Hospital in Halifax, an ironmonger's shop, a bookseller's, a law office, and a wholesaler's business in Boston. Following these apprenticeships, he was sent to the Halifax Grammar School, where he re-

Oliver Goldsmith (Queen's University Archives)

mained till his father secured him a post in the commissariat in 1810.

Oliver Goldsmith served in the commissariat for forty-five years, retiring in 1855 with the rank of assistant commissary general. His service included twenty-three years in Halifax, eleven in Saint John, four in Hong Kong, five in St. John's, Newfoundland, and one in Corfu. These periods of service were broken twice by short intervals on half pay.

In 1822 the Garrison Amateur Theatre opened in Halifax. Goldsmith was involved with it from the start, playing the part of Tony Lumpkin in his forebear's *She Stoops to Conquer*

(1773) and composing an address in heroic couplets for the opening of the theater. His career as a poet began with this effort and culminated in 1825 with the publication in London of *The Rising Village*.

The poem, consisting of some six hundred lines in heroic couplets, is a response to and continuation of *The Deserted Village*. Early in the poem, Goldsmith invokes the spirit of his great-uncle, and throughout there are echoes and allusions that point up contrasts between the old and the new. The poem moves from the rugged conditions the settlers found on arrival, through the subduing of the wilderness and the Indians, to an extended portrayal of village life. Goldsmith does not appear to have shared his namesake's distrust of mercantilism and individual enterprise, but he does introduce into his idyll elements of disorder and vice to make his picture truer. Over a hundred lines are devoted to the narrative of Flora and Albert, a pathetic story of broken vows, which, though it mitigates the poem's prevailing optimism, by no means dispels it altogether. Although the poem's graceful couplets lack the warmth, richness, and fine modulation of the older poem's verse, they do speak eloquently and at times vividly, particularly in the depiction of village types and institutions. Recent critical studies have shown that the poem is not as simple as it appears and that if studied in close conjunction with *The Deserted Village* it reveals ironies and ambivalences its creator may not have been conscious of when composing.

Following a discouraging reception of his first published effort, Goldsmith wrote little verse. In 1834 a second volume appeared, containing in addition to a slightly shortened version of *The Rising Village* eighteen largely occasional pieces. These show Goldsmith's skill in the handling of various verse forms and in eloquent, if conventional, expression.

Upon his retirement in 1855 Goldsmith made his home with his surviving sister in Liverpool, England. There he died in 1861, leaving among his papers a short and largely accurate autobiography.

Oliver Goldsmith has a secure place in Canadian letters and not just a historical one. His achievement in *The Rising Village* was a modest one. The poet's own modesty speaks in the voice and gives the poem its charm, but the poem rewards close study as a truly fine expression of life and attitudes in its time.

References:

Kenneth J. Hughes, "Oliver Goldsmith's 'The Rising Village,'" *Canadian Poetry*, 1 (Fall / Winter 1977): 27-43;

W. J. Keith, "The Rising Village Again," *Canadian Poetry*, 3 (Fall / Winter 1978): 1-13;

Gerald Lynch, "Oliver Goldsmith's *The Rising Village*: Controlling Nature," *Canadian Poetry*, 6 (Spring / Summer 1980): 35-49;

Desmond Pacey, "The Two Goldsmiths and Their Villages," *University of Toronto Quarterly*, 21 (October 1951): 27-38.

George Monro Grant
(22 December 1835 - 13 May 1902)

Susan Jackel
University of Alberta

BOOKS: *Ocean to Ocean* (Toronto: Campbell, 1873; London: Low, Marston, Low & Searle, 1873; revised and enlarged edition, 1877; modern reprint, Toronto: Coles, 1970);

The Religions of the World (Toronto: Methodist Book and Publishing House, 1894; London: Black, 1894; New York: Revell, 1894; revised and enlarged edition, New York: Randolph, 1895);

Joseph Howe (Halifax: MacKinlay, 1904).

OTHER: *Picturesque Canada*, 2 volumes, edited by Grant (Toronto: Art Publishing, 1875).

SELECTED PERIODICAL PUBLICATIONS–
UNCOLLECTED: "Education and Co-Education," *Rose Belford's Canadian Monthly and National Review,* 3 (November 1879): 509-518;

"The Relation of Religion to Secular Life," *Rose Belford's Canadian Monthly and National Review,* 5 (December 1880): 614-624;

"*Canada and the Canadian Question*: A Review," *Week,* 8 (1 May and 15 May 1891);

"Current Events," *Queen's Quarterly,* 1-8 (1893-1898).

The three dominant strands of Canadian public life in the later nineteenth century–religion, education, and national self-definition–merged in the life and influence of George Monro Grant. That influence was based on Grant's leadership in the Presbyterian Church, his twenty-five years (1877-1902) as principal of Queen's University, Kingston, and his lectures and writings on Canada's national development and role in the British Empire. Said by his admirers to occupy a rank comparable to that of Henry Ward Beecher in the United States, Grant lived to the full his conviction that the university and the church were vital forces in the coming-of-age of Canadian democracy.

Born at Albion Mines, Nova Scotia, Grant attended Pictou Academy and West River Seminary near his birthplace and then spent six years at Glasgow University in Scotland. Ordained a minister of the Church of Scotland after a brilliant university career, he returned to his homeland in 1860. Three years later he was summoned to the pulpit of St. Andrew's Church, Halifax. Then began Grant's lifelong involvement in higher education; he was instrumental in the reorganization in 1863 of Dalhousie University as a provincial, nondenominational institution and was elected to the first board of governors, a post he held until 1885.

In 1872 Grant acted as secretary to Sandford Fleming's expedition across Canada to map out a route for the projected Canadian Pacific Railway. Grant's description of that summer journey from Toronto to the Pacific coast, only two years after Canada's acquisition of the huge territories of Rupert's Land from Great Britain, was published in 1873 as *Ocean to Ocean,* a classic of travel writing and an important milestone in Canadian awareness of the hitherto-unknown regions lying between the Great Lakes and the Rocky Mountains. Grant's firsthand inspection of the prairies confirmed his belief in Canada's destiny as a transcontinental nation. "Since that journey," he wrote thirty years later, "I have never doubted the future of Canada." Hence his firm rejection of the argument advanced by Goldwin Smith in *Canada and the Canadian Question* (1891) that the commercial and political union of all North America was both inevitable and desirable, in the interests of Anglo-Saxon union. Instead, Grant countered, Canada should seek to confirm her attachment to Great Britain within an imperial federation.

Grant's tenure at Queen's enabled that university to survive a prolonged period of crisis and reorganization in Ontario's nascent system of higher education. In his 1877 installation address Grant exhorted Queen's students to aspire toward an "homage to truth, [with] the knowledge

Grant as principal of Queen's University, a post he held for twenty-five years (Queen's University Archives)

that truth is the peculiar possession of no one sect or party." For Grant the road to truth lay in all branches of study: medicine and science as well as divinity and moral philosophy. Darwinian evolutionary theory and the higher biblical criticism held no terrors for him; "piety and learning are both dishonoured when even for a moment it is imagined that there is any incompatibility between them," he adjured the students. Nor was truth to be the peculiar possession of one sex alone. Grant was in the forefront in advocating higher education for women and officiated in 1878 when the first woman student graduated from Queen's.

Grant's views on a wide range of issues were disseminated by his admiring students at Queen's, many of whom became teachers or ministers in Ontario and throughout the country; by the many public lectures and speeches he gave as an educator and a leader in the councils of the Presbyterian Church; and by his contributions over a thirty-year period to several of Canada's most widely read periodicals, notably the *Cana-*

dian Monthly and National Review, the *Canadian Magazine*, the *Week*, the *Toronto Globe*, and the *Canadian Methodist Magazine*. In the mid 1890s he regularly surveyed "Current Events" in *Queen's Quarterly*. He edited and wrote parts of the two-volume *Picturesque Canada* (1875), and in 1882 contributed a chapter on "Churches and Schools in the North-West" to John Macoun's *Manitoba and the Great North-West*. A charter member of the Royal Society of Canada in 1882, Grant served as its president in 1901.

In 1894 Grant published his comparative study *The Religions of the World*. This volume demonstrates Grant's overriding ecumenism, the same spirit that sustained his drive for Presbyterian union in the 1870s and underlay his hopes for the union of all the Christian churches in Canada, and eventually of all Christendom. In a similar vein was his belief in the ultimate reconciliation of all the English-speaking peoples of the world, toward which imperial federation was to be but a first step. Grant was a founding member in 1884 of the Imperial Federation League of Canada, and he joined his friend George Parkin in giving and publishing lectures on this topic throughout the 1890s.

George Monro Grant's enduring reputation as a writer rests on his travel book, *Ocean to Ocean*. There, in the beguiling persona of "the Secretary," he leads his readers to share his wonderment and rising excitement at the western region's manifest invitation to agricultural settlement. Discreetly in the background, but nonetheless persistently and artfully pursued, are Grant's arguments in favor of building the Canadian Pacific Railway, in order that "a continuous line of loyal provinces" may fill the gap between Manitoba and British Columbia and so ward off the threat of absorption by the United States.

Grant's book thus becomes more than the record of a summer jaunt across Canada and emerges as a coherent statement of political and moral vision, and an important document in Canadian cultural history.

References:

Carl Berger, *The Sense of Power: Studies in the Ideas of Canadian Imperialism* (Toronto: University of Toronto Press, 1970);

William L. Grant and Frederick Hamilton, *Principal Grant* (Toronto: Morang, 1904);

David Jackel, "*Ocean to Ocean*: G. M. Grant's 'Round Unvarnish'd Tale,'" *Canadian Literature*, 81 (Summer 1979): 7-23.

John Gyles

(1680 - 1755)

Neil K. Besner
University of Winnipeg

BOOK: *Memoirs of odd adventures, strange deliverances, etc. in the captivity of John Gyles, Esq., commander of the garrison on Saint George River, in the district of Maine. Written by Himself* (Boston: Printed & sold by S. Kneeland & T. Green, 1736); republished as *Nine Years A Captive, or John Gyles' Experience among the Malicite Indians, from 1689 to 1698*, edited by James Hannay (Saint John, N.B.: Daily Telegraph Steam Job Press, 1875).

John Gyles's brief but compelling first-person account (1736) of his nine years as a captive–the first six among the Malicite Indians (Etchemins) of the Saint John River, the last three bound over to the French–is among the most vivid and informed of the captivity narratives from this period. Divided into eight chapters, the whole piece is some thirty-five pages long, documenting Gyles's experiences beginning with his capture as a boy of nine, continuing with his forced travels in the Saint John River area with the Malicites, and recounting the hardships

and abuses he shared and suffered with them. James Hannay, editor of the 1875 version of Gyles's memoirs, speaks of the "simple and truthful quaintness" of the narrative, remarking that it is "the only authentic narrative that is known to exist of any lengthened residence among the savage tribes of Acadie during the seventeenth century, the period of their greatest power and greatest activity." Gyles's descriptions of the Indian, writes Hannay, show him "stripped of his paint and feathers and without those romantic surroundings amid which writers of poetry and some historians have delighted to depict him." Hannay's description of Gyles's narrative attests to the particular value assigned to this kind of tale: like the travel journals of explorers such as Samuel Hearne, Alexander Mackenzie, Alexander Henry, or David Thompson, captivity narratives were looked to for documentary truth, for an objective record of the writers' experiences–at the same time that the captivity narrative, a kind of subgenre of the adventure story, conforms in the shape of its plot, style, attention to detail,

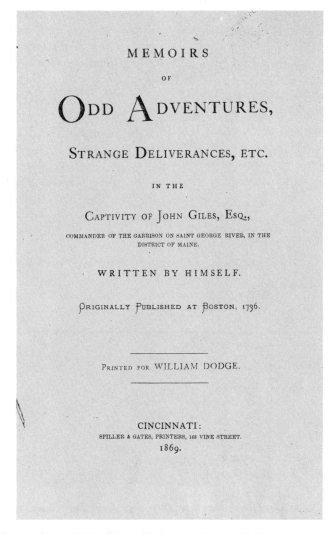

MEMOIRS

OF

ODD ADVENTURES,

STRANGE DELIVERANCES, ETC.

IN THE

CAPTIVITY OF JOHN GILES, ESQ.,

COMMANDER OF THE GARRISON ON SAINT GEORGE RIVER, IN THE
DISTRICT OF MAINE.

WRITTEN BY HIMSELF.

ORIGINALLY PUBLISHED AT BOSTON, 1796.

PRINTED FOR WILLIAM DODGE.

CINCINNATI:
SPILLER & GATES, PRINTERS, 168 VINE STREET.
1869.

Title page for an 1869 edition of Gyles's only book (with his name misspelled)

and apparent verisimilitude to the conventions of the fictional form.

Gyles devotes separate chapters to the kind of treatment he and other prisoners sometimes received (chapter 2, for example, is called "Of the Abusive and Barbarous Treatment Which Several Captives Met With From the Indians"); to Malicite beliefs and superstitions (chapter 5: "Of Their Familiarity With and Frights from the Devil, etc"); to a catalog of some of their quarry (chapter 6: "A Description of Several Creatures Commonly Taken by the Indians on St. Johns River"); to their preparations for battle (chapter 7: "Of Their Feasting. Before They Go to War"); and to his time with the French (chapter 8: "Of My Three Years Captivity With the French"). In Gyles's introduction, he explains how the narrative came to be published: "These private memoirs were collected from my minutes, at the ear-

nest request of my second consort, for the use of our family, that we might have a memento ever ready at hand, to excite in ourselves gratitude and thankfulness to God; and in our offspring a due sense of their dependence on the Sovereign of the universe, from the precariousness and vicissitudes of all sublunary enjoyments."

Most sources suggest that John Gyles was born in 1680, the date consistent with his record of his capture at the age of nine on 2 August 1689. He was born in Pemaquid, Maine. His father was Thomas Gyles, and John had two older brothers, a younger brother, and a younger sister. His father was shot several times during the 1689 Indian attack and died the same day, killed when it became clear he was too weak to travel. James, one of the older brothers, Gyles reports, "was, after several years' captivity, most barbarously tortured to death by the Indians";

Thomas, the other older brother, escaped in a fishing vessel. Gyles's mother and his two younger siblings were released after several years, but his mother died before Gyles returned home.

Gyles was taken prisoner in the second year of the second "Indian war" (1688-1698), also known as King William's War; as Hannay explains, "It was a ruinous contest. All the Indian tribes eastward of the Merrimack, including the Micmacs, took part in it. Every town and settlement in Maine except Wells, York, Kittery, and the Isle of Shoals was over-run. A thousand white people were killed or taken prisoners and an untold number of domestic animals destroyed. Like nearly every other war, which the Indians have waged against the Whites, the latter were responsible for its origin."

Gyles's skill as a writer should not be underestimated, despite his stance as merely a truthful, ordinary recorder of his extraordinary experience. He successfully maintains a dispassionate and detached viewpoint, even when describing events that horrify him, and his more intimate reflections are also couched in conventional language, so that his narrative as a whole retains its purportedly objective distance, while at the same time conveying, in precise, vivid, and at times chilling detail, the texture of the Indian life he observed and in which he was forced to participate.

After his release in June 1698 Gyles served the government of New England in various capacities, as cited in detail in the appendix with which he closes his memoirs. Having gained a good command of Indian languages, he worked at various times as an interpreter and fought in 1707 in the war that had broken out in 1701. He helped build Fort George at Pejepscot (Brunswick, Maine) and became commander of the fort until 1725. Gyles was married twice, to Ruth True in 1703, and Hannah Heath in 1722; he died in Roxbury—now part of Boston—in 1755. His services to the government, distinguished though they were, remain unmemorable in print, matters of record fixed in their time. Gyles's memoirs, however, transform his experience in a way that belies and transcends both Gyles's purported documentary intentions and the conventions of the form, rendering his lived experience into literary adventure.

Reference:

James Hannay, Introduction to *Nine Years a Captive, or John Gyles' Experience among the Malicite Indians, from 1689 to 1698* (Saint John, N.B.: Daily Telegraph Steam Job Press, 1875).

Thomas Chandler Haliburton

(17 December 1796 - 27 August 1865)

Richard A. Davies
Acadia University

See also the Haliburton entry in *DLB 11: American Humorists, 1800-1850*.

BOOKS: *A General Description of Nova Scotia*, anonymous (Halifax: Royal Acadian School, 1823);

An Historical and Statistical Account of Nova-Scotia, 2 volumes (Halifax: Joseph Howe, 1829);

The Clockmaker; or, The Sayings and Doings of Samuel Slick, of Slickville, anonymous, first series (Halifax: Joseph Howe, 1836; London: Richard Bentley, 1837; Philadelphia: Carey, Lea & Blanchard, 1837; modern edition, Toronto: McClelland & Stewart, 1958); second series (London: Richard Bentley, 1838; Philadelphia: Carey, Lea & Blanchard, 1838); third series (London: Richard Bentley, 1840; Philadelphia: Lea & Blanchard, 1840);

The Bubbles of Canada (London: Richard Bentley, 1839; Philadelphia: Lea & Blanchard, 1839);

A Reply to the Report of the Earl of Durham, anonymous (London: Richard Bentley, 1839 ; Halifax, 1839; modern edition, Ottawa: Golden Dog Press, 1976);

The Letter-Bag of the Great Western; or, Life in a Steamer (Halifax: Howe, 1840; London: Richard Bentley, 1840; Philadelphia: Lea & Blanchard, 1840; modern edition, Toronto: University of Toronto Press, 1973);

The Attaché; or, Sam Slick in England, anonymous, first series (London: Richard Bentley, 1843; Philadelphia: Lea & Blanchard, 1843); second series (London: Richard Bentley, 1844; Philadelphia: Lea & Blanchard, 1844);

The Old Judge; or, Life in a Colony, anonymous (London: Henry Colburn, 1849; New York: Stringer & Townsend, 1849; modern edition, Ottawa: Tecumseh, 1979);

The English in America, anonymous, 2 volumes (London: Colburn, 1851; republished as *Rule and Misrule of The English in America* (London: Colburn, 1851; New York: Harper, 1851);

Thomas Chandler Haliburton

Sam Slick's Wise Saws and Modern Instances; or, What He Said, Did, or Invented, anonymous (London: Hurst & Blackett, 1853; Philadelphia: Blanchard & Lea, 1853); republished as *Wise-Saws; or, Sam Slick in Search of a Wife* (New York: Stringer & Townsend, 1855);

Nature and Human Nature, anonymous (London: Hurst & Blackett, 1855; New York: Stringer & Townsend, 1855);

An Address on the Present Condition, Resources and Prospects of British North America, Delivered by Special Request at the City Hall, Glasgow, on the 25th March, 1857 (Montreal: Lovell, 1857; London: Hurst & Blackett, 1857);

The Season-Ticket (London: Richard Bentley, 1860; modern edition, Toronto: University of Toronto Press, 1973);

Speech of the Hon. Mr. Justice Haliburton, M.P., in the House of Commons on Tuesday, the 21st of April, 1860, on the Repeal of the Differential Duties on Foreign and Colonial Wood (London: Edward Stanford, 1860).

Collection: *The Sam Slick Anthology*, edited by R. E. Watters (Toronto: Clarke Irwin, 1969).

OTHER: *Traits of American Humor, by Native Authors*, 3 volumes, edited by Haliburton (London: Colburn, 1852);

The Americans at Home; or, Byeways, Backwoods, and Prairies, 3 volumes, edited by Haliburton (London: Hurst & Blackett, 1854).

All his life, Thomas Chandler Haliburton was proud of being a second-generation Nova Scotian. Haliburton's grandfather William H. Haliburton, a New England planter, settled in Nova Scotia in 1761. The grandfather's early fortunes were somewhat checkered. Haliburton's father, William Hersey Otis Haliburton, a successful lawyer, judge, businessman, and politician, placed the family fortunes on a surer footing with a prudent second marriage to Susannah Boutineau Francklin Davis, the daughter of a former lieutenant-governor of the province, Michael Francklin. W. H. O. Haliburton's first wife (Thomas Chandler Haliburton's mother), Lucy Chandler Grant Haliburton, had died in 1797, several months after Thomas was born.

Thomas Chandler Haliburton began his writing career with a description and a history of his province. Then, at the age of thirty-nine, while a circuit judge of the Inferior Court of Nova Scotia, he penned the first of several collections of comic, satiric, and descriptive sketches. The invention of his most celebrated comic character, Sam Slick the clockmaker, gained Haliburton a loyal and international readership. Any in-depth consideration of Haliburton's extensive body of writing must examine his relationships to early American comic traditions of tall-tale telling, from which he took his inspiration, and to early nineteenth-century travel books that sought to introduce the New World to the Old, as well as the influence of well-established exponents of the literary sketch, such as Washington Irving. However, much can be learned from a straightforward survey of Haliburton's literary career. Even though he eventually retired to England from Nova Scotia in 1856, the collections of sketches that form the cornerstone of his present-day literary reputation—the first series of *The Clockmaker* (1836), *The Old Judge* (1849), and *Sam Slick's Wise Saws* (1853)—are firmly grounded in the life of Nova Scotia.

Haliburton was born (on 17 December 1796) and educated in Windsor, Nova Scotia. He graduated with a B.A. from King's College, Windsor, in 1815. On a visit to his stepmother's family in England in 1815 and 1816, he met and married Louisa Neville at Henley-on-Thames, Oxfordshire. They returned to Nova Scotia and in 1817 began a family. Over the next fifteen years, they had five daughters, three sons, and three other children who died at an early age. In 1818 Haliburton bought a house and land at Avondale, near Windsor, which his wife named "Henley Farm." He intended to venture into gypsum mining, but the plan was short-lived. Instead, Haliburton commenced business under the wing of his lawyer father. In October 1819, Thomas Haliburton applied to be a notary public, and in 1821 he moved to Annapolis Royal, the old provincial capital, where he practiced law for the next eight years. Deprived of much of a social life in what was then a quiet backwater, Haliburton started to write, publishing (anonymously) his *General Description of Nova Scotia* in 1823.

The *General Description* and the two history volumes that followed it are essential reading for those who wish a full understanding of the thematic concerns of the first series of *The Clockmaker*. The *General Description* was written to correct opinions of Nova Scotia in the United Kingdom, to undeceive potential immigrants. Haliburton said it was written in haste, yet it is an informative account of the state of Nova Scotia in 1823, full of his personal comments on the past, present, and future of his native province: "All that the Province requires is capital and population," he wrote.

His legal work in Annapolis brought him regularly into contact with Abbé Jean-Mandé Sigogne at Clare, as well as Judge Peleg Wiswall (and his nephew G. K. Nichols) at Digby. The judge encouraged Haliburton to work on a full-length history of the province of Nova Scotia,

Louisa Neville, Haliburton's first wife, whom he married in 1816. She died in 1841.

which Haliburton eventually published in 1829. To some extent the delay in its appearance was caused by his election to the legislature as M.L.A. for Annapolis County in 1826. These were exciting and exacting years for Haliburton. In the legislature he was both relished and feared as an orator. He frequently found himself at odds with the ruling oligarchy, the Council of Twelve; and his championing of educational reform, Catholic emancipation, and Thomas McCulloch's Pictou Academy were highlights of a brief political career. All speeches of the legislature, at this time, were reported in full by the indefatigable new editor of the *Novascotian* newspaper, Joseph Howe. Furthermore, Howe celebrated the conjunction of himself, Haliburton, and several other kindred spirits in a column entitled "The Club." Howe's fictional portrait of Frank Halliday, lawyer of Annapolis, seems to be modeled on Haliburton.

In the midst of establishing his legal career, raising an ever-expanding family, and enduring the hurly-burly of political life, Haliburton managed to complete his second work, *An Historical*

and Statistical Account of Nova-Scotia (1829). To compile his two-volume history, for which he received public commendation, Haliburton enlisted the help of many friends and notable men of his day to ensure that his topographical and historical accounts of localities were up-to-date and accurate. One of his closest advisers was Judge Wiswall. The result is readable and interesting, especially his sensitive account of the deportation of the Acadians in 1755. The years from 1762 until 1828, he claimed, afforded "no materials for an historical narrative." At Wiswall's suggestion Haliburton closed the first volume with "A Chronological Table of Events," a personal selection of significant events in this period of the province's history. Volume 2 is a more extensive version of the *General Description*, with more elaborate accounts of landscape in the regions discussed and more detailed discussion of subjects that interested him: the Shubenacadie canal scheme (which ended in failure), Pictou Academy, gypsum mining at Windsor, education at Annapolis, the Annapolis Iron Mining Company (in which he invested), fishing at Digby (based on "notes of conversations which I have held with persons engaged in it, and committed to paper at the time"), King's College at Windsor, and the law courts. Unlike its predecessor, the *Historical . . . Account* argued that Nova Scotia, in 1829, did not need immigrants.

The history appeared at a significant moment for Haliburton, coinciding with the reorganization of his life consequent upon the death of his father in July 1829. Haliburton was appointed, by the same council he had attacked in the legislature, to the judgeship of the inferior court of common pleas for the middle division of Nova Scotia, left vacant by his father. He returned with his family to Windsor, where he lived for the next twenty years. Haliburton once estimated that his job as a circuit judge meant that he was away from home, on average, one hundred twenty days in the year. He therefore built "Clifton" as a retreat to which he could return after the rigors of the open road. When at home, he superintended the quarrying of gypsum on his property, presided over the Avon Bridge Company (which successfully built a bridge across the nearby Avon river), and was one of the town's leading citizens.

It is against this background of his early life and his historical work in the 1820s that one can place the sudden emergence of Haliburton's first series of *The Clockmaker*. The first twenty-one sketches were serialized by Howe in the *Novascotian* from September 1835 to February 1836 and then revised, added to, and published anonymously, in their entirety (then thirty-three sketches), in response to popular demand. The work opens with the narrator meeting Sam Slick as they are both on horseback riding near Fort Lawrence in Colchester County, Nova Scotia. They strike up a conversation and travel together to Windsor, talking all the way. The book is the narrator's record of his conversations with Slick, a vendor of clocks, who does most of the talking as befits his Yankee identity, his vocation, and his comic character. Haliburton created Slick by combining various humorous traditions in American frontier literature with the character of the stage Yankee, a popular figure of the day. Haliburton adapted this comic character to his own purposes, using Slick to "wipe up the Bluenoses considerably hard," for neglecting opportunities to develop the potential of their province. At the same time, he did not (in Slick's words) "let off the Yankees so very easy neither." There is much clever irony in the first series, for Sam both vaunts and exposes the "go-ahead" civilization he represents by the things that he says. The portrayal of the shrewd Yankee clock pedlar, who deals as much in "soft sawdur and human natur'" as in clocks, becomes a study of the impact of mechanized progress (embodied by Slick) on a traditional, agrarian society (Nova Scotia). The book is marred only by what Northrop Frye has described as Haliburton's display of "ego" whenever he drops his fictional mask and begins to exhort the reader with italicized moral imperatives.

The first series was published in England by Richard Bentley without Haliburton's knowledge. It distracted the London reading public of 1837 from the current wave of Pickwick mania, and the book had a considerable sale. As compensation Bentley sent Haliburton a silver platter with his name incorrectly inscribed on it! Although Haliburton was flattered, he was more concerned with negotiating with Bentley to publish the second series (which he had already written prior to his visit to England in 1838 and 1839).

The second series (1838) works much like the first. The narrator (or the "Squire," as Slick calls him) and Slick continue their travels together from Windsor, via Digby and Shelburne, along the Chester Road into Halifax. The landscape and people they observe prompt Sam to expand upon all manner of American topics as well as Nova Scotia. An important development in this series is Slick's recollection of conversations with Rev. Hopewell, his old minister back home in Slickville, Onion County, Connecticut. Hopewell is a ninety-five-year-old Church of England minister whose experience of life covers "a considerable space of colony time." He is a loyalist who has serious reservations about the direction in which American society, politics, religion and civilization have gone since the Revolution. Haliburton thought the introduction of Hopewell was a stroke of genius. His intention was to qualify Slick's view of the United States by means of a sharp contrast with Hopewell's yearnings for a lost America. Armed with the triumvirate of Slick, Hopewell, and the Squire, Haliburton makes a personal exploration of the crosscurrents of American and British influences in Nova Scotian life. All three characters, in turn, reflect aspects of Haliburton's own outlook.

At the opening of the third series (1840), the Squire revisits the ruin of the duke of Kent's lodge on the shores of the Bedford Basin in Halifax. He is about to set out on his third journey with Slick, the destination being Slickville, Connecticut, en route to New York and eventually England. The chapter is one of the most eloquent in Haliburton's work. In the third series Slick manages, despite his excesses, to develop his friendship with the Squire. Criticism of Slick only increases when Rev. Hopewell is present as a contrast, and such criticism is noticeably absent until the companions arrive in Slickville. In chapter 18, "The Old Minister," once again Rev. Hopewell's prerevolutionary, pro-British, and premechanistic view of America takes precedence over Slick's vigorous championing of the virtues of mechanism and progress. Hopewell prophesies British loss of control over her colonies and likens the situation to a barrel without hoops. He accompanies the Squire and Slick to England, where Slick, as a reward for his literary achievements, has been appointed attaché at the court of St. James.

Between the second and the third series of *The Clockmaker*, Haliburton wrote *The Bubbles of Canada* (1839). The work was written while Haliburton was in England and completed on 24 December 1838. It was intended as a "sketch of the origin, progress, and present state of agitation in Lower Canada," detailing the events leading up to the rebellion of 1837 and concluding with the appointment of John George Lambton, Lord Durham, as commissioner. The form of the book is a series of eleven letters, addressed to

Haliburton and his second wife, Sarah Harriet, at Gordon House, their rented mansion outside London (by permission of the Nova Scotia Museum)

Haliburton's new friend, James Haliburton, the Egyptologist (no relation). Thomas Haliburton admitted: "I could command neither the time nor the materials . . . to do it properly." The book's main argument was that the conciliatory attitude of the British government toward the French Canadians had led to rebellion. While still in England and in response to the publication of Lord Durham's *Report on the Affairs of British North America* (1839), Haliburton wrote seven letters to the *Times*, signing them "By a Colonist." He published the letters in a pamphlet entitled *A Reply to the Report of the Earl of Durham* (1839), part of the conservative opposition to the report.

Between the third series of *The Clockmaker* and the first series of its continuation, *The Attaché*, Haliburton wrote a work he felt would amuse many, *The Letter-Bag of the Great Western; or, Life in a Steamer* (1840). The *Great Western* steamship, the brainchild of Isambard Kingdom Brunel, was launched at Bristol in July 1837. During his stay in England during 1838 and 1839, Haliburton tried to interest its directors to call at Halifax. The ship's letterbag had actually been stolen by a young reporter on the ship's arrival in Boston in 1838, and the idea of making a reader privy to the contents of such a letterbag

struck Haliburton as having comic and satiric potential. Haliburton includes letters written by a wide variety of classes, ethnic groups, and characters. For example, there are letters (in appropriate idiom) from an actress, a black steward, a military captain, a naval officer, a butcher, a Quaker, a New Brunswicker, an abolitionist, a cadet, a lawyer's clerk, a traveler, a stoker, a stockholder, a servant, a French passenger, an old hand, an American citizen, and so on. There are twenty-seven letters, and their subjects are not confined to life on a steamer. *The Letter-Bag* is not rated highly as a work of fiction; it tends to be a grab bag of comic effects. Nevertheless, the work relates interestingly to an ongoing dialectic within Haliburton's fiction between the need for mechanical progress and the consequences of it for the quality of human life. Unlike much of the contemporary wonder at the *Great Western*, Haliburton's portrayal of life in a steamer is far from flattering.

In 1841 the inferior courts of common pleas in Nova Scotia were abolished. Haliburton was appointed to the supreme court of Nova Scotia, which took over the duties of the inferior courts. The achievement was marred, first, by a squabble with the Nova Scotia government over his salary and pension rights and, in the second place, by the sudden death of his wife, Louisa, in November 1841. Haliburton continued his writing career but against a background of financial problems–relating to gypsum dealings–and the death, in 1847, of his musically gifted son Tom in a lunatic asylum in Boston. Two visits to England, one in 1843 and the other ten years later, help to chart his middle years. The visit of 1843 did nothing to lift his spirits. Indeed it was hurried and unsatisfactory, even though it coincided with the publication of *The Attaché*. In contrast, the visit of 1853 was, according to Haliburton, one of the happiest times of his life. He met the woman who was to become his second wife, and his stay coincided with the success of *Sam Slick's Wise Saws*.

However, *The Attaché* proved to be a failure, a literary cul-de-sac. Haliburton openly masqueraded as the Squire, revealed now as Thomas Poker, retired member of the Nova Scotia bar. The idea of the work was to turn a critical eye on the English and redress some of the imbalance caused by English laughter at the first three *Clockmakers*. The first *Attaché* is an account of the journey of the Squire, Slick, and Hopewell from Liverpool to London; the second *Attaché* is almost a journal of Haliburton's experiences in England in 1843. It was published a year later. In both books the Squire becomes an observer of Slick and Hopewell in their new surroundings, trying as best he can to reconcile their different views of life. *The Attaché* was a commercial disaster for Richard Bentley, and the reason is not hard to discern: Haliburton's knowledge of English society was superficial.

It was only when he was back home and about his ordinary business that Haliburton realized this and rekindled his creative spirit to good effect. He started writing a series of sketches that became known as *The Old Judge; or, Life in a Colony*. These sketches was serialized in *Fraser's Magazine* from 1846 to 1847. The group of sketches was subsequently enlarged and transposed for book publication in 1849. *The Old Judge* is considered by many to be Haliburton's finest achievement.

The narrator is a visitor to Nova Scotia who is introduced to the province through two further pairs of eyes, those of Squire Barclay (a lawyer, whose tone is sometimes cynical) and Judge Sanford (an "old Tory"), both residents of Illinoo (i.e., Windsor). The narrator takes the pulse of Nova Scotian life by means of these two knowledgeable guides. Eventually, through Barclay, the narrator meets Stephen Richardson, a ring-tailed roarer figure, a woodsman, "a sort of oddity, a kind of privileged person," whose personality dominates the main portion of the work, entitled "The Keeping Room of An Inn; or, Judge Beler's Ghost." The entire volume is filled with odd and fascinating tales of Nova Scotian life, such as "The Lone House," a sad story celebrating the pioneer spirit. Richardson is a source of many stories, a living embodiment of Nova Scotia's primitive pioneering past. He has seen the old Judge's ghost, which comes to represent the departed spirit of the past. The effect of the tales told by Barclay, Richardson, and Sanford is an encomium of colonial life in the past against which the present–symbolized by such irritations as the modern doorbell and itinerant Yankees–seems lacking. The work reaches a poignant climax, not in the official conclusion on "Colonial Government," tagged on at the end, but in the evocation of Nova Scotia's proud, primitive, and superstitious past in the chapters entitled "The Seasons, or Comers and Goers" and "The Witch of Inky Dell."

In 1851 Haliburton published a successful historical work, *The English in America*, in two volumes. It is a connected history of the American colonies from their earliest days to 1851, designed to argue that the first two republics in New England are the origin of almost every institution now existing in the United States. The book also purports to be an introduction to the "complicated mechanism and simple action of the American Federal Constitution." It is a readable and well-organized work.

Haliburton's friendship with Bentley, his English publisher, had broken up in 1843. Ten years later Bentley healed the breach in their relations. Haliburton, nevertheless, continued to publish his books with Henry Colburn, Bentley's rival, and then with Colburn's successors, Hurst and Blackett, until he published with Bentley once more in 1860. Among the works Haliburton published with Colburn and with Hurst and Blackett were two sets of humorous American stories, *Traits of American Humor* (1852) and *The Americans at Home* (1854). Haliburton had been collecting tall tales and yarns for years, culling them from magazines and newspapers. The preface to *Traits of American Humor* reveals how widely read Haliburton was in the literature of ring-tailed roarers. A comparison between the figures in these tales and Sam Slick should inform a reader as to the differences between the traditional tall tales and the use to which Haliburton had put them.

Alongside these compilations, Haliburton published a further revival of Sam Slick, *Sam Slick's Wise Saws and Modern Instances*. He revised the format that had not worked well in *The Attaché*, nearly dispensed with the figure of the Squire (who becomes an unseen editor), and writes his book as Sam Slick's journal. Sam is a commissioner of fisheries, appointed by the president of the United States, to investigate the fisheries of Nova Scotia, which are being neglected by the Nova Scotians. Sam sails up and down the South Shore of Nova Scotia in the *Black Hawk*, and his journal is full of finely observed vignettes of rural and maritime life of the day. Haliburton's propensity to lecture his reader is transmuted into distillations drawn from Sam's experience of life and labeled "wise saws." Haliburton's confidence in his own literary powers experienced a resurgence in this work. Sam is portrayed as a man who has traveled widely, examined human nature the world over, and can deliver the fruits of his reflections on life in general by means of his reactions to Nova Scotians in particular. Some critics argued that Haliburton was making "soup out of the bones" of his popular character, but this is unfair. Only in the continuation, *Nature and Human Nature* (1855), does the newly discovered energy flag, the digressions become forced, or the prosy intrusions (Sam's "meditations") become prolonged. *Sam Slick's Wise Saws* was a popular work and continued a relationship between Haliburton and his reading public that had developed into a lifelong friendship.

In 1853 Haliburton spent a happy summer in England, and in 1854 his last unmarried daughter married. In 1856 he moved to England, married Sarah Harriet Williams, a widow he had met in 1853, and settled, not in Shropshire, where she lived, but in Gordon House, a rented mansion in the salubrious London suburb of Isleworth, Middlesex. His new life was a busy one. He can hardly be said to have retired. The Haliburtons circulated in London society and took an active interest in local affairs. Haliburton revealed new political ambitions, becoming an active platform speaker on colonial subjects. Oxford University awarded him an honorary D.C.L., and his revived friendship with Bentley extended to acting as his literary and legal adviser. All his life Haliburton had enjoyed good eating, drinking, and the company of kindred spirits

who enjoyed talking and smoking. It was not surprising, then, that he should be afflicted with a severe attack of gout, which laid him low for several months in 1858. What is surprising was his sudden entry into Parliament, as Conservative M.P. for the pocket borough of Launceston in North Cornwall, effected (he claimed) at three days' notice. Although his neighbor in Isleworth was the duke of Northumberland, who controlled politics in the Cornish borough, Haliburton claimed he was not the duke's nominee but sought to represent the four million people of North America, who had no voice in the imperial Parliament. Haliburton was elected unopposed, although he did face vigorous opposition in the borough from those who were cynical of his entry into Parliament by means of the back door of a borough that had survived the 1832 Reform Act. Haliburton was, nevertheless, a conscientious M.P.

He renewed his writing career in 1858 and 1859 by penning *The Season-Ticket*, in serial form, for the *Dublin University Magazine* (published as a book in 1860). *The Season-Ticket* was supposedly the journal of Squire Shegog, the narrator, who travels from London to Southampton by train with a season ticket. As might be expected, this is a mere peg on which Haliburton hangs a multitude of topics that come under discussion by the book's central characters, Cary (an Irishman), Senator Lyman Boodle, George Peabody (a ringtailed roarer), and the narrator himself. Disorder (or "gallimaufry" as the Squire calls it) is rampant. The book often serves merely as a vehicle for Haliburton's opinions. Haliburton ranges far and wide in his subject matter, although the majority of topics have an American concern. There are fine passages on steamships, travelers, clubmen, and funerals, but the absence of the Nova Scotian landscape and life has much to do with the work's failure. Nonetheless, *The Season-Ticket* should be read by all those who admire the achievement of *The Clockmaker* and *The Old Judge*. Haliburton fully intended to continue the series, but Bentley did not publish the book anonymously, as Haliburton had requested, and Haliburton angrily claimed that his pen had been knocked from his hand. It is apparent that Haliburton had hoped to construct another blind from which he could take satirical potshots at the world. One feels that the book's value rested in its being therapy for the aging writer. The lifelong conflict within Haliburton's work between fic-

Haliburton in London, circa 1860 (photograph by Mayall; from D. J. Pound, The Drawing-Room Portrait Gallery of
Eminent Personages, *1860)*

tion and polemic ended with the victory of polemic.

In 1863 Haliburton's health failed, and he notified his constituents at Launceston that he would not seek reelection. Parliament was dissolved in July 1865. On 27 August Haliburton died. The last years had been busy ones. He had launched himself into some new business interests, such as the Canada Land and Emigration Company, of which he became chairman. The company helped settle what is now Haliburton County in Northern Ontario. He crossed the Atlantic twice in successive years (1860 and 1861). Although not a rich man, he could look back from the vantage point of his Thames-side villa on a full life as a famous author, two stints as an active politician, and a life of devoted service as a

judge, and reflect with pride on his achievements. The London Post Office Directory of 1862 listed him erroneously as Sir Thomas Chandler Haliburton, bestowing on him a fictitious knighthood. Further bibliographical, biographical, and critical work on Haliburton is needed. The Carleton University Centre for the Editing of Early Canadian Texts plans to publish the first three *Clockmakers* in a scholarly edition. There is a strong desire among recent critics to explore and confront the problematic and paradoxical values at the heart of Haliburton's work.

Letters:

Richard A. Davies, ed. *The Letters of Thomas Chandler Haliburton* (Toronto: University of Toronto Press, 1988).

Biographies:

V. L. O. Chittick, *Thomas Chandler Haliburton ("Sam Slick"). A Study in Provincial Toryism* (New York: Columbia University Press, 1924);

Stanley McMullin, *Thomas Chandler Haliburton and His Works* (Downsview, Ont.: ECW, 1989).

References:

Walter S. Avis, "A Note on the Speech of Sam Slick," in *The Sam Slick Anthology*, edited by R. E. Watters (Toronto: Clarke Irwin, 1969), pp. xix-xxix;

Richard W. Bailey, "Haliburton's Eye and Ear," *Canadian Journal of Linguistics*, 26 (1981): 90-101;

Richard A. Davies, ed., *On Thomas Chandler Haliburton, Selected Criticism* (Ottawa: Tecumseh, 1979);

Janice Kulyk Keefer, *Under Eastern Eyes. A Critical Reading of Maritime Fiction* (Toronto: University of Toronto Press, 1987), pp. 44-48;

Darlene Kelly, "Thomas Haliburton and Travel Books about America," *Canadian Literature*, 94 (1982): 25-38;

R. D. Macdonald, "Thomas Chandler Haliburton's 'Machine in the Garden': Applying Leo Marx's Criticism of America to Haliburton's Clockmaker," *Canadian Review of American Studies*, 19 (1988): 165-181;

Tom Middlebro', "Imitatio Inanitatis: Literary Madness and the Canadian Short Story," *Canadian Literature*, 107 (Winter 1985): 189-193;

Katharine Morrison, "In Haliburton's Nova Scotia: 'The Old Judge or Life in a Colony,' " *Canadian Literature*, 101 (1984): 58-68;

Bruce Nesbitt, Introduction to *Thomas Chandler Haliburton: Recollections of Nova Scotia*, edited by Nesbitt (Ottawa: Tecumseh, 1984), pp. 1-8;

W. H. New, *Dreams of Speech and Violence* (Toronto: University of Toronto Press, 1987), pp. 35-42;

M. G. Parks, Introduction to *The Old Judge* (Ottawa: Tecumseh, 1979), pp. i-xvii;

M. Brook Taylor, "Thomas Chandler Haliburton as a Historian," *Acadiensis*, 18 (1984): 50-68;

Frank Tierney, ed., *The Thomas Chandler Haliburton Symposium: Reappraisals* (Ottawa: University of Ottawa Press, 1985).

Papers:

The largest single collection of letters can be found at the Houghton Library, Harvard University. However, the Public Archives of Nova Scotia in Halifax is also a rich source of materials relating to Haliburton.

Susan Frances Harrison

(24 February 1859 - 5 May 1935)

Carole Gerson
Simon Fraser University

BOOKS: *Crowded Out! And Other Sketches*, as Seranus (Ottawa: Evening Journal, 1886);

The Canadian Birthday Book, as Seranus (Toronto: Robinson, 1887);

Pine, Rose and Fleur de Lis (Toronto: Hart, 1891);

The Forest of Bourg-Marie (London: Arnold, 1898; Toronto: Morang, 1898 [i.e., 1899]);

In Northern Skies and Other Poems, as Seranus (Toronto, 1912);

Ringfield (Toronto: Musson, 1914; London: Hodder & Stoughton, 1914);

Songs of Love and Labor, as Seranus (Toronto, 1925);

Later Poems and New Villanelles (Toronto: Ryerson, 1928);

Four Ballads and a Play, as Seranus (Toronto, 1933);

Penelope, and Other Poems, as Seranus (Toronto, 1934).

As a poet, novelist, journalist, lecturer, musician, and composer, Susan Frances Harrison was a prominent cultural figure in central Canada during the last decades of the nineteenth century, known particularly for her interest in French Canada. Music was her first love; in 1888 Agnes Ethelwyn Wetherald reported that "musical composition, were it not for the great difficulties attending it, would be [Harrison's] preferred ideal profession." Her frustration at not being able to arrange for the publication or performance of "Pipandor," the opera on which she worked with F. A. Dixon for two years, is reflected in the title story of her first book, *Crowded Out! And Other Sketches* (1886).

Harrison was born Susan Frances Riley in Toronto on 24 February 1859, the daughter of John and Frances Riley, and educated there and in Montreal, where at the age of sixteen she reportedly began to publish poetry in the *Canadian Illustrated News* under the pseudonym "Medusa." As "Gilbert King" she is said to have published some songs, and as the "Rambler" she may have written occasional journalism in Toronto, but her usual pen name was "Seranus," derived from a misreading of her signature, "S. Frances." In 1879 she married John W. F. Harrison, a British-born organist and choirmaster. For seven years they lived in Ottawa, where her writing activities included correspondent work for the *Detroit Free Press*, and John (according to Duncan Campbell Scott) transformed the musical life of the city. They then moved to Toronto, their home for the rest of their lives, where they raised two sons.

Harrison demonstrated her versatility in her many literary and musical activities. For six months, in 1886 and 1887, she was music critic of the *Week* and for a time its acting editor and literary editor; for twenty years she served as principal of the Rosedale Branch of the Toronto Conservatory of Music; and for many years she edited and wrote for the *Conservatory Monthly*. In 1887 she brought out *The Canadian Birthday Book*, a popular diary-cum-anthology of Canadian verse in English and French. She published prose and poetry in many English and American periodicals, including the *New England Magazine* and the *Pall Mall Magazine*, and in 1893 she conducted literature classes in her home. During 1896 and 1897 she presented a series of well-received lecture recitals on "The Music of French Canada," thereby participating in the current popularity of French-Canadian folk life and history–to which she herself had contributed with her poems and stories, and which she would reinforce with the publication of her two novels, *The Forest of Bourg-Marie* (1898) and *Ringfield* (1914).

Although Harrison claimed (in a 23 February 1916 letter to E. J. Hathaway), "I am a realist, a modern of the moderns. *My* Montreal is not the easy historical one of some writers," her version of Quebec is tinged with the romance typical of turn-of-the-century English-Canadian literary interpretations of the lower province. In the opening "Down the River" section of her collection of poems, *Pine, Rose and Fleur de Lis* (1891), she invites her readers to travel "Far from flat Ontario" to a "province old and quaint," where "The Old

Susan Frances Harrison

World and the New World meet" in a culture of cheerful peasants and Gothic shadows. Gothicism is especially powerful in *The Forest of Bourg-Marie*, in which a contemporary conflict between American materialism and French-Canadian traditionalism tragically unfolds in an impenetrable forest replete with a crumbling seigneurial manor house, a superhuman woodsman, and a hunchbacked singer. Like William Kirby in *The Golden Dog* (1877), Harrison writes elegiacally of a regime whose romantic qualities are largely the creation of an Upper Canadian quest for a distinctive historical identity. The vigor of the writing in *The Forest of Bourg-Marie* (which took ten years to find a publisher) even earned the admiration of the New York *Nation* (2 March 1899), which often gave short shrift to romantic fiction. In some of Harrison's stories and her second novel, the mythic nature of her conception of Quebec is expressed through the fate of English visitors who encounter terror, madness, and death, occasionally in the form of beguiling women behind whom hovers a decadent Catholicism. Most protracted is the story of Joshua Ringfield (in

Ringfield), a Methodist minister destroyed by his infatuation with a French-Canadian actress descended from an ancient noble family, and by her lover, an alcoholic remittance man.

Much of Harrison's best prose is to be found in her first book, *Crowded Out! And Other Sketches,* a potpourri of ten deftly composed tales and one novella set in locales ranging from Europe to the Canadian Northwest, describing interesting phases of Canadian life. Most are recounted by male narrators; all reveal Harrison's dexterity with detail and her ability to achieve a tonal balance of irony and sentimentality. Her best poetry, scattered among her various publications (most of them pamphlets), is light in texture, often in the form of the villanelle or the sonnet, and usually about French-Canadian or proletarian life.

Harrison did not grow rich from her creative writing; although Hodder and Stoughton paid her one hundred pounds for *Ringfield*, she was continually in search of journalistic work and had to underwrite the publication of *Later Poems and New Villanelles* (1928) in the Ryerson Chapbook series. Encouraging toward and encouraged by her fellow Canadian writers, she felt especially sympathetic toward Isabella Valancy Crawford. While literary editor of the *Week,* Harrison had the unpleasant task of regretfully informing Crawford that they didn't pay for poetry. Two weeks after the latter's death, Harrison published in the *Week* a warm appreciation of her work (24 February 1887), and later wrote "A Monody" (*Week,* 27 December 1889) to her memory. Letters from the last decade of Harrison's life indicate that, like Crawford, she left many manuscripts. Unlike Crawford, however, Harrison's unpublished work has not been preserved, her published work is out of print and difficult to obtain, and her once-substantial position in the literary life of her country is now all but forgotten.

References:
Duncan Campbell Scott, "At the Mermaid Inn" [8 April 1893], in *At the Mermaid Inn,* edited by Barrie Davies (Toronto: University of Toronto Press, 1979), p. 292;

Agnes Ethelwyn Wetherald, "Some Canadian Literary Women–I. Seranus," *Week,* 5 (22 March 1888): 267-268;

Margaret Whitridge, "The Distaff Side of the Confederation Group: Women's Contribution to Early Nationalist Canadian Literature," *Atlantis,* 4 (Autumn 1978): 30-39;

Marjory Willison, "Mrs. J. W. F. Harrison–'Seranus,'" *Canadian Bookman,* 14 (July-August 1932): 80-81.

Papers:
Harrison's correspondence is housed in the Thomas Fisher Rare Book Room, University of Toronto Library; the National Archives of Canada; the W. D. Lighthall Papers, Rare Book Department, McGill University Library; and the Queen's University Archives, Kingston, Ontario.

Julia Catherine Hart
(10 March 1796 - 28 November 1867)

Mary Jane Edwards
Carleton University

BOOKS: *St. Ursula's Convent, or, The Nun of Canada* (Kingston, Upper Canada [Ont.]: Hugh C. Thomson, 1824; modern edition, Sackville, N.B.: Mount Allison University, 1978); *Tonnewonte; or, The Adopted Son of America* (Watertown, N.Y.: James Q. Adams, 1824-1825).

SELECTED PERIODICAL PUBLICATION—
UNCOLLECTED: "Scenes from an Unpublished Work. The Three Courtships of Chas. McDonald," *New Brunswick Reporter and Fredericton Advertiser,* December 1848 and January 1849.

Julia Catherine Hart is chiefly remembered as the author of *St. Ursula's Convent* (1824), according to Douglas Lochhead, "the first Canadian work of fiction written by a native-born Canadian and published in what is now Canada."

Hart was born Julia Catherine Beckwith on 10 March 1796, the daughter of Nehemiah Beckwith, a Protestant, and his wife, the former Julie-Louise Lebrun de Duplessis, who had been brought up a Roman Catholic. The Beckwith family, originally from Yorkshire, had migrated to Connecticut in the seventeenth century. About 1780 Nehemiah Beckwith, who also had relatives in Nova Scotia, moved to New Brunswick, where one of his business partners was Benedict Arnold. Julie-Louise Beckwith was the daughter of a Frenchman who had come to New France in 1755 and had stayed after it was ceded to Great Britain in 1763. When Julie-Louise married Nehemiah, she was working in Fredericton as governess to the children of Thomas Carleton, the lieutenant-governor of New Brunswick. Julia Catherine was born in Fredericton, but her family's connections in Connecticut, Nova Scotia, and Quebec, the family's mixture of nationality, religion, and social rank, and its involvement in such historical events as the Seven Years' War helped shape both her life and her fiction.

As a child Hart visited her mother's relatives in Quebec, and when she began her first

Julia Catherine Hart (C 345, National Archives of Canada)

novel, she chose as her subject one that had been—as she says in the preface—"suggested to [her] during a residence in the Canadas." *St. Ursula's Convent* is set in Quebec, France, and England in the last decades of the eighteenth century and has as its chief character Julia de la Valiere, a native of Rouen, France. When the novel opens, Julia is Mother St. Catherine, a "good nun" at the Ursuline Convent in Quebec. The main plot of the story concerns Mother St. Catherine's reunion with her husband, children, and sister and her return with them to France. These events, however, are complicated by several other stories of love and adventure, including the apparent death of the nun's husband while fighting for the French in the Seven Years' War, his residence with Quakers at Philadelphia, and his imprisonment in a Mexican silver mine.

Hart actually began this "production" at seventeen, when she was visiting her father's relatives "in the delightful vale of Cornwallis, . . . the Garden of Nova Scotia." It was not published, however, until 1824, when she was twenty-eight. By then Hart's father had drowned (1815), and she had moved to Kingston, Upper Canada (Ontario). Here in the early 1820s she ran a "Young Ladies' Seminary," and on 3 January 1822 at the Parish Church of St. George she married George Henry Hart.

It was probably her husband's business as a bookbinder and stationer that finally led to the printing of *St. Ursula's Convent* by Hugh C. Thomson, the publisher of Kingston's *Upper Canada Herald*. Subscriptions were sought to help defray expenses, and 165 copies were sold by the time the novel went to press. Hart added her preface dated "Kingston, U.C. March 1st, 1824," and a dedication to the countess of Dalhousie, wife of the governor of Lower Canada.

One subscriber was Samuel Hull Wilcocke, who reviewed *St. Ursula's Convent* in the *Scribbler*, his Montreal periodical, on 8 July 1824. He included the novel in "those heaps of inane 'reviewer's miseries.'" Other contemporary reviewers were equally negative, the *Canadian Magazine* (May 1824) declaring that "'The Quintessence of Novels and Romances' . . . would have been a far more appropriate epithet" than *St. Ursula's Convent*. All, however, noted its interest for Canadians.

Hart's second novel, *Tonnewonte*, was published in New York state (1824-1825), probably after the Harts had moved to Rochester. Set in the United States and France, it tells the story of Theodore, a Frenchman who eventually must choose between an aristocratic life with his natural relatives in his native country and a democratic life as a hardworking farmer with adopted relatives on the American frontier in Tonnewonte, New York. Theodore, after fighting against Napoleon at Waterloo, finally decides to return to the greater freedom and happiness of America.

In the introduction to *Tonnewonte*, Hart takes up the question of the alleged superiority of Europe to America and its effects on the literary productions of "all Americans, Canadians, Nova-Scotians, New Brunswickers, Yankees, etc." She hoped that her novel would help induce "some Americans of superior talents, to devote

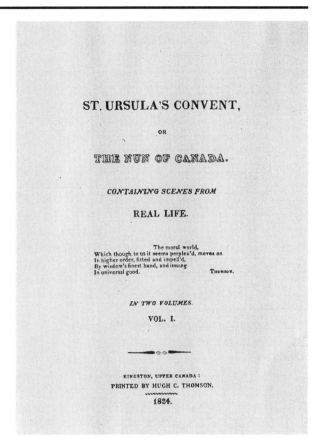

Title page for Hart's first book, the first Canadian novel printed in Canada

their abilities to the general service and amusement of their countrymen." In fact, in this second novel Hart's own talents seem superior to those displayed in *St. Ursula's Convent*. Despite the absence of a psychologically intriguing alter ego figure like the nun Julia, *Tonnewonte*'s plot is tighter; its American setting more deftly described; and its chief Connecticut Yankee characters, the Marvins–this time named after Beckwith relatives–more subtly presented.

In 1831, the year of the last published edition of *Tonnewonte*, the Harts left Rochester for Fredericton, where George Henry Hart worked in the New Brunswick Crown Lands Office. There Mrs. Hart, in addition to raising several children, wrote a third novel, "Edith, or The Doom." She made various attempts to have it published in the 1840s and 1850s, but only a relatively brief excerpt ever appeared. "Scenes from an Unpublished Work. The Three Courtships of Chas. McDonald" was published by the *New Brunswick Reporter and Fredericton Advertiser* in December 1848 and January 1849.

On 29 November 1867 the same newspaper briefly noted the death and funeral of "Julia C. B. Hart, wife of Geo. H. Hart." There was no mention, however, of her fiction, an omission that is fairly typical of Hart's lack of popular and critical recognition as a creative writer. This neglect is undoubtedly partly deserved. For despite her use of family traditions and "scenes from real life," her novels fail ultimately to entertain and instruct in an appealing, memorable way, although amusement and moral improvement were clearly her aims. Still, "that Power" that finally guided Hart's characters to "the blessings of prosperity" (as she says in *St. Ursula's Convent*) also cast her in the seminal role of first Canadian novelist.

References:

C. L. Bennet, "An Unpublished Manuscript of the First Canadian Novelist," *Dalhousie Review,* 43 (1963): 317-332;

Philéas Gagnon, "Le Premier Roman canadien de sujet par un auteur canadien et imprimé au Canada," *Proceedings and Transactions of the Royal Society of Canada,* second series 6 (1900): 121-132;

Douglas Lochhead, Introduction to *St. Ursula's Convent or The Nun of Canada* (Sackville, N.B.: Mount Allison University, 1978), pp. 1-9;

Lilian M. Beckwith Maxwell, "The First Canadian Born Novelist," *Dalhousie Review,* 31 (1951): 59-64.

Papers:

The University of New Brunswick Archives, Fredericton, New Brunswick, holds the manuscript of "Edith, or The Doom" and other material relevant to Hart.

Robert Hayman
(August 1575 - November 1629)

David Galloway
University of New Brunswick

BOOK: *Quodlibets* (London: Printed by Elizabeth All-de for Roger Michell, 1628).

Robert Hayman's book of epigrams, *Quodlibets*, published in London in 1628 and never reprinted, is probably the first book of verse in English to be written in what is now Canada. The quality of the verse falls far below that of Ben Jonson's epigrams and even below that of John Harington's, but the book is valuable in that it supplies information, not available elsewhere, about people who settled, or promoted settlements, in Newfoundland in the second and third decades of the seventeenth century.

Hayman, the second of five children and eldest son of Nicholas and Alice Gaverocke Hayman, was baptized at Wolborough, Devon, on 14 August 1575. The Haymans and Gaverockes were prosperous landowners. Robert's mother died when he was a child; she was buried on 3 April 1578. Four months later, on 4 August, Robert's father married Amis Balle. Sometime between the late summer of 1578 and the early summer of 1579 the Haymans moved to the nearby town of Totnes, where they prospered. Nicholas Hayman became a member of Parliament for the town in October 1586 and mayor in 1589. His wife, Amis, however, had died, being buried on 15 May 1586. Thus Robert lost both his mother and stepmother when he was quite young. Presumably Robert went to Totnes Grammar School, but there is no record of his having been there, because the earliest extant school records are for the late nineteenth century.

On 15 October 1590 Robert Hayman matriculated at that haven of Devonshire students, Exeter College, Oxford, where, according to Anthony à Wood in his *Athenae Oxoniensis* (1691-1692), he was "noted for his ingenuity and pregnant parts" and was "valued by several persons who were afterwards eminent." He completed requirements for a B.A. in 1596 and then followed a sound Devonshire tradition by enrolling to study law at Lincoln's Inn, London. It is doubtful that he ever completed his studies, however. After Lincoln's Inn he seems to have studied at the University of Poitiers, because a letter, dated 1 July 1600, from his father to Robert Cecil, asks that Cecil find employment for his "eldeste sonne Robert," who has studied at "poyttiers in ffraunce." Whether Cecil found employment for Robert is not known.

The Hayman family had moved to Dartmouth in 1591 or 1592, where Nicholas married his third wife, Joyce Blackaller, on 25 September 1591 and seems to have been just as prominent and prosperous as he had been in Totnes. However, Nicholas died in the spring of 1606 and was buried in Dartmouth on 27 April. Joyce followed him to the grave on 25 February 1608. In the meantime, on 21 May 1604, Robert had married Grace Spicer, the daughter of a prominent Exeter merchant, in St. Petrock's Church, Exeter, but no more information about the marriage has come to light.

In the early years of the seventeenth century Hayman seems to have lived in Bristol, where his brother-in-law, John Barker, was a prosperous merchant interested in trade with the New World. Bristolian John Guy had been first governor of the Cuper's Cove colony in Newfoundland in 1610, and Barker, when he was master of the Society of Merchant Venturers, was one of the leaders in arranging for the settling of the land in Newfoundland called Bristol Hope from 1617 to 1618. Hayman may have gone to Newfoundland about this time or a few years later.

Quodlibets, from Hayman's own pen, is the main source of information about his visits to Newfoundland. Of the 357 epigrams in the book, "All of them composed and done at Harbor-Grace . . . in Newfoundland," about one hundred are addressed to famous and obscure men and women of the day, and of these about half refer to people directly concerned with the Newfoundland settlements. The title page says that Hayman was "Sometimes Gouernour of the Planta-

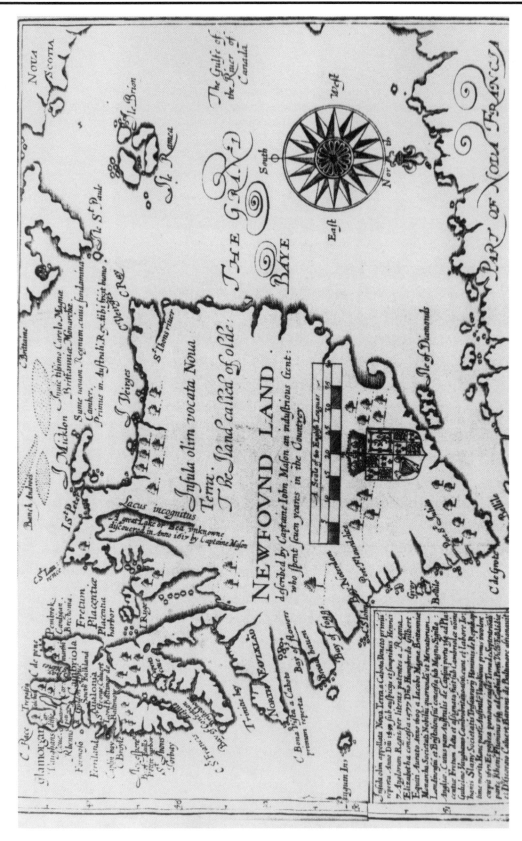

A map of Newfoundland as it was when Robert Hayman lived there and wrote Quodlibets *(1628). Based on descriptions by colonist John Mason, this map was published in* The Golden Fleece *(1626), by Hayman's Oxford acquaintance Sir William Vaughan, another early colonist.*

tion there," but it is doubtful that he ever had any official appointment as governor.

Quodlibets is dedicated to Charles I, and about the same time as it was published Hayman wrote a letter to the duke of Buckingham asking him to bring to the king's attention "A Proposition of Profitt and Honor" that Hayman had written pointing out the advantages to the kingdom of royal support for the colonization of Newfoundland. *Quodlibets* and the "Proposition" add up to a desperate plea to save the colony. They stress its natural resources–fish, minerals, furs, and timber– and its salubrious climate. Hayman praises people who have shown enthusiasm for the colony, but is annoyed at the delays and hesitations of the first planters and those who go there merely for personal gain and quick profits. England should send out the right people, and in an appeal to the universities of Oxford and Cambridge, he urges them (in *Quodlibets*) to "Send forth your Sonnes unto our *New Plantation*; / Yet send such as are *Holy, wise*, and *able*." In fact, with royal support and loyal, industrious people, Newfoundland could be "The hopefull'st, easiest, healthi'st, just plantation / That ere was undertaken by our *Nation*."

Perhaps the assassination of Buckingham on 29 August 1628 and the king's increasing preoccupation with Parliament helped to put an end to Hayman's hopes for royal support. Although in the "Epistle Dedicatorie" to *Quodlibets* he had said that he had "nowe growne dull and aged," at the age of fifty-three he formed a little company and sailed for Guiana in November 1628. In November 1629 he died of a fever on an expedition up the River Wyapoko (now the Oyapock). His servant, Thomas Duppe, and three or four Indians of the Narrack tribe buried him by the water's edge.

In his epigrams Hayman, like other epigrammatists of the period–John Harington, John Davies, and John Weever–provides a wealth of information, satiric and didactic, on the life and personalities of the time. For the most part, however, he is a plodding versifier who recognizes ad nauseam his own limitations, and to Ben Jonson

he writes: "My Epigrams come after yours in time; / So doe they in conceipt, in forme, in Ryme. . . . / There never had beene better Verses writ, / As good as *yours*, could I have ruled it." Nevertheless, Hayman's charming tribute to Francis Drake, which recalls a childhood meeting with the great seaman on "*Totnes* long Street," is beginning to find its way into anthologies: "A faire red *Orange* in his hand he had, / He gave it me, whereof I was right glad, / Takes and kist me, and prayes, *God blesse my boy*; / Which I record *with comfort* to this day." Modest as Robert Hayman's contribution to Canadian literature was, he saw the possibility that his "few bad unripe Rimes" might be the beginnings of a cultural life in Canada that would produce far greater poets than he.

References:

Robin Endres, "Robert Hayman's 'Quodlibets,' " *Canadian Literature*, 73 (Summer 1977): 68-78;

David Galloway, "Robert Hayman (1575-1629): Some Materials for the Life of a Colonial Governor and First 'Canadian' Author," *William and Mary Quarterly*, third series 24 (January 1967): 75-87;

F. J. C. Hearnshaw, "The Death of Robert Hayman, 1629," *English Historical Review*, 34 (1919): 590-591;

M. H. M. Mackinnon, "Parnassus in Newfoundland: The First Fruits of Britaniola," *Dalhousie Review*, 32 (Spring 1952): 110-119;

Allan Pritchard, "From These Uncouth Shores: Seventeenth-Century Literature of Newfoundland," *Canadian Literature*, 14 (Autumn 1962): 68-78;

G. C. Moore Smith, "Robert Hayman and the Plantation of Newfoundland," *English Historical Review*, 33 (1918): 21-36.

Papers:

Some of Hayman's correspondence, including "A Proposition of Profitt and Honor," is in Egerton MS. 2541, fol. 63-169, at the British Library.

Samuel Hearne
(1745 - November 1792)

Victor G. Hopwood
University of British Columbia

BOOKS: *A Journey from Prince of Wales's Fort, in Hudson's Bay, to the Northern Ocean* (London: A. Strahan & T. Cadell, 1795; Philadelphia: Joseph & James Crukshank, 1802); modern edition, edited by J. B. Tyrell (Toronto: Champlain Society, 1911; New York: Greenwood, 1968); another modern edition, edited by R. G. Glover (Toronto: Macmillan, 1958);

Journals of Samuel Hearne and Philip Turner, edited by Tyrell (Toronto: Champlain Society, 1934).

When Samuel Hearne, on foot, reached the central Arctic shore of North America in 1771, he finished a centuries-old will-o'-the-wisp of the European imagination–a navigable Northwest Passage through or north of the Americas from Europe to Asia–until it was recently revived by giant tankers and icebreakers. Explorers such as James Cook and John Franklin continued to be instructed to search for it, but the testimony is more to the stubbornness of myths than to the inconclusiveness of Hearne's evidence. For the rest of his life Hearne worked on *A Journey from Prince of Wales's Fort, in Hudson's Bay, to the Northern Ocean*, which was published posthumously in 1795. It is among the most engaging of travel books: lucid and, as appropriate, informative, dramatic, ironic, or amusing. For travelers in British North America, his work is the prototype in style and structure of explorers' and traders' journals transformed into narratives.

Hearne was born in London in 1745. After his father, Samuel, an engineer, died in 1748, Hearne's mother, Diana, moved to Dorset with him and his sister. Although his mother did her best to obtain an education for her son, the young Hearne had no interest in book learning, although he showed talent for sketching. At eleven or twelve years of age he went to sea as a servant to Capt. Alexander Hood (later an admiral). After seeing action in the Seven Years' War, Hearne left the British Navy in 1763. Three

Samuel Hearne

years later he entered the service of the Hudson's Bay Company as a mate on one of its coasting vessels, whaling out of Prince of Wales's Fort (Churchill) and trading with the "Esquimaux" (Inuit).

In 1769 Hearne was directed to travel to the shore of the Northern (Arctic) Ocean to find the truth of a rumored copper mine, a navigable river, and a northwest passage from Hudson Bay. After two failures Hearne drew the conclusions necessary for success–to travel without white companions, to attach himself to a band of Chipewyan hunters (women, children, and all), and to follow them in their nomadic wanderings,

Illustrations by Hearne for his Journey from Prince of Wales's Fort, in Hudson's Bay, to the Northern Ocean *(1795):*
"A North West View of Prince of Wales Fort" and "A Winter View in the Athapuscow Lake" (Great Slave Lake)

directing himself toward his goal as feasible. Hearne was helped to this judgment by his main companion on the successful journey, Matonabbee, a Chipewyan leader of great prestige. Hearne's portrait of this friendly patriarch who had from five to eight wives is shrewd, three-dimensional, and sympathetic. Matonabbee's solution to Hearne's difficulties was to work within the gender division of labor among hunters: "For, when all the men are heavy laden, they can neither hunt nor travel to any considerable distance; and in case they meet with success in hunting, who is to carry the produce of their labour? Women . . . also pitch our tents, make and mend our clothing, keep us warm at night; and . . . as they always stand cook, the very licking of their fingers in scarce times, is sufficient for their subsistence." As a result Hearne set out in early December 1770 with Matonabbee as his guide. Hearne grasped his adviser's point: although Hearne does not say so explicitly, it is possible to read between the lines that he not only had a woman to cook and sew but also to warm him at night.

Hearne's first attempts and the first months of his third try took him west across the country later described in Farley Mowat's 1952 book, *The People of the Deer*. (Mowat later paid tribute to his predecessor by writing a popular version of Hearne's narrative: *Coppermine Journey*, 1958.) Hearne's party then turned north toward the Arctic Ocean. They gathered forces as they went, in spite of Hearne's expostulations, to raid the Inuit they expected to meet. Near the mouth of the Coppermine River, at a place Hearne named Bloody Falls, the Chippewa Indians fell upon the tents of a helpless band of Inuit while Hearne "stood neuter in the rear." Hearne's description is often quoted, partly because it is so graphic, but also because Europeans and Anglo-Saxon North Americans have a passion for scenes showing the savagery of peoples other than themselves. John Newlove concludes his 1968 poetic tribute, "Samuel Hearne in Wintertime," by echoing the passage: "There was that Eskimo girl / at Bloody Falls, at your feet // Samuel Hearne, with two spears in her, / you helpless before your helpers, // and she twisted about them like / an eel, dying, never to know."

At the mouth of the river, Hearne made observations (notoriously erroneous). Then the party turned to the copper mines, a disappointment. On the return journey to Hudson Bay, Hearne added Great Slave Lake to his list of first sights for a white man.

A

J O U R N E Y

FROM

Prince of Wales's Fort, in Hudſon's Bay,

TO

THE NORTHERN OCEAN.

UNDERTAKEN

BY ORDER OF THE HUDSON'S BAY COMPANY.

FOR THE DISCOVERY OF

COPPER MINES, A NORTH WEST PASSAGE, &c.

In the Years 1769, 1770, 1771, & 1772.

By S A M U E L   H E A R N E.

LONDON:

Printed for A. STRAHAN and T. CADELL:
And Sold by T. CADELL Jun. and W. DAVIES, (Succeſſors to
Mr. CADELL,) in the Strand.

1795

Title page for Hearne's account of his major expeditions, the first important Canadian exploration narrative

Shortly after his return to Prince of Wales's Fort in 1772 Hearne was sent inland by the Hudson's Bay Company to found Fort Cumberland. In 1776 he was made governor of the renamed Fort Prince of Wales, which in 1782 was attacked by ships of France, the ally of revolutionary America. Hearne, recognizing superior odds, surrendered to Admiral de la Pérouse, a famous navigator and author. La Pérouse returned the partly completed manuscript of Hearne's narrative on the condition that he finish and publish it.

In 1783 Hearne returned to Hudson Bay, where he built Fort Churchill. In 1784 an apprentice, David Thompson, age fourteen, arrived at Churchill, where he copied some pages of Hearne's manuscript. The freethinking Hearne baited the orthodox apprentice. Thompson also certainly learned of Hearne's defects as a surveyor. The consequence was Thompson's dislike, a sad result, since the two men actually shared many admirable qualities. However, Thompson likely learned from Hearne about the scope in North America for exploration and natural history. The youth also had before him a model of writing on exploration and encounters with new people and environments.

Ill health forced Hearne's retirement in 1786 to England, where he continued work on his narrative. On 18 October 1792, Hearne concluded the sale of his manuscript for the very good price of two hundred pounds. In November he died of dropsy.

Hearne's concluding chapter on the creatures of the North expands on the information he had already communicated to Thomas Pennant for the latter's pioneering *Arctic Zoology* (1784). Hearne was a fine naturalist. He was also a keen iconoclast, delighting in deflating myths, such as the belief that the beaver used its tail as a trowel.

On publication Hearne's book caught the imagination of Britain, Europe, and America, being quickly translated into German, Dutch, Swedish, French, and Danish, as well as being reprinted in Ireland and the United States. Its observations on Indian life strongly impressed William Wordsworth and Samuel Taylor Coleridge. Echoes of Hearne's description of the aurora borealis appear in the poetry of both. Since then Hearne's accounts of the customs and beliefs of the Chipewyans have found their way into modern writings on religion, myth, and anthropology. Hearne's illustrations have been often reproduced. The historian John B. Brebner gives an admirable summary of Hearne's work: "Hearne was blessed with an odd, judicious literary artistry which enabled him to write what is one of the classics of the literature of exploration, not only because it is an illuminating account of the country, its natural history and its inhabitants, but also because it conveys unconsciously a portrait 'in the round' of a very likeable and inquisitive, if somewhat timorous, man." "Timorous" rings a bit odd when describing a man who endured such hardship and faced such risks. However, it suits the way Hearne accomplished his epic journey, not by thrusting ahead like Alexander Mackenzie or John Franklin, but by adapting his ways to the Chipewyans, complying with their needs and wishes. Hearne learned from the Chipewyans to be philosophical about difficulties. He also seems to have picked up a touch of French philosophical skepticism, especially about the final value of heroics.

Reference:

John Bartlett Brebner, *The Explorers of North America, 1492-1806* (London: Black, 1933), pp. vii, 325-333, 335-336, 361, 364, and 370-371.

Charles Heavysege

(1816 - 14 July 1876)

Sandra Djwa
Simon Fraser University

BOOKS: *The Revolt of Tartarus: A Poem* (London: Simpkin, Marshall, 1852; revised edition, Montreal: Privately published, 1855);

Sonnets (Montreal: Rose, 1855);

Saul: A Drama in Three Parts (Montreal: Rose, 1857; revised edition, London: Low, 1859; Boston: Fields, Osgood, 1869);

Count Filippo; or, The Unequal Marriage: A Drama in Five Acts (Montreal: Dawson, 1860);

Jephthah's Daughter (Montreal: Dawson, 1865; London: Low & Marston, 1865);

The Advocate: A Novel (Montreal: Worthington, 1865);

Saul and Selected Poems by Charles Heavysege, edited by Sandra Djwa (Toronto: University of Toronto Press, 1976).

SELECTED PERIODICAL PUBLICATIONS— UNCOLLECTED: "Jezebel," *New Dominion Monthly*, 1 (January 1868): 224-231;

"The Dark Huntsman," *Canadian Monthly and National Review*, 10 (August 1876): 134-136.

Charles Heavysege, a popular verse dramatist in his day, is now best known not for his poetry, but for the critical commentary about it. For the critic Northrop Frye, Heavysege's poem *Jephthah's Daughter* (1865) is the quintessence of whatever is "Canadian" in Canadian literature; for the novelist Robertson Davies, Heavysege is the quintessence of dullness in Canadian writing. In Davies's satire *Leaven of Malice* (1954), the protagonist "Saul" becomes representative of the Canadian scholarly industry, which Davies dubs "Amcan." The fact that both critic and satirist isolate Heavysege for comment is indicative of his importance in Canadian literature. Heavysege was one of the first of the Anglo-Canadian poets to achieve international recognition; he paved the way for later poets such as Charles Sangster and Charles G. D. Roberts. Heavysege is well worthy of study when compared with any of his North American contemporaries, or for that matter with the lesser but significant figures of the En-

glish Romantic revival such as Thomas Beddoes.

Heavysege was reportedly born in 1816 in Huddersfield, Yorkshire. Describing his childhood, as noted by Lawrence J. Burpee, he remarked (in an October 1860 letter to Charles Lanman) that he was "religiously brought up" and "taught to consider not only the theatre itself, but dramatic literature, even in its best examples, as forbidden things. Hence, when a boy, it was only by dint of great persuasion that I covertly obtained from my mother some few pence weekly for a cheap edition of Shakespeare that was then being issued in parts." Heavysege became an apprentice woodcarver and eventually established his own business in Liverpool, but in 1853 he immigrated to Canada. There in Montreal he worked as a journeyman carver for the firm of J. and H. Hilton and for the Grand Trunk Railway. Later that year Heavysege became a reporter for the Montreal *Transcript* and eventually joined the staff of the *Daily Witness*. His sixteen years in newspaper journalism were interrupted only by a brief return to woodcarving, during which time he wrote *Jephthah's Daughter*.

His first book, *The Revolt of Tartarus* (1852), a six-book epic in the manner of John Milton's *Paradise Lost* (1667), drew heavily on Milton's theology and on Shakespearean diction. But the young man who attended the public theaters and who once wanted to become an actor had absorbed the prevailing Romantic spirit of the times. Within the Miltonic cosmology of *The Revolt of Tartarus* as within the biblical narratives of *Saul* (1857) and *Jephthah's Daughter*, one finds strong assertions of Romantic individualism and religious doubt. There are two versions of Heavysege's first dramatic poem. The first, bearing his name, was published in London and Liverpool in 1852; the second, considerably edited, appeared anonymously in Montreal in 1855. This poem prefigures Heavysege's subsequent concerns; the poem's protagonist, the rebellious Satan, draws from the Satan of Milton's *Paradise Lost* and from the Lucifer of Lord Byron's *Cain* (1822). Although *The Revolt of Tartarus* does present the Romantic Promethean rebel, Heavysege does not carry to full tragic intensity Byron's assertion of a capricious God functioning in a Manichaean universe. Satan's claim that evil holds equal power with God is recognized as a transparent fiction, even by those new Adams whom he tempts to disobedience. Grotesquely attempting the sexual temptation of Eve, he is described as "harlotlike, rub[bing] in / The glory of the morn upon his cheek." Byron's gigantic rebel has become a lesser being, a palpable sinner.

The primary source of Heavysege's major work, the drama *Saul*, is the familiar account in the first book of Samuel. Heavysege provides a Romantic justification, that of the cruel Jehovah, for Saul's spiritual rebellion, and this rebellion is further excused by a secondary theme of the political conflict of king and priest. By providing such rationales, Heavysege presents Saul as the noble villain of Romantic, heroic tragedy. Yet in dramatic context both justifications are undercut: politically, it is demonstrated that the fabric of society falls apart when the king disobeys God; spiritually, Saul's revolt is categorized as Luciferian. Early in the play Saul confesses his "proud imagination [and] rash impatience," and both pride and rashness precipitate his downfall, when he usurps the role of the priest, Samuel, and becomes, in his own final condemnation of Jehovah, "the Omnipotent's accuser."

The romance and verbal wit of *Count Filippo; or, The Unequal Marriage* (1860) differs substantially from the martial rhetoric of *Saul*. Here we find the substance of Shakespearean tragicomedy. There is tragedy in the role of the courtier, Gallantio, as Iago-Pander, and the freshness of a Romeo-and-Juliet romance in the encounter between Hylas and Volina, Filippo's restless young wife. Comedy is present in skillful double entendres such as: "It is man, / Not horse, you want,—a lover in a husband. / Wherefore does yours not squire you through the glades?" The narrative source of this Italianate tale is Vittorio Alfieri's *Filippo* (1789). When the aged Filippo leaves the court to arrange a marriage for the unwilling Hylas, Gallantio urges Hylas to seduce Volina. The witty sexual comedy of the first third of the play abruptly turns to tragedy when Volina returns Hylas's affection only to recognize that both have fallen irreparably from God's grace. By presenting the aged Filippo as a good man who recognizes the validity of Volina's defense, and through his use of a framing structure of Christian atonement, Heavysege transforms revenge tragedy into Christian drama. Nonetheless, conventional Victorian morality prevails in the conclusion when Filippo, Hylas, and Volina, all equally repentant, are dispatched to the cloister.

In his long narrative poem *Jephthah's Daughter*, Heavysege returns to a theme similar to that of the earlier *Saul*: the struggle of Jephthah (Judges 11:31), the great—but in Heavysege's characterization, "rash"—Israelite leader who vows to Jehovah that if granted victory against the enemy he will sacrifice whoever comes first from his household to greet him on his return from battle. When to his horror his daughter meets him, the distraught Jephthah attempts to revoke his oath. The central scene, in which Jephthah asks God to release him from the vow, has been quoted by Frye as characteristic of the attitude to nature in Canadian poetry. Waiting for a sign from heaven, Jephthah hears:

The hill-wolf howling on the neighbouring height,
And the bittern booming in the pool below.
Some drops of rain fell from the passing cloud,
That sudden hides the wanly shining moon,
And from the scabbard instant dropped his sword,
And, with long, living leaps and rock-struck clang,
From side to side, and slope to sounding slope,
In gleaming whirls swept down the dim ravine
(Ill omen!): and, mute trembling, as he stood
Helmless (to his astonished view), his daughter,
All in sad disarray, appeared.

However, the landscape of this poem is not Canadian but rather a landscape derived from literature, in this case Alfred, Lord Tennyson's "Morte d'Arthur" (1842). Like Sir Bedivere, Jephthah is described as a man who must be rebuked until he keeps his promise: "No ransom may there be, no compromise." The omen of the falling sword followed by the sudden manifestation of his daughter (an ironic reversal of the biblical Abraham story and the ram Jephthah had arrogantly demanded of God), suggests that Heavysege is evoking the stern Old Testament Jehovah. From this perspective it is not directly Canadian nature but rather the biblical God of nature that responds to Jephthah.

Heavysege also wrote some shorter poems, many of which are now unavailable: "The Dark Huntsman," a conventional set piece on the approach of death, was published in the *Canadian Monthly and National Review* (August 1876); "Jezebel" (*New Dominion Monthly*, January 1868) is a dramatization of the biblical account of the infamous queen, and the description of the death of Jezebel, her bones licked by dogs, has a macabre vitality. He also published a novel, *The Advocate*

(1865), a potboiler of unassimilated Gothic elements.

Heavysege was highly celebrated in the 1860s and 1870s. Canada had little in the way of a national literature, and he had been acclaimed as the major poet of the Dominion, the leading dramatist of British North America. Coventry Patmore, writing anonymously in the *North British Review* (August 1858), commented that his major work, *Saul*, was "one of the most remarkable English poems ever written out of Great Britain." In the nationalist 1920s critics disparaged Heavysege's poetry on the grounds that he was not really a Canadian writer, although he continued to be read by poets like W. W. E. Ross, Ralph Gustafson, and A. J. M. Smith. The dominant critical approach to Canadian poetry, Frye's influential theory of a cruel Canadian nature, rests partly on Heavysege's poetry. Today his crude but vigorous poetry is underrated by Canadian criticism.

References:

Lawrence J. Burpee, "Charles Heavysege," *Transactions of the Royal Society of Canada*, second series, 7 (1901): II, 19-60;

Sandra Djwa, Introduction to *Saul and Selected Poems by Charles Heavysege* (Toronto: University of Toronto Press, 1976), pp. ix-lxvii;

Northrop Frye, "The Narrative Tradition in English Canadian Poetry" [1946], in his *The Bush Garden: Essays in the Canadian Imagination* (Toronto: Anansi, 1971), pp. 150-151.

Alexander Henry

(August 1739 - 4 April 1824)

Neil K. Besner
University of Winnipeg

BOOK: *Travels and Adventures in Canada and the Indian Territories, Between the Years 1760 and 1776* (New York: Riley, 1809); revised and edited by James Bain (Boston: Little, Brown, 1901; Toronto: Morang, 1901); revised and edited by Milo Milton Quaife (Chicago: Donnelly, 1921; Edmonton: Hurtig, 1969).

Alexander Henry, the Elder–so named to distinguish him from his son, Alexander, and from his nephew, Alexander Henry, the Younger, who also kept memorable journals of his twenty-three years in the fur trade with the North West Company–is remembered today principally for his account of sixteen important years in his life and in Canadian history. *Travels and Adventures in Canada and the Indian Territories, Between the Years 1760 and 1776* was first published in 1809 and has since been published and reprinted in many versions, some of them abridged, with the first edition edited and corrected by an unknown hand to smooth the rough edges of Henry's style. The importance of Henry's account of his travels, which he divided into two parts, lies not so much in its documentary accuracy–there are errors in chronology, and his estimates of distances between points in his travels are sometimes inaccurate–as in its vivid portrayal of Henry's experiences as the second Englishman (Henry Bostwick was the first) to travel from Montreal via the Ottawa River, Lake Nippissing, and the French River to Michilimackinac (Mackinaw City, Michigan) in order to trade with the Indians. Henry's account of his adventures, including his observations of the Indian character and way of life, is celebrated as a classic adventure tale; in particular, his first-hand recollection of the infamous massacre at Fort Michilimackinac on 2 June 1763–from which Henry barely escaped with his own life–is the most vivid rendition in Canadian writing of what has become a legendary episode. This section of Henry's journal has also been drawn

upon by other writers in their historical and fictional reconstructions of this period–by the American historian Francis Parkman (*The Conspiracy of Pontiac*, 1851), for example, and Canada's first native-born novelist, John Richardson, in his best-known work, *Wacousta* (1832). On the strength of *Travels and Adventures*, Henry is usually grouped with four other writers of roughly the same period whose works are essentially shaped as documentary accounts of travel and exploration in Canada: Samuel Hearne, Alexander Mackenzie, David Thompson, and Capt. John Franklin.

Henry was born in New Brunswick, New Jersey, in August 1739 to English parents: Alexander Henry, a merchant, and Elizabeth Henry. His life in Canada began when, at the age of twenty, he traveled as a supplier to the British forces on their advance to Montreal in 1760. Montreal's surrender on 8 September opened the country to English traders, and in 1761, guided by Etienne Charles Campion, Henry traveled by canoe to Michilimackinac, the central trading post in the region. The Indians at this time were still allies of the French and suspicious of the English; Henry therefore (unsuccessfully) attempted to disguise himself as a French trader but was eventually "adopted" as a brother by Wawatam, an Ojibway chief, and was able to trade with both the French and the Indians.

The massacre at Michilimackinac was precipitated by the Ottawa chief Pontiac, who led an Indian uprising in 1763 against the British in the Northwest. The Indians' ruse to gain entrance to the fort has also become part of the lore about this incident: outside of the enclosure, the Chippewa and Saakie tribes began a fierce game of "baggatiway," or as the French in Canada called it at the time, "le jeu de la crosse," from which lacrosse derives. On the pretext of retrieving a ball that had fallen inside the fort, the Indians rushed in and attacked the English. Henry ran to the house of Charles Langlade, where he hid for a time before being discovered; he was threatened with death several times but was rescued by

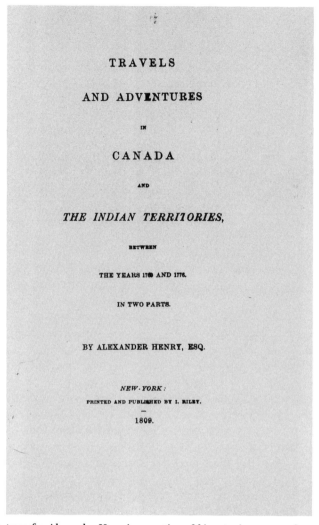

TRAVELS

AND ADVENTURES

IN

CANADA

AND

THE INDIAN TERRITORIES,

BETWEEN

THE YEARS 1760 AND 1776.

IN TWO PARTS.

BY ALEXANDER HENRY, ESQ.

NEW-YORK:
PRINTED AND PUBLISHED BY I. RILEY.
—
1809.

Title page for Alexander Henry's narrative of his experiences as a fur trader

Wawatam. Henry then lived with Wawatam and his family for almost one year, moving with them on their rounds of fishing and hunting.

Henry's account of the attack at Michilimackinac is vivid and immediate, although his description of the Indians is steeped in the conventional language and style of the period: "Through an aperture, which afforded me a view of the area of the fort, I beheld, in shapes the foulest and most terrible, the ferocious triumphs of barbarian conquerors. The dead were scalped and mangled; the dying were writhing and shrieking, under the unsatiated knife and tomahawk; and, from the bodies of some ripped open, their butchers were drinking the blood, scooped up in the hollow of joined hands, and quaffed amid shouts of rage and victory. I was shaken, not only with horror, but with fear. The sufferings which I witnessed, I seemed on the point of experiencing."

Although the passages recalling this episode are the ones most often cited from *Travels and Adventures*, the work also remains interesting for Henry's many detailed observations of Indian customs, for his accounts of his extensive travels in the upper Great Lakes region, and, in part 2, his journeys on Lake Superior and into the Canadian Northwest, where he traveled in 1775 with Peter Pond and Joseph and Thomas Frobisher in a bid to challenge the Hudson's Bay Company's hold on trading in the area.

Pursuing his interests in fur trading in the Northwest, Henry traveled to England and France in 1776, and returned to England in 1778, 1780, and 1781, eventually settling in Montreal, where he became a merchant but remained involved in the fur trade. In the 1780s and 1790s Henry was active in helping the North West Company ship furs to China, an enterprise that had become involved in the fur trade; in 1812 brought him into contact with John Jacob Astor, the noted American merchant. In 1785 Henry married Julia Ketson; their daughter Julia had been born in 1780, and four sons, Alexander, William, Robert, and John, were born between 1782 and 1786. The year of his marriage he was also one of the nineteen founders of the famous Beaver Club of Montreal, and he served as a justice of the peace from 1794 to 1821. By the time he wrote *Travels and Adventures*, a new generation

Henry was appointed "vendue master and auctioneer for the district of Montreal." He died in Montreal at the age of eighty-five in 1824; the travels and adventures that he had so vividly recreated had taken place over sixty years earlier. Nearly 230 years later, his experiences, recollected in a narrative that has itself been transformed by later historians and novelists alike, resonate as faint but persistent echoes and trace the filaments of legend in the contemporary Canadian imagination.

Sophie Almon Hensley

(31 May 1866 - 10 February 1946)

Gwendolyn Davies
Acadia University

BOOKS: *Poems*, as Sophie M. Almon (Windsor, N.S.: Anslow, 1889);
A Woman's Love Letters (New York: Tait, 1895);
Love & Company (Limited), as John Wernberny and Another (New York: Tait, 1897), republished under the names J. Try-Davies and Mary Woolston (Montreal: Brown, 1901);
Princess Mignon: A Musical Play in Three Acts, founded on one of Andrew Lang's fairy tales, as Almon Hensley (New York: Kenworthy, 1900);
The Heart of a Woman, as Almon Hensley (New York & London: Putnam's, 1906);
Woman and the Race, as Gordon Hart (Westwood, Mass.: Ariel, 1907);
Love and the Woman of Tomorrow (London: Drane's, 1913);
The Way of a Woman, and Other Poems (San Diego: Canterbury, 1928).

A descendant of Cotton Mather and Increase Mather, Sophie Almon Hensley began her writing career as a literary protégée of Charles G. D. Roberts. Her periodical contributions consolidated her reputation in the 1880s and 1890s, and her essays and books on feminism and social issues brought her to the attention of both Canadian and American audiences.

Born in Bridgetown, Nova Scotia, the daughter of the Reverend Henry Pryor Almon and Sarah Frances DeWolf Almon, Sophie was reportedly educated abroad at St. Monica's, Warminster, Wiltshire, and at Miss Watson's School in Paris. While she was living at "Fairfield," her family home in Windsor, Nova Scotia, she came under the literary tutelage of Roberts, just appointed to the faculty of the University of King's College in 1885. Roberts encouraged her poetic contributions to the *Week*, the *King's College Record*, the *Dominion Illustrated Monthly*, the *Current*, and a variety of other North American periodicals. Her first collection, *Poems*, was printed privately in April 1889, the same month in which she married barrister Hubert A. Hensley in Halifax. Included in *Poems* is "There Is No God," one of two Hensley poems selected by Douglas Sladen for his *Younger American Poets* (1891) and singled out by him in his introduction.

A letter from Hensley to Montreal litterateur William Douw Lighthall (in the McGill University Archives) indicates that she and her husband were planning to leave Nova Scotia to sail the world by yacht for several years and earn their living by their pens. This plan may not have materialized. Certainly by the early 1890s the Hensleys were residents of New York, where her second volume of verse, *A Woman's Love Letters*, was published in 1895. Exploring stages of dream, doubt, misunderstanding, and even death in the speaker's relationship with a lover, Hensley reveals the tensions between the sexes that would also be the subject of the 1897 novelette *Love & Company (Limited)*, published as being by "John Wernberny and Another" but attributed to Hensley in several reliable contemporary publications. Its plot revolves around two diaries in which a man and a woman record an experiment to make one fall in love with the other. The joke backfires when the pair genuinely fall in love and become separated, but they are accidentally and successfully reunited ten years later. Reprinted in 1901 in Montreal under different pseudonyms (J. Try-Davies and Mary Woolston), *Love & Company (Limited)* presents bibliographical problems. Canadian critic Carole Gerson has explored this area and Hensley's alleged authorship of the novel *A Semi-Detached House* (Montreal, 1900) in *Canadian Notes & Queries*, number 39.

In 1900 Hensley collaborated with her husband in writing *Princess Mignon*, a musical play in three acts based on one of Andrew Lang's fairy tales. However, her work became increasingly socially oriented as she involved herself in progressive causes. Described by *Who's Who In New York* in 1904 as "a radical and fearless speaker and thinker," Hensley became an organizer and president of the New York City Mother's Club, president of the Society for the Study of Life, secretary of the New York State Assembly of Mothers, a member of the Society for Political Study and of the New York Press Club, associate editor of *Health: A Home Magazine Devoted to Physical Culture and Hygiene*, and an active supporter of feminist and child welfare causes. Her 1906 collection of poems, *The Heart of a Woman*, makes it clear that women can be passionate, not dutifully submissive, lovers, and that mother love may vie with romantic love. *Woman and the Race*, written under the pseudonym Gordon Hart, went into two editions (1907, 1911) and explored social and moral questions consistent with Hensley's New York interests. However, it was in *Love and the Woman of Tomorrow* (1913), dedicated to her husband and published after living in London for several years, that Hensley most clearly defined her feminist sensibility. It is during this period that Hensley probably became associated with Christabel Pankhurst and her mother. Pointing out that the fight for women's political recognition had led to a leveling of social inequality,

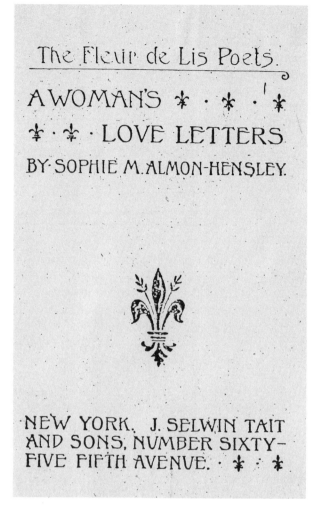

Title page for Hensley's second poetry collection. The first book published under her married name, it explores tensions between the sexes.

Hensley attacks convention in the book by arguing that not all women are suited to being mothers, that those who want to be mothers without entering marriage should not be discouraged, and that women with their newfound freedom to do any work should not feel pressured to marry. The book ranges frankly over sexual, economic, and social issues and represents a synthesis of Hensley's feminist and social views.

At least one other collection of verse, *The Way of a Woman, and Other Poems* (1928) was published during Hensley's lifetime. A frequent world traveler, she nonetheless returned to her summer home in Barton, Nova Scotia, as often as possible. A letter to Roberts from "Quiet Waters," Barton, on 21 August 1935 (in the University of New Brunswick Library) indicates that she continued to write poetry as she grew older: "I am thinking of collecting the verses written here and making a little volume, 'Songs of St. Mary's Bay.' Our bay is as yet unsung." With members of her family she moved to the island of Jersey in 1937, but was forced to flee when the Nazis invaded the Channel islands in 1940 and commandeered her house. She died in Windsor, Nova Scotia, on 10 February 1946. Always an elegant woman and an independent thinker, Hensley wore a knickerbocker suit in an age when women

did not yet wear slacks or shorts; she spoke fearlessly on the social issues dear to her heart; and, according to Henry James Morgan, she always saw herself on the international scene as "a Canadian in thought, feeling, and expression."

Reference:
Henry James Morgan, *The Canadian Men and Women of the Time* (Toronto: Briggs, 1898).

Abraham S. Holmes
(1821? - 4 March 1908)

Mary Lu MacDonald

BOOK: *Belinda, or The Rivals* (Detroit: Bagg & Harmon, 1843; modern edition, Toronto: Alcuin, 1970).

One of the earliest Upper Canadian novelists, Abraham S. Holmes was the son of Rev. Ninian Holmes, a Methodist minister who had retired from the Detroit circuit to teach and farm in Upper Canada (Ontario), and of his wife, Elizabeth, née Newkirk, daughter of one of the earliest settlers in the Western District. Abraham was probably born on their farm in Raleigh Township in 1821. The year can only be deduced by counting backward from the age he gave to census takers in later life.

Holmes's one novel and the few poems and letters to the editor scattered through the *Chatham Gleaner* and the *Western Herald* are all youthful works. He is not known to have published anything after 1846. Like so many other young Canadian men of his time, Holmes seems to have stopped writing when he began his professional career. He settled in Chatham, where he practiced law. It is difficult to sort out biographical details since there was more than one Abraham Holmes living in that city, but Holmes the author seems always to have signed himself "Abraham S." In the 1851 census his religion is given as Congregational and in 1861 as Church of England—a not uncommon movement away from the Methodism of

his upbringing. At least as late as the 1871 census he was unmarried. There is no mention of a widow or children in his obituary, and a nephew was appointed administrator of his estate. In Chatham today he is remembered as one of the cofounders of that city's public library.

Holmes's novel, *Belinda, or The Rivals* (1843), is a unique work in the body of early Canadian literature. Some writers have seen it as an unintentionally comic imitation of the sentimental novel of seduction; others have seen it as a relatively sophisticated spoof of the genre. Supporters of each view have produced textual evidence to prove their point. In the book's own day, only one review, generally favorable, is known to have been published. That review took it as a straightforward "unpretending tale" (*Chatham Journal*, 28 October 1843).

Only one copy of the original edition is known to have survived. When the historian F. C. Hamil read it in the Burton Historical Collection of the Detroit Public Library he found a note, evidently written in the nineteenth century and pasted in the back, which provided a key to the names of the principal protagonists. Hamil was able to establish that these people had indeed all lived in the Chatham district and that the supposed original of Belinda, Hester Ann Richardson of the Talbot Settlement, had died in 1840, shortly after her marriage. The note subse-

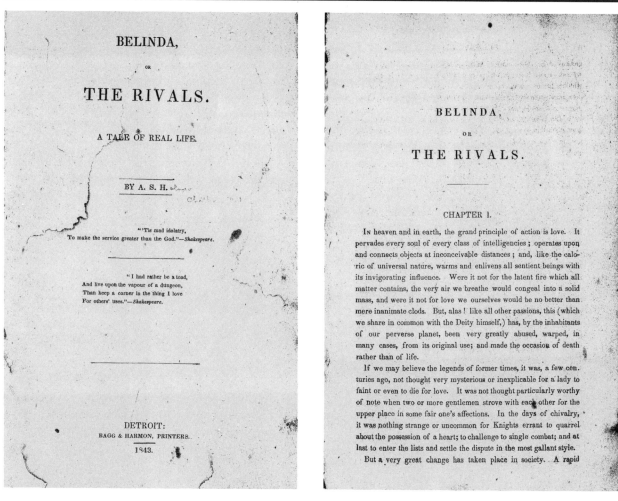

BELINDA,

OR

THE RIVALS.

A TALE OF REAL LIFE.

BY A. S. H.

"'Tis mad idolatry,
To make the service greater than the God."—*Shakespeare.*

" I had rather be a toad,
And live upon the vapour of a dungeon,
Than keep a corner in the thing I love
For others' uses."—*Shakespeare.*

DETROIT:
BAGG & HARMON, PRINTERS.
1843.

BELINDA,

OR

THE RIVALS.

CHAPTER I.

In heaven and in earth, the grand principle of action is love. It pervades every soul of every class of intelligencies ; operates upon and connects objects at inconceivable distances ; and, like the caloric of universal nature, warms and enlivens all sentient beings with its invigorating influence. Were it not for the latent fire which all matter contains, the very air we breathe would congeal into a solid mass, and were it not for love we ourselves would be no better than mere inanimate clods. But, alas ! like all other passions, this (which we share in common with the Deity himself,) has, by the inhabitants of our perverse planet, been very greatly abused, warped, in many cases, from its original use; and made the occasion of death rather than of life.

If we may believe the legends of former times, it was, a few centuries ago, not thought very mysterious or inexplicable for a lady to faint or even to die for love. It was not thought particularly worthy of note when two or more gentlemen strove with each other for the upper place in some fair one's affections. In the days of chivalry, it was nothing strange or uncommon for Knights errant to quarrel about the possession of a heart; to challenge to single combat; and at last to enter the lists and settle the dispute in the most gallant style.

But a very great change has taken place in society. A rapid

Title page and first page of text from the only known copy of the first edition of Holmes's novel (Burton Historical Collection, Detroit Public Library)

quently disappeared. The one contemporary review makes no mention of the possibility that Holmes's claim to having produced a "true narrative" was anything other than the conventional disclaimer of genteel fiction writers.

Belinda, the principal protagonist, is not the poor female victim of seduction, but rather the beautiful, selfish seducer of a series of young men. Disgraced after a broken engagement, Belinda again finds a public role and social acceptance as an enthusiastic speaker at religious gatherings. Among those who seek her advice is a married man, a merchant who "seldom looked an honest man in the face." His wooing of Belinda, and her acceptance, all in terms of pious and sanctimonious platitudes about divine love and morality, is a minor masterpiece of satire that must certainly have been intentional. Fortunately for Belinda, a young man conveniently besotted with her charms appears on the scene and, despite all

warnings and family opposition, marries her. Six weeks later Belinda produces a son. Although her husband forgives her, no one else does. She goes into a decline and, after a suitable edifying deathbed repentance, dies.

The narrator's voice is one of the charms and problems of the novel. By turns sophisticated and naive, bathetic and straightforward, sympathetic and disapproving, it leads the reader through a decade of Belinda's life. The focus is almost entirely on people, all of whom are portrayed from outside. Belinda is both a coquette and a hypocrite. While the author did not approve her treatment of men, it is her religious hypocrisy that the narrator's voice most strongly condemns. There are two frequently quoted paragraphs of scenic description, but in general the action is not specific to Canada West. The same events could have taken place in any rural community. Because so much of the detail appears to be deliberately exaggerated it is difficult to know whether the glimpse afforded of this particular society is accurate or not.

Perhaps the novel's greatest contribution to Canadian literary history comes from its resistance to simple labels. It is not a "pioneer" novel. The author, at least a third-generation North American, is writing in assured acceptance, and criticism, of what he perceives as an established society. There are no lyrical passages describing Canadian scenery and manners for the benefit of European readers, because the author was writing for his own community, not for outsiders. There are no Indians. The protagonists are not quaint or exotic; they are ordinary human beings whose

activities and emotions are common to many societies. The novel is evidence that early-nineteenth-century Canadian literature was more complex than twentieth-century Canadians have come to believe.

References:

Marilyn Davis, "Anglo-Boston Bamboozled on the Canadian Thames," *Journal of Canadian Fiction*, 2 (Summer 1973): 56-61;

F. C. Hamil, "A Pioneer Novelist of Kent County," *Ontario History*, 39 (1947): 101-113;

C. F. Klinck, Introduction to *Belinda, or The Rivals* (Toronto: Alcuin, 1970).

Joseph Howe

(13 December 1804 - 1 June 1873)

Thomas B. Vincent
Royal Military College of Canada

BOOKS: *The Speeches and Public Lectures of the Hon. Joseph Howe*, edited by William Annand, 2 volumes (Boston: Jewett, 1858); revised and edited by J. A. Chisholm (Halifax: Chronicle, 1909);
Poems and Essays (Montreal: Lovell, 1874);
The Heart of Howe, edited by D. C. Harvey (Toronto: Oxford University Press, 1939);
Western and Eastern Rambles: Travel Sketches of Nova Scotia, edited by M. G. Parks (Toronto: University of Toronto Press, 1973).

OTHER: "Sable Island," in *Sable Island*, by J. Bernard Gilpin (Halifax: Wesleyan Conference, 1858).

SELECTED PERIODICAL PUBLICATION—
UNCOLLECTED: "The Locksmith of Philadelphia," *Bentley's Miscellany*, 5 (1839).

Joseph Howe was a man of many talents, most of which he pursued with considerable distinction and success. He is most widely remembered as the leading politician of nineteenth-century Nova Scotia: he won responsible gov-

ernment for the province; served in its legislature through three decades (ultimately as premier); fought Confederation, but subsequently represented Nova Scotia in the federal parliament and became a minister of the federal government; in the end, he died at Government House, while serving as lieutenant governor of Nova Scotia. Moreover, his political life did not simply amount to struggles for power and authority; he was also a driving force behind Nova Scotia's economic development, contributing significantly to the building of railroads and the management of Atlantic fisheries. At the same time, particularly in the earlier part of his life, he was deeply concerned with the social and cultural character of the province. He was trained as a newspaperman, and under his editorship the *Novascotian* became a major instrument in articulating the social and cultural values of his society as it emerged from protective colonialism to responsible self-government. Howe contributed to that process directly through his own poetry and prose and indirectly through the encouragement he gave others and through his efforts as publisher to give local literary talent access to Nova Scotia readers.

Joseph Howe (lithograph by C. G. Crehen, 1854, from an 1851 portrait by T. Debaussy)

Howe was born in Halifax on 13 December 1804, the son of John Howe and his second wife, Mary Edes Howe. He came from a family of printers and newspapermen, so not unexpectedly his father and older brother took him into the family business as an apprentice at the age of thirteen. By the time he was sixteen he was writing reasonably competent verse and publishing it anonymously in various Halifax newspapers. From 1820 to 1825 he seriously considered becoming a poet. Looking back in later life he wrote, in a 26 May 1845 *Novascotian* editorial, "Politics was the termagant matron to whom we were married—Poetry was our first love, for whom we have ever since kept a corner of our heart; and, faith, we are not sure that it was not that small corner that preserved all the rest green and vigorous."

It was the newspaper business, not politics, that first displaced poetry as his prime interest. In January 1827 he and his cousin James Spike purchased the *Weekly Chronicle* (owned by an uncle, William Minns) and renamed it the *Acadian*. Within a year, however, a larger prize came

on the market. In December 1827 Howe bought the *Novascotian* from George Renny Young and soon turned it into the leading newspaper in the province. During this time he continued to write occasional lyrics for newspaper publication but made no pretentions to becoming a serious poet. His role lay in encouraging others, as he made clear in the 26 May 1845 editorial: "Though God has not vouchsafed to us the power 'to build the lofty rhyme,' nor the leisure to linger long upon even the lower slopes of Parnassus, he has given us . . . an abiding faith in the high vocation to which others have been called. . . . " In Howe's view literature was an integral part of developing a truly civilized society in colonial Nova Scotia, "blending the memories of the past with the prophetic anticipations of the future." Literature was a vehicle of vision and a means of nurturing man's best sentiments: "But for the poetic spirit, pervading and permeating through our very existence, by this time we should have been a savage—or a dead, dull clod of the political valley, without as much vitality as a turnip." Through his

Howe in the late 1860s (photograph by Notman; Public Archives of Nova Scotia)

newspaper and press, he actively promoted the work of Griselda Tonge, Alexander McDougall, Henry Clinch, Mary Jane Katzmann, Thomas Haliburton, John McPherson, and many others, in an effort to develop a tradition of local literature.

In spite of his preference for things cultural, Howe himself was drawn into the political arena as a result of a libel suit brought against him in 1835 by the government over a politically sensitive letter he published in the *Novascotian*. At his trial, he personally argued for freedom of the press, won his acquittal, and created a political base in the process. He was elected to the provincial assembly the following year and through the 1840s fought for responsible government for Nova Scotia. By 1848 that fight was won and Howe turned his attention to railway building. Through the 1850s he was involved in bitter partisan politics and in railway development; he

reached the height of his provincial political career serving as premier from 1860 to 1863.

The issue of the mid 1860s was Confederation, and Howe led opposition forces in Nova Scotia. As a "repeal" candidate, Howe ran and won election to the federal parliament in 1867. But by 1869 Howe recognized that Confederation would remain and accepted a position in the federal cabinet as secretary of state for the provinces. He served as a federal minister until his appointment to the lieutenant governorship of Nova Scotia in April 1873, two months before his death.

Howe's poetic output consisted for the most part of occasional lyrics and songs, with some didactic and descriptive verse. The two poems Howe considered his most serious works were "Melville Island" and "Acadia." The first, published in the *Weekly Chronicle*, 6 January 1826 (collected in *Poems and Essays*, 1874), is a reflective, philosophical poem dealing with the human condition in the historical and topographical context of a former prison site near Halifax. It demonstrates how things familiar to Nova Scotians may be viewed as part of universal human experience, and by implication argues that the experiences of life in Nova Scotia are not isolated and remote from the main stream of reality. "Acadia" (first published in *Poems and Essays* but probably written in the early 1830s) is also dominated by historical and topographical concerns but ultimately projects a vision of a brighter future in patriotic, sociopolitical terms. There is more of Howe the politician and less of Howe the philosopher in this poem. Unfortunately the social and political vision vested in the poem seems blurred and inconclusive, probably because the poem was left incomplete.

Howe's prose works, while competently written, are limited in their interests. His political works deal with issues that are now only of historical concern; his one known work of fiction, "The Locksmith of Philadelphia" (*Bentley's Miscellany*, 1839), is weak and flat. He appears at his best in the informal essay style of *Western and Eastern Rambles* (1973), which describe his travels through different parts of Nova Scotia. These pieces ran serially in the *Novascotian* from 1828 to 1831 and were partially patterned on William Cobbett's *Rural Rides* (1830). They describe the terrain, the people, and the way of life in rural Nova Scotia.

Howe's literary career, while limited and overshadowed by his political career, was nonetheless a significant part of the cultural growth of Nova Scotia in the 1830s and 1840s. But as a stimulus to literary activity, as a kind of cultural broker, he played an even more vital role in developing a sense of cultural cohesiveness and self-awareness in the society of early-nineteenth-century Nova Scotia. In Howe's eyes cultural and political growth moved together in a healthy society. "Responsibility" was not simply a matter of acquiring power; it was a question of social maturity that manifested itself as much in cultural activity as in political activity.

Bibliography:

T. B. Vincent, *Joseph Howe: Chronology of the Poems* (Kingston, Ont.: Loyal Colonies, 1980).

Biographies:

J. A. Roy, *Joseph Howe* (Toronto: Macmillan, 1935);

J. M. Beck, *Joseph Howe* (Kingston, Ont.: McGill-Queen's University Press, 1982).

Papers:

Howe's papers are at the Public Archives of Nova Scotia, Halifax; the National Archives of Canada, Ottawa; and at Harvard University.

John Hunter-Duvar

(29 August 1821 - 25 January 1899)

Paul Matthew St. Pierre
Simon Fraser University

BOOKS: *John à Var, Gentilhomme et Troubadour, His Lais* (Boston: Hodges, 1874);

The Enamorado: A Drama (Summerside, P.E.I.: Graves, 1879);

De Roberval, A Drama; also The Emigration of the Fairies, and The Triumph of Constancy, A Romaunt (St. John, N.B.: McMillan, 1888);

The Stone, Bronze and Iron Ages: A Popular Treatise on Early Archaeology (London: Sonnenshein / New York: Macmillan, 1892);

Annals of the Court of Oberon (London: Digby Long, 1895);

Hernewood: The Personal Diary of Col. John Hunter Duvar, June 6 to September 17, 1857; The Story of Anne of Hernewood, a Fascinating Lady; and The Emigration of the Fairies, edited by L. George Dewar (O'Leary, P.E.I., 1979).

John Hunter-Duvar (Public Archives of Prince Edward Island)

A master of the esoteric in verse and of the eccentric in life, John Hunter-Duvar is among the most curious of nineteenth-century Canadian writers, his writing itself often a kind of historical curiosity. His reputation in Canadian literature lies less in his books than in excerpts from them and in individual poems he placed in little magazines including the *Dominion Illustrated Monthly* and periodicals such as the *Maritime Monthly*, occasional verse that has since found its way into standard Canadian poetry anthologies and thus effectively turned an amateur into a literary figure of representative exception. His most qualitatively exceptional (and frequently anthologized) works are indeed his only works dealing emphatically with Canada as a fit place for poetic expression, *De Roberval* and *The Emigration of the Fairies* (published together in 1888) offering historically and fantastically romantic treatments of the rite of passage from Old World to New. Even his voluminous unpublished manuscripts are predominantly cosmic in character, quite independent of their place and time of composition.

As a transplanted British gentleman and amateur scholar who served his adopted country as a soldier and a civil servant, Hunter-Duvar regarded literature as essentially a recreational activity of early retirement and a re-creational activity in a large private library. Indeed, privacy was his Muse. Even though his writings circumnavigated the world of literature in tradition and convention, they did not find a haven in the actual (nor even in the romanticized) place of Canada, their place of departure, because to Hunter-Duvar Canada was concentrated into the island-within-the-island of his Prince Edward Island estate of

Hernewood and the microcosm of imagination into which he transformed it.

Born on 29 August 1821, the first son of John and Agnise Strickland Hunter, John Hunter, Jr. (who later added Duvar on his own), received his initial education in Newburgh, Scotland, his birthplace, and his higher education at Edinburgh University and possibly at the University of Aberdeen and the Sorbonne. In 1848 he married Anne Carter, a woman from Leamington, England, and thus entered into the first of a series of mysteries that would make up his life. The exact identity of Anne remains unclear, but the legend surrounding the squire and bard of Hernewood identifies her as an illegitimate cousin of Queen Victoria, forced into the respectability of marriage and into the role of a remittance woman. A note scribbled onto the back of Hunter-Duvar's will by a granddaughter provides the only documentary evidence to date for this sinister line to monarchy. A second mystery concerns the children of Anne and John Hunter: two died in childhood and, of the two who managed to reach adulthood, one became a writer whose permanent disappearance in New York in 1884 shocked the family; the other enjoyed a relatively peaceful existence in Charlottetown, P.E.I.

John Hunter, Jr., made his first contact with Canada shortly after leaving university, as a British correspondent and agent with the Associated Press of New York, shipping out his dispatches in sealed tins via the Cunard line to Halifax. Beginning in 1849 he made several trips to Canada before finally settling in Prince Edward Island in 1857, having made what would prove to be an irreversible progression from Halifax to Charlottetown, to Summerside, to Alberton, and ultimately to the Hernewood estate that was to be his kind of personal retreat house. (After having encountered a prominent Haligonian named John Hunter, he had his own name officially changed to John Hunter-Duvar by an 1859 act of parliament, the new surname having associations with the *troubadours et trouvères* and with the protagonist of his first collection of verse, *John à Var*, 1874.) Hunter-Duvar served as a militia officer in the Volunteer Force of Prince Edward Island until 1877, with the exception of the years 1863 to 1868, which he spent in the Halifax Artillery, becoming a justice of the peace upon his return to the island. Between 1879 and 1889 he held the position of dominion inspector of fisheries for the province.

Although he had earlier published articles on wildlife and ecology and had placed individual poems in such journals as the *Dominion Illustrated* and the *Maritime Monthly*, Hunter-Duvar did not publish his first book, *John à Var*, until middle age. The book virtually disappeared for the next century. This rare work is his most characteristic in its preoccupation with medieval concepts of poet and poetry, with lyrical form, regular meter, and rhythmic delivery, and with the precise bibliographic orientation of his private library of the obscure and the arcane. Intended for private circulation, the book positions its troubadour character and authorial persona within the intimacy of courtly verse. The series of songs concludes with "John à Var's Last Lai," in which the poet realizes that "Life may be joyous, even if life is death" and, in communion with his verse itself, "Dying as echo dies / Faint and more faint." In their romantically nostalgic perspective on the Middle Ages nudging the Renaissance, the poems making up the collection are somewhat too characteristically Victorian, but they do assume a special significance as expressions of Hunter-Duvar's consuming poetic interests and of the poetics that would be the foundation of all his remaining verse.

During his brief tenure as editor of the *Summerside Progress* (1875-1879), Hunter-Duvar composed his next book of verse, *The Enamorado* (1879), a poetic drama based on the historical life of a latter-day troubadour of fifteenth-century Spain, Mazias of Gallacia, and on the tragic intrigue in the court of Castilian Henry III. In its intermarriage of history and romance and in its perpetuation of Renaissance and Restoration dramatic forms and formulae, the play is typical of Hunter-Duvar's poetic output during what might be seen as the decade of his literary maturity (1879-1888). In his second important verse drama, *De Roberval*, the classic love triangle of *The Enamorado* becomes more complex and original, a ménage of an explorer, his homeland, and his new world. A somewhat respectful dedication to Algernon Charles Swinburne in *The Enamorado* is replaced in *De Roberval* with a much more heroic dedication to John A. Macdonald. Set in the expansive sixteenth-century court of Francis I, the latter play focuses on the "little king of Vimieu," Jean François de la Roque, Seigneur de Roberval, and on his expeditionary role in early Canadian colonization. Ultimately de Roberval must choose between his separate loyalties to king and to Canada, a decision that gives Hunter-Duvar occasion for some of his best verse:

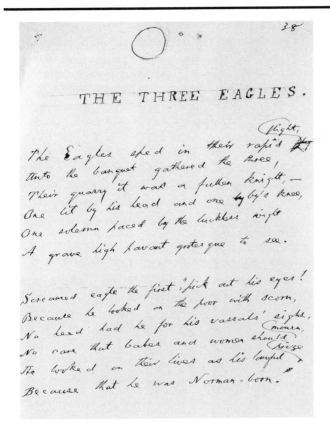

First page of Hunter-Duvar's manuscript for a poem that was collected in John à Var (1874); and the printed version, which
he pasted on a larger sheet and illustrated with pen and ink (Public Archives of Prince Edward Island)

This is the land where I had hoped to live,
And where I would have no regret to die.
A touch of tenderness, a clasp of grief,
Fingers the inner tendrils of my heart.
I have dreamed dreams that wanted but due time
To grow material and reality;
These for a time must yet remain in sleep.

The action of both this and the earlier work is essentially verbal, emphasizing that they are more dramatic poetry than poetic drama, that they are closet drama accommodating an exchange of beautifully formal speeches quite removed from life.

The two long poems published with *De Roberval* are somewhat more removed and considerably less moving. *The Emigration of the Fairies* is an allegory of Hunter-Duvar and his wife's passage from England to Canada, a mock-heroic account of the fantastic voyage of the fairies from the Old World to the New and of their settling at Hernewood, in Hunter-Duvar's library and lyrics. The poem is an important piece of Prince Edward Island folkloric literature and a good example of the poet's whimsically comic mode. In a later work, *Annals of the Court of Oberon* (1895), Hunter-Duvar conducted a Swiftian analysis of

Hernewood's fairy society, offering a satire on Anglo-Canadian Victorian mores and institutions. The other *De Roberval* companion piece, *The Triumph of Constancy*, is a romance about a faithless knight-errant, Sir Pallinor, who encounters his black white-magician wife in a series of seductive disguises before finally returning to her and to marital fidelity. Virtually all Hunter-Duvar's poems are the product of his thirty years of retirement in his crypto-library, neatly hidden away on the seven-hundred-acre Hernewood estate, which the poet, eccentrically sporting monocle and walking stick, professed to believe was the home of the fairies, as real to him as romantic fantasy itself.

The majority of Hunter-Duvar's works (including personal letters) remain in manuscript form in the Public Archives of Prince Edward Island. Besides the one scientific treatise Hunter-Duvar published, *The Stone, Bronze and Iron Ages* (1892), there are two incomplete scientific manuscripts, "Arctic Explorations" and "Footprints of the Peoples," together totaling more than one thousand pages. The Hunter-Duvar papers also contain two completed novels: "Meluran," a science fantasy about a Faustian count of sixteenth-century Venice, who in his quest for knowledge loses his daughter and spends the next three centuries searching for her around the globe; and "The Romance of the Second Empire," a Dickensian tale of socially star-crossed lovers in the France of Louis Napoleon, a story Hunter-Duvar finished shortly before his death. A third work of fiction survives in manuscript form, "Madame de Phillippippon," a novelette. Among Hunter-Duvar's poetic works are an eighty-thousand-line narrative satire in ottava rima (a fragment entitled "Atlantis") and a translation of a medieval Italian troubadour romance, "The Seven Lays of Lancelot." The most ambitious and impressive of Hunter-Duvar's unpublished projects is "The Drama at Linkum Hall," a cycle of seven plays (only the first three of which remain among the papers): "A Chance Father," "Call the Guard," "Fin de Siècle," "An Appic Lion," "Captain Hamlet," "Shepherdesses All," and "The Wrong Man." Hunter-Duvar illustrated many of his manuscripts with his own pen-and-ink drawings.

The little oeuvre of John Hunter-Duvar reveals far less about Canada and Canadian literature than about "A man who, with a harmless eccentricity, / In a rude country life sought his felicity" (*The Emigration of the Fairies*). Yet it is precisely within this unassuming oddity that his contribution to Canadian life and letters is to be found.

Bibliography:

Stephen C. Campbell, "John Hunter-Duvar: A Bibliographical Introduction, Checklist of His Works, and Selected Bibliography," M.A. thesis, University of New Brunswick, 1966.

Douglas Smith Huyghue

(23 April 1816 - 24 July 1891)

Gwendolyn Davies
Acadia University

BOOKS: *Argimou. A Legend of the Micmac*, as Eugene (Halifax: Courier, 1847); modern edition, edited by Gwendolyn Davies (Sackville, N.B.: Mount Allison University, 1977); *Nomades of the West; or, Ellen Clayton*, 3 volumes (London: Bentley, 1850).

SELECTED PERIODICAL PUBLICATIONS–
UNCOLLECTED: "Recollections of Canada. The Scenery of the Ottawa," *Bentley's Miscellany* (1849): 489-497;

"A Winter's Journey," *Bentley's Miscellany* (1849): 630-638;

"My First Winter in the Woods of Canada," *Bentley's Miscellany* (1850): 152-160;

"Forest Incidents–Recollections of Canada," *Bentley's Miscellany* (1850): 472-477.

Writer, artist, civil servant, and amateur anthropologist, Douglas Smith Huyghue enjoyed a career that spanned two continents. Known in Canada primarily as a novelist and a defender of native culture, Huyghue enjoyed a reputation in Australia as an artist and eyewitness to the Eureka Stockade uprising in the Ballarat goldfields in 1854.

Born in Charlottetown, Prince Edward Island, where his father, Lt. Samuel Huyghue, was stationed with the British Army, Samuel Douglas Smith Huyghue was christened in honor of the province's governor, Charles Douglas Smith. By 25 October 1817 his father was a half-pay officer living in Saint John, New Brunswick. Douglas Huyghue was probably educated at the Saint John Grammar School, but by November 1840 he seems to have been living in Halifax, where he submitted poetry to the *Halifax Morning Post & Parliamentary Reporter* under the pseudonym "Eugene." However, between October 1841 and January 1843 he was back in Saint John and, using the same pseudonym, was actively contributing poetry, short fiction, and an essay to the *Amaranth*, a literary periodical in that city. His novel *Argimou. A Legend of the Micmac* was serialized in the *Amaranth* between May and September 1842 and was sufficiently popular to be republished in book form in Halifax in 1847 and in serial form in the *Saint John Albion* in 1859-1860. The first Canadian novel to describe the 1755 expulsion of the Acadians, *Argimou* is also one of the first Canadian novels to denounce the process of cultural assimilation and deracination that had taken place as European settlement had intruded on native society. "We are the sole and only cause of their overwhelming misery, their gradual extinction," Huyghue's narrator notes of the Micmac and Milecete in the opening section of the novel, and in ensuing chapters Huyghue punctuates a rousing adventure story and romance with his hero's comparison of Indian life "unrestrained by penal codes, or chains, or strong dungeons" to so-called "civilized" society with its hypocrisy, conventionality, and dedication to progress. Huyghue's stock characterization, passionate prose, and reliance on coincidence tend to undermine the artistic strengths of his novel, but his dramatization of moral and historical issues, his integration of climate and geography into the plot, and his challenge to social complacency all make *Argimou* an important novel in pre-Confederation Canada.

Huyghue's interest in romantic primitivism and his celebration of "natural man" found practical expression in his association in the early 1840s with New Brunswick's Commissioner of Indian Affairs, Moses Henry Perley, and in his involvement in May 1843 in organizing an exhibition of Indian artifacts for a grand bazaar in Saint John sponsored by the Mechanics' Institute. His appointment in 1843 to the Boundary Commission surveying the line separating New Brunswick, Quebec, and Maine gave him expanded opportunities to experience both forest living and association with native peoples, for in his capacity as commissary agent, he set up a winter supply camp at Lake Isheganelshegek on the northwest branch of the Saint John River, traveled overland to Quebec, and journeyed the Saint John River by canoe. These experiences inform "A Winter's

ARGIMOU

A

LEGEND OF THE MICMAC

By "Eugene"

Halifax, N. S.

PRINTED AT THE MORNING COURIER OFFICE

1847

Title page for the first Canadian novel describing the forced exile of the Acadians

Journey," "My First Winter in the Woods of Canada," and "Forest Incidents–Recollections of Canada," three of four essays on Huyghue's appreciation of the Canadian wilderness published in *Bentley's Miscellany* of London in 1849 and 1850.

Huyghue completed his appointment with the Boundary Commission around 1845 and left New Brunswick for London in the late 1840s. He not only placed his four essays on the Canadian wilderness with *Bentley's Miscellany* but also published a three-volume novel, *Nomades of the West; or, Ellen Clayton,* with Bentley's in 1850. Outlining in the preface of this novel the same concerns about Indian deracination that had informed *Argimou,* Huyghue ended his preface with a plea for his novel: "It presents them [the Indians] to the reader as they were before their ranks were

thinned, or their spirit broken by aggression. May it awaken his sympathies in their behalf, and would that it might impel the spirit of philanthropy, which is the redeeming feature of the age, to devise some plan to rescue those perishing tribes."

Although the *Morning Post* of London described *Nomades of the West* as "a very pleasant book, with some vivid sketches of Indian life" (15 February 1850), the novel was not a financial success. Huyghue's failure to succeed in London as a writer undoubtedly led to his immigrating to Australia on the *Lady Peel* in 1852. Landing in Melbourne, he joined the permanent staff of the civil service and in August 1853 was appointed as a clerk in the Office of Mines in the Ballarat goldfields. Here he witnessed the Eureka Stockade uprising in 1854, recording his impressions in a watercolor, "The Eureka Stockade," now held by the Ballarat Fine Arts Gallery, in a series of other published illustrations, and in an unpublished memoir, "The Ballarat Riots," as "Pax" (Mitchell Library, State Library of New South Wales). Although Huyghue "could not shake off for many years a forlorn sense of exile" (as he wrote in "The Ballarat Riots"), he remained in Australia for the rest of his life. He held various civil service posts in Ballarat and Graytown and eventually moved to a position in the Department of Mines in Melbourne in 1876, two years before he retired in that city. Correspondence in the Reynell Eveleigh Johns Papers in the State Library of Victoria indicates that Huyghue maintained a creative interest in literature and natural history until his death in 1891.

Douglas Smith Huyghue once described his career as "chequered," but throughout it he maintained a consistent interest in Indian culture and social justice. From a Canadian perspective, his novels still stand as some of the earliest literary statements of social conscience written before Confederation.

References:

Gwendolyn Davies, Introduction to *Argimou. A Legend Of The Micmac* (Sackville, N.B.: Mount Allison University, 1977), pp. i-xiv;

A. W. Grieg, "Letters from Australian Pioneers," *Victorian Historical Magazine* (December 1927): 60-68–includes illustrations by Huyghue;

Janice Kulyk Keefer, *Under Eastern Eyes* (Toronto: University of Toronto Press, 1987), pp. 28, 68, 110-116;

Alan McCulloch, *Artists of the Australian Goldrush* (Melbourne: Lansdowne, 1977), pp. 39, 41, 114a, 116, 121-122, 139-140;

W. B. Withers, *History of Ballarat* (Ballarat, Australia, 1870).

Anna Jameson
(19 May 1794 - 17 March 1860)

Clara Thomas
York University

BOOKS: *A First or Mother's Dictionary for Children* (London: W. Darton, 1810-1830);

Cadijah; or, The Black Palace. A Tragedy (London, 1825);

Diary of an Ennuyée (London: H. Colburn, 1826; Philadelphia: E. Littell, 1826);

The Loves of the Poets, 2 volumes (London: Colburn, 1829); republished as *Memoirs of the Loves of the Poets* (Boston: Russell, Odiorne, 1833);

Memoirs of Celebrated Female Sovereigns, 2 volumes (London: Colburn & Bentley, 1831; New York: J. & J. Harper, 1832);

Characteristics of Women, 2 volumes (London: Saunders & Otley, 1832; New York: Saunders, 1832; enlarged edition, London: Saunders & Otley, 1833; enlarged again, 1836; New York: Saunders & Otley, 1837); republished as *The Heroines of Shakespeare* (New York: Wiley, 1846); republished as *Shakespeare's Heroines* (London: Bell, 1913; New York: Burt, 192-?);

The Beauties of the Court of King Charles the Second (London: H. Colburn, 1833; Philadelphia: Carey & Hart, 1834);

Visits and Sketches at Home and Abroad, 4 volumes (London: Saunders & Otley, 1834; New York: Harper, 1834);

Sketches of Germany (Frankfurt am Main: C. Jugel, 1837);

Winter Studies and Summer Rambles in Canada, 3 volumes (London: Saunders & Otley, 1838; New York: Wiley & Putnam, 1839; modern edition, Toronto: McClelland & Stewart, 1923);

Sketches of Italy (Frankfurt am Main: C. Jugel, 1841);

Anna Jameson (watercolor portrait; by permission of the Metropolitan Toronto Library, J. Ross Robertson Collection)

A Handbook to the Public Galleries of Art In and Near London (London: Murray, 1842);

Companion to the Most Celebrated Private Galleries of Art in London (London: Saunders & Otley, 1844);

Memoirs and Essays Illustrative of Art, Literature, and Social Morals (London: Bentley, 1846; New York: Wiley & Putnam, 1846);

Winter Journey to Niagara, an 1837 ink drawing by Jameson (by permission of the Royal Ontario Museum)

Sacred and Legendary Art, 2 volumes (London: Longman, Brown, Green & Longmans, 1848; Boston: Houghton, Mifflin, 1857);

Legends of the Monastic Orders (London: Longman, Brown, Green & Longmans, 1850; Boston & New York: Houghton, Mifflin, n.d.);

Legends of the Madonna (London: Longman, Brown, Green & Longmans, 1852; New York: Bowman, n.d.);

A Commonplace Book of Thoughts, Memories, and Fancies (London: Longman, Brown, Green & Longmans, 1854; New York: Appleton, 1855);

A Hand-Book to the Courts of Modern Sculpture (London: Bradbury & Evans, 1854);

Sisters of Charity (London: Longman, Brown, Green & Longmans, 1855; enlarged edition, 1855; Boston: Ticknor & Fields, 1857);

The Communion of Labour (London: Longman, Brown, Green, Longmans & Roberts, 1856);

Sketches of Art, Literature, and Character (Boston: Ticknor & Fields, 1857);

Memoirs of Early Italian Painters (London: Murray, 1859; Boston & New York: Houghton, Mifflin, 1894);

Studies, Stories, and Memoirs (Boston: Ticknor & Fields, 1859);

The History of Our Lord as Exemplified in Works of Art, by Jameson and Elizabeth Rigby, Lady Eastlake, 2 volumes (London: Longman, Green, Longman, Roberts & Green, 1864; New York: Longmans, 1890).

Editions and Collections: *Mrs. Jameson's Works*, 10 volumes (Boston: Ticknor & Fields, 1866);

The Writings on Art of Anna Jameson, edited by Estelle M. Hurll, 5 volumes (Boston: Houghton, Mifflin, 1896);

Early Canadian Sketches, edited by G. H. Needler (Toronto: Burns & MacEachern, 1958).

In a long, nineteenth-century writing career Anna Jameson established a durable reputation in three fields: art history, feminism, and travel writing. She is recognized as a pioneer art historian for her *Sacred and Legendary Art* (1848). Her various writings on women, particularly *Characteristics Of Women* (1832), her public lectures in 1855 and 1856 on working opportunities for women, and her influence as adviser and mentor on a group of influential early feminists assure her a place in the history of the women's movement in England. Her *Winter Studies and Summer Rambles in Canada* (1838), written after a nine-month stay in 1836-1837, has remained a classic in Canada.

Robert Sympson Jameson, the author's husband (portrait by J. W. L. Forster; by permission of the Law Society of Upper Canada)

Born in Ireland in 1794, Anna Murphy (later Jameson) took up her first post as governess, to the four small sons of the marquis of Winchester, in 1810 when she was sixteen. In 1819 she began an engagement with the Rowles family that first opened up the possibilities of travel writing to her. She accompanied them to the Continent in 1821, quickly becoming an avid traveler, a connoisseur of art galleries, and an intrepid sightseer. Back home in 1822 she became governess to the Littleton children, a post she retained until her marriage in 1825. While there she wrote her first works, including *Much Coin, Much Care*, a drama for children that was collected in *Visits and Sketches at Home and Abroad* (1834).

Robert Sympson Jameson of Ambleside, who became Upper Canada's first vice-chancellor—the province's highest legal post—and the first speaker of the legislature after the union of the Canadas, had courted Anna since before her continental trip in 1821. Though there was a strange, intermittent incompatability between them that they both recognized, they shared a love of literature and literary society, and for the first years of their marriage Jameson encouraged his wife's

writing ambitions. *Diary of an Ennuyée* (1826), a romanticized and fictionalized version of her first European trip, ends with the death of its heartbroken narrator-heroine. The book, its plan derived from Mme. (Anne) de Staël's popular novel *Corinne* (1807), was a sentimental Childe Harold's journey for adventure-hungry young ladies. It was a great success, and Jameson became the celebrity of the hour in London society.

By 1829 when her husband left England for a judgeship in Dominica, Jameson was making no secret of her unhappiness in marriage; she was also committed to a life of writing and travel. Her *Loves of the Poets* was published in 1829, *Memoirs of Celebrated Female Sovereigns* in 1831, and *The Beauties of the Court of King Charles the Second* in 1833. These books were designed for the great and growing multitude of women who were voracious in their appetite for entertaining and pleasantly improving reading material, and Jameson took every opportunity to stress the necessity for improved education for women. In 1832 her *Characteristics of Women*, a study of Shakespeare's heroines, made her name on the Continent and in the United States as well as in England. On a trip to Germany after its publication she was the center of an admiring group that included Ludwig Tieck and August Wilhelm von Schlegel, and she began a lifelong friendship with Ottilie von Goethe, the well-known poet's daughter-in-law. Her *Visits and Sketches at Home and Abroad* is basically the record of a continental trip taken in 1829. For it, as for her future works, Jameson was now assured of a reading public—she had become an established authoress.

In the fall of 1836 she reluctantly came to Canada to join her husband, who had become attorney general of Upper Canada (later Ontario). He had begun to build a house in Toronto in which to receive his wife, and he very much wanted her presence to confirm his own social stability in Toronto's tight little society. Anna had long since accepted their incompatibility; furthermore, she thoroughly enjoyed the life of a successful writer and a cosmopolitan traveler—and, as always, her own family needed her financial assistance. Life in Upper Canada held no attractions whatever for her; she came only because social and financial necessity dictated that she must. She stayed only nine months, from December 1836 to August 1837, but she did make a successful book out of her experiences.

Winter Studies and Summer Rambles in Canada is the account of the frigid winter of 1836-1837 spent in Toronto–"a little ill-built town on low land, at the bottom of a frozen bay. . . . I did not expect much, but for this I was not prepared"– and a summer tour through the southwestern part of the province, up to Sault Ste. Marie, and back to Toronto by way of Lake Huron and Manitoulin Island. The attraction of the first section, "Winter Studies," lies in the sharpness of Jameson's observations on society and politics in the young colony rather than in the unhappy picture she paints of herself as an unwilling outsider. In contrast, "Summer Rambles" is distinguished by her vivacity and adaptability as an enthusiastic traveler who formed quick, warm relationships with all manner of people. The critical and popular success of the book in both England and the United States confirmed her reputation as a writer to be taken seriously, though her outspoken remarks on the pettiness and pretentiousness of colonial society won her no admirers among Upper Canada's social elite.

In the last two decades of her life, Jameson's massive compendium of Christian art was her major work. Lavishly illustrated by her own drawings and etchings and those of her niece, Geraldine Macpherson, the series' final two volumes (*The History of Our Lord*, 1864) were completed after her death by her friend Elizabeth Rigby, Lady Eastlake, wife of Sir Charles Eastlake, the director of the National Gallery. *Sacred and Legendary Art*, as the entire series is usually called, is of continuing interest to art historians, particularly the volume *Legends of the Madonna* (1852).

In her last years Jameson spoke freely, and in public, on the crying need for expanded educational and employment opportunities for women. She was a potent influence on a group of ardent young feminists, among them Emily Faithfull and Bessie Raynor Parkes, who founded *The Englishwoman's Journal*, and Barbara Bodichon, one of the founders of Girton College. Anna Jameson's many works, particularly the many editions of *Characteristics of Women* and *Sacred and Legendary Art*, helped to form and direct popular taste in England and North America, both in her own day and considerably beyond it.

Letters:

Anna Jameson, Letters and Friendships, edited by Beatrice Erskine (London: Unwin, 1915; New York: Dutton, 1916);

Letters of Anna Jameson to Ottilie von Goethe, edited by G. H. Needler (London & New York: Oxford University Press, 1939).

Biographies:

Geraldine Macpherson, *Memoirs of the Life of Anna Jameson . . . by Her Niece* (London: Longmans, Green, 1878);

Clara Thomas, *Love and Work Enough: The Life of Anna Jameson* (Toronto: University of Toronto Press, 1968; London: Macdonald, 1968).

Reference:

Marian Fowler, *The Embroidered Tent: Five Gentlewomen in Early Canada* (Toronto: Anansi, 1982), pp. 137-180.

Papers:

The Goethe and Schiller Archives, Weimar, hold 410 letters to and from Ottilie von Goethe. The Wellesley College Library holds 78 letters to and from Elizabeth Barrett Browning. The Yale University Library houses 30 letters to and from Anna Jameson, and the Houghton Library, Harvard, has 26 letters from Jameson to various other people.

John Rodgers Jewitt

(21 May 1783 - 7 January 1821)

Neil K. Besner
University of Winnipeg

BOOKS: *A Journal, Kept at Nootka Sound* (Boston: Printed for the author, 1807); enlarged edition, edited by Norman L. Dodge (Boston: Goodspeed, 1831);

A Narrative of the Adventures and Sufferings, of John R. Jewitt; Only Survivor of the Crew of the Ship Boston, During a Captivity of Nearly Three Years Among the Savages of Nootka Sound: With an Account of the Manners, Mode of Living, and Religious Opinions of the Natives, by Jewitt and Richard Alsop (Middletown, Conn.: Loomis & Richards, 1815; modern edition, Toronto: McClelland & Stewart, 1974; Ramona, Calif.: Ballena, 1975; another modern edition, edited by Hilary Stewart, Vancouver: Douglas & McIntyre, 1987).

If John Rodgers Jewitt had complied with his father's wishes that he become a surgeon's apprentice, his life might have been unexceptional. By convincing his father, a blacksmith in Boston, England, to accept him as an apprentice to his trade in 1797, Jewitt unknowingly embarked on a course that six years later would find him spared from a massacre but wounded and taken captive by the Nootka Indians on the west coast of North America. The necessarily terse journal that Jewitt secretly kept from March 1803 to July 1805 while he lived with the Nootkas–written with the ink he made from the juice of berries–became the starting point for *A Narrative of the Adventures and Sufferings, of John R. Jewitt,* written by Richard Alsop (one of the best-known of a group of writers called the "Connecticut Wits") after he became fascinated by Jewitt's journal and interviewed Jewitt extensively over the course of a year. *A Narrative* was published in 1815, ten years after Jewitt's escape and the year of Alsop's death. Jewitt's *Journal,* published in 1807, was a pamphlet of forty-eight pages; Alsop's version is about two hundred pages long and is consciously modeled on Daniel Defoe's *Robinson Crusoe* (1719), providing us with a fascinating case study of how the literary conventions of the captivity

tale and the adventure story reshape a purportedly documentary account. At the same time, the details Jewitt reported in his *Journal* and, presumably, in his conversations with Alsop, give us a rich and complex portrait of the Nootkas and their chief, Maquinna. The *Narrative* proved popular enough to go through some nineteen editions before 1940 and to be translated into German in 1928; the latest editions in Canada (1987) and the United States (1975) attest to its continuing interest for contemporary readers.

Jewitt was born on 21 May 1783 in Boston, England, where he was educated in a private academy. In 1798 the family moved to Kingston-upon-Hull, where Jewitt's father worked in the shipyards. Four years later Jewitt sailed with Capt. John Salter on the *Boston,* an American ship, on a fur-trading voyage to the northwest coast of North America, arriving at Nootka Sound, on the west coast of Vancouver Island, British Columbia, on 12 March 1803. Jewitt was taken on by Salter as an armorer; his skills at repairing weaponry and working with iron were noted by Chief Maquinna on his visits to the *Boston.* Relations between Maquinna and Salter deteriorated when Maquinna returned a fowling piece Salter had given him as a gift, claiming that it was defective. Salter, angered, threw it down and called in Jewitt to repair it. On 22 March 1803 Maquinna and his men attacked the ship, killing all of the crew except for Jewitt and an American sailmaker from Philadelphia, John Thompson, whose life Jewitt saved by claiming Thompson was his father.

Jewitt and Thompson, eventually accepted and trusted enough by Maquinna to serve sometimes as his bodyguards, lived a split life with the Nootkas, trying on one hand to preserve their Christian practices and beliefs, and on the other being initiated into Nootka customs. In 1804, at Maquinna's insistence, Jewitt married a Nootka woman, the seventeen-year-old daughter of Chief Upquesta. Jewitt's report of the marriage in his *Journal,* in an entry dated 10 September 1804, is

Nootka Sound, on the west coast of Vancouver Island, and the Spanish-established settlement there, as they appeared before the Indian massacre of March 1803 (by permission of the Ministerio de Asuntos Exteriores, Madrid)

a paragraph in length; Alsop's version runs some six pages. In the *Journal,* Jewitt's account is quite straightforward, revealing his ambivalence and his pragmatic resolve to make the best of the situation:

> This day our chief bought a wife for me, and told me that I must not refuse her, if I did he would have both Thompson and myself killed. The custom of the natives on their being married is that the man and his wife must not sleep together for ten nights immediately succeeding their marriage. It is very much against my inclination to take one of these heathen for a partner, but it will be for my advantage whilst I am amongst them, for she has a father who always goes fishing, so that I shall live much better than I have at any time heretofore.

Alsop's reconstruction heightens the sense of Jewitt's ambivalence, dramatizing the tension between European and Indian norms, celebrating the Indian princess's beauty but also pointing out that "her complexion was, without exception, fairer than any of the women," and closing with Jewitt's reflections on his position: "With a partner possessing so many attractions, many may be apt to conclude, that I must have found myself happy, at least comparatively so; but far otherwise was it with me, a compulsory marriage with the most beautiful and accomplished person in the world, can never prove a source of real happiness, and in my situation, I could not but view this connection as a chain that was to bind me down to this savage land, and prevent my ever again seeing a civilized country."

In July 1805 the *Lydia,* commanded by Capt. Samuel Hill, arrived in Nootka Sound after Hill had learned of Jewitt's presence there, and Hill contrived to lure Maquinna aboard and then to hold him hostage to secure Jewitt and Thompson's release. Jewitt and Thompson remained on the *Lydia* for nearly two years, sailing to China with a cargo of furs, and reaching Boston, Massachusetts, in June 1807.

After Alsop published *A Narrative,* Jewitt sold copies of the book as he traveled around New England, hawking it from a handcart and singing "The Poor Armourer Boy," a song in five

verses commemorating his adventure. He also performed in James Nelson Barker's successful stage adaptation, *The armourer's escape; or, three years at Nootka,* in Philadelphia in 1817. Jewitt married Hester Jones in Boston on 25 December 1809; his wife and children lived in Middletown, Connecticut, Alsop's hometown, while Jewitt continued traveling around New England. On 7 January 1821 Jewitt died at the age of thirty-seven in Hartford, relatively unknown, although the *Narrative* had already appeared in six editions.

Little else is known about Jewitt's life after his return from captivity, save for a suggestion that Alsop found him a reticent interview. According to Karl P. Harrington, Theodore Dwight, Alsop's nephew, recalled that his uncle "had a peculiar taste for adventures and drew from Jewitt his story during repeated interviews, but complained of the difficulties he encountered from the small capacity of the narrator. 'If he had been a Yankee,' he used to say, 'I could have done much better.'" Dwight also recalls that Alsop "afterwards expressed a fear that he had done Jewitt more harm than good, for [Jewitt] became unsettled in his habits by his wandering life in selling the book." Jewitt's literary legacy, however—one of the earliest accounts of European contact with the Indians of the Pacific Coast—remains clearly valuable today; and the story of the evolution of *A Narrative,* from its origins in Jewitt's *Journal* to Alsop's more consciously literary reconstruction, is as fascinating in its way as are the rich details of Jewitt's memorable report of his captivity.

References:

Karl P. Harrington, *Richard Alsop: "A Hartford Wit"* (Middletown, Conn.: Wesleyan University Press, 1969);

Maurice Hodgson, "Initiation and Quest: Early Canadian Journals," *Canadian Literature,* 38 (Autumn 1968): 29-40;

Edmond S. Meany, Jr., "The Later Life of John R. Jewitt," *British Columbia Historical Quarterly,* 4 (1940): 143-161;

Hilary Stewart, Annotations to *A Narrative of the Adventures and Sufferings, of John R. Jewitt* (Vancouver: Douglas & McIntyre, 1987).

Adam Kidd
(1802? - 6 July 1831)

Mary Lu MacDonald

BOOK: *The Huron Chief, and Other Poems* (Montreal: Herald and New Gazette, 1830); modern edition [of *The Huron Chief* alone], edited by D. M. R. Bentley (London, Ont.: Canadian Poetry, 1987).

In a social milieu that still considered literature as a leisure occupation for ladies and gentlemen, Adam Kidd stood out for several reasons. Although he did publish anonymously and under a pseudonym he, in effect, mocked that gentlemanly convention by openly acknowledging authorship almost immediately. He was also only the second writer in the Canadas (now Ontario and Quebec) to break with the socially accepted convention of anonymity by having his name printed on the title page of a book of his own work. He tried, unsuccessfully, to make a living by writing. Kidd was a *poète engagé* whose personality and experience illuminate everything he wrote, although he lived in a community that valued authors who kept a respectable distance between themselves and their work. Had he lived longer, he might or might not have been a great poet, but he certainly would always have been an interesting one.

Kidd was born (probably in 1802) in Tullynagee, Northern Ireland, the son of Alexander Kidd (his mother's name unknown). There is no concrete evidence as to when he arrived in Canada. He may have immigrated with his father about 1818 or arrived at any time between then and 1824, when he first began to publish lyrics in the *Quebec Mercury*.

He was accepted by George Mountain, bishop of Quebec, for tutoring as one of a group doing preparatory studies for the Church of England priesthood, but was dismissed as unfit for the ministry. It seems obvious that he was, indeed, temperamentally unsuited to a clerical role; however, scholarly views of the termination of his theological studies have been influenced by marginal notes in the copy of the *The Huron Chief* in the Baldwin Room of the Metropolitan Toronto Reference Library. The library's copy was

Adam Kidd (pen-and-ink drawing by Edwin Heaton; by permission of the Metropolitan Toronto Public Library)

the property of a Kidd contemporary, Rev. Job Deacon, whose handwritten comments that Kidd was "first attracted by a squaw" and fell from "a Mountain" because of his "own foolish wayward inclination" have led modern scholars to put two and two together and assume that the dismissal was because of involvement with an Indian girl. There is no evidence to support this hypothesis, but it seems to fit the persona the poet created for himself. Certainly he appears to have loved, poetically, the many young women to whom his lyrics are often dedicated.

Kidd's whereabouts and means of support in the next few years are matters for conjecture. He seems to have done some traveling, since the datelines to various poems place him on both the Ottawa and St. Lawrence rivers, and also to have been in Montreal, where he was associated with the radical Irish newspaper the *Vindicator*. His poetry, usually signed by the pseudonym Slievegallin, appeared in several newspapers and in the Philadelphia periodical the *Irish Shield*. In 1829 he began a tour through Upper Canada (Ontario) to gather subscriptions for his projected book, the formal prospectus for which had appeared in June. Kidd's journey through Upper Canada is relatively easy to follow since he contacted the newspaper office in each community. The editors obligingly mentioned him in positive terms, along with the title of his planned book and a note as to where subscriptions could be left.

After the publication of *The Huron Chief* in February 1830, the book was widely noticed and, except for one article in the *Montreal Gazette*, generally praised. One of Kidd's principal sources had been James Buchanan's *Sketches of the History, Manners, and Customs of the North American Indians* (1825); however, Kidd did not approve of Buchanan's proposal (he was the British consul in New York) to allow the United States free navigation of the St. Lawrence River, and he attacked Buchanan on this subject in a footnote. In early March two of Buchanan's sons and another man attacked Kidd with cudgels on the street in Montreal. The poet seems to have defended himself with the aid of passersby and escaped with only his dignity hurt. Letters to the editor in Montreal papers presented various versions of the affair in which one or the other party emerged as the victor.

In the summer of 1830 Kidd again traveled to Upper Canada, presumably delivering copies of his book, and also doing promotional work for a projected new work on the "tales and traditions" of North American Indians, to be centered on the life of a famous chief, Red Jacket. Kidd's health deteriorated rapidly. While in Kingston in October he suffered a lung hemorrhage. When well enough to travel, early in the new year, he returned to Quebec to prepare for a sea voyage that might restore his health, but he died of tuberculosis in Quebec City early in July 1831.

Perhaps because of the title poem's subject matter, as well as Kidd's romantic life story and antiestablishment reputation, *The Huron Chief* has received more attention from modern critics than other works by "one book" authors of the early nineteenth century. The actual events of the long poem are simple. The poet-narrator travels to the Lake Huron area, where he encounters the wise Chief Skenandow and his band, who live in idyllic natural surroundings. Whites attack. Their leaders are captured but released at Skenandow's insistence. They return to ambush and kill all the Indians, including Skenandow. The text includes much information about Indian history and customs, derived from various sources, as well as an extensive description of the Great Lakes area. The poet, as an oppressed outsider, identifies completely with his Indian subjects. Skenandow is almost the archetype of the "noble savage," a familiar figure in European literature of the late eighteenth and early nineteenth centuries, and the scenery, complete with ruins, fits European criteria for romantic beauty. The poet proudly acknowledged his debt to Lord Byron and the Irish poet Thomas Moore.

Thirty-seven short poems complete the volume. Some of these are on Irish subjects, five are elegies, and almost half are dedicated to various women. Kidd's eighteen uncollected poems, published in newspapers, maintain about the same balance. The most frequently quoted of those in the book are poems that celebrate Byron and the exiled Napoleon.

Kidd was a competent poet who used varied verse forms to great effect in his longer works. When he identified with a subject, as with Byron, Napoleon, and the Indians, and when he had actually seen the places he described, the strength of his emotional response is so winning that the reader readily accepts minor poetic flaws. One wonders what he would have achieved as a poet had he lived beyond the age of twenty-nine.

References:

D. M. R. Bentley, Introduction and notes to *The Huron Chief* (London, Ont.: Canadian Poetry, 1987);

C. F. Klinck, "Adam Kidd–an Early Canadian Poet," *Queen's Quarterly*, 65 (Autumn 1958): 495-506.

William Kirby

(13 October 1817 - 23 June 1906)

Patricia Monk
Dalhousie University

BOOKS: *The U. E., A Tale of Upper Canada* (Niagara, Ont., 1859);

The Chien D'Or. The Golden Dog: A Legend of Quebec (New York & Montreal: Lovell, Adam, Wesson, 1877); revised as *The Golden Dog (Le Chien D'or): A Romance of Old Quebec* (Toronto: American News, 1925); abridged by D. C. Woodley (Toronto: Macmillan, 1944);

Canadian Idylls (Welland, Ont.: Tribune, 1884);

Annals of Niagara (Welland, Ont.: Tribune, 1896);

Reminiscences of A Visit to Quebec. July, 1839 (N.p., 1903).

William Kirby reportedly (according to Lorne Pierce) arrived in Canada with only a rifle and a trunkful of books, and this luggage accurately represents his personality. In his career, literature is consistently wrenched into the service of political activity. The results, not always happy as far as the literary works are concerned or effective as far as the political activity is concerned, add up to an unambiguous portrait of a man of letters who, without having any particular talent as a writer of either prose or verse, nevertheless managed to produce one of the most popular books of his time.

Born on 13 October 1817 in Kingston upon Hull, in the North Riding of Yorkshire, England, William Kirby was the fourth child and only son of John and Charlotte Kirby. He arrived with his family in the United States as a youngster of fifteen. His father found work as a journeyman tanner in Cincinnati, and he apprenticed Kirby to the same trade, as well as inculcating into the boy his own Tory principles (which can be summed up as "Fear God and honour the King"). In his free time, Kirby managed to study with Alexander Kinmont, a well-known local teacher, educating himself informally but thoroughly in classical and modern languages and in English literature. In his privately printed *Reminiscences of A Visit to Quebec. July, 1839* (1903), Kirby records his agitation at the prospect of an American invasion of Canada, following the unsuccessful rebellions in

Upper and Lower Canada in 1837, and cites this as his reason for leaving the United States for Canada in 1839. After brief visits to Niagara (later to be renamed Niagara-on-the-Lake), Toronto, and Montreal, he arrived in Quebec City for the visit that is the subject of *Reminiscences*. He records that he was "in love with the old capital" and "might easily have been persuaded to stay there forever." In fact, he returned almost at once to Niagara and settled there, first as a tanner, and later as editor of the *Niagara Mail*, one of the several local newspapers. He married Eliza Whitmore, daughter of an important and well-connected local family, in 1847 and spent the rest of his life, until his death in 1906, with her and their two sons in Niagara.

Although there is no indication of any previous attempts to write seriously for publication, Kirby began to write and publish verse and prose almost as soon as he was settled in Niagara. His first known publication is the poem "On the Sickness and Retirement of His Excellency Lord Metcalfe from the Government of Canada, November 1845," which was first published in the *Niagara Chronicle* and later reprinted in *Canadian Idylls* (1884). Apart from this poem and his major works, his output consisted largely of broadsheets and pamphlets (often privately printed). To judge from the samples available, his prose is stylistically unremarkable, and his verse is flat-footed.

Kirby's first major work, however, was a poem, *The U*[nited]. *E*[mpire]., *A Tale of Upper Canada*, which appeared in 1859, although the author's preface claims it was written in 1846. Curiously, Kirby's name does not appear on the title page. Beginning as a pastoral tale of the experience of emigration from England to Canada, complete with a glowing eulogy of life in the Ontario bush, the poem mutates to an epic narrative of the Loyalist opposition to the Mackenzie rebellion in 1837, celebrating the heroism of those who took part in "Prescott fight." The poem, which follows the fortunes of Walwyn and his

William Kirby in 1880 (C 5312, National Archives of Canada)

sons Ethwald and Eric, is rambling and discursive, so that it is sometimes difficult to keep track of what is happening, or where, and who is speaking. Part of this discursiveness is due to a reluctance to leave anything out: for example, two long interpolated narratives–one by Ranger John (concerning his early experiences) and one by an escaped black slave from the United States (concerning the torments he has suffered and the loss of his wife and children)–while they are both interesting in themselves, slow down the development of the main story. Moreover, Kirby has encumbered himself with much of the paraphernalia of classical and Renaissance epic narrative. He begins, for example, with an invocation to his "woodland Muse" and employs, so far as his command of language will permit, an archaic and po-

etic diction. He does take, however, a rather slapdash attitude to other epic conventions–by his choice of couplets as the verse form (for his "Cantos" turn out to be groups of stanzas, and the stanzas in turn are merely groups of couplets) and by choosing to begin not in medias res, as convention would suggest, but at the end (so that the whole thing is in flashback, which does not add to its clarity). Beyond this, the poem is hampered by sheer linguistic ineptitude (there are lines that would suggest to the uninstructed reader that English was not Kirby's native language), as well as by a very poor ear for rhythm. Nevertheless, however clumsy it may appear in execution, *The U. E.* is unmistakably a sincere and passionate exposition of the Tory Loyalist vision of the nation of Canada–its people and its land, and their part in

JOHN KIRBY
1863

CHARLOTTE KIRBY

WILLIAM KIRBY
1850

MRS. WILLIAM KIRBY
1884

Kirby with his parents and wife, Eliza, née Whitmore (from Lorne Pierce, William Kirby: The Portrait of a Tory
Loyalist, *1929)*

the "United Empire"–that inspired both Kirby and those for whom he wrote.

Much the same vision forms the foundation for *The Chien D'Or* (1877), the work for which Kirby is chiefly remembered. This text has had rather a complex history, to the extent that no definitive edition is yet available, since Kirby had no chance to correct the first edition, and subsequent editions were altered by publishers' editors (chiefly by condensing it). Dealing with *The Chien D'Or* requires a certain amount of critical caution, for calling it a novel, as most critics tend to do, invites comparisons that can only do the work great injustice, since the term is commonly used to include works to which *The Chien D'Or* bears only a very distant relationship. What Kirby writes in *The Chien D'Or*, and what he suggests by his subtitle *A Legend of Quebec*, is a classic example of the prose romance, whose great practitioners were Sir Walter Scott and Alexandre Dumas, and whose antecedents are such works as Sir Philip Sidney's *Arcadia* (1590) and Robert Greene's *Pandosto* (1588), not the novels of Daniel Defoe, Samuel Richardson, and Henry Fielding. Nevertheless, Kirby differs from Scott. Whereas Scott, who was a novelist as well as a "romancer," carried over the skills developed in his novels–such as *Heart of Midlothian* (1818)–into his romances–such as *Ivanhoe* (1819)–Kirby is clearly a romancer pure and simple: someone in the grip of a compulsion to tell a story, but without the necessary artistic talents, techniques, or disci-

Kirby in 1860 (from Lorne Pierce, William Kirby: The Portrait of a Tory Loyalist, *1929)*

plines to produce a great work of literary art.

In his story of the ill-fated love of Amélie de Repentigny for the brave and noble Colonel Philibert, son of the Bourgeois Philibert (an important and influential merchant), in the early days of New France, Kirby indiscriminately incorporates history, legend, and pure fiction. Characteristically, in accordance with its nature as a romance, the story is remote in setting (in this case, remoteness is achieved by going back in time); loose in structure (the narrative moves slowly, indirectly, and does not consistently build toward the climactic death of the Bourgeois Philibert at the hands of Le Gardeur, Amélie's brother); full of digressions (even in the modern, shortened edition Kirby can take as much as seven pages of small print to introduce a minor character such as Caroline de St. Castin); and melodramatic in plot (for Le Gardeur's impulsive killing of the Bourgeois inevitably leads to the separation of Amélie and her fiancé and to her death from grief). The characters are idealized (Amélie and Colonel Philibert are paragons of virtue and honor); stereotyped

in their arrangement as pairs of opposites (the good Amélie and the wicked Angélique, the good Bourgeois and the wicked Intendant, the good Pierre Philibert and the weak, rather than wicked, Le Gardeur); and sentimentalized (especially in the character of the "wronged" Caroline de St. Castin).

The ethic of the story is governed by the code of chivalry that demands that the women be "virtuous" and the men "honorable," which produces not only a certain rigidity and lifelessness about the good characters but also a certain amount of irony where Angélique (a greedy, ambitious murderess, who is nevertheless virtuous because she is sexually pure) and the members of the Grand Company (*La Friponne,* followers of the Intendant) are concerned. It is hard to say whether Kirby appreciated this irony, or whether he simply took it over as part of the borrowed chivalric tradition. The romance characteristics, which must be considered faults if judged by the criteria applicable to the novel, are, however, precisely the qualities that enabled *The Chien D'Or* to seize the popular imagination in Kirby's own time and even today render it quite readable. For the romance, at least in its more naive manifestations, is primarily a transmitter of the writer's passion for his subject, and Kirby's subject was one in which he saw all the ideals of his political convictions, literary background, and personal temperament acted out. *The Chien D'Or* presents itself, therefore, as the vision of a passionate imagination that desired to share its vision and strove to do so to the best of its limited artistic ability.

While working on *The Chien D'Or,* as well as subsequently to its publication, Kirby had continued to write and publish verse, which appeared either in newspapers and periodicals, or as broadsheets or pamphlets. By 1884 the quantity and the quality of these poems appeared to the poet to merit a more permanent incarnation, and the collected poems appeared as a volume under the title *Canadian Idylls* (a second edition followed ten years later). The term "idylls," which may perhaps suggest Tennyson's *Idylls of the King* (1859), is somewhat misleading, for although Kirby's longer poems (for example, "The Queen's Birthday") in the volume have been described as narrative, they are not narrative in the same sense as Tennyson's *Idylls* but instead are discursive anecdotes arranged in a complicated interlocking pattern. The volume includes, in addition to the longer poems, some shorter poems (such as "The

Sparrows"), eighteen sonnets on various subjects, and a few translations. A poetic style similar to that of *The U. E.* characterizes the longer poems, and the sonnets are approximately Petrarchan, with considerable freedom of rhyme scheme in the sestet, revealing, regrettably, that in many instances, Kirby's ear for the sound of what he was writing is somewhat less than perfect. There is, however, in these poems a quality similar to the quality of the storytelling of *The Chien D'Or*. They are "naive"–innocent of irony and aesthetic distance–and hence reveal the poet's personality, with brutal candor, by reason of their lack of artistic skill (since without such skill, no poetic persona can plausibly be constructed).

The poems and *The Chien D'Or* of William Kirby are naturally of considerable interest to the literary historian, for they are valuable indicators of the temper of the times at a crucial moment in Canadian history. Nevertheless, their intrinsic interest is not only historical. They are also important to the student of form, for Kirby's attempts to accommodate his Canadian experience within his European models illustrate precisely the stylistic problems of early Canadian literature, which other, more skilled, writers and poets were to solve. Above all, however, Kirby's literary efforts enable us to encounter through them his unique personality. There is a certain endearing gallantry about his attempts to enrich the society that was his ideal by creating monuments to it in literature, as well as a solid Yorkshire stubbornness in his persistent efforts to master a medium that was not natural to him.

Letters:

Alfred, Lord Tennyson and William Kirby: Unpublished Correspondence, edited by Lorne Pierce (Toronto: Macmillan, 1929).

Biographies:

William Renwick Riddell, *William Kirby* (Toronto: Ryerson, 1923);

Lorne Pierce, *William Kirby: The Portrait of a Tory Loyalist* (Toronto: Macmillan, 1929).

Louis-Armand de Lom d'Arce, Baron de Lahontan

(9 June 1666 - 1715?)

Camille R. La Bossière
University of Ottawa

BOOKS: *Nouveaux Voyages de Mr le baron de Lahontan, dans l'Amérique Septentrionale* (The Hague: Frères l'Honoré, 1703; revised and enlarged edition, The Hague: Charles Delo, 1706);

Mémoires de l'Amérique Septentrionale, ou La Suite des voyages, volume 2 of *Nouveaux Voyages* (The Hague: Frères l'Honoré, 1703); translated with *Nouveaux Voyages* as *New Voyages to North-America* (London: Printed for H. Bonwicke, T. Goodwin, M. Wotton, B. Tooke & S. Manship, 1703);

Supplément aux voyages du baron de Lahontan, ou l'on trouve des dialogues curieux entre l'auteur et un sauvage de bon sens qui a voyagé, volume 3 of *Nouveaux Voyages* (The Hague: Frères l'Honoré, 1703); revised by Nicolas Gueudeville as *Dialogues de Monsieur le baron de Lahontan et d'un sauvage, dans l'Amérique* (Amsterdam: Veuve de Boeteman / London: D. Mortier, 1704);

Collection Oakes. Nouveaux Documents de Lahontan sur le Canada et Terre-Neuve/New Documents by Lahontan Concerning Canada and New Foundland [French and English on opposite pages in same volume], edited by Gustave Lanctôt (Ottawa: Patenaude, 1940).

Editions: *New Voyages to North America* [the 1703 translation of volumes 1 and 2 of *Nouveaux Voyages*], enlarged by Reuben Gold Thwaites, 2 volumes (Chicago: McClurg, 1905);

Dialogues Curieux . . . et Mémoires de l'Amérique Septentrionale [volumes 2 and 3 of *Nouveaux Voyages*], edited by Gilbert Chinard (Baltimore: Johns Hopkins Press / Paris: Margraff / London: Oxford University Press, 1931);

Voyages [selections from the 3 volumes of *Nouveaux Voyages*], edited by Stephen Leacock (Ottawa: Graphic, 1932);

Dialogues avec un sauvage [volume 3 of *Nouveaux Voyages*], edited by Maurice Roelens (Paris: Sociales, 1973).

Louis-Armand de Lom d'Arce, Baron de Lahontan, is chiefly remembered for his contribution to the Enlightenment ideology of "the noble savage." While the notions promoted by Lahontan do not originate with him, the currency that his sometimes inventive writings enjoyed throughout eighteenth-century Europe assures him of a place in cultural history. His accounts of the New World continue to find a sympathetic readership among ethnologists and historiographers of a mind with Jules Michelet. According to Maurice Roelens, Lahontan's privileging of "la vie sauvage" (the untamed life), over a life of artificial constraint, advances "la fraternelle identité de l'homme" (the brotherly identity of man).

Born on 9 June 1666 in Mont-de-Marsan, France, in the Basses-Pyrénées, Lahontan was the only child of Isaac de Lom d'Arce, second Baron de Lahontan, and Jeanne-Françoise née Le Fascheux de Couttes, the sister of a curate well known at the Court. The death of Isaac, an accomplished but fiscally imprudent engineer, left mostly debts and lawsuits for the son to inherit in 1674. Having to look to his own future, Lahontan joined the Régiment de Bourbon as a cadet; and, in the hope of gaining more rapid promotion, he requested a transfer to the Marine Guard in 1681. It was as a marine lieutenant that Lahontan, at age seventeen, sailed from La Rochelle to Quebec in the troopship *Tempête*, arriving in November 1683.

The story of Lahontan's life in North America is well stocked, thanks in great part to his account of it in *Nouveaux Voyages . . . dans l'Amérique Septentrionale* (1703). Lahontan spent his first winter in New France billeted at Beaupré, whiling away the months reading classical authors and hunting with a party of Algonquin youths. He was ordered to Ville-Marie (Montreal) in the summer of 1684 and participated in the disastrous expedition to Fort Frontenac (Kingston) led by Lefèbvre de La Barre. After a winter at Ville-Marie and a posting to the nearby Fort Chambly, Lahontan was assigned to Boucherville, where he

Frontispiece and title page for the second edition (1706) of Lahontan's major work, originally published in 1703

remained till the spring of 1687. Reading Anacreon, Homer, Lucian, and Petronius, and hunting with the Algonquin, in whose language he came to acquire some fluency, continued to be his principal winter occupations. Late in the summer of 1687 Lahontan took part in the Marquis de Denonville's campaign against the Iroquois. Immediately thereafter, and much to his frustration, Lahontan's leave to return home to attempt a salvage of what remained of the family estate was canceled. Instead Lahontan was assigned the command of Fort Saint Joseph (near Port Huron, Michigan), where he arrived, after a near-fatal sightseeing excursion at Niagara

Falls, in September of 1687.

The following spring and summer found Lahontan away from his command. While at Michillimakinak, on the north shore of Lake Huron, he had occasion to hear from survivors of Sieur de La Salle's ill-fated Louisiana expedition; and during an otherwise profitless raid against the Iroquois, he met Kondiaronk (whose sobriquet was "Le Rat"), the wily Huron chief who succeeded in subverting French efforts to bury the hatchet with the Five Nations in 1688 and who would come to serve as the model for the enlightened Adario of Lahontan's *Dialogues Curieux* (in *Supplément aux voyages*, 1703). In response to the news of Iroquois incursions that greeted Lahontan's return to his command, he ordered the burning of Fort St. Joseph and retired to Michillimakinak. In the period from September 1688 to May 1689, according to Lahontan's *Nouveaux Voyages*, he explored the Wisconsin and Mississippi rivers, and discovered La Rivière Longue, with its peoples, the Eokoros, the Esanapes, and the Gnacsitares.

Lahontan found his way back to Quebec in October 1689, where he spent the winter as a guest in the chateau of the new governor, Louis de Buade de Frontenac. Another cancellation of his leave to return home seriously disappointed Lahontan the following spring. While his understanding of *les sauvages* made Lahontan too valuable to spare, his awareness of the perils attendant on heading a delegation of peace to the Five Nations prompted him to decline the mission proposed by Frontenac. Instead Lahontan continued to serve as the governor's companion. In October 1690 he witnessed the defeat of William Phipps at Quebec; and, to his delight, he was entrusted with dispatches announcing that victory to the French court.

The high expectations Lahontan brought home with him aboard the *Fleur-de-Mai* met with disappointment. A knighthood (Order of St. Lazarus) and a promotion to the rank of captain of a company of marines gave little consolation to a Lahontan bedeviled by lawyers and chagrined by his orders to return to New France before the coming of winter. Nor did Lahontan find pleasing, finally, the prospect of the marriage arranged for him by Frontenac in the Quebec winter of 1691-1692. At the last moment, he declined the hand of Geneviève d'Amours. The late summer of 1692 saw Lahontan's return voyage to France with his plan for the defense of the Great Lakes. On the way his ship, the *Sainte-Anne*, put in at Plaisance (Placentia, Newfoundland), where Lahontan led a group of Basque fishermen in their efforts to repel an incursion by five English ships. The valor shown in that engagement earned Lahontan a promotion to king's lieutenant; but this latest advancement also brought with it a posting to Placentia. And the refusal of his ambitious plan of defense did nothing to diminish Lahontan's frustration. Unhappy at Placentia, Lahontan responded imprudently to his unjust treatment at the hands of its governor, M. de Brouillan, who subsequently submitted a report that seriously compromised Lahontan before the home authorities. Fearing eventual arrest and imprisonment in the Bastille, Lahontan secretly fled Newfoundland for Portugal, arriving at Viana in January 1694.

Relatively little is known of Lahontan's life as an expatriate. Visits to Copenhagen and Hamburg followed a voyage from Portugal to Holland in 1694. That same year, he offered to supply the French government with valuable information on Louisiana. But that intelligence, on examination by officials, was judged to be inauthentic. During the late 1690s Lahontan found himself lost in a maze of ambiguous allegiances. He volunteered to spy for France while in Spain, and submitted two memoirs, "Abrégé instructif des affaires du Canada" and "Ebauche d'un projet pour enlever Kebec et Plaisance" (both published in *Collection Oakes*, 1940), to British Secretary-of-War William Blathwayt. It was also during this period that Lahontan spent the better part of a year in a Swedish prison. As he asked himself in "L'Auteur au Lecteur," written in London (and published in the 1931 edition of *Dialogues Curieux*), "Quelle route suivray-je donc pour me tirer du Labirinte où je me trouve?" (What path will I follow then to take me out of the labyrinth where I find myself?) While at The Hague in 1702, he deposited with a local bookseller the manuscript he had developed from notes taken during his years in North America. The three volumes that publicized Lahontan's life of displacement and discovery and thus made his name appeared in the following year.

The first of the three volumes, *Nouveaux Voyages . . . dans l'Amérique Septentrionale*, dedicated to Frederick IV of Denmark, consists of twenty-five letters that purport to have been written in the period 1683-1694. The chronicle they give of life in New France is salted with witticisms, chiefly at the expense of Aristotle's logic, the learned professions, the Jesuits, women, and zealous curates. In letter 14 Lahontan relates his famous "Voyage à la Rivière Longue," which belongs, in the view of Roelens, to "la tradition du *Voyage imaginaire*." *Mémoires de l'Amérique Septentrionale*, the second volume, is a journal of Lahontan's observations on that country's peoples, institutions, customs, geography, flora, and fauna. The frontispiece, picturing an Amerindian brandishing a bow and arrow and standing with one foot on a code of law, the other on a crown and scepter, allegorizes Lahontan's ruling theme: "*Et leges et sceptra territ*" (To the terror of laws and kings). As Gilbert Chinard points out, the idea underlying Lahontan's *Mémoires* corresponds to Jean-Jacques

NEW

VOYAGES

TO

North-America.

Giving a full Account of the Customs, Commerce, Religion, and strange Opinions of the Savages of that Country.

WITH

POLITICAL REMARKS upon the Courts of *Portugal* and *Denmark*, and the Present State of the Commerce of those Countries.

Never Printed before.

WRITTEN

By the Baron LAHONTAN, Lord Lieutenant of the *French* Colony at *Placentia* in *Newfoundland*: Now in *England*.

VOL. II.

LONDON:

Printed for H. *Bonwicke* in St. *Paul's* Church-yard ; T. *Goodwin*, M. *Wotton*, B. *Tooke* in *Fleetstreet* ; and S. *Manship* in *Cornhil*, 1703.

Title page for volume 2 of the first translation of Lahontan's
Nouveaux Voyages

Rousseau's famous dictum: "l'homme qui pense est un animal dépravé" (the thinking man is a perverted animal). The third volume, *Supplément aux voyages*, includes the best known of Lahontan's writings, *Dialogues Curieux entre l'auteur et un sauvage de bon sens*. Here the Huron *philosophe* Adario reduces to rubble the weak arguments in favor of Christianity and European civilization advanced by the mock persona of Lahontan. In the revised edition of 1704, prepared by Nicolas Gueudeville (an ex-Benedictine and a convert to Protestantism), Adario's French is made more elegant, his creed more obviously deistic, and his polemic more strident.

The three volumes brought Lahontan fame. They went through thirteen editions in fourteen years, were widely translated, and found favor with a large segment of the European intelligentsia. As a celebrated author Lahontan was warmly received during visits to Hanover, Denmark, and England. A friendly correspondence with Gottfried Wilhelm Leibniz, begun in 1710, added luster to his achievement. While Leibniz found Adario's adversary in *Dialogues Curieux* something of a straw man, he did vouch for the reliability of Lahontan as an eyewitness. Less critical of the cogency of that work as philosophy, Pierre Bayle responded altogether sympathetically to the persona and rationalized primitivism of Lahontan. Given the baron's celebrity, the scarcity of information available on his later years is remarkable. According to the sketchy historical record, Lahontan died at the court of the elector of Hanover, not long before 1716.

The value of Lahontan's books to freethinking authors remained relatively high throughout the eighteenth century. Delisle de la Drevetière, for example, drew from Lahontan's writings material for his *L'Arlequin Sauvage* (1721), a play much admired by Rousseau, as did Alain-René Lesage for his satirical picaresque novel, *Aventures du chevalier Beauchêne* (1732). François Chateaubriand, too, found in Lahontan's work congenial matter and ideas for his novels, and this in spite of the characterization he gave of the author of *Dialogues Curieux*—"ignorant et menteur" (uninformed and mendacious)—in his *Génie du Christianisme* (1802). For those writers of the Enlightenment who, like Denis Diderot, drew from Lahontan's books evidence to affirm the moral superiority of "la vie sauvage" to the life of "l'homme qui pense," the substantial veracity of the adventurous baron's testimony remained a certainty.

References:

Gilbert Chinard, Introduction to *Dialogues Curieux* (Baltimore: Johns Hopkins Press / Paris: Margraff / London: Oxford University Press, 1931), pp. 5-72;

Gustave Lanctôt, *Faussaires et faussetés en histoire canadienne* (Montreal: Variétés, 1948), pp. 96-129;

Maurice Roelens, Introduction to *Dialogues avec un sauvage* (Paris: Sociales, 1973), pp. 7-81;

J.-Edmond Roy, "Le Baron de Lahontan," *Mémoires de la Société Royale du Canada*, 12 (1895): 63-192.

Anne Langton

(24 June 1804 - 10 May 1893)

Clara Thomas
York University

BOOKS: *The Story of Our Family* (Manchester: Sowler, 1881);

Langton Records, Journals and Letters from Canada, 1837-1846, edited by Ellen Josephine Philips (Edinburgh: Clark, 1904);

A Gentlewoman in Upper Canada: The Journals of Anne Langton, edited by H. H. Langton (Toronto: Clarke, Irwin, 1950).

The letters and sketches of Anne Langton collected in *A Gentlewoman in Upper Canada* (1950), edited and published by her great-nephew, H. H. Langton, are a vivid record of the daily life of an immigrant family of means living on a farm in Sturgeon Lake, Ontario, from 1837 to 1846. With her father, her mother, and Aunt Alice, her mother's sister, Langton came to Canada to join her brother John, who had immigrated and taken up land in 1833. She had been born on 24 June 1804 at Farfield Hall in Yorkshire, the second child of Thomas and Ellen Currer Langton. Her father, for twenty years a merchant trading out of Russia, for another half-dozen years a traveler in Europe with his family, decided in 1834, because of business reverses, to join his son John in Upper Canada. Another son, William, remained in England, the successful manager of a bank in Manchester. H. H. Langton included letters from Mr. and Mrs. Langton and John in the book he assembled, but the journals his great-aunt kept, later to be sent home to William and his family, make up the bulk of the book, and it is her personality that dominates its pages.

Unlike most settlers' records, Anne Langton's journals present her as a willing, even eager, immigrant. She was well educated, partly in Swiss schools, and particularly trained in sketching, watercoloring, and miniature painting, for Thomas Langton had given his children every educational advantage until his financial reversals. When John reported his progress in clearing and settling near Peterborough in Canada and his lively hopes for the future, she entered into the

Anne Langton (self-portrait; by permission of the Anne Langton Committee, Fenelon Falls, Ontario; Langton Collection)

family expedition to join him with an enthusiasm that seldom flagged and never, even under adverse circumstances, disappeared, certainly not in the reports she sent home to England. Her journals, therefore, have a constant ring of irrepressible good humor, adaptability, and high hopes that make them unique in the literature of settlement. Her devotion to her family and particularly to her brother was the cornerstone of her life, and after the death of her parents, Thomas in 1838 and Ellen in 1846, she remained contentedly with him and his family, except for visits to friends and relatives overseas, until her death in Toronto on 10 May 1893. John, who left the Peterborough district in 1855, retired in Toronto after a distinguished career of twenty-three years in the civil service. He was the first auditor of the provinces of Upper and Lower Canada, vice-chancellor of the University of Toronto from

Langton in the 1880s (512752, Archives of Ontario; Langton Collection)

1856 to 1860, and first auditor for the Dominion of Canada after Confederation in 1867.

All her life Anne Langton remained an indefatigable artist. Some of her work illustrates *A Gentlewoman in Upper Canada*, and more of it is to be found in the Fenelon Falls Public Library and in Ontario's provincial archives. Her trained, observant eye made her an excellent recorder of the details of everyday living, of food and furnishings, methods of farming and housekeeping, entertainment, and in a good-natured, chatty, sometimes ironic way, of the people she met. Her journals are rich in the minutiae of living that made up the fabric of her days, and they bring the past vividly and visually to life. Sometimes she wrote with irony, but never with malice, as when she commented on a large family of new neighbors, the Dunsfords: "Hitherto I fancy that we have more English elegancies about us than most of our neighbors, but the Dunsfords, I expect, will quite eclipse us, for they, it is said, are bringing a carriage out with them. I hope they do not forget to bring a good road too."

Though her days were full of the hard work of pioneer housekeeping she found time to teach any children who came to her, and in 1840, with a small legacy, she purchased the land for the first public school in the district. She also established the first neighborhood circulating library, making the family collection of twelve hundred volumes available to the few subscribers in Fenelon Falls, Sturgeon Lake, and Bobcaygeon. When brother John was away she became surrogate preacher for their little community, and later, after moving with John and his family to Peterborough, she played the organ and led the choir in St. John's Anglican church–this despite increasing deafness. In 1879 she wrote *The Story of Our Family* (1881) for private circulation among her nieces and nephews. Then, safe in the assurance of her brother's success and her assured place in his family, she could and did admit the difficulties of the early days on the uncleared land: "I never shall forget my feeling of despair at that time.... Now, it did seem a rash step for such a party to come out to such a place, but we were very careful in writing home to say as little of our difficulties as possible." Anne Langton is unique in Canada's literary past for the insouciant gallantry of tone that is a hallmark of her journals.

References:

Marian Fowler, *The Embroidered Tent: Five Gentlewomen in Early Canada* (Toronto: Anansi, 1982), p. 211;

John Langton, *Early Days in Upper Canada*, edited by William A. Langton (Toronto: Privately printed, 1926);

Thomas Langton, *Letters of Thomas Langton to Mrs. Hugh Hornby 1815-1818* (Manchester: Privately printed, 1900);

Barbara Williams, *Anne Langton: Pioneer Woman and Artist* (Peterborough, Ont.: Peterborough Historical Society, 1986).

Pamphile Lemay

(5 January 1837 - 11 June 1918)

Barbara Godard
York University

BOOKS: *Essais poétiques* (Quebec: Desbarats, 1865);

Deux Poèmes couronnés par l'Université Laval (Quebec: Delisle, 1870);

Catalogue de la bibliothèque de la Législature de Québec (Quebec: Lévis, 1873);

Les Vengeances (Quebec: Darveau, 1875); republished as *Tonkourou* (Quebec: Darveau, 1888); republished as *Les Vengeances: Poème rustique* (Montreal: Granger, 1930);

Les Vengeances: Drame en six actes (Quebec: Bossue-Lyonnais, 1876);

Le Pèlerin de Sainte-Anne, 2 volumes (Quebec: Darveau, 1877; abridged edition, 1 volume, Montreal: Beauchemin, 1893);

Picounoc le maudit, 2 volumes (Quebec: Darveau, 1878; modern edition, Montreal: HMH, 1972);

La Chaîne d'or (Quebec: Darveau, 1879);

Une Gerbe (Quebec: Darveau, 1879);

Fables canadiennes (Quebec: Darveau, 1882; revised, 1891; revised again, Montreal: Granger, 1903; abridged, 1925);

Petits Poèmes (Quebec: Darveau, 1883);

L'Affaire Sougraine (Quebec: Darveau, 1884);

Rouge et bleu (Quebec: Darveau, 1891);

Fêtes et corvées (Lévis, Que.: Roy, 1898);

Contes vrais (Quebec: Soleil, 1899; revised and en-

larged edition, Montreal: Beauchemin, 1907);

Les Gouttelettes (Montreal: Beauchemin, 1904);

Les Epis: Poésies fugitives et petits poèmes (Montreal: Guay, 1914);

Reflets d'antan (Montreal: Granger, 1916).

PLAY PRODUCTIONS: *Les Vengeances*, Quebec, L'Academie de Musique, 1876;

Rouge et bleu, Quebec, L'Academie de Musique, 26 April 1889.

TRANSLATIONS: Henry Wadsworth Longfellow, *Evangeline* (Quebec: Delisle, 1870); revised and enlarged as *Evangeline et Autres Poèmes de Longfellow* (Montreal: Guay, 1912);

William Kirby, *Le Chien D'or* (Quebec: Etendard, 1884).

Easily the most prolific and varied of the "Ecole de 1860," the beachhead of romanticism in Quebec, Pamphile Lemay developed the religious and nationalistic themes of his contemporaries in a more intimate form. Whether probing the heart or celebrating the hearth, Lemay's poetry differs from the public verse then in vogue. His lyrical evocations of the Quebec countryside have been cherished by readers. Long esteemed

by critics for his sonnets, in *Les Gouttelettes* (The Droplets, 1904), Lemay is more recently being acclaimed as a storyteller, his skill demonstrated in *Contes vrais* (True Tales, 1899).

The eldest of fourteen children, Léon-Pamphile Lemay was born 5 January 1837 at Lotbinière, Quebec, the son of a merchant farmer, Léon Lemay, and his wife, Louise Auger Lemay. After primary school with the Frères des Ecoles Chrétiennes at Trois Rivières and preparatory studies with the notary of Lotbinière, Lemay began his classical studies at the Séminaire de Québec in 1846. On completion in 1850 he experienced a period of uncertainty, abandoning legal studies in order to earn a living, holding a variety of jobs in the United States and Canada until he felt a call to the priesthood. However, he was later obliged to leave the seminary at the University of Ottawa because of stomach problems that gave him pain all his life. Literature became his

pulpit. In 1860 he resumed his study of the law in the same class as the poet Louis Fréchette. Both worked as translators for the legislative assembly at Quebec. In 1865 Lemay married Celima Robitaille, with whom he had fourteen children. Called to the bar in 1865, but no longer interested in practicing, he found a government sinecure as a translator for Parliament in Ottawa. This same year he published his first volume of verse, *Essais poétiques,* which begins with his translation of Longfellow's *Evangeline,* later published in a separate book (1870).

Alphonse Lamartine's facile musicality and prolix lyricism, according to Romain Legaré, mark the some eight thousand lines of Lemay's apprentice work; his themes are seen in embryo: nature, the poet's soul, his love of his native country and its traditions, and hymns to God. An individual poetic personality, characterized by depth of thought, originality of image, correctness of language, and sobriety of style, is lacking. The difficulties stem from his ignorance of French versification. Lemay acknowledged the problem in his preface and by revising his work through successive editions. New titles are deceptive, for often they are revised work. For example, *La Chaîne d'or* (The Gold Chain, 1879), was revised and included in *Une Gerbe* (A Sheaf, 1879) and again in *Petits Poèmes* (1883).

In 1867 Lemay became parliamentary librarian at Quebec, a post he occupied for twenty-five years while turning his spiritual energy to poetry. This same year he was the first winner of a poetry contest at Laval University with his entry "La Découverte du Canada," a poem in the epic mode of Fréchette about the war against the Indians. He first used here the motif of the Christian miracle–from François Chateaubriand's *Les Martyrs* (1809) and *Les Natchez* (1826)–a subject to be reworked in his narratives over the next decade. In 1869, with another patriotic poem, "Hymne pour la fête nationale des Canadiens français," he won the same Laval competition.

Working hard at the library, where he published a catalog (1873), Lemay was equally productive in his poetry, publishing a long narrative in verse, *Les Vengeances* (The Revenges, 1875; republished as *Tonkourou,* 1888), a popular success that marked a turning point in Quebec poetry. This period must have been exciting in Crémazie's Quebec bookshop, where the literati gathered and Lemay gave readings. This heroic poem, as Camille Roy later said, seemed to embody the poet's dream to represent all phases of life from the bloody and tragic episodes of 1837 to the picturesque manners of daily life in rural Lotbinière, thus initiating a new realism. A didactic poem illustrating sin and redemption, the work deals with the separation of parents and children and the coincidences of fate leading to their union, which reveal that "heaven has its secrets: its greatness crushes us." Indian vengeance, the kidnapping of a child, is contrasted to the Christian miracle, which reunites the good characters and brings evil Tonkourou, the Indian villain, to repentance. The conflict of these forces had dramatic potential, as Lemay realized in adapting the poem for the stage the following year. On 12 April 1876 it received an amateur production in Quebec City and played sporadically until 1929.

The narrative was further developed in *Le Pèlerin de Sainte-Anne* (The Pilgrim of Saint-Anne, 1877), its sequel *Picounoc le maudit* (Picounoc the Cursed, 1878), and *L'Affaire Sougraine* (The Sougraine Affair, 1884), which were the first detective novels in French Canada. The later books rework the basic themes of the poem: the unforeseen return of the main character to his family after months or years of forced absence, following treacherous intrigues based on the greed of others; the unexpected reunion of family; and the forced marriage motivated by greed or passion. Hypocrisy is unmasked, vice punished, and good rewarded: after a struggle and a thousand digressions happiness is obtained. *Picounoc le maudit* alone has been reedited. In introducing it, contradicting nineteenth-century criticism that had decried a lack of vivacity and a heaviness of style, Anne Gagnon underlines Lemay's strengths in his use of language and his subtle humor. All concur, however, in finding the novel interesting, his characters being powerful, archetypal figures.

The 1880s was a period of experimentation for Lemay. He wrote for the stage three weak comedies and produced *Fables canadiennes* (1882), which compares unfavorably with its model, Jean de la Fontaine's *Fables* (1668-1694). Nonetheless he was a founding member of the Royal Society of Canada in 1882 and in 1888 was awarded an honorary doctorate from Laval. Perhaps his most significant work at this time was in the essay; one written for St. Jean Baptiste Day in 1880 proclaims the sacred nature of the writer's function—to lead his people toward God and help them maintain their culture. This culture he saw manifested in the work and celebrations of the people, which he elaborated, documenting them in *Fêtes et corvées* (Holidays and Bees, 1898), wherein

he advances a theory of history that was to shape his final works.

In 1899 appeared Lemay's masterpiece in prose, his *Contes vrais*. Like his friend Fréchette, he turned to a style in which his digressions are accommodated in the form of oral narrative, tale embedded within tale as narrators exchange stories. Though the marvelous and supernatural elements of the folktale are to be found in these stories, Lemay places his legends in real places and within the context of real historical events. Moreover, he demystifies the fantastic, "Le Loupgarou" (The Werewolf) ending on a note of skepticism. Legaré, consequently, has seen Lemay as one of the first Quebec realists. The variety of his stories and the vivacity of his style made this book a favorite. The book was enlarged through three editions.

The change heralded in *Contes vrais* was confirmed in his acknowledged poetic masterpiece, *Les Gouttelettes*, a collection of sonnets characterized by their restraint and simplicity, responding thus to the new Parnassian poetry. Lemay's subject matter remains familiar, religious or rustic scenes transfused with emotion. His taste for dreaming and habit of moral meditation are here mated with a mature technique to produce delicate poetry. Lemay's strength, according to Maurice Hébert, lies in these miniatures (rather than in his frescoes), which he traces lovingly with the fine point of his brush (pen).

In 1910, having been honored with the rosette of an officer of L'Instruction Publique of France, Lemay returned to the region he nostalgically wrote of, to the home of his son-in-law. Here he produced two more volumes of verse before dying on 11 June 1918 at the age of eighty-one. He was buried in the habit of an associate of St. Francis of Assisi, indicating that his desire to be a priest had remained with him, only partially submerged in his writing.

As well as producing some of the most enduring and readable poetry of the late nineteenth and early twentieth centuries, Lemay inaugurated a movement of regionalist poetry, poetry of the soil, that extended to the work of Alfred Desrochers and Felix-Antoine Savard.

References:

Maurice Hébert, "L'Oeuvre poétique de Pamphile Lemay," *Canada Français* (January 1937): 487-507;

Romain Legaré, "Essais Poétiques," in *Dictionnaire des oeuvres litteraires du Québec,* edited by Maurice Lemire, volume 1 (Montreal: Fides, 1978), p. 223;

Legaré, "Evolution littéraire de Pamphile Lemay," in *Archives des lettres canadiennes*, volume 1 (Montreal: Fides, 1961);

Camille Roy, *A l'ombre des érables* (Quebec: Action Sociale, 1924).

James MacPherson Le Moine

(24 January 1825 - 5 February 1912)

Carole Gerson
Simon Fraser University

BOOKS: *Ornithologie du Canada*, 2 volumes (Quebec: Fréchette, 1860, 1861);

The Legendary Lore of the Lower St. Lawrence [poems] (Quebec: Mercury, 1862);

Maple Leaves: A Budget of Legendary, Historical, Critical, and Sporting Intelligence, 7 volumes (Quebec: Hunter, Rose, 1863-1906);

Les Pêcheries du Canada (Quebec: Atelier, 1863);

Album canadien; histoire, archeologie-ornithologie (Quebec: Presses Mécaniques, 1870);

L'Album du touriste (Quebec: Côté, 1872);

Quebec, Past and Present (Quebec: Coté, 1876);

The Chronicles of the St. Lawrence (Montreal: Dawson / Rouses Point, N.Y.: Lovell, 1878);

Origin of the Festival of Saint-Jean-Baptiste. Quebec, Its Gates and Environs (Quebec: Morning Chronicle, 1880);

Picturesque Quebec: A Sequel to Quebec Past and Present (Montreal: Dawson, 1882);

Monographies et esquisses (Quebec: Gingras, 1885);

Chasse et pêche au Canada (Quebec: Hardy, 1887);

Historical Notes on Quebec and Its Environs (Quebec: Darveau, 1887; enlarged, 1890);

The Explorations of Jonathan Oldbuck (Quebec: Demers, 1889);

The Legends of the St. Lawrence (Quebec: Holiwell, 1898);

The Port of Quebec (Quebec: Chronicle, 1901).

James M. Le Moine (C 37828, National Archives of Canada)

The bilingual son of an English-Canadian mother, Julia Ann MacPherson Le Moine, and a French-Canadian father, Benjamin Le Moine, James MacPherson Le Moine devoted much of his life to recording the history, folklore, and natural features of Quebec in more than fifty volumes and pamphlets, the majority of them in English. His popular books of legends and anecdotes acquainted English-speaking readers with the romantic side of French Canada and inspired the writing of many historical romances, among them William Kirby's *The Chien D'or. The Golden Dog* (1877). A desultory chronicler rather than a systematic historian, Le Moine nonetheless won the friendship of Francis Parkman and in 1897 he was knighted for his literary services.

Le Moine was born in Quebec City on 24 January 1825. His father, a descendant of one of the few noble families to settle in New France in the seventeenth century, died when James was three years old. He was adopted by his maternal grandfather, Daniel MacPherson, a United Empire Loyalist who eventually settled in a Quebec seigneurial manor. Le Moine was educated in French—first at the village school, then at the Petit Séminaire of Quebec. While indentured to a leading barrister of the Quebec bar he helped found the Institut Canadien in 1847. In 1856 he married Harriet Atkinson. He practiced law from 1850 until 1869, when he was appointed inspector of inland revenue for the district of Quebec, a position he held until he retired in 1899.

Le Moine's first publications were on ornithology, an interest developed in his boyhood and later reinforced by the bird life on his rural estate, Spencer Grange, just outside Quebec City. Here he assembled a private museum of ornithological specimens, historical writings, and artifacts. He began to publish works on history in the 1860s, in 1863 producing the first of his seven volumes of *Maple Leaves*. In 1865 a copy of this book of sketches and essays was purchased by Kirby while on a visit to Quebec City from his home in Niagara. Excited by Le Moine's chapters on Chateau Bigot, The Golden Dog, and La Corriveau, Kirby eventually produced his ponder-

ous historical romance, *The Chien D'Or*, praised in nineteenth-century Canada as the finest Canadian novel.

Several decades later Le Moine was consulted by Gilbert Parker, who was searching for a suitably romantic subject for a historical novel on Quebec. Le Moine directed Parker to the fourth volume of *Maple Leaves* (1873), which contained a sketch of the adventures of Maj. Robert Stobo that became the source of Parker's best-seller *The Seats of the Mighty* (1896). For his continuing efforts to recover and popularize French-Canadian legends and history, Le Moine was occasionally likened to Sir Walter Scott, though, unlike Scott, he left the writing of fiction to others.

During his long life Le Moine belonged to more than a score of Canadian, American, and European historical and cultural societies. He was a founding member of the Royal Society of Canada, serving as first president of the French section and from 1894 to 1895 as president of the society itself. Although several detractors accused him of plagiarizing from other historical and travel writers and of writing badly, Le Moine was highly regarded by most English and French Canadians for his activities as an antiquarian, naturalist, and man of letters.

Bibliography:

Raoul Renault, *Bibliographie de Sir James-M. Le Moine* (Quebec: Brousseau, 1897).

References:

Anonymous, Obituary of Le Moine, *Proceedings and Transactions of the Royal Society of Canada*, third series 6 (1912): v-vii;

Bernard Muddiman, "The Grape Festivals at Spencer Grange," *Canadian Magazine*, 40 (April 1913): 501-511.

Anna Leonowens

(5 November 1834 - 19 January 1914)

Gwendolyn Davies
Acadia University

BOOKS: *The English Governess at the Siamese Court* (London & Cambridge, Mass.: Trübner, 1870); republished as *Siam and the Siamese* (Philadelphia: Coates, 1897);

The Romance of the Harem (Philadelphia: Porter & Coates, 1872); republished as *The Romance of Siamese Harem Life* (London: Trübner / Boston: Osgood, 1873); modern edition published as *Siamese Harem Life* (London: Barker, 1952; New York: Dutton, 1953);

Life and Travel in India (Philadelphia: Porter & Coates, 1884);

Our Asiatic Cousins (Boston: Lothrop, 1889).

OTHER: *The Art Movement in America*, edited by Leonowens (New York: Century, 1887).

In the popular mind Anna Leonowens is probably most often associated with *Anna and the King of Siam*, the 1946 film based on Margaret Landon's 1944 biography, the book that also served as the basis for the 1951 musical *The King and I*, filmed in 1956. However, Leonowens was known in her own time not only as the author of two books on Siam but also as a sometime travel writer, supporter of social and feminist causes, cofounder of the Victoria School of Art and Design in Halifax, and lecturer in Sanskrit at McGill University in Montreal.

Born in Carnarvon, Wales, on 5 November 1834, Anna Harriette Crawford (her married name to be Leonowens) remained in Wales for her education when in 1840 her father, Capt. Thomas Maxwell Crawford, was transferred to India, eventually to become aide-de-camp to William Hay MacNaughton, commander of the British forces sent to control Sikh unrest. A year later her father was ambushed and hacked to death on the Lahore border. Her mother's second marriage to a British official in the Public Works Department at Poona brought Anna little happiness when she joined the couple in 1849, and in 1850 she began the first of her famous travels when she accompanied Rev. George Percy

Anna Leonowens (portrait from the Halifax Herald, *19 June 1897)*

Badger and his wife on a tour of Damascus, Jerusalem, and the Nile—in an effort to escape the dominance of her stepfather and his plans to marry her to a middle-aged merchant of his choice. On her return to Bombay in 1851, she defied her stepfather and married the man of her choice, a young officer, Maj. Thomas L. Leonowens, who held a staff appointment in the commissariat of-

"Procession to eradicate the evil influence of witchcraft," an illustration (based on a photograph by Sarah Bradley) for Leonowens's Romance of the Harem *(1872), showing King Mongkut of Siam astride a bull*

fice. After the deaths of her mother and the Leonowens's first baby a year later, Anna Leonowens set sail for England with her husband, only to be shipwrecked off the Cape of Good Hope. Taken to New South Wales, she lost her second baby in childbirth. Between 1853 and 1856 the Leonowens lived in London and had two more children. In 1856 they were posted to Singapore and were living there when the Indian Mutiny broke out in 1857. Anna Leonowens lost several relatives in the mutiny and was left penniless after the failure of Indian banks. However, her granddaughter, Anna Harriet Leonowens Fyshe, noted years later that Anna had supported the Indian cause, feeling that Britain had no moral right to control India, a nation capable of governing itself, or to send missionaries to convert Buddhists and Hindus.

Disaster struck Leonowens again in 1859, when her husband died of sunstroke after participating in a tiger hunt. His fellow officers had two of the tiger's claws set in a gold brooch, and

Fyshe recalled in 1962 that "I cannot remember ever seeing her without this unusual ornament, which she wore every day for the remaining years of her long life." After establishing a school for officers' children in Singapore, in 1862 Leonowens accepted an invitation from King Mongkut of Siam (Thailand) "to undertake the education of our beloved royal children." Her subsequent five years in the Siamese court teaching the King's sixty-four children and some of his many wives formed the basis of her two most famous books, *The English Governess at the Siamese Court* (1870) and *The Romance of the Harem* (1872).

The English Governess at the Siamese Court, published three years after Leonowens left Thailand because of ill health, gives a vivid insight into the opposition, court intrigues, and cultural differences that made the life of the new teacher extremely difficult. The romance and exoticism of the country also inform the book, but a modern reader is struck by Leonowens's sense of outrage

Leonowens with her son, Louis (left), and some of her Siamese pupils (illustration by Margaret Ayer for Margaret Landon's
Anna and the King of Siam, *1943)*

at the indignities imposed on human beings by slavery, concubinage, and absolute monarchy. Her highly developed sense of injustice often made her an intermediary in disputes between palace authorities and the oppressed, and she earned the nickname "The White Angel," particularly for her influence on her pupil Prince Chulalongkorn who some thirty years later would abolish slavery when he was king. Leonowens often found herself in conflict with King Mongkut and the prime minister, however, both of whom emerge from the book as complex, intelligent men who nonetheless ruled subordinates with tyranny and cruelty. So angry were the Siamese authorities when the book came out that they refused to pay the legacy that King Mongkut had left Leonowens, and they tried to prevent the book from being widely circulated in the United States. It was an immediate success, however, and won for Leonowens the admiration of such American writers as Oliver Wendell Holmes, Henry Wadsworth Longfellow, Ralph Waldo Emerson, and Harriet Beecher Stowe.

Both *The English Governess at the Siamese Court* and *The Romance of the Harem* were written in the United States while Leonowens taught school on Staten Island and lectured on her experiences. As with the first book, *The Romance of the Harem* drew on the social experiences and characters of Leonowens's years in Siam. However, it focused more directly on the situation of individual women, some of whom she had mentioned in the earlier book (such as Tuptim, a palace concubine) and some of whom she had heard about in stories in Siam. While the title suggests "romance," the book in fact reveals Leonowens's feminist sensibility and her sense of horror at the absence of dignity and freedom in the lives of the women she had met.

In 1876 Leonowens moved to Halifax, Nova Scotia, when her son-in-law, Thomas Fyshe, was appointed cashier and manager of the Bank of Nova Scotia. In Halifax, Leonowens continued to be active, traveling to New York at one point to help in the establishment of the Berkeley School for Boys and in 1881 going to Russia to write a series of articles on the country for the *Youth's Companion*. Studying Russian as she crossed the Atlantic, Leonowens traversed Russia from St. Petersburg to Archangel to Odessa. In a letter to her family in May 1881 she predicted that someday in Russia there would be "a sudden revolution of the most fearful character" and so impressed editor Perry Mason of the *Youth's Companion* with her articles that he offered her a position in Boston. Leonowens's desire to be near her family took her back to Halifax, however, and it was there that she wrote her 1884 travelogue, *Life and Travel in India*. Filled with reminiscences of friends, family, and locations that she and her husband had known, the book also reveals Leonowens's deep love for the history, countryside, and people of India. Although it includes conventional descriptions such as that of the Taj Mahal, it is enlivened by Leonowens's vivid pictorial style (as in the phrase "a fat, sun-burnt, frowzy-looking man"), sense of detail, and narrative pace. This book was followed in 1889 by *Our Asiatic Cousins* in which Leonowens turned to the history of the Mongolians, the life of Confucius, and the people of the Korean peninsula to explore the social and religious themes that had also informed her earlier works.

During her residence in Halifax from 1876 to 1897, Leonowens was active in the founding of the Pioneer Book Club, the Shakespeare Society, and, in 1887, the Victoria School of Art and Design (now the Nova Scotia College of Art and Design, where a gallery is named in Leonowens's honor). Her interest in North American art movements and in putting "before the Nova Scotia public what had been done and is being done in the far-off Western cities of the United States by the establishment of Schools of Art and Design" led to her 1887 publication of *The Art Movement in America*, a collection of three articles reprinted from the *Century Magazine* of August, October, and November 1886. Leonowens was also active in her Halifax years in supporting the countess of Aberdeen in founding a Local Council of Women, in advocating various social causes to better the conditions of women and children, and in furthering the fight for women's enfranchisement.

In 1897, when Thomas Fyshe became associate general manager of the Merchant's Bank of Canada in Montreal, Leonowens moved to Leipzig so that her granddaughter Anna could study piano. En route to Germany she accepted an invitation to visit her former pupil, now the King of Siam, in London. The personal connection with Siam had also been continued years before by her son's having accepted a post at the Siamese court, marrying the daughter of a Siamese princess, and sending his children home to his mother in Halifax for an education. After several years in Germany, Anna Leonowens rejoined the family circle in Montreal, giving her last lecture in Sanskrit at McGill when she was seventy-five. Each day until she was eighty she read in Sanskrit and translated into English her beloved *Rig Veda*.

Leonowens's vivid style, acute social sense, and narrative skill made her a much-read author in the late Victorian period. She brought a liberal worldview, sense of tolerance, and worldliness to her writing unusual for a woman of the Victorian era, and she made very personal contributions to Canadian artistic, social, and feminist circles.

Biographies:
Anonymous, "Her Farewell to Halifax," *Halifax Herald*, 19 June 1897, p. 12;

Margaret Landon, *Anna and the King of Siam* (Toronto: Longmans, Green, 1944);

Ruth Blake, "Anna of Siam Lived in Canada," *Maritime Advocate and Busy East* (January 1951): 9-12;

Anna Harriet Leonowens Fyshe, "Anna, from the Unpublished Memories of Anna Harriet Leonowens Fyshe," *Chatelaine*, 35 (January 1962): 32-33, 60, 62, 64;

Phyllis R. Blakeley, "Anna of Siam in Canada," *Atlantic Advocate* (January 1967): 41-45.

Reference:
E. R. Forbes, "Battles in Another War: Edith Archibald and the Halifax Feminist Movement," in his *Challenging the Regional Stereotype* (Fredericton: Acadiensis, 1989), pp. 67-89.

Rosanna Eleanor Leprohon

(12 January 1829 - 20 September 1879)

Mary Jane Edwards
Carleton University

BOOKS: *Le Manoir de Villerai,* translation by E. L. DeBellefeuille of "The Manor House of De Villerai" (Montreal: Plinguet, 1861);

Antoinette De Mirecourt; or, Secret Marrying and Secret Sorrowing (Montreal: Lovell, 1864; modern edition, Toronto: McClelland & Stewart, 1973; critical edition, edited by John C. Stockdale, Ottawa: Carleton University Press, 1989);

Armand Durand; or, A Promise Fulfilled (Montreal: Lovell, 1868);

The Poetical Works of Mrs. Leprohon (Montreal: Lovell, 1881).

OTHER: Edward Hartley Dewart, ed., *Selections from Canadian Poets,* includes five poems by Leprohon (Montreal: Lovell, 1864; modern edition, Toronto: University of Toronto Press, 1973).

SELECTED PERIODICAL PUBLICATIONS–
UNCOLLECTED: "Ida Beresford," *Literary Garland,* new series 6 (1848): 15-24, 71-77, 106-114, 157-178, 230-238, 269-278, 321-328, 371-381, and 410-424;

"The Manor House of De Villerai. A Tale of Canada Under the French Dominion," *Family Herald* (Montreal), 16 November 1859 - 8 February 1860; modern edition, edited by John R. Sorfleet, *Journal of Canadian Fiction,* 34 (1985);

"Clive Weston's Wedding Anniversary," *Canadian Monthly and National Review,* 2 (1872): 97-111, 193-208;

"Who Stole the Diamonds?," *Canadian Illustrated News,* 2 January-9 January 1875;

"A School-Girl Friendship," *Canadian Illustrated News,* 25 August-15 September 1877.

In the middle decades of the nineteenth century, Rosanna Eleanor Mullins Leprohon wrote poems, short stories, and novels. Her most important works are "The Manor House of De Villerai" (*Family Herald,* 1859-1860; translated as

Le Manoir de Villerai, 1861), *Antoinette De Mirecourt* (1864), and *Armand Durand* (1868), three novels based on her extensive knowledge of, and close association with, French-Canadian culture.

Leprohon was the second child of Francis and Rosanna Mullins. Francis, an Irish immigrant, became a wealthy merchant in Montreal, so his daughter had many privileges, including that of being educated at the Convent of the Congregation. In "A Touching Ceremony" (1859; collected in *Poetical Works,* 1881) Leprohon commemorated this "beloved Institution in which the happy days of [her] girlhood were passed" and, in the 1869 poem "On the Death of the Same Reverend Nun" (also in *Poetical Works*), honored the nuns who taught her there and evidently encouraged her to write. One of the first poems she published in the *Literary Garland* (November 1846), John Lovell's monthly periodical, described "The Young Novice" of the title, who "renounced a fleeting world, to give herself to God."

From 1846 until 1851, when the *Literary Garland* ceased publication, Leprohon's poems, short stories, and serialized novels appeared regularly there and received favorable notices. In 1848, for example, in *Victoria Magazine,* Susanna Moodie praised Leprohon's "Ida Beresford," a short novel then being serialized, as "a story written with great power and vigor" that augured for its "still very young" writer "a bright wreath of fame."

Fame, however, eluded Leprohon for another decade. After marrying Dr. Jean-Lukin Leprohon at the Parish Church of Notre Dame, Montreal, on 17 June 1851, she went to live at St. Charles on the Richelieu, where her husband had a medical practice, and within a year had the first of their thirteen children. Although both the birth and early death of this child occasioned poems, for the next few years Leprohon published little. Nevertheless, her marriage to a descendant of an old French-Canadian family and her residence at St. Charles among people whose ancestors had fought for the French during the

Seven Years' War, and who themselves had witnessed events in the rebellion of 1837, proved seminal for her development as a writer.

In 1859 Leprohon, living again in Montreal, began publishing a new serialized novel, which told the story of Blanche de Villerai, the wealthy, beautiful, and virtuous heiress of "The Manor House of De Villerai," situated on the banks of the Richelieu. Engaged to Gustave de Montarville by her parents, she eventually frees Gustave so he can marry Rose Lauzon, a farmer's daughter from Villerai whom he truly loves. Although motifs such as a childhood engagement resemble aspects of Leprohon's earlier fiction, the setting of the main events of Blanche's story is New France between 1756 and 1760. Thus for the first time in her fiction Leprohon used a Canadian setting and depicted events of crucial importance in Canadian history. She depicted these events, furthermore, from the point of view of French Canadians, an angle rarely found in early English-Canadian literature.

Leprohon's second French-Canadian novel, *Antoinette De Mirecourt,* is set in Montreal just "after the royal standard of England had replaced the fleur-de-lys of France." Antoinette, a young French-Canadian, Roman Catholic heiress, who has come to Montreal to visit her married cousin, seems to fall in love with Major Audley Sternfield, a British officer stationed there, and secretly marries him in a Protestant ceremony. The result—much "secret sorrowing"—allows Leprohon both to moralize about the importance of young girls obeying the wise teachings of the Roman Catholic Church and the reasonable wishes of parents, and to explore English-French relations in Canada.

In 1864, when John Lovell published *Antoinette De Mirecourt,* the renewed nationalism of French Canadians and the desire of many English Canadians to create a new nation were already bearing political and cultural fruit. Thus when Leprohon had Antoinette marry a second time, to an (albeit Roman Catholic) Englishman, Sternfield having been killed in a duel, she was quite clearly making a statement about the possibility of a new English-French culture emerging in Canada.

In her novel *Armand Durand,* Leprohon presented other aspects of French-Canadian society. Armand, the son of a poor, French, yet aristocratic mother and a prosperous French-Canadian farmer, leaves the country to be educated in Montreal and eventually becomes a lawyer and politi-

cian. His birth, education, and career are typical of many French Canadians. The complications in his life stem from a jealous brother and a thoughtless marriage to Délima Laurin, a frivolous woman. Only her death in childbirth frees him to marry Gertrude de Beauvoir, whom he has long loved, and to fulfill his early promise.

Leprohon continued to publish poems and short stories throughout the 1870s. Her stories are usually set in Canada, but they do not normally deal with specifically Canadian themes. Rather, they concentrate on such topics as the nature of friendship and marriage, the importance of education for women, and the worth of intelligence and morality as compared to wealth and beauty.

In 1864 five poems by Leprohon were included in the first anthology of English-Canadian poetry, Edward Hartley Dewart's *Selections from Canadian Poets,* and in 1867 Leprohon was described by Henry Morgan in *Bibliotheca Canadensis,* an early biographical dictionary, as someone who had done "more almost than any other Canadian writer to foster and promote the growth of a national Literature." In 1881, two years after her death, an edition of her *Poetical Works* was published. After that, although the French translations of each of her three "essentially Canadian" novels continued to be republished, Leprohon's reputation gradually diminished, and her role as a seminal writer of fiction in English dealing with French-Canadian subjects went unrecognized. Since 1970, however, the life and works of Rosanna Eleanor Mullins Leprohon have been frequently noted and increasingly praised by critics and scholars of both English- and French-Canadian literature, and new editions of her works have been published.

References:

Elizabeth Brady, "Towards a Happier History: Women and Domination," in *Domination,* edited by Alkis Kontos (Toronto: University of Toronto Press, 1975), pp. 17-31;

Mary Jane Edwards, "Essentially Canadian," *Canadian Literature,* 52 (Spring 1972): 8-23;

Edwards, "Rosanna Leprohon," in her *The Evolution of Canadian Literature in English: Beginnings to 1867* (Toronto: Holt, Rinehart & Winston, 1973), pp. 265-266;

Carole Gerson, "Three Writers of Victorian Canada," in *Canadian Writers and Their Works,* volume 1, edited by Robert Lecker, Jack David, and Ellen Quigley (Downsview, Ont.: ECW, 1983), pp. 195-199;

Carl F. Klinck, Introduction to *Antoinette De Mirecourt* (Toronto: McClelland & Stewart, 1973), pp. 5-14;

John Stockdale, Introduction to *Antoinette De Mirecourt* (Ottawa: Carleton University Press, 1989), pp. xvii-lviii.

Marc Lescarbot
(circa 1570 - 1642)

Renate Usmiani
Mount St. Vincent University

BOOKS: *Les Muses de la Nouvelle France* (Paris: J. Millot, 1609)–includes *Le Théâtre de Neptune,* translated by Harriette Taber Richardson as *The Theatre of Neptune in New France* (Boston: Houghton Mifflin, 1927);

Histoire de la Nouvelle France (Paris: Jean Milot [*sic*], 1609; revised and enlarged edition, 1611; enlarged again, Paris: A. Perier, 1617); translated by "P. E." as *Nova Francia, or The Description of that Part of New France, which Is One Continent with Virginia* (London: Printed for A. Hebb, 1609); translated by W. L. Grant and published with the original 1617 text as *The History of New France,* 3 volumes (Toronto: Champlain Society, 1907, 1911, 1914);

La Conversion des sauvages (Paris: Jean Millot, 1610);

Le Tableau de la Suisse et autres alliez de la France és hautes Allemagnes (Paris: Adrian Perier, 1618).

Collection: *Marc Lescarbot,* edited by René Baudry (Montreal & Paris: Fides, 1968).

PLAY PRODUCTION: *Le Théâtre de Neptune,* Port Royal, Nova Scotia [staged at the harbor], 14 November 1606.

Marc Lescarbot has made his mark in several widely divergent areas, as historiographer, theatrical producer, and poet. His *Histoire de la Nouvelle France* (1609) provides the first in-depth view of the New World: including accounts of the major voyages of exploration; life in the colonies, with descriptions of Indian tribes as well as flora and fauna; and an analysis of the philosophical, moral, religious, and socioeconomic implications of the concept of colonization. His *Théâtre de Neptune,* an aquatic spectacle staged at Port Royal in 1606 (and published in *Les Muses,* 1609), represents the first European theatrical venture to take place on the North American continent, while his collection of poetry, *Les Muses de la Nouvelle France,* although of dubious literary merit, constitutes the first body of French-language poetry predominantly written in the New World.

Lescarbot was born in about 1570 in Vervins, Picardy, and educated in Paris, where he practiced law beginning in 1599; but his main interests lay outside the legal profession. A Renaissance man in the Rabelaisian tradition, he loved good company and good cheer, composed verses, sang, and played several musical instruments. His humanistic education had made him familiar with Hebrew and the literatures of Greece and Rome, but he also took a lively interest in contemporary scientific endeavors, especially medicine and geography. Always eager for new experiences, he was delighted when Jean de Poutrincourt invited him to join his expedition to Acadia. To his mother, who objected, the thirty-six-year-old Lescarbot addressed a respectful letter apologizing for his filial disobedience, then left.

The expedition sailed from La Rochelle in May 1606, arriving at Port Royal two months

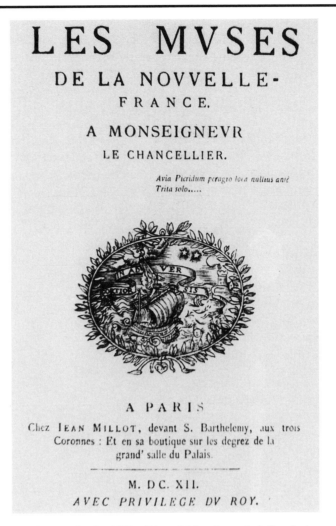

LES MVSES
DE LA NOVVELLE-
FRANCE.

A MONSEIGNEVR
LE CHANCELLIER.

Avia Pieridum peragro loca nullius anté
Trita solo.....

A PARIS
Chez IEAN MILLOT, devant S. Barthelemy, aux trois
Coronnes : Et en sa boutique sur les degrez de la
grand' salle du Palais.

M. DC. XII.
AVEC PRIVILEGE DV ROY.

Title page for the 1612 edition of Marc Lescarbot's first book

later. Lescarbot settled happily into the habitation built by Pierre de Monts the preceding year, calling it "the most beautiful spot God created on this earth." He developed a veritable passion for gardening ("often, in Springtime, I would still be at it in the moonlight") and explored the surroundings of the fort. Because of the friendly relations between the French and the Souriquois Indians of the region, he was able to make close contacts and gather information about their way of life, customs, songs, and language. All this material was later incorporated into his *Histoire de la Nouvelle France,* thus making it the first methodical ethnographic treatise on North America.

During an absence of Poutrincourt, Lescarbot was left in charge of the fort. There, he composed and produced *Le Théâtre de Neptune,* a spectacle that was, according to the title page, "presented upon the waves of Port Royal the fourteenth day of November, sixteen hundred and

six, on the return of the Sieur de Poutrincourt from the Armouchiquois country." A masque rather than a drama, *Le Théâtre de Neptune* echoes the classical Naumachia, as well as the Renaissance custom of triumphal royal entries. It opens with a solemn greeting by Neptune, splendidly robed and seated on a raft drawn by six Tritons: "Hail to you, Sagamos [the Souriquois word for 'chief'], rest and remain awhile!" Neptune glorifies both Poutrincourt and King Henry IV of France and gives his divine approval to the colonial venture. In a lighter vein the six Tritons repeat similar ideas, with one of them providing some comic relief. Next, four Frenchmen disguised as Indians approach in a canoe bearing gifts. A musical finale, followed by trumpets and cannon salute, concludes the festivities on the water. As he enters the habitation, the returning leader is once more welcomed, now by a jolly companion promising an abundance of food and drink. In a postscript to the work, the author apologizes for the poor quality of his verses, but nevertheless submits them to the reader, "because they serve as part of our history and to show that we lived joyously."

Lescarbot returned to France in September 1607, full of enthusiasm and convinced of the enormous potential of the colonies for the mother country. Eager to convey his newly gained knowledge as well as his ideas, he wrote the *Histoire de la Nouvelle France* in feverish haste: by 28 February 1609 the first edition of the book was off the press. It proved immensely popular, went through three successive editions in France, and was subsequently translated into English and German.

There are essential differences between Lescarbot's history and the accounts of Samuel de Champlain, who covers basically the same material (Champlain's chronicle, however, stops in 1607, while Lescarbot's goes to 1615); while Champlain is purely factual, Lescarbot's work is imaginatively written, more sophisticated, and more personal. Three main topics are covered: the voyages of exploration; life in the New World; and principles of colonialism. The main interest of the work lies in Lescarbot's description of the Acadian venture, based on his own experience and expanded through firsthand witnesses, which makes it an invaluable documentary source. His descriptions of the Indians in particular go far beyond those of Champlain and give a graphic view of Indian life from birth to death. He also examines the morality of taking over the Indians' lands and eventually justifies the colonizing process by referring to Divine Right, by which the earth belongs to the "children of God," who should, however, not use their God-

given rights to exterminate the "savages" (as the Spaniards did) but rather allow them to benefit from the moral and cultural liberation of Christianization. Setting up a colonial empire should serve three noble purposes: the greater glory of God; the greater glory of France; and economic relief for an overcrowded homeland.

Lescarbot had hoped to put some of his ideas into practice; but although he offered his services to the king many times, he was never granted another post in the New World. He served as companion to the French ambassador to Switzerland in 1613 and 1614; in 1619 he married Françoise de Valpergues and was made Commissaire de la Marine. Family and professional concerns took up the rest of his life. His name, however, remains linked to the *Histoire de la Nouvelle France*, which has become a classic of colonial literature.

References:

Romeo Arbour, "Le Théâtre de Neptune de Marc Lescarbot," in *Archives des lettres canadiennes*, volume 5: *Le Théâtre canadien-français* (Montreal: Fides, 1974), pp. 21-31;

René Baudry, Introduction to *Marc Lescarbot*, edited by Baudry (Montreal & Paris: Fides, 1968);

H. P. Biggar, "The French Hakluyt: Marc Lescarbot of Vervins," *American Historical Review*, 6 (July 1901): 671-692;

Jean-Pierre Houlé, "Marc Lescarbot," in *Centenaire de L'Histoire du Canada de F.-X. Garneau* (Montreal: Société Historique, 1945), pp. 165-170;

J. Clarence Webster, "The Classics of Acadia," *Canadian Historical Association, Annual Report* (1933): 6-8.

John Lesperance

(1835? - 10 March 1891)

Richard Duprey
Emerson College

BOOKS: *One Hundred Years Ago. An Historical Drama of the War of Independence*, anonymous (Montreal: Minerva, 1876); French edition, *Il y a cent ans* (Montreal: Beauchemin & Valois, 1876);

The Bastonnais: Tale of the American Invasion of Canada 1775-76 (Toronto: Bedford, 1877); French edition, *Les Bastonnais* (Montreal: Beauchemin, 1896);

Toque bleue: A Christmas Snowshoe Sketch (Montreal: Dawson, 1882).

OTHER: William Douw Lightall, ed., *Songs of the Great Dominion*, includes 3 poems by Lesperance (London: Scott, 1889).

SELECTED PERIODICAL PUBLICATIONS– UNCOLLECTED: "American and Canadian Sonnets," *Rose-Belford's Canadian Monthly*, 3 (November 1879): 449-455;

"The Poets of Canada," *Royal Society of Canada Proceedings and Transactions*, first series 2 (23 May 1884): 31-44.

John Lesperance, a man whose fictions may possibly have spilled beyond his writing into the substance of his life, was born in St. Louis, Missouri, probably in 1835. Principally a journalist, working for several Canadian papers, Lesperance claimed he had obtained an education on the Continent and had served in the Confederate Army, stories that have turned out to be dubious at best.

What was certain about Lesperance was that he did succeed in creating a single interesting novel; a short, fanciful holiday piece about the romances of young people; and a collection of poetry that went unpublished as a freestanding work but found partial publication in several periodicals. And he *did* offer considerable support as a journalistic editor and public speaker for the notion of developing the phenomenon of the Canadian writer.

After studying at St. Louis University in his hometown and withdrawing from a course of studies for the priesthood (which began in the Society of Jesus' novitiate at Florissant, Missouri, and took him to other American cities and abroad), Lesperance, of French descent, moved to Saint-Jean, Quebec, in the mid 1860s. He married Parmelle Lacasse in 1866 and began his long career as a journalist and editor by taking a job on the *News and Frontier Advocate*.

It is in regard to these early years of his life that Lesperance created the aforementioned degree of ambiguity, claiming to have studied at the universities of Heidelberg and Paris and to have served as a soldier for the Confederacy in the American Civil War. This seems to be at odds with evidence that he was in the Society of Jesus during the war, serving in Kentucky, Missouri, New York, and Belgium as a Jesuit scholastic before being discharged from the society for reasons of ill health.

After establishing himself in Saint-Jean as a journalist, Lesperance acquired a new position in Montreal. There, from 1873 to 1880, he edited the *Canadian Illustrated News*, and for several years in the 1880s, under the pseudonym Laclede, he wrote a weekly column for the *Gazette*. In 1888, having worked for a time as a provincial immigration officer, he became the first editor of the *Dominion Illustrated News*.

Lesperance had an appreciative eye for literary talent in others and as editor he published works of poetry and fiction by new writers. For instance, he published for the first time Charles Mair's "Last Bison" and "Kanata" in the *Dominion Illustrated*.

He was elected a founding member of the Royal Society of Canada in 1882. At its annual meetings Lesperance read papers such as "The Literature of French Canada" (1883) and "The Poets of Canada" (1884).

He published a popular work of fiction in his hometown when the story "My Creoles," a fictionalized, autobiographical memoir of the Missis-

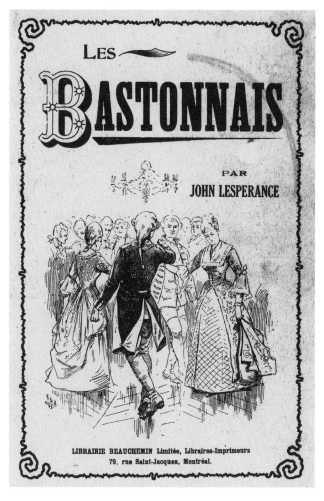

Title page for the 1896 French edition of Lesperance's 1877 novel, a tale of war and romance in Quebec City

sippi Valley, was serialized in the *St. Louis Republican* in 1878. Subsequently the same work was serialized in the *Canadian Illustrated News.* "Rosalba; or Faithful to Two Loves. An Episode of the Rebellion of 1837-38" was published in the *Canadian Illustrated News* in 1870 under the pseudonym Arthur Faverel. The latter work treats English-French relations by focusing on the marriages of a French Canadian girl first to a *Patriote* and then to an English Canadian Loyalist. Lesperance's affection for the French Canadians clearly emerges from the work. Although he wrote in English, his works were frequently translated into French, for they manifested considerable understanding and sympathy for *les habitantes.*

His novel, *The Bastonnais* (1877), is his most important work. Though both sentimental and mannered in the fashion of the day, Lesperance describes well the country of his immigrant choice, and he holds relentlessly to the story, which not only deals with the ill-fated U.S. take-

over of Quebec City but with complicated love affairs between two interesting couples. Both women, Pauline Belmont and Zulma Sarpy, are French Canadians, while one of the young males, Roderick Hardinge, is a lieutenant in the Quebec Militia, sworn to uphold the Crown, and the other, Cary Singleton, is an officer in the American occupying force. Their lives, as well as those of Pauline's noble father and an engaging French Canadian named Batoche, are bound up in the tumult and acrimony of the brief occupation of Quebec by the "Bastonnais."

Lesperance here, too, manifests a great deal of empathy for the French Canadians, and he also describes the "Bastonnais" invaders–as the Quebecois called those rebelling against British authority in New England and southward–in a rather heroic manner: "Arnold's men stood like a spectral army on the heights of Levis, but unlike spectres they did not vanish in the full glare of light. After gazing their fill on the renowned city, which they had come so far to see—its beetling citadel, its winding walls, its massive gates, the peaked roofs of its houses, the tall steeples of its churches, the graceful campaniles of its numerous convents—they set actively to the work of attack which remained as a culmination of their heroic march through the wilderness. The enchantment of distance had now vanished and the reality of vision was now before them."

Among Lesperance's other works is *Toque bleue: A Christmas Snowshoe Sketch* (1882), which uses the courtship of two young couples to describe the activities of the "Old Montreal" and other snowshoe clubs during the winter of 1872-1873. Lesperance also prepared a collection of verse, apparently called "The Book of Honour," but it does not seem to have been printed. William Douw Lighthall included three poems by him in *Songs of the Great Dominion* (1889).

Lesperance wrote eloquently on Canadian poetry. Two of these pieces are "The Poets of Canada" (1884) and "American and Canadian Sonnets" (1879). Additionally, he wrote and spoke in public on the phenomenon of authorship in Canada, working toward a Canadian literature. An example of his ideas is the following excerpt from a paper he read at the Kuklos Club in Montreal on 17 February 1877:

Different men have different ways of testing the progress of a country. My test is the progress of its literature. The deduction is easily made. Where there is an active commerce, there is a free circulation of money; where money is plentiful, a surplus is devoted to education. Education creates a demand for books and the different forms of reading, and to meet this demand publishers eagerly come forward, backed by a host of writers in the divers[e] walks of letters. In a financial crisis the book trade is the first to suffer. In an era of financial prosperity literature always flourishes.

Tried by this standard, there is no question that Canada is rapidly progressing. Twenty years ago, as I am informed schools were scanty; colleges and academies were few, and making only faint beginnings; special courses were unknown, and the people had little to read beyond newspapers and political pamphlets. Now, all this is changed. The common school system is estab

lished everywhere with results that obtain even European commendation; there are colleges and universities mounted on a fair footing; a spirit of inquiry pervades all classes, and the consequence is that Canada is fast laying the foundation of a literature of her own. This is a matter for congratulation. Science, letters and the arts are the triple crown of a people. Dr. Johnson has said that "the chief glory of a nation lies in its authors."

Unusually, Lesperance gave evenhanded attention to French and English writers. In his editorial work and in his critical efforts, he published and spoke well of writers such as Charles Mair and François-Xavier Garneau, as well as Thomas Haliburton, Charles Sangster, Susanna Moodie, and Rosanna Leprohon. At one point it appears that Lesperance turned his attention to drama with an officially nonattributed work, *One Hundred Years Ago* (1876), a play set in the American Revolution and dealing with themes similar to those of *The Bastonnais*.

Lesperance, though not a major figure and to a large extent forgotten, exerted a certain influence in Canadian letters. He encouraged other writers, helping to create a notion that writers of Upper Canada and Lower Canada had a degree of common interest.

Bibliography:
Mary Jane Edwards, "Fiction and Montreal, 1769-1885: A Bibliography," *Papers of the Bibliographical Society of Canada*, 8 (1969): 61-75.

References:
Anonymous, *"The Bastonnais* par John Lesperance," *Opinion Publique*, 8 (5 April 1877): 167;
Mary Jane Edwards, "Essentially Canadian," *Canadian Literature*, 52 (1972);
Edwards, Paul Denham, and George Parker, *The Evolution of Canadian Literature in English: 1867-1914* (Toronto: Holt, Rinehart & Winston, 1973), pp. 16-24;
William B. Faherty, *Better the Dream: St. Louis University and Community, 1818-1968* (St. Louis, 1968).

George Longmore

(1793? - 8 August 1867)

Tracy Ware
Bishop's University

BOOKS: *The Charivari or Canadian Poetics,* as Launcelot Longstaff (Montreal, 1824; modern edition, Ottawa: Golden Dog, 1977);

Tales of Chivalry and Romance, anonymous (Edinburgh: James Robertson, 1826);

The War of the Isles (London: W. Cadell / Edinburgh: W. Blackwood, 1826);

Mathilde: or, The Crusaders, an Historical Drama, in Five Acts (Edinburgh: W. Blackwood, 1827);

The Spirit of the Age (Cape Town, 1837);

The Missionary (Cape Town, 1839);

Don Juan (Cape Town, 1850);

Byzantium: A Poem, in Two Cantos (Cape Town, 1855);

Prince Alfred's Welcome. A Song in Commemoration of the Prince's Visit to South Africa (Cape Town, 1860);

The Pilgrims of Faith, in Three Cantos (Cape Town: Robertson, 1860).

SELECTED PERIODICAL PUBLICATION–
UNCOLLECTED: "Euphrosyne–A Turkish Tale," *Canadian Review and Literary and Historical Journal* (July 1824).

George Longmore is one of those writers whose significance for Canadian literature is disproportionate to the time he spent in Canada. Although only two of his many poems are set in Canada, Longmore is important because of his considerable merit and because of his participation in noteworthy literary trends. *The Charivari* (1824) is the finest of the early Canadian responses to Lord Byron, and *Tecumthe* (written in 1824 and included in *Tales of Chivalry and Romance,* 1826) is the first treatment of its titular hero.

The details of Longmore's career and canon are still somewhat obscure because of a dearth of biographical information, the difficulty of obtaining most of his works, and also because of the anonymous and pseudonymous publication of his early volumes. Until the 1979 scholarship of Mary Lu MacDonald, both his Canadian poems were mistakenly attributed to Levi Adams. Longmore was born in Quebec City, probably in 1793, the son of George and Christina Latitia Longmore, his father a doctor. He lived there until entering the Royal Staff Corps in 1809. His experience overseas in the Peninsular War became the basis for *The War of the Isles* (1826). After returning to Canada around 1820, he lived as an officer in Montreal, then the site of much literary activity. There Longmore wrote *The Charivari* and the poems (including *Tecumthe*) later collected in his *Tales of Chivalry and Romance.* He left Canada in 1824 to become surveyor general of Mauritius. The date of his marriage and the maiden name of his wife, Elizabeth, are unknown, but we do know that the marriage occurred before his departure from Canada and that the Longmores eventually had three daughters. In 1834 the family moved to South Africa, where he held the positions of magistrate and aide-de-camp, and where he continued to publish poetry. After a period of unemployment and, in 1846, bankruptcy, he served as a sergeant at arms (from 1854) and librarian (from 1857) until his death in 1867. Elizabeth died in 1863, and Longmore married Jane Catherine Hide three months before he died.

The cosmopolitanism of his career is reflected in the varied settings, subjects, and styles of his poetry. In *The Charivari,* advertised as a poem "after the manner of *Beppo*" and published under the pseudonym Launcelot Longstaff, he applies the techniques of Byronic satire to the literary and social life of Montreal. A charivari was a colorful local custom, according to which newlyweds of advanced age were aroused from their sleep by a boisterous and occasionally unruly crowd. Baptisto, the mock-heroic bridegroom, demonstrates exemplary common sense in placating the crowd, and as the poem ends he returns to bed. The full title, *The Charivari or Canadian Poetics,* implies that this charivari is also an emblem of the state of early Canadian poetry and, therefore, that the literary digressions in the poem

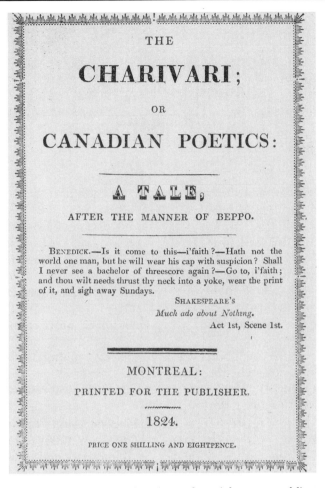

THE

CHARIVARI;

OR

CANADIAN POETICS:

A TALE,

AFTER THE MANNER OF BEPPO.

BENEDICK.—Is it come to this—i'faith?—Hath not the
world one man, but he will wear his cap with suspicion? Shall
I never see a bachelor of threescore again?—Go to, i'faith;
and thou wilt needs thrust thy neck into a yoke, wear the print
of it, and sigh away Sundays.
SHAKESPEARE'S
Much ado about Nothing.
Act 1st, Scene 1st.

MONTREAL:

PRINTED FOR THE PUBLISHER.

1824.

PRICE ONE SHILLING AND EIGHTPENCE.

Title page for Longmore's first book, a Byronic satire on the social customs and literary life of Montreal

("Oh, what a motley group of bards to war at," says the narrator near the opening) are more relevant than they first seem. Furthermore, other details connect the poem with the defeat of the Union Bill of 1822, which would have joined Upper and Lower Canada. Longmore suggests that this defeat can be overcome if common sense like that shown by his protagonist leads to terms of union more equitable to the French. Throughout the poem's 179 ottava rima stanzas, in his conversational manner, obtrusive rhymes, intentional bathos, and witty digressions, in his allusions, and in his explicit critical remarks, Longmore shows a sophisticated understanding of Byron. In so doing he brought a healthy irreverence to Canadian literature.

Longmore published an essay on Byron in *Tales of Chivalry and Romance*, an anonymously published volume later admired by Dante Gabriel Rossetti. The first and last poems in the book, "To the Author of *Waverly*" and "Elegy, On the Death of Lord Byron," point to two important influences on Longmore. For Canadian readers, however, the most interesting poem here is *Tecumthe, A Poetical Tale in Three Cantos*. Relying as Longmore did on oral sources, he is historically inaccurate, but his poem is nonetheless internally consistent. For Longmore the War of 1812 is one of the "gory tales" of "Destructive War." Though he presents the battles of this war, he is also interested in an allegorical contrast of the "art" of the whites to the "ruder virtues" of the Indians. This contrast is then revealed as a false one, an "imperfect choice" of "sophistry." While his sense of human futility is stated repeatedly, his reference to "the purer goal, / Where Faith and justice sway the soul" suggests the ideal of a synthesis that Tecumthe might have achieved if he possessed the "polish'd mind / Civilization's wand supplies."

Longmore is beginning to emerge as one of the more important of the pre-Confederation poets. His *Charivari* offers some provocative insights into early Canadian culture, and his *Tecumthe* compares favorably with John Richardson's *Tecumseh or the Warrior of the West* and Charles Mair's *Tecumseh: A Drama*.

References:

Carl F. Klinck, "*The Charivari* and Levi Adams," *Dalhousie Review*, 40 (Spring 1960): 34-42;

Mary Lu MacDonald, "Further Light on a Life: George Longmore in Cape Colony," *Cana-*

dian Poetry, 24 (Spring/Summer 1989): 62-77;

MacDonald, "George Longmore: A New Literary Ancestor," *Dalhousie Review*, 59 (Summer 1979): 265-285;

Tracy Ware, "George Longmore's *The Charivari*: A Poem 'After the Manner of *Beppo*,'" *Canadian Poetry*, 10 (Spring/Summer 1982): 1-17.

John Keast Lord

(1818 - 9 December 1872)

Bryan N. S. Gooch
University of Victoria

BOOKS: *The Naturalist in Vancouver Island and British Columbia*, 2 volumes (London: Bentley, 1866);

At Home in the Wilderness, as The Wanderer (London: Hardwicke, 1867; republished under author's name, London: Hardwicke & Bogue, 1876).

John Keast Lord, about whose life certain details are a matter of speculation, grew up in Tavistock, Devon, received a medical education at St. Bartholomew's Hospital (London), and subsequently (in 1844) a diploma from the Royal Veterinary College. Lord's education was evidently not narrow; he clearly developed a skill not only in animal medicine but in zoology and classification, as well as an informed interest in virtually all parts of the natural world. He was obviously well read—his literary references are telling clues. Though he returned to a veterinary practice in Tavistock, the call of distant climes was too strong to be resisted. After surviving a shipwreck on Anticosti Island in the Gulf of St. Lawrence, he apparently served on a Greenland whaler, later found his way to Quebec (not for the first time in the grip of cholera), and thence to Bruce County, Ontario, where he spent a winter at the copper mines, as well as to Arkansas and west to Minnesota and the eastern approaches to the Rocky Mountains. He was a strong, large, bushy-

bearded adventurer in a wild and often hostile country.

That Lord styled himself as "The Wanderer"–as author of *At Home in the Wilderness* in 1867–was not inappropriate. But the Wild West did not hold him. He returned to England only to go out as a veterinary surgeon in the Osmanli Horse Artillery to the Crimean conflict (1854-1856) and, after a brief sojourn in England, was drawn again to North America in 1858, this time to British Columbia and the American Northwest (with a quick trip to northern California). He served as a veterinary surgeon and naturalist to the British North American Land Boundary Commission, which was charged, like its American counterpart, with surveying and clearing the borderline (on the 49th parallel) between what was to become Canada and the United States. The first chapter of *The Naturalist in Vancouver Island and British Columbia* (1866) describes his trip across the Atlantic by paddle steamer, the crossing of the isthmus of Panama by train, and the paddle steamer voyage up the West Coast to Victoria, a trip made specifically for the purpose of participating in commission work.

While his sojourn in the West was both fascinating and valuable to him from a scientific point of view, it was relatively brief. He returned to London in 1861. In 1863 he appeared–in the dress of a western pioneer/trapper–to give lectures in

Engraving courtesy of the National Library of Canada

the Egyptian Hall, Piccadilly, on "The Canoe, the Rifle and the Axe." Subsequently, he left for the Mediterranean (1868-1869) to carry out scientific and archaeological work in Egypt, Arabia, and along the western shore of the Red Sea, under the aegis of the viceroy of Egypt, returning to England and finally taking up an appointment in 1872 as the first manager of the Brighton Aquarium, in which post he served only a short time; he died in December of that year.

Lord was clearly an avid and effective chronicler of his numerous experiences, and the results of his journeys were preserved both in the numerous remarkable and thorough collections of fauna and other artifacts (with impeccable documentation, given the period) deposited in the British Museum and in the prose accounts of his experiences, contributions to the extensive and growing range of travel literature. His two books

on North America gained him a place among the important mid-century writers of the new country; they combine lively reporting of day-to-day adventures and travel in a new, rough, and exciting country, with detailed comments on the terrain and vast array of wildlife as well as the animals in his charge.

The Naturalist in Vancouver Island and British Columbia carries a slightly misleading title, for it concerns not only Lord's ventures and observations on what was to be the Canadian side of the boundary but also his excursions into American territory as far south as Sacramento and Stockton to obtain mules for the commission and drive them north to Fort Colville. Further, while the title suggests primarily a scientific focus, the text is a happy mélange of stories about pioneer life and the range of species coming under Lord's gaze. Part of the excitement is generated by the

217

sometimes understated accounts of hair-raising adventures with obstacles both animal and human (including hostile Indians, on occasion), and part of it by the infectious enthusiasm Lord displays in his discovery of new species and his genuine pleasure in collecting and preparing specimens for the museum. The reader is treated, then, to an account that lies at once in the realm of colonial travel literature and the area of burgeoning and important scientific record; and what makes it all so approachable is Lord's fluid, clear, and pleasant, discursive style, which is marked on many occasions by high humor, by a sense of mischief and fun, and by an evident delight in what he is doing, a pleasure that manages to underplay a great deal of the very real physical hardship. Lord neither complains nor laments, despite obvious difficulties; he copes, and he does so with energy and a clear mind. The written record is valuable as a scientific and historical document; it is also valuable as a literary document and was obviously designed to appeal to a broad audience in England in his day. His purpose is stated clearly enough in the preface: "the Author has purposely avoided any definite system of arrangement, preferring a pleasant gossip, chatting, as it were, by the fireside about North-Western wilds." He wants to supply what he calls the "missing link" in volumes about Vancouver Island and British Columbia (at the time two separate colonies), offering details not only about natural history–about genera and species–but about the *habits* of the wildlife.

That he fulfills his promise is often demonstrated. Of Victoria in the throes of gold-rush crowds on their way north he remarks: "The rattle of the dice-box, the droning invitation of the keepers of the monte-tables, the discordant sounds of badly-played instruments, angry words, oaths too terrible to name, roistering songs with noisy refrains, were all signs of the golden talisman that met me on every side. . . . " The same descriptive vigor is applied to the stickleback: "one of the most voracious little gourmands imaginable, devourer of everything, and cannibals into the bargain; tearing their wounded comrades into fragments, they greedily swallow them." He reports with some mischievous glee his theft of the severed head of an Indian chief (a battle token) from under the noses of the victorious tribe–he wanted it as a specimen, since the shape of the skull had been altered by flattening. Remarks on the lowly clam are equally graphic: "there is nothing poetical about [it], and its habits

are anything but clean; grovelling in the mud, and feeding on the veriest filth it can find, appears to be the great pleasure of its life; [its] stomach is a kind of dust hole, into which anything and everything finds ready admission." Certain of the anecdotes in these volumes are reprints of material published earlier–his trip to Fort Rupert appeared, for example, in *Once A Week* (24 June 1865). Obviously he gained a good deal of literary mileage from his exploits. Despite his claim to lack of arrangement, the book holds together well–the reader simply has to keep in mind the rough chronology–and the frequent interludes to describe a "new" muskrat, Clark's crow, a "new" cicada, or the yellow-haired porcupine are not disturbances but part of the delight.

At Home in the Wilderness, published in 1867 under the pseudonym "The Wanderer" and later republished under Lord's own name, carries a revealing subtitle: "what to do there and how to do it: a handbook for travellers and emigrants." Like *The Naturalist*, this book is based largely on Lord's Boundary Commission experiences and deals with virtually all the practical problems of survival in the bush; his subjects include tents, bedding, clothing, guns, edible berries, house-building, rattlesnakes, deer ticks, managing pack trains, and crossing rivers. Once more, the style is pleasant and congenial: Lord has the happy knack of talking directly to his reader and offering personal advice. In discussing crossing a river with baggage, for instance, he remarks: "you must tie up the things in a buffalo skin– remember I told you never to travel without one strapped to the back of the saddle." The geography noted in this volume also ranges outside the Northwest to the southern United States (including Texas), and though the object is practical, the advice is in anecdotal form in many instances and provides interesting vignettes–the description of a rodeo (a primitive and somewhat grisly affair) is a case in point. And here, too, he draws on earlier material; his account of the breeze-flies and their effect on mules also appears in *The Naturalist*. Books of this kind were numerous–even Susanna Moodie's *Roughing It in the Bush* (1852) is a member of the group–and clearly had their place in a day when prospective immigrants needed to be prepared for life in the wilds, where nature often did not give greenhorns a second chance of survival. And the books have their place for the modern reader who wants to come to grips with the nature of pioneer life and the appearance of the land in the late 1850s and 1860s.

The Naturalist and *At Home* are such vivid accounts of early life in the West that they must find a secure position in the ranks of significant colonial literature. Here one does not encounter an imperial traveler who looks down his nose to cast aspersions on the roughness of the country or its inhabitants, but a highly articulate and, indeed, brilliant scientific vagabond whose reputation as naturalist and storyteller has been grossly undervalued during the last century and a quarter.

References:

Anonymous, "John Keast Lord, F. Z. S." *Leisure Hour*, 1 November 1870, pp. 696-699;

J. W. Eastham, "John Keast Lord," *Museum Notes* (Vancouver), 2 (May 1927): 3-7; (December 1927): 3-8.

Alexander Mackenzie

(1763 - 12 March 1820)

Victor G. Hopwood
University of British Columbia

BOOKS: *Voyages from Montreal, on the River St. Laurence, through the Continent of North America, to the Frozen and Pacific Oceans; in the Years 1789 and 1793*, edited by William Combe (London: Cadell & Davies, 1801; New York: G. F. Hopkins, 1802); modern edition, edited by J. W. Garvin (Toronto: Radisson Society of Canada, 1927);

The Travels of Capts. Lewis & Clarke, by Order of the Government of the United States, Performed in the Years 1804, 1805, & 1806 (Philadelphia: Hubbard Lester, 1809);

The Journals and Letters of Sir Alexander Mackenzie, edited by W. Kaye Lamb (London: Cambridge University Press / Toronto: Macmillan, 1970).

In 1802 the *Edinburgh Review* called attention to Alexander Mackenzie's *Voyages from Montreal* (1801) in a way that anticipates and defines the response of most readers. The reviewer points out how "the idea of traversing a vast and unknown continent . . . gives an agreeable expansion to our conceptions; and the imagination is insensibly engaged and inflamed." The statement reaches beyond Mackenzie to most worthwhile exploration literature.

Alexander Mackenzie, born in Stornoway, Scotland, in 1763, the only son and oldest child of Kenneth and Isabella Mackenzie, immigrated

Alexander Mackenzie (portrait by Thomas Lawrence; by permission of the National Gallery of Canada, War Memorials Collection).

with his family to America. As his father was a Royalist, Alexander was sent to Montreal, where

First page of a letter from Mackenzie to John Sullivan, Under Secretary of State for the British Department of War and the Colonies. One of only a few extant autograph letters by Mackenzie, it refers to a proposed union of the XY and North West companies, which occurred in 1804 (by permission of the Public Record Office, London).

after a brief schooling he entered the fur trade in 1779 as a countinghouse clerk. After five years he went west as a trader. In 1787 his concern was absorbed into the North West Company, with Mackenzie becoming a *bourgeois* (partner). He was sent to Fort Chipewyan in the Athabasca district (now in Alberta) to join and then replace the irascible American Peter Pond, who had been involved in the deaths of two other traders. From Pond, whom the Nor'Westers squeezed out, Mackenzie undoubtedly got his ideas of the possibility of a route that led to either the Pacific or the Arctic and could open a fur trade in China.

In 1789, with his young cousin Roderic Mackenzie looking after trade and logistics in Athabasca, Mackenzie made his first great exploration–to the Arctic by the river later named for him. He is dubiously said to have called it "the River Disappointment" because it reached the sea too far north to open a route to the Pacific; he certainly called it "the Grand River."

In 1793, with Roderic again minding his base, Mackenzie carried out his even more venturesome and arduous journey to the Pacific. Not far from what is now Bella Coola, British Columbia, he wrote his most famous and typically laconic words: "I now mixed up some vermillion in melted grease, and inscribed, in large characters, on the South-East face of the rock on which we had slept last night, this brief memorial– 'Alexander Mackenzie, from Canada, by land, the twenty-second of July, one thousand, seven hundred and ninety-three'" (*The Journals and Letters*, 1970). He had completed the first crossing of North America in its continental width.

Mackenzie's *Voyages from Montreal* brought fame for him and for his explorations. Two months later he was knighted. Mackenzie himself asked only "the approbation due to simplicity and to truth" (*The Journals and Letters*), a request generally allowed by posterity. Only occasionally does he indulge in rhetoric or fancy writing, although this may in part come from his editor, William Combe, the author of *Doctor Syntax*. The real force of Mackenzie's writing comes from his energetic practicality. Indeed, *Voyages from Mon-*

treal has an epic quality, but with the absence of epic similes. Mackenzie himself had the bravery, persistence, keenness of observation, inventiveness, wariness, and diplomacy of Odysseus; in addition, he was honest; he also avoided violence, never firing a hostile shot in all his journeys among Indians.

Mackenzie's *Voyages from Montreal* is essentially his own, a slight reworking of the journals of his two explorations. However, his failure to admit the contribution of others to both his explorations and his book reveals an egotistic lack of feeling in a generally admirable man. Pond gets no credit for his ideas; nor Roderic for his support or for writing the long introduction on the history of the fur trade; nor David Thompson for drawing the maps or for contributing the many geographical locations in the introduction.

Marshall Bernadotte had *Voyages from Montreal* specially translated for Napoleon, who was interested in finding a back route for a diversionary expedition against Canada. Thomas Jefferson bought a copy. No doubt it spurred him on to establish the Lewis and Clark expedition, which Mackenzie later reported on (1809).

After leaving the West in 1794, Mackenzie continued until the end of his life to be involved in struggles for control of the fur trade, first for the North West Company, then for the Hudson's Bay Company. He married Geddes Mackenzie in 1812. Still a relatively wealthy man, he died in Scotland on 12 March 1820.

Letters:

The Journals and Letters of Sir Alexander Mackenzie, edited by W. Kaye Lamb (London: Cambridge University Press / Toronto: Macmillan, 1970).

Biography:

Roy Daniells, *Alexander Mackenzie and the North West* (London: Faber & Faber, 1969).

Reference:

Roy Daniells, "The Literary Relevance of Alexander Mackenzie," *Canadian Literature*, 38 (Autumn 1968): 19-28.

Charles Mair
(21 September 1838 - 7 July 1927)

Norman Shrive
McMaster University

BOOKS: *Dreamland and Other Poems* (Montreal: Dawson / London: Low & Marston, 1868);

Tecumseh, A Drama (Toronto: Hunter, Rose / London: Chapman & Hall, 1886);

Tecumseh, A Drama and Canadian Poems (Toronto: Briggs, 1901); enlarged edition, edited by J. W. Garvin (Toronto: Radisson Society, 1926 [i.e., 1927]);

Through the Mackenzie Basin; A Narrative of the Athabasca and Peace River Treaty Expedition of 1899 (Toronto: Briggs, 1908; London: Simpkin, Marshall, Hamilton, Kent, 1908).

Edition: *Dreamland and Other Poems, Tecumseh: A Drama*, edited by Norman Shrive (Toronto: University of Toronto Press, 1974).

SELECTED PERIODICAL PUBLICATIONS–
UNCOLLECTED: "The New Canada," *Canadian Monthly and National Review*, 8 (July and August 1875): 2-8, 156-164;

"The American Bison," *Transactions of the Royal Society of Canada*, first series 2 (1890): 93-108.

Charles Mair

Charles Mair is of considerable significance in both Canadian literature and history. Less than a year after Confederation he published the appropriately entitled *Dreamland* (1868), Canada's first important collection of poetry. In 1886 *Tecumseh* appeared, a patriotic verse drama that was an almost sensational success, in Toronto at least. But he is equally notable, in some quarters notorious, for his melodramatic role in the Riel insurrection at Red River in 1869 and 1870, from which he narrowly escaped with his life. During his long life he was an avid if eventually disillusioned nationalist.

Mair's paternal grandparents were Scottish immigrants to Lanark, Upper Canada (later Ontario), in 1824, his father in 1831; Mair was born there on 21 September 1838, the son of James and Margaret Mair. Until he was thirty he lived in Lanark and nearby Perth, obviously much influenced by the romantic if culturally primitive life of the timber trade and by the family's general merchandising businesses. Mair attended Queen's medical school for one year in 1856 (where he probably met John Schultz of later Red River notoriety) and began contributing reviews, verse, and nature articles to the *Montreal Transcript* and the *British American Magazine*. By 1868 he had become much concerned with the territories of the Northwest and their possible future as part of a Canadian nation or, ominously, of American expansionist policies. In May of that year he was in Ottawa, seeing his first collection of poems, *Dreamland*, through the press, and while there he met the four other young men with whom he was to form the so-called "Canada First party"–Henry J. Morgan, Robert G. Haliburton, George T. Denison, and William A. Foster. Mair also came to the attention of William McDougall, minister of public works and one of the key figures in negotiating the transfer of the Northwest territories of the Hudson's Bay Company to Canada. With these men Mair became a dedicated nationalist.

Dreamland contains thirty-three poems, mostly short lyrics, with titles such as "Innocence," "Our Beautiful Land by the Sea," and "Stanzas from the Heart" reflecting the book's highly romantic flavor and debt to John Keats, Percy Bysshe Shelley, Edgar Allan Poe, and Algernon Charles Swinburne. Its quality is very uneven. Some lines convey an imaginative sensitivity, a real capacity to see and depict minute details of the animals and birds of the woods; others are ludicrous, even grotesque, in Mair's attempts to be "literary," and betray his youthful reading and the more unsophisticated aspects of life in Lanark. The book was widely reviewed in Canada, the United States, and England, with transatlantic differences of critical opinion being marked by unstinted praise in Toronto and Montreal and the opposite in London. Copies are today rare, partly because all but two hundred were destroyed in a fire at the Ottawa binding house at the time of publication.

Just as the book appeared, McDougall, slated to be lieutenant-governor of the new territory when it became part of Canada, asked Mair to go to Red River and write articles for the Montreal and Toronto papers extolling the virtues of the new country and encouraging immigration to it. Although often brilliant, these reports' sometimes tasteless references to the Métis aggravated already tense feelings in the settlement–Mair was even physically assailed. By Christmas 1869 he, Schultz, and others were imprisoned in Fort Garry and even threatened with death by the insurgent Louis Riel, but by mid January Mair had escaped and, after a quite incredible journey across the frozen wastes of North Dakota, arrived in Toronto to help incite the public outcry against Riel.

In September 1869 Mair had married Elizabeth MacKenney, and after comparative peace returned to Red River. They lived first in Portage la Prairie, then, in 1877, moved to Prince Albert, on the North Saskatchewan River. There Mair engaged in fur trading, general merchandising, and land speculation, hoping to emulate the prosperity of Schultz in Winnipeg and eventually find the security and time necessary for a protracted period of writing. By 1882 he was reasonably prosperous, but once again the West began to fear the possibility of insurrection. Drought and frost were followed by a drop in property values.

The plight of the Indians and the Métis began to assume ominous proportions. Ottawa continued to delay any clear policy about development and land entitlement. Mair therefore moved his family to Windsor, Ontario, where he composed his verse drama, *Tecumseh*, interrupted temporarily while he joined the militia regiment of his old friend Denison in the North-West Rebellion of 1885.

"I am conscious that it is a great work," Mair wrote to his wife on 19 February 1886, when *Tecumseh* was published (Mair Papers, Queen's University). There is no doubt about Mair's purpose–to reflect and inculcate a great national spirit. But it is hardly a "great" work. For five acts of twenty-eight scenes, which, if acted, would require at least four hours, the play presents a pageant of stylized and highly rhetorical history, Mair's version of the three-sided struggle for the North-American continent, the War of 1812.

During the period depicted, three heroes, Tecumseh, Gen. Isaac Brock, and Lefroy ("a poet-artist, enamoured of Indian life"), vie for supremacy not only with invading Americans (including "Yankee ruffians") but also with traitors in their own camps: Tecumseh's villainous brother the Prophet and Brock's cowardly subordinate commander, Col. Procter. Since the play is a tragedy, the final curtain falls on a scene of desolation–Tecumseh is dead, Procter has ignominiously retreated, the Americans have won the important battle of Moraviantown, and the Indian maiden Iena (the love interest) is carried away lifeless in the arms of the distraught Lefroy. Brock, however, has died gloriously in victory at Queenston Heights, Tecumseh has achieved immortality even in failure, and the Canadian reader is obviously expected to realize that the ultimate outcome of the war was an American defeat.

As with *Dreamland*, Mair's *Tecumseh* reflects an inconsistency of quality, an unsureness of poetic and dramatic principles. The subordination of such principles to those of ardent nationalism and of sentimental melodrama results in a literary curiosity. But the critics acclaimed the work as Canada's outstanding artistic achievement. It was quickly and completely sold out.

As he had done in 1870, Mair returned to the West, hoping to prosper in business and to continue writing. Several patriotic pieces appeared in journals and newspapers, and in 1889 he was elected to the Royal Society of Canada and submitted a paper on the "American Bison," a remark-

Mair with his son Cecil in 1883 (Queen's
University Archives)

Mair's wife, Elizabeth Louise (née MacKenney), whom he married in September 1869

The Chain.

Once from the bitter page of Doubt it hapt
    That, wearily, I turned me to the wall, .
And, lo! there, in the hearth's dull embers, all
    The self-same thoughts which harrowed me seemed mapt.
    But near were coiled a cat and kitten, lapt
In furry dream; then next, where lay in thrall
Of slumber softer than a feather's fall
    Dear wife and babe, I stood in silence rapt.

Dendless chain of being and of love,
    · O paths and pathos of mysterious sleep,,
    Ye pointed to a world yet undescried!
Strange calm befell me, light as from above,
    And thoughts which man can neither yield nor keep:
    My heart was filled, my house was glorified!

                                                    C. Mair
                                                    - 1888.

Fair copy of one of Mair's romantic poems (Queen's University Archives, Lorne Pierce Collection; by permission of the Estate of Elizabeth L. [Mair] Jamieson)

Charles Mair (Queen's University Archives; Lorne Pierce Collection)

able reflection of the clarity, the richness of metaphor, and the detailed knowledge that had characterized the best of his letters to the *Globe* in 1869, and a plea for the preservation of a vanishing species "which has been of great service on our continent . . . and whose extinction would be a disgrace to civilized man." Within a few years the Canadian government brought the only available buffalo herd from Montana to a sanctuary recommended by Mair: Wainwright Park, Alberta.

By 1892, however, Mair's hope for prosperity in the West had faded; as the economic depression grew, his land speculations and failing general-store business in Prince Albert placed him heavily in debt. He opened a store in Kelowna, British Columbia, but to no avail. Then, in 1898, he secured a minor appointment as an immigration agent in Clifford Sifton's ministry of the interior. For almost twenty-five years—until he was in his eighties—Mair conducted the settlers, now pouring in, to their new farms in

Manitoba, Saskatchewan, Alberta, and British Columbia, and prepared much of the department's descriptive literature. He began this new career in Winnipeg, then went to Lethbridge, Alberta, and then to Fort Steele, British Columbia, where he retired in 1921.

During this period he published, in 1901, *Tecumseh, A Drama and Canadian Poems*, a collection of his two previous works (with revisions to *Dreamland* to make it more "Canadian") and other pieces that had appeared in periodicals. It went virtually unnoticed and was a financial failure. Then, in 1908, *Through the Mackenzie Basin* appeared, the record of a trip he had made in 1899 as English secretary of the Scrip Commission, and a confirmation that Mair had not lost his vigorous prose style. In the 1920s John W. Garvin made an earnest attempt to revive interest in Mair through his Master-Works series, but the Mair volume, which appeared in April 1927 (dated 1926), was a pretentious failure. Mair died shortly afterward, on 7 July, in Victoria, British Columbia, and was buried beside his wife (who died in 1906) in Ross Bay Cemetery. They had had five daughters and two sons, of whom three daughters and a son survived their father.

A. J. M. Smith wrote in 1966 that "Mair . . . was not a very attractive character nor a consistent one," that he "was the willing victim of the colonists' desire to demonstrate that they could produce a poet of as good a class as those of the old world and who therefore must write in the language of the old world." The two small communities in which Mair lived a major part of his life give additional emphasis to this assessment. *Dreamland* reflects weaknesses particularly relevant to an environment of backwoods Upper Canada and to a conception of the writer's craft gained from a reading of the more romantic, the more "manly" of the recognized British authors. By the time he had embarked upon *Tecumseh*, Mair had become a practicing patriot, had been involved, indeed, in one of the most stirring events in Canada's political history. His concept of nationalism, therefore, not only permeates the drama; it provides its raison d'être. He is, perhaps, the best example Canadians have of the confusing of national sentiment with literary merit, of the personal and artistic inability either to separate them or to combine them into aesthetic unity.

Biography:

Norman Shrive, *Charles Mair: Literary Nationalist* (Toronto: University of Toronto Press, 1965).

References:

John Matthews, "Charles Mair," *Canada's Past and Present: Our Living Tradition*, fifth series (Toronto: University of Toronto Press, 1965), pp. 78-101;

A. J. M. Smith, "A Fatal Mistake," *Canadian Literature*, 27 (Winter 1966): 59-61.

Papers:

Mair's papers, including correspondence to and from him, are in the Denison Papers, Public Archives of Canada, Ottawa, and in the Garvin Papers and Mair Papers at Queen's University Library, Kingston, Ontario.

Thomas McCulloch

(1776 - 9 September 1843)

Gwendolyn Davies
Acadia University

BOOKS: *Popery Condemned by Scripture and the Fathers* (Edinburgh: J. Pillans, 1808);

Popery Again Condemned by Scripture and the Fathers (Edinburgh: A. Neill, 1810);

Colonial Gleanings: William and Melville (Edinburgh: W. Oliphant, 1826);

A Memorial from the Committee of Missions of the Presbyterian Church of Nova Scotia, to the Glasgow Society for Promoting the Religious Interests of the Scottish Settlers in British North America (Edinburgh: Oliver & Boyd, 1826);

Calvinism, the Doctrine of the Scriptures (Glasgow: Collins, 1849);

Letters of Mephibosheth Stepsure (Halifax: Blackadar, 1860 [i.e., 1862]); modern edition published as *The Stepsure Letters* (Toronto: McClelland & Stewart, 1960); another modern edition, edited by Gwendolyn Davies as *The Mephibosheth Stepsure Letters* (Ottawa: Carleton University Press, 1990).

OTHER: "Auld Eppie's Tales" [unpublished novel], edited by Heather MacFadgen, B.A. thesis, Mount Allison University, 1981.

An educator, clergyman, and writer, Thomas McCulloch was a major force in shaping the intellectual, religious, and cultural life of Nova Scotia in the first four decades of the nineteenth century. As the guiding power behind Pictou Academy and as the first principal of Dalhousie College, he did much to further the cause of liberal education in the province and to extend higher learning to those outside the established church. His endeavors on behalf of Secessionist Presbyterians led to his training an indigenous ministry, while his letters, sermons, and fictional sketches reveal his untiring efforts to challenge the patronage and complacency of colonial society. Often portrayed by his antagonists as an unbending and waspish man, McCulloch in fact recognized the efficacy of humor in translating moral works into successful agents of reform. His *Letters of Mephibosheth Stepsure* (1860; first pub-

lished serially in the *Acadian Recorder*, 22 December 1821 - 29 March 1823) illustrates the effectiveness of his earthy, tongue-in-cheek satire in exposing human follies and foibles, and has joined Thomas Chandler Haliburton's "Sam Slick" sketches (1835-1853) as classic expressions of nineteenth-century Canadian humor.

Born in 1776 in the parish of Neilston in Renfrewshire, Scotland, McCulloch was the son of Michael McCulloch, a master block-printer, and Elizabeth Neilson McCulloch. After attending the University of Glasgow to study medicine, McCulloch entered the Secessionist Divinity Hall at Whitburn and in 1799 was ordained a minister of the Secession Church at Stewarton, near Glasgow. He remained there in a disciplined round of parish activities and self-study (Oriental languages, literature, and British Constitutional history) until just before his 1803 departure for Canada and Prince Edward Island. After wintering in Pictou, Nova Scotia, he accepted that town's call to establish a Presbyterian congregation there and did not proceed to Prince Edward Island as planned.

Throughout his clerical career in Pictou, McCulloch was embroiled in controversies that divided the Secessionist Church in Nova Scotia from the Church of Scotland, and these differences eventually complicated McCulloch's attempts to sustain an institution of higher learning in Pictou for the education of dissenters. However, his most immediate obstacle in establishing Pictou Academy was the reluctance of His Majesty's Council to support non-Anglican colleges, and between 1805 and 1838 McCulloch fought for the cause of Pictou Academy at home and abroad with varying degrees of success.

A permanent building for the academy was finally opened in 1818, and for the next two decades dissenters came from all over the region to study under the man who was not only introducing a Scottish system of education into higher learning in Nova Scotia but was also becoming increasingly renowned as a lecturer on both science

*Most affectionately yours
Thomas McCulloch*

and theology. By 1822 McCulloch had already received honorary doctorates from Union College in Schenectady and the University of Glasgow in recognition of his contributions as a churchman, educator, and naturalist, and he brought to Pictou Academy standards of teaching and a program of study as rigorous as those found in contemporary Scottish universities. Thus, although Pictou Academy was never officially designated a college because of its secessionist Presbyterian affiliation, it did much to provide a highly educated new middle class for the Maritime region. From its halls professionals were to venture forth to challenge the social, political, and religious hegemony enjoyed by the province's old colonial hierarchy.

Closely related to McCulloch's work as an educator and clergyman was the theological and creative writing in which he was engaged in the 1808-1833 period. His *Popery Condemned* and *Popery Again Condemned* were published in Edinburgh in 1808 and 1810 respectively in direct response to a Protestant-Roman Catholic controversy raging in Halifax at the time. While McCulloch's mustering of patristic, scriptural, and historical evidence in the defense of Protestantism earned him the qualified respect of the Anglican bishop Charles Inglis, it did little in the long run to soften the council's opposition to Pictou Academy.

McCulloch's religious writing was often a direct extension of his active involvement in provincial affairs and so was his creative work. The letters of "Mephibosheth Stepsure," originally published anonymously (1821-1823), were rooted in McCulloch's deep concern over the manners and morals of Nova Scotian society and attacked everything from the get-rich-quick mentality of

The Thomas McCulloch House in Pictou, Nova Scotia, where McCulloch lived from 1803 to 1838

new settlers to the false values of Halifax and its satellite small towns. To mask his message, McCulloch employed a persona, Mephibosheth Stepsure, an outspoken farmer who prided himself on having overcome poverty, servitude, and two clubfeet. With a Bible in one hand and a hoe in the other, Stepsure acerbically berates those who do not follow his example of sobriety, diligence, and thrift. As part of his philosophy, he advocates staying at home, lashing out at those who choose to "gad about" instead of "stepping sure."

To enliven his moral message, McCulloch filled his sketches with characters who represent vices, such as Mr. Tipple, Miss Sippit, Ehud Slush, Yelpit, Puff, and the Goslings, but the real strength of the interconnected letters lies in the author's subtle treatment of the central figure, Stepsure. Suggesting at the beginning of the sketches that Stepsure is the moral exemplar against whom the entire community is to be measured, McCulloch later reveals his self-righteous little protagonist to be as corruptible as the neighbors he criticizes. Thus while the satire in the letters operates on one level by having Stepsure act

as an agent of satire, it functions on another by increasingly making the persona the subject of the author's irony. By the end of book 1 of the sketches, the gratingly pompous Stepsure is hiding his undignified, lame feet behind a green cloth, courting the Halifax magistrates he once professed to despise, and signing himself "Mephibosheth Stepsure, Gentleman."

The effectiveness of McCulloch's satire on the corruption of rural values in the New World can be measured by the reaction the *Letters of Mephibosheth Stepsure* provoked. Years later, as reported by William McCulloch, the author's son, one old Nova Scotian was to recall that "we looked with great anxiety for the arrival of the *Recorder,* and on its receipt used to assemble in the shop of Mr.– to hear 'Stepsure' read, and pick out the characters, and comment on their foibles, quite sure that they and the writer were among ourselves. Great was often the anger expressed, and threats uttered against the author if they could discover him." The editors of the *Acadian Recorder* praised the satires for painting "with such inimitable truth the thoughtless, luxurious, and ex-

McCulloch's resignation from Pictou Academy on the occasion of his being named principal of Dalhousie in Halifax
(Collection of the McCulloch family)

travagant habits of our population" (11 May 1822), and encouraged McCulloch in his plan to publish more letters. The most interesting of these later letters (book 2) are those that present a mock-heroic confrontation among Apollo, Stepsure, and the Halifax critic Censor. The responses to Censor, in their play on epic conventions, earthy imagery, and spoofing of romanticism, give new evidence of McCulloch's versatility as a creative writer.

The local success of the Stepsure letters encouraged McCulloch to send them to Scotland (as he said in a 10 November 1822 letter to his friend Rev. John Mitchell in Glasgow) in the hope that "some bookseller who deals in light wares might sometime or other consent to publish them as a sketch of American manners." Although William Blackwood was willing to issue them in revised form in his magazine, he turned down the book, with McCulloch's suggested title of "Chronicles of our Town, or, a Peep at America," because of the explicitness of some of the Swiftian humor and the particularity of the Nova Scotia setting. However, memories and scattered

copies of the original newspaper version of the sketches continued to keep Stepsure alive in the public mind in the Maritimes for several years thereafter. (McCulloch was to write Mitchell–in the 10 November 1822 letter–"I would have sent you a printed copy but these were so thumbed that such a thing could not be got.") But it was not until 1862–nineteen years after McCulloch's death–that the original sixteen letters were to appear in book form in Halifax (with 1860 on the title page).

With their episodic structure, stock figures, direct address, and socially conscious protagonist, the letters of Mephibosheth Stepsure employ many of the conventions of popular fiction familiar to McCulloch in his youth in Scotland. His next literary endeavor, published in Edinburgh in 1826, also reflects the influence of the author's eighteenth-century literary education. Consisting of a pair of moral tales entitled "William" and "Melville," *Colonial Gleanings* was written, as McCulloch states in the preface, "for the information of those parents and children in Britain, who found their hope of happiness upon the acquisition of wealth in foreign lands." "Melville" also appeared in the *Novascotian* (September-October 1826) and, with its emphasis on the temptations facing new settlers, echoes many of the concerns articulated in the Stepsure satires. The hero (Melville) is shown to be an ideal Scottish youth, conscious of his responsibility to his family and filled with good intentions about succeeding in the New World. Nonetheless, he is attracted to the vices of Nova Scotia's provincial capital, Halifax; gradually, drinking, gambling, and business expediency destroy the virtue that was once there.

As in the Stepsure sketches, the urban area is shown to be a Vanity Fair, and Melville, who has emigrated on the same ship as William, is shown to be as susceptible to the spiritual perversion of the garrison town as his fellow countryman. The protagonists of *Colonial Gleanings* both repent before they die, but not before McCulloch has meticulously traced every stage of their downfalls. Essentially a moralist in his fiction, the author seemed determined to reveal to Nova Scotians how subtle and seemingly insignificant were the turning points in their lives. In this sense, he provided an explanation for individual misfortune never found in Haliburton's more famous "Sam Slick" sketches.

In spite of their regional references and a few allusions to Scottish history, "William" and "Melville" never transcend the didactic limitations imposed upon them by their genre. However, with his next novel, written in 1828 and 1829, McCulloch turned to something less predictable, writing to his friend Mitchell in Glasgow on 16 January 1828, "I hope it will be read and amuse. I have begun with the days of popery and intend to carry on through three volumes without meddling with any thing but popery and the progress of Lollardism in the west of Scotland, not forgetting a due quantity of witches, kelpies, and other gods whom our fathers worshipped." The (unpublished) result, "Auld Eppie's Tales," is an ambitious work set in McCulloch's boyhood area of Neilston and unfolding in part through the filtered narrative voice of Auld Eppie. As in Sir Walter Scott's work, the rustics speak in a broad Scots dialect and the upper classes in precise English, although McCulloch's portrayal of the Covenanters is far more sympathetic than that in Scott's *Tales of My Landlord* (1819). To dramatize Scottish history, McCulloch felt it most appropriate to focus the novel on the region he knew best, and for this reason Paisley

Abbey and its monks play an important role in the work.

Although McCulloch had expectations that Blackwood would publish "Auld Eppie's Tales," McCulloch suggested in an 18 May 1829 letter that the volumes were rejected because "there is too much dirt in them." Moreover, although McCulloch had planned "Auld Eppie's Tales" as an answer to Scott's *Tales of My Landlord,* Blackwood clearly wanted to avoid comparisons with Scott's work. In some bitterness McCulloch observed to Mitchell (18 May 1829) that he had "never intended to be an imitator of Sir Walter" and in fact was convinced "that the kind of information and humour which I possessed would have enabled me to vindicate where he was misrepresented and also to render contemptible and ludicrous what he has laboured to dignify."

In the period following the composition of "Auld Eppie's Tales," McCulloch was actively involved in politics over the future of Pictou Academy and felt, according to a 3 December 1829 letter, that he had "too many irons in the fire to engage in any literary undertakings." By 1833, however, he had again composed a series of sketches, some of them commemorating his cherished colleague Dr. James McGregor, whom he had already developed as a character in *Colonial Gleanings.* McCulloch offered this book to Oliphant's of Edinburgh for fifty guineas, indicating at the same time that he was writing a four-hundred-page novel set in 1669, before the murder of Archbishop James Sharp. Oliphant was evidently not interested in the novel, for a letter written by McCulloch on 18 July 1834 (to Mitchell) announces somewhat bitterly that he can no longer "bear pace with the judgment of the public" and will henceforth cease writing.

Also discouraging McCulloch from continuing a literary career at this time were the political events surrounding the final demise of Pictou Academy as an institution of higher learning. With his first educational experiment collapsing, in 1838 McCulloch accepted the principalship of the fledgling Dalhousie College in Halifax. In the five remaining years of his life he not only brought to Dalhousie the fundamentally Scottish, practical system of education he had established in Pictou but also developed for the university an ornithological collection almost as fine as that which John James Audubon had admired at Pictou Academy in 1833. After his death in 1843 McCulloch was remembered as an outstanding educator, churchman, and author, and it became increasingly obvious over the years that his sly and subtle Stepsure letters had laid a foundation for Canadian literary humor. "The tone of his humour," noted Northrop Frye in the 1960 edition of *The Stepsure Letters*, "quiet, observant, deeply conservative in a human sense, has been the prevailing tone of Canadian humour ever since."

Bibliography:
Douglas G. Lochhead, "A Bibliographical Note," in *The Stepsure Letters* (Toronto: McClelland & Stewart, 1960), pp. 156-159.

Biographies:
William McCulloch, *Life of Thomas McCulloch, D.D.* (Truro, N.S.: Privately printed, 1920);

Frank Baird, "A Missionary Educator: Dr. Thomas McCulloch," *Dalhousie Review*, 52 (1972-1973): 611-618;

Marjorie Whitelaw, *Thomas McCulloch, His Life and Times* (Halifax: Nova Scotia Museum, 1985).

References:
M. R. Audobon, "Account of Visit With Rev. Thomas McCulloch," in *Audobon And His Journals* (London: Nimmo, 1897), pp. 435-436;

Gwendolyn Davies, " 'A Past of Orchards': Rural Change in Maritime Literature Before Confederation," in *The Red Jeep and Other Landscapes*, edited by Peter Thomas (Fredericton: Goose Lane, 1987), pp. 35-43;

Northrop Frye, Introduction to *The Stepsure Letters* (Toronto: McClelland & Stewart, 1960), pp. iii-ix;

D. C. Harvey, *An Introduction to The History of Dalhousie University* (Halifax: McCurdy, 1938), pp. 148-165;

John A. Irving, "The Achievement of Thomas McCulloch," in *The Stepsure Letters* (Toronto: McClelland & Stewart, 1960), pp. 150-156;

Janice Kulyk Keefer, *Under Eastern Eyes* (Toronto:
University of Toronto Press, 1987), pp. 39-45, 67-68;

Harrison S. Lewis, "Some Canadian Audobonia," *Canadian Field Naturalist*, 47 (December 1933): 162-172;

Robin Mathews, "The Stepsure Letters: Puritanism and the Novel of the Land," *Studies in Canadian Literature*, 7, no. 1 (1982): 127-138;

Stanley E. McMullin, "In Search of the Liberal Mind: Thomas McCulloch and the Impulse to Action," *Journal of Canadian Studies*, 23 (Spring/Summer 1988): 68-85;

George Patterson, *A History of the County of Pictou, Nova Scotia* (Montreal: Dawson, 1877; modern edition, Belleville, Ont.: Mika, 1972), pp. 267-269, 321-361;

Beverly Rasporich, "The New Eden Dream: The Source of Canadian Humour: McCulloch, Haliburton, and Leacock," *Studies in Canadian Literature*, 7, no. 2 (1982): 227-240;

J. Robertson, *History of the Secession Church of Nova Scotia and Prince Edward Island from Its Commencement in 1765* (Edinburgh: Johnston, 1847);

Vincent Sharman, "Thomas McCulloch's Stepsure: The Ruthless Presbyterian," *Dalhousie Review*, 52 (1972-1973): 618-628;

Marjorie Whitelaw, "Thomas McCulloch," *Canadian Literature*, 68-69 (Spring/Summer 1976): 138-147;

B. Anne Wood, "The Significance of Calvinism in the Educational Vision of Thomas McCulloch," *Vitae Scholasticae*, 4 (Spring-Fall, 1985): 15-30.

Papers:
The McCulloch Papers and Letters, MGI: volumes 550-555, are in the Public Archives of Nova Scotia, Halifax. Others are deposited in the Maritime Conference Archives of the United Church of Canada, Atlantic School of Theology, Halifax, and in the Dalhousie University Archives.

Thomas D'Arcy McGee

(13 April 1825 - 7 April 1868)

Neil K. Besner
University of Winnipeg

BOOKS: *Eva MacDonald; A Tale of the United Irish-men and Their Times* (Boston: Brainard, 1844);

Historical Sketches of O'Connell and His Friends (Boston: Donahoe & Rohan, 1845);

Gallery of Irish Writers. The Irish Writers of the Seventeenth Century (Dublin: Duffy, 1846; modern edition, New York: Lemma, 1974);

A Memoir of the Life and Conquests of Art Mac-Murrogh, King of Leinster (Dublin: Duffy, 1847);

A History of the Irish Settlers in North America (Boston: American Celt, 1851); republished as *A History of the Irish Settlers in America* (Dublin, 1870);

A Popular History of the Irish Settlers in North America (Boston, 1852);

A History of the Attempts to Establish the Protestant Reformation in Ireland, and the Successful Resistance of That People (Boston: Donahoe, 1853);

The Catholic History of North America (Boston: Donahoe, 1855);

A Life of the Rt. Rev. Edward Maginn, Coadjutor Bishop of Derry (New York: O'Shea, 1857; enlarged edition, 1858);

Canadian Ballads, and Occasional Verses (Montreal: Lovell, 1858);

Sebastian; or The Roman Martyr (New York: Sadlier, 1860?);

A Popular History of Ireland: From the Earliest Period to the Emancipation of the Catholics, 2 volumes (New York & Montreal: Sadlier, 1863, 1864; republished in one volume, Glasgow: Cameron, Ferguson, 1864);

Speeches and Addresses Chiefly on the Subject of British American Union (London: Chapman & Hall, 1865);

Notes on Federal Governments, Past and Present (Montreal: Dawson, 1865);

The Poems of Thomas D'Arcy McGee, edited by Mary Anne Sadlier (New York: Sadlier / Boston: Brady, 1869);

Engraving of Thomas D'Arcy McGee published in the 18 April 1871 issue of Canadian Illustrated News *(photograph by Henderson; C 54336, National Archives of Canada)*

1825–D'Arcy McGee–1925; A Collection of Speeches and Addresses, edited by Charles Murphy (Toronto: Macmillan, 1937).

Thomas D'Arcy McGee's life included interesting contradictions. An Irishman whose most passionate and enduring attachments were to the history and literature of his own country, he was the most ardent Canadian nationalist among the Fathers of Confederation. A man celebrated in Ca-

234

McGee's wife, Mary Theresa (née Caffrey), whom he married on 13 July 1847

nadian politics and cultural life as the finest public speaker of his day, McGee was by all accounts physically unprepossessing, even an ugly man; it was his voice, and not his appearance, that compelled his audiences. As a teenager, his first celebrated speeches were for temperance; in his adult life he had serious drinking problems. In his early twenties he was a founding member of the revolutionary group known as Young Ireland, participating in the unsuccessful revolt against England in 1848; twenty years later he would repeatedly denounce any Irish plan for armed rebellion as pure folly. As a young man he was attacked by the Irish Catholic clerisy and press in the United States when he came to America and tried to found newspapers that took a different nationalist line than that of the Church; subsequently he turned about-face to affirm his deep faith in Catholicism as the bedrock of his life. A man revered by many for his political and personal integrity, he was reviled by his enemies

as a callow opportunist. He was a prolific poet whose verse was celebrated in Ireland as among the finest of the age, yet some of his work might strike the contemporary reader as repetitive and formulaic. A man whose public life is fully documented in several lengthy biographies, and who was widely praised as a warm, congenial, engaging personality, McGee also led a private and domestic life that is, curiously, scantily known. The most ironic of all of these contradictions is the one that shapes his life story into a tragedy: a man famous for his genius at working compromises and reconciling factions in the fractious politics of his times, he was assassinated by a Fenian. McGee had passionately denounced this group for years and had been harassed by them in turn.

McGee was born on 13 April 1825 in Carlingford, County Louth, Ireland. His father, James McGee, a coastguardsman, was transferred to Wexford in 1833, when McGee was eight; his mother, Dorcas Catherine Morgan McGee, was seriously hurt during the ride to Wexford over rough roads and died of her injuries soon after. In 1842, when his father remarried in Wexford, McGee and his sister, Dorcas Catherine, sailed for the United States on 7 April–twenty-six years to the day before McGee's assassination in Ottawa. They arrived in Boston on 4 June 1842. In a story that may be apocryphal but nicely confirms McGee's widely praised powers as an orator, Isabel Skelton, his first biographer, tells of his first speech in North America: walking around during the Fourth of July celebration in Boston, McGee jumped up on a cart and instantly commanded the attention of a crowd for half an hour. Skelton writes that, twenty years later during the Civil War, Gen. Ben Butler, an eyewitness, told McGee's brother of the incident: " 'Who is it?' he said was the question asked by every one. 'Oh,' said one in the crowd, 'he is a little curly-headed Paddy.' 'I wish to God, then,' replied another, 'that such little curly-headed Paddies as that would come to us by whole shiploads; any country may feel proud of that youth.' "

The next day, McGee landed a job with the *Boston Pilot*, the leading Irish-American newspaper of the day, reporting on the turbulent events in Ireland and on the acclaimed speeches of Daniel O'Connell, the Irish "Liberator," leader of the repeal movement (advocating dissolution of Ireland's union with England) and the subject of one of McGee's first books, *Historical Sketches of O'Connell and His Friends* (1845). O'Connell's and others' admiration for McGee's writing in the *Pilot*–O'Connell, according to Skelton, referred to McGee's work as "the inspired writings of a young exiled Irish boy in America"–secured McGee a job with the *Freeman's Journal*, an Irish newspaper, to contribute reports from London. So McGee returned to Ireland in August 1845 at the age of twenty to prepare to move to London and begin the second and more important phase of his career as a writer.

Before traveling to England, McGee met and spent time in Dublin with Gavin Duffy, one of the founders of a new, strongly nationalist Irish newspaper, the *Nation*. Although McGee wrote for the *Freeman's Journal*, he soon became fascinated with the works of Irish writers he read in the British Museum and began to spend much of his time writing "Letters from London" columns for the *Nation*. His work for that paper led to his dismissal from the *Freeman's Journal* in 1846, to his passionate embracing of the more

avowedly nationalist Irish line of the *Nation*, and to his return to Dublin. One of the chief projects of the paper was to publish a series of volumes called *The Library of Ireland*, designed to reacquaint the Irish with their own cultural heritage; McGee adopted this as one of his own lifelong aims and wrote the last of the twenty-two volumes in the series, *A Memoir of the Life and Conquests of Art MacMurrogh* (1847).

Just as McGee returned to Dublin, the terrible effects of Ireland's worst famine, due largely to the failure of the 1845 potato crop, were heightening tensions and generating calls for more radical solutions to Ireland's political problems. McGee joined a group known as Young Ireland that broke with O'Connell, opposed his calls for moderation, advocated the Repeal of the Union by revolution, and finally spearheaded the unsuccessful revolt of 1848. McGee's role in the revolution was to travel to Scotland and organize the several hundred Irish volunteers assembled there. On 22 July 1848 McGee, evading surveillance, traveled to Scotland via Londonderry. In Scotland, McGee read a description of himself in a London newspaper, the *Hue and Cry*, which–as quoted by Skelton–provides a vivid sketch of McGee's appearance at the time: "Thomas D'Arcy McGee–connected with *The Nation* newspaper, twenty-three years of age; five foot three inches in height; black hair, dark face, delicate, pale, thin man, dresses generally black shooting coat, plaid trousers, light vest." On his return to Ireland via Belfast, McGee went into hiding for ten days, posing as a vacationing student and preparing for the arrival of the men from Scotland; but the revolt having failed in the south of Ireland, McGee was forced to escape on a ship to America. Helped in Londonderry by Bishop Edward Maginn (who later became the subject for McGee's 1857 biography), McGee disguised himself in a clerical suit and breviary, passed through enemy lines, and sailed on the *Shamrock* to New York.

McGee's several years in Ireland between his two sojourns in the United States were crucial in strengthening his deeply felt connections with Irish history, literature, and culture. His connections with Duffy and the other founders of Young Ireland, his newspaper work, his already promising careers as a poet, orator, and historian, the real beginnings of his life in politics–all these strands can be traced to McGee's years in Ireland during this vital period in its history. It was also during this period that McGee married Mary

McGee at his desk in Ottawa in 1867 (National Archives of Canada)

Caffrey on 13 July 1847; they had four daughters and one son. Some of McGee's finest poetry is inspired by his love for his wife. In the opening stanzas of "Memories" (collected in *The Poems*, 1869), McGee powerfully evokes the twin senses of exile he felt upon leaving Ireland and his wife in 1848:

> I left two loves on a distant strand,
> One young and fond and fair and bland;
> One fair, and old, and sadly grand—
> My wedded wife and my native land.
>
> One tarrieth sad and seriously
> Beneath the roof that mine should be;
> One sitteth sybil-like by the sea,
> Chanting a grave song mournfully.

McGee's second stay in the United States, from 1848 to 1857, was not nearly as rewarding as the first; on several counts these were the most troubled years of his life. First, his youthful enthusiasm for the American democracy he had embraced so fully on his first stay was now dissipated by his witnessing the squalid conditions in which hundreds of thousands of newly arrived Irish immigrants lived in the cites on the eastern seaboard. Second, his struggles to establish two newspapers–the *New York Nation* and the *American Celt*–brought him into bitter conflict with other Irish interests in America, principally with the Catholic hierarchy, led by powerful figures such as the Catholic bishop of New York, John Hughes, who, originally a strong supporter of Young Ireland, bitterly denounced the group after its ignominious defeat. Writing in the *Freeman's Journal*, Hughes attacked McGee and the *Nation* in a series of articles; McGee in turn blamed the Irish defeat on the Catholic clergy.

McGee's conflicts with the clergy on one hand and, on the other, with more radical Irish groups–chief among them, the Fenians–hastened the failure of both his newspapers.

McGee was also rapidly becoming disillusioned with the political realities of the democracy he had earlier applauded, as he saw the inexperienced immigrants being manipulated by various groups to buy their votes but being excluded from any real chance at gaining a foothold in America. Another major concern for McGee was the threat of assimilation of the immigrants' children, whom he saw losing their Irish heritage and culture. This danger was one of the influences that led McGee back to Catholicism and contributed to his decision to move to Montreal in 1857.

During this period in the United States, McGee was also very active as a writer. In *A Popular History of the Irish Settlers in North America* (1852) McGee strongly advocates establishing night schools to educate the immigrants–a project he was much involved with in Boston and New York–in order to prepare them for life in America: "Next to intemperance, ignorance is the emigrant's worst foe." McGee also wrote a history of the Protestant reformation in Ireland (1853) and *The Catholic History of North America* (1855)–two subjects that preoccupied him at this point in his life.

In 1854 McGee had gone on a lecture tour of Canada, and in 1855 he had written editorials in the *American Celt* encouraging Irish immigration to Canada–editorials that angered his Irish-American opponents, who called him a hypocrite. In 1857, at the age of thirty-two, he made the final and most definitive move of his life, relocating to Montreal, where he had been invited to found another newspaper, the *New Era*, which first appeared in May 1857. Aside from McGee's attraction to this new venture and to Canada as a better place for Irish immigration, however, he was attracted mainly by the prospect of a political career in Canada, and this was to be his principal occupation for the last ten years of his life. In Canada he established once and for all his fame as the finest speaker of his day and as a politician who, while never sacrificing his principles or misrepresenting the wishes of his constituency, had a genius for reconciliation and compromise that was crucial to the arguments for Confederation that he championed for the few years before his assassination.

McGee's funeral procession in Montreal, 1868 (National Archives of Canada)

McGee's early responses to Canada are best captured in the only book of poetry he published during his lifetime, *Canadian Ballads, and Occasional Verses* (1858). The poems, like much of McGee's work, draw their inspiration from history; perhaps the best known of them is his seven-part narrative "Jacques Cartier," a stirring account of Cartier's voyage of discovery from Saint Malo to the New World and back. But the major work that McGee wrote in Canada, and the one that he had in fact been preparing to write all his life, was his two-volume *Popular History of Ireland* (1863, 1864). Skelton praises this work's scrupulous balance and impartiality, its broad scope, and, aside from its evenhanded treatment of Ireland's history, its value as "a synopsis in chronological order of Irish literature from the very earliest days, down through a more comprehensive treatment of seventeenth and eighteenth century writings." It was widely praised in Ireland.

McGee began his political life in Canada in 1857 as one of the elected members of Parliament from Montreal, supported largely by the powerful Irish Catholic constituency. Very quickly McGee found that he had to use all his skills to navigate the turbid crosscurrents of the Canadian political life of the day: elected from Lower Canada, with its majority of Catholics, to sit in Upper Canada, with its majority of Protestants, McGee had to balance the demands of his constituency against those of Orange (Protestant) Toronto. McGee first sat as an Independent, but eventually joined the Reform ranks led by George Brown, publisher of the *Globe* and initially an enemy of McGee's. He sat in Opposition from 1858 until 1862, when he became president of the council in the Reform government of John Sandfield Macdonald and L. V. Sicotte. In this position he was a strong advocate of the development of intercolonial railways, stretching east to the Maritime provinces and west toward British Columbia across the vast territory overseen by the Hudson's Bay Company.

But Macdonald dropped McGee from his cabinet in 1863, partly for political expediency and partly because McGee's drinking problem had alienated him from Macdonald. McGee sat again as an Independent, elected to represent Montreal West. In March 1864 McGee became minister of agriculture in the cabinet of the John A. Macdonald government; his most important role, however, was as a member of the crucial Charlottetown Conference in 1864. From this point until his death, McGee was a tireless and eloquent proponent of Confederation and became known as its most able spokesman.

Meanwhile the Fenians, McGee's longtime bitter enemies, had for years been agitating against what they perceived as the treason and cowardice of his moderate position on the Irish question. When McGee traveled to Ireland in the spring of 1885 as the minister of immigration, he made a major speech in Wexford that alienated many of his longtime Irish supporters, such as Duffy, because he appeared to them to be too harsh in his condemnation of Young Ireland and its platform. This incident added to the ranks of McGee's enemies in Canada and Ireland.

In 1867, while McGee was on a trip to Rome and Paris, Macdonald dropped him and Charles Tupper from the cabinet, replacing them both with E. F. Kenny, an Irish-Catholic Conservative from Nova Scotia, in order to allay unease about balanced representation; McGee returned as a backbencher. From October 1867 to February 1868 illness kept McGee confined to his house in Montreal, but this interlude allowed him to return to his literary vocation more singlemindedly. Among other works, he composed a novel–an "Irish-American tale," he called it–that he was arranging to have published anonymously and that he described as "a pretty thick volume of about six hundred and fifty pages." Skelton notes, however, that this manuscript has unfortunately been lost.

The tragic end of McGee's life is the most infamous and most written about political assassination in Canadian history. On 7 April 1868 McGee left the House of Parliament in Ottawa after a long session in which he had spoken warmly in defense of Charles Tupper, who was absent. McGee was to return home to Montreal the next day to spend Easter with his family, and some Montreal friends were to commemorate his birthday by giving his wife a portrait of McGee painted by Bell Smith. McGee said good night to several colleagues and walked down Metcalfe Street to Sparkes Street, where he was rooming at a boarding house. When McGee bent down to put his key in the door, he was shot once in the back of the head and died almost immediately. Patrick James Whelan, a Fenian, was arrested, tried, and found guilty of the crime; he was hanged on 11 February 1869.

McGee's funeral in Montreal, the largest that had ever been seen in the city, testified to his enormous popularity with virtually all of the city's diverse population. Two services were held for him, at St. Patrick's and at Notre Dame. And the tributes from all parties of government attested to his stature across Canada, irrespective of political affiliations. He died just short of his forty-third birthday, the third youngest of the thirty-three Fathers of Confederation. Given the astonishing span of his achievements in such a short lifetime, it is difficult to imagine what he might have accomplished had he lived another thirty years. As it stands, the range of McGee's contributions to the political and cultural life of the country he lived in for less than a quarter of his life is virtually unmatched by any other figure of his time.

Biographies:
Isabel Skelton, *The Life of Thomas D'Arcy McGee* (Gardenvale, Ont.: Garden City Press, 1925);

Josephine Phelan, *The Ardent Exile: The Life and Times of Thos. D'Arcy McGee* (Toronto: Macmillan, 1951).

References:
Bill Kirwin, *Thomas D'Arcy McGee: Visionary of the Welfare State in Canada* (Calgary: University of Calgary Faculty of Social Welfare, 1981);

Josephine Phelan, *The Ballad of D'Arcy McGee: Rebel in Exile* (Toronto: Macmillan, 1967);

T. P. Slattery, *The Assassination of D'Arcy McGee* (Toronto & Garden City, N.Y.: Doubleday, 1968).

James McIntyre

(1827 - 5 March 1906)

Bruce Nesbitt

BOOKS: *Musings on the Banks of Canadian Thames. Including Poems on Local, Canadian and British Subjects, and Lines on the Great Poets of England, Ireland, Scotland and America, with a Glance at the Wars in Victoria's Reign* (Ingersoll, Ont.: Rowland, 1884);

Poems (Ingersoll, Ont.: Chronicle, 1889);

The Rise and Progress of the Canadian Cheese Trade and Descriptive Poems and Tales [bound with the second edition of *Poems*] (Ingersoll, Ont.: Chronicle, 1891).

Collection: *Oh! Queen of Cheese: Selections from James McIntyre, the Cheese Poet*, edited by Roy A. Abrahamson (Toronto: Cherry Tree, 1979).

Perhaps English Canada's best-known bad poet, James McIntyre, is noteworthy for his verse celebration of the dairy industry. He was also one of the main subjects of William Arthur Deacon's *Four Jameses* (1927), a satiric study of mediocre Canadian literature.

Born in Forres, Morayshire, Scotland, McIntyre immigrated to Canada West, now Ontario, either in 1841 or after 1843; details of his early life are obscure. After some years probably spent as a farm laborer and later as a furniture dealer in St. Catherines, by 1858 he had established himself as an undertaker and a manufacturer and retailer of furniture in Ingersoll, where he would remain until his death. He had two children by his wife, Euphemia Fraser: Alexander, who died in 1876 after injuries sustained in his father's furniture factory, and Kate, who would herself pub-

James McIntyre (C 12569, National Archives of Canada)

lish a volume of execrable verse (*Rhymes Right or Wrong of Rainy River*, 1926), some written in defense of her father's poetry. Twenty years after his death she recalled him as a "Caledonian Bard, forty years a Free Mason and fifty years an

Oddfellow, holder of all Veteran Jewels, Illuminated Adresses, Grand Master's Buckskin Apron, Ac. [sic]" (*Bracebridge Gazette*, 23 December 1926).

An occasional newspaper contributor of "rhymes on local subjects" beginning in at least 1858, McIntyre published his first collection of verses a quarter century later on topics (other than those listed in the full title of *Musings*, 1884) as various as Methodist Union, the typewriter, potato bugs, and electric light. His most celebrated accomplishment proved to be his "Ode on the Mammoth Cheese Weighing over 7000 Pounds"; after its appearance McIntyre was moved to thank his acquaintances (in *Musings*) "who so highly appreciate the Cheese Ode" and, ambiguously, "the cheese buyers of the town who so liberally have assisted to render it a success." He would later observe, in *Poems* (1889), that Joachin Miller "hailed me as 'my dear poet of the Canadian pasture fields,' and he said I did wisely in singing of useful themes."

The headnote to McIntyre's second volume, the *Poems*, accurately reflects his major interests: "Fair Canada is our Theme, / Land of rich cheese, milk and cream." In *Musings* he had grappled with some aspects of literary nationalism: contrasting Robert Burns's use of Halloween, for example, with Canadian winter sports, or noting that thanks to lacrosse, "if a foe invade; we can / Drive them back with clubs Canadian." Fully the first half of *Poems*, however, deals exclusively with Canadian subjects, including six poems on Canadian authors and fourteen "dairy sketches." McIntyre's final collection in his lifetime (1891) is more heterogeneous, ranging from his much-derided "The Canadian Patriotic Hen," through a prediction of a future ten-ton cheese, to a prose essay on the cheese trade. It is also a bibliographical curiosity and, as such, usually overlooked. McIntyre had retained half the unbound sheets of *Poems*; paginating *The Rise and Progress of the Canadian Cheese Trade* consecutively after the index to *Poems*, he then had the two works bound together.

With the exception of Deacon's remarkable parody of academic literary criticism, most Canadian critics have either utterly ignored McIntyre or dismissed him as an eccentric. His generous modern editor, Roy A. Abrahamson, has termed him "the Chaucer of Cheese."

References:

Roy A. Abrahamson, "Introducing James McIntyre," in *Oh! Queen of Cheese: Selections from James McIntyre, the Cheese Poet* (Toronto: Cherry Tree, 1979), pp. 5-9;

William Arthur Deacon, "James McIntyre: The Cheese Poet," in his *The Four Jameses* (Ottawa: Graphic, 1927; revised edition, Toronto: Ryerson, 1953), pp. 41-82;

Doug Fetherling, Introduction to *The Four Jameses*, by Deacon (Toronto: Macmillan, 1974), pp. 7-15;

Kate McIntyre Ruttan, *Rhymes Right or Wrong of Rainy River* (Orillia, Ont.: Times, 1926).

Alexander McLachlan
(24 May 1818 - 20 March 1896)

Elizabeth Waterston
University of Guelph

BOOKS: *The Spirit of Love, and Other Poems* (Toronto: Cleland, 1846);
Poems (Toronto: Geikie, 1856);
Lyrics (Toronto: Armour, 1858);
The Emigrant, and Other Poems (Toronto: Rollo & Adams, 1861);
Poems and Songs (Toronto: Hunter, Rose, 1874);
Songs of Arran (Edinburgh: Mackenzie & Storrie, 1889);
The Poetical Works of Alexander McLachlan (Toronto: Briggs, 1900; facsimile, Toronto: University of Toronto Press, 1974).

Called "the Canadian Burns" in his own time, Alexander McLachlan lived humbly but not inconspicuously. Six volumes of poetry were published in his lifetime; his work was anthologized, recited in schools, praised by Ralph Waldo Emerson, Henry David Thoreau, Henry Wadsworth Longfellow, and other Americans, and revered by an influential group of Canadians including Thomas D'Arcy McGee, George Brown, and George Monro Grant. McLachlan achieved this surprising fame partly because of contemporary hunger for a "native bard" and partly because of his strong lyric expression of pioneer attitudes.

Born in Johnstone, in the Clyde Valley of Scotland, on 24 May 1818 to a rigorously Calvinist mother (Jane Sutherland McLachlan) and a Chartist and Temperance-activist father (Charles McLachlan), McLachlan became an apprentice in a Glasgow tailor shop and began writing radical verses. He followed his immigrant family to Upper Canada in 1840. His father's sudden death left the young Scot with a half-cleared farm near Caledon (northwest of Toronto). He failed as a farmer, eventually settling on a one-acre holding in Erin village, with his wife (his cousin Clamina). He worked as a part-time tailor, writer, and lecturer at Mechanics' Institutes. In 1846 *The Spirit of Love* was published, presenting his poetic meditations on liberty, labor, nature, and science.

Alexander McLachlan

Poems (1856) celebrates Scottish memories; *Lyrics* (1858) adds Canadian rhymes on contemporary politics, and strikes more tender notes: love for birds and animals, for eccentric neighbors, and for Clamina and the bairns (children). The McLachlans had a total of eleven, one of whom died in infancy.

A longer episodic poem, *The Emigrant* (1861) moves from the first trials of pioneering—homesickness, sabbath in lonely woods, fire in a solitary clearing—to first comforts: family love, faithful animals, and the companionship of books. McLachlan had been wresting a pioneer's living from his small homestead for a family now including three sisters and his mother. But *The Emigrant* is general history, too, forceful and dignified.

McLachlan was in demand as a lecturer, a sort of Ontario version of Thomas Carlyle, John Ruskin, and Ralph Waldo Emerson, who all influenced his ideas about work, duty, and art. The government sent him in 1862 to speak in Britain on emigration. In 1864 Edward H. Dewart, in *Selections from Canadian Poets*, a still-important anthology, ranked McLachlan with Charles Sangster, calling them the best two poets in the colonies.

Friends subscribed enough money to publish his next book, *Poems and Songs* (1874). Intimate, intense, concentrating on homely incidents, as in "Sparking" and "The Picnic," the poems celebrate a New World achievement of Robert Burns's dreams of democracy. (True to his family tradition, though, McLachlan eschewed those other Burnsian notes, bawdiness and drunkenness.)

In 1877 the poet moved near Orangeville, Ontario. Toronto admirers, convening a testimonial dinner in 1890, presented him with twenty-one hundred dollars. The death of his farmer son Alexander in 1895 forced a move into Orangeville; McLachlan died there the next year.

In the introduction to the posthumous *Poeti-cal Works* (1900), the anonymous editors (friends of the family) compared him to Longfellow, Tennyson, Wordsworth, and Burns. Critics today mock such comparisons. But a strong beat and social energy give McLachlan's verses permanent appeal to ordinary readers. Stalwart, combative, and tender, McLachlan struck a peculiarly Canadian combination of notes: protest and loyalty; and unbroken affection for the "old country" but rising enthusiasm for the new one.

Biography:

Anonymous, "Biographical Sketch," in *The Poetical Works* (Toronto: Briggs, 1900; facsimile, Toronto: University of Toronto Press, 1974), pp. 17-28.

References:

Edward H. Dewart, Introduction to *Selections from Canadian Poets* (Montreal: Lovell, 1864), pp. xvii-xviii;

E. Margaret Fulton, Introduction to the facsimile of *The Poetical Works of Alexander McLachlan* (Toronto: University of Toronto Press, 1974).

John Wedderburn Dunbar Moodie

(7 October 1797 - 22 October 1869)

Carole Gerson
Simon Fraser University

BOOKS: *Memoirs of the Late War: Comprising the Personal Narrative of Captain Cooke . . . the History of the Campaign of 1809 in Portugal, by the Earl of Munster; and a Narrative of the Campaign in Holland, by Liet. W. D. Moodie,* 2 volumes–volume 2 by Moodie (London: H. Colburn & R. Bentley, 1831);

Ten Years in South Africa: Including a Particular Description of the Wild Sports of That Country, 2 volumes (London: R. Bentley, 1835);

The Victoria Magazine, by J. W. D. and Susanna Moodie and others (Belleville, Ont., September 1847-August 1848; collected edition, Vancouver: University of British Columbia Press, 1968).

Scenes and Adventures as a Soldier and Settler During Half a Century (Montreal: Lovell, 1866).

OTHER: "The Village Hotel," "The Land-Jobber," and "Canadian Sketches," in *Roughing It in the Bush,* by Susanna Moodie, second edition (London: Bentley, 1852).

The husband of Susanna Strickland Moodie, John Wedderburn Dunbar Moodie was a minor author whose talents and writings have been overshadowed by those of his wife. Characterized by her (in *Roughing It in the Bush,* 1852) as "the poet, the author, the musician, the man of books, of refined taste and gentlemanly habits" who braved the privations of pioneer life in an unsuccessful bid to attain for his children the material comforts that eluded them in Great Britain, he recorded his Canadian experiences in the three chapters he contributed to the second edition of *Roughing It in the Bush* (also 1852), and in the introduction to his own *Scenes and Adventures as a Soldier and Settler During Half a Century* (1866), a collection of previously published pieces.

Moodie was born in the Orkney Islands of Scotland on the family estate, Melsetter, the fourth son of Maj. James Moodie, Ninth Laird of Melsetter, and Elizabeth Dunbar Moodie. In

John Wedderburn Dunbar Moodie (photograph by William Notman)

1813, at the age of sixteen, Dunbar, as he was called, followed the family tradition of military service by joining the army as a second lieutenant in the 21st Royal North British Fusiliers and was wounded the following year in the Netherlands. Three years later the continuing deterioration of the Moodie family fortunes prompted Benjamin, the eldest son, to establish a colony of Scottish emigrants in South Africa; in 1819 Benjamin was joined by his younger brothers Donald and Dunbar, the latter now a retired officer on half pay. Moodie's experiences at the Cape are described in his first major publication, *Ten Years in South Africa* (1835). Like *Roughing It in the Bush,* this account of colonial life, directed to British readers by a seasoned settler, offers a compen-

Moodie and his wife, Susanna, with an unidentified friend at the Moodies' cottage in 1860 (Province of Ontario Archives)

dium of geographical description, personal adventures, humanitarian social analysis, and advice to prospective emigrants. Favorably reviewed in both the *Athenaeum* and the *Quarterly Review* and profitable for Moodie, *Ten Years in South Africa* lacks the lively style and distinctive personal tone that have kept Mrs. Moodie's books in print, and has been virtually ignored by scholars of history and literature.

After returning to England in 1829, Moodie met Susanna Strickland at the home of Thomas Pringle, secretary of the Anti-Slavery Society; they married in 1831. The following year, when the Moodies decided that emigration was the only solution to their poor economic prospects, Dunbar's inclination to return to South Africa was opposed by his wife, who was sufficiently disturbed by her husband's account of having been attacked by an elephant to decide that she preferred the untried terrain of North America to the wild creatures of the Cape.

As soon as they settled near Cobourg, Upper Canada (Ontario), Moodie began the Canadian phase of his literary career by contributing his elephant hunt narrative to the *Cobourg Star* in 1832. However, in the unexpectedly harsh physical and social environment of the Douro bush (near present-day Peterborough, Ontario) where Moodie took a grant of uncleared land in 1834, literary interests quickly yielded to the more pressing issue of elementary survival. Moodie was appointed sheriff of Victoria District, Upper Canada, in 1839, after his wife petitioned Lieutenant Governor George Arthur for a position in recognition of her husband's service to the crown during the rebellion of 1837-1838, and was then able to move his family to Belleville. Here the Moodies resumed their literary efforts in the pages of the *Literary Garland* (Montreal), to which Dunbar contributed several poems and essays during the 1840s, and in their first joint publishing venture, the *Victoria Magazine* (1847-1848).

Founded, as Moodie said, with "the hope of inducing a taste for polite literature among the working classes," this monthly publication contained essays, poems, stories, and puzzles, mostly written by the Moodies themselves. In addition to drawing from his previously published South African material, Dunbar composed light essays, Norse ballads, and "Papers on Practical Jokes"; however, despite a subscription list of nearly five hundred names, the "literary philanthropists" could not find a publisher to see their magazine through its second year.

When Susanna Moodie prepared the sketches that were compiled as *Roughing It in the Bush*, she relied on her husband's three informative chapters, "The Village Hotel," "The Land Jobber," and "Canadian Sketches," to supply the details of personal history and factual analysis that set the context for her own colorful anecdotes. Unfortunately, these chapters reached her London publisher, Richard Bentley, too late for inclusion in the first edition of 1852 (although they did find their way into *Bentley's Miscellany*). They were added to the second edition later that year but were dropped from the 1871 revised edition, from which nearly all later versions of the book have been derived, with the result that, to the modern reader, Mrs. Moodie has appeared to be evasive about many aspects of her personal life, and Mr. Moodie's voice has been silenced. Fortunately, these chapters have been restored in two recent editions of the book (Carleton University Press, 1988, and New Canadian Library, 1989). In his first two chapters, Moodie presents the two errors that contributed to his family's subsequent financial difficulties—namely selling his commission in the army and investing in ultimately worthless steamboat stock—as the result of both his own naiveté and the deceitfulness of agents who preyed upon newly arrived immigrants. The chapter "Canadian Sketches" presents an optimistic description of the economy and society of Upper Canada, beginning with a general overview of the development of responsible colonial government, then focusing on a factual analysis of Belleville life, ranging from economic statistics to instructions for building a plank road.

During the 1850s the Moodies were greatly interested in spiritualism. Dunbar conducted experiments that he carefully recorded in a special diary, along with messages received during seances. This diary is now at the National Library of Canada.

The last decade of Moodie's life was shadowed by misfortune. In 1861 he suffered from partial paralysis on his left side, and in 1863 he was forced to resign from his position as sheriff for having made an inappropriate arrangement with a deputy—an arrangement for collecting fees that Moodie claimed was common practice, but for which he was persecuted by his political enemies. Subsequently an agreement under which he and his wife would be supported by their eldest son fell through; left to their own resources, the elderly and ailing Moodies tried to live by their pens. Dunbar was able to earn about six hundred dollars by assembling some of his earlier writings into a little book published by subscription, *Scenes and Adventures as a Soldier and Settler During Half a Century*, for which he wrote a bitter introduction declaring that his immigration to Canada had been his "*first* mistake."

Since his death in 1869 Moodie's name has been preserved from utter obscurity only because of the remarkable woman he married. In his writings one can see that he shared the cultural and social values that informed Susanna's work: strong opposition to slavery, faith in the power of literature and education to reform society, and liberal support for the reordering of social classes that occurs in a frontier environment, coupled with the view that pioneering was not an appropriate venture for gentlefolk like themselves.

Biography:
Edmund H. Burrows, *The Moodies of Melsetter* (Cape Town & Amsterdam: A. A. Balkema, 1954).

References:
Carole Gerson, "Mrs. Moodie's Beloved Partner," *Canadian Literature*, 107 (Winter 1986): 34-45;

Susanna Moodie, *Letters of a Lifetime*, edited by Carl Ballstadt, Elizabeth Hopkins, and Michael Peterman (Toronto: University of Toronto Press, 1985).

Papers:
The Robert Baldwin Papers, Metropolitan Toronto Library, include letters from Moodie. A few other items are in the Traill Family Papers, National Archives of Canada. Other letters and papers—including Dunbar's "spiritualism" album—are in the Moodie-Strickland-Vickers-Ewing Family Papers, National Library of Canada.

Susanna Moodie
(6 December 1803 - 8 April 1885)

Carl Ballstadt
McMaster University

BOOKS: *Happy Because Good* (London: Dean, n.d.);

The Little Prisoner; or, Passion and Patience (London: Dean & Munday, n. d.);

The Little Quaker; or, The Triumph of Virtue (London: Cole, n.d.);

Profession and Principle (London: Dean & Munday, n.d.);

Rowland Massingham (London: Dean & Munday, n.d.);

Spartacus. A Roman Story (London: Newman, 1822);

Hugh Latimer; or, The Schoolboy's Friendship (London: Newman, 1828);

Patriotic Songs, by Moodie and Agnes Strickland (London: Green & Soho, 1830);

Enthusiasm, and Other Poems (London: Smith & Elder, 1831);

The Victoria Magazine by Susanna and J. W. D. Moodie and others (Belleville, Ont., September 1847-August 1848; collected edition, Vancouver: University of British Columbia Press, 1968);

The Little Black Pony, and Other Stories (Philadelphia: Collins, 1850);

Roughing It in the Bush; or, Life in Canada, 2 volumes (London: Bentley, 1852; New York: Putnam, 1852; revised edition, Toronto: Hunter, Rose, 1871; modern edition, Toronto: McClelland & Stewart, 1962; another modern edition, Ottawa: Carleton University Press, 1988);

Life in the Clearings versus the Bush (London: Bentley, 1853; New York: DeWitt & Davenport, 1854; modern edition, Toronto: Macmillan, 1959);

Mark Hurdlestone, 2 volumes (London: Bentley, 1853; New York: DeWitt & Davenport, 1853);

Flora Lyndsay; or, Passages in an Eventful Life, 2 volumes (London: Bentley, 1854; New York: DeWitt & Davenport, 1855);

Matrimonial Speculations (London: Bentley, 1854);

Geoffrey Moncton; or, The Faithless Guardian (New York: DeWitt & Davenport, 1855); republished as *The Moncktons. A Novel*, 2 volumes (London: Bentley, 1856);

The World Before Them. A Novel, 3 volumes (London: Bentley, 1868 [i.e., 1867]);

George Leatrim; or, The Mother's Test (Edinburgh: Hamilton, 1875).

OTHER: *The History of Mary Prince*, edited by Moodie (London: Westley, 1831);

Negro Slavery Described by a Negro: Being the Narrative of Ashton Warner, a Native of St. Vincent's, edited by Moodie (London: Smith & Elder, 1831).

SELECTED PERIODICAL PUBLICATIONS–
UNCOLLECTED: "Sketches From the Country. No. I. The Witch of East Cliff," *La Belle Assemblée*, new series 6 (July 1827): 15-19;

"Sketches From the Country. No. II. The Two Fishermen," *La Belle Assemblée*, new series 6 (September 1827): 109-114;

"Sketches From the Country. No. III. Naomi," *La Belle Assemblée*, new series 6 (December 1827): 247-251;

"Sketches From the Country, No. IV. The Dead Man's Grave," *La Belle Assemblée*, new series 7 (February 1828): 51-55;

"Sketches From the Country, No. V. Old Hannah; or, The Charm," *La Belle Assemblée*, new series 9 (January 1829): 21-24;

"Canadian Sketches: Old Woodruff and His Three Wives," *Literary Garland*, new series 5 (January 1847): 13-18;

"The Walk to Dummer," *Literary Garland*, new series 5 (March 1847): 101-109;

"Our Borrowing," *Literary Garland*, new series 5 (May 1847): 197-205;

"Tom Wilson's Emigration," *Literary Garland*, new series 5 (June and July 1847): 283-286, 293-303;

Susanna Moodie (Collection of the J. F. Killough family, Castlegar, British Columbia)

"Uncle Joe and His Family," *Literary Garland*, new series 5 (August and September, 1847): 363-368, 423-429;

"Brian the Still Hunter," *Literary Garland*, new series 5 (October 1847): 460-466;

"Scenes in Canada. A Visit to Grosse Isle," *Victoria Magazine*, 1 (September 1847): 14-17;

"Scenes in Canada. No. II. First Impressions. Quebec," *Victoria Magazine*, 1 (November 1847): 65-68;

"Rachel Wilde, or Trifles From the Burthen of a Life," *Victoria Magazine* (January-July, 1848): 113-115, 126-128, 156-159, 183-187, 212-214, 234-237, 250-252.

Susanna Moodie's importance in Canadian literary history derives partly from her promi-nence as a contributor to the *Literary Garland*, the most successful literary periodical in the British North American provinces in the mid nineteenth century, but mostly from the quality of her classic settlement narrative *Roughing It in the Bush* (1852) and its first sequel, *Life in the Clearings* (1853). The former work in particular has received much attention from Canadian critics and has been controversial. Some early reviewers took exception to its negative views of Canada and its declared intent to discourage British gentlefolk from immigrating to the country, but it is a complex and engaging book that has often been perceived as much more than a guide to prospective emigrants. In 1972 Margaret Atwood's book of poems *The Journals of Susanna Moodie* brought Moodie to increased prominence through its presentation of an apt model of Canadian experience and a collective Canadian psyche. Concurrent with and subsequent to Atwood's poetic portrait, critics have attempted to define the generic and structural nature of *Roughing It in the Bush* and to probe the complexities of the narrator's personality in order to explain its literary durability and its haunting power. Although *Roughing It* alone secures for the author an enduring place in Canadian literary history, Moodie did in fact create a trilogy of immigrant experience, from the initial preparations and the voyage out depicted in *Flora Lyndsay* (1854) to the appraisal of Canadian towns and institutions in *Life in the Clearings*. Together these works present a vivid sense of the trials and accomplishments in pioneer and colonial life.

Susanna Strickland Moodie was born near Bungay, Suffolk, England, on 6 December 1803, the sixth daughter of Thomas and Elizabeth Homer Strickland. Her father had been the manager of the Greenland Dock, on the south bank of the Thames, but he retired and moved with his family to East Anglia sometime between January 1802 and December 1803. For some months they resided near Norwich, but by the time of Susanna's birth they were living at Stowe House on the Waveney near the town of Bungay. In 1808 the Stricklands bought Reydon Hall, about a mile from the coastal village of Southwold in Suffolk. They also retained a house in Norwich, where Thomas Strickland usually spent the winter months accompanied by some members of the family while the others remained at Reydon. As a child and young woman, therefore, Moodie experienced rural, coastal, and urban life, and her early writing reflects these varied settings. The pedagogical interests of her father, the availability of his well-stocked library, the tutorship of her elder sisters, and the relative isolation of Reydon Hall were the chief factors in the education and literary preparation of Moodie. By the time of their father's death in April 1818, she and her sisters were developing their literary skills and, following his death, pursued literary careers by writing natural history, moral and historical tales for children, and sketches, stories, and poems for periodicals and the elegant annuals. Eventually the name of Strickland was well known in English and international literary circles, the chief architect of their fame being Agnes Strickland, who, with the collaboration of her sister Elizabeth, produced *Lives of the Queens of England* (1840-1848) and many other biogra-

phies of royal persons, which proved popular in Britain and the United States.

Moodie's writing for children and her poems reflect the religious cast of her own personality. She developed close friendships with Dissenters and Quakers in Suffolk and underwent a conversion experience at the Congregational Chapel in the nearby community of Wrentham, much to the distress of her staunchly Anglican elder sisters. Many of her tales are marked by the language of religious enthusiasm, conversions, and death-bed repentances, while others, notably *Spartacus* (1822), evidence her admiration of heroic leaders.

Enthusiasm, and Other Poems (1831), a collection of her early work, also reveals her religious orientation. The theme that pervades the volume is that of the poet as prophet issuing warnings about the transitory nature of earthly pleasures and the waywardness of the ego, and declaring the need for humility and faith. The long title poem (more than four hundred lines) dismisses all human enthusiasms, except for devotion to God and His word, as ultimately unrewarding. Nevertheless, parts of that poem and others in the volume reveal the author's own delight in nature and the meditation it inspires. Her own enthusiasm, her desire for vision, and her emulation of Byronic rhythms and diction give ample evidence of her own compatibility with aspects of the Romantic movement.

During the late 1820s several literary contacts became important to the development of Moodie's career. James Bird, a Suffolk poet, probably encouraged her interest in Suffolk lore and legend, his own favorite subject. Her admiration of Mary Russell Mitford led to correspondence with her and to the writing of rural sketches in the manner of Mitford's *Our Village* (1824). Thomas Harral, another Suffolk writer and editor, provided an outlet for the rural sketches and other work in *La Belle Assemblée*, a fashionable London journal for ladies. But Thomas Pringle, secretary to the Anti-Slavery Society, was the most influential. He fostered an interest in humanitarian issues in Moodie, introduced her to his circle of writers in London, and gave her an opportunity to review contemporary works.

With respect to her Canadian career, two facets of Moodie's early work are particularly significant. The "Sketches from the Country" that appeared in *La Belle Assemblée* in 1827, 1828, and 1829, devoted to unusual Suffolk characters and local legends, provided a model for her later atten-

The First Mine in Ontario at Marmora, *a watercolor by Moodie (C 174, National Archives of Canada)*

tion to backwoods customs and characters, with emphasis on realistic detail, dialect, and humor. Another literary exercise that encouraged objectivity in her writing was the transcription of slavery narratives, which she did while residing at Pringle's home. Two such narratives, *The History of Mary Prince* and *Negro Slavery Described by . . . Ashton Warner*, were published in 1831. Besides fostering a movement toward the presentation of plausible detail in her own writing, they show her humanitarian awakening and set the stage for issues she was to address in her Canadian works.

In April 1831 she married Lt. John Wedderburn Dunbar Moodie, an officer on half pay and a writer, whom she met at Pringle's home. After living in London for a short time, they moved to Southwold and then decided that immigration to Canada offered the only hope of a secure future for themselves and the children they wished to have. They sailed for Canada from Edinburgh on 1 July 1832 and, following their arrival in late August, purchased a cleared farm near Cobourg in Hamilton township, Upper Canada (Ontario), where they lived for a year and a half before moving to the backwoods north of Peterborough to be closer to Mrs. Moodie's sister Catharine Parr Traill and her brother Samuel

Strickland. Much of the backwoods life was uncongenial to the temperaments and tastes of the Moodies. Lt. Moodie found partial release from the trials of such a life by serving in the militia during and following the Mackenzie Rebellion of 1837, and late in 1839 he was appointed sheriff of the Victoria District. The family, including five children, moved to Belleville early in 1840. Two more children were born in Belleville and two of the Moodies' children died there in the 1840s.

Susanna Moodie was not entirely inactive as a writer during her eight years as a pioneer wife. She submitted some items, chiefly poems, to American and Canadian periodicals and sent some poems home to England as well. She may even have begun writing her Canadian sketches while in the backwoods, but in any case she did begin to write for the *Literary Garland* of Montreal beginning in late 1838, and much of her work appeared in that journal during the next twelve years. She was one of the principal contributors, submitting serialized novels based on English life, several of them expansions of earlier short work, poems on Old World and Canadian subjects, and most important, a series of six "Canadian

Sketches" that formed the nucleus of *Roughing It in the Bush*.

For one year, from September 1847 to August 1848, the Moodies also edited the *Victoria Magazine* for Joseph Wilson of Belleville. They wrote much of the material themselves and received contributions from her siblings Catharine, Samuel, and Agnes as well. The periodical was to be a medium for the education of farmers and mechanics, but it included historical tales, Old World romances, essays on practical jokes, discourses on moral issues, several articles on South Africa, where Lt. Moodie had lived for ten years, and two more "Canadian Sketches." Its chief importance now is that it reflects the Moodies' own diverse interests and is the repository of a serialized, autobiographical story, "Rachel Wilde" (1848), which gives glimpses of Mrs. Moodie's childhood and her romantic and impulsive personality.

The large volume of "English" fiction she contributed to the *Garland* indicates both the importance to her of her English past as a resource for themes and subjects, and her willingness to satisfy a popular literary taste. Although a few items reflect life in a Suffolk parish as her early rural sketches had done, the bulk of her work is religious romance marked by melodramatic and gothic excesses. It is a highly conventional literature characterized by the affective states of heroes, heroines, and unscrupulous villains, all presented with an excess of stock epithets and metaphors.

Following the demise of the *Garland* in 1851, Moodie explored the prospect of publishing her work in book form and the first to receive her attention was the "Canadian Sketches." She sent a manuscript to John Bruce, an antiquarian and friend to the Moodies living in London, and he took it to Richard Bentley, who agreed to publish it. Moodie did not correspond with Bentley until after the publication of *Roughing It in the Bush* early in 1852, at which time she offered him the manuscript of *Mark Hurdlestone* (1853) and told him of several other works she had ready as books.

Roughing It in the Bush, which in its original edition contains three chapters by her husband, is her most significant book, stylistically and topically a radical departure from her "English" fiction. It is a settlement narrative consisting of sketches in a basically chronological order and reflecting the Moodies' experience of and responses to the culture shock, the trials, and the pleasures of immigration and pioneer life, from the arrival at Grosse Isle, the quarantine station in the St. Lawrence, to their departure from the backwoods in 1840. The book derives its vitality from the encounter of cultured, refined persons with rude, harsh, and elemental human and natural forces, but in spite of the often bitter experiences, Moodie is distanced enough in the telling to depict her adversaries and her own behavior with humor and restraint. In addition she offers sober reflections on the hazards of immigration and compensatory praise of Canada as a haven for the poor and a potentially great country.

The declared main theme of the book is that men and women of refinement and economic means ought not to attempt to settle in the backwoods, that to do so is likely to be ruinous as it was for the Moodies. Rather such persons should settle on cleared farms or take up opportunities for investment and business in the New World. Such a theme, of course, pertains to the time in which the book was written and published, but *Roughing It* is diverse and complex, and transcends–through compelling narrative, modulation of style, the complexities of the narrator's personality, and richness of imagery–the specific, limited theme. Ultimately the book offers an ironic vision of life. Such a reading may be derived from attention to patterns of incident and imagery. In the opening chapters entry into the uncivilized land is associated with death, imprisonment, disease, and decay: cholera is the "phantom of the journey"; "the graves of pine frown down in hearse-like gloom upon the mighty river"; and the narrator's feeling is "nearly allied to that which the condemned criminal entertains for his cell–his only hope of escape being through the portals of the grave." Such images are frequent–even the last sentence of the book expresses the hope that "the secrets of the prison-house" have been revealed–and they are also consistent with much of Moodie's other work, especially her poems. The principal reliefs from oppression are exhilarated responses to the splendors of nature or indulgence in memories of the pastoral English home, but every high point of emotion or reverie is disturbed by some intrusion of the mundane, the absurd, the grotesque, or the incidence of death. "The land of all our hopes" becomes a land of suffering and poverty. The negative images together with the general decline in the Moodies' fortunes make *Roughing It* an ironic narrative that challenges the optimism of the immigration accounts that she had

Susanna Moodie (engraving based on a drawing by John Elphick)

read before her departure.

Conversely, however, periods of misfortune or suffering are always followed by some positive experience. Poverty itself is declared ennobling: there is always "light springing up in the darkness," and "a new state of things . . . [is] born out of that very distress." The narrative proclaims personal growth and the strengthening of religious faith; the Moodies battle their pride in order to reconcile themselves to the truths of their condition and the positive aspects of the land they inhabit. Eventually they discover wonders within the forest prison, take excursions that elevate mood, and recognize that the waters that at first appalled them are superior to "muddy English rills"–and a challenging subject to the poet. Furthermore, in her rendition of a large gallery of characters, Moodie offers a conception of man as an unfulfilled creature. The most pervasive manifestation of this is that people are almost always identified with animals or seen in association with them. She gives accounts of encounters with wolves and bears, sometimes associating herself

or others with the innocent victim, the deer, but more often people are seen as hawks, snakes, ravens, pigs, wolves, and bears. In her outlook "human nature has more strange varieties than any one menagerie can contain," and man is "a half-reclaimed savage" who is slowly being transformed "into the beauteous child of God."

Roughing It found favor with the public, as is evidenced by the number of editions required. Bentley issued three editions in the 1850s, and there were several issues of an American edition also in the 1850s. A Canadian edition did not appear until 1871, but it renewed interest in the work and more Canadian and American editions followed. Early reviewers generally admired Moodie's lively style and humor and the graphic detail of her accounts. Through the years the book has been valued both as a social document and as a work of literature. Recently, the variety of critical approaches to *Roughing It* has testified to its literary complexity. Carl Klinck began the debate with his observation in the introduction to the New Canadian Library edition (1962) that

Moodie "was on her way to fiction," as "she dramatized her vision of herself." Essentially the debate has focused on the nature of the book and whether or not it is a work of art. Carl Ballstadt and Marian Fowler have examined its derivation from English forms, the former seeing its origins in Mary Russell Mitford's *Our Village* and the latter exploring its affinities with English gothic novels. T. D. MacLulich deals with it as a version of the Robinson Crusoe fable, noting its psychological richness, and R. D. MacDonald finds that it has a structure based on alternating styles and reiterated versions of the failure of British gentlefolk in the backwoods. David Jackel and David Stouck both take exception to the idea that *Roughing It* is a work of art, Jackel challenging its romantic excesses and its imitative qualities while Stouck dwells on the preoccupation with death and suffering, seeing in the book a prototype of repeated and pervasive aspects of the Canadian imagination.

Moodie's relationship with the Bentley firm, although short, was highly productive in its first phase. After *Roughing It*, *Life in the Clearings* and *Mark Hurdlestone* were published, and three more books—*Flora Lyndsay*, *Matrimonial Speculations* (1854), and *Geoffrey Moncton* (1855)—soon followed. Of these, only *Life in the Clearings* and *Flora Lyndsay* seem to merit analysis by the modern critic. The others are marred by excessive of religious romance and awkwardness of structure.

Flora Lyndsay was thought of by Moodie as "the real commencement of Roughing It," and indeed it functions as the first part of a trilogy on emigration and settlement that ends with *Life in the Clearings*. It is a highly autobiographical novel that begins with discussions of emigration by a young British couple and follows them through decision, preparation, the hardship of departure, and the voyage to Canada. But its literary value resides chiefly in sketches of characters the author knew in Suffolk and encountered in various stages of her journey. On several occasions in this novel and in *Life in the Clearings* Moodie writes of her "love of the ridiculous" and her "delight in the study of human character," and it is these preferences that she especially realizes in *Flora Lyndsay*. She shows herself to be a close observer of human appearance, mannerisms, and language, and is able to render both the pathetic and the amusing and ridiculous in convincing vignettes and dramatic encounters. Unfortunately she lapses from her skill as a realistic portraitist to include in the novel a long melodramatic tale,

"Noah Cotton," which does not feature her strengths. Although *Flora Lyndsay* is an episodic novel of character rather than plot, it does convey a sense of both the tedium and the hazards of the ocean voyage, the trauma of leaving the homeland, and the excitement of arrival off Canadian shores. It is also rich with autobiographical detail, including glimpses of Moodie's literary career and her romantic enthusiasm for grandeur in nature.

That enthusiasm is also given voice in the climactic arrival at Niagara Falls in *Life in the Clearings*, a book generated by the success of *Roughing It* and by Bentley's request that she update her story by giving an account of life in the towns of Canada at mid century. A voyage from Belleville to Niagara, the fulfillment of a long-standing desire, functions as a frame within which to place sketches and essays. In choosing such a frame Moodie may well have had in mind Anna Jameson's *Winter Studies and Summer Rambles in Canada* (1838), or even Margaret Fuller's *Summer on the Lakes* (1844). Some of Moodie's chapters on character had been intended for *Roughing It*, being derived from backwoods experience or the journey inland, and some appeared earlier in periodicals, but the majority stem from her life in Belleville and visits to other communities via the Niagara voyage. In dealing with the institutions and traits of a young society she is able to amplify her view of human progress by conveying a sense of the vitality and liberty of the people and celebrating the advancement resulting from their mechanical genius and industrious habits. Although the book does not possess the novelistic complexity of *Roughing It*, probably because the focus is on institutions with Moodie more often the detached observer, it is a personal perspective so that one is still aware of her fascination with extremes of human behavior, her religious outlook, and her conviction that education is the true wealth of countries and individuals. She also takes the opportunity to defend herself against charges of an anti-Canadian and anti-Irish bias, leveled against her because of *Roughing It*, and to assert her love for the country resulting from the years of "comfort and peace" she had enjoyed since leaving the bush.

From 1838 to 1854 Moodie's literary career had been prolific, but thereafter she did not do much writing. The demise of the *Garland* in 1851 and the relative unavailability of other outlets must have been a factor, although mention of American literary figures in her letters suggests that she may have continued to send work to the United States. Certainly she was disappointed by the Canadian reception of her work and wrote to Bentley (on 8 October 1853) that *Flora Lyndsay* would be her last work on Canada because she was "sick of the subject and it awakens ill feelings in others." She may also simply have been exhausted. Financial difficulties led her to submit work to Bentley again in the mid 1860s, but only one book, *The World Before Them* (1868), was published by him. Occasional pieces also appeared in Canadian periodicals of the 1860s and 1870s, and *George Leatrim* (1875) was published in Edinburgh.

The 1860s were trying years for the Moodies. Her husband lost his shrievalty in 1863 and was unable to gain another position. They gave up their stone cottage on Bridge Street in Belleville and moved out of town to a smaller dwelling, where Mrs. Moodie–as she told Bentley in a September 1866 letter–resumed a "long neglected talent," doing paintings of flowers, which she sold for from one to three dollars each to provide some small income. Her husband's health was in decline, and following his death in October 1869, she lived for various periods with either her daughter Katie or her son Robert, mostly in Toronto, where she died in 1885.

Throughout her life Moodie maintained an active correspondence with family members, friends, and literary associates in Canada, Britain, and the United States. In letters that are extant she gives evidence of a lively intelligence and a broad range of literary, social, and political interests, and often testifies to the strong emotional and intellectual relationship she enjoyed with her husband. They obviously kept abreast of literary affairs as their means permitted, reading English, American, and Canadian works of the time.

Although Moodie wrote much poetry, some of it on Canadian subjects, and often embellished her prose work with poetic epigraphs and resolutions, her literary strength was the realistic and dramatic sketch. The memorable gallery of characters and the accounts of crises that she presents in *Roughing It* and related works indicate that her talent as a writer was best realized in short narratives in which she repressed her romantic sensibility. One wishes that she had more often resisted the impulse to create Old-World romance and allowed what she called (in *Flora Lyndsay*) her "love of the ridiculous" and her "delight ... [in] human character" to manifest themselves. This is not to say that *Roughing It in the Bush* is without

unity, for it does possess chronological order, persistent patterns of imagery, and development in the narrator, but its genesis was a series of "Canadian Sketches" and some of its best parts have the economy and design of short stories.

Letters:

Susanna Moodie: Letters of a Lifetime, edited by Carl Ballstadt, Elizabeth Hopkins, and Michael Peterman (Toronto: University of Toronto Press, 1985).

References:

Carl Ballstadt, Introduction to *Roughing It in the Bush* (Ottawa: Carleton University Press, 1988), pp. xvii-1x;

Ballstadt, "Proficient in the Gentle Craft," *Copperfield*, 5 (1974): 101-109;

Ballstadt, "Susanna Moodie and the English Sketch," *Canadian Literature*, 51 (Winter 1972): 32-38;

Ballstadt, Elizabeth Hopkins, and Michael Peterman, " 'A Glorious Madness': Susanna Moodie and the Spiritualist Movement," *Journal of Canadian Studies*, 17 (Winter 1982-1983): 88-100;

Marian Fowler, "*Roughing It in the Bush*; a Sentimental Novel," in *The Canadian Novel: Beginnings*, edited by John Moss (Toronto: New Canada, 1980), pp. 80-96;

William Gairdner, "Traill and Moodie: Two Realities," *Journal of Canadian Fiction*, 1 (Spring 1972): 35-42;

Janet Giltrow, " 'Painful Experience in a Distant Land': Mrs. Moodie in Canada and Mrs. Trollope in America," *Mosaic*, 14 (Spring 1981): 131-144;

David Jackel, "Mrs. Moodie and Mrs. Traill and the Fabrication of a Canadian Tradition," *Compass*, 6 (1979): 1-22;

Carl Klinck, Introduction to *Roughing It in the Bush* (Toronto: McLelland & Stewart, 1962), pp. ix-xiv;

R. D. MacDonald, "Design and Purpose," *Canadian Literature*, 51 (Winter 1972): 20-31;

T. D. MacLulich, "Crusoe in the Backwoods: A Canadian Fable?," *Mosaic*, 9 (1976): 115-126;

Robert McDougall, Introduction to *Life in the Clearings* (Toronto: Macmillan, 1959), pp. vii-xxiii;

Gerald Noonan, "Susanna and Her Critics: A Strategy of Fiction for *Roughing It in the*

Bush," *Studies in Canadian Literature*, 5 (Fall 1980): 280-289;

Michael Peterman, "Susanna Moodie (1803-1885)," in *Canadian Writers and Their Works*, edited by Robert Lecker, Jack David, and Ellen Quigley (Toronto: ECW, 1983), I: 63-104;

David Stouck, " 'Secrets of the Prison House'; Mrs. Moodie and the Canadian Imagination," *Dalhousie Review*, 54 (1974): 463-472;

Clara Thomas, "The Strickland Sisters," in *The Clear Spirit: Twenty Canadian Women and Their Times*, edited by Mary Quayle Innes (Toronto: University of Toronto Press, 1966), pp. 42-73.

Papers

Moodie's letters and other papers are in the Susanna Moodie Collection, National Archives of Canada, MG 29, D 100; the Patrick Hamilton Ewing Collection of Moodie-Strickland-Vickers-Ewing Family Papers, National Library of Canada; the John Glyde Papers, Suffolk County Public Records Office, Ipswich, England; and the Richard Bentley Archives in the collections of the British Library and the University of Illinois at Urbana.

Emily Murphy

(14 March 1868 - 26 October 1933)

Donna Coates
University of Calgary

BOOKS: *The Impressions of Janey Canuck Abroad*, as Emily Ferguson (Toronto, 1902);

Janey Canuck in the West, as Ferguson (London: Cassell, 1910; modern edition, Toronto: McClelland & Stewart, 1975);

Open Trails, as Janey Canuck (London & New York: Cassell, 1912; London & Toronto: Dent, 1920);

Seeds of Pine, as Canuck (London & New York: Hodder & Stoughton, 1914; Toronto: Musson, 1922);

The Black Candle (Toronto: Allen, 1922; London: Hurst & Blackett, 1926);

Our Little Canadian Cousin of the Great Northwest (Boston: Page, 1923);

Bishop Bompas (Toronto: Ryerson, 1929).

SELECTED PERIODICAL PUBLICATIONS–
UNCOLLECTED: "What is Wrong With Marriage?," *Western Home Monthly* (July 1928);

"Do Women Oppose War?," *Canadian Home Journal* (November 1930): 7, 50, 55, 59;

"Women and the Priesthood," *Canadian Home Journal* (March 1931).

It is difficult to say whether Emily Murphy, née Ferguson, is best known as the first woman appointed police magistrate in the British Empire, the woman who instigated the lengthy struggle to have Canadian women declared "persons," the author of the first comprehensive book on drug addiction in North America, or as "Janey Canuck," a writer with a considerable literary reputation for her books of travel sketches. It is clear, though, that whether she was crusading for social reform, championing the rights of women, or documenting her observations, Murphy approached each task with unflagging energy and passionate dedication.

Murphy's distinguished family background undoubtedly contributed to her success as a leader. Her mother, Emily Jemima Ferguson, was the daughter of Ogle R. Gowan, founder of the Orange Order in Canada, and her father, Isaac Ferguson, a well-to-do landowner and businessman, was a cousin of one of the chief justices of Ontario. One of six children, the author was born on 14 March 1868, at Cookstown, Ontario, and raised in a family in which boys and girls were encouraged to share responsibilities equally. Emily's four brothers took up traditional careers:

Emily Murphy (by permission of the University of Waterloo)

three became lawyers (one becoming a supreme court judge), and the other a doctor. In keeping with the family's social position, Emily was sent to the Bishop Strachan School in Toronto.

While at school she met Arthur Murphy, an Anglican divinity student eleven years her senior, and married him on 23 August 1887. From all accounts, their relationship was a happy one, marred only by the tragic deaths in early childhood of two of their four daughters. Arthur Murphy's restless nature drove him to seek new careers and new adventures, and possessing an extraordinary ability to make the best of any situation in which she found herself, Emily cheerfully complied with the changes.

In spite of her youth, Murphy fit well into her role as parson's wife. Her warm, friendly manner and genuine concern for others endeared her to Arthur's western Ontario parishioners, and while undertaking a variety of church-related activities, she began to display a flair for organizing groups of women to work together on projects. Liberated from many domestic and reli-

gious duties after Arthur was appointed a missionary preacher, Murphy began to record her itinerant experiences, a habit she continued when Arthur was invited, in 1898, to preach in England and Germany. In 1902 Murphy's account of their journey was published as *The Impressions of Janey Canuck Abroad*. Murphy took her fictional name from the popular Canadian cartoon figure, Jack Canuck; like him, Janey is self-confident and nationalistic. The book is dedicated to Janey's amiable fellow traveler, the Padre, who is obviously modeled on Arthur Murphy.

Although the book was poorly proofread and printed and did not reach a large audience, it did earn praise for its lively tempo, entertaining style, and honest depiction of social problems. For while the insatiably curious Janey delights in tourist attractions, describes them in detail, and generally finds the British way of life agreeable, she is most "impressed" by the poverty and degradation she witnesses all around her. In what were to become characteristic inquiries, she angrily questions who is responsible and asks what can be done to alleviate such misery. The trip overseas served to raise Murphy's social consciousness.

Upon the couple's return to Toronto in 1899, Murphy contributed articles to the *National Monthly of Canada* and later became its women's editor. However, after a series of family traumas–both Emily and Arthur contracted typhoid and their daughter died of diphtheria–they were advised medically to seek a change of environment. In 1903 they moved to Swan River, Manitoba, where Arthur had already purchased a small, unsurveyed timber limit. While helping him manage the property, Murphy continued to contribute to the *National Monthly*, wrote many book reviews for the *Winnipeg Tribune*, and acted as literary editor for the *Winnipeg Telegram* from 1904 to 1912.

That Murphy loved her new home is evident in *Janey Canuck in the West* (1910). Adoring the natural, wide-open spaces and believing that the harsh conditions of a frontier society bring out the best in people, Janey expresses sympathy for easterners who lead merely "canned" lives. What consistently draws her, though, is the heterogeneity of the population. Roaming through the countryside on horseback, she explores Indian settlements and Doukhobor villages, and visits with farmers in their fields. She staunchly defends immigrants' cultural differences, arguing that they should be applauded, not criticized, for they are making valuable contributions to the building of a new land.

Subsequent Janey Canuck books evoke similar themes. In *Open Trails* (1912), Janey travels from the West to Minnesota and eastern Canada, making frequent comparisons between Americans and Canadians and eastern and western Canadians. The book concludes with a glimpse into Janey's eastern-Canadian childhood. In *Seeds of Pine* (1914), Janey travels to the northern outpost Grouard's Landing, recounts Indian legends and the events of the Helpman expedition to the Klondike, and describes the workings of an Alberta coal mine.

Murphy's truthful rendering of Canadian pioneering life during the first decade of the century made her books–particularly *Janey Canuck in the West* and *Open Trails*–immensely popular. One reviewer in Montreal's *Family Herald and Weekly Star* (4 January 1928) suggested that Murphy wrote such accurate pictures of Canadian life on the prairies that she "lured thousands of settlers to the western provinces" and that her books

gave "class and distinction to Canadian literature."

Murphy's conversational, somewhat discursive style does make the West come alive. Murphy's first biographer, Byrne Hope Sanders, finds that she did not aim for style but "wrote as she spoke and spoke as she thought."

In the introduction to the 1975 edition of *Janey Canuck in the West*, Isabel Bassett notes that Murphy's style reflects the "free, no-nonsense, no-frills attitude of the West," but Bassett expresses annoyance at Murphy's tendency to quote her favorite bits of poetry. On the other hand, in the introduction to the Sanders biography, Murphy's friend Nellie McClung praises her encyclopedic mind, her "ability to collect and co-ordinate knowledge," and her "gift of expression which, at its best, was not surpassed by anyone in her generation." A voracious reader and lover of the clever turn of phrase, Murphy wrote many herself: for example, " 'The hand that rocks the cradle rules the world' is a prodigious untruth. Women's sphere is still flattened at the poles," and "the distinguishing mark of a really fine woman is loyalty to her sex."

Murphy contributed more to the development of the West than a chronicling of her own experiences, however. Through her efforts, the Swan River community gained a hospital and a library. Ever quick to spot a need and then attack it with vigor, Murphy rapidly made her mark in Edmonton, where Arthur decided to move in 1907 to engage in land speculation. While writing the Janey Canuck volumes, Murphy also inaugurated movements for the establishment of the Victorian Order of Nurses, municipal hospitals, and public playgrounds, helped women become elected as school trustees, campaigned strenuously for women's suffrage, and was instrumental in the passage of the Alberta Dower Act in 1911. She also found time to be the president of the Women's Canadian Club and of the Edmonton branch of the Local Council of Women.

On the strength of her suggestion that female offenders should be tried in the presence of women, Murphy was appointed police magistrate in 1916. Believing, according to Christine Mander, that "wicked people were only good material that was badly damaged," she consistently stressed compassion and rehabilitation over punishment, and worked to change unjust laws. As magistrate, Murphy was shocked by the many drug addicts she encountered, and appalled by the linkage between illegal drugs and crime. Feeling strongly that Canadians should be aware of the prevalence of addiction, and in spite of threats on her life, she conducted exhaustive research into the problem, publishing her findings initially as a series of articles in *Maclean's Magazine* and then, after an expression of public interest, more comprehensively in *The Black Candle* (1922). The first book of its kind, it had considerable influence. Some provinces adopted several of Murphy's recommendations on how to control the drug trade and how to treat addicts. Considered an authority, Murphy lectured throughout Canada and the United States, and the League of Nations purchased copies of the book for its committee on the narcotics traffic.

On her first day as police magistrate, Murphy was stunned to have her jurisdiction challenged on the grounds that she was not legally a "person." Only qualified persons–men–were eligible to hold public office under common law; women could not, therefore, sit in the senate, either. Murphy's thirteen-year effort to have the laws changed was thwarted several times, including a defeat in the supreme court of Canada. But she and the four prominent Alberta women she had gathered together to fight with her carried their petition to the highest court of appeal, the judicial committee of the privy council in England, and on 18 October 1929 the "Famous Five" won the right for Canadian women to be declared "persons." In 1930 Murphy was pleased to see a woman appointed to the senate, but disappointed that neither she nor any of the other "Famous Five" achieved that honor.

Deprived of time to write, Murphy nonetheless did manage to write one book for children, *Our Little Canadian Cousin of the Great Northwest* (1923), which provides, among other things, a brief history of the North West Mounted Police. In 1929 she published *Bishop Bompas*, a small book principally for use in schools, about an Anglican clergyman who spent forty years as a missionary in the Arctic Circle. When Murphy resigned as magistrate in 1931, she intended to resume her writing career full-time, but she died on 26 October 1933 without publishing any other major works.

Emily Murphy firmly believed that women could and should combine home and public life, that public-spirited women made the best wives, mothers, and daughters. Sanders quotes Murphy as saying, "The only truly contented women are those who have both a home and a profession." As wife, mother, judge, lecturer, writer, and political activist, Murphy was her own best example of that combination.

Biographies:
Byrne Hope Sanders, *Emily Murphy: Crusader* (Toronto: Macmillan, 1945);
Grant MacEwan, "Emily Murphy: Captain of the Famous Five," in his *And Mighty Women Too: Stories of Notable Western Canadian Women* (Saskatoon, Sask.: Western Producer, 1975), pp. 127-137;
Donna James, *Emily Murphy* (Don Mills, Ont.: Fitzhenry & Whiteside, 1977);
Christine Mander, *Emily Murphy: Rebel* (Toronto: Simon & Pierre, 1985).

Papers:
A collection of Murphy's papers is held at the City of Edmonton Archives.

Jonathan Odell

(25 September 1737 - 25 November 1818)

Gwendolyn Davies
Acadia University

See also the Odell entry in *DLB 31: American Colonial Writers, 1735-1781*.

BOOKS: *The American Times: A Satire. In Three Parts*, as Camillo Querno (London: Printed for the author & sold by W. Richardson, 1780); published with *The Cow-Chace*, by John André (New York: Printed by James Rivington, 1780);

The Loyal Verses of Joseph Stansbury and Doctor Jonathan Odell, edited by Winthrop Sargent (Albany: Munsell, 1860).

OTHER: Pierre Augustin Boissier de Sauvages, *Directions for the Breeding and Management of Silk-Worms*, translated, with a preface, by Odell (Philadelphia: Printed by J. Cruckshank & I. Collins, 1770);

"Verses on the Late Dr. Franklin," in *The Works of William Smith, D.D.*, 2 volumes (Philadelphia: Maxwell & Fry, 1803), I: 92;

Winthrop Sargent, ed., *The Loyalist Poetry of the Revolution*, includes poems by Odell (Philadelphia: Collins, 1857).

A physician, Church of England clergyman, poet, and wit, Jonathan Odell of New Jersey emerged as one of the Tories' most trenchant satirists during the American War of Independence. When on 14 June 1776 he composed an ode to the king's birthday for a group of captured English officers, he provoked a series of reactions that culminated in his fleeing to New York and eventually becoming a Loyalist refugee in the newly created province of New Brunswick in British North America (Canada).

Odell's reaction to the war was a natural result of his social and educational background. Born on 25 September 1737 in Newark, New Jersey, of Massachusetts Bay stock (the son of John and Temperance Dickinson Odell), he received his M.A. from the College of New Jersey (Princeton), where his grandfather had been the first president. After a sojourn in the West Indies as a British Army surgeon, Odell entered Anglican orders in England in 1767 and returned to Burlington, New Jersey, as an S.P.G. (Society for the Propagation of the Gospel) missionary. Even before insurrection broke out in 1775, Odell's poetry, published under the pseudonyms "Veridicus" and "Yorick," warned of religious and political ideologies in America that would breed anarchy. In spite of yearning for peace and order, Odell found himself increasingly the target of Tory hunters. By the end of 1776 he was obliged to leave his wife, Ann, and three children and become a refugee. Taking refuge in New York, Odell served at various times as chaplain to the Loyalist forces, superintendent of the printing presses and periodical publications, intermediary in the Benedict Arnold conspiracy, and translator and secretary to Guy Carleton, commander in chief of the British forces. With his property in New Jersey confiscated, Odell proceeded to London at war's end in 1783 to seek preferment. He was appointed provincial secretary, registrar of records, and clerk of the council in the new province of New Brunswick and settled in Fredericton, the capital, in 1784.

Throughout the 1777-1783 period Odell's public and private verse had grown increasingly caustic about the morality of the rebel cause. *The American Times* (1780) is typical of Odell's major literary statements on "foul Sedition's" destruction of the country. Opening the three-part poem with an image of social disorder ("The awl, the needle, and the shuttle drops; / Tools change to swords, and camps succeed to shops"), Odell denounces political corruption and irresponsibility ("The state is rotten, rotten to the core, / 'Tis all one bruize, one putrefying sore"). The poet's role in the midst of this chaos is "to stigmatize the fraud," first by castigating the revolution's leaders and then by exposing democracy as the false harlot she really is. The result is an acidic and impassioned poem, which ends with a vision of order returning to the land only when British authority is reestablished.

Jonathan Odell

The disciplined couplets and vigorous rhymes of *The American Times* made this and other political poems by Odell powerful weapons in the Loyalist cause. However, after his move to New Brunswick, Odell turned to satire again only during the War of 1812, preferring instead to write on the domestic and patriotic issues that were pertinent to his life as a colonial official.

The geographical dispersal of literary Loyalists in their new country militated against their having any unified literary influence, but the precedent set by Odell is often quoted in discussions of the literary flowering of Fredericton (as exemplified by Charles G. D. Roberts and Bliss Carman) in the 1880s. Odell died in Fredericton in 1818 and is buried under an inscription describing him as "religious," "loyal," and "charitable." However, at the height of his writing career, the latter quality never distracted Odell from denouncing the Revolution as the hypocrisy and outrage he always felt it to be.

Bibliography:

Thomas B. Vincent, *Jonathan Odell: An Annotated Chronology of The Poems 1759 - 1818* (Kingston: Loyal Colonies Press, 1980).

Biography:

Cynthia Dubin Edelberg, *Jonathan Odell: Loyalist Poet of the American Revolution* (Durham: Duke University Press, 1987).

References:

P. S. Cafferty, "Loyalist Rhapsodies: The Poetry of Stansbury and Odell," Ph.D. dissertation, George Washington University, 1971;

Ann Gorman Condon, *The Envy of the American States: The Loyalist Dream for New Brunswick* (Fredericton: New Ireland Press, 1984);

Cynthia Dubin Edelberg, "The Shaping of a Political Poet: Five Newfound Verses of Jonathan Odell," *Early American Literature*, 18 (Spring 1983): 45-70;

Lewis Leary, "Francis Hopkinson, Jonathan Odell, and 'The Temple of Cloacina': 1782," *American Literature*, 15 (1943-1944): 183-191;

Books from Odell's library, miniatures of him and his wife, family letter seals, and the manuscript for an 1804 poem dedicated to Thomas Carleton, governor of New Brunswick, entitled "He comes!" (by permission of the New Brunswick Museum; from Ann G. Condon's Loyalist Dream for New Brunswick, *1984)*

Kenneth Rede, "A Note on the Author of *The Times,*" *American Literature,* 2 (1930): 79-82;

Moses Coit Tyler, *The Literary History of the American Revolution,* volume 2 (New York: Putnam's, 1897), pp. 98-129;

Thomas B. Vincent, "Jonathan Odell's Satire on the American Participation in the Battle of Queenston Heights," *Signum* (May 1974): 32-43;

Vincent, *Narrative Verse Satire in Maritime Canada,*

1779-1814 (Ottawa: Tecumseh, 1978), pp. 173-185.

Papers:

Odell's papers and letters are in the New Brunswick Museum, Saint John; the Public Archives of Nova Scotia, Halifax; the Provincial Archives of New Brunswick, Fredericton; and the Archives of the United Societies for the Propagation of the Gospel, London, England.

Gilbert Parker

(23 November 1860 - 6 September 1932)

Carole Gerson
Simon Fraser University

BOOKS: *The Chief Factor* (New York: Trow Directory, 1892);

Round the Compass in Australia (London: Hutchinson, 1892);

Pierre and His People (London: Methuen, 1892; New York: Wayside, 1893);

Mrs. Falchion, 2 volumes (London: Methuen, 1893; New York: Home, 1893; Toronto: Copp, Clark, 1898);

The Trespasser (New York: Appleton, 1893; Toronto: Copp, Clark, 1898);

The Translation of a Savage (New York: Appleton, 1893; London: Methuen, 1894; enlarged, New York: Appleton, 1898);

A Lover's Diary: Songs in Sequence (Cambridge, Mass. & Chicago: Stone & Kimball / London: Methuen, 1894); republished in *Embers; A Lover's Diary* (New York: Scribners, 1913);

The Trail of the Sword (New York: Appleton, 1894; Toronto: Copp, Clark, 1898); translated as *Femme ou Sabre* (Quebec: Carrel, 1898);

An Adventurer of the North (Chicago: Stone & Kimball, 1895; London: Methuen, 1895); republished as *A Romany of the Snows* (New York: Stone & Kimball, 1896; Toronto: Copp, Clark, 1898);

When Valmond Came to Pontiac; The Story of a Lost Napoleon (Chicago: Stone & Kimball, 1895; London: Methuen, 1895);

The Pomp of the Lavilettes (Boston & New York: Lamson, Wolffe, 1896; London: Methuen, 1897);

The Seats of the Mighty (New York: Appleton, 1896; London: Methuen, 1896; Toronto: Copp, Clark, 1896);

The Battle of the Strong (Boston & New York: Houghton, Mifflin, 1898; London: Methuen, 1898; Toronto: Copp, Clark, 1898);

Born with a Golden Spoon (New York: Doubleday & McClure, 1899);

The Liar (Boston: Brown, 1899); republished as *An Unpardonable Liar* (Chicago: Sergel, 1900);

The Lane That Had No Turning (New York: Doubleday, 1900; London: Heinemann, 1900);

The Right of Way (New York & London: Harper, 1901; London: Heinemann, 1901; Toronto: Copp, Clark, 1901);

Donovan Pasha, and Some People of Egypt (New York: Appleton, 1902; London: Heinemann, 1902; Toronto: Copp, Clark, 1902);

Old Quebec, the Fortress of New France, by Parker and Claude G. Bryan (New York & London: Macmillan, 1903; Toronto: Copp, Clark, 1903);

Cumner's Son and Other South Sea Folk (London: Heinemann, 1904; New York & London: Harper, 1910);

A Ladder of Swords (New York & London: Harper, 1904; London: Heinemann, 1904; Toronto: Copp, Clark, 1904);

The Weavers (New York & London: Harper, 1907; Toronto: Copp, Clark, 1917);

Embers: Being A Book of Verses (Plymouth: Brendon, 1908); republished in *Embers; A Lover's Diary* (New York: Scribners, 1913);

Northern Lights (New York & London: Harper, 1909; Toronto: Copp, Clark, 1909);

The Works of Gilbert Parker, 23 volumes (New York: Scribners, 1912-1923);

The Judgement House (New York & London: Harper, 1913; Toronto: Copp, Clark, 1913);

You Never Know Your Luck: Being the Story of a Matrimonial Deserter (New York: Doran, 1914; London & New York: Hodder & Stoughton, 1915);

The Money Master (New York: Harper, 1915);

The United States and This War (London: Darling, 1915);

The World in the Crucible (New York: Dodd, Mead, 1915; London: J. Murray, 1915);

The World for Sale (New York & London: Harper, 1916; Toronto: Gundy, 1916);

Wild Youth, and Another (Philadelphia & London: Lippincott, 1919; Toronto: Copp, Clark, 1919);

Gilbert Parker, circa 1913

No Defence (Philadelphia & London: Lippincott, 1920; Toronto: Copp, Clark, 1920);

Carnac's Folly (Philadelphia & London: Lippincott, 1922); republished as *Carnac* (London: Hodder & Stoughton, 1922; Toronto: Copp, Clark, 1922);

The Power and the Glory (New York & London: Harper, 1925);

Tarboe (New York & London: Harper, 1927; Toronto: Copp, Clark, 1927);

The Promised Land (London: Cassell, 1928; New York: Stokes, 1929).

During the two decades surrounding the turn of the century, Gilbert Parker enjoyed international fame as a novelist who romanticized Quebec and the Canadian Northwest and as a public figure who spoke for Canada and the British empire. In 1902 he was knighted for his writing, and in 1903 he placed fourth (behind Wilfrid Laurier, Lord Strathcona, and Charles Tupper) in a Montreal newspaper poll listing the greatest living Canadians. Yet today the dozens of British, American, and Canadian editions of his more than thirty books gather dust in secondhand bookstores, and his fiction is usually dismissed as facile and unrealistic. An eloquent speaker and a fastidious dresser, Parker was occasionally denigrated as a social and political climber for cultivating powerful literary and political friends, particularly in England, where he served as M.P. for Gravesend for eighteen years (1900-1918). However, he was a sincere, hardworking patriot who may have accomplished his most lasting work not as a writer but as director of American propaganda for the British during World War I.

Horatio Gilbert George Parker was born on 23 November 1860 in the small lumbering town of Camden East (Canada West, now Ontario) to Joseph and Samantha Jane Simmons Parker, both of English, Loyalist descent. As a young man he cast his net into a variety of streams before settling on writing as a career, and he tried several kinds of writing before concentrating on fiction.

Parker's wife, Amy, in her court presentation dress, 1902

Initially he trained and worked as a teacher. At the age of twenty-one he was drawn to the church, and after qualifying for the deaconate in the Church of England he entered Trinity College, Toronto, to study for the ministry. At the same time, he was hired by Trinity as professor of elocution. After several terms as a divinity student, he became a professor of elocution at Queen's University, Kingston, keeping up his religious activities and also giving well-attended public readings. In 1885 he again changed course, withdrawing from the church and publishing his first poems in periodicals. To recover from the stress of illness, overwork, and the death of a brother, early in 1886 Parker embarked on a voyage to the South Seas, acquiring a wide range of experiences that were to reappear in his fiction.

Parker launched his literary career in Aus-

tralia, where he lived from mid 1886 until the end of 1889. He first won attention as an elocutionist, then was hired by the *Morning Herald* of Sydney, fulfilling assignments that brought him into direct contact with many phases of Australian life. In 1888, when he wrote his first play, a successful adaptation of Johann Wolfgang von Goethe's *Faust*, which was performed for seven weeks, the *Herald* declared him "one of the most prominent writers in Australia."

Hoping to collect his Australian articles into a book (eventually published in 1892 as *Round the Compass in Australia*), Parker sailed early in 1890 for London, which was to be his home for the rest of his life. During the winter of 1890 he abandoned his efforts to publish his "Pike Pole Sketches on the Madawaska," several of which had previously appeared in the Sydney *Mail*, and instead began to work on the first of his many stories of the Canadian Northwest without ever having been there. That spring, while on a four-month visit to North America, he set aside several weeks to cross Canada by train, catching at least a glimpse of the region he was to use so successfully in his fiction. He also traveled to New York, where Bliss Carman gave him an important break by accepting "The Patrol of the Cypress Hills," the first of his Pretty Pierre stories, for the *Independent*, where it appeared on 29 January 1891.

By 1892 Parker hit his stride as a writer. He participated in the current vogue for fiction about the inhabitants of exotic and distant locales, established by Rudyard Kipling's stories of India and Bret Harte's tales of the American frontier, by being the first to exploit the Canadian North and West. *Pierre and His People* (1892), a collection of sentimental and sensational tales unified by the recurring figure of Pretty Pierre, the romantic Métis gambler, was an immediate success at home and abroad. Its great appeal lay in its novel assortment of characters: Mounted Police, Indians, missionaries, and displaced Europeans with mysterious connections. British critics, as quoted by John Coldwell Adams, praised Parker's picturesque settings and presentation of "the atmosphere of an unfamiliar state of life"; however, it was not long before some Canadians recognized that "Parker's Northwest is as much like the real thing as a peacock is like a Moor hen, and as for that preposterous Pierre, with his everlasting cigaret and his graceful insouciance–such a half-breed as that could hardly escape the Lieutenant Governorship of the Territories" (*Toronto Evening Standard*, 2 June 1898).

During the 1890s Parker was remarkably prolific, publishing much of his fiction in periodicals before it appeared in book form. He continued his Pretty Pierre stories in *An Adventurer of the North* (1895; also titled *A Romany of the Snows*) and expanded his fictional territory to include French Canada in *When Valmond Came to Pontiac* (1895), *The Pomp of the Lavilettes* (1896), and *The Lane That Had No Turning* (1900). Other novels, *Mrs. Falchion*, *The Trespasser*, and *The Translation of a Savage* (all 1893), describe the intermingling of Europeans and Canadians in various locales. This theme might have led Parker toward a realistic analysis of national characteristics and social and class structures in the manner of Sara Jean-

nette Duncan, had he preferred literary realism to popular romance.

Parker's greatest success of the decade was in historical romance. *The Trail of the Sword* (1894), based on the adventures of Pierre Le Moyne D'Iberville, served as a warm-up to his best-seller, *The Seats of the Mighty* (1896). In 1892, while on a visit to Quebec, Parker had asked James Le Moine to suggest a topic for a novel and had been directed to the memoirs of Maj. Robert Stobo. Four years later appeared Parker's version of the adventures of the Scotsman who had been imprisoned by the French at Quebec during the Seven Years' War; the tale was enhanced with predictable embellishments such as a pure-hearted heroine, a demented prophetess, and a scintillating villain. *The Seats of the Mighty* was the first of Parker's novels to appear in a Canadian edition (the first of several to be published by Copp, Clark in Toronto), and it proved so popular that Parker was invited by Herbert Beerbohm Tree to prepare a stage version to celebrate both the founding of his new theater in London and Queen Victoria's Diamond Jubilee. The play first opened in late 1896, in the United States, where its failure did not halt Parker's meteoric rise to wealth and respectability. In 1895 he had married Amy Vantine, a New York heiress; in 1899 he was awarded an honorary degree by Trinity College, Toronto, where he had both taught and studied; and in 1900, with his royalties rumored to be seven thousand pounds a year, he contested and won a seat in the British Parliament, representing Gravesend for the Conservatives.

During his early years in office, Parker avidly supported the Imperialist wing of the governing Conservatives, endorsing Joseph Chamberlain's policy of greater tariff protection within the empire. Parker's own contribution toward closer ties between the mother country and the colonies included organizing the first Colonial Universities Conference in 1903, serving as chairman of the South African Association in 1904, and accompanying Wilfrid Laurier to the inaugural ceremonies when Saskatchewan and Alberta joined Confederation in 1905. However, he solicited in vain to be named successor to the aging Lord Strathcona as Canadian High Commissioner in London. Parker's literary output diminished only slightly during this busy decade. *The Right of Way* (1901), recounting the adventures of Charley Steele, an English-Canadian lawyer who defends a French-Canadian woman accused of murdering her husband, topped the best-seller list in the

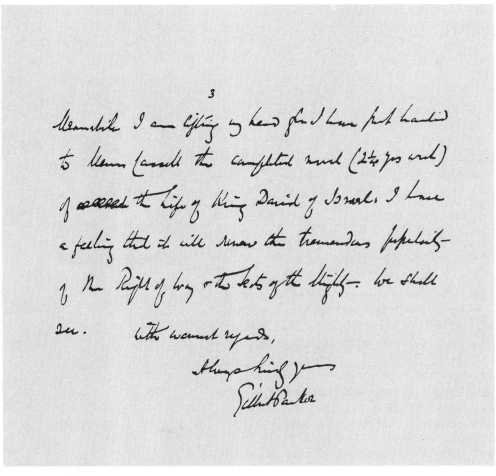

Last page of a 22 May 1928 letter from Parker to Charles G. D. Roberts, mentioning Parker's version of the story of David, published later that year as The Promised Land *(from John Coldwell Adams,* Seated with the Mighty, *1979)*

United States, selling twenty-five thousand copies in a period of two weeks. He set *Donovan Pasha* (1902) and *The Weavers* (1907) in Egypt, where he had traveled, and in *Cumner's Son* (1904) he collected earlier tales of the South Seas. The Channel Islands, another vacation spot, provided the setting for a historical romance, *A Ladder of Swords* (1904), and he returned to the Canadian region that had first brought him fame with *Northern Lights* (1909).

Despite the defeat of the British Conservatives in 1906, Parker remained busy politically. He had little sympathy with the Suffragettes, declaring, according to Adams, "When women in England get the vote, I shall take the veil." Honors continued to befall him. In 1909 he was chosen president of the Sir Walter Scott Society in Edinburgh; in 1912 Laval University conferred upon him a Doctorate of Letters, and Scribners commenced the Imperial Edition of his works,

for which he wrote lengthy introductions; in 1913 he produced another best-seller, *The Judgement House*.

Upon the outbreak of World War I, Parker assumed a position of new importance, covertly heading the British campaign to foster American support for the British side. Drawing upon his personal network of literary and journalistic acquaintances, his immense energy, his respectable public image, and funds from the Foreign Office, Parker superintended a subtle strategy that helped shape American public opinion by supplying material to major and local newspapers, maintaining contact with influential educators and professional men, and constantly analyzing the views expressed by the American press. These efforts were rewarded in June 1915, when he was elevated to the rank of baronet. During the war he managed to publish several more novels, drawing on a backlog of previously completed manuscripts.

Gilbert Parker (charcoal sketch by Kathleen Shackleton; C 104529, National Archives of Canada)

Exhausted after the war, Parker resigned his parliamentary seat and retired from active public service. On a visit to North America in 1920 to attend the Imperial Press Conference in Ottawa, he also went to Hollywood, where some of his books were being filmed and the studios were trying to attract audiences by cultivating eminent authors. After a short stint as a screenwriter attempting to adapt his own books, Parker returned to England. None of his later novels matched his earlier successes. *Carnac's Folly* (also published as *Carnac*, 1922), his conservative rebuke of the labor movement, met with as little praise as *The Power and the Glory* (1925), his historical romance of Sieur de La Salle, and *The Promised Land* (1928), his retelling of the biblical story of King David.

After the death of his wife in 1925 (they

had no children), Parker continued to travel extensively. His 1929 visit to his younger brother in Oakland, California, so impressed him with the state that he planned to live there permanently. In 1930 he returned to England to settle his affairs. He died there two years later before completing his move to the United States.

On 28 May 1928 Parker wrote to Charles G. D. Roberts: "Long after you and I are gone our work will be read and admired, for I unhesitatingly say that you were the first poet of eminence in Canada, and apart from William Kirby I was the first writer of fiction, but Kirby's work was not known throughout the world as mine is. . . ." Nearly sixty years after his death, Parker (unlike Roberts) is neither read nor admired. Almost all his work is out of print, and he is all but ignored by literary scholars, who find his romanticized portrait of Canada false, his style artificial, his characters unrealistic, and his plots melodramatic. Yet he was the first Canadian writer to make a comfortable living by his pen, and the extent of his popularity clearly indicates that he understood the taste and temperament of turn-of-the-century readers, many of whom liked implausible fiction written in pretentious language and authors who performed well as public figures.

Biography:

John Coldwell Adams, *Seated with the Mighty: A Biography of Sir Gilbert Parker* (Ottawa: Borealis, 1979).

References:

George Friden, *The Canadian Novels of Sir Gilbert Parker: Historical Elements and Literary Techniques* (Upsala, Sweden: Upsala University Press, 1953);

Mahmoud Manzalaoui, "Months of the Sevenfold Nile: English Fiction and Modern Egypt, in *Studies in Arab History*, edited by Derek Hopwood (London: Macmillan, 1990), pp. 131-150;

J. R. Sorfleet, "Fiction and the Fall of New France: William Kirby vs. Gilbert Parker," *Journal of Canadian Fiction*, 2 (Summer 1973): 132-146;

Elizabeth Waterston, "Gilbert Parker and His Works," in *Canadian Writers and Their Works*, Fiction Series, volume 2, edited by Robert Lecker, Jack David, and Ellen Quigley (Downsview, Ont.: ECW, 1989), pp. 106-156.

Papers:

The Queen's University Archives, Kingston, Ontario, holds a collection of Parker's papers, including correspondence. The Gilbert Parker Collection of the National Archives of Canada holds letters dated 1892 to 1900.

Moses Henry Perley

(31 December 1804 - 17 August 1862)

George L. Parker
Royal Military College of Canada

BOOKS: *Reports on Indian Settlements, &c.* (Fredericton: Simpson, 1842);

Reports Relating to the Project of Constructing a Railway, and a Line of Electro-magnetic Telegraph (Fredericton: Simpson, 1847);

Report on the Fisheries of the Gulf of St. Lawrence (Fredericton: Simpson, 1849);

Report on the Sea and River Fisheries of New Brunswick, within the Gulf of Saint Lawrence and Bay of Chaleur (Fredericton: Simpson, 1850);

Report upon the Fisheries of the Bay of Fundy (Fredericton: Simpson, 1851);

A Hand Book of Information for Emigrants to New-Brunswick (Saint John: Chubb, 1854; London: Stanford & Wilson, 1857);

On the Early History of New Brunswick, edited by W. F. Ganong (Saint John: Barnes, 1891).

OTHER: "The Progress of New Brunswick, with a Brief View of Its Resources, Natural and Industrial," in *Eighty Years' Progress of British North America*, by Perley, H. Y. Hind, and others (Toronto: Stebbins, 1863), pp. 542-653.

SELECTED PERIODICAL PUBLICATIONS–
UNCOLLECTED: "Sporting Sketches of New Brunswick," *Amaranth* (Saint John), 1: "The Lawyer and the Black Ducks" (March 1841): 81-85; "The White Spectre of the Weepemaw" (May 1841): 129-134; "The Indian Regatta" (June 1841): 185-189; "The Bear and the Lumberman" (July 1841): 215-221; "La Belle Tolotah" (October 1841): 288-296;

"Report on the Forest Trees of New Brunswick," *Simmonds Colonial Magazine and Foreign Miscellany* (London), 11 (May-August 1847): 129-155, 314-324, 412-429.

Writer, lawyer, entrepreneur, and civil servant, Moses Henry Perley was that rare combination who is equally at home in literature and science, in the lecture hall, the government office, and the woods, hunting and fishing. He was, in

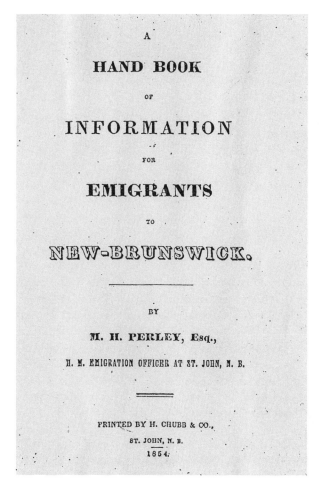

Title page for one of Perley's government publications. He was Her Majesty's Emigration Officer for New Brunswick from 1843 to 1858.

short, like several other New Brunswick writers, for whom urban and wilderness life interpenetrated.

Perley was born in Maugherville, New Brunswick, on New Year's Eve 1804, the son of Moses and Mary Perley (cousins as well as man and wife), and educated in nearby Saint John. He married Jane Ketchum in 1829 and was called to the bar in 1830. Instead of practicing law, he was active in business ventures during the 1830s but found time to contribute letters to local newspapers on the state of the New Brunswick economy and the plight of the Malecite and Micmac Indians, who reciprocated his interest by making him an honorary chief. In 1837 he helped establish the Saint John Mechanics' Institute, and later in life he founded (in 1860) the Natural History Society of New Brunswick.

Perley's writing career blossomed in the 1840s in the form of reports he prepared for the provincial government. His appointment as unsalaried commissioner of Indian affairs (1841) was the result of his well-known association with the Indians. In four magazine articles entitled "Sporting Sketches of New Brunswick"–first published in the *London Sporting Review* and reprinted in 1841 in the *Amaranth*, the first magazine in New Brunswick–he recounts humorously and self-effacingly his duck-hunting and fishing exploits. Although these were written to attract British sportsmen to New Brunswick, Perley himself loved to live and dress like the Indians, from whom, he believed, the white man had much to learn. Perley "goes native" in a characteristic Canadian way, keeping his feet in both camps. In 1842 he issued the *Reports on Indian Settlements, &c.*, recommending improved health and education services to protect the Indians' way of life.

While he remained a spokesman for Indian rights through the 1840s, his vast knowledge of natural resources led to his appointments as emigration officer for New Brunswick (1843), railway commissioner to England (1847), and fisheries investigator (1848). In 1849 he traveled more than nine hundred miles, five hundred of them by canoe. He provided three reports on the fisheries of the Gulf of St. Lawrence and the Bay of Fundy; these were reissued in one volume in 1852, *Reports on the Sea and River Fisheries of New Brunswick*. From his statistics emerge a sympathy and affection for the fishermen he interviewed, as they described their social life and their work. Perley displays the novelist's curiosity about human nature, along with the artist's selection of telling detail. The province rewarded him with the post of fisheries commissioner in 1854.

His investigations and recommendations had created enemies, though, and a new reform government in 1858 fired him as emigration officer, while he was allowed to retain his fisheries post. In 1861 he became editor of a new Saint John newspaper, the *Colonial Empire*, which criticized the province's handling of crown lands and supported colonial union and railway expansion. In 1862 he was sent to Labrador to survey the fisheries, became seriously ill, and died at sea on 17 August aboard H.M.S. *Desperate*.

As one of New Brunswick's first natural historians, Perley advocated proper management of natural resources. Like his more famous contemporaries, Thomas Chandler Haliburton, Susanna Moodie, and Catharine Parr Traill, he was most comfortable with nonfictional prose forms such as the personal essay and travel and sporting sketches. Like them, he accurately recorded the warp and woof of everyday life with his highly visual style. The gentleness, compassion, and irony of his persona reminds one of a later writer, Stephen Leacock, but he is without Leacock's satire. Perley is perhaps the best unknown prose writer of nineteenth-century Canada.

Biography:

Philip Cox, "Life of Moses Henry Perley, Writer and Scientist," *Miramichi Natural History Association Proceedings* (Chatham, N.B.), 4 (1905): 33-40.

References:

W. S. MacNutt, *New Brunswick, A History: 1784-1867* (Toronto: Macmillan, 1963), pp. 230, 244, 300-301, 303;

George L. Parker, "Literary Journalism Before Confederation," *Canadian Literature*, 68-69 (Spring-Summer 1976): 88-100;

L. F. S. Upton, "Indian Affairs in Colonial New Brunswick," *Acadiensis*, 3 (Spring 1973-1974): 3-26.

Papers:

Perley's papers, personal correspondence, and scrapbook are housed in the New Brunswick Museum, Saint John. His government correspondence is contained in dozens of New Brunswick lieutenant governors' letterbooks in the Public Archives of New Brunswick, Fredericton.

Pierre Petitclair

(13 October 1813 - 15 August 1860)

Leonard E. Doucette
University of Toronto

BOOKS: *Griphon ou La Vengeance d'un valet* (Quebec: Cowan, 1837);
Une partie de campagne (Quebec: Savard, 1865).

PLAY PRODUCTIONS: *La Donation*, Quebec City, 16 November 1842;
Une partie de campagne, Quebec City, 22 April 1857.

OTHER: "Une Aventure au Labrador," "La Somnambule," and *La Donation*, in *Le Répertoire national*, edited by James Huston, volume 2 (Montreal: Lovell & Gibson, 1848); *La Donation* translated by L. E. Doucette, *Canadian Drama*, 14, no. 1 (1988): 41-78.

SELECTED PERIODICAL PUBLICATIONS– UNCOLLECTED: "Le Revenant," *Canadien*, 27 July 1831, p. 1;
"L'Erable," *Canadien*, 23 May 1836, p. 1;
"Le Bon Parti," *Télégraphe*, 24 March 1837, p. 1;
"Sombre est mon âme comme vous," *Fantasque*, 1 October 1839, p. 81;
"Pauvre Soldat! Qu'il doit souffrir!," *L'Artisan*, 28 November 1842, p.1;
"A Flore," *L'Artisan*, 12 December 1842, p. 1;
"Le Règne du Juste," *L'Artisan*, 2 January 1843, p. 1.

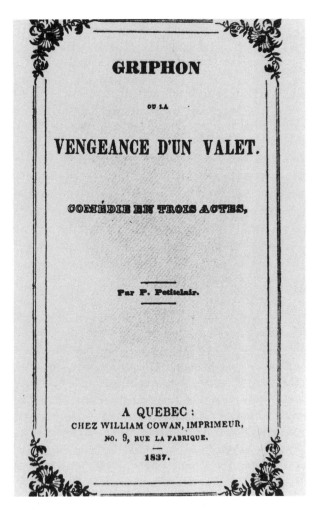

Title page for Pierre Petitclair's first book, a three-act comedy that was never performed, probably due to its appearance at the outbreak of the Patriote Rebellion (1837-1838)

A dramatist, poet, and author of short stories, Pierre Petitclair was the first native French Canadian to have a play published (*Griphon*, 1837) and the first to have a play performed *and* published (*La Donation*, 1842; 1848). It is for these pioneering achievements that he is best remembered today.

Born to illiterate parents–Pierre and Cécile Moisan Petitclair–in the small farming community of St-Augustin de Portneuf, near Quebec City, Petitclair attended the newly established local primary school and the Petit Séminaire de Québec. He abandoned formal studies at the age of sixteen, working thereafter in a notary's office before accepting, in late 1837, a permanent position as tutor to the children of a large merchant family (the Labadies) established in Labrador. Literature remained an avocation for Petitclair for the rest of his life, almost all of which was spent on the remote North Shore (he died at Pointe-au-Pot, Labrador), with only occasional visits to Quebec City.

The titles of five of his plays are known, but only three have survived. *Griphon* appeared at the outset of the Patriote Rebellion of 1837-1838, which perhaps explains why the play was never performed. A three-act comedy with strong farcical elements, it is derivative of both Molière and Shakespeare, and directly reminiscent of college theater of the type then in vogue in Quebec. A beginner's play, it is deficient in structure, repeating the same devices with diminishing effect. It does, however, demonstrate real promise in its manipulation of character and situation, and in its convincing use of a colorful local idiom. *La Donation*, by contrast, is heavily influenced by contemporary European melodrama, the first example of such influence on French-Canadian theater. First performed by the controversial troupe Les Amateurs Typographes, in Quebec City on 16 November 1842, it was published the following month in successive issues of the newspaper *L'Artisan* and later collected by James Huston in *Le Répertoire national* (1848). A comedy of intrigue, it pits a shameless confidence man against a gullible Quebec merchant, the latter being saved only by a dramatic *coup de théâtre*. The play's two well-balanced acts are effective, and it was twice revived in the 1850s, with considerable success.

Apart from its melodramatic flavor, the significant difference between this work and *Griphon* is its topical Canadian element, with direct reference to recent political events in Lower Canada. *Une partie de campagne*, written in 1856 and published posthumously in 1865, is even more topical and is exempt from the melodramatic excesses that mar *La Donation*. A two-act comedy of manners visibly influenced by Scribe, it satirizes the blind anglophilia of its protagonist, a young Quebecois who sets out to sever all his roots, even in the French language. This is an obvious and primary threat, then as now, to French-Canadian culture, so "William" (as part of his infatuation with things English, he has changed his name from "Guillaume") must be punished in exemplary fashion. His intemperateness is more than counterbalanced by the moderation and charm of the other characters including, surprisingly, the two anglophones in the play. First performed by amateurs in Quebec City on 22 April 1857, *Une partie de campagne* is deservedly recognized as Petitclair's finest play.

His two published stories are distinguished by a predilection for the macabre, typical of contemporary European romanticism. "Le Revenant" (1831), composed in rhymed alexandrine verse, recounts how a condemned prisoner escapes by taking the place of a corpse being removed in a coffin. In amusing detail it describes the effects of his sudden "resurrection" on the gullible folk who have come to mourn. "Une Aventure au Labrador" (1840; collected in 1848) is remarkable chiefly for its detailed descriptions of the remote and inaccessible region where it is situated. The tale itself is formulaic: a hunter is overcome by a fierce snowstorm and then assailed by ghosts and demons, which in the end are revealed to be mere products of his harassed imagination.

The seven poems now attributed to Petitclair are diverse in format and theme. They include a stilted description of nature ("L'Erable," 1836); a comic drinking-song in six couplets ("Le Bon Parti," 1837); three romantic poems dealing with unrequited love ("La Somnambule," 1848; "Sombre est mon âme comme vous," 1839; and "A Flore," 1842); a surprising panegyric ("Le Règne du Juste," 1843) addressed to Governor-General Charles Bagot; and the bathetically patriotic "Pauvre Soldat! Qu'il doit souffrir!" (1842). Pierre Petitclair's reputation rests not on his poetry but on his significant contribution to the development of indigenous dramaturgy and short fiction in French Canada.

Biography:

Jean-Claude Noël, "Pierre Petitclair, sa vie, son oeuvre et le théâtre de son époque," Ph.D. dissertation, Université d'Ottawa, 1975.

References:

L. E. Doucette, "Pierre Petitclair's *La Donation* and its Place in Canadian Theatre History," in *Canadian Drama/L'Art dramatique canadien*, 14, no. 1 (1988): 34-40;

Doucette, *Theatre in French Canada: Laying the Foundations, 1606-1867* (Toronto: University of Toronto Press, 1984), pp. 116-121, 126-129, 182-186;

Jean-Claude Noël, "Le Théâtre de Pierre Petitclair," in *Archives des lettres canadiennes*, volume 5 (Montreal: Fides, 1976), pp. 127-136.

Joseph Quesnel

(15 November 1746 - 3 July 1809)

John E. Hare
University of Ottawa

BOOK: *Colas et Colinette ou le Bailli dupé. Comédie en trois actes et en prose, mêlée d'ariettes* (Quebec: John Neilson, 1808).

PLAY PRODUCTION: *Colas et Colinette ou le Bailli dupé*, Montreal, Théâtre de Société, 14 January 1790.

OTHER: Michael Gnarowski, ed., *Quelques Poèmes et chansons selon les manuscrits dans la Collection Lande*, includes poems and songs by Quesnel (Montreal: McGill University, 1970).

SELECTED PERIODICAL PUBLICATIONS— UNCOLLECTED: *L'Anglomanie, Barre du Jour*, 1, nos. 3-5 (1965): 113-141;
Les Républicains français, Barre du Jour, 25 (1970): 64-88.

Joesph Quesnel (Archives Nationales du Québec)

Joseph Quesnel is remembered as the author and composer of the first operetta written and performed in Canada, probably the first in North America. He was born on 15 November 1746 in Saint Malo, France, to Isaac and Pélagie Duguen Quesnel. It seems that Quesnel visited South America and the Orient before entering his uncle's shipping firm in Bordeaux. In the fall of 1779 Quesnel was sent to the United States with a cargo for the Revolutionary Army. However, the ship was captured by the Royal Navy, and Quesnel found himself in Halifax. Having obtained a passport from Frederick Haldimand, the governor-general, he went to Montreal, where he entered the firm of Maurice Blondeau, a fur trader, and married Blondeau's stepdaughter, Marie-Josephte Deslandes, the following year. Quesnel took an active part in the cultural life of Montreal, playing in amateur theatrical companies and composing music for the church.

In 1788 he returned to Bordeaux to claim his inheritance and to make arrangements for importing wine with his brother who had taken his place in his uncle's firm. During his stay he attended many performances at the Grand Théâtre and sketched out an operetta. On his return to Montreal he founded a theater company with several of his friends. In January 1790 they produced *Colas et Colinette ou le Bailli dupé*, an operetta in three acts, which became his best-known work. During the following years, Quesnel became obsessed with the desire to write and compose. Around 1795 he had amassed enough wealth to retire to Boucherville, a small village about thirty miles from Montreal. His passion for poetry led him to complain more and more bitterly about the lack of interest of his compatriots in his work. However, he published very little, and most of his work circulated in manuscript. His operetta, although printed in 1808, was not put on the market until 1812 and then only the libretto, because John Neilson had been unable to print the music. A definitive edition of his works would contain thirty or so poems and five dramatic works as well as the music for two of them.

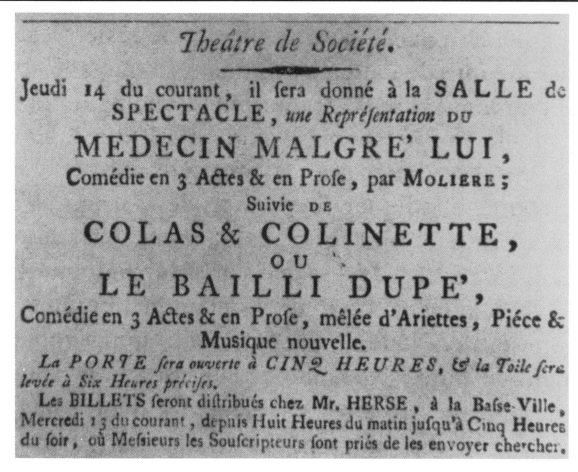

Advertisement for the first performance of Quesnel's major work (from the Gazette de Montréal, *7 January 1790)*

Such a volume has yet to be published.

Colas et Colinette, with its fourteen vocal parts, takes its inspiration from French works of the period. The five characters are the usual stereotypes of the eighteenth-century theater: the village lovers–Colas, a rather naive young man, and Colinette, a pretty orphan; M. Dolmont, the village squire and guardian of the young girl; the Bailiff, who in order to marry Colinette takes advantage of Colas's gullibility by having him sign an enlistment when he thinks he is signing a marriage contract; and finally, L'Epine, a rustic valet whose colorful speech adds to the comedy.

L'Anglomanie, a one-act verse comedy written in 1802 (but not published until 1965), must be considered Quesnel's most important work. It shows how the predominant political and economic role of the English in Quebec since 1760 had influenced the social structure of the former French-Canadian aristocracy. Thinking to please the governor, who had been invited to dinner, the squire takes on English manners. On the advice of his son-in-law, an officer in a British regi-

ment, he refuses to invite anyone who is too French, even his own mother. In the end, the governor decides not to come since the squire's family will not be there. Another play, in the satirical vein, attributed to Quesnel is *Les Républicains français* (published in 1970). Set in Paris at the height of the Terror, it is a parody in which a whole society is attacked through the actions of six members of the lower order being shown in the worst light possible. It serves as a refutation of revolutionary ideas circulating at that time.

Quesnel's poetry is mainly circumstantial and descriptive; his charming songs "A Boucherville" and "Stances sur mon jardin a Boucherville" recall the simple pleasures of his pastoral retreat. For this eighteenth-century man poetry sometimes takes on a didactic or philosophical tone. In his first poem, "A M. Panet," he chides his friend for his faith in Jean-Jacques Rousseau and Voltaire, and he describes with a light touch the eccentricities of his contemporaries. He remained preoccupied with the role of the writer in society and wrote three long poems on this subject: "Epître à Labadie," in which he describes how his early works were received in Montreal; "Le Dépit ridicule," which satirizes his ridiculous attempts to read a sonnet to his neighbors in Boucherville; and finally, "La Nouvelle Académie. Songe," in which he dreams of a literary academy in Quebec. His political poems are perhaps of more interest. In 1799 Quesnel was pro-British on account of his hatred for the French Revolution (in "Songe agréable"); however, in 1803 he spoke out against "L'Anti-français," those who seem to hate everything French. Finally, in 1806, he wrote "Les Moissonneurs," symbolizing the racial conflict in Quebec as a harvest in which the Quebecois can never overtake the English no matter how hard they work.

As a writer Quesnel left an indelible impression on the cultural elite of his day in Quebec, and even two decades after his death his name was often held up as a model. A disciple of Nicolas Boileau-Despréaux, Pierre de Ronsard, and Molière, he served as a link between Quebec and France in a period when the Quebecois were just beginning to overcome the traumatic experience of the 1760 conquest.

References:

Baudoin Burger, *L'Activité théâtrale au Québec (1765-1825)* (Montreal: Parti-Pris, 1974), pp. 199-215;

John E. Hare, *Anthologie de la poésie québécoise du XIXe siècle (1790-1890)* (Montreal: HMH, 1979), pp. 21-35;

Hare, "Joseph Quesnel et l'anglomanie de la classe seigneuriale au tournant du XIXe siècle," *Co-Incidences*, 6 (1976): 23-31;

David M. Hayne, "Le Théâtre de Joseph Quesnel," in his *Le Théâtre canadien-Français* (Montreal: Fides, 1976), pp. 109-117.

John Richardson

(4 October 1796 - 12 May 1852)

Leslie Monkman
University of Guelph

BOOKS: *Tecumseh; or, the Warrior of the West*, anonymous (London: R. Glynn, 1828);

Ecarté; or, The Salons of Paris, 3 volumes (London: H. Colburn, 1829; republished in 2 volumes, New York: G. Long, 1829; revised edition, 1 volume, New York: Dewitt & Davenport, 1851);

Frascati's; or, Scenes in Paris (London: Colburn & Bentley, 1830; Philadelphia: Carey & Hart, 1836);

Kensington Gardens in 1830 (London: Marsh & Miller, 1830);

Wacousta; or, The Prophecy, 2 volumes (London: T. Cadell / Edinburgh: W. Blackwood, 1832; Philadelphia: Key & Biddle, 1833; revised edition, 1 volume, New York: Dewitt & Davenport, 1851); modern critical edition published as *Wacousta, or The Prophecy: A Tale of the Canadas*, edited by Douglas Cronk (Ottawa: Carleton University Press, 1987);

Journal of the Movements of the British Legion (London: E. Wilson, 1836); revised as *Movements of the British Legion, with Strictures on the Course of Conduct Pursued by Lieutenant-General Evans* (London: Simpkin, Marshall, 1837);

Personal Memoirs of Major Richardson (Montreal: Armour & Ramsay, 1838);

The Canadian Brothers; or, The Prophecy Fulfilled, 2 volumes (Montreal: Armour & Ramsay, 1840; modern edition, Toronto: University of Toronto Press, 1976); revised as *Matilda Montgomerie; or, The Prophecy Fulfilled* (New York: Dewitt & Davenport, 1851);

War of 1812 (Brockville, Ont., 1842); enlarged edition, edited by Alexander Clark Casselman (London: Musson, 1902; Toronto: Historical Publishing, 1902);

Eight Years in Canada (Montreal: Cunningham, 1847; London: Simmonds & Ward, 1847);

The Guards in Canada; or, The Point of Honor (Montreal: Cunningham, 1848);

The Monk Knight of St. John (New York: Dewitt & Davenport, 1850);

Hardscrabble; or, The Fall of Chicago (New York: Dewitt & Davenport, 1851);

Wau-Nan-Gee; or, The Massacre at Chicago (New York: Long, 1852);

Westbrook, The Outlaw; or, The Avenging Wolf (New York: Dewitt & Davenport, 1853);

Tecumseh and Richardson; The Story of a Trip to Walpole Island and Port Sarnia, edited by A. H. U. Colquhoun (Toronto: Ontario Book, 1924);

Major John Richardson's Short Stories, edited by David Beasley (Penticton, B.C.: Theytus, 1985).

SELECTED PERIODICAL PUBLICATIONS–
UNCOLLECTED: "A Canadian Campaign, by a British Officer," *New Monthly Magazine*, 17 (December 1826): 541-548; 19 (February 1827): 162-170; (March 1827): 248-254; (May 1827): 449-457; (June 1827): 538-551;

"Jack Brag in Spain, by Mr. Hardquill," *New Era*, 1 (June 1841 - February 1842);

"Recollections of the West Indies," *New Era*, 2 (March 1842 - June 1842);

"A Trip to Walpole Island and Port Sarnia," *Literary Garland*, 7 (January 1849): 17-26;

"The Sunflower, A True Tale of the North-West," *Graham's Magazine*, 37 (November 1850): 285-292;

"The North American Indian," *Copway's American Indian*, 1 (July 1851): 1;

"Captain Leslie; or The Generous Foe. A Tale of the Revolutionary War," *Sunday Mercury*, 13 (16 November 1851): 1.

Frustrated by his contemporaries' failure to acknowledge his literary accomplishments, John Richardson argued near the end of his life that Canada, alone among nations, offered no honors to its writers. In a bitter message to future generations, Richardson asks in *Eight Years in Canada* (1847) "that should a more refined and cultivated taste ever be introduced into the matter-of-

John Richardson (C 31606, National Archives of Canada; Kingsford Collection, 487 PDP)

fact country in which I have derived my being, its people will decline to do me the honor of placing my name in the list of their 'Authors'. I certainly have no particular ambition to rank among their future 'men of genius', or to share in any posthumous honor they may be disposed to confer upon them." In death as in life, Richardson's wishes have been denied, and he is now honored not only as an important nineteenth-century journalist and historian but also as the major novelist of pre-Confederation Canada and the first Canadian-born novelist to achieve international recognition.

Born on 4 October 1796 in Queenston, Ontario, Richardson was the second child of Robert Richardson, an assistant surgeon with the Queen's Rangers at nearby Fort George, and Madeleine Askin Richardson, the daughter of a wealthy pioneer merchant of Detroit, John Askin. Most of his childhood was spent in Amherstburg, Ontario, after his father was named surgeon to the adjacent garrison at Fort Malden in 1802. Rich-

ardson's mother died in 1811, and a year later at the age of fifteen he began the military career that he would intermittently pursue for the next twenty-five years by enlisting as a gentleman volunteer with the 41st Regiment of the British Army, then engaged in war with the United States.

Two events brought Richardson's activities in the War of 1812 to a climax: before the beginning of the Battle of Moraviantown in 1813, Tecumseh, the leader of the Indian forces allied with the British, shook the hand of the sixteen-year-old, and in that same battle Richardson was captured by the American forces. After a year's imprisonment in the United States, he returned to Canada in October 1814. In the following summer he sailed to Europe to join the forces opposing Napoleon. Upon his arrival he was promoted to the rank of lieutenant although the Battle of Waterloo had been fought while he was crossing the Atlantic. After a brief interval as a half-pay officer, Richardson was assigned to the Queen's Regiment and posted to the West Indies, where he

ECARTE;

OR,

THE SALONS OF PARIS.

BY MAJOR RICHARDSON,

AUTHOR OF " WACOUSTA," " HARDSCRABBLE, ETC.

Title page for the 1851 revision of Richardson's novel about the War of 1812 and Parisian gambling

spent the next two years. In 1818 he returned to England as a half-pay lieutenant. Relatively little is known of the next decade of his life, but during this period he began his career as a writer.

Tecumseh; or, the Warrior of the West (1828) is the earliest published volume that can definitely be attributed to Richardson. Written in Byronic ottava rima, this narrative poem in four cantos honors the Shawnee chief whom Richardson had long revered. A preface insists that the poem "is the production of a Soldier—of one who aspires not to the high pinnacle of poetical fame; but whose ardent wish it has been to rescue the name of a hero from oblivion." Several early reviewers and subsequent critics have suggested that even this assessment of the work's poetic merit may be generous. Thus, William Riddell, the author of the first book-length study of Richardson's life and works, introduces his examination of the

poem by noting that "nothing is said which could not be equally well said in prose form; the verse reads like so much prose cut into lengths; the whole work is a typical example of 'machine made poetry.' "

Each of the three works that followed the publication of *Tecumseh* examines aspects of the English and French society in which Richardson apparently moved after his return to Europe in 1818. *Ecarté* (1829), although drawing on Richardson's experience as a captive during the War of 1812 for one of its episodes, uses the gambling salons of Paris as a focus, as does its successor, *Frascati's* (1830). *Kensington Gardens* (1830), identified on its title page as "a satirical trifle," owes a good deal to Lord Byron's *Don Juan* in its attempt to satirize the cavaliers and ladies of London. The conclusion to Richardson's single canto of fifty-eight stanzas promises further comment and disclosures in subsequent cantos unless the poet's muse should fall victim to "some snarling critic or reviewer / Who pins her to the earth with iron skewer." The absence of any continuation of the poem suggests that Richardson may have been forced to recognize that poetry was not his métier.

Richardson's early fiction met with little more success. *Ecarté* is a three-volume novel based on what the narrator claims to be "experience and an intimate knowledge of facts" concerning the gaming houses or "salons d'écarté" of Paris. Tracing the corruption, decline, and redemption of two young Englishmen exposed to the temptations of gambling and of Paris, the novel repeatedly insists that moral instruction rather than the diversion of romance is its primary concern: "these facts are revealed, not with a view to pamper the vitiated appetites of the voluptuous, or to excite the imaginations of the depraved, but with the sole object of exposing and denouncing vice." Despite such assertions, the novel met with a mixed critical reception and a limited readership. *Frascati's* takes its title from one of the gambling salons mentioned in *Ecarté* and addresses similar concerns. The weakness of both novels is identified in an anonymous review of *Frascati's* in the *New Monthly Magazine* in 1830: "Gamblers and gambling-houses, their fearful occupations . . . the awful end that too frequently awaits them, have been recently made familiar to us through more effective channels. . . . A single anecdote might be related, that would more 'warn and scare' the young and the thoughtless, than the many pages through which it has been our duty to wade." Both novels are finally of interest primarily in their anticipation of some of the thematic concerns and structural problems in Richardson's later works.

Just as 1813 marked the high point of Richardson's early military career, 1832 marked a second climax in both personal and literary terms. In April of that year, he married Maria Drayson of Waltham Abbey (an earlier marriage to another Englishwoman, Jane Marsh, in 1825 apparently ended with her unrecorded death); and in December, *Wacousta; or, The Prophecy* was published. In this, his most successful novel, Richardson, under the acknowledged influence of James Fenimore Cooper, turned for his setting to the North American frontier. The attacks made on the British forts at Detroit and Michilimackinac by Pontiac's massed Indian tribes in 1763 provide the background of *Wacousta*, and imposed on this

historical framework is a fictional plot combining elements of gothic and sentimental romance in a narrative of love, betrayal, and revenge. The protagonist forsakes his European past, aligning himself with the savagery associated with the Indians in order to take his revenge against a man who once betrayed his trust. Richardson's theme in the novel is that "man, naturally fierce and inexorable, is alone the enemy of his own species," and the conflicts between English soldiers and their French, Scottish, and Indian opponents finally mirror more powerful psychological oppositions between reason and passion, love and hatred. In contrast to the reception of Richardson's earlier novels, reviews of *Wacousta* were favorable. A dramatized version played in New York with great success within a year of the novel's publication–and James Reaney's melodrama based on the novel was published as *Wacousta!* in 1979. In 1858 *Wacousta* was published in a German translation. Many subsequent editions in English have made it Richardson's most widely read and frequently published work, though Douglas Cronk's 1987 critical edition is the only reliable text, correcting many previous errors.

Despite the recognition as a writer that the publication of *Wacousta* brought to him, Richardson returned to active military service in July 1835 by enlisting in the British Auxiliary Legion formed to support the queen of Spain against the threat of civil war. Although he was promoted to the rank of captain and later to that of major in this conflict, Richardson's return to military life was not an unqualified success. Three volumes detail his sense of injustice in the face of intrigues and incompetence among his superiors: *Journal of the Movements of the British Legion* (1836) offers a defense of the British action in Spain and of the legion's commander. But after the discovery that he had been ignored in a list of promotions, Richardson published a second version in 1837 as *Movements of the British Legion, with Strictures on the Course of Conduct Pursued by Lieutenant-General Evans*. *Personal Memoirs of Major Richardson* (1838) continued his attacks on DeLacy Evans as did a satiric novel for which Richardson could not find a publisher, "Jack Brag in Spain."

Richardson's *Personal Memoirs* were published in Montreal rather than London since in the spring of 1838 he had returned to Canada after an absence of twenty years. Commissioned by the *Times* of London to write a series of articles on political affairs in Canada, Richardson lost his contract when his sympathies with the

Title page for the revised edition (1851) of Richardson's most popular novel, an adventure set on the American frontier and reminiscent of tales by James Fenimore Cooper

new governor-general, John George Lambton, Lord Durham, increasingly conflicted with the editorial stance of the *Times*. Richardson had come to Canada hoping for an official appointment that would remove his financial worries, but in his pursuit of such a position over the next decade, he repeatedly encountered difficulties reminiscent of his military history in Spain, difficulties attributable in part to his own irascible personality. In the absence of a government pension, he attempted to make a living as a writer by contributing to the newly established *Literary Garland* in Montreal and by establishing weekly newspapers in Brockville, Ontario (the *New Era; or Canadian Chronicle*, 1841-1842), Kingston (the *Canadian Loyalist or Spirit of 1812*, 1843-1844), and Montreal (the *Weekly Expositor*, 1846). In these periodicals Richardson serialized several of his own works, including "Recollections of the West In-

dies" and "Jack Brag in Spain," but the major publication of this period was *The Canadian Brothers* (1840), the sequel to *Wacousta* that he had begun writing in 1832.

The Canadian Brothers continues Richardson's preoccupation with humanity's thirst for revenge. Set two generations later than *Wacousta*, *The Canadian Brothers* has the historical background of the War of 1812. Just as Pontiac appears as a secondary character in the earlier novel, General Brock, Captain Barclay, and Tecumseh lend an air of historical verisimilitude to this sequel, but many of the most convincing details derive from Richardson's own experiences in the war. Contemporary reviews in Canadian journals praised the novel, but readers ignored it, thereby intensifying Richardson's conviction that Canada offered no rewards to its artists. Similar public apathy greeted his *War of 1812* (1842), the first of a projected three-volume series. A substantial part of this work had been published in the *New Monthly Magazine* in 1826 and 1827, while Richardson was living in London, and in his *New Era* in 1842, but the dream, expressed in his preface, of a series of school texts that would educate Canadian students on "the gallant deeds performed by their Fathers" was not fulfilled. Only one volume was published.

When Richardson's long-awaited government appointment finally arrived in May 1845, it brought little relief to him in a year that also saw the death of his wife. His tenure as superintendent of police on the Welland Canal lasted less than a year and was filled with disputes, charges, and counter charges (detailed in the letters in *Correspondence*, 1846). Relieved of his duties, Richardson prepared for publication his volume of autobiography *Eight Years in Canada*, in which he examines both his own career from 1838 to 1847 and the colonial administrations of that period. The title page to *The Guards in Canada; or, The Point of Honor* (1848) announces the volume as a sequel to *Eight Years in Canada*, but in fact it simply documents the duels and various affairs of honor that punctuated Richardson's career. In 1848 Richardson made his last trip to the landscapes of his childhood and published an account of his visit as "A Trip to Walpole Island and Port Sarnia" in the *Literary Garland* of January 1849 (the account being separately published as *Tecumseh and Richardson* in 1924).

In search of literary opportunities not evident in Canada, Richardson apparently left Canada in October 1849 and spent the rest of his life in New York City. There he published his last four novels, as well as *Matilda Montgomerie* (1851), a new edition of *The Canadian Brothers* with references hostile to the United States removed. The novels of this final period have evoked favorable comment from David Beasley, the author of the only book-length biography of Richardson and the editor of his short stories, but other critics have viewed them more harshly, as Richardson's attempts to attract American readers of popular fiction by intensifying the gothic, sensual, and sentimental elements of his works. *The Monk Knight of St. John* (1850), "a tale of the Crusades," is a gothic romance that Beasley suggests is concerned with "the mystery of love." Other critics, such as Desmond Pacey, have dismissed it as a lurid potboiler that skirts the boundaries of pornography in its exploration of a tension between "the grossness of sensuality" and "the refined

and tender voluptuousness which livens the soul."

The other novels of this period return to the conventions of frontier fiction exploited more successfully in earlier works. *Hardscrabble; or, The Fall of Chicago* (1851) and *Wau-Nan-Gee; or, The Massacre at Chicago* (1852) are the first two novels of a projected trilogy based on events surrounding an Indian massacre of the inhabitants of Fort Dearborn in 1812. Begun while Richardson was still living in Montreal, both books attempt to combine elements of history and romance in a manner more successfully achieved in *Wacousta*. *Hardscrabble* establishes the historical and physical setting and introduces Maria Heywood, the heroine whose experiences unify the trilogy. *Wau-Nan-Gee*, dedicated by Richardson to the Americans "who were then our enemies" in 1812, includes more dramatic incidents than its predecessor and was described in a contemporary review in the *Literary Gazette* as "a powerfully drawn picture of Indian warfare–its cruelties, its atrocities, and also its strange wild romance." Richardson notes in *Wau-Nan-Gee* that the composition of the final volume of the trilogy would "depend on the interest with which its predecessors shall have been received," but his death followed *Wau-Nan-Gee*'s publication within two weeks. Apart from a few short stories, essays, and a pamphlet defending Lola Montes, Richardson's last work was *Westbrook, The Outlaw; or, The Avenging Wolf*, serialized along with *Wau-Nan-Gee* in the *Sunday Mercury* in 1851 and published the year after his death. Like its immediate predecessors, *Westbrook* is a narrative of violence and revenge on the 1812 frontier, exploiting the conventions of sensational gothic and adventure fiction.

One of the most interesting passages in *Westbrook* reiterates Richardson's view of Canada as a "semi-barbarous province, which, even at the present day, when *affecting* a position among the nations of the earth, cannot boast in literature of three native authors, while it compels even those to court a strange soil for the harvest that awaits the man of talent and application in every portion of the civilized world." Embittered by the failure of his countrymen to acknowledge his legitimate claims as a man of letters, Richardson died penniless and was buried in an unmarked grave. A century later he has been accorded the honors that he sought so much of his life and is now regarded by many as the major anglophone novelist of pre-Confederation Canada.

Letters:

Correspondence (Submitted to Parliament) between Major Richardson ... and the Honorable Dominick Daly (Montreal: Donoghue & Mantz, 1846).

Bibliography:

William Morley, *A Bibliographical Study of Major John Richardson* (Toronto: Bibliographical Society of Canada, 1973).

Biographies:

Desmond Pacey, "A Colonial Romantic, Major John Richardson, Soldier and Novelist, Part I: The Early Years," *Canadian Literature*, 2 (Autumn 1959): 20-31; "Part II: Return to America," *Canadian Literature*, 3 (Winter 1960): 47-56;

David Beasley, *The Canadian Don Quixote* (Erin, Ont.: Porcupine's Quill, 1977).

References:

Carl Ballstadt, *Major John Richardson. A Selection of Reviews and Criticism* (Montreal: Lawrence M. Lande Foundation, 1972);

Alexander Clark Casselman, Introduction and notes to Richardson's *War of 1812* (London: Musson, 1902; Toronto: Historical Publishing, 1902);

Michael Hurley, "Wacousta: The Borders of Nightmare," in *The Canadian Novel: Beginnings*, edited by John Moss (Toronto: New Canada, 1980); pp. 60-69;

R. Jones, "Wacousta or the Curse," *Black Moss*, second series 1 (Spring 1976): 41-74;

Robert Lecker, "Patterns of Deception in *Wacousta*," *Journal of Canadian Fiction*, 19 (1977): 77-85;

Gaile McGregor, *The Wacousta Syndrome* (Toronto & Buffalo: University of Toronto Press, 1985);

Leslie Monkman, "Richardson's Indians," *Canadian Literature*, 81 (Summer 1979): 86-94;

William Riddell, *John Richardson* (Toronto: Ryerson, 1923).

Louis Riel

(22 October 1844 - 16 November 1885)

Glen Campbell

University of Calgary

BOOKS: *L'Amnistie* (Montreal: Nouveau Monde, 1874);

Poésies religieuses et politiques (Montreal: L'Etendard, 1886; modern edition, St. Boniface, Man.: Editions des Plaines, 1979).

Collections: *Louis Riel: Poésies de jeunesse*, edited by Gilles Martel, Glen Campbell, and Thomas Flanagan (St. Boniface, Man.: Editions du Blé, 1977).

The Collected Writings of Louis Riel / Les Ecrits complets de Louis Riel, edited by George F. G. Stanley and others, 5 volumes (Edmonton: University of Alberta Press, 1985).

As leader of the Métis in the Red River Rebellion of 1869-1870 and the North-West Uprising of 1884-1885, Louis Riel played a pivotal role in the history of western Canada. Heralded as the father of the province of Manitoba, he nevertheless remains one of Canada's most controversial historical figures. Although his political and religious activities have been well documented, it is only recently that his talents as a poet have become more widely known. With the exception of a small booklet of eight poems published by his family a few months after his execution, his verse long remained largely in obscurity.

In 1966 the Public Archives of Manitoba acquired several boxes of documents that had been stored in the Riel family home at St. Vital. In the boxes were many of Riel's unpublished poetry manuscripts, including a notebook filled with poems that he had written during his student days in Montreal. This discovery made possible a much more extensive appraisal of his literary merits and revealed that the poetry of the later years is greatly overshadowed by the inspirational and artistic qualities of the youthful verse.

Louis Riel was born on 22 October 1844 in St. Boniface, Manitoba, the son of Louis and Julie Lagimodière Riel. His maternal grandmother, Marie-Anne Gaboury, is said to have been the first married white woman to settle in western Canada. Riel's Indian ancestry came by

Louis Riel, circa 1873 (C 2048, National Archives of Canada)

way of his paternal great-grandmother, who was a Montagnais-Chipewyan. In 1858 Riel was chosen by the Bishop of St. Boniface, Alexandre Taché, to study with the Sulpician fathers at the College of Montreal. Taché made the necessary educational and financial arrangements, having recognized the natural talents and potential of the young lad. It was hoped that Riel, after completing his years in the seminary, would return to become the first Métis priest of the Red River settlement.

Riel, circa 1884 (R-A2294, Saskatchewan Archives Board, Regina)

Although Riel did well scholastically in his early years in Montreal, he was later asked to leave the seminary because of unauthorized absences from his classes. The reason for his frequent truancy was that he had fallen in love and was contemplating marriage. The priesthood was not to be in his destiny, and a similar fate would befall his romance with Marie-Julie Guernon. The parents of the young Montreal girl refused to grant permission for the marriage because of Riel's racially mixed background. The reason for the refusal of the Guernon family, long a subject of speculation, is confirmed in one of his early (circa 1865) poems: "Ma fille est trop tranquille / Pour avoir un bandit ... / Comptez-vous interdit" (My girl is too gently bred / To marry

an outcast ... / Count yourself out [*The Collected Writings*, volume 4, 1985]).

Riel left eastern Canada unfulfilled: he had not become a priest, he had not married the girl he wanted, nor had he found gainful employment. When he returned to Red River in 1868, he put the luster back on his tarnished image by entering the political arena. His creation of a provisional government, his efforts at bringing Manitoba into Confederation, his exile, his involuntary psychiatric confinement, his years in the United States (he became an American citizen on 16 March 1883), his involvement in the events in Saskatchewan in 1884 and 1885, and, finally, his execution for treason on 16 November 1885, have all been carefully documented and are well

Sculpture of Riel by Marcien Lemay and Etienne Gaboury (1967)

known to students of Riel's life.

Less known are his poems. The corpus of Riel's poetry includes fables, songs, love poems, letters in verse, and political and religious compositions. Of the more than five hundred sheets of poetic works uncovered to date, the verse written during the youthful years, especially that composed in the style of the French Romantics, is undoubtedly the best. Had this early artistic bent been allowed to develop further, Riel might possibly have earned a higher niche for himself in the realm of Canadian literature. As it is, the majority of his poems will likely be read not for their inherent aesthetic qualities but rather for their historical or biographical interest. In the verse of the later years, for instance, heavy religious overtones mar the quality of many of the compositions. Numerous poems of this period are either written in praise of or in condemnation of various individuals who crossed Riel's path.

About eighty percent of the manuscripts

are written in French, the rest in English, except for one poem in Latin. The latter, "Incendium," is a seventy-eight-line work, couched in epic style, that describes the great Montreal fire of the summer of 1852. Quite likely composed for a class at the seminary, it is loosely based on Virgil's description of the destruction of Troy in book 2 of the *Aeneid*. Riel's English poetry, which is generally inferior to that written in his mother tongue, was composed mainly in the final two or three years of his life, when he was in closer contact with anglophone communities.

It is interesting, but perhaps not surprising, to note that Riel's poetic output increased during lulls in his political activities. There are, for example, few compositions dating from the periods of the two rebellions. On the contrary, there are many that come from the times of his confinement in Beauport asylum in Quebec or in prison in Regina. Even the week that Riel spent in the

285

Choteau County jail in Montana saw hundreds of lines of verse flow from his pen.

It was with the fable genre that Riel first tried his hand at composing poetry. Under the tutelage of the Sulpician fathers, he received a solid knowledge of classical and neoclassical authors, including Aesop, Phaedrus, and Jean de La Fontaine. Since most of his fables date from his student years, it is reasonable to assume that some of them may have originally been composed for class assignments, he and his fellow classmates being encouraged to imitate classical models while attempting their own poetic compositions. It is evident that from his predecessors, Riel borrowed the format of the genre, stock characters and traits, themes, and other archetypal elements. While not attaining their high degree of art, he nonetheless displays a definite originality. In his work, the fable evolves to capture nineteenth-century Canadian reality. Not only does he update the genre by adding local color, he personalizes it as well by altering classical prototypes to conform to his own artistic and moral temperament.

Certain of the fable themes are traditional, but Riel often reworks them to illustrate some specific event or circumstance. One such example is found in "Le Chat et les Souris" (The Cat and the Mice, in *The Collected Writings*, volume 4), in which a group of mice is being systematically decimated by an omnipotent and tyrannical cat. Even though the basic idea for the narrative is classical, the rest of the fable displays Riel's creative abilities. Instead of trying to bell the cat as in the traditional model, the mice group themselves in military formation and set out to destroy their foe. At the height of the battle between these mortal enemies, Riel's poem takes on almost epic proportions, its alexandrines being far removed from the terse style of the Roman or Greek fable. In the end, because of their unified maneuvers, the mice triumph over their formidable adversary.

In "Le Chat et les Souris" the characters represent allegorically the founding peoples of the Canadian confederation, the cat personifying the Anglo-Saxon conqueror, the mice, the oppressed francophone nation. Riel incorporates into this work a strong element of the French-Canadian nationalism that was most apparent in the Quebec society of the time.

The final line of the poem, "Le bon droit est ainsi toujours vengé" (Thus one's rightful cause is always vindicated), is highly indicative of Riel's way of thinking and marks a clear departure from classical tradition. In the latter, the moral stems from natural law, the strongest or the cleverest defeating their inferior opponents. The moralizing in Riel's fables is very different and is heavily influenced by Roman Catholic dogma. Might does not necessarily make right in his poems; victory goes to the most virtuous. Divine justice oversees all worldly events, and punishes or rewards according to a preconceived moral plan.

Considering all that the classical fable had to offer, it is apparent that Riel was most strongly attracted by its didactic aspect. It allowed him to create a literary universe built on the themes of immanent and distributive justice. It allowed him to create a world not as it is but as it should be, where the good are always rewarded and the wicked always punished, and where victims of oppression could liberate themselves from abuses of power. If Riel overpersonalized the fable genre and deviated from its original intent, it is only because his artistic talents were overwhelmed by his religious and moral zealousness.

Throughout the rest of his poetry, Riel strayed little from the moral point of view expressed in his earlier works. In an untitled poem penned in 1879 (in *The Collected Writings*, volume 4), for instance, during the period of his exile in the United States, he directed a long (481-line), scathing attack against Canada's first prime minister, John A. Macdonald, whom he considered a mortal enemy. He had never forgiven Macdonald for having reneged on his promise to grant an unconditional amnesty to all those who had participated in the Red River Rebellion and for having forced him to spend five years in exile. He was convinced that the prime minister was waging a personal vendetta against him. Riel wanted him to feel remorse because, as he states, "Vous m'avez mangé, comme un vampire" (You have sucked the life from me like a vampire). The poem continues:

L'horizon, tout le ciel m'apparaissait vermeil.
Vous avez accablé de soucis mon jeune âge.
Et vous êtes sur moi comme un épais nuage
Qui dérobe à mes yeux la clarté du soleil

(The horizon, the entire sky appears vermilion to
  me.
You have overwhelmed my youthful years with
  anxiety.

Riel's grave in Saint-Boniface, Manitoba

And you hang over me like a heavy cloud
   Hiding the sunlight from my eyes).

Even if the Métis leader's poetry often leaves something to be desired from an artistic point of view, there is certainly no lack of emotional intensity to it. Riel writes from the heart. Whatever his theme, his sincerity in treating it is unquestionable. Whatever his cause, his commitment to it is total. Whether he is agonizing over his decision to leave the priesthood, or castigating the conduct of certain political foes, or even when he is advocating the establishment of a theocratic Métis republic in the Northwest, he does so with the utmost passion. His position is generally extremist, because with Riel there is no middle ground, no room for compromise. Although his religious and political theories are elaborated elsewhere in his writings, his poetry serves to highlight them with great emotion.

Whatever epithet one attaches to his name,

there is no doubt that Louis Riel is one of the most fascinating figures from Canada's past. Opinions about him, and his actions, differ markedly. His poetry, on which his complex, often enigmatic self is imprinted, should not be overlooked in helping form these opinions. Because of the autobiographical nature of much of the verse, one can witness Riel the historical figure being observed by Riel the creative artist, the latter commenting on events in which he has participated or on contemporaries with whom he has come in contact. It is a penetrating and intimate view of Riel's inner being. The image that emerges is not always flattering but it is at least worthy of respect. It shows a self-righteous, hypersensitive individual who, considering himself divinely inspired, tried to right what he perceived to be the wrongs of the world. He devoted his life to causes in which he sincerely believed, and he eventually sacrificed himself while fighting for the betterment of his people: "Je suis le bien-public. Je

suis venu de Dieu. / Et je dépends du vrai ... "
(I am the public good. I have come from God. /
And I am answerable to the truth ... [Untitled,
circa 1873, in *The Collected Writings*, volume 4]).

Biographies:
Joseph Kinsey Howard, *Strange Empire, a Narrative of the Northwest* (New York: Morrow,
1952); republished as *Strange Empire: Louis*

Riel and the Métis People (Toronto: Lewis &
Samuel, 1974);
George F. G. Stanley, *Louis Riel* (Toronto: Ryerson, 1963);
Thomas Flanagan, *Louis "David" Riel: "Prophet of
the New World"* (Toronto: University of Toronto Press, 1979);
Gilles Martel, *Le Messianisme de Louis Riel* (Waterloo: Wilfrid Laurier University Press, 1984).

Adolphe-Basile Routhier

(8 May 1839 - 27 June 1920)

Leonard E. Doucette
University of Toronto

BOOKS: *Causeries du Dimanche*–includes *La Senti-
nelle du Vatican* (Montreal: Beauchemin & Va-
lois, 1871);
Portraits et pastels littéraires, as Jean Piquefort (Que-
bec: Brousseau, 1873);
En Canot; Petit Voyage au Lac Saint-Jean (Quebec:
Fréchette, 1881; Paris: Casterman, n.d.);
A travers l'Europe, Impressions et paysages, 2 vol-
umes (Quebec: Delisle, 1881, 1883);
Les Echos (Quebec: Delisle, 1882);
A travers l'Espagne, Lettres de voyage (Quebec: Côté,
1889);
Les Grands Drames (Montreal: Beauchemin, 1889);
Conférences et discours, 2 volumes (Montreal: Beau-
chemin, 1889, 1904);
De Québec à Victoria (Quebec: Demers, 1893);
La Reine Victoria et son jubilé (Quebec: Darveau,
1898);
Québec et Lévis à l'aurore du XXe siècle (Montreal:
Champlain, 1900); translated (anonymously)
as *Quebec: A Quaint Mediaeval French City in
America at the Dawn of the XXth Century* (Montreal: Montreal Printing, 1904);
Le Centurion (Quebec: Action Sociale, 1909; Paris
& Lille, France: Société St-Augustin, Desclée, De Brouwer, 1909); translated by Lu-
cille P. Borden as *The Centurion: A Romance
of the Time of the Messiah* (St. Louis: Herder,
1910);

Adolphe-Basile Routhier (Archives Nationales du Québec)

De l'homme à Dieu (Quebec: Garneau / Lille,
France: Desclée, De Brouwer, 1912);
Paulina (Quebec: Franciscaine, 1918);
Montcalm et Lévis (Quebec: Franciscaine, 1918);

Des causes de nullité des contrats (Quebec: Charrier & Dugal, 1942).

PLAY PRODUCTION: *La Sentinelle du Vatican*, Collège de Ste-Anne-de-la-Pocatière, 8 December 1869.

SELECTED PERIODICAL PUBLICATIONS–
UNCOLLECTED: "Les Voix du monde," *Foyer Canadien*, 4 (1866): 525-531;

"Le Premier de l'an 1869," *Revue Canadienne*, 6 (1869): 52-56;

"La Sentinelle du Vatican," *Courrier du Canada*, 28 February 1870, pp. 1-2;

"Au pays du soleil," *Nouvelles Soirées Canadiennes*, 1 (1882): 63-73, 103-117, 256-267, 297-315;

"Lettre d'un volontaire du 9ᵉ Voltigeurs, campé à Calgary," *Mémoires de la Société Royale du Canada*, 3 (1885): 29-34;

"L'Idylle des ranches," *Revue Canadienne*, 29 (1893): 19-29;

"Mon Journal de voyage," *Revue Canadienne*, 3 (1909): 411-424;

"Le Dualisme canadien," *Mémoires de la Société Royale du Canada*, 9 (1915): xlix-lvii;

"Souvenirs d'enfance," *Revue Canadienne*, 25 (1920): 161-167, 248-254, 362-368.

Adolphe-Basile Routhier is best remembered now for his patriotic poem "O Canada" (in *Les Echos*, 1882), which, set to the music of Calixa Lavallée, has become the national anthem. Essayist, journalist, poet, novelist, historian, playwright, and lecturer, he was considered in his day to be a major author and one of the most eloquent spokesmen for the cultural and political aspirations of French Canada.

Born to Charles and Angéline Lafleur Routhier in the tiny village of St-Placide, Quebec, on 8 May 1839, Routhier completed classical studies at the Collège de Ste-Thérèse before entering the law school of Laval University in Quebec City. A brilliant scholar, he accepted a professorship of civil law and, later, international law at Laval soon after his admission to the bar in 1861. The following year he married Marie-Clorinde Mondelet. An unsuccessful *Bleu* (Conservative) candidate in the federal election of 1873, he was appointed to Quebec's superior court, eventually (in 1904) becoming chief judge of that body. He also served briefly as lieutenant-governor of Quebec and as president of the Saint-Jean-Baptiste Society and of the Royal Society of Canada.

Despite this intense professional activity, Routhier found time to publish sixteen books (several translated into other languages), nine brochures, and countless journalistic pieces in a literary career that lasted more than fifty years. His first major work, *Causeries du Dimanche* (Sunday Conversations, 1871), is a collection of articles on religion, politics, history, and literary criticism, most of which had already appeared in the newspaper *Courrier du Canada*. In this work the conservative, ultramontanist views that would infuse all his subsequent writing are already clearly formulated. In *Portraits et pastels littéraires* (Portraits and Literary Pastels, 1873), published under the pseudonym Jean Piquefort, Routhier attacked various contemporary French-Canadian authors and critics, notably L.-H. Fréchette, Hubert LaRue, Joseph Mermette, and H.-R. Casgrain, castigating them for their liberal, "modernist" tendencies. Surprised by the vigor of their reaction, the author soon turned to less contentious topics. *Les Echos*, a collection of forty-nine poems (many previously published in newspapers), added a new dimension to his literary reputation. The titles of the volume's three subdivisions faithfully reflect its inspiration and intent: "Les Echos évangéliques," the first section, glorifies the life and works of Jesus, with much attention to biblical detail and language; "Les Echos patriotiques" is intensely conservative and Catholic; "Les Echos domestiques" is more personal, but no less traditional in inspiration. In general Routhier sacrifices feeling to form, naturalness of expression to rhetoric. Critical reaction was mixed.

He was also an indefatigable traveler, and the accounts of his journeys fill five published volumes. *En Canot* (1881), despite its local focus (it describes a trip the author took with friends in the Lac St-Jean area of Quebec in 1880), was the first of his books to be published abroad (in Paris) as well as in Canada. *A travers l'Europe* (2 volumes; 1881, 1883) recounts, in some eight hundred pages, his travels in England, Ireland, Scotland, France, and Italy. Along with predictable descriptions of countryside, cities, and cultural monuments, the author offers historical background and philosophic reflection in what is as much a personal diary as a guide for actual or armchair travelers. *A travers l'Espagne* (1889) describes in epistolary form a trip to Spain and North Africa in 1883-1884. Here again, personal reflections on history, literature, politics, and religion abound. Routhier was particularly fascinated with North Africa, describing its customs

Letter from Routhier to Abbé Thomas Hamel regarding Routhier's first book (Archives du Petit Séminaire de Québec) and culture in lyrical terms. *De Québec à Victoria* (1893), the account of a journey on Canada's recently completed transcontinental railway, is hastily composed and overtly proselytizing, seeking to encourage French-Canadian colonization of the newly accessible West.

Routhier's interest in history is evident in his essays, poems, and travel literature. It comes to the fore in his study *Québec et Lévis à l'aurore du XXᵉ siècle* (1900), the first of his works to be translated into English (1904). Conservative to the point of simplicity, the text is memorable for the beauty of its illustrations rather than for its historical insight. *La Reine Victoria et son jubilé* (1898) is even more traditionalist, not surprising in a French-Canadian author knighted (in 1911) by the British crown. The author's love of history is put to better use in his prose fiction, in *Le Centurion* (1909) and *Paulina* (1918), both set in early Christian times. *Le Centurion*, a "Romance of the Time of the Messiah," saw three editions in France, as well as translations into Italian, Hungarian, English (1910), and Spanish within two years of its publication in Quebec. Influenced by contemporary novels such as *Ben Hur* (1880) and *Quo Vadis?* (1896), Routhier's text is more proselytizing, to the extent that the love theme it introduces is of tertiary importance, behind the author's evangelistic zeal and his fascination with historical and geographical detail. Even more tendentious in tone and intent, *Paulina* portrays the persecution and martyrdom by fire of the eponymous Christian heroine, paralleling them with the fiery but pagan death (in the eruption of Vesuvius in 79 A.D.) of the prince who loves her. This novel attracted less international attention, although it was published in Spanish in 1926.

Routhier's only other work of fiction is *Montcalm et Lévis*, published in 1918. A drama in five acts dealing with the two French military leaders of the losing campaign for New France, it was never performed. Didactic and verbose, it remains an interesting paradigm for the nationalistic, ultramontanist approach to history that was for so long central to French-Canadian culture. Another play, *La Sentinelle du Vatican* (The Sentry of the Vatican), published in his *Causeries du Dimanche*, espouses the papal cause in the Vatican's struggle against Garibaldi. It was performed by students at the Collège de Ste-Anne-de-la-Pocatière on 8 December 1869.

Perhaps better than anyone, Adolphe-Basile Routhier encapsulated the ideals of French-Canadian intellectuals of his day. His contemporaries appreciated his pervasive rhetoric and his firm patriotism and unwavering loyalty to traditional religious, social, and literary values. Precisely these characteristics make his work seem dated and inaccessible today.

References:

Elie-J. Auclair, *Sir Adolphe Routhier: Son Oeuvre d'homme de lettres* (Montreal: Arbour & Dupont, 1921);

Henry Morgan, *The Canadian Men and Women of the Time* (Toronto: Briggs, 1912), p. 97.

Mary Anne Sadlier

(31 December 1820 - 5 April 1903)

Michèle Lacombe
Trent University

BOOKS: *Tales of the Olden Times: A Collection of European Traditions* (Montreal: Lovell, 1845);

The Red Hand of Ulster; or, the Fortunes of Hugh O'Neill (Boston: Donahoe, 1850);

Willy Burke; or, the Irish Orphan in America (Boston: Donahoe, 1850);

Alice Riordan; the Blind Man's Daughter (Boston: Donahoe, 1851);

New Lights; or, Life in Galway (New York: Sadlier, 1853; Montreal: Excelsior Catholic, 1903);

The Blakes and the Flanagans: A Tale Illustrative of Irish Life in the United States (Dublin: Duffy, 1855; New York & Boston: Sadlier, 1858);

The Confederate Chieftains: A Tale of the Irish Rebellion of 1641 (New York: Sadlier, 1860; London: Cameron & Ferguson, 18-?);

Julia; or, The Gold Thimble: A Drama for Girls (New York: Sadlier, 1861);

Elinor Preston; or, Scenes at Home and Abroad (New York: Sadlier, 1861);

Bessy Conway; or, the Irish Girl in America (New York: Sadlier, 1862);

The Lost Son (New York: Sadlier, 1862);

Old and New; or, Taste versus Fashion (New York & Boston: Sadlier, 1862);

The Daughter of Tyrconnell: A Tale of the Reign of James the First (New York & Boston: Sadlier, 1863);

The Fate of Father Sheehy: A Tale of Tipperary Eighty Years Ago (New York & Boston: Sadlier, 1863; enlarged edition, Dublin, 1881);

The Hermit of the Rock: A Tale of Cashel (New York: Sadlier, 1863);

The Talisman: A Drama in One Act; Written for the Young Ladies of the Ursuline Academy, East Morrisania (New York: Sadlier, 1863);

Con O'Regan; or, Emigrant Life in the New World (New York: Sadlier, 1864);

Confessions of an Apostate (New York: Sadlier, 1864);

The Old House by the Boyne; or, Recollections of an Irish Borough (New York & Montreal: D. & J. Sadlier, 1865; Dublin, 1888);

Secret, A Drama Written for the Young Ladies of St.

Mary A. Sadlier

Joseph's Academy, Flushing, L. I. (New York: Sadlier, 1865);

Aunt Honor's Keepsake. A Chapter from Life (New York: Sadlier, 1866);

A New Catechism of Sacred History (New York: Sadlier, 1866);

The Heiress of Kilorgan; or, Evenings with the Old Geraldines (New York & Boston: Sadlier, 1867);

MacCarthy More; or, The Fortunes of an Irish Chief in the Reign of Queen Elizabeth (New York: Sadlier, 1868);

Maureen Dhu, the Admiral's Daughter (New York & Boston: Sadlier, 1870);

The Invisible Hand: A Drama in Two Acts (New York: Sadlier, 1873);

Purgatory: Doctrinal, Historical and Poetical (New York: Sadlier, 1886);

Catholic School History of England (New York: Sadlier, 1891);

Stories of the Promises, by Sadlier and her daughter [Anna Teresa Sadlier] (Montreal: Sadlier, 1895?);

The Minister's Wife, and Other Stories (New York: Wildermann, 1898);

O'Byrne; or, The Expatriated (New York: Wildermann, 1898);

Short Stories (New York: Wildermann, 1900).

OTHER: *The Poems of Thomas D'Arcy McGee*, edited by Sadlier (New York: Sadlier / Boston: Brady, 1869);

The Young Ladies' Reader, edited by Sadlier (New York: Sadlier, 1875);

"Mary Anne Sadlier," in *A Round Table of the Representative American Catholic Novelists*, edited by Eleanor C. Donnelly (New York & Cincinnati: Benziger, 1897).

SELECTED PERIODICAL PUBLICATIONS–
UNCOLLECTED: "A Venetian Sketch," as M. A. M., *Literary Garland* (October 1845): 477;

"Life," as M. A. M., *Literary Garland* (November 1845): 522;

"The Winds," as M. A. M., *Literary Garland* (December 1845): 551;

"The Old and the New Year," as M. A. M., *Literary Garland* (January 1846): 48;

"The Village Bell," as M. A. M., *Literary Garland* (February 1846): 83;

"Evening in the Woods," as M. A. M., *Literary Garland* (December 1846): 550;

"Catharine of Aragon to her Husband," as M. A. M., *Literary Garland* (January 1847): p. 22;

"The Jewess of Moscow," as M. A. M., *Literary Garland* (February-May 1847): 65-72, 121-128, 178-184, 227-230;

"A Peep into the Dominions of Pluto," as M. A. S., *Literary Garland* (November 1847): 504-506;

"Presentiment," as M. A. S., *Literary Garland* (January-May 1848): 25-34, 86-92, 119-128, 179-185, 203-209;

"The Fortunes of Brian Mulvaney and his Wife Oonah," as M. A. S., *Literary Garland* (June 1848): 329-334;

"Maiden Tower, a Tradition of the Middle Ages," as M. A. S., *Literary Garland* (July-September 1848): 329-334, 382-388, 425-432;

"The Nameless Tomb," as M. A. S., *Literary Garland* (October-November 1848): 469-476, 510-519;

"Autobiography of an Irish Earl of the Eighteenth Century," as M. A. S., *Literary Garland* (June 1851): 271-278.

A Victorian woman writer whose voluminous fiction has escaped canonization, Mary Anne Sadlier was famous in her day for didactic, sentimental romances promoting the causes of Catholicism and Irish culture in North America. Henry J. Morgan (early editor of biographical dictionaries) and Thomas D'Arcy McGee (her lifelong friend, whose poems she edited for publication upon his death) both thought her unsurpassed as author of "the romance of Irish immigration." A characteristic blend of pious Catholic precepts and hard-earned awareness of the plight of unschooled immigrant girls, her American novels are particularly worth a second glance. The Irish historical romances, for their part, found an appreciative audience and, together with the Bible and Catholic school texts, helped create the prosperity of her husband's and brother-in-law's publishing firm, D. & J. Sadlier and Company. Mary Anne Sadlier joined well-known authors such as Susanna Moodie and more prolific but less famous writers such as May Agnes Fleming in achieving a wide readership in both Europe and North America, as evidenced by the ubiquitous serializations, reprints, and pirated editions of her work.

Born Mary Anne Madden on 31 December 1820, she immigrated to Montreal via Saint John, New Brunswick, from Cootehill, County Cavan, Ireland, in 1843 following the death of her merchant father and her own consequent impoverishment. She had been privately tutored in Ireland, publishing in *La Belle Assemblée* at an early age. While her Catholic faith was always deep and sincere, her father's death and her own subsequent immigration contributed greatly to her fatalistic outlook on life. *Tales of the Olden Times: A Collection of European Traditions* (1845), published by subscription when the author was experiencing financial difficulty, represents a farewell to her fatherland and to the more frivolous outlook of her youth, a keynote also struck in the occasional verse she sold to the *Literary Garland* at this time.

Mary Anne Madden's marriage to James Sadlier in 1846 relieved her financial concerns and enabled her to indulge her writing inclinations under the guise of suitably didactic purposes. The brothers James and Denis Sadlier's bookbinding business, begun in 1837, had by 1860 developed into the preeminent publisher of Bibles and school texts for North America's Catholic population of three million. The success of their firm, with offices in Montreal, New York, and Boston, was largely due to the popularity of Mrs. Sadlier's novels. In the fourteen years between her marriage and her move to New York in 1860, she produced six children and six novels. Her reputation was made with the serialization in 1850 of her first novel, *The Blakes and the Flanagans*, in McGee's *American Celt*, a journal subsequently purchased by the Sadliers and edited (like its successor the *New York Tablet*) by Mrs. Sadlier. Its plot based on the debate about the separate schools, the novel saw at least two Germanlanguage editions in 1857 and 1866. For a while Patrick Donahoe, editor of the *Boston Pilot*, serialized and reprinted her fiction, but from 1853 the Sadliers published virtually all her work, and the publishing house grew in direct proportion with her output.

After James's death in 1869, she took over management of the family firm until Denis's death in 1885, by which time his own financial worries had led to straitened circumstances for the company. With the death in Rome, also that year, of her favorite son, the Jesuit priest François Xavier Sadlier, personal and financial tragedies led her back to Montreal to live with her daughter Anna Teresa Sadlier, herself a novelist of some repute in the United States. Having ceased writing, Mrs. Sadlier devoted herself to benevolent work with such charitable institutions as the Home for Friendless Girls, only to lose control of the family firm, along with all her copyrights, to New York nephew William Sadlier in 1895. Seeing her in yet further reduced circumstances, concerned friends that year created "the Sadlier Testimonial Fund" and obtained for her Notre Dame University's Laetare Medal for her literary contributions and Pope Leo XIII's special blessing in recognition of her services to the Church.

After her death in 1903 Sadlier's novels, like the publishing house associated with them, passed into obscurity. While it is impossible to reassess all her publications in this allotted space, a brief mention of *Elinor Preston* (1861) and *Bessy Conway* (1862) might summarize her strengths and weaknesses as a popular novelist of immigration. *Elinor Preston* is the first of Sadlier's many novels about suffering womanhood to employ a first-person narrator, as well as the only one (to my knowledge) to focus on upper-middle-class values and perspectives, and one of her few stories set in Canada. Despite the divergence between the heroine's early death in a state of single blessedness and the author's own lengthy career as a matriarch and public figure, this is probably the most autobiographical of Sadlier's works, and one that offers a telling commentary on the plight of the genteel lady immigrant. However, it is rather disjointed, and the interest does not lie in its melodramatic plot so much as in its documentary digressions and the observations of the narrator / heroine: "The flight of years–few but heavyladen with sorrow and reverse–has crushed the buoyant spirit and withered the roseate cheek, and dimmed the sparkling eye of the ball-room belle; and I sit as demurely, day after day, hammering the alphabet into thick little skulls, as though I had been all my life a 'school-ma'am,' as a female teacher is, oddly-enough, called in the neighboring Republic [the United States]."

The tone is a peculiar mixture of Catharine Parr Traill and Susanna Moodie. When Elinor gradually comes to love the flora and fauna of rural Quebec differently but as deeply as those of her native land, or when she makes judicious use of spoken English to celebrate, not without condescension, the common sense and superior survival skills of the less educated female immigrant, it is not difficult to detect the influence of these two famous gentlewomen on Sadlier's characteristically Irish-Catholic version of the pre-Confederation fictionalized autobiography.

Bessy Conway tells of a poor Tipperary farm girl who immigrates alone to work as a domestic servant in New York City. Characteristically surmounting the strong temptations open to such vulnerable young women, Bessy (unlike Elinor) thrives in America. Bessy's virtue and hard work rescue her impoverished parents from indigence and despair. Urban evils are emphasized only to be contrasted to rural oppression "back home." Aging or foolish parents' wishes are often problematic at the same time that their will is to be obeyed. Sadlier offers a moral rather than a political allegory of the contradictory experience of immigration and acculturation experienced by the least privileged of Sadlier's generation of Irish Catholics in the new world, rather innocently claiming to offer her reader sanctity rather than suspense. Simple, working-class women and their shared values are celebrated.

Despite all the happy endings, there is much in the documentary mode, especially in Sadlier's fiction about domestic servants, and a rendering of the social climate sufficient to rescue her novels from the obscurity to which she has been relegated by social historians more interested in Harriet Beecher Stowe or by political historians more preoccupied with Thomas D'Arcy McGee. As a Canadian and a woman, Mary Anne Sadlier restricted her activities to maternal feminism. Catholicism provided her with a suitable venue for her own kind of nationalism, a literary venture attuned to the time and place in which she flourished.

References:

Dorsey Kleitz, "D. and J. Sadlier and Company," in *Dictionary of Literary Biography 49: American Literary Publishing Houses, 1638-1899, Part 2: N-Z* (Columbia, S.C.: Bruccoli Clark / Detroit: Gale, 1986), pp. 409-410;

Michèle Lacombe, "Frying Pans and Deadlier Weapons: The Immigrant Novels of Mary Anne Sadlier," *Essays on Canadian Writing*, 29 (Summer 1984): 96-116.

Papers:

Thomas D'Arcy McGee's letters to Sadlier and other papers are in the Sadlier Papers, National Archives of Canada.

Charles Sangster

(16 July 1822 - 9 December 1893)

Paul Matthew St. Pierre
Simon Fraser University

BOOKS: *The St. Lawrence and the Saguenay, and Other Poems* (Kingston, Ont.: Creighton & Duff / New York: Orton & Mulligan, 1856);
Hesperus, and Other Poems and Lyrics (Montreal: Lovell, 1860; London: Trubner, 1860);
Our Norland (Toronto: Copp, Clark, 189-?);
Norland Echoes and Other Strains and Lyrics, edited by Frank M. Tierney (Ottawa: Tecumseh, 1976);
The Angel Guest and Other Poems, edited by Tierney (Ottawa: Tecumseh, 1977).

If Charles Sangster had had the good fortune to be born later and to be recognized as a Confederation poet instead of classified as a pre-Confederation poet, he might enjoy the reputation of Charles G. D. Roberts, Bliss Carman, Duncan Campbell Scott, and Archibald Lampman–provided, that is, he had been able to respond to the historical moment as they did. Because Sangster is now acknowledged as a precursor of the new voices of the new country, however, his poetry is still assigned a well-deserved place of importance in Canadian literary history. A native of Kingston, Ontario (then Upper Canada)–Canada's first capital and the home of its first prime minister, John A. Macdonald–Sangster had humble beginnings and an unremarkable, unfortunate life. Throughout his life he was just as concerned with making ends meet practically as with making words meet poetically.

His Scottish heritage and his military background (his grandfather was a British Army sergeant and a United Empire Loyalist, and his father worked for the Navy Department in Kingston and around the Great Lakes) perhaps prepared him to endure the misfortunes and hardships that began to follow him from his birth on 16 July 1822. He was the son of James and Anne Ross Sangster, who had moved to Kingston from Prince Edward Island about 1802. His twin sister died in infancy, and his father died when Sangster was only two years old. As a result, his

Charles Sangster (C 6372, National Archives of Canada)

formal education was rudimentary. Sangster left school (and home) in 1837 to take a job with the Ordnance Department at Fort Henry in Kingston, where he worked at various tasks until 1849, including filling cartridges during the rebellion of 1837.

Among the poems he composed during these years, submitting some of them to Kingston newspapers either anonymously or under pseudonyms, are many that were to make up the only volumes published in his lifetime: *The St. Lawrence and the Saguenay* (1856) and *Hesperus* (1860). By the time these books appeared, Sangster had completed a rigorous literary apprenticeship, working part-time for the *British Whig* newspaper while he was with the Ordnance Department, later full-time as editor of the *Amherstburg Courier* (briefly during 1849), and as subeditor of the *Whig* (where he performed various duties throughout the 1850s). He later worked as a reporter for the *Kingston Daily News*, beginning in 1864. Throughout these tenures he contributed verse to several publications. But by the mid 1860s Sangster's personal health and his poetic abilities had begun their rapid and irreversible decline, causing his reputation, for a long time, to rest primarily on his first two volumes, the work of his youth and vitality, each book appearing in a year when he married (in 1856 to Mary Kilborn, who died eighteen months later; and in 1860 to Henrietta Charlotte Mary Meagher, a seventeen-year-old who was to bear him four children). The coincidence of marriage and publication in Sangster's life seems to fit with his predilection for sonnets, lyrics, and other love poems.

Both volumes drew unusually favorable reviews, citing Sangster's original poetic insight and his singular contribution to Canadian literature. *The St. Lawrence and the Saguenay* consists mainly of sentimental love poems and of poetic descriptions of nature, with the exception of the title poem, an imaginative, ambitious, demanding exploration of the narrator's journey from Lake Ontario along the St. Lawrence and the Saguenay rivers in southern Quebec. Accompanied and inspired by a fanciful, nymphlike figure, the speaker offers a series of interpretations of the countryside and of his voyage in order to reveal his personal quest for poetic beauty and truth and their parallels with man's basic journey through life: "Yes, here the Genius of Beauty truly dwells. / I worship Truth and Beauty in my soul. / The pure prismatic globule that upwells / From the blue deep; the psalmy waves that roll / Before the hurricane; the outspread scroll / Of heaven, with its written tomes of stars; / The dewdrop on the leaf: These I extol, / And all alike— each one a Spirit-Mars, / Guarding my Victor-Soul above Earth's prison bars." Through a sequence of comparable reflections that are at once introspective and empirical, Sangster comes to a realization of "How unutterably deep and strong is Human Love." "The St. Lawrence and the Saguenay" clearly stands out from among the other poems in the volume, which are more conventional in their subject matter and more regular in their rhythm and meter.

Although *Hesperus* won a very favorable critical response from a public anxious to see Sangster repeat or better the accomplishment of his previous collection, its actual aesthetic and poetic accomplishment is slightly inferior, seemingly presaging the imminent decay of the poet and his abilities. Once again the principal work is the title poem, "Hesperus: A Legend of the Stars," in which Sangster describes a kind of dream vision in which he and his wife Mary contemplate the evening sky so intensely that their "spirits seem / Absorbed in the stellar world," and they are able to detect an angelic chorus recounting the tale of the birth of the evening star, Hesperus. The mystical experience seems to fulfill them, and at the poem's conclusion they are ecstatically meditating upon the "Known Unknown." The last stanza contains some of Sangster's most interesting poetry: "Still on the Evening Star / Gazed we with steadfast eyes, / As it shone / On its throne / Afar, / In the blue skies. / No longer the charioteers / Dashed through the gleaming spheres; / No more the evangels / Rehearsed the glad story; / But, in passing, the angels / Left footprints of glory. . . . " In the rest of the collection Sangster is mainly concerned with historical and ethereal subjects that sometimes seem beyond his abilities, although the sonnet sequence with which he concludes the book ("Sonnets Written in the Orillia Woods, August 1859") is noteworthy for the control and specificity of its development.

In 1860 Sangster took a job with the Post Office Department, to which in the 1870s he was to attribute the declines in his health and talents, leading to his physical breakdown in 1875 and to the development of a chronic nervous condition during the 1880s. Between 1886 and 1889 Sangster set about putting his literary life into order—particularly since his physical life seemed destined to remain in disorder—making revisions to his published poems and compiling two volumes of previously unpublished verse: *Norland Echoes and Other Strains and Lyrics* and *The Angel Guest and Other Poems*, both published posthumously (in 1976 and 1977 respectively). The only other work to appear under Sangster's name— again posthumously, the evidence seems to suggest—is the poem *Our Norland*, an undated chapbook.

After his death in 1893 in Kingston, Sangster's work quickly slipped into obscurity, his manuscripts remaining safe but unread at McGill University. However, their rediscovery in 1957 began a slow critical and historical process vindicating his reputation as an important pre-Confederation poet and as a precursor of a national literature.

References:

R. P. Baker, "Charles Sangster," in his *A History of English-Canadian Literature to the Confederation* (Cambridge, Mass.: Harvard University Press, 1920), pp. 159-165;

Arthur S. Bourinot, "Charles Sangster," in *Leading Canadian Poets*, edited by W. P. Percival (Toronto: Ryerson, 1948), pp. 202-212;

E. H. Dewart, "Charles Sangster, the Canadian Poet," *Canadian Magazine*, 7 (May 1896): 28-34;

W. D. Hamilton, *Charles Sangster* (New York: Twayne, 1971);

John Macklem, "Who's Who in Canadian Literature: Charles Sangster," *Canadian Bookman*, 10 (July 1928): 195-196;

Desmond Pacey, "Charles Sangster," in his *Ten Canadian Poets* (Toronto: Ryerson, 1958), pp. 1-33;

Donald Stephens, "Charles Sangster: The End of an Era," in *Colony and Confederation: Early Canadian Poets and Their Background*, edited by George Woodcock (Vancouver: University of British Columbia Press, 1974), pp. 54-61.

Papers:
Sangster's papers are in the Osler Library, McGill University, Montreal, and in the National Archives in Ottawa.

Elizabeth Simcoe
(September 1762 - 11 January 1850)

Clara Thomas
York University

BOOK: *The Diary of Mrs. John Graves Simcoe*, edited by J. Ross Robertson (Toronto: Briggs, 1911); revised and enlarged as *Mrs. Simcoe's Diary*, edited by Mary Quayle Innis (Toronto: Macmillan, 1965).

In 1791 Elizabeth Posthuma Gwillim Simcoe began the diary of her Canadian experience as wife of John Graves Simcoe, a soldier, country gentleman, and member of Parliament who had just been appointed Upper Canada's first lieutenant governor. She was both an orphan and an heiress. Her father, Lt.-Col. Thomas Gwillim, had died seven months before her baptism at Whitchurch, Herefordshire, on 22 September 1762, and her mother, Elizabeth Spinkes Gwillim, died within hours after her birth. Her exact birthdate remains unknown. She was cared for by Samuel and Margaret Graves, her aunt and uncle. Admiral Graves was the godfather of John Graves Simcoe. When she was sixteen Elizabeth married

Lt.-Col. Simcoe, fourteen years her senior and a veteran of the war in America, and with him lived as country gentry on a large estate, Wolford Lodge, near Honiton in Devonshire. They eventually had eleven children.

A tiny woman, no more than five feet tall, Elizabeth Simcoe was well educated by the standards of her day. She spoke French and German, sketched and painted watercolors with unusual talent, and enjoyed thoroughly both an active social life with plenty of visiting and dancing and one that included a good deal of healthy open-air activity. She was excited by her husband's appointment to Canada, and though she had to leave behind four of their six young children, taking only two-year-old Sophia and the baby, Francis, with her, she embarked for Canada with lively anticipation. Diary and letter writing were obsessive features of her daily activities: "I have us'd myself from my Infancy to Read after I am in Bed, it is grown so habitual to me that I cannot sleep with-

*Elizabeth Simcoe (miniature by Mrs. Burgess, 1799;
C 81931, National Archives of Canada)*

out a dose of Literature . . . & generally catching every thought which accidentally floats on my Brain, I commit it to paper."

The Simcoes spent the winter of 1791 in Quebec City, then moved, arriving on 25 July at Newark (now Niagara-on-the-Lake) in Upper Canada (Ontario) after a six-week journey. Based at Niagara, but spending time in York (Toronto) and in journeys throughout the southern peninsula of Upper Canada and back to Quebec, Mrs. Simcoe recorded her impressions and opinions until their departure for England in July of 1796. Intermittently in poor health ever since his early campaign in America, her husband was preparing to take over the command of British forces in India in 1806, when he was ordered to join the fleet off Portugal, became ill en route, and died. Elizabeth lived on until 11 January 1850, an autocrat to her nine surviving children, particularly to her daughters, whom she insisted remain with her.

While in Canada, Elizabeth Simcoe kept two diaries: in the first, a series of small books, she re-

corded daily, on-the-spot events; she then rewrote, deleting or expanding, into large blank books that she sent back to Wolford Lodge to be read to her daughters there. The manuscript, together with some sketches, watercolors, and letters, is now in the Ontario Archives. Simcoe was proud of her husband, his position, and hers, and her diary reflects her satisfaction with her life in Canada as well as her keen appreciation of the land, its possibilities, and its diversity. In fact, in 1796, as she approached her English home once again, she wrote, "the fields looked so cold, so damp, so chearless [*sic*], so uncomfortable from the want of our bright Canadian Sun that the effect was striking & the contrast very unfavourable to the English climate."

As well as being the "Governor's Lady" and outranked only by Lady Maria Dorchester, wife of Guy Carleton, Baron Dorchester, the commander-in-chief of the Canadas, she was, of course, and knew she was, a temporary resident only. She could enjoy the novelties of society in a new land and even of living in a tent, as the Simcoes did at York, with a traveler's tolerance. True, it was a superior kind of tent, twenty-two feet by thirteen, with a floor, windows, and a door, papered and painted, built on a wooden framework and boarded up on the outside for warmth. At Quebec she established a pattern that was hers throughout, dancing, playing cards, taking tea, gossiping, and making expeditions on foot and by sleigh with the members of the small and close-knit official society, finding everything stimulating and pleasurable except the excessive heat in the houses, about which she complained. When she deemed something of particular interest, such as her visit to the Ursuline Convent, she enlarged upon it, in this case describing the nuns' varied occupations.

She was young, vigorous, brave, and country-bred, an indefatigable sketcher, thinking nothing of long walks if the goal was likely to be "picturesque," for she had, as she said, "the picturesque eye" and looked at all she saw with her sketchbook in mind. At York she instituted picnics as a popular society pastime and displayed a distinctly bizarre taste for enjoyment of the spectacle of fiercely burning wood. She was an enthusiastic reporter of the natural world in all its manifestations, from rattlesnakes to blossoming orchards, and her talent for the telling detail gives her writing its lasting appeal. She was not universally popular, some contemporary critics calling her excessively rank-conscious, demanding, and formal, but for her part she was ready to accept both the land and its inhabitants, particularly the Indians, with remarkable equanimity, even enthusiasm. Since 1965, when the complete diary was first published, it has been a classic text, valued for the vivid personality it reveals as much as for the flavor of its time and the range of its information.

Biography:

Mary Beacock Fryer, *Elizabeth Posthuma Simcoe, 1762-1850* (Toronto: Dunburn, 1989).

References:

Marian Fowler, *The Embroidered Tent: Five Gentlewomen in Early Canada* (Toronto: Anansi, 1982), pp. 7-51;

John Ross Robertson, Introduction to *The Diary of Mrs. John Graves Simcoe* (Toronto: Briggs, 1911), pp. 1-34.

Burrows Willcocks Arthur Sleigh
(1821 - 1869)

Eva H. Seidner
University of Toronto

BOOKS: *The Outcast Prophet: A Novel* (London: Newby, 1847);

Pine Forests and Hacmatack Clearings; or, Travel, Life, and Adventure in the British North American Provinces (London: Bentley, 1853).

"My first breath was drawn on the shores of the mighty St. Lawrence," wrote B. W. Arthur Sleigh in the preface to *Pine Forests and Hacmatack Clearings* (1853), his book of "travel, life and adventure," "and I may perhaps therefore claim the right of feeling and expressing a deep interest in Canadian affairs." Born in 1821 in Lower Canada (Quebec), Sleigh was the son of the physician William Willcocks Sleigh and his wife, Sarah Campbell Sleigh. He received his early education in England, but in 1834 returned to Lower Canada and there studied for the next four years. At the age of twenty-one Sleigh enrolled in the Second West India Regiment and bought his lieutenancy in Jamaica in 1844. The following year he transferred, again by purchase, to the 77th Foot Regiment, with which he arrived in Halifax, Nova Scotia, in 1846, moving on to Quebec in September of that year.

It was during this time, in order to "pass away . . . the tedium of . . . a couple of stupid stations in the Canadas and neighbouring provinces," that Sleigh wrote *The Outcast Prophet: A*

Novel (1847). Copies are extremely rare; indeed, the title has until recently escaped the attention of bibliographers. It is a romantic tale of adventure in the North American wilderness, very much in the narrative tradition of Sir Walter Scott and James Fenimore Cooper. Set in the 1770s near the Thousand Islands region of Canada, and in the wilds of America, the romance features the dark and fair heroines, disguised and wandering heirs, noble savages, doomed lovers, and happy endings common in the popular fiction of the time. In addition Sleigh inadvertently provides insight into many equally familiar social and racial prejudices, some of which he earnestly tries to explain on "scientific" grounds. His Esquimaux, for example, are an "inferior" race, their minds and bodies "locked in their icy boundaries," while his Indians, freely roaming a "luxuriant country," rejoicing in an "unrivaled clime," may possess some of the attributes of the "cultivated and classic European." Throughout, the romance, law, order, and the discipline of British army life are extolled.

By June of 1848 Sleigh had sold his military commission and returned to civilian life in England. He became, as he says in *Pine Forests and Hacmatack Clearings*, "proprietor over forty-five miles of country" by purchasing 100,000 acres of land–seven townships–in King's County, Prince

PINE FORESTS

AND

HACMATACK CLEARINGS;

OR,

Travel, Life, and Adventure,

IN THE

BRITISH NORTH AMERICAN PROVINCES.

BY

LIEUTENANT-COLONEL SLEIGH, C.M.,

LATE OF HER MAJESTY'S 77TH REGIMENT.

Second Edition.

LONDON:
RICHARD BENTLEY, NEW BURLINGTON STREET,
Publisher in Ordinary to Her Majesty.
1853.

Title page for the second edition of Sleigh's autobiography

Edward Island. Returning to Canada to live the life of the landed gentry, he eventually became a justice of the peace and a lieutenant-colonel in one of the local militia regiments. He spent much time amid the relative refinements of Halifax. In 1851 he traveled in the United States, a country that he pronounced possessed of an "aggrandizing spirit" highly threatening to "her Majesty's magnificent colonial possessions in British North America," and a place where "the Mob" held sway. The following year he started a steamship service from New York to Quebec, but was forced by the exorbitant costs of the insurance to abandon the enterprise. He sold his huge Maritime estate and again returned to England.

His *Pine Forests and Hacmatack Clearings* was the product of his travels, military experiences, civil service, and ill-fated marine business venture. As its subtitle, *Travel, Life and Adventure in the British North American Provinces*, suggests, the author describes everything from a tedious stagecoach ride to a perilous crossing of the icebound Northumberland Straits and introduces the reader to persons from every social and economic level. His book is filled with descriptions, anecdotes, and gossip, and is especially interesting in its accounts of government corruption and ineptitude, and the rascalry of the local population. Sleigh's aim, as stated in the preface, was to strengthen and preserve the empire, to inspire her majesty's "Ministers to enact legislation to keep the British North American Colonies as appendages to the British Crown . . . through the [introduction of] institutions more suited to their advanced state of progress." He believed that the appointment in Canada of a governor general, a royal viceroy, was essential to the maintenance of the empire. "Lose Canada," he warned, "and the West Indies are lost also."

Unfortunately Sleigh's ambitious schemes in England met with as little success as had those in Canada. He served as publisher of first the *British Army Dispatch*, which began publication in 1853 and which he soon sold. In 1855 he became one of the publishers of a penny daily, the *Daily Telegraph*, which fared well initially, but which he also sold after incurring ruinous debts. Three times he tried to win election to the House of Commons, each failure deepening his financial distress. By 1857 he was bankrupt and withdrew entirely from public life. He died in Chelsea, England, in 1869.

References:

Eva Seidner, "Outcast No Longer: An Early Canadian Romance Reinstated—B. W. A. Sleigh's *The Outcast Prophet*," *Canadian Literature*, 107 (December 1985);

P. B. Waite, "Crossing Northumberland Straits in March, 1852," *Dalhousie Review*, 42 (1962-1963): 55-67.

Goldwin Smith

(13 August 1823 - 7 June 1910)

Susan Jackel
University of Alberta

BOOKS: *Irish History and Irish Character* (Oxford: Parker, 1861); revised as *Irish History and the Irish Question* (New York: McClure, Phillips, 1905);

Rational Religion (Oxford: Wheeler / London: Whittaker, 1861);

Lectures on the Study of History (Oxford: Parker, 1862; New York: Harper, 1866; Toronto: Adam, Stevenson, 1873);

Does the Bible Sanction American Slavery? (Cambridge: Sever & Francis, 1863);

The Empire. A Series of Letters (Oxford: Parker, 1863);

A Plea for the Abolition of Tests in the University of Oxford (Oxford: Wheeler & Day, 1864);

The Civil War in America (London: Simpkin, Marshall, 1866);

Three English Statesmen (London: Macmillan, 1867; New York: Harper, 1867);

Cowper (New York: Harper, 1880; London: Macmillan, 1880);

Lectures and Essays (Toronto: Hunter, Rose, 1881; New York: Macmillan, 1881);

False Hopes (New York: Lovell, 1883);

A Trip to England (Toronto: Robinson, 1888; New York: Macmillan, 1888);

Life of Jane Austen (London: Scott, 1890);

Canada and the Canadian Question (London & New York: Macmillan, 1891; Toronto: Hunter, Rose, 1891; modern edition, Toronto: University of Toronto Press, 1971);

The Moral Crusader, William Lloyd Garrison (New York & London: Funk & Wagnalls, 1892);

Essays on Questions of the Day (New York & London: Macmillan, 1893);

The United States: An Outline of Political History, 1492-1871 (New York & London: Macmillan, 1893);

Oxford and Her Colleges (London & New York: Macmillan, 1894);

Guesses at the Riddle of Existence (New York & London: Macmillan, 1897);

Shakespeare: The Man (Toronto, 1897; New York:

Goldwin Smith

Doubleday & McClure, 1899);

The United Kingdom: A Political History, 2 volumes (Toronto: Copp, Clark, 1899; New York & London: Macmillan, 1899);

Commonwealth or Empire (Toronto: Tyrrell, 1900; enlarged edition, New York & London: Macmillan, 1902);

In the Court of History (Toronto: Tyrrell, 1902);

My Memory of Gladstone (London: Unwin, 1904; Toronto: Tyrrell, 1904);

In Quest of Light (New York & London: Macmillan, 1906);

No Refuge but in Truth (New York & London: Putnam, 1908; Toronto: Tyrrell, 1908);
Reminiscences, edited by Arnold Haultain (New York: Macmillan, 1910).

For more than half a century, on two continents, Goldwin Smith played the part of controversialist, man of letters, and intellectual gadfly. His nom de plume in Canada, "Bystander," reflected his habitual preference for observation and comment over direct political action. Yet he made an important contribution to Canadian public life through his many journalistic activities and his unremitting insistence on the need for informed, independent thought among the reading and voting public.

Born on 13 August 1823 in Reading, England, the son of a well-to-do physician, Smith grew up among rural scenes and figures redolent of the novels of Henry Fielding: fox-hunting parsons and farmers who "ploughed with four horses [and] voted with the Squire," as Smith says in *Reminiscences* (1910). He was educated at Eton and then Oxford, graduating in 1845 with first class honors and many prizes.

Although called to the bar in 1847, Smith preferred the life of a man of letters. In 1846 he had become fellow and then tutor at University College, Oxford, but during this period he also established his reputation as a journalist, joining the staff of the Peelite *Morning Chronicle* in 1850. When the *Saturday Review* began publication in 1855, Smith headed the list of contributors. He wrote also for the *Fortnightly Review* and the *Times*, and his incisive analysis and epigrammatic style marked him as a potential candidate for Parliament.

Smith's political sympathies were with the Manchester School of Bright, Cobden, and Mill. Out of these sympathies came *The Empire* (1863), a collection of Smith's letters to the Liberal *Daily News* on the subject of emancipating England's colonies. There Smith wrote: "I am no more against Colonies than I am against the solar system. I am against dependencies, when nations are fit to be independent. . . . While she remains a province, Canada is insensibly blending with the United States. . . . There is but one way to make Canada impregnable, and that is to fence her round with the majesty of an independent nation."

Appointed Regius Professor of History at Oxford in 1858, Smith resigned in 1866, joining the staff of the newly established Cornell University in 1868. Three years later he moved to To-

ronto to be with relatives. There in 1875 he married Harriet Boulton, widow of a prominent Toronto Loyalist and mistress of the Grange, a stately residence that seemed to Smith and his many visitors like a bit of old England.

Smith's involvement in the public discussions of the new Canadian Confederation began within weeks of his arrival in Toronto. In January 1872 the *Canadian Monthly and National Review* was launched, and the following month Smith contributed the first of many articles signed "Bystander," offering wide-ranging and perspicacious commentary on books, events, and issues in Canada and abroad.

By 1874 Smith was firmly established at the center of Canada's intellectual life, so that when the National Club was formed in that year by adherents of the Canada First movement, Smith was the natural choice for president of the club. Despite high hopes, the club soon foundered; its house organ, the *Nation*, largely written and underwritten by Smith, lasted only from April 1874 to the fall of 1876.

Intensely devoted to the principle of independent journalism free of party affiliations and ad hominem attack, Smith was utterly at odds with the prevailing partyism and rabid personalism of nineteenth-century-Canadian newspaper life. Nevertheless he persisted, first through the *Bystander*, which he produced virtually single-handedly, with intermissions, from 1880 to 1883, and then in the *Week*, for which he wrote "Bystander" columns from 1883 to 1888. Smith established this latter periodical as "an independent journal of literature, politics and criticism," and through it he dealt impartial blows at both the leading political parties, while continuing his penetrating surveys of British, American, and European public affairs.

Smith's most controversial views, and the ones that isolated him from the majority of his Canadian readers over the long run, were on Canada's destiny as a nation. Although sanguine during his early years in Toronto over the prospects of there emerging a distinct and enduring Canadian political and cultural nationality, he was disillusioned by the collapse of the Canada First movement in the mid 1870s, and his pessimism grew with the years. By 1889 he was advocating commercial union with the United States in the pages of his newly revived *Bystander*, and his case for the eventual amalgamation of the two North American countries was made at length in *Canada and the Canadian Question* (1891). His argu-

Smith at Eton, 1841 (portrait by Margaret Sarah Carpenter; by permission of the Art Gallery of Toronto, Goldwin Smith Collection)

ments were countered by G. M. Grant in a review in the *Week* (May 1891).

By now in his seventies Smith was nonetheless still sympathetic to radical causes. In 1896 he bought a controlling interest in the *Weekly Sun*, the newspaper of the Ontario Patrons of Industry, where for the next thirteen years regular "Bystander" columns appeared. All this time, moreover, from the 1860s until well after the century's turn, Smith was also publishing books and pamphlets on literary figures (William Cowper, Jane Austen, and Shakespeare), political histories of the United States and Great Britain, *Essays on Questions of the Day* (1893), and a volume called *Irish History* (1861; enlarged in 1905)–these being only a handful of his many publications.

Perhaps the title of his last book published in his lifetime sums up Smith's credo, however: *No Refuge but in Truth*, published in 1908, two years before his death at 86. Opinionated, reserved, seldom swayed by contrary facts or argu-

ments, "the Sage of the Grange" nevertheless earned the respect and gratitude of Canadian intellectuals and journalists, however unpopular his views often made him among the citizens of his adopted city (and Smith's advocacy of commercial union drew a virulent response from ultraloyal Toronto Tories). In his writing, Goldwin Smith set a standard of civility, independence, and analytical rigor, not to mention lucidity and wit, that contributed immeasurably to the maturation of periodical publishing in Canada.

Letters:

A Selection from Goldwin Smith's Correspondence, compiled by Arnold Haultain (London: Laurie, 1913; Toronto: McClelland & Goodchild, 1913; New York: Duffield, 1913).

Biographies:

Arnold Haultain, *Goldwin Smith, His Life and*

Facsimile of a paragraph from the manuscript for Smith's Reminiscences, *1910 (published in the first edition of that book)*

Opinions (Toronto: McClelland & Goodchild, 1912);

Elisabeth Wallace, *Goldwin Smith: Victorian Liberal* (Toronto: University of Toronto Press, 1957).

References:

Carl Berger, Introduction to *Canada and the Canadian Question* (Toronto: University of Toronto Press, 1971);

Berger, *The Sense of Power: Studies in the Ideas of Canadian Imperialism* (Toronto: University of Toronto Press, 1970);

Malcolm Ross, "Goldwin Smith," in *Our Living Tradition: Seven Canadians*, edited by Claude Bissell (Toronto: University of Toronto Press, 1957), pp. 29-47;

George Stewart, Jr.

(26 November 1848 - 26 February 1906)

George L. Parker
Royal Military College of Canada

BOOKS: *The Story of the Great Fire in St. John, N.B. June 20th, 1877* (Toronto: Belford / Detroit: Craig & Taylor, 1877);

Evenings in the Library: Bits of Gossip about Books and Those who Write Them (Toronto: Belford / Boston: Lockwood, Brooks, 1878 [i.e, 1877]);

Canada Under the Administration of the Earl of Dufferin (Toronto: Rose-Belford, 1878; London: Low, Marston, Searle & Rivington, 1878);

Essays from Reviews (Quebec: Dawson, 1892);

Essays from Reviews, Second Series (Quebec: Dawson, 1893).

OTHER: "Frontenac and his Times," in *Narrative and Critical History of America*, edited by Justin Winsor (Boston & New York: Houghton, Mifflin, 1885), IV: 317-368;

"Literature in Canada," in *Canadian Leaves: History, Art, Science, Literature, Commerce; A Series of New Papers Read before the Canadian Club of New York*, edited by G. M. Fairchild, Jr. (New York: Thompson, 1887), pp. 129-144.

SELECTED PERIODICAL PUBLICATIONS–
UNCOLLECTED: "Canadian Literature," *Stewart's Literary Quarterly Magazine*, 3 (January 1870): 403-407;

"Letters in Canada," *Week*, 4 (16 June 1887): 461-462;

"Brief Notes on the Present Condition of Historical Studies in Canada," *Papers of the American Historical Society*, 5 (1890): 71-74;

"Literature in French Canada," *New England Magazine*, new series 3 (September 1890): 16-20;

"Views of Canadian Literature," *Week*, 11 (30 March 1894): 415-416;

"Work of Francis Parkman," *New England Magazine*, new series, 20 (August 1899): 704-711;

"Literary Reminiscences," *Canadian Magazine*, 17 (June 1901): 163-166;

"Popular Songs of Old Canada," *Living Age*, 246 (15 July 1905): 162-167.

George Stewart, Jr., devoted much of his career as editor and man of letters to the promotion of a national culture based on the history and the literature of both English and French Canadians. Born on 26 November 1848 in New York City, he came to Canada in 1851 with his parents (George and Elizabeth Dubuc Stewart) and received his education in London, Canada West (now Ontario), and Saint John, New Brunswick. At sixteen he began the *Stamp Collector's Monthly Gazette* (1865-1867), the first Canadian periodical devoted to philately, then dropped it to establish *Stewart's Literary Quarterly Magazine* (1867-1872). As the only literary periodical at the time of Confederation, it quickly achieved national recognition. Stewart's aim was to counter the flood of "trashy" weeklies, "immoral" monthlies, and dime novels from the United States by providing a forum for Canadian writers. Reviewing Charles Mair's *Dreamland and Other Poems* (1868), he said, "It is time we had a literature of our own. . . . Without a national literature what is a nation?" (January 1869). While the Canadian reprint industry flourished on British and American best-sellers, local professional authorship was barely remunerative, even though many Canadians published abroad. His own *Literary Quarterly* survived because his publisher, George James Chubb, whom Stewart called "the John Murray of St. John," agreed to take no profits from the venture. The quarterly published fiction, poetry, biographical sketches, and criticism of British poetry.

After selling his quarterly in 1871 (it became the *New Brunswick Quarterly* after January 1872), Stewart served first as city editor of the *Saint John Daily News* and then as literary and dramatic editor of the *Weekly Watchman*. In 1877 he published his magazine sketches on contemporary authors as *Evenings in the Library* (with 1878 on the title page); much of his later reputation was due to reworked lectures on some of the same subjects: Ralph Waldo Emerson, Henry

George Stewart, Jr.

David Thoreau, Henry Wadsworth Longfellow, Thomas Carlyle, Alfred, Lord Tennyson, and Matthew Arnold, all of them major presences in late-nineteenth-century Canada.

In May 1878 he moved to Toronto as editor of *Rose-Belford's Canadian Monthly*, the country's most distinguished magazine of literature and current affairs, and introduced both the illustrated article and serialized fiction by Americans, where previously only British and Canadian authors had been serialized. But his publishers, Rose-Belford (the Canadian pirates of Mark Twain's works), refused to pay him royalties for his *Canada Under the Administration of the Earl of Dufferin* (1878), which they claimed was done as part of his editorial work, and he lost a court case against them. He resigned in April 1879 to take over editorship of the *Quebec Daily Chronicle*, a position he held until 1896. In this post he was an Independent in his political positions.

In the next quarter century he contributed many literary and historical articles to magazines in Canada, the United States, and Britain, as well as to prestigious publications such as Justin Winsor's *Narrative and Critical History of America* (1884-1889), Daniel Appleton's *Cyclopaedia of American Biography*, the *Encyclopaedia Britannica*, and William and Robert Chambers's *Encyclopedia*. These activities brought him international recognition: he became the first Canadian member of the International Literary Congress in 1879; gained membership in the Prince Society, Boston, and honorary membership in the Athenaeum Club, London; and was awarded honorary degrees by Laval, McGill, and Bishop's universities, and King's College. He was also a charter member of the Royal Society of Canada and secretary of its English section for many years.

At a time when Canadian literature was facing crucial economic and cultural strains, Stewart worked for improved international copyright laws, publicized contemporary French-Canadian authors for American and English-Canadian audiences, and maintained (against considerable opposition at the time) that American and Canadian literatures were distinct entities from British literature. Even today, when he is almost unknown, his style and judgments retain their graceful and colloquial force.

Biography:

Carol Fullerton, "George Stewart, Jr., a Nineteenth-Century Canadian Man of Letters," *Papers of the Bibliographical Society of Canada*, 25 (1986): 83-108–includes bibliography.

References:

"Deceased Members," *Proceedings and Transactions of the Royal Society of Canada*, second series, 12 (1906): vii-viii;

Marilyn G. Flitton, Introduction to her *Index to the Canadian Monthly and National Review and to Rose-Belford's Canadian Monthly and National Review 1872-1882* (Toronto: Bibliographical Society of Canada, 1976), pp. xviii-xix;

"George Stewart," in *The Canadian Men and Women of the Time*, edited by H. J. Morgan (Toronto: Briggs, 1898), pp. 969-970;

J. Russell Harper, *Historical Directory of New Brunswick Newspapers and Periodicals* (Fredericton: University of New Brunswick, 1961), pp. 89, 90-91.

Papers:

Stewart's papers are housed at the National Archives of Canada, Ottawa (MG 27, I.I. 25); the Thomas Fisher Rare Book Library, University of Toronto; and the Metropolitan Toronto Central Library.

Samuel Strickland

(6 November 1804 - 3 January 1867)

Michael A. Peterman
Trent University

BOOK: *Twenty-Seven Years in Canada West; or, The Experience of an Early Settler*, edited by Agnes Strickland, 2 volumes (London: Bentley, 1853).

Samuel Strickland is perhaps best known today as the younger brother of two of Canada's most important nineteenth-century writers, Catharine Parr Traill and Susanna Moodie. However, it is as one of the earliest settlers in the Peterborough and Lakefield areas, as a member of the Canada Company staff that helped to settle the Guelph and Goderich areas, and as author of his own settler's memoir, *Twenty-Seven Years in Canada West* (1853), that he most deserves attention.

The first son and seventh child of Thomas and Elizabeth Strickland, he was born on 6 November 1804 in Suffolk, England, raised at Reydon Hall near Southwold, and educated at Valpy's Grammar School in Norwich. In the wake of his father's financial reversals and death (1818), Strickland was called upon increasingly to help in the management of and farming at Reydon Hall. An active young man much given to cricket and hunting, he was not long in measuring the limits of his long-range prospects at Reydon. Thus, in 1825 at the age of 21, he took up an invitation from close family friends and immigrated to the small settlement of Darlington in Upper Canada (now Ontario), bent upon achieving financial independence as a colonist and enjoying the outdoor life so prominent in accounts of the New World.

An old friend of his father, Col. James Black, had himself escaped problems in London by immigrating with his large family. At Darlington, near Lake Ontario, Black served as postmaster, local magistrate, and colonel in the second battalion of the Durham militia. Years later during the Rebellion and postrebellion period, he received another government appointment as customs officer at Port Colborne on the strategic Welland Canal. Black welcomed young Strickland, happy to have the advantage of his energy, his practical knowledge of farming, and his amiable companionship in his home. Strickland was happy there, too, growing close to Black's daughter Emma. Assessing the opportunities available to him given his limited resources, Strickland opted to purchase land north of the expensive Lake Ontario front. Talk of a canal system linking Lake Ontario to Lake Huron and the West led him in May 1826 to buy property on the Otonabee River near the incipient village of Peterborough and adjacent to the holdings of two of the most prominent settler-developers in the area, Thomas A. Stewart and Robert Reid. Married by then to Emma Black, he left his pregnant, young wife in Darlington while he struggled to clear some of his land and build a log house. Emma, however, died shortly after the birth of their son, and Strickland, some fifty miles away by foot, arrived in Darlington in time only for her funeral.

The deaths of Emma and, a few years later, of his son effectively terminated his initial connection in Canada. Returning to his Otonabee land, he boarded with Reid's family and found companionship in Reid's daughter, Mary, whom he married in 1827. But neither good friends nor a new wife could redress the problems of the land-rich, capital-poor young man, however great his expectations. It cost too much simply to employ laborers to help in the clearing of land so deep in the backwoods. Faced with such pressures, Strickland took the initiative of seeking out John Galt in York (Toronto) and managed to gain a position with the Canada Company. A jack-of-all-trades, as competent in practical dentistry as in road making, Strickland was given an outdoor job at Guelph superintending among other things the building of bridges and the allotment of supplies. Working closely with Charles Prior and in particular the ebullient William "Tiger" Dunlop, Strickland was in the employ of the company from 1828 to 1831. From Guelph he was transferred to the Goderich settlement, where he took

Samuel Strickland (3203 38363, Archives of Ontario)

a leading role in the development of that community as well.

In his memoir, Strickland emphasizes two "blunders" he regretted. The first was leaving the Canada Company, though with Galt removed from his position and an unsympathetic new administrator in place, Strickland's chances of continued employment were not strong. The second was selling his Peterborough property in the excitement of news about development of a canal system north of Peterborough. Whatever the case, Strickland did sell and moved to land in Douro Township at Selby (Lakefield). Now a man of experience, influence, and some capital, he took a leading role in the development of the area, engaging in his own farming, land dealing, and lumbering. He encouraged immigration and settlement—including the moves to Canada of his two married sisters—served in various official, mag-

isterial, and military positions, helped to develop local roads, mills, bridges, and other improvements, and with his wife, Mary, raised a large family. In all his doings he was a staunch conservative, Anglican, and loyal Englishman.

In 1852, after Mary died delivering their thirteenth child, Strickland took his widowed daughter Maria to England. On this first return to his native land, he renewed acquaintances with Katherine Rackham of Suffolk, to whom he was wed in 1855 during a second visit. In 1853, while still in England, and urged on by his sister Agnes, herself a renowned biographer and poet, he set out to prepare the manuscript of his one and only book. Written in the immediate wake of Susanna Moodie's *Roughing It in the Bush* (1852) and at a great distance from Canada and available records, it is a kind of orchestrated family antidote to Moodie's book, which Agnes and her English sisters found "disgusting" and "vulgar." Agnes edited *Twenty-Seven Years* and made sure that it contained several of her own poems and that it projected a rather prissy image of her likable, rough-and-ready brother. The result is an odd blend of adventures and joie de vivre with sentimental homily, genteel restraint, and extensive padding borrowed from available sources in the Strickland library. The hard-drinking, funloving, venturesome pioneer is, thus, too often lost in the interventions of his editor.

While the book did not sell as well as expected, it was well reviewed and added considerably to Strickland's prestige, helping him not only in his business relations but also in his rather pretentious scheme to provide agricultural training in rural Canada to green, young Englishmen. His later years were those of a successful progenitor and settler. Moodie rightly called him "the Father and founder of the village of Lakefield." His sons gradually took over and expanded his business interests while he dedicated himself increasingly to good works, such as the building of Lakefield's first Anglican church. It was early in 1867, the year of Confederation, that, after returning from a third trip to England, Strickland succumbed to the effects of diabetes, having helped to see several areas of Upper Canada through their "colonial dawn."

Letters:

Susanna Moodie: Letters of a Lifetime, edited by Carl Ballstadt, Elizabeth Hopkins, and Michael A. Peterman (Toronto: University of Toronto Press, 1985).

References:

Audrey Morris, *Gentle Pioneers: Five Nineteenth-Century Canadians* (Toronto: Hodder & Stoughton, 1968);

Una Pope-Hennessy, *Agnes Strickland, Biographer of the Queens of England* (London: Chatto & Windus, 1940).

Papers:

Records pertaining to Strickland's work with the Canada Company are in the Public Archives of Ontario. An unpublished essay on Strickland is included in the Edwin Guillet Papers, Trent University Archives, Peterborough, Ontario.

Benjamin Sulte

(17 September 1841- 6 August 1923)

Kathleen L. Kellett
University of Toronto

BOOKS: *Les Marchés de la ville de Trois-Rivières* (Trois-Rivières, Que.: Bergeron, 1868);

Les Laurentiennes (Montreal: Senécal, 1870);

Histoire de la ville des Trois-Rivières et de ses environs (Montreal: Senécal, 1870);

L'Expédition militaire de Manitoba, 1870 (Montreal: Senécal, 1871);

Le Canada en Europe (Montreal: Senécal, 1873);

La Caverne de Wakefield (Montreal: Burland-Desbarats, 1875);

Le Collège de Rimouski: Qui l'a fondé? (Ottawa: Bureau, 1876);

Mélanges d'histoire et de littérature (Ottawa: Bureau, 1876);

Au coin du feu: Histoire et fantaisie (Quebec: Blumhart, 1877);

Chronique trifluvienne (Montreal: Canadienne, 1879);

Chants nouveaux (Ottawa: *Le Canada*, 1880);

Album de l'histoire des Trois-Rivières (Montreal: Desbarats, 1881);

Histoire des Canadiens-Français 1608-1880: Origine, histoire, religion, guerres, découvertes, colonisation, coutumes, vie domestique, sociale et politique, développement, avenir, 8 volumes (Montreal: Wilson, 1882-1884);

Histoire de Montferrand, l'athlète canadien (Montreal: Camyré & Braseau, 1884);

Situation de la langue française au Canada: Origines, modifications, accent, histoire: Situation présente, avenir (Montreal: Générale, 1885);

Histoire de Saint-François-du-Lac (Montreal: L'Etendard, 1886);

Pages d'histoire du Canada (Montreal: Granger, 1891);

Causons du pays et de la colonisation: Entretiens, as Joseph Amusart (Montreal: Granger, 1891);

Pages d'histoire: Collection de mémoires préparés pour la Société Royale du Canada, de 1895 à 1905, by Sulte and Narcisse-E. Dionne (Ottawa: Royal Society, 1895-1905);

Histoire de la milice canadienne-française, 1760-1897 (Montreal: Desbarats, 1897);

La Langue française en Canada (Lévis, Que.: Roy, 1898);

La Bataille de Châteauguay (Quebec: Renault, 1899);

A History of Quebec, Its Resources and People, by Sulte, C. E. Fryer, and L. O. David, 2 volumes (Montreal & Toronto: Canada History, 1908);

Historiettes et fantaisies (Montreal: Pigeon, 1910);

Mélanges historiques: Etudes éparses et inédites, 21 volumes, edited by Gérard Malchelosse (Montreal: Ducharme & Garand, 1918-1934);

Des Contes, edited by Malchelosse (Montreal: Ducharme, 1925); enlarged as *Mélanges littéraires*, 2 volumes (Montreal: Ducharme, 1925, 1926).

OTHER: "La Poésie Française en Canada: Revue historique par Benjamin Sulte," in *La Poésie française au Canada*, edited by Louis H. Taché (St. Hyacinthe, Que.: *Courrier de St-Hyacinthe*, 1881), pp. 5-37;

"Des Trois-Rivières à Machiche avant 1760," in *Histoire de la Paroisse d'Yamachiche (Précis historique)*, by Napoléon Caron (Trois-Rivières, Que.: Ayotte, 1892), pp. 278-297;

John Castell Hopkins, *Histoire populaire du Canada*, translated by Sulte (Philadelphia & Chicago: Winston, 1901);

Joseph Elzéar Bellemare, *Histoire de la Baie-Saint-Antoine, dite Baie-du-Febvre, 1683-1911*, with notes by Sulte (Montreal: *La Patrie*, 1911);

Marie de l'Incarnation, *Lettres historiques*, compiled by Sulte (Quebec: L'Action Sociale, 1927).

The Quebec writer and historian Benjamin Sulte amazed his contemporaries by his inexhaustible energy and his voluminous production. To avoid wasting time, while walking down the street he would compose poems that he referred to as "vers à pattes" (verse on foot). Never bothering with a rough draft, Sulte found it most efficient to write approximately thirty articles at the same

Benjamin Sulte

time, rather than going through all his notes to write just one. In 1886 the *Revue Canadienne* honored him with a special centenary banquet celebrating their publication between 1864 and 1886 of one hundred of his articles. By the end of his life Sulte had published more than thirty-five hundred articles as well as a long list of books.

Born in Trois-Rivières, Quebec, on 17 September 1841 to Benjamin and Marie-Antoinette Lefebvre Sulte, he developed a strong work ethic at an early age through necessity. His father, a navigator, died in a shipwreck when young Benjamin was only six years old, and thus the boy was obliged to break off his formal studies to go to work at the age of ten. Sulte first worked as a delivery boy in the store of his aunt, Sophia Sulte, and then went on to various other jobs, including store clerk, bookkeeper, and shopkeeper. Largely self-taught, he began to participate in the cultural life of Trois-Rivières, writing verse and founding with his friends the Cercle Littéraire of

Trois-Rivières. In 1863 he enrolled in the militia and in 1865 went to military school in Quebec to become a captain. In 1866, at the end of his military service, Sulte went to Ottawa, where he served a brief stint as the editor of the journal *Le Canada*. He started work as a translator in 1867 in the federal government, first for the House of Commons and later for the newly established Department of Militia and Defense, where he worked until his retirement in 1903. In 1871 he married Augustine Parent, the daughter of Etienne Parent, then under secretary of state. Both of their children died shortly after birth.

Sulte devoted his days to his work as a translator, but his evenings were free for study and for writing. A very social individual, he was a founding member and one-time president of the Royal Society of Canada and also a member of various historical societies in Canada and the United States. As his fame as a historian grew, he was frequently asked to give lectures, an activity at which he excelled. In 1916 he was awarded the honorary degree of doctor of laws by the University of Toronto.

From his very beginning as a historian, Sulte gave special attention to his hometown, Trois-Rivières, treated, for example, in *Les Marchés de la ville de Trois-Rivières* (The Markets of the city of Trois-Rivières, 1868) and *Histoire de la ville des Trois-Rivières* (1870), a book that was to find few buyers. Sulte deplored this lack of interest that prevented him from producing the full-scale history of Trois-Rivières that he had planned, but with his extra notes, he wrote *Chronique trifluvienne* (Three-Rivers Chronicle, 1879). The people of Trois-Rivières came to appreciate Sulte in his lifetime, surprising him agreeably in 1917 by asking for his portrait for a gallery to honor prominent citizens. Upon his death in 1923 Trois-Rivières paid tribute to him with a civic funeral.

Sulte's most ambitious work is his *Histoire des Canadiens-Français 1608-1880* (1882-1884). This study excited much controversy because of its criticism of the Jesuits. In particular, Joseph Charles Taché attacked it vehemently in *Les Histoires de M. Sulte* (1883). Later generations would focus their criticism on its lack of synthesis as well as its chaotic presentation of events. Sulte's strength lies in the less ambitious studies, where he gave free rein to his love of detail. A good collection of his shorter pieces can be found in *Mélanges d'histoire et de littérature* (1876) and in the twenty-one-volume *Mélanges historiques* (1918-1934), edited by Sulte's disciple, Gérard Malchelosse, which includes several short studies, a few of them in English, on subjects as diverse as the seigneurial system, the politicians George-Etienne Cartier and Louis-Joseph Papineau, the history of Trois-Rivières, and the history of maple syrup.

Sulte expressed his patriotism not only in his historical writings but also in his poetry. His first book of poems, *Les Laurentiennes* (1870), often celebrates Quebec and its history especially through its heroes, be they individuals such as the historian François-Xavier Garneau or groups such as French-Canadian pioneers, missionaries, loggers, and craftsmen. In addition to many songs and some occasional verse, this volume contains Sulte's translations of five sonnets by Shakespeare and of several other English poems as well as English versions of two of his own poems. *Chants nouveaux* (1880) communicates the same values of patriotism, hard work, and Christian faith as *Les Laurentiennes* but also contains many lighter

poems, which, though cheerful, are little more than doggerel.

Sulte also wrote short stories, most of which were compiled by Malchelosse in *Des Contes* (Some Tales, 1925), enlarged as *Mélanges littéraires* (two volumes, 1925, 1926). The stories in the first volume of *Mélanges littéraires* are identical to those in *Des Contes*. Many of these are comic tales, including "Une chasse à l'ours" and "Mordant mordu." Sulte sometimes introduces a supernatural element in his stories, either as an illusion, as in "Le Loupgarou" and "L'Esprit frappeur," or as an authentic phenomenon, as in "Le Rêve du capitaine." In the second volume of *Mélanges littéraires*, the moralistic tales "Sans tambours ni trompettes" and "Une Récompense honnête" preach the importance of hard work and honesty respectively. Other more entertaining tales include "Beugnot," about a con man masquerading as a count in North America, and the anecdote "Mystification," about two French Canadians in Paris bewildering the French by speaking in Canadian place names.

It almost appears that Sulte intended to assure his place in posterity by the sheer bulk of his publications. His poems are generally too didactic for modern tastes, though his short stories may have a more lasting appeal. He should be remembered primarily as a historian who, despite his limited vision of Quebec history, contributed greatly to historiography in Canada by unearthing a tremendous amount of historical information and by stimulating his compatriots' interest in the past.

Bibliographies:

Gérard Malchelosse, *Benjamin Sulte et son oeuvre: Essai de bibliographie des travaux historiques et littéraires (1860-1916) de ce polygraphe canadien, précédé d'une notice biographique* (Montreal: Pays Laurentien, 1916);

Aurélien Boivin, "Benjamin Sulte," in his *Le Conte littéraire québécois au XIXᵉ siècle* (Montreal: Fides, 1975).

Biographies:

L.-O. David, "Benjamin Sulte," *Souvenirs et biographies, 1870-1910* (Montreal: Beauchemin, 1911), pp. 257-264;

Francis-J. Audet, "Benjamin Sulte," *Bulletin des Recherches Historiques*, 32 (June 1926): 337-347;

Albert Tessier, "Dans l'intimité de Benjamin Sulte," *Cahiers des Dix*, 21 (1956): 159-177;

Victor Morin, "Benjamin Sulte intime," *Cahiers des Dix*, 27 (1962): 177-186.

References:

Lucie Béliveau, "Benjamin Sulte et l'Outaouais," *Asticou*, 7 (June 1971): 5-13;

Hervé Biron, "Benjamin Sulte intime," *Culture*, 3, no. 1 (1942): 3-16;

Jean Feron, "Benjamin Sulte et son oeuvre," *La Vie Canadienne: Littérature et Littérateurs* (sup-

plement to *Le Roman Canadien*), 49 (January 1931): 53-56; 50 (February 1931): 57-64;

Jules-S. Lesage, "Benjamin Sulte," in his *Propos littéraires: Ecrivains d'hier*, 2 volumes (Quebec: L'Action Catholique, 1933), II: 60-71;

"Le Premier Centenaire de la Revue Canadienne," *Nouvelles Soirées Canadiennes*, 6 (1887): 544-562;

Joseph Charles Taché, *Les Histoires de M. Sulte: Protestation* (Montreal: Cadieux & Derome, 1883).

Joseph-Charles Taché

(24 December 1820 - 16 April 1894)

Jack Warwick
York University

BOOKS: *De la tenure seigneuriale en Canada, et Projet de commutation* (Quebec: Lovell & Lamoureux, 1854); English edition published as *The Seignorial Tenure in Canada, and Plan of Commutation* (Quebec: Lovell & Lamoureux, 1854);

Le Pléiade rouge, as Gaspard LeMage (Montreal: Minerve, 1855);

Esquisse sur le Canada considéré sous le point de vue économiste (Paris: Bossange, 1855); English edition published as *Sketch of Canada, Its Industrial Condition and Resources* (Paris: Bossange, 1855);

Le Canada et l'Exposition Universelle de 1855 (Toronto: Lovell, 1856);

Des Provinces de l'Amérique du Nord et d'une union fédérale (Quebec: Brousseau, 1858);

Le Défricheur de langue. Tragédie bouffe en trois actes et trois tableaux, by Taché and François-Alexandre-Hubert Larue, collaborating as Isidore de Méplats (Quebec, 1859);

Notice historiographique sur la fête célébrée à Québec, le 16 juin 1859 (Quebec: Brousseau, 1859);

Trois Légendes de mon pays (Montreal: Beauchemin & Valois, 1871);

Forestiers et Voyageurs (Montreal: Saint-Joseph, Ca-

dieux & Derome, 1884; modern edition, Montreal: Fides, 1946);

Les Sablons (Montreal: Saint-Joseph, Cadieux & Derome, 1885; modern edition, Tours, France: Mame / Montreal: Granger, 1930).

Joseph-Charles Taché was one of the most vigorous founders of the Patriotic School of Quebec, the literary movement which transformed writing from a sporadic occurrence into a distinctive French-Canadian tradition. His activities extended from his own writing to founding and directing periodicals and writing articles in defense of Canadian language and culture. At the same time, he was a medical practitioner, distinguished journalist, member of Parliament, and deputy minister. Both as politician and as author, he was a passionate defender of traditional French-Canadian values, which he largely identified with language, religion, and folklore, but also with forest industries and economic development. He is best remembered for his arch-conservative but sympathetic representation of backwoods life and his love of the forests, lakes, and rivers.

Joseph-Charles Taché (C 1496, National Archives of Canada)

Taché, born on 24 December 1820 in Kamouraska, about one hundred miles from Quebec City, was the son of Charles Taché, captain in an elite militia regiment, and Henriette Boucher de la Broquerie Taché; his uncle, Etienne-Paschal Taché, was distinguished in military, medical, and political life. Joseph-Charles studied at the village school and at the Quebec Seminary (the only existing type of secondary school and not necessarily training for the priesthood). In 1844 he qualified to practice medicine; he was awarded the then-unusual M.D. thirty-four years later. Taché's practice, in Rimouski, Lower Canada (now Quebec), included regular visits to lumber camps. In 1847 he married Françoise Lepage, the daughter of a local farmer, and was elected, as a Conservative, to the House of Assembly, where he began writing political correspondence for his constituency. In 1854 he published his first book, a long brochure expressing his views on proposed reforms in the land tenure system. He had actively participated in the debate and per-

suaded the major landowners (seigneurs) to accept commuting their privileged system. However, his compromise did not satisfy the Liberals, whom he attacked in a pamphlet entitled *Le Pléiade rouge* (1855).

Representing Canada at the Paris Exposition Universelle in 1855, Taché campaigned to encourage French-speaking immigrants to Canada. From this he developed his *Esquisse sur le Canada* (1855), and attracted enough interest in France to be elected to the legion of honor. In 1857, after ten years in electoral politics, Taché founded the journal *Le Courrier du Canada*, not only to advance his political views, but also to encourage the nascent literature of his country. Here he published Henri-Raymond Casgrain's first stories; they were versions of traditional French-Canadian folktales. He himself wrote articles proposing a union of the then-separate provinces of British North America (which became Canada in 1867 after Confederation); these essays were collected and published in volume form (*Des Provinces*) in 1858. Taché's arguments did much to prepare the Confederation.

The year 1861 saw the first volume of *Les Soirées Canadiennes*, the first all-literary periodical in Canada, dominated by Taché, whose orientation thus had long-term effects in literature. Preliminary discussion had included two conflicting views: Canada should have a French-language publication open to all French literature, or else the journal should be strongly national, fostering distinctively Canadian material such as folklore. Taché had his way and practically filled the first volume with three folktales inspired by regional folklore.

Taché's *Trois Légendes de mon pays* was published as a book in 1871. The three independent stories are firmly welded together by authorial comment that stresses the genius of French Canada and the triumphant progress of Christianity. They depict the Indians of the Gaspé peninsula, whose historic misfortunes and proud resistance are chronicled with admiration in two stories, while the third, set in Taché's own time, appeals to Christian pity for Indians as victims of superstition. Each story is based on an incident remembered in local tales and in place-names such as Massacre Island. Taché's theory that primitive art has led him to natural truths, however sketchy, constitutes a striking new assessment of folk myths.

In 1863 *Les Soirées Canadiennes* published the entire text of Taché's *Forestiers et Voyageurs* (issued as an independent volume in 1884). The same basic ideas are present: simple folks are wiser than intellectuals because they are closer to the truth of nature; there is a Canadian character linked to Canadian geography; these truths find their synthesis in the folktale, which is essentially moral and Christian. Taché's art has here developed: the idealized figure of the backwoodsman, for example, is often free from the author's doctrinaire purposes and even quite humorous. Nevertheless, the main story line brings the loosely connected episodes together in a glorious conversion that symbolizes the triumph of French-Canadian Catholicism over English-Canadian secular authority. Taché works into his narrative considerable documentary detail about the last days of the fur trade, the rising lumber trade, and other forest occupations. At the same time, his version of a lumber camp may be read as a manifesto for the autocratic society dear to Taché's heart. Yet Old Michel, the main character, a poacher, runaway criminal, voyageur, trapper, and lumberman, is depicted as a lovable rogue; his presentation seems astonishingly like a stand for personal freedom. Old Michel is also a fervent Catholic, but he has never hesitated to mix with superstitious Indians and practice their magic for his trap line. In defiance of logical consistency, Taché creates a humorously complex world.

Taché continued to seek written forms for oral legends, sometimes using verse narrative, sometimes mixing documentary, personal, and legendary material, but always stressing the fusion of language, memory, and place. *Les Sablons* (1885) is of particular interest, being a by-product of his report to the government on the possibility of establishing a new penal colony on the uninhabited Sable Island. His forthright expression of opinions never wavers, as he attacks both Benjamin Sulte for anticlericalism and Father Casgrain for dubious appropriation of copyright income.

Taché literally put Canada on the cultural map, both by his dynamic promotion and by his own imaginative fusion of voice and place. He placed the French-Canadian backwoodsman, including rebellious aspects of the character, firmly among the heroic collective figures of his people. However, his best work has never been translated into English. Taché himself was not free from the contradictions that are seen in Old Michel–though Taché tried to fit him into a mold that suited a middle-class public. The roguish individualist is nonetheless outstanding, and his inherent contradictions are a valid part of Taché's complex worldview. Anglophobe and federalist, primitivist and classicist, moralizing and humorous, conservative and maverick, Taché captured the essentials of his time in highly readable fiction.

Biography:

Eveline Bossé, *Joseph-Charles Taché (1820-1894): Un grand représentant de l'élite canadienne-française* (Quebec: Garneau, 1974).

Reference:

Jack Warwick, *The Long Journey* (Toronto: University of Toronto Press, 1968), pp. 53-57 and 108-111.

Jules-Paul Tardivel

(2 September 1851 - 24 April 1905)

Virginia A. Harger-Grinling
Memorial University of Newfoundland

BOOKS: *Vie du Pape Pie IX, ses oeuvres et ses douleurs* (Quebec: Duquet, 1878);

L'Anglicisme, voilà l'ennemi (Quebec: Canadien, 1880);

Mélanges; ou, Recueil d'études religieuses, sociales, politiques et littéraires, 3 volumes: volume 1 (Quebec: Vérité, 1887); volumes 2 and 3 (Quebec: Demers, 1901, 1903);

Notes de voyages en France, Italie, Espagne, Irlande, Angleterre, Belgique et Hollande (Montreal: Senécal, 1890);

Polémique à propos d'enseignement, by Tardivel and C.-J. Magnan (Quebec: Demers, 1894);

Pour la patrie (Montreal: Cadieux & Derome, 1895); translated by Sheila Fischman as *For My Country* (Toronto & Buffalo: University of Toronto Press, 1975);

La Situation religieuse aux Etats-Unis (Montreal: Saint-Joseph, Cadieux & Derome, 1899; Lille & Paris: Desclée, De Brouwer, 1900);

La Langue française au Canada (Montreal: Revue Canadienne, 1901).

Jules-Paul Tardivel (Archives Nationales du Québec)

Although not much of any length has been written about Jules-Paul Tardivel, he stands out as a controversial figure difficult to evaluate in his own time or today. Depending on the critic's inclinations, Tardivel has been variously interpreted as one of the greatest journalists of his era, a man imbued with a messianic nationalism for his adopted land, Quebec, and, conversely, as a religious fanatic, as one of the first writers to prostitute religion and patriotism as sources of inspiration, and as a precursor of racist novelists.

Born on 2 September 1851 in Covington, Kentucky, of a metropolitan French father, Claudius Tardivel, and an English mother converted to Catholicism, Isabella Brent Tardivel, he was raised in a religious atmosphere by Julius and Frances Brent, an uncle and an aunt. Tardivel had no real knowledge of the French language until in 1869, of his own choosing, he went to study at Saint-Hyacinthe Seminary in Quebec. He returned briefly to the United States after completing his studies but, transformed at that point into a Francophile, was totally disillusioned with his birthplace and departed once more for Saint-Hyacinthe, where he married Henriette Brunelle in 1874. After some difficulties he succeeded in establishing himself as a journalist, working for various papers including *La Minerve* and *Le Canadien*. With the help of a small legacy and following the invitation of Father Zacharie Lacasse, who wished to see a basically Catholic newspaper in existence, Tardivel became the editor, director, and owner of *La Vérité*; the first issue appeared on 14 July 1881, and he continued to publish the paper until his death in 1905.

La Vérité was associated from its beginning with Tardivel and was to become the principal organ for French-Canadian nationalism, Catholicism, and the defense of the French language and French minority rights in Canada. His paper had the constant support of the Jesuits (as did Tardivel in all his undertakings), and in spite of a distribution of only three thousand copies per issue, it was widely used in colleges and schools, contributing to the promulgation of the ultramontane doctrine prevalent in Quebec at that time. That is not to say that Tardivel did not have his share of adversaries. His bitter attacks on the French liberals of Quebec and France, on modern decadence–exemplified, for him, by current fiction and theater–and on the Freemasons, whom he considered totally godless agents of subversion, caused him to have many critics.

Apart from his newspaper articles, some of which are collected in the three volumes of *Mélanges* (1887-1903), he published *Notes de voyages* (1890), which, while revealing his prejudices, is a good work of geographic journalism; his one novel, *Pour la patrie* (1895), which has little aesthetic value; his two nationalistic speeches in defense of the French language (1880 and 1901); his first long publication, *Vie du Pape Pie IX* (1878), a work that indicates the importance of the papacy in the eyes of French Canada; and other less important works. Given the anti-Protestant and less obvious anti-Semitic biases in *Pour la patrie*, its influence is easy to misinterpret. Essentially a fantasy about cultural federalism in the year 1945, it presents a time when Canada is run by masonic satanists intent on subverting Quebec, but whose machinations are overcome by a pure-hearted Catholic M.P. and by divine intervention.

In spite of his prejudices and limitations, or perhaps because of them, Tardivel expressed the spirit of the majority of French Canadians of that period. While perhaps aesthetically limited, there is no doubt that he was a perspicacious analyst of language and thought, and is to be considered one of the main influences on his adopted compatriots in the late nineteenth century.

References:

Pierre Savard, *Jules-Paul Tardivel, La France et les Etats-Unis 1851-1905* (Quebec: Presses de l'Université Laval, 1967);

A. I. Silver, Introduction to *For My Country*, Sheila Fischman's translation of *Pour la patrie* (Toronto & Buffalo: University of Toronto Press, 1975), pp. vi-xl.

David Thompson

(30 April 1770 - 10 February 1857)

Victor G. Hopwood
University of British Columbia

BOOKS: *New Light on the Early History of the Greater Northwest. The Manuscript Journals of Alexander Henry . . . and of David Thompson*, edited by Elliot Coues, 3 volumes (New York: Harper, 1897);

David Thompson's Narrative of His Explorations in Western America, 1784-1812, edited by J. B. Tyrell (Toronto: Champlain Society, 1916); revised and edited by Richard Glover (Toronto: Champlain Society, 1962); revised as *Travels in Western North America, 1784-1812*, edited by Victor G. Hopwood (Toronto: Macmillan, 1971);

David Thompson's Account of His First Attempt to Cross the Rockies, edited by F. W. Howay (Kingston, Ont.: Queen's University, 1933);

Journals Relating to Montana and Adjacent Regions, 1808-1812, edited by M. Catherine White (Missoula, Mont.: Montana State University Press, 1950).

Just as the British-American War of 1812 began, David Thompson, a leading North American mapmaker, explorer, and travel writer, went to Montreal for the first and only time. Forty-two years old, he had completed explorations and surveys of the West from Hudson Bay to the mouth of the Columbia, from the Mississippi and the Missouri to Lake Athabasca. Five years later he began an additional eleven strenuous years as astronomer (surveyor) for the British side in the British-American survey of the Canada-U.S. boundary, working on the Ontario section, stretching between St. Regis (near Montreal) and the Lake of the Woods. After the American astronomer resigned, Thompson acted for both powers. John J. Bigsby, a physician attached as naturalist and secretary to the British commission, described Thompson and his story-telling ability: "He was plainly dressed, quiet, and observant. . . . His speech betrayed the Welshman. . . . No living person possesses a tithe of his information respecting the Hudson's Bay countries. . . . Never mind his Bunyan-like face and cropped hair; he has a

very powerful mind, and a singular faculty of picture-making. He can create a wilderness and people it with warring savages, or climb the Rocky Mountains with you in a snow-storm, so clearly and palpably, that only shut your eyes and you hear the crack of the rifle, or feel the snow-flakes melt on your cheeks as he talks."

The qualities that Bigsby noted in Thompson's conversation are preeminently to be found in the prose of *David Thompson's Narrative of His Explorations in Western America, 1784-1812* (1916). A later version, based mainly on the same manuscripts but with both additions and omissions, is called *Travels in Western North America, 1784-1812* (1971); Thompson always called the book his "Travels." In it Thompson displays his unsurpassed direct knowledge; his ability to go directly to the heart of events, scenes, situations, or characters; his imagination, perhaps Celtic; and the overtones of his speaking voice, that of a skilled raconteur who has perfected his phrasing through scores of tellings.

David Thompson was born in London, England, on 30 April 1770 to parents almost certainly Welsh. His father, also named David, died when Thompson, the older of two sons, was two, leaving the widowed mother, Ann, to raise the two infants. At seven Thompson was fortunate in being admitted to an excellent charity school–the Grey Coat Hospital in the Westminster area of London. Practical and religious instruction was central, science and mathematics were emphasized, and the atmosphere was friendly and liberal. Thompson tells in his *Narrative* of the reading the students shared: "Those which pleased us most were the Tales of the Genii, the Persian and Arabian Tales, with Robinson Crusoe and Gulliver's Travels."

The young Thompson was prepared to become a naval officer, but the peace of 1783 between Britain and the United States closed off the intended career. Instead he was apprenticed as a clerk to the Hudson's Bay Company, arriving on the bay in 1784 at Fort Churchill on the

The David Thompson postage stamp

southern edge of the tundra, where he spent his first winter in the New World. Here he met both Indians and Inuit.

Samuel Hearne was then governor at Churchill. The fourteen-year-old Thompson regrettably formed a low opinion of Hearne, a notable Arctic explorer and writer who was as free-thinking as Thompson, his apprentice, was devout. However, Thompson did copy a part of the manuscript of Hearne's *Journey to the Northern Ocean* (1795), finding in it, no doubt, some idea of the opportunities for exploration in the wild interior of North America. He also had before him a classic of narrative style and a model structure for presenting the journeys, the life, and the background of exploration. At sixteen the apprentice's duties and training took him inland to the prairies, where at times he kept accounts and trade journals, the keeping of daily records being the basis of his later writing.

In his second year inland Thompson was sent to the limit of white penetration to live with the Peigan Indians and learn their language and customs. The Peigans were among the last Indians of Canada and the United States to submit to European control. He wintered in the tent of a very old leader, Saukamappee, who told of customs, traditions, and events going back to his child-

hood. Thompson's retelling, in his *Narrative*, of Saukamappee's reminiscences takes one back to the first decades of the eighteenth century, earlier and deeper than any other literary source for the lives and minds of the martial peoples of the Great Plains before the white man came.

Saukamappee introduced Thompson to Kootenae Appee, the war chief, with whom he formed a permanent friendship. After Thompson, Kootenae Appee is the central character of the *Narrative*; their relationship forms one of the book's main unifying threads. Their meeting is memorable, with a dimension approaching myth: "On entering the tent [Kootenae Appee] gave me his left hand, and I gave him my right hand, upon which he looked at me, and smiled as much as to say a contest would not be equal; at his going away the same took place. . . . [Saukamappee later said] If one of our people offers you his left, give him your left hand, for the right hand is no mark of friendship, this hand wields the Spear, draws the Bow, and the trigger of the gun; it is the hand of death. The left hand is next to the heart, and speaks truth and friendship, it holds the shield of protection, and is the hand of life."

A winter later, just before Christmas, hauling firewood for Buckingham House on the Sas-

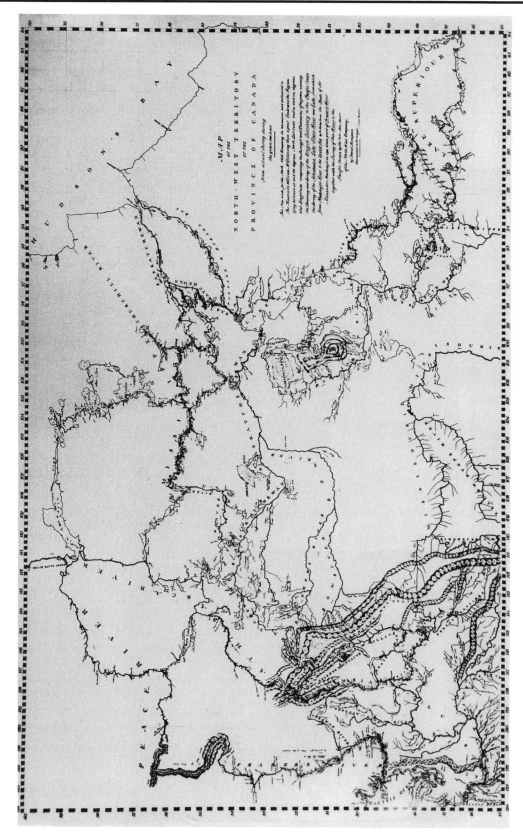

Thompson's "Map of the North-West Territory of the Province of Canada, from Actual Survey During the Years 1792 to 1812"
(redrawing by Jack McMaster; Archives of Ontario)

katchewan River, Thompson broke his right leg. Still an invalid, in the spring he was sent down the river by canoe to Cumberland House, where in his second winter of illness he met Philip Turnor, the earliest scientific explorer in the North American interior. Turnor, as Thompson notes in his *Narrative*, was "one of the compilers of the Nautical Almanac and a practical astronomer" and taught Thompson astronomical surveying, including how to keep weather records, field books, and the appropriate journals. Thompson was soon a proficient surveyor, partly a result of hard study: "By too much attention to calculations in the night, with no other light than a small candle my right eye became so much inflamed that I lost its sight." But sclerotitis rather than Thompson's industrious practicing of astronomical observation and calculation was the cause of the problem. In any case, his basic education was now complete. His profession was learned from an "excellent master of the science"; his character was set; and he had found his purpose in life–scientifically to map and explore the almost unmapped wilderness around him. He was also blind in one eye and had a game leg.

When Thompson returned to Hudson Bay in the spring of 1790, he made his first survey, that of the Nelson or lower Saskatchewan River, and he began the series of journals he kept up until he was eighty at least. In his lifetime Thompson wrote an estimated ten million words of notes, journals, reports, letters, and narratives. Of these documents, about half can be found today in archives.

For seven years beginning in 1790 Thompson traded and surveyed faithfully for the Hudson's Bay Company. Although promoted rapidly and paid well, he chafed under the policies and conflicts of the "Company," which restrained him almost completely from "going upon discovery." In this period, however, he did perfect his wilderness skills and his fluency in the Nahathaway (Cree) and Déné (Chipewyan) languages. He also expanded his intellectual world: he studied works on astronomy, navigation, surveying, mathematics, and natural science; he read books of sermons and theology; more important, perhaps, he acquired a book on rhetoric; and he also purchased, among other works, John Milton's *Paradise Lost* (1667), a reprint of Samuel Johnson's *Rambler* (1750-1752), and selections from the *Spectator* (1711-1712).

In 1797 Thompson left what he called the "mean and selfish" Hudson's Bay Company and joined its great rival from Montreal, the North West Company, called the "pedlars from Quebec" by H.B.C. employees but referred to by Thompson as gentlemen of "liberal and public spirit."

Thompson's first assignment for the "Nor'-Westers" took him four thousand miles in ten months. In the last months of 1797 he traveled from Grand Portage on Lake Superior to central Saskatchewan and on south to the villages of the now-extinct agricultural Mandan Indians on the Missouri, of whom, in his *Narrative*, he leaves one of the earliest, liveliest, and most authoritative accounts.

In January of the following year he returned from the Mandan villages to the Red River posts of the North West Company. He then mapped the headwaters of the Red, Mississippi, and St. Louis river systems. He determined the Mississippi's source as Turtle Lake (but surveys a century later favored nearby Lake Itasca). Thompson then canoed around and mapped Lake Superior. At Sault Ste. Marie he met the trader, explorer, and author Alexander Mackenzie, who said Thompson "had performed more in ten months than he [Mackenzie] expected could be done in two years" (as reported in Thompson's *Narrative*). Sometime after this Thompson drew the maps for Mackenzie's *Voyages from Montreal to the Frozen and Pacific Oceans* (1801). He also provided Mackenzie with most of the astronomical positions included in the book.

On 10 June 1799 at Isle à la Crosse, Thompson married Charlotte Small, daughter of a Cree woman and Patrick Small, a bourgeois (partner) of the North West Company. Charlotte was three months short of fourteen, and the marriage was without benefit of clergy, as there were none available. In an early manuscript of his *Narrative*, in a passage later deleted, but included in *Travels*, Thompson attributes to the assistance of his "lovely wife" much of his knowledge of the beliefs of the Nahathaways, she being fluent in both Cree and English (Thompson himself taught her to read and write English).

From 1798 to 1806 Thompson traded, surveyed, and explored extensively east of the Rocky Mountains, especially along the upper reaches of those rivers whose passes lead into the Rockies: the Bow, the North Saskatchewan, the Athabasca, and the Peace. In the summer of 1807 Thompson crossed the mountains by

Howse Pass. Some Peigan Indians blocking his way had been diverted south by the killing in 1806 on the upper waters of the Missouri of two confederate Blackfeet by Meriwether Lewis and William Clark. Later in 1807 Thompson built Kootenae House north of the 49th parallel near the source of the Columbia. (His later transmountain posts–Kullyspell House, Salish House, and Spokane House–were south of that line.)

While wintering at Kootenae House, Thompson was besieged by hostile Peigans. By diplomacy and with the help of his old friend Kootenae Appee, Thompson won a temporary truce. At this point in his *Narrative* Thompson writes about Indian oratory, perhaps also commenting on his own ideals of style: "The speeches of the Indians on both sides of the mountains are in plain language, sensible to the purpose. . . . I have never heard a speech in the florid, bombastic style I have often seen published as spoken to white men."

A well-known anecdote (in his *Narrative*) from one of Thompson's many crossings of the Rockies reveals his story-telling method. He proceeds by brief grammatical units, conversational in tone. At the same time, he shows his attitude to Indians and to the morality of the fur trade:

> I was obliged to take two kegs of alcohol, overruled by my partners . . . for I had made it a law to myself that no alcohol should pass the mountains in my company, and thus be clear of the sad sight of drunkenness and its many evils. But these gentlemen insisted upon alcohol being the most profitable article that could be taken for the Indian trade. In this I knew they had miscalculated; accordingly, when we came to the defiles of the mountains, I placed the two kegs of alcohol on a vicious horse, and by noon the kegs were empty and in pieces, the horse rubbing his load against the rocks to get rid of it. I wrote to my partners what I had done, and that I would do the same to every keg of alcohol, and for the next six years I had charge of the fur trade on the west side of the mountains no further attempt was made to introduce spirituous liquors.

Descriptions of areas explored, such as the country from the Great Lakes to the Missouri, form the major sections of his *Narrative*. Individual journeys usually make up parts of such large blocks. The final and most dramatic region described is the northern half of the Columbia Basin or Oregon Territory. This section contains the story of Thompson's greatest journey, his final exploration in 1810 and 1811 of the Colum-

bia River to its mouth on the Pacific Ocean. The importance of the journey for Thompson was scientific, the completion of the explorations for his great maps of the West and of Oregon. As such, the journey is the climax of the *Narrative* and the pinnacle of Thompson's career as an explorer.

Thompson's way across the Rockies was again blocked by the Peigans in 1810. As a result, he turned north and crossed the Rockies by a new route, Athabasca Pass, which for half a century was the main trade route from Canada to the Columbia. A supplementary version of Thompson's story of his evasion of the Peigans in the *Narrative* is given by Alexander Henry in *New Light on the History of the Greater Northwest* (1897).

After his journey to the Pacific, Thompson in returning up the Columbia raised a British flag and posted a British territorial claim at the junction of the Snake and the Columbia. In the following year Thompson completed the survey of the Columbia from its mouth to its source, and completed the similar survey of its tributaries, the Kootenai and Pend Oreille rivers. He also journeyed to Flathead Lake. Near Missoula, Montana, he made observations joining his traverses to those of Lewis and Clark at a final basic position. The framework of his maps was now complete. In 1812 he left the Northwest never to return, going down to Montreal, to see civilized Canada for the first time, twenty-eight years after leaving London forever.

In Montreal, Thompson's first act was to solemnize his marriage. He also acted as an ensign in the reserve in the defense of Montreal in the War of 1812. For the army he built cedar canoes of a pattern he had invented on his voyage to the Pacific, thus becoming the first manufacturer of canoes using European methods of boat building. He also designed a frame for carrying cannons in the wilderness, quoting in his specifications Blaise Pascal on the advantages of carrying in the upright position. His most important activity was working on his maps of the West.

An early sketch of his map of the West from Hudson Bay to the mouth of the Columbia was delivered in 1813 to the North West Company, which published it in England in an 1816 pamphlet without Thompson's permission or any acknowledgment. A similar map hung in the "Nor'Westers'" great hall at Fort William, where it was seen by Ross Cox, who described it in *The Columbia River* (1832), expressing admiration for its size, detail, and accuracy. This map was among the papers taken by Lord Selkirk when he seized

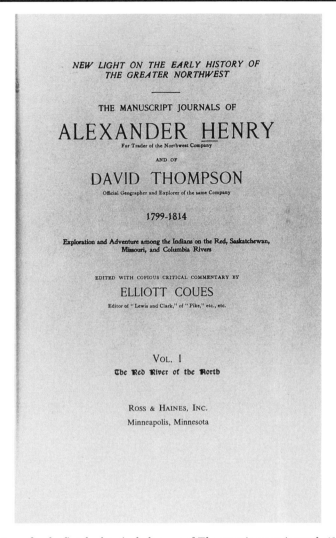

Title page for the first book to include some of Thompson's many journals (1897)

Fort William in 1816. Thompson's two 1813 maps were the basis for a generation of much of the information in published maps of Oregon and the Canadian West. Another map, drawn in 1814 and now in the Ontario Archives, is the best known of Thompson's maps, providing the basis for a map published by the government of Upper Canada in 1857, which was the only source until the twentieth century for much information on parts of western Canada and the Pacific Northwest.

The Treaty of Ghent, which ended the War of 1812, provided for a survey settling the Canada-U.S. boundary as far west as the Lake of the Woods. From 1816 to 1828, Thompson's time was taken up with the western (Ontario) section of the boundary. Although Thompson came out of the West a relatively wealthy man, he was bank-

rupt by the 1830s. The reasons included his having lost money in the bankruptcy of the company established to settle the debts of the North West Company when it merged with the Hudson's Bay Company in 1821. Another reason was Thompson's inability to collect money owed him in certain business ventures. This latter problem was deepened by his absence from direct control of his affairs for all the summers he was on the boundary survey. From 1833 to 1845 Thompson earned his living mainly as a surveyor, the commissions growing fewer and smaller as he grew older. By 1842 he was destitute. In 1843 he worked on his final set of maps of the West and the Oregon, sending them to the British Foreign office in the hope they would be used in negotiations on the Oregon boundary. They were not. The Hudson's Bay Company provided a modified copy of one of Thompson's 1813 maps.

In his seventies, no longer able to earn a decent living as a surveyor, Thompson at last turned his full attention to an old project, the writing of his *Narrative*. His work was made difficult not only by old age and illness but by poverty. He tried without success in 1844 to arrange for publication by subscription. His journals show he corresponded with Washington Irving. Thompson-family tradition has it that Irving was interested in publishing the book but that Thompson was not satisfied with Irving's terms for acknowledgment.

On 24 February 1848, Thompson was led, completely blind, by one of his daughters to an eye surgeon, who successfully treated both eyes, the left for cataract, the right for sclerotitis. Afterward he told the doctor that he saw a star with his right eye for the first time in sixty years. In July of the following year Thompson almost died of cholera.

Throughout the late 1840s Thompson worked on his *Narrative*. He also tried his hand at short fiction. Two fictional passages are included in the *Narrative* but are not usually recognized as such. One describes a battle between the Peigans and the interior Salish; the other tells of a ruse used by Kootenae Appee. These are probably the earliest Canadian fiction about life in and across the Rockies. They may well have been an attempt at juvenile-oriented fiction, likely a response to R. M. Ballantyne's *Hudson's Bay* (1848).

In 1851, eighty years old, Thompson appears to have given up the struggle to write; he bundled up his journals and other manuscripts in preparation for moving out of Montreal to live with one of his daughters. Family tradition indicates that Thompson's old age was peaceful, the old man continuing to read and to observe the stars for astronomical time. He died on 10 February 1857, followed by his wife three months later. It has become a tradition that Thompson was buried in a pauper's grave; the plot, however, was paid for by a son-in-law. In 1927 J. B. Tyrrell was responsible for having a monument erected on the grave.

Tyrrell, himself a notable geographer, explorer, surveyor, and editor, was mainly responsible for bringing Thompson's work out of obscurity, and in particular for the first publication of Thompson's *Narrative*. His knowledgeable verdict on Thompson as explorer and mapmaker is that David Thompson is "the greatest practical land geographer the world has ever produced." Since 1916 a similar recognition of Thompson's preeminence among the writers of travel literature has slowly but unmistakably emerged. He belongs in the company of such authors as Hearne, Friedrich Humboldt, Lewis and Clark, Charles Darwin, Henry Walter Bates, and Vilhjalmur Stefansson. Among such writers only James Cook is Thompson's peer in miles of journeying and years of exploring and observing; only Knud Rasmussen is his equal in the sensitive recording of the world, mind, and speech of hunting peoples.

Thompson's writing has been a source for several modern works. There have been some short biographies, including those for juveniles, based on the *Narrative*, the best of which is Kerry (Edgar A.) Wood's *The Mapmaker* (1955). Parts of Thompson's *Narrative* have also been incorporated into a speculative and anachronistic novel, Elizabeth Clutton-Brock's *Woman of the Paddle Song* (1972), supposedly an autobiography of Thompson's wife. John Newlove uses Saukamappee's description from the *Narrative* of Peigan-Shoshone war in "The Pride," a poem on the Indian roots of Canadian awareness of the earth. Marion Smith has written a long poem in free verse called *Koo-koo-sint* (1976) based on Thompson's *Narrative*. Her title is taken from the name that Alexander Ross in *Adventures of the First Settlers on the Columbia River* (1849) says the interior Salish gave Thompson. The name refers to the stars, and means, presumably, "star man" or "the man who looks at the stars." Smith's book is a powerful poetic abstract of the *Narrative*. In all the above works and much other writing on Thompson, the power of Thompson's language is evident—almost without exception, writers on Thompson find themselves inescapably bound to his very words.

Bibliography:

M. Catherine White, Bibliography, in *David Thompson's Journals Relating to Montana and Adjacent Regions, 1808-1812*, edited by White (Missoula, Mont.: Montana State University Press, 1950).

References:

Anonymous, *Inventory of David Thompson's Journals* (Toronto: Ontario Department of Public Records, 1969);

John J. Bigsby, *The Shoe and Canoe*, 2 volumes (London: Chapman & Hall, 1950);

Elliott Coues, Introduction to *New Light on the Early History of the Greater Northwest. The Manuscript Journals of Alexander Henry . . . and of*

David Thompson, edited by Coues, 3 volumes (New York: Harper, 1897);

John Hess, "Mackenzie and Thompson in Canada's Vastness," in his *Into the Wilderness* (Washington: National Geographic Society, 1978), pp. 88-123;

Victor G. Hopwood, "Centenary of an Explorer: David Thompson's 'Narrative' Re-consid-ered," *Queen's Quarterly* (Spring 1957): 41-48;

Hopwood, "New Light on David Thompson," *Beaver* (Summer 1957): 26-31;

William Kaye Lamb, Introduction to Gabriel Franchère's *Journal of a Voyage on the North-west Coast of North America*, edited by Lamb (Toronto: Champlain Society, 1969).

Thomas Phillips Thompson

(25 November 1843 - 22 May 1933)

Ramsay Cook
York University

BOOKS: *The Future Government of Canada* (St. Catherines, Ont.: Leavenworth's, 1864);

The Political Experiences of Jimuel Briggs, D.B., at Toronto, Ottawa and Elsewhere (Toronto: Flint, Morton, 1873);

The Politics of Labor (New York: Belford, Clarke, 1887);

The Labor Reform Songster (Philadelphia: Journal of the Knights of Labor, 1892);

Leasehold Arbitrations: How the System of Renewal Awards Results in Practical Confiscation (Toronto: James & Williams, 1896).

Thomas Phillips Thompson studied law but devoted his life to writing and social activism. He published poetry, satire, social criticism, and reports and essays on topics ranging from the Irish question, imperialism, and spiritualism to natural resources, the labor question, free thought, and agricultural protest. Though he lived until his ninetieth year his most important writing was accomplished, and his outlook established, by the beginning of the twentieth century.

Thompson was born in Newcastle-on-Tyne, England, on 25 November 1843. At the age of fourteen he joined his Quaker parents, William and Sarah Thompson, in their immigration to Canada. After brief stops in Belleville and Lindsay the family settled in St. Catherine's, Canada West (now Ontario). There Thompson finished his formal education, read law, and moved into journalism. He was married twice, first to Delia Florence Fisher in 1871 and, after her death in 1897, to her sister Edith in 1900.

Thompson began his journalistic career in the exciting years when the proposed Confederation of British North America (Canada) dominated political debate. As a reporter for the *St. Catherine's Post* he covered that debate and joined in it. He was only twenty-one when he published a well-considered polemic entitled *The Future Government of Canada* (1864), in which he took issue with two of the most important features of the Confederation scheme. First he insisted that the new nation should be a republic not a monarchy, the latter being condemned as European and conservative and thus unsuited to the conditions of progressive North America. He remained a republican all his life. Secondly he denounced the provisions that legalized French in the new constitution. He considered the French a defeated, backward people who should not be allowed to stand in the way of the progress that the English symbolized. Thompson later revised this opinion when he discovered that the French Canadians shared his anti-imperialism, and he took up their defense.

In 1867 Thompson moved to Toronto, where he was employed first by the *Daily Telegraph* and then by the *Mail*. At the latter paper his capacity for satire and mimicry quickly won him attention. Under the nom de plume of Jimuel Briggs, D.B. (dead beat), of Coboconk University, he published a series of letters to the "Coboconk *Irradiator*" in which he poked fun at well-known personalities, politicians, and the orthodoxies of the age. George Brown of the *Globe* was a favored target. Together with many other young men who had expected Confederation to create a more heady national feeling, Thompson supported the Canada First movement in the 1870s. But he found Goldwin Smith's associates too staid and English, and he was soon attacking them in the *National,* his first venture into independent journalism. That lively weekly publicized political debate, religious controversy, agricultural unrest, and the beginnings of the demand for women's rights. But the paper proved a precarious venture, and in 1876 Thompson moved to Boston, where he worked for several newspapers, contributed to the American *Punch,* and dispatched articles to Toronto. Boston was in intellectual ferment: dissenters and conservatives debated the meaning of the new science and the new industrialism. Thompson rapidly assimilated many of the radical nostrums of the day, especially those advanced in Henry George's *Progress and Poverty* (1879). When Thompson returned to Toronto in 1880 his lifetime preoccupation had been defined–the labor question. He had become a labor reformer and an antimonopolist.

In 1880 he joined the *Globe* (his nemesis Brown now dead), with an assignment to cover the Irish Land League controversy. He soon became involved in social, religious, and labor reform activities, especially with the Knights of Labor who were unionizing Canadian and U.S. workers at an unprecedented rate. In 1883 he joined the newly founded *Toronto News* and was able to give freer expression to his radicalism since the paper's owner, E. E. Sheppard, hoped to win the readership of the working class. But Thompson also had another outlet, the *Palladium of Labor,* the Knights' weekly published in Hamilton from 1883 to 1887. Under the pseudonym Enjolras he expounded George's ideas about the inequalities of industrial society and urged such reforms as the single tax, municipal ownership of public utilities, shorter hours and higher wages, and the need for workers to unionize. In 1887 many of these ideas were brought together and systematized in *The Politics of Labor.* Writing in a more sober fashion than was usual for him, Thompson developed an indictment of monopo-

listic capitalism, a system in which the rich grew richer and fewer while the poor multiplied and lived in misery. Thompson argued that it was the system rather than the individual that was at fault and needed reform. He advocated a new economic order in which human needs took precedence over the demands of the market, one in which the monopolies that dominated society would be transferred from private to public ownership. The book includes Thompson's finest poem, "The Political Economist and the Tramp," which satirized the social Darwinist theories that supposedly gave scientific sanction to unfettered economic competition. The theories of George had thus been modified into a socialism that had much in common with Edward Bellamy's utopia *Looking Backward* (1887).

In these same years Thompson's religious beliefs also underwent a significant shift. Born a Quaker, he had become a religious skeptic in the 1870s and a leader of the free-thought movement that developed in the climate of Darwinian science and biblical criticism. But in 1890 Thompson discovered, along with many Bellamyites and Fabians, the new religion of theosophy. This attempt to combine the best of all the world's religions emphasized ethical conduct and the gradual building of the heavenly kingdom on earth, while rejecting the harsh theology of sin, predestination, and retribution. The cosmopolitan liberalism of theosophy appealed to Thompson's optimistic nature and his active social conscience. In such poems as "Always with You" (*Grip,* 22 April 1893), he attacked the orthodox churches as part of the economic establishment and demanded instead the preaching of a gospel of social reform. Single taxers, Bellamyite socialists, theosophists, and social gospel Protestants formed the core of the reform movement that mushroomed during the depression years of the 1890s.

Thompson's eclecticism meant that he supported almost every reform group. In 1891 he established the *Labor Advocate,* and when that periodical failed after only a year he joined his friend George Wrigley, editor of the *Farmers Sun,* in which he continued to advocate radical social reform. In these years he also contributed poems and paragraphs to J. W. Bengough's brilliant satirical weekly *Grip.* But he did more than write. With Wrigley he became a leading figure in an effort to form a political coalition between the Knights of Labor and the Patrons of Industry, the farmers' organization. The effort ultimately failed and the election of the Liberals in 1896 and the gradual return of prosperity left the ground for social radicalism somewhat barren.

During the next decades Thompson continued to write for a great variety of publications both at home and abroad, including *Citizen and Country*, the *Western Clarion*, and the *Toiler*. He also accepted employment as a correspondent for the *Labour Gazette*, published by the newly established federal Department of Labour and presided over by the young Mackenzie King, an acquaintance of Thompson's from his university days. In 1902 Thompson became an organizer for the Ontario Socialist League and ran unsuccessfully for office on several occasions. Above all he remained a dissenter, opposing Canadian participation in the Boer War and criticizing the Robert Borden government's policies during World War I. To the end of his life he remained what he called a class-conscious socialist.

After World War I Thompson retired to Oakville, Ontario, where he continued to read and write and began to cultivate a large, luscious garden. However, his eyesight faltered and he was blind for nearly ten years before he died of a stroke on 22 May 1933.

Thomas Phillips Thompson was Canada's first systematic, radical intellectual of the industrial age. His outlook and his love of versification are both exemplified by a stanza from a poem in *The Labor Reform Songster* (1892):

> Not by canon nor by sabre
> > Not by flags unfurled,
> Shall we win the rights of labor,
> > Shall we free the world.
> Thought is stronger far than weapons,
> > Shall we stay the course?
> It spreads its onward circling waves
> > And ever gathers force.

References:

Jay Atherton, Introduction to *The Politics of Labor* (Toronto & Buffalo: University of Toronto Press, 1975);

Ramsay Cook, *The Regenerators: Social Criticism in Late Victorian Canada* (Toronto: University of Toronto Press, 1987), pp. 152-171;

Russell Hann, "Brainworkers and the Knights of Labor: E. E. Sheppard, Phillips Thompson and the *Toronto News* 1883-1887," in *Essays in Canadian Working Class History*, edited by Gregory S. Kealey and Peter Warrian (Toronto: McClelland & Stewart, 1976), pp. 35-57.

Papers:

The T. Phillips Thompson Papers are in the National Archives of Canada, Ottawa.

Catharine Parr Traill

(9 January 1802 - 26 August 1899)

Michael A. Peterman
Trent University

BOOKS: *The Tell Tale: An Original Collection of Moral and Amusing Stories* (London: Harris, 1818);

Disobedience; or, Mind What Mama Says (London: Woodhouse, 1819);

Reformation; or, The Cousins (London: Woodhouse, 1819);

Little Downy; or, The History of a Field Mouse: A Moral Tale (London: Dean & Munday, 1822);

The Flower Basket; or, Poetical Blossoms (London: Newman, c. 1825);

Prejudice Reproved; or, The History of the Negro Toy-Seller (London: Harvey & Darton, 1826);

The Young Emigrants; or, Pictures of Life in Canada (London: Harvey & Darton, 1826);

The Juvenile Forget-Me-Not; or, Cabinet of Entertainment and Instruction (London: Hailes, 1827);

The Keepsake Guineas; or, The Best Use of Money (London: Newman, 1828);

Amendment; or, Charles Grant and His Sister, published with *The Little Prisoner* by Susanna Strickland [Moodie] (London: Dean & Munday, 1828);

The Step-Brothers. A Tale (London: Harvey & Darton, 1828);

Sketches from Nature; or, Hints to Juvenile Naturalists (London: Harvey & Darton, 1830);

Sketchbook of a Young Naturalist; or, Hints to the Students of Nature (London, 1831);

Narratives of Nature, and History Book for Young Naturalists (London: Lacey, 1831);

The Backwoods of Canada: Being Letters from the Wife of an Emigrant Officer (London: Knight, 1836; modern edition, Toronto: McClelland & Stewart, 1929); enlarged as *Canada and the Oregon. The Backwoods of Canada* (London: Nattali, 1846);

The Canadian Crusoes: A Tale of the Rice Lake Plains, edited by Agnes Strickland (Boston: Woolworth, Ainsworth, 1852; London: Hall, Virtue, 1852; modern edition, Toronto: McClelland & Stewart, 1923; another modern edition, edited by Rupert Schieder, Ottawa: Carleton University Press, 1986); re-

Catharine Parr Strickland (later Traill), circa 1825 (miniature by Thomas Cheesman; collection of Miss Kathleen McMurrich, Thornhill, Ontario)

published as *Lost in the Backwoods. A Tale of the Canadian Forest* (London & New York: Nelson, 1882);

The Female Emigrant's Guide, and Hints on Canadian Housekeeping, 2 volumes (Toronto: Maclear, 1854); republished in 1 volume as *The Canadian Settler's Guide* (Toronto: Old Countryman, 1855; London: Stanford, 1860); enlarged as *The Canadian Emigrant Housekeeper's Guide* (Toronto: Lovell & Gibson, 1862);

Lady Mary and Her Nurse; or, A Peep into the Canadian Forest (London: Hall, Virtue, 1856); republished as *Stories of the Canadian Forest; or, Little Mary and Her Nurse* (New York & Boston: Francis, 1857); republished again as *Afar in the Forest; or, Pictures of Life and Scenery in the Wilds of Canada* (London: Nelson, 1869);

Canadian Wild Flowers (Montreal: Lovell, 1868);

The Infant's Prayer-Book; with Texts and Simple Hymns for Infant Minds (Toronto: Rowsell, 1873);

Studies of Plant Life in Canada; or, Gleanings from Forest, Lake and Plain (Ottawa: Woodburn, 1885); revised as *Studies of Plant Life in Canada: Wild Flowers, Flowering Shrubs, and Grasses* (Toronto: Briggs, 1906);

In the Forest; or, Pictures of Life and Scenery in the Woods of Canada (London: Nelson, 1886; London & New York: Nelson, 1890);

Pearls and Pebbles; or, Notes of an Old Naturalist (Toronto: Briggs, 1894);

Cot and Cradle Stories, edited by Mary Agnes Fitzgibbon (Toronto: Briggs, 1895).

SELECTED PERIODICAL PUBLICATIONS–
UNCOLLECTED:
"The Mill of the Rapids: A Canadian Sketch," *Chambers' Edinburgh Journal*, 7 (1838): 322-323;

"Love of Flowers," *Literary Garland*, new series 1 (1843): 41-42;

"The Two Widows of Hunter's Creek," *Home Circle*, 21 July 1849, pp. 33-35;

"The Settlers Settled; or, Pat Connor and His Two Masters," *Sharpe's London Journal*, 10 (1849): 107-110, 137-142, 274-277, 335-340;

"Forest Gleanings" (nos. I-XIII), *Anglo-American Magazine*, 1-3 (1852-1853);

"A Glance Within the Forest," *Canadian Monthly and National Review*, 6 (1874): 48-53;

"Voices from the Canadian Woods: The White Cedar," *Canadian Monthly and National Review*, 9 (1876): 491-494.

Catharine Parr Traill has a greater importance in nineteenth-century Canadian letters than her work as a whole would seem to justify. Mistrusting fiction (which she felt satisfied the imagination while seducing the judgment) and feeling little aptitude for poetry, she was at her best in writing discursively about subjects she deemed to be useful to her readers. In particular, as in *The Backwoods of Canada* (1836), she made the problems of the female settler in Canada and the description of Canadian flora and fauna her concerns. While these topics may seem today small cause for a literary reputation, they were subjects about which she knew a great deal and to which she brought a geniality, openness, and thoughtfulness that distinguish her observations. In England, had she remained, she would likely have become a minor contributor to what W. J. Keith has called "the rural tradition" in English prose. In Canada she became something far more important–a recorder and a namer. Like her sister, Susanna Moodie (author of *Roughing It in the Bush*, 1852, and *Life in The Clearings*, 1853), who was more romantic and emotional by temperament, Traill left a body of writing that has proven an important resource to students of the history, social conditions, culture, early botanical descriptions, and literature of Upper Canada (now Ontario).

Born to Thomas and Elizabeth Homer Strickland in Kent, England, on 9 January 1802, Catharine saw her life alter dramatically in the spring of 1832 when she married Lt. Thomas Traill, a widowed, retired military officer. Within a week they immigrated to Canada, settling in the rugged bush country north of Peterborough (Ontario). Before that point her life had been tied to rural Suffolk and the quiet, cultivated domesticity of the Strickland family at Reydon Hall. It was to Suffolk that her parents took their five daughters (Susanna and two sons were later born there) when Thomas Strickland retired from a lucrative docks-management position in London. First at Stowe House (1804-1808) and thereafter at Reydon Hall, Strickland sought to implement his forward-looking scheme of educating his daughters in subject matter then thought appropriate only for boys–geography, mathematics, and so on. He insisted upon scientific observation and the practical application of learning to life. With a sternness characteristic of the times, he advocated self-reliance and personal responsibility in work and at play. His regimen left an indelible mark on his children. Indeed, most of

Traill's conservative and puritan views have their roots in her father's teaching and personal influence. From him she learned as well a deep affection and respect for the rural life; till her death she treasured his copy of Izaak Walton's *The Compleat Angler* (1653) from which he had read to her during fishing excursions.

Illness and financial reversals, however, took Strickland increasingly away from his educative plans and his family. His death in 1818 was a tremendous blow; not only did the family lose its remarkable leader but they were forced to cope with more straitened conditions. The children rallied around their mother in a brave attempt to maintain face. All the daughters but one wrote, and several were skilled painters. Catharine was in fact the first to be published, though her older sisters, Elizabeth and Agnes, who later gained fame as biographers of English royalty, were the most sophisticated and advanced in their writing, soon achieving prominence. Catharine, Susanna, and Jane Margaret for the most part confined themselves to writing simple moral tales for children and placing tales, sketches, and occasional poems in the popular gift-book annuals of the day.

Traill's early writing (most of which was published without her name) is generally consistent with her Canadian work, both in values and format. For various publishers, most notably the Quaker firm of Harvey and Darton, she produced several didactic narratives, including *Disobedience; or, Mind What Mama Says* (1819), *Reformation; or, the Cousins* (1819), *Little Downy; or, the History of a Field-Mouse* (1822), *Prejudice Reproved; or, the History of the Negro Toy-Seller* (1826), *The Young Emigrants; or, Pictures of Life in Canada* (1826), *The Keepsake Guineas; or, The Best Use of Money* (1828), and *Sketchbook of a Young Naturalist* (1831). Misbehavior, lying, slovenliness, neglect of duty, and racial prejudice are her typical concerns in these pious and cautionary stories. Her most interesting works of the period, however, stick closely to natural facts and manifest a conscious link to rural writers from Virgil and Walton to Mary Russell Mitford and Gilbert White. In *Narratives of Nature* she articulates her confidence in nature's ability to provide moral guidance and inspiration: "Nothing that exists in the animal, vegetable, or mineral world is unworthy of our attention: a close investigation of the works of nature will afford an increase of amusement and of instruction. Every object that we examine bears in it the impress of a divine origi-

nal. . . ." *Little Downy*, likely her most popular story, reflects this outlook, and *Sketchbook of a Young Naturalist* blends recollections of the Strickland children's pets, outdoor hobbies, and rural adventures with pieces of natural history culled from encyclopedias and other references.

As Traill's characteristic juxtaposition of personal experience and natural observation is prefigured in her early work, so in *The Young Emigrants* she seems to have almost anticipated her own immigration to and interest in Canada. Clearly the idea of vigorously and dutifully meeting the challenges of a new and independent life fascinated her. Drawing upon letters from family friends who had emigrated and perhaps from her brother Sam (who left for Upper Canada in 1825), she follows the movements of the exemplary Clarence children from England to Canada, amplifying her descriptions of place and scene by paraphrasing such available sources as John Howison's *Sketches of Canada* (1821). Though the narrative is often pious and didactic and the children more like elderly ministers than youths, it celebrates the values of English resolution and resourcefulness much as Traill would do in *The Backwoods of Canada* and *The Canadian Crusoes* (1852).

A lover of rural quietness and the family circle, Catharine stayed happily at Reydon through her twenties. It was only with the failure of her two-year engagement to Francis Harral (the break was not clear until late in 1831) that she had the chance to travel around England and began to spend some time in London. Early in 1832, she met Lt. Traill, a man from Orkney who was a close friend of Susanna's husband, J. W. D. Moodie. After being married in May, the Traills almost immediately left for Canada to take up Traill's military land grant entitlement and to seek a financial independence not possible for them in England. The Strickland family was displeased by Catharine's choice of husband and by the rapid pace of events.

In Upper Canada the Traills lived in the backwoods some forty miles north of Cobourg. Settling at first at Lake Katchawanook (north of present-day Lakefield) close to her enterprising brother, Sam, they had help and a social life sufficiently congenial to ease their adjustment to pioneer living. Mrs. Traill wrote positively of the experiences of their first three years in *The Backwoods of Canada*. Continuing financial pressures, however, took their toll on the couple. They sold their backwoods farm in 1839 and,

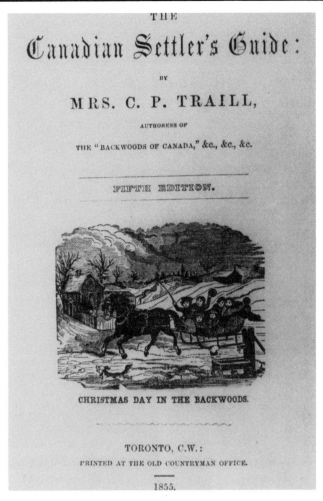

THE

Canadian Settler's Guide:

BY

MRS. C. P. TRAILL,

AUTHORESS OF

THE "BACKWOODS OF CANADA," &c., &c., &c.

FIFTH EDITION.

CHRISTMAS DAY IN THE BACKWOODS.

TORONTO, C.W.:

PRINTED AT THE OLD COUNTRYMAN OFFICE.

1855.

Title page for the 1855 edition of Traill's handbook for pioneers, originally published as
The Female Emigrant's Guide *(1854)*

from then until 1846, lived in various places in and around Peterborough, often on the edge of poverty. They then spent eleven years in the Rice Lake vicinity, still typically in straitened circumstances. In all the Traills had nine children, two of whom died in infancy, during these years.

At Rice Lake they suffered their worst calamity, the burning of their home, Oaklands, in 1857. Thomas Traill, it seems, never emotionally recovered from the event. He died in 1859. After his death, with the help of her family and a small British government grant, Mrs. Traill was able to move into her own home, "Westove," in Lakefield to be close to some of her children and other relatives. During these quiet and more leisurely years her range of correspondence (with literary figures such as William Kirby and scientists such as John Macoun) widened, and she continued to write a great deal besides. Much of this late-written material, particularly her reminiscences

about her English years and the Strickland family, was not published. It is part of the Traill Family Collection in the Public Archives of Canada, Ottawa.

A woman of extraordinary goodwill and patience, Traill suffered much in her pioneering years but seldom flagged in her energy or convictions. *The Backwoods of Canada*, which went through numerous editions and was translated into French and German, reveals the strength of her middle-class, English values even as it offers one of the most perceptive personal accounts of early settlement in Upper Canada. Comprised of "letters" home to her mother, sisters, and friends, the book follows the Traills from England to the bush and provides occasion for Traill to describe in detail various landscapes, the effects of the seasons, the habits of local Indians, bush customs, her domestic arrangements, and the botanical life around her. At the same time,

Traill in 1884 (photograph by Topley; PA-802715, National Archives of Canada)

it offers detailed practical advice to female settlers, not only concerning preparations for emigration but also about how to make use of available resources in the bush. Though committed to ideals of civilization and beauty that owed much to the eighteenth century, Traill was open to experience and the exigencies of change. Like her character Richard Clarence in *The Young Emigrants* she accepts the premise that "whatever is, is right." Refusing to look backward with regret, she undertakes to allow for violations of her taste, to adapt herself cheerfully, and to understand the reasons behind the conditions that disturb her. In this spirit she notes in the final letter, "My husband is becoming more reconciled to the country, and I daily feel my attachment to it strengthening. The very stumps that appeared so odious, through long custom, seem to lose some of their hideousness. . . ."

Though Traill's "bush" sketches and narratives appeared (with the help of her sister Agnes) in various British magazines, including *Sharpe's London Journal*, the *Home Circle*, and *Chamber's*

Edinburgh Journal during the 1830s and 1840s, her next book, *The Canadian Crusoes*, did not come out until 1852. It is the tale of three adolescents (Catharine, her brother Hector, and her cousin Louis) who get lost in the woods south of Rice Lake during an early stage in the area's settlement, and who, through discipline, economy, and adaptation, survive for two years, managing even to convert an abandoned Mohawk girl to Christianity in the process. *The Canadian Crusoes* has not, however, worn as well as *The Backwoods of Canada*. Its strengths, which include Traill's careful attention to the details of survival and her understanding of Rice Lake's topography and Indian history, are not in themselves enough to compensate for its melodramatic plotting and the wooden piety and goodness of her characters. Traill does, however, make the landscape a major force in the novel and shows that the descendants of solid European stock can turn it to their advantage without stooping to what she saw as the unregenerate impulses of the Indian.

Traill's remaining work must be more

briefly summarized. In 1854 she produced a useful addendum to *The Backwoods of Canada* entitled *The Female Emigrant's Guide, and Hints on Canadian Housekeeping* (republished as *The Canadian Settler's Guide* a year later). A collection of recipes, practical advice, and anecdotes, it established her, in Clara Thomas's phrase, as "the Mrs. Beeton of nineteenth century Canada" (Introduction to the 1969 edition). *Lady Mary and Her Nurse* (1856) combines narrative with observations of nature to interest very young children. Not insignificantly, Traill's continuing interest in botany led to the writing and publication of *Canadian Wild Flowers* (1868) and the much more ambitious *Studies of Plant Life in Canada* (1885), for which she was much praised by several eminent scientists. Both books were based on over forty years of record keeping and research. Indeed, one of her plant discoveries, *Lastria marginalis Traillae*, includes her name. Two late collections, *Pearls and Pebbles* (1894) and *Cot and Cradle Stories* (1895), include sketches of nature and personal reminiscences.

While few of Catharine Parr Traill's works have generated much twentieth-century critical attention, her place in early Canadian literary history has been attested to by literary scholars, writers, and historians. She is in fact a special presence, as Margaret Laurence's use of her in *The Diviners* (1974) suggests. Often she is seen as the objective, optimistic, forward-looking counterpart of her sister, Susanna Moodie, their two views seeming to stand as representative ways of responding to Upper Canada's landscape and social conditions. On her behalf it needs also to be noted that she thought of herself less as a literary figure than as a children's writer and friendly counselor of pioneering women and their society. If she was naive in her view of human nature and civilization, if she treated nature selectively rather than comprehensively, she still stood firmly for values that were to her consequential and incontestible. Rooted in these English middle-class views, her most important book, *The Backwoods of Canada*, is not only one of the classic accounts of pioneering in Upper Canada but also, as David Jackel has said, a book that reveals "the real strengths of [Canada's] British inheritance."

Biography:
Sara Eaton, *Lady of the Backwoods: A Biography of Catharine Parr Traill* (Toronto: McClelland & Stewart, 1969).

References:
Carl Ballstadt, "The Literary History of the Strickland Family," Ph.D. dissertation, University of London, 1965;

Jean Murray Cole, "Catharine Parr Traill," in *Portraits: Peterborough Area Women Past and Present*, edited by Gail Corbett (Woodview, Ont.: Homestead Studios, 1975);

William D. Gairdner, "Traill and Moodie: The Two Realities," *Journal of Canadian Fiction*, 2, no. 3 (1973): 75-81;

David Jackel, "Mrs. Moodie and Mrs. Traill, and the Fabrication of a Canadian Tradition," *Compass*, 6 (1979): 1-22;

W. J. Keith, *The Rural Tradition: A Study of the Nonfiction Prose Writers of the English Countryside* (Toronto: University of Toronto Press, 1974);

Audrey Morris, *The Gentle Pioneers* (Toronto: Hodder & Stoughton, 1968);

G. H. Needler, *Otonabee Pioneers: The Story of the Stewarts, the Stricklands, the Traills and the Moodies* (Toronto: Burns & MacEachern, 1953);

Michael A. Peterman, " 'Splendid Anachronism': The Record of Catharine Parr Traill's Struggles as an Amateur Botanist in Nineteenth-Century Canada," in *Re(dis)covering Our Foremothers*, edited by Lorraine McMullen (Ottawa: University of Ottawa Press, 1990), pp. 173-185;

Lloyd M. Scott, "The English Gentlefolk in the Backwoods of Canada," *Dalhousie Review*, 39 (1959): 56-69;

Clara Thomas, Introduction to *The Canadian Settler's Guide* (Toronto: McClelland & Stewart, 1969);

Thomas, "Journeys to Freedom," *Canadian Literature*, 51 (1972): 11-19;

Thomas, "The Strickland Sisters," in *The Clear Spirit*, edited by Mary Q. Innis (Toronto: University of Toronto Press, 1966), pp. 42-73.

Papers:
The Traill Family Collection of papers is held in the National Archives of Canada, Ottawa, and some of Traill's letters to Francis Stewart are in the Baldwin Room of the Metropolitan Toronto Library.

Joseph-Patrice Truillier-Lacombe

(20 February 1807 - 6 July 1863)

Mary Lu MacDonald

BOOK: *La Terre Paternelle* (Montreal: Beauchemin & Valois, 1871; modern edition, Montreal: HMH, 1972).

Joseph-Patrice Truillier-Lacombe was born near present-day Oka, Quebec, on 20 February 1807, the son of a merchant, François-Xavier Truillier-Lacombe, and his wife Marie-Geneviève Adhémar Truillier-Lacombe. His father's business, situated on Lake of Two Mountains at the beginning and end of the fur-trade routes, must have given the young Patrice some understanding of the life of a voyageur, which one of his protagonists, Charles Chauvin, was later to follow. However, it would appear that a life of adventure and hardship was not for Lacombe himself, since he was a prize-winning student at the Collège de Montréal and then entered the profession of notary. After several years of practice on his own, he became business agent of the Society of Saint Sulpice in Montreal in 1832 and remained in their employ until his death. Lacombe married a widow, Léocadie Boucher, in 1835. They had no children. All the obituaries refer to him as a respectable man of great integrity and literary interests.

His literary reputation has suffered from the fact that there is not the faintest hint in his biography that he even approached the archetype of the romantic young writer; indeed, he was almost forty when his one novel was published (appearing in installments in *L'Album Littéraire* in February 1846). He left no papers that might illuminate his thoughts and feelings, so the image of the cautious, dry notary, who worked all his adult life for the Sulpicians, has dominated the critical view of his work.

His short novel, far more complex than it appears on the surface, was the first to introduce many themes that later became common in French-Canadian literature, but Lacombe is generally not given more than token credit for the innovative qualities of *La Terre Paternelle* (published in book form in 1871). In a romantic age Lacombe wrote an essentially realistic novel. The story is set in the region he knew as a child and the city in which he lived as an adult. The basic plot line is quite simple: the younger son of a prosperous farmer leaves home to become a voyageur; so, to keep the elder son on the land, the father gives him the farm. Bankruptcy follows, and the family moves into Montreal, where father and son support the family as water carriers. After ten years of poverty and hunger the elder son dies and, for lack of money, is refused winter burial or any tolling of bells to mark his death. The younger son then reappears with money, the farm is repurchased, and the Chauvin family, sadder but wiser, recommence their rural life.

La Terre Paternelle is the first of the French-Canadian *romans de la terre* (novels of the land), but it differs in many respects from those that followed. The opposition of the evil town to the happy countryside is certainly there, and the former is depicted as the center of negative individualism, while the latter operates as a positive collectivity. However, in the Chauvin family, neither the older generation nor the younger is depicted as understanding the value of rural life, and the father is shown to be the greater fool in giving his land to his son during his lifetime and then in trying to succeed as a merchant, a business about which he knew absolutely nothing. It is the younger generation, in the person of Charles Chauvin, who, wiser after his years in the woods, saves the family and ensures their happy resettlement on their old farm.

Many have noted the anticlericalism of the novel's Montreal segment, in which a priest refuses a church funeral for the eldest son, Joseph, unless his father pays a minimum of ten piastres for the tolling of one bell. Since the family is too poor to pay, Joseph is taken straight to the charnel house with no religious service. However, even in the sections set in the country, although the neighbors are shown congregating on the church steps for the community's unofficial weekly meeting, nothing is written that would attribute value to what goes on inside the church itself.

*The Collège de Montréal, as it appeared when Truillier-Lacombe was a student there (drawing by J. Drake, circa 1826;
by permission of the Bibliothèque Municipale de Montréal)*

Another theme, that of the wanderer, which also became common in French-Canadian literature, found expression in *La Terre Paternelle*. The case of Charles is not archetypal, since it is almost by accident that he signs on as a voyageur, and when he returns it is with money and a desire to settle down on the farm. He is not by nature a permanent wanderer and outsider, but rather a young man looking for adventure who, having found more hardship than fun in the experience, rejects a wandering life in favor of a settled one.

Lacombe's realistic narrative style results in vivid descriptions of particular scenes in both town and country, and the omniscient narrator intervenes in the last pages to defend the novel's happy ending as being more true to *canadien* life than the murders and suicides that ended contemporary European novels. Lacombe's secure use of realism shows the maturity of French-Canadian culture, even in the very early years of Canadian literary history.

References:

Antoine Sirois, "Espace et temps dans *La Terre Paternelle*," *Journal of Canadian Fiction*, 2 (Summer 1973): 62-64;

André Vanasse, Preface to *La Terre Paternelle* (Montreal: HMH, 1972), pp. 11-27.

Roger Viets

(9 March 1738 - 15 August 1811)

Thomas B. Vincent
Royal Military College of Canada

BOOKS: *A Serious Address and Farewell Charge to the Members of the Church of England in Simsbury and the Adjacent Parts* (Hartford, Conn.: Hudson & Goodwin, 1787);

A Sermon Preached in St. Andrew's Church, Simsbury (Hartford, Conn.: Hudson & Goodwin, 1787);

Annapolis Royal, anonymous (Halifax: A. Henry, 1788);

A Sermon, on the Duty of Attending the Public Worship of God (Hartford, Conn.: Hudson & Goodwin, 1789);

A Sermon Preached to the Ancient and Worshipful Society of Free and Accepted Masons (Halifax: John Howe, 1792);

A Sermon, Preached at Sissaboo, Now Called Weymouth, in Nova Scotia (Saint John, N.B.: John Ryan, 1799);

A Sermon, Preached Before the Lodge of Free and Accepted Masons, at Granby (Hartford, Conn.: Hudson & Goodwin, 1800);

A Sermon, Preached in St. Peter's Church, in Granby (Hartford, Conn.: Hudson & Goodwin, 1800).

Roger Viets was one of the well-educated clergy who came to Maritime Canada in the wake of the American Revolution and contributed significantly to the cultural and spiritual development of late-eighteenth-century Nova Scotia. He made a respectable contribution to the sermon literature of his day, but his place in Canadian literary history arises from the fact that in 1788 he published the first separate work of poetry (*Annapolis Royal*) to appear in what is now Canada.

Viets came from a respected Connecticut family. The second child of John and Lois Phelps Viets, he was born at Simsbury (later called Granby) on 9 March 1738. After graduation from Yale in 1758, he assisted the local Church of England clergyman at Simsbury as a lay reader for several years before sailing to London to complete his theological training. Viets was ordained on 17 April 1763 and appointed Church

of England missionary at Simsbury. He married Hester Botsford on 19 November 1772, and they had eight children, five of whom lived to maturity. In pre-Revolutionary Connecticut, he was a popular priest, but as political emotions heightened in the 1770s, his unbending support for royal authority and the established church made him a target for the ire of the rebel faction. In 1776 he was jailed at Hartford on suspicion of having aided a group of fugitive British officers.

After the Peace of 1784 it became impossible for Viets to remain in Simsbury. In December 1785 he was assigned to Digby, Nova Scotia, and in May 1786 went to inspect his new charge. Upon arrival he set about his ministerial duties and in the autumn returned to Connecticut to gather his family. The following June he moved them to Digby. Hester Viets died on 25 April 1800, and he married Mary Pickett, a widow, in 1802; there were no children from this second marriage. Viets remained at Digby until his death on 15 August 1811. A leading cleric in Nova Scotia, he did not lose touch with his friends back in Connecticut, and returned on several occasions to preach to his old congregation. During these years, seven of his sermons were published, five in Connecticut and two in Maritime Canada.

Viets's sermons fall into two categories: those which focus on particular theological subjects and those designed for special occasions, dealing with broader social and moral questions. In his theological sermons, Viets was very orthodox, adhering closely to eighteenth-century Anglican doctrine. Nonetheless, these sermons are a skillful blend of logic and persuasive rhetoric and reflect a strong evangelical sentiment underlying the formal subject matter. Similarly, in Viets's occasional sermons, the reader must look past the surface rhetoric to find the fuller meaning. An interesting example is the valedictory sermon *A Serious Address and Farewell Charge* (1787), which he delivered to his Connecticut congregation before departing with his family to Nova Scotia. On the surface the sermon functions as an apologia for

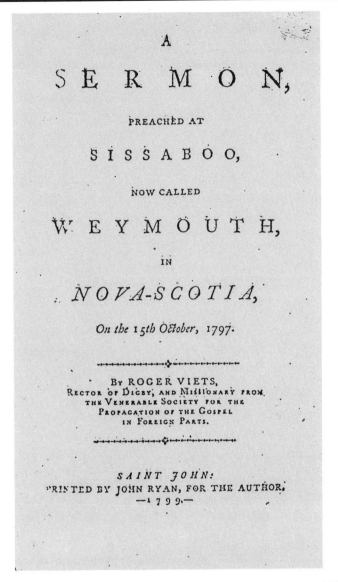

A

SERMON,

PREACHED AT

SISSABOO,

NOW CALLED

WEYMOUTH,

IN

NOVA-SCOTIA,

On the 15th October, 1797.

By ROGER VIETS,
RECTOR OF DIGBY, AND MISSIONARY FROM
THE VENERABLE SOCIETY FOR THE
PROPAGATION OF THE GOSPEL
IN FOREIGN PARTS.

SAINT JOHN:
PRINTED BY JOHN RYAN, FOR THE AUTHOR.
—1799.—

Title page for one of Viets's many sermons, only seven of which were published

his actions, but in the process it presents a reasoned condemnation of the social, political, and ideological circumstances that have compelled him to seek a new home. The sermon projects an attractive and logically convincing model of communal life incorporating all the central features of eighteenth-century conservative ideology relating to social order and human contentment. He envisions a society founded on common sense and common decency, where people live in harmony with one another and with nature, guided by universal moral propriety, reinforced by the spirit of their Christian faith. At the heart of this social vision lies a concept of order in which authority and responsibility are distributed in a hierarchical fashion and the whole is harmonized through the principle of duty. Duty involves both the acceptance of distributed authority and the responsible exercising of it. As such, it has the force of personal obligation but is directed toward communal well-being. Against the background of political upheaval in late-eighteenth-century America, Viets's views function as an implicit condemnation of the democratic principles of individual freedom and self-realization that fueled the revolutionary imagination; further, they act as a judgment on the inherent instabilities of a society founded upon such self-interested principles.

Viets's poem *Annapolis Royal*, published at Halifax, was aimed directly at Nova Scotians and therefore presents his social vision more openly and confidently. By turning to poetry, he is able to approach his subject through imaginative description rather than argument. The poem employs the conventions of eighteenth-century topographical verse and all the elements of the pastoral tradition associated with it. This allows him to begin with an idealized description of the natural setting, one that explicitly emphasizes order and harmony as the principles shaping the world of the poem, and around which all civilized reality is organized. When the narrator moves on from natural description to depict the characteristics of the emerging social reality in Loyalist Nova Scotia, his imaginative logic is carried forward on this central, governing concept of order and harmony. The order and harmony of the pastoral landscape is matched by the social, political, and emotional contentment of the Loyalist community; indeed, the two pictures of order and harmony are really one, for contented man and benevolent nature partake of the same divinely conceived creation. Not surprisingly the poetic vision is made complete by ultimately focusing on the spiritual quality of life at Annapolis Royal. Viets draws on the imagery of choir music and religious worship to connect the projected harmony between man and nature with the spiritual harmony that flows from a benevolent God. In the end the reader is left with a poetic vision that fuses the natural, human, and divine elements of reality into a universal, logical, imaginative structure from which rational man can draw comfort. The whole is symbolized by Annapolis Royal, the city of royal Queen Anne, a community that epitomizes traditional neoclassical ideals and conservative sociopolitical values in both its imagined

form and its historical reality. As a poetic symbol, it articulates and confirms the meaning of Nova Scotia and the meaning of Loyalism.

As a cultural document Viets's poem offers comfort to a displaced people facing great physical hardship and social deprivation. It deals imaginatively not with what is but with what will be, given the social, cultural, moral, and religious principles on which this community was founded. But, more important, it is also a confirmation that the Loyalists have chosen the right side of the ideological issue. They are part of a greater reality, one which flows from the divinely ordered pattern of creation and which found its fullest expression in eighteenth-century English life. Essentially the poem presents a vision of civility in a time of doubt. Although these people have been forced to begin their lives anew in a remote part of the civilized world, they are not cast into outer darkness. In their imaginations they carry the seeds of eighteenth-century European civilization, which they must nurture in their communal lives and make real in their cultural history. In this context the poem is itself both an early blossom and a sign of promise.

Viets's contributions to Canadian literature, though brief, represent more than a historical footnote. *Annapolis Royal* is important and revealing. Viets also left behind the largest collection of eighteenth-century manuscript sermons in Maritime Canada.

Papers:
Viets's unpublished sermons are housed at the University of King's College, Halifax, and at the National Archives of Canada in Ottawa.

Agnes Ethelwyn Wetherald

(26 April 1857 - 9 March 1940)

Carole Gerson
Simon Fraser University

BOOKS: *An Algonquin Maiden: A Romance of the Early Days of Upper Canada,* by Wetherald and Graeme Mercer Adam (New York: Lovell, 1886; Montreal: Lovell, 1887; London: Low, Marston, Searle & Rivington, 1887);

The House of the Trees and Other Poems (Boston & New York: Lamson, Wolfe, 1895);

Tangled in Stars (Boston: Badger, 1902);

The Radiant Road (Boston: Badger, 1904);

The Last Robin: Lyrics and Sonnets (Toronto: Briggs, 1907); also published as *Poems, Lyrics and Sonnets* (Toronto: Musson, n. d.);

Tree-Top Mornings (Boston: Cornhill, 1921);

Lyrics and Sonnets, edited by John W. Garvin (Toronto: Nelson, 1931).

OTHER: *The Garden of the Heart: A Garland of Verses,* by Wetherald, Edith Thomas, Harriet Prescott Spofford, and others (Boston: Badger, 1903);

The Collected Poems of Isabella Valancy Crawford, edited by John W. Garvin, introduction by Wetherald (Toronto: Briggs, 1905).

An active and congenial member of the Canadian literary community for more than fifty years, Agnes Ethelwyn Wetherald was best known for her journalism and poetry which appeared in many Canadian and American newspapers and periodicals. Professionally and in private life she associated and corresponded with some of the leading literary figures of the 1890s, including Wilfred Campbell, Edward William Thomson and Duncan Campbell Scott; today her name is scarcely remembered, and her only work to have been recently republished is, ironically, the one she least wanted to preserve.

Raised as a member of the Society of Friends, Agnes Ethelwyn Wetherald was born in Rockwood, Ontario, the sixth of the eleven children of William Wetherald and Jemima Harris Balls Wetherald. When she was seven her father, founder and principal of Rockwood Academy, became superintendent of Haverford College, near Philadelphia; a few years later the family moved to a fruit and dairy farm at Chantler, near Fenwick, on the Niagara Peninsula. This was to be the poet's home for most of her life, the farm being run by some of her nine brothers after her father became a Quaker minister. Wetherald was educated at the Friends Boarding School at Union Springs, New York, and at Pickering College in Ontario. She sold her first poem when she was seventeen to *St. Nicholas Magazine* and published a series of stories in *Rose-Belford's Canadian Monthly* from 1880 to 1882. But she did not write seriously until 1886, when she began to contribute essays and sketches to the *Toronto Globe* under the pseudonym Bel Thistlethwaite, the maiden name of her paternal grandmother. During the next three years she also contributed poetry and prose to the *Week,* including a series of articles on Canadian literary women, and collaborated with Graeme Mercer Adam on her only piece of extended fiction, *An Algonquin Maiden: A Romance of the Early Days of Upper Canada* (1886).

At Wetherald's request, no mention of this book appeared in John W. Garvin's introduction to her collection *Lyrics and Sonnets* (1931). The embarrassing qualities of this historical romance (which was republished by the University of Toronto Press in 1973) were aptly summarized by two of Wetherald's contemporaries, Sara Jeannette Duncan, who commented rather acidly in the *Week* on the style of Wetherald's "aerial writing," and Pauline Johnson, who, in "A Strong Race Opinion on the Indian Girl in Modern Fiction" (*Toronto Sunday Globe,* 22 May 1892), focused on the unreality of Wanda, the unfortunate maiden whose ill-fated love for a white man leads to tragedy.

In the fall of 1889 Wetherald was invited by John Cameron to move to London, Ontario, to write for the *London Advertiser* and for a new feminist monthly, *Wives and Daughters,* which ran for three years. During this period of professional journalism she found herself increasingly drawn to poetry, which she began to publish in a wide

Agnes Ethelwyn Wetherwald

range of Canadian and American periodicals, including *Scribner's, Outlook,* the *Chap-Book,* and the *Detroit Free Press.* Like many Canadian writers of the 1890s, she contributed to the *Youth's Companion* (Boston) when Edward William Thomson became its fiction editor. In 1894 she published more poems in the *Companion* than any other poet; these became the basis of her first book of poetry, *The House of the Trees* (1895). Her involvement in the American publishing business increased during the winter of 1895-1896, when she worked in Philadelphia as an editorial assistant on the *Ladies' Home Journal,* and then with Charles Dudley Warner and Forrest Morgan on *A Library of the World's Best Literature,* for which she may have moved to Hartford, Connecticut. She also lived for several years in St. Paul.

Afraid that employment as a proofreader would "crush out whatever repressed spontaneous growth of my own was still surviving," as she

said in "Reminiscences," her foreword to *Lyrics and Sonnets,* Wetherald returned to Fenwick to work on the farm and her writing. Unmarried, she eventually adopted a little girl, Dorothy, born in 1910. The first years of the twentieth century were her most productive decade, with the publication of three books of poetry. Wetherald's mastery of rhyme and meter is evident in her sonnets and her concise lyrics celebrating love and nature, some of which were written from the tree house where she slept on hot summer nights. The best of her poems are musical, restrained, and precise, and are equal to much of the work of her better-known Canadian contemporaries such as Archibald Lampman, Bliss Carman, and Duncan Campbell Scott. On occasion ("The Humming-Bird," "The World Well Lost") her themes and images recall the poetry of Emily Dickinson, whose "unerring fastidiousness" she praised in *Wives and Daughters.*

Wetherald's later work does not show developments in form or content. She continued to write about the regenerative powers of nature and the birth and death of love without any apparent temptation to experiment with free verse or unconventional topics. She also produced a volume of children's verse, *Tree-Top Mornings* (1921), which was written for her adopted daughter, Dorothy. A letter from the late 1920s describing an unidentified period of her life includes a tantalizing reference to "an anonymous novel, for which [E. W. Thomson] found publication." Wetherald named Ralph Waldo Emerson, Matthew Arnold, and Elizabeth Barrett Browning as some of her influences; her close Canadian literary acquaintances included Laura Durand, literary editor at the *Globe*, and the poets Helena Coleman and Marjorie Pickthall, with whom she vacationed in 1911. She responded appreciatively to the poetry of Isabella Valancy Crawford and in 1905 wrote an introduction to Crawford's *Collected Poems*, edited by Garvin, who later edited and introduced her own *Lyrics and Sonnets*, a gathering of all the verse she wished to preserve. At the end of her life Ethelwyn Wetherald was remembered as much for the warmth and dignity of her personality as for the charm of her poetry, and was praised by her contemporaries as "a genuine and indigenous Canadian Singer."

References:

John W. Garvin, Introduction to Wetherald's *Lyrics and Sonnets* (Toronto: Nelson, 1931), pp. v-xviii;

Margaret Whitridge, "The Distaff Side of the Confederation Group: Women's Contribution to Early Nationalist Canadian Literature," *Atlantis*, 4 (Autumn 1978): 30-39.

Papers:

Some of Wetherald's letters are in the Lorne Pierce Collection in the Queen's University Archives, Kingston, and others are in the M. O. Hammond Papers at the Archives of Ontario, Toronto.

William Henry Withrow

(6 August 1839 - 12 November 1908)

Paul Matthew St. Pierre
Simon Fraser University

BOOKS: *Intemperance: Its Evils and Their Remedies* (Napanee, Ont.: Henry, 1869);

The Physiological Effects of Alcohol (Toronto, 1870);

The Catacombs of Rome, and Their Testimony Relative to Primitive Christianity (New York: Nelson & Phillips, 1874; London: Hodder & Stoughton, 1876);

The Bible and the Temperance Question (Toronto: Rose, 1876);

A History of Canada for the Use of Schools and General Readers (Toronto: Copp, Clark, 1876);

A Popular History of the Dominion of Canada from the Discovery of America to the Present Time (Boston & Portland: Russell, 1878; revised edition, Toronto: Briggs, 1885; revised again, Toronto: Briggs, 1888; revised again, Toronto: Briggs, 1893);

Worthies of Early Methodism (Toronto: Rose, 1878);

The Romance of Missions (Toronto: Rose, 1879);

The King's Messenger; or, Lawrence Temple's Probation: A Story of Canadian Life (Toronto: Methodist Book, 1879);

Great Preachers, Ancient and Modern (Toronto: Briggs, 1880);

Neville Trueman, the Pioneer Preacher: A Tale of the War of 1812 (Toronto: Briggs, 1880; London: Wesleyan Methodist Sunday School Union, 1886); republished as *A Victory and Its Cost; or, Neville Trueman, the Pioneer Preacher: A Tale of the War of 1812* (London: Wesleyan Methodist Sunday School Union, 1893);

A Canadian in Europe: Being Sketches of Travel in France, Italy, Switzerland, Germany, Holland and Belgium, Great Britain and Ireland (Toronto: Rose-Belford/Briggs, 1881);

Valeria, the Martyr of the Catacombs: A Tale of Early Christian Life in Rome (Toronto: Briggs, 1882; New York: Phillips & Hunt, 1882; London: Woolmer, 1883);

Life in a Parsonage; or, Lights and Shadows of the Itinerancy (London: Woolmer, 1885; Toronto: Methodist Mission Rooms, 1886);

An Abridged History of Canada, published with *An Outline History of Canada*, by G. Mercer Adam (Toronto: Briggs, 1887);

Our Own Country: Canada Scenic and Descriptive (Toronto: Briggs, 1889);

Barbara Heck: A Tale of Early Methodism in America (Toronto: Methodist Mission Rooms, 1895; Cincinnati: Cranston & Curtis/New York: Hunt & Eaton, 1895; London: Kelly, 1897);

Makers of Methodism (Toronto: Briggs, 1898; New York: Eaton & Mains, 1898; London: Kelly, 1903);

Beacon Lights of the Reformation (Toronto: Briggs, 1899);

Religious Progress in the [Nineteenth] *Century* (London & Philadelphia: Linscott, 1900; Toronto & Philadelphia: Linscott, 1902);

The Underground Railway (Ottawa: Hope, 1902).

OTHER: Egerton Ryerson, *Canadian Methodism: Its Epochs and Characteristics*, preface by Withrow (Toronto: Briggs, 1882);

Byron Laing, *What Harm Is There in It?*, introduction by Withrow (Toronto: Briggs, 1885);

W. H. Poole, *Anglo-Israel, or, The Saxon Race Proved to Be the Lost Tribes of Israel*, introduction by Withrow (Toronto: Briggs, 1889);

China and Its People, edited by Withrow (Toronto: Briggs, 1894);

A Harmony of the Gospels: Being the Life of Jesus in the Words of the Four Evangelists, arranged by Withrow (Toronto: Briggs, 1894; New York: Hunt & Eaton, 1894);

W. E. H. Massey, *The World's Fair Through a Camera: And How I Made My Pictures*, introduction by Withrow (Toronto: Briggs, 1894);

The Native Races of North America, edited by Withrow (Toronto: Briggs, 1895);

The Nineteenth Century Series, 26 volumes, edited by Withrow, Charles G. D. Roberts, J. Castell Hopkins, and T. S. Linscott (London: Linscott, 1900-1905);

Joseph Hamilton, *Our Own and Other Worlds*, introduction by Withrow (London: Kelly, 1905);

William Henry Withrow

Hamilton, *The Spirit World*, introduction by Withrow (New York: Revell, 1906).

William Henry Withrow was a minister in the Methodist church who dedicated his life to exemplifying the spirit of the Bible within his community and to recording the activities of Methodist missionaries, writers, and preachers in Canada and in Britain. Whether he wrote fiction, history, travel books, or biographies, he instilled in his writing his absolute faith in Methodism, at the same time respecting the traditions of other Christian denominations.

Withrow was born in Toronto on 6 August 1839. His father, James Withrow, was a Nova Scotian of United Empire Loyalist descent; his mother, Ellen Sanderson Withrow, was originally from Ireland. William received his early education at the Toronto Academy. He then attended Victoria College, Cobourg (the Methodist college of the University of Toronto), becoming a Method-

ist minister in 1862 and receiving B.A. (1863), M.A. (1864), and D.D. (1880) degrees. He was elected a fellow of the Royal Society of Canada in 1884, an honor that proved to be more a promise of writing to come than unqualified recognition of writing completed.

His earliest work was pastoral and pedantic. In three pamphlets of mainly sociological interest today, Withrow addressed himself to alcohol abuse and to the social question and Christian virtue of temperance; these are *Intemperance: Its Evils and Their Remedies* (1869), *The Physiological Effects of Alcohol* (1870), and *The Bible and the Temperance Question* (1876). Of much greater scholarly merit is his study of underground Christianity, *The Catacombs of Rome, and Their Testimony Relative to Primitive Christianity* (1874). Comprising more than five hundred pages of anthropological data, sociological exposition, and theological exegesis, the book is a substantial contribution to atavistic church history. Based on this study and his minis-

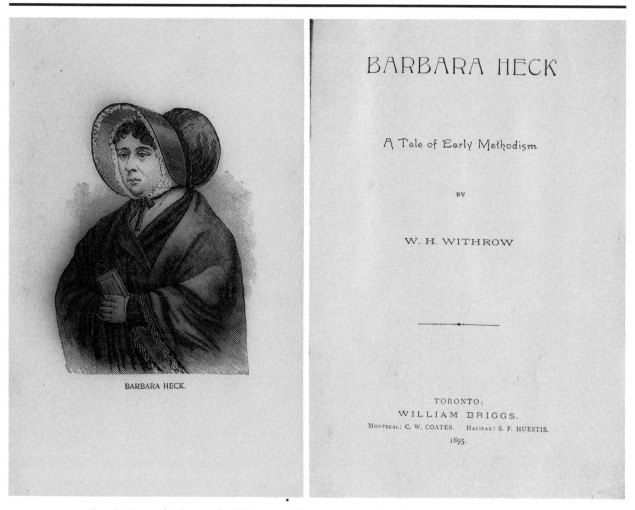

BARBARA HECK

A Tale of Early Methodism

BY

W. H. WITHROW

TORONTO:
WILLIAM BRIGGS.
MONTREAL: C. W. COATES.   HALIFAX: S. F. HUESTIS.
1895.

Frontispiece and title page for Withrow's 1895 novel, whose title character is a devout Methodist

terial work in Ontario and Quebec, Withrow was appointed editor of the *Canadian Methodist Magazine* in 1874, a position he held through 1906.

He next wrote two histories, one instructional–*A History of Canada for the Use of Schools and General Readers* (1876)–the other celebratory: *A Popular History of the Dominion of Canada from the Discovery of America to the Present Time* (1878). These patriotic works were followed by two travel narratives recounted from Canadian perspectives, featuring some of his most lucid descriptive writing. In *A Canadian in Europe* (1881) Withrow conducts his reader on a talking tour mainly through Italy and England: the book is remarkable for its descriptions of Leonardo da Vinci's "injured" "Last Supper" and of the monuments of London. *Our Own Country* (1889) is an ambitious outsiders' trek to Canada's faraway places and activities, coast-to-coast, with engrav-

ings illustrating every other of its six hundred pages.

Withrow wrote five historical novels, including plots with real historical figures and in which fictional characters are placed in historical situations. *The King's Messenger; or, Lawrence Temple's Probation: A Story of Canadian Life* (1879) features some lively descriptions of logging operations. In a wilderness of rough loggers, the eponymous character finds his faith and resolve tested severely: "Lawrence was not without spiritual contests also as well as conflicts with the giants of the forest, and the former were the more desperate and deadly of the two. To live a godly life amid these godless men–for so far as he knew none of them had any personal experience of religion– was no slight task." *Neville Trueman, the Pioneer Preacher: A Tale of the War of 1812* (1880) is decidedly conspicuous in its lack of preaching. *Valeria,* the Martyr of the Catacombs: A Tale of Early Christian Life in Rome (1882) makes a good fictional complement to The Catacombs of Rome. Life in a Parsonage; or, Lights and Shadows of the Itinerancy (1885) shows the sedentary and the peripatetic in the Methodist ministry. Barbara Heck: A Tale of Early Methodism in America (1895) is a rather flat fictionalized biography. These parables of proper Christian conduct are openly didactic and moralistic; they are Bible stories meant to edify. Withrow's purpose in writing them seems to have been to recognize in simple characters and stories counterparts to John Wesley, his followers, and their celebrated lives.

His biographies of Methodists of accomplishment and substance in turn complement his fictional celebration of ordinary characters somewhat dwarfed by dogmatic history. Worthies of Early Methodism (1878), Great Preachers, Ancient and Modern (1880), Makers of Methodism (1898), and Beacon Lights of the Reformation (1899) single out major figures in Methodist church history and feature ardent commemorative writing. Withrow has only unstinting praise for Charles Wesley, for example: "Between his conversion and death Charles Wesley wrote nearly seven thousand hymns, filling thirteen octavo volumes of five hundred pages each, exceeding all the poetry of Watts, Cowper and Pope put together. He wrote on an average nearly three hymns a week for fifty years. And the number of his hymns is only equalled by their range and variety, span-

ning as they do the sublime empyrean from the first cry of a new-born babe to the last shout of a dying spirit." As a chronicler and judge of church history, Withrow reached his zenith in his encyclopedic Religious Progress in the [Nineteenth] Century (1900), as ambitious a work in its own right as his Popular History of the Dominion of Canada.

A sometimes overlooked work by Withrow, but a crowning personal achievement, is his biography of Christ in the form of a scripture paraphrase: A Harmony of the Gospels: Being the Life of Jesus in the Words of the Four Evangelists (1894). Although the story remains that of the original version, the arrangement is all Withrow's own.

William Henry Withrow died in Toronto on 12 November 1908. His books sold well during his life; several were published simultaneously in Canada, the United States, and Britain, but Withrow is a minor figure in Canadian literary history. However, he figures prominently in Canadian religious history. Although his works are long out of print, they continue to be of interest to students of Canadian history, travel literature, Methodism, and missionary and community life.

Reference:

The Literary History of Canada: Canadian Literature in English, volume 1, edited by Carl F. Klinck (Toronto: University of Toronto Press, 1965), pp. 232, 263, 308, 309, 322.

Supplementary Reading List

Atlantic Provinces Literature Colloquium. Saint John, New Brunswick: Atlantic Canada Institute, 1977.

Atwood, Margaret. *Survival: A Thematic Guide to Canadian Literature*. Toronto: Anansi, 1972.

Avis, Walter, and others. *A Concise Dictionary of Canadianisms*. Toronto: Gage, 1973.

Bailey, A. G. *Culture and Nationality: Essays*. Toronto: McClelland & Stewart, 1972.

Baillargeon, Samuel. *Littérature canadienne-française*, third edition, revised. Montreal & Paris: Fides, 1960.

Baker, Ray Palmer. *A History of English-Canadian Literature to the Confederation*. Cambridge, Mass.: Harvard University Press, 1920.

Ballstadt, Carl, ed. *The Search for English-Canadian Literature*. Toronto & Buffalo: University of Toronto Press, 1975.

Beaudoin, Réjean. *Naissance d'une littérature*. Montreal: Boréal, 1988.

Bélisle, Louis-Alexandre. *Dictionnaire général de la langue française au Canada*. Quebec: Bélisle, 1957.

Bélisle. *Dictionnaire nord-américaine de la langue française*. Montreal: Beauchemin, 1979.

Beraud, Jean. *350 Ans de théâtre au Canada français*. Montreal: Cercle du Livre de France, 1958.

Berger, Carl. *The Sense of Power*. Toronto: University of Toronto Press, 1970.

Berger. *The Writing of Canadian History*. Toronto: Oxford University Press, 1976.

Bissell, C. T., and R. L. McDougall, eds. *Our Living Tradition*, 4 volumes. Toronto: University of Toronto Press, 1957-1965.

Boivin, Aurélien. *Le Conte littéraire québécois au 19e siècle: Essai de bibliographie critique et analytique*. Montreal: Fides, 1975.

Bourinot, John George. *Our Intellectual Strength and Weakness*. Montreal: F. Brown, 1893; republished, Toronto: University of Toronto Press, 1973.

Brown, E. K. *Responses and Evaluations: Essays on Canada*. Toronto: McClelland & Stewart, 1977.

Brunet, Berthelot. *Histoire de la littérature canadienne-française*. Montreal: L'Arbre, 1946.

Brym, Robert J., and Bonnie J. Fox. *From Culture to Power: The Sociology of English Canada*. Toronto: Oxford University Press, 1989.

Buitenhuis, Peter. *The Great War of Words: British, American, and Canadian Propaganda and Fiction 1914-33*. Vancouver: University of British Columbia Press, 1989.

Burnet, Jean. *"Coming Canadians": An Introduction to a History of Canada's Peoples.* Toronto: McClelland & Stewart, 1968.

The Canadian Encyclopedia, second edition, 4 volumes. Edmonton: Hurtig, 1985.

Capone, Giovanna. *Canada: il villaggio della terra.* Bologna: Pàtron Editore, 1978.

Cappon, Paul, ed. *In Our House: Social Perspectives on Canadian Literature.* Toronto: McClelland & Stewart, 1978.

Cleverdon, Catherine Lyle. *The Woman Suffrage Movement in Canada.* Toronto: University of Toronto Press, 1950.

Codignola, Luca, ed. *Canadiana.* Venice: Marsilio, 1978.

Collet, Paulette. *L'Hiver dans le roman canadien français.* Quebec: Laval, 1965.

Collin, W. E. *The White Savannahs.* 1936; republished, Toronto & Buffalo: University of Toronto Press, 1975.

Colombo, John Robert. *Colombo's Canadian Quotations.* Edmonton: Hurtig, 1974.

Colombo, comp. *Colombo's Canadian References.* Toronto, Oxford & New York: Oxford University Press, 1976.

Colombo and others, comps. *CDN SF & F: A Bibliography of Science Fiction and Fantasy.* Toronto: Hounslow, 1979.

Cook, Ramsay. *The Regenerators: Social Criticism in Late Victorian English Canada.* Toronto & Buffalo: University of Toronto Press, 1985.

Costisella, Joseph. *L'Esprit révolutionnaire dans la littérature canadienne-française de 1837 à la fin du 19e siècle.* Montreal: Beauchemin, 1968.

Daymond, Douglas. *Towards a Canadian Literature,* volume 1. Ottawa: Tecumseh, 1984.

Daymond, and Leslie Monkman, eds. *Canadian Novelists and the Novel.* Ottawa: Borealis, 1981.

Dictionary of Canadian Biography, 12 volumes, ongoing. Toronto: University of Toronto Press, 1966-

Dooley, D. J. *Moral Vision in the Canadian Novel.* Toronto: Clarke, Irwin, 1981.

Dostaler, Yves. *Les Infortunes du roman dans le Quebec du XIXe siècle.* Montreal: HMH, 1977.

Doyle, James. *North of America: Images of Canada in the Literature of the United States, 1775-1900.* Toronto: ECW, 1983.

Ducrocq-Poirier, Madeleine. *Le Roman canadien de langue française de 1860 à 1958.* Paris: Nizet, 1978.

Dudek, Louis, and Michael Gnarowski, eds. *The Making of Modern Poetry in Canada.* Toronto: Ryerson, 1967.

Duffy, Dennis. *Gardens, Covenants, Exiles: Loyalism in the Literature of Upper Canada/Ontario.* Toronto: University of Toronto Press, 1982.

Duhamel, Roger. *Manuel de littérature canadienne-française*. Montreal: Renouveau Pédagogiques, 1967.

Egoff, Sheila. *The Republic of Childhood*. Toronto: Oxford University Press, 1967.

Fairbanks, Carol. *Prairie Women: Images in American and Canadian Fiction*. New Haven & London: Yale University Press, 1986.

Falardeau, Jean-Charles. *Imaginaire social et littérature*. Montreal: HMH, 1974.

Fowke, Edith. *Canadian Folklore*. Toronto: Oxford University Press, 1988.

Fowke, and Carole Henderson Carpenter, comps. *A Bibliography of Canadian Folklore in English*. Toronto & Buffalo: University of Toronto Press, 1981.

Fowke and Carpenter, eds. *Explorations in Canadian Folklore*. Toronto: McClelland & Stewart, 1985.

Frye, Northrop. *The Bush Garden: Essays on the Canadian Imagination*. Toronto: Anansi, 1971.

Frye. *Divisions on a Ground*. Toronto: Anansi, 1982.

Gagnon, Serge. *Quebec and Its Historians*, 2 volumes, translated by Jane Brierly. Montreal: Harvest House, 1982, 1985.

Gauvin, Lise, and Laurent Mailhot. *Guide culturel de Québec*. Montreal: Boréal Express, 1982.

Gerson, Carole. *A Purer Taste: The Writing and Reading of Fiction in English in Nineteenth-Century Canada*. Toronto, Buffalo & London: University of Toronto Press, 1989.

Gnarowski, Michael. *A Concise Bibliography of English-Canadian Literature*. Toronto: McClelland & Stewart, 1973.

Godard, Barbara, ed. *Gynocritics/Gynocritiques: Feminist Approaches to Canadian and Quebec Writing*. Toronto: ECW, 1987.

Goldie, Terry. *Fear and Temptation: The Image of the Indigene in Canadian, Australian, and New Zealand Literatures*. Kingston, Ont., Montreal & London: McGill-Queen's University Press, 1989.

Gross, Konrad, and Wolfgang Kloss, eds. *English Literature of the Dominions*. Würzburg: Königshausen & Neumann, 1981.

Guillaume, Pierre, Jean-Michel Lacroix, and Pierre Spriet, eds. *Canada et canadiens*. Bordeaux: Presses Universitaires de Bordeaux, 1984.

Hall, Roger, and Gordon Dodds. *Canada: A History in Photographs*. Edmonton: Hurtig, 1981.

Halpenny, Francess G., ed. *Editing Canadian Texts*. Toronto: Hakkert, 1975.

Harper, J. Russell. *Painting in Canada: A History*. Toronto: University of Toronto Press, 1970.

Harris, R. Cole. *The Historical Atlas of Canada*, volume 1 (to 1800). Toronto: University of Toronto Press, 1987.

Harrison, Dick. *Unnamed Country: The Struggle for a Canadian Prairie Fiction*. Edmonton: University of Alberta Press, 1977.

Harrison, ed. *Crossing Frontiers*. Edmonton: University of Alberta Press, 1979.

Hayne, David M., and Marcel Tirol. *Bibliographie critique du roman canadien-français, 1837-1900*. Toronto: University of Toronto Press, 1968.

Heath, Jeffrey M., ed. *Profiles in Canadian Literature*, volumes 1-4. Toronto & Charlottetown: Dundurn, 1980-1982.

Hébert, Chantal. *Le Burlesque au Québec*. Montreal: HMH, 1981.

Hébert, Pierre. *Le Journal intime au Québec*. Montreal: Fides, 1988.

Hinchcliffe, Peter, ed. *Family Fictions in Canadian Literature*. Waterloo, Ont.: University of Waterloo Press, 1988.

Innis, Mary Quayle, ed. *The Clear Spirit: Twenty Canadian Women and Their Times*. Toronto: University of Toronto Press, 1966.

Jones, D. G. *Butterfly on Rock*. Toronto: University of Toronto Press, 1970.

Kallmann, Helmut, and others. *The Encyclopedia of Music in Canada*. Toronto: University of Toronto Press, 1981.

Keith, W. J. *Canadian Literature in English*. London & New York: Longman, 1985.

Keitner, Wendy, ed. *"Surveying the Territory"* and *"Staking Claims,"* Canadian issues of *Literary Criterion*, 19, 3-4 (1984) and 20, 1 (1985).

King, Thomas, and others, eds. *The Native in Literature*. Toronto: ECW, 1988.

Klinck, Carl F., ed. *Literary History of Canada*, 3 volumes, second edition. Toronto: University of Toronto Press, 1976.

Kline, Marcia B. *Beyond the Land Itself: Views of Nature in Canada and the United States*. Cambridge, Mass.: Harvard University Press, 1970.

Kröller, Eva-Marie. *Canadian Travellers in Europe 1851-1900*. Vancouver: University of British Columbia Press, 1987.

Laflamme, Jean, and Rémi Tourangeau. *L'Eglise et le théâtre au Québec*. Montreal: Fides, 1979.

Lecker, Robert, and Jack David, eds. *The Annotated Bibliography of Canada's Major Authors*, 6 volumes, ongoing. Downsview, Ontario: ECW, 1979-   .

Lecker and David, eds. *Canadian Writers and Their Works*, 10 volumes, ongoing. Toronto: ECW, 1983-

Lee, Dennis. *Savage Fields: An Essay in Literature and Cosmology*. Toronto: Anansi, 1977.

Léger, Jules. *Le Canada français et son expression littéraire*. Paris: Nizet & Bastard, 1938.

Legris, Renée, and others. *Le Théâtre au Quebec 1825-1980: Repères et perspectives*. Montreal: VLB, 1988.

Lemieux, Louise. *Pleins feux sur la littérature de jeunesse au Canada français*. Montreal: Leméac, 1972.

Lemire, Maurice. *Les Grands Thèmes nationalistes du roman historique canadien-français*. Quebec: Presses de l'Université Laval, 1970.

Lemire, ed. *Dictionnaire des oeuvres littéraires du Quebec*. Montreal: Fides. Volume 1 (*Des Origines à 1900*, 1978); volume 2 (*1900 à 1939*, 1980).

Lewis, Merrill, and L. L. Lee. *The Westering Experience in American Literature*. Bellingham, Wash.: Western Washington University Press, 1977.

Lewis, Paula Gilbert, ed. *Traditionalism, Nationalism, and Feminism: Women Writers of Quebec*. Westport, Conn. & London: Greenwood Press, 1985.

Lochhead, Douglas, comp. *Bibliography of Canadian Bibliographies*, second edition, revised and enlarged. Toronto: University of Toronto Press, 1972.

Lortie, Jeanne d'Arc. *La Poésie nationaliste au Canada français (1606-1867)*. Quebec: Presses de l'Université Laval, 1975.

MacLulich, T. D. *Between Europe and America*. Toronto: ECW, 1988.

MacMechan, Archibald. *Headwaters of Canadian Literature*. Toronto: McClelland & Stewart, 1924.

MacMurchy, Archibald. *Handbook of Canadian Literature (English)*. Toronto: Briggs, 1906.

Mailhot, Laurent. *La Littérature québécoise*. Paris: Presses Universitaires de France, 1974.

Mandel, Eli, ed. *Contexts of Canadian Criticism*. Chicago & London: University of Chicago Press, 1971.

Marshall, Tom. *Harsh and Lovely Land: Major Canadian Poets and the Making of a Canadian Tradition*. Vancouver: University of British Columbia Press, 1979.

Mathews, Robin. *Canadian Literature: Surrender or Revolution*. Toronto: Steel Rail, 1978.

Matthews, John. *Tradition in Exile*. Toronto: University of Toronto Press / Melbourne: Cheshire, 1962.

May, Cedric. *Breaking the Silence: The Literature of Quebec*. Birmingham, U.K.: University of Birmingham, 1981.

McConnell, R. E. *Our Own Voice: Canadian English and How It Is Studied*. Toronto: Gage, 1979.

McGregor, Gaile. *The Wacousta Syndrome: Explorations in the Canadian Langscape*. Toronto, Buffalo & London: University of Toronto Press, 1985.

McKillop, A. B. *Contours of Canadian Thought*. Toronto: University of Toronto Press, 1987.

McKillop. *A Disciplined Intelligence*. Montreal: McGill-Queen's University Press, 1979.

McKillop, ed. *Contexts of Canada's Past: Selected Essays of W. L. Morton*. Toronto: Macmillan, 1980.

McMullen, Lorraine, ed. *Twentieth Century Essays on Confederation Literature*. Ottawa: Tecumseh, 1977.

Moisan, Clément. *L'Age de la littérature canadienne*. Montreal: HMH, 1969.

Monkman, Leslie. *A Native Heritage: Images of the Indian in English-Canadian Literature*. Toronto: University of Toronto Press, 1981.

Moss, John. *Patterns of Isolation in English Canadian Fiction*. Toronto: McClelland & Stewart, 1974.

Moss. *A Reader's Guide to the Canadian Novel*. Toronto: McClelland & Stewart, 1981.

Moss. *Sex and Violence in the Canadian Novel*. Toronto: McClelland & Stewart, 1977.

Moss, ed. *Beginnings*. Toronto: NC Press, 1980.

Moyles, R. G., and Doug Owram. *Imperial Dreams and Colonial Realities: British Views of Canada 1880-1914*. Toronto, Buffalo & London: University of Toronto Press, 1988.

Narasimhaiah, C. D., ed. *Awakened Conscience*. New Delhi: Sterling, 1978.

Neuman, Shirley, and Smaro Kamboureli, eds. *A Mazing Space: Writing Canadian Women Writing*. Edmonton: Longspoon/NeWest, 1986.

New, W. H. *Among Worlds: An Introduction to Modern Commonwealth and South African Fiction*. Erin, Ont.: Porcépic, 1975.

New. *Dreams of Speech and Violence: The Art of the Short Story in Canada and New Zealand*. Toronto, Buffalo & London: University of Toronto Press, 1987.

New. *A History of Canadian Literature*. London: Macmillan, 1989.

New, comp. *Critical Writings on Commonwealth Literatures: A Selective Bibliography to 1970, With a List of Theses and Dissertations*. University Park: Pennsylvania State University Press, 1975.

New, ed. *Dramatists in Canada: Selected Essays*. Vancouver: University of British Columbia Press, 1972.

New, ed. *Literary History of Canada*, volume 4. Toronto: University of Toronto Press, 1990.

New, ed. *A Political Art*. Vancouver: University of British Columbia Press, 1978.

Northey, Margot. *The Haunted Wilderness: The Gothic and Grotesque in Canadian Fiction*. Toronto & Buffalo: University of Toronto Press, 1976.

OKanada. Ottawa: Canada Council, 1982.

O'Leary, Dostaler. *Le Roman canadien-français*. Montreal: Cercle du Livre de France, 1954.

Olinder, Britta, ed. *A Sense of Place: Essays in Post-Colonial Literatures*. Göteburg: Gothenburg University Press, 1984.

Pacey, Desmond. *Creative Writing in Canada*, second edition, revised. Toronto: Ryerson, 1961.

Pacey. *Essays in Canadian Criticism 1938-1968*. Toronto: Ryerson, 1969.

Pacey. *Ten Canadian Poets*. Toronto: Ryerson, 1958.

Pache, Walter. *Einführung in die Kanadistik*. Darmstadt: Wissenschaftliche Buchgesellschaft, 1981.

Paradis, Suzanne. *Femme fictive, femme réelle: Le Personnage féminin dans le roman féminin canadien-français, 1884-1966*. Quebec: Garneau, 1966.

Parker, George L. *The Beginnings of the Book Trade in Canada*. Toronto & Buffalo: University of Toronto Press, 1985.

Paul-Crouzet, Jeanne. *Poésie au Canada*. Paris: Didier, 1946.

Petrone, Penny. *Northern Voices: Inuit Writing in English*. Toronto, Buffalo & London: University of Toronto Press, 1988.

Petrone, ed. *First People, First Voices*. Toronto: Ryerson, 1927.

Pierce, Lorne. *An Outline of Canadian Literature*. Toronto: Ryerson, 1927.

Polk, James. *Wilderness Writers*. Toronto: Clarke, Irwin, 1972.

Rabb, J. D. *Religion and Science in Early Canada*. Toronto: Frye, 1988.

Rashley, R. E. *Poetry in Canada: The First Three Steps*. Toronto: Ryerson, 1958.

Reid, Dennis. *A Concise History of Canadian Painting*. Toronto, Oxford & New York: Oxford University Press, 1973.

Rhodenizer, V. B. *A Handbook of Canadian Literature*. Ottawa: Graphic, 1930.

Ricou, Laurence R. *Vertical Man/Horizontal World*. Vancouver: University of British Columbia Press, 1973.

Riedel, Walter E. *Das Literarische Kanadabild*. Bonn: Bouvier, 1980.

Riemenschneider, Dieter, ed. *The History and Historiography of Commonwealth Literature*. Tübingen: Gunter Narr Verlag, 1983.

Rièse, Laure. *L'Ame de la poésie canadienne-française*. Toronto: Macmillan, 1955.

Ripley, C. Peter, ed. *The Black Abolitionist Papers*, volume 2 (Canada: 1830-1865). Chapel Hill: University of North Carolina Press, 1986.

Ross, Malcolm. *The Impossible Sum of Our Traditions: Reflections on Canadian Literature*. Toronto: McClelland & Stewart, 1986.

Roy, Camille. *Manuel d'histoire de la littérature canadienne de langue française*. Quebec: L'Action Sociale, 1918.

Rutherford, Paul. *A Victorian Authority: The Daily Press in Late Nineteenth-Century Canada*. Toronto & Buffalo: University of Toronto Press, 1982.

Sarkonak, Ralph, ed. "The Language of Difference: Writing in QUEBEC(ois)," special issue of *Yale French Studies*, no. 65 (1983).

Shortt, S. E. D. *The Search for an Ideal.* Toronto & Buffalo: University of Toronto Press, 1976.

Sirois, Antoine. *Montréal dans le roman canadien.* Montreal: Didier, 1970.

Smith, A. J. M. *Towards a View of Canadian Letters.* Vancouver: University of British Columbia Press, 1973.

Smith, ed. *Masks of Poetry.* Toronto: McClelland & Stewart, 1962.

Staines, David, ed. *The Canadian Imagination.* Cambridge, Mass.: Harvard University Press, 1977.

Stevenson, Lionel. *Appraisals of Canadian Literature.* Toronto: Macmillan, 1926.

Stich, K. P., ed. *Reflections: Autobiography and Canadian Literature.* Ottawa: University of Ottawa Press, 1988.

Story, G. M., and others, eds. *Dictionary of Newfoundland English.* Toronto: University of Toronto Press, 1982.

Stouck, David. *Major Canadian Authors.* Lincoln: University of Nebraska Press, 1984.

Stratford, Philip. *Bibliography of Canadian Books in Translation: French to English and English to French. Bibliographie de livres canadiens traduits de l'anglais au français et du français à l'anglais.* Ottawa: CCRH, 1977.

Stuart, E. Ross. *The History of Prairie Theatre.* Toronto: Simon & Pierre, 1984.

Sutherland, Fraser. *The Monthly Epic: A History of Canadian Magazines 1789-1989.* Toronto: Fitzhenry & Whiteside, 1989.

Taylor, Charles. *Six Journeys: A Canadian Pattern.* Toronto: Anansi, 1977.

Thomas, Clara. *Our Nature–Our Voices: A Guidebook to English-Canadian Literature.* Toronto: New Press, 1972.

Tougas, Gérard. *Histoire de la littérature canadienne-française.* Paris: Presses Universitaires de France, 1960. Translated by Alta Lind Cook as *History of French-Canadian Literature.* Toronto: Ryerson, 1966.

Toye, William, ed. *The Oxford Companion to Canadian Literature.* Toronto: Oxford University Press, 1983.

Trudel, Marcel. *L'Influence de Voltaire au Canada,* 2 volumes. Montreal: Fides, 1945.

Turnbull, Jane-M. *Essential Traits of French-Canadian Poetry.* Toronto: Macmillan, 1938.

Viatte, Auguste. *Histoire littéraire de l'Amérique française des origines à 1950.* Quebec: Presses Universitaires Laval, 1954.

Wagner, Anton, ed. *The Brock Bibliography of Published Canadian Plays in English 1766-1978.* Toronto: Playwrights, 1980.

Waldon, Freda Farrell. *Bibliography of Canadiana Published in Great Britain, 1519-1763.* Revised and edited by William F. E. Morley. Toronto: National Library of Canada/ECW, 1990.

Wardhaugh, Ronald. *Language & Nationhood: The Canadian Experience.* Vancouver: New Star, 1983.

Warwick, Jack. *The Long Journey: Literary Themes of French Canada.* Toronto: University of Toronto Press, 1968.

Waterston, Elizabeth. *Survey: A Short History of Canadian Literature.* Toronto: Methuen, 1973.

Waterston and others. *The Travellers–Canada to 1900: An Annotated Bibliography of Works Published in English from 1577.* Guelph, Ont.: University of Guelph, 1989.

Watters, R. E. *A Check List of Canadian Literature and Background Material 1628-1950,* revised edition. Toronto: University of Toronto Press, 1972.

Winks, Robin W. *The Myth of the American Frontier.* Leicester: Leicester University Press, 1971.

Woodcock, George. *Canada and the Canadians.* Toronto: Macmillan, 1970.

Woodcock. *Odysseus Ever Returning: Essays on Canadian Writers and Writing.* Toronto: McClelland & Stewart, 1970.

Woodcock, comp. *Colony and Confederation: Early Canadian Poets and Their Background.* Vancouver: University of British Columbia Press, 1974.

Woodcock, ed. *The Canadian Novel in the Twentieth Century.* Toronto: McClelland & Stewart, 1975.

Wyczynski, Paul, and others. *Archives des lettres canadiennes.* Montreal: Fides. No. 2 (*Ecole littéraire de Montréal,* 1972); no. 3 (*Roman,* 1971); no. 4 (*Poésie,* 1969); no. 5 (*Théâtre,* 1976).

Contributors

Carl Ballstadt .... *McMaster University*
Neil K. Besner .... *University of Winnipeg*
Glen Campbell .... *University of Calgary*
Donna Coates .... *University of Calgary*
Ramsay Cook .... *York University*
Gwendolyn Davies .... *Acadia University*
Richard A. Davies .... *Acadia University*
Sandra Djwa .... *Simon Fraser University*
Leonard E. Doucette .... *University of Toronto*
James Doyle .... *Wilfrid Laurier University*
Richard Duprey .... *Emerson College*
Mary Jane Edwards... *Carleton University*
David Galloway .... *University of New Brunswick*
Carole Gerson .... *Simon Fraser University*
Robert Gibbs .... *University of New Brunswick*
Barbara Godard.. *York University*
Bryan N. S. Gooch .... *University of Victoria*
John E. Hare .... *University of Ottawa*
Virginia A. Harger-Grinling .... *Memorial University of Newfoundland*
Victor G. Hopwood .... *University of British Columbia*
Susan Jackel... *University of Alberta*
Kathleen L. Kellett .... *University of Toronto*
Eva-Marie Kröller.. *University of British Columbia*
Camille R. La Bossière... *University of Ottawa*
Michèle Lacombe .... *Trent University*
Julie LeBlanc .... *Carleton University*
Mary Lu MacDonald .... *Halifax, Nova Scotia*
I. S. MacLaren... *University of Alberta*
David R. Mawer .... *Saint Paul University*
Lorraine McMullen.. *University of Ottawa*
Kathy Mezei.. *Simon Fraser University*
Patricia Monk .... *Dalhousie University*
Leslie Monkman.. *University of Guelph*
Bruce Nesbitt.. *Rockcliffe Park, Ontario*
George L. Parker .... *Royal Military College of Canada*
John Parr.. *Winnipeg, Manitoba*
Michael A. Peterman .... *Trent University*
Harry Prest.. *Camrose Lutheran University College*
Paul Matthew St. Pierre .... *Simon Fraser University*
Eva H. Seidner.. *University of Toronto*
Norman Shrive .... *McMaster University*
John Stockdale.. *Laval University*
Clara Thomas .... *York University*
Dawn Thompson .... *University of British Columbia*
Renate Usmiani .... *Mount St. Vincent University*
Thomas B. Vincent.. *Royal Military College of Canada*
Anton Wagner .... *York University*
Tracy Ware .... *Bishop's University*

Jack Warwick..*York University*
Elizabeth Waterston ....*University of Guelph*
Lorraine Weir...*University of British Columbia*

Cumulative Index

Dictionary of Literary Biography, Volumes 1-99
Dictionary of Literary Biography Yearbook, 1980-1989
Dictionary of Literary Biography Documentary Series, Volumes 1-7

Cumulative Index

DLB before number: *Dictionary of Literary Biography,* Volumes 1-99
Y before number: *Dictionary of Literary Biography Yearbook,* 1980-1989
DS before number: *Dictionary of Literary Biography Documentary Series,* Volumes 1-7

A

D

G

N

Q

R

S

U

V

W

Cumulative Index

Y

(Continued from front endsheets)

71: *American Literary Critics and Scholars, 1880-1900,* edited by John W. Rathbun and Monica M. Grecu (1988)

72: *French Novelists, 1930-1960,* edited by Catharine Savage Brosman (1988)

73: *American Magazine Journalists, 1741-1850,* edited by Sam G. Riley (1988)

74: *American Short-Story Writers Before 1880,* edited by Bobby Ellen Kimbel, with the assistance of William E. Grant (1988)

75: *Contemporary German Fiction Writers,* Second Series, edited by Wolfgang D. Elfe and James Hardin (1988)

76: *Afro-American Writers, 1940-1955,* edited by Trudier Harris (1988)

77: *British Mystery Writers, 1920-1939,* edited by Bernard Benstock and Thomas F. Staley (1988)

78: *American Short-Story Writers, 1880-1910,* edited by Bobby Ellen Kimbel, with the assistance of William E. Grant (1988)

79: *American Magazine Journalists, 1850-1900,* edited by Sam G. Riley (1988)

80: *Restoration and Eighteenth-Century Dramatists,* First Series, edited by Paula R. Backscheider (1989)

81: *Austrian Fiction Writers, 1875-1913,* edited by James Hardin and Donald G. Daviau (1989)

82: *Chicano Writers,* First Series, edited by Francisco A. Lomelí and Carl R. Shirley (1989)

83: *French Novelists Since 1960,* edited by Catharine Savage Brosman (1989)

84: *Restoration and Eighteenth-Century Dramatists,* Second Series, edited by Paula R. Backscheider (1989)

85: *Austrian Fiction Writers After 1914,* edited by James Hardin and Donald G. Daviau (1989)

86: *American Short-Story Writers, 1910-1945,* First Series, edited by Bobby Ellen Kimbel (1989)

87: *British Mystery and Thriller Writers Since 1940,* First Series, edited by Bernard Benstock and Thomas F. Staley (1989)

88: *Canadian Writers, 1920-1959,* Second Series, edited by W. H. New (1989)

89: *Restoration and Eighteenth-Century Dramatists,* Third Series, edited by Paula R. Backscheider (1989)

90: *German Writers in the Age of Goethe, 1789-1832,* edited by James Hardin and Christoph E. Schweitzer (1989)

91: *American Magazine Journalists, 1900-1960,* First Series, edited by Sam G. Riley (1990)

92: *Canadian Writers, 1890-1920,* edited by W. H. New (1990)

93: *British Romantic Poets, 1789-1832,* First Series, edited by John R. Greenfield (1990)

94: *German Writers in the Age of Goethe: Sturm und Drang to Classicism,* edited by James Hardin and Christoph E. Schweitzer (1990)

95: *Eighteenth-Century British Poets,* First Series, edited by John Sitter (1990)

96: *British Romantic Poets, 1789-1832,* Second Series, edited by John R. Greenfield (1990)

97: *German Writers from the Enlightenment to Sturm und Drang, 1720-1764,* edited by James Hardin and Christoph E. Schweitzer (1990)

98: *Modern British Essayists,* First Series, edited by Robert Beum (1990)

99: *Canadian Writers Before 1890,* edited by W. H. New (1990)